Cambodia

John J. Horton is Deputy Librarian of the University of Bradford and was formerly Chairman of its Academic Board of Studies in Social Sciences. He has maintained a longstanding interest in the discipline of area studies and its associated bibliographical problems, with special reference to European Studies. In particular he has published in the field of Icelandic and of Yugoslav studies, including the two relevant volumes in the World Bibliographical Series.

Robert A. Myers is Associate Professor of Anthropology in the Division of Social Sciences and Director of Study Abroad Programs at Alfred University, Alfred, New York. He has studied post-colonial island nations of the Caribbean and has spent two years in Nigeria on a Fulbright Lectureship. His interests include international public health, historical anthropology and developing societies. In addition to *Amerindians of the Lesser Antilles: a bibliography* (1981), *A Resource Guide to Dominica, 1493-1986* (1987) and numerous articles, he has compiled the World Bibliographical Series volumes on *Dominica* (1987), *Nigeria* (1989) and *Ghana* (1991).

Ian Wallace is Professor of German at the University of Bath. A graduate of Oxford in French and German, he also studied in Tübingen, Heidelberg and Lausanne before taking teaching posts at universities in the USA, Scotland and England. He specializes in contemporary German affairs, especially literature and culture, on which he has published numerous articles and books. In 1979 he founded the journal *GDR Monitor*, which he continues to edit under its new title *German Monitor*.

Hans H. Wellisch is Professor emeritus at the College of Library and Information Services, University of Maryland. He was President of the American Society of Indexers and was a member of the International Federation for Documentation. He is the author of numerous articles and several books on indexing and abstracting, and has published *The Conversion of Scripts and Indexing and Abstracting: an International Bibliography*, and *Indexing from A to Z*. He also contributes frequently to *Journal of the American Society for Information Science*, *The Indexer* and other professional journals.

Ralph Lee Woodward, Jr. is Professor of History at Tulane University, New Orleans. He is the author of *Central America, a Nation Divided*, 2nd ed. (1985), as well as several monographs and more than seventy scholarly articles on modern Latin America. He has also compiled volumes in the World Bibliographical Series on *Belize* (1980), *El Salvador* (1988), *Guatemala* (Rev. Ed.) (1992) and *Nicaragua* (Rev. Ed.) (1994). Dr. Woodward edited the Central American section of the *Research Guide to Central America and the Caribbean* (1985) and is currently associate editor of Scribner's *Encyclopedia of Latin American History*.

VOLUME 200

Cambodia

Helen Jarvis

Compiler

CLIO PRESS
OXFORD, ENGLAND · SANTA BARBARA, CALIFORNIA
DENVER, COLORADO

British Library Cataloguing in Publication Data

Jarvis, Helen
Cambodia. – (World bibliographical series; v. 200)
1. Cambodia – Bibliography
I. Title
016.9′596

ISBN 1–85109–177–7

ABC-CLIO Ltd.,
Old Clarendon Ironworks,
35A Great Clarendon Street,
Oxford OX2 6AT, England.

ABC-CLIO Inc.,
130 Cremona Drive,
Santa Barbara,
CA 93117, USA.

Designed by Bernard Crossland.
Typeset by Columns Design Ltd., Reading, England.
Printed and bound in Great Britain by Bookcraft (Bath) Ltd., Midsomer Norton.

THE WORLD BIBLIOGRAPHICAL SERIES

This series, which is principally designed for the English speaker, will eventually cover every country (and some of the world's principal regions and cities), each in a separate volume comprising annotated entries on works dealing with its history, geography, economy and politics; and with its people, their culture, customs, religion and social organization. Attention will also be paid to current living conditions – housing, education, newspapers, clothing, etc. – that are all too often ignored in standard bibliographies; and to those particular aspects relevant to individual countries. Each volume seeks to achieve, by use of careful selectivity and critical assessment of the literature, an expression of the country and an appreciation of its nature and national aspirations, to guide the reader towards an understanding of its importance. The keynote of the series is to provide, in a uniform format, an interpretation of each country that will express its culture, its place in the world, and the qualities and background that make it unique. The views expressed in individual volumes, however, are not necessarily those of the publisher.

VOLUMES IN THE SERIES

1 *Yugoslavia*, Rev. Ed., John J. Horton
2 *Lebanon*, Rev. Ed., C. H. Bleaney
3 *Lesotho*, Rev. Ed., Deborah Johnston
4 *Zimbabwe*, Rev. Ed., Deborah Potts
5 *Saudi Arabia*, Rev. Ed., Frank A. Clements
6 *Russia/USSR*, Second Ed., Lesley Pitman
7 *South Africa*, Rev. Ed., Geoffrey V. Davis
8 *Malawi*, Rev. Ed., Samuel Decalo
9 *Guatemala*, Rev. Ed., Ralph Lee Woodward, Jr.
10 *Pakistan*, David Taylor
11 *Uganda*, Rev. Ed., Balam Nyeko
12 *Malaysia*, Ian Brown and Rajeswary Ampalavanar
13 *France*, Rev. Ed., Frances Chambers
14 *Panama*, Eleanor DeSelms Langstaff
15 *Hungary*, Thomas Kabdebo
16 *USA*, Sheila R. Herstein and Naomi Robbins
17 *Greece*, Richard Clogg and Mary Jo Clogg
18 *New Zealand*, R. F. Grover
19 *Algeria*, Rev. Ed., Richard I. Lawless
20 *Sri Lanka*, Vijaya Samaraweera
21 *Belize*, Second Ed., Peggy Wright and Brian E. Coutts
23 *Luxembourg*, Rev. Ed., Jul Christophory and Emile Thoma
24 *Swaziland*, Rev. Ed., Balam Nyeko
25 *Kenya*, Rev. Ed., Dalvan Coger
26 *India*, Rev. Ed., Ian Derbyshire
27 *Turkey*, Merel Güçlü
28 *Cyprus*, Rev. Ed., P. M. Kitromilides and M. L. Evriviades
29 *Oman*, Rev. Ed., Frank A. Clements
30 *Italy*, Lucio Sponza and Diego Zancani
31 *Finland*, Rev. Ed., J. E. O. Screen
32 *Poland*, Rev. Ed., George Sanford and Adriana Gozdecka-Sanford
33 *Tunisia*, Allan M. Findlay, Anne M. Findlay and Richard I. Lawless
34 *Scotland*, Eric G. Grant
35 *China*, New Ed., Charles W. Hayford
36 *Qatar*, P. T. H. Unwin

37 *Iceland*, Rev. Ed., Francis R. McBride
38 *Nepal*, John Whelpton
39 *Haiti*, Rev. Ed., Frances Chambers
40 *Sudan*, Rev. Ed., M. W. Daly
41 *Vatican City State*, Michael J. Walsh
42 *Iraq*, Second Ed., C. H. Bleaney
43 *United Arab Emirates*, Frank A. Clements
44 *Nicaragua*, Rev. Ed., Ralph Lee Woodward, Jr.
45 *Jamaica*, Rev. Ed., K. E. Ingram
46 *Australia*, Second Ed., I. Kepars
47 *Morocco*, Rev. Ed., Anne M. Findlay and Allan M. Findlay
48 *Mexico*, Rev. Ed., George Philip
49 *Bahrain*, P. T. H. Unwin
50 *The Yemens*, G. Rex Smith
51 *Zambia*, Anne M. Bliss and J. A. Rigg
52 *Puerto Rico*, Elena E. Cevallos
53 *Namibia*, Rev. Ed., Stanley Schoeman and Elna Schoeman
54 *Tanzania*, Rev. Ed., Colin Darch
55 *Jordan*, Ian J. Seccombe
56 *Kuwait*, Rev. Ed., Frank A. Clements
57 *Brazil*, Rev. Ed., John Dickenson
58 *Israel*, Second Ed., C. H. Bleaney
59 *Romania*, Andrea Deletant and Dennis Deletant
60 *Spain*, Second Ed., Graham Shields
61 *Atlantic Ocean*, H. G. R. King
62 *Canada*, Ernest Ingles
63 *Cameroon*, Mark W. DeLancey and Peter J. Schraeder
64 *Malta*, John Richard Thackrah
65 *Thailand*, Michael Watts
66 *Austria*, Denys Salt with the assistance of Arthur Farrand Radley
67 *Norway*, Leland B. Sather
68 *Czechoslovakia*, David Short
69 *Irish Republic*, Michael Owen Shannon
70 *Pacific Basin and Oceania*, Gerald W. Fry and Rufino Mauricio
71 *Portugal*, P. T. H. Unwin
72 *West Germany*, Donald S. Detwiler and Ilse E. Detwiler
73 *Syria*, Ian J. Seccombe
74 *Trinidad and Tobago*, Frances Chambers
75 *Cuba*, Jean Stubbs, Lila Haines and Meic F. Haines
76 *Barbados*, Robert B. Potter and Graham M. S. Dann
77 *East Germany*, Ian Wallace
78 *Mozambique*, Colin Darch
79 *Libya*, Richard I. Lawless
80 *Sweden*, Leland B. Sather and Alan Swanson
81 *Iran*, Reza Navabpour
82 *Dominica*, Robert A. Myers
83 *Denmark*, Kenneth E. Miller
84 *Paraguay*, R. Andrew Nickson
85 *Indian Ocean*, Julia J. Gotthold with the assistance of Donald W. Gotthold
86 *Egypt*, Ragai N. Makar
87 *Gibraltar*, Graham J. Shields
88 *The Netherlands*, Peter King and Michael Wintle
89 *Bolivia*, Gertrude M. Yeager
90 *Papua New Guinea*, Fraiser McConnell
91 *The Gambia*, David P. Gamble
92 *Somalia*, Mark W. DeLancey, Sheila L. Elliott, December Green, Kenneth J. Menkhaus, Mohammad Haji Moqtar, Peter J. Schraeder
93 *Brunei*, Sylvia C. Engelen Krausse and Gerald H. Krausse
94 *Albania*, Rev. Ed., Antonia Young
95 *Singapore*, Stella R. Quah and Jon S. T. Quah
96 *Guyana*, Frances Chambers
97 *Chile*, Harold Blakemore
98 *El Salvador*, Ralph Lee Woodward, Jr.
99 *The Arctic*, H. G. R. King
100 *Nigeria*, Robert A. Myers
101 *Ecuador*, David Corkhill
102 *Uruguay*, Henry Finch with the assistance of Alicia Casas de Barrán
103 *Japan*, Frank Joseph Shulman
104 *Belgium*, R. C. Riley
105 *Macau*, Richard Louis Edmonds
106 *Philippines*, Jim Richardson
107 *Bulgaria*, Richard J. Crampton
108 *The Bahamas*, Paul G. Boultbee
109 *Peru*, John Robert Fisher
110 *Venezuela*, D. A. G. Waddell

111 *Dominican Republic*, Kai Schoenhals
112 *Colombia*, Robert H. Davis
113 *Taiwan*, Wei-chin Lee
114 *Switzerland*, Heinz K. Meier and Regula A. Meier
115 *Hong Kong*, Ian Scott
116 *Bhutan*, Ramesh C. Dogra
117 *Suriname*, Rosemarijn Hoefte
118 *Djibouti*, Peter J. Schraeder
119 *Grenada*, Kai Schoenhals
120 *Monaco*, Grace L. Hudson
121 *Guinea-Bissau*, Rosemary Galli
122 *Wales*, Gwilym Huws and D. Hywel E. Roberts
123 *Cape Verde*, Caroline S. Shaw
124 *Ghana*, Robert A. Myers
125 *Greenland*, Kenneth E. Miller
126 *Costa Rica*, Charles L. Stansifer
127 *Siberia*, David N. Collins
128 *Tibet*, John Pinfold
129 *Northern Ireland*, Michael Owen Shannon
130 *Argentina*, Alan Biggins
131 *Côte d'Ivoire*, Morna Daniels
132 *Burma*, Patricia M. Herbert
133 *Laos*, Helen Cordell
134 *Montserrat*, Riva Berleant-Schiller
135 *Afghanistan*, Schuyler Jones
136 *Equatorial Guinea*, Randall Fegley
137 *Turks and Caicos Islands*, Paul G. Boultbee
138 *Virgin Islands*, Verna Penn Moll
139 *Honduras*, Pamela F. Howard-Reguindin
140 *Mauritius*, Pramila Ramgulam Bennett
141 *Mauritania*, Simonetta Calderini, Delia Cortese, James L. A. Webb, Jr.
142 *Timor*, Ian Rowland
143 *St. Vincent and the Grenadines*, Robert B. Potter
144 *Texas*, James Marten
145 *Burundi*, Morna Daniels
146 *Hawai'i*, Nancy J. Morris and Love Dean
147 *Vietnam*, David Marr and Kristine Alilunas-Rodgers
148 *Sierra Leone*, Margaret Binns and Tony Binns
149 *Gabon*, David Gardinier
150 *Botswana*, John A. Wiseman
151 *Angola*, Richard Black
152 *Central African Republic*, Pierre Kalck
153 *Seychelles*, George Bennett, with the collaboration of Pramila Ramgulam Bennett
154 *Rwanda*, Randall Fegley
155 *Berlin*, Ian Wallace
156 *Mongolia*, Judith Nordby
157 *Liberia*, D. Elwood Dunn
158 *Maldives*, Christopher H. B. Reynolds
159 *Liechtenstein*, Regula A. Meier
160 *England*, Alan Day
161 *The Baltic States*, Inese A. Smith and Marita V. Grunts
162 *Congo*, Randall Fegley
163 *Armenia*, Vrej Nersessian
164 *Niger*, Lynda F. Zamponi
165 *Madagascar*, Hilary Bradt
166 *Senegal*, Roy Dilley and Jerry Eades
167 *Andorra*, Barry Taylor
168 *Netherlands Antilles and Aruba*, Kai Schoenhals
169 *Burkina Faso*, Samuel Decalo
170 *Indonesia*, Sylvia C. Engelen Krausse and Gerald H. Krausse
171 *The Antarctic*, Janice Meadows, William Mills and H. G. R. King
172 *São Tomé and Príncipe*, Caroline S. Shaw
173 *Fiji*, G. E. Gorman and J. J. Mills
174 *St. Kitts-Nevis*, Verna Penn Moll
175 *Martinique*, Janet Crane
176 *Zaire*, Dawn Bastian Williams, Robert W. Lesh and Andrea L. Stamm
177 *Chad*, George Joffé and Valérie Day-Viaud
178 *Togo*, Samuel Decalo
179 *Ethiopia*, Stuart Munro-Hay and Richard Pankhurst
180 *Punjab*, Darshan Singh Tatla and Ian Talbot
181 *Eritrea*, Randall Fegley
182 *Antigua and Barbuda*, Riva Berleant-Schiller and Susan Lowes with Milton Benjamin
183 *Alaska*, Marvin W. Falk
184 *The Falkland Islands*, Alan Day
185 *St Lucia*, Janet Henshall Momsen

186 *Slovenia*, Cathie Carmichael
187 *Cayman Islands*, Paul G. Boultbee
188 *San Marino*, Adrian Edwards and Chris Michaelides
189 *London*, Heather Creaton
190 *Western Sahara*, Anthony G. Pazzanita
191 *Guinea*, Margaret Binns
192 *Benin*, J. S. Eades and Chris Allen
193 *Madrid*, Graham Shields
194 *Tasmania*, I. Kepars
195 *Prague*, Susie Lunt
196 *Samoa*, H. G. A. Hughes
197 *St. Helena, Ascension and Tristan da Cunha*, Alan Day
198 *Budapest*, Mátyás Sárközi
199 *Lisbon*, John Laidlar
200 *Cambodia*, Helen Jarvis
201 *Vienna*, C. M. Peniston-Bird
202 *Corsica*, Grace L. Hudson
203 *Amsterdam*, André van Os
204 *Korea*, J. E. Hoare

Contents

Preface

Angkor, *Angkar* and *angko* are the three quintessential themes of Cambodian history. *Angkor* refers to the glory of the past civilization that flourished from the 9th to the 14th centuries; *Angkar* (the Organization) was the name used by the Khmer Rouge and its leaders during its reign of terror from 1975-79; and *angko* means harvested rice – the staff of life for the majority of Cambodians. The literature on Cambodia is dominated by the first two of these three themes, but it is the third that has the most meaning for Cambodians, although precious little has been written about it. How to select around 1,000 items to reflect adequately the balance of these three themes was the challenge I faced in compiling this bibliography.

In accordance with the format of the World Bibliographical Series, I have set out to select from across all fields of knowledge English-language (or Western European-language) items likely to be of interest to the ubiquitous or perhaps imaginary 'informed general reader', giving emphasis to publications likely to be available in a good public library. The final selection derived from two further intentions: to reflect what has been published on Cambodia; and to provide some greater depth of coverage in areas of my own interest and expertise, in order to give a distinctive character to the bibliography.

If the bibliography were to mirror the proportions of the existing corpus of Cambodiana, then it would contain little outside that which concerned colonial scholars, particularly, of course, those from France, who overwhelmingly concerned themselves with archaeology, religion, philology and literature, and whose approach was dominated by what may today be regarded as orientalism. Even when balanced by my other two concerns, these kinds of works still make up a substantial proportion of the bibliography, as it would be a great pity to exclude items of considerable scholarship in an attempt to create an artificial equilibrium of subject coverage. The sections on science and technology, and on economics, for instance, are in contrast relatively slight.

I have gone into greater depth in several areas reflecting my own fields of interest. One is that of contemporary politics and history, as I have had the privilege and the pain of observing the country at first hand as it has moved from the People's Republic of Kampuchea, through the State of Cambodia and the installation of the United Nations Transitional Authority in Cambodia (UNTAC) to the re-establishment of the Kingdom of Cambodia, both before and after the July 1997 upheavals. I have given particular attention to the issue of the crimes of the Khmer Rouge as I am the Consultant on Documentation to Yale University's Cambodian Genocide Program. Another area of emphasis in the bibliography is the representation of Cambodia in contemporary Western literature and film. It is generally quite hard to find such material, given the tendency for libraries not to assign subject headings to fiction, but there can be few better ways to prepare oneself for a visit, or to gain an understanding of a country and its myths and mysteries as well as those others have fabricated about it than through its image as depicted in literary or visual works. Finally, I have given perhaps somewhat more than expected coverage of materials relating to libraries and archives and publishing in Cambodia as since 1987 I have been actively participating in the attempt to rebuild that sector, particularly at the National Library of Cambodia.

Arrangement

In all, the bibliography has thirty-eight sections. By far the largest is History, which contains some 174 items, divided into period subsections. Clearly, many items potentially fall into more than one section. In instances where the content is highly significant in more than one category, the item has been given a main listing under one subject category such as History, and then cross-referenced in another, such as Law. In the main I have preferred to place items according to subject rather than form hence a bibliography on refugees is primarily noted and annotated under Overseas Populations, and a legal dictionary under Law, and also given a summary listing under the form section, such as Bibliography or Languages, respectively. Where a book has appeared in a film version, or vice versa, it appears both under the chapter relevant to its subject and under Films, as is the case also for the few items (such as newspapers) that also have an Internet version, since these are considered to be distinct and independent forms of publication (although several items whose Internet version was found only after the manuscript was in press have the electronic version noted in the annotation to the print edition). Most items in the bibliography are given several listings in the subject index to assist the reader in finding related works that may have been placed in sections other than that first consulted.

Where possible, the latest edition of a work has been listed, with a note indicating its earlier publication details, including its original title for translations, or in cases where the title has changed.

Methodology

There are two ways of going about the task of compiling a bibliography. One, as described by David Marr in his introduction to the *Vietnam* volume in this series, is to go from the known, in his case from his own bookshelves through ever-widening circles of libraries, bibliographies and references. I chose the opposite approach of first building a database of as many bibliographic records as I could obtain (beginning with some 4,000 from the Australian Bibliographic Network), and selecting from these the items to include. Individual items were assigned one of five orders of priority as well as a subject classification and, over the course of the project, they rose into, and fell from, the category one priority that eventually formed the bibliography. It was surely my years in information management and database development that led me to take this approach, of particular appeal because it would lead to a significant pool of records (more than 6,000 by the project's end) to be given to the National Library of Cambodia to assist in its own cataloguing efforts.

The second aspect of the project involved finding the items provisionally assigned priority one. Some were close at hand on my own bookshelves or in libraries in Sydney, chiefly the University of Sydney, the State Library of New South Wales and the University of New South Wales. A large number were to be found in Canberra in the National Library of Australia and the Australian National University. A further subset was obtained for me on inter-library loan or consulted at more distant locations, particularly the École Française d'Extrême-Orient (EFEO – French School of Far Eastern Studies) and Sorbonne libraries in Paris and Cornell University in Ithaca, New York, as well as the National Library of Cambodia and National Museum of Cambodia in Phnom Penh. Finally, some books were lent to me by friends and colleagues.

Only after tracking down the items was I able to confirm or reject their provisional status, and decide whether to proceed with preparing annotations. Some items were later discarded from the bibliography even though an annotation had been prepared, because it was felt that a different, especially a more recent, publication was more appropriate for inclusion.

Acknowledgements

Many people have helped me during the course of the preparation of this bibliography, and they deserve my heartfelt thanks. Some alerted me to significant titles; some helped track them down; and others drafted annotations particularly in their areas of expertise. Serge Thion worked like a dervish over the early days of 1997 with a number of French titles. His knowledge of things Cambodian and of French attempts to describe and analyse them over more than 100 years, combined with his acerbic wit and firm opinions, have, I think, given something special, particularly to the anthropological and early historical accounts. Peter Annear contributed particularly on development and economics; Sally Low on politics and human rights; and my daughter Mina (Minnie O'Shea) focused on art, but ranged widely through travel, maps and miscellanea. Bronwen Phillips combed indexes of film and literature to find many more titles than I had been aware of, and she looked at their plots through postmodern eyes. Peter Arfanis and Rosanna Barbero tracked down and reported on a number of titles from Phnom Penh, and Rosanna also carried out the initial categorization of items by subject and by priority for inclusion. James Gerrand and Milton Osborne both lent me precious items from their own collections.

On the production side Nereida Cross wove her usual magic with database structure, importing of records and formatting the output. Rahmat Fattahi pulled the subject index into shape, while Barbara Law helped with the author and title indexes, as well as tracking down some Internet sites. My mother, Olwen Tudor Jones, spent weeks on end proofreading and correcting the manuscript, as well as translating French titles and typing up the Chronology. The administrative staff of the School of Information, Library and Archive Studies of the University of New South Wales (Christine McBrearty, Jennie Lynch and Ray Locke) helped me meet the many pressing deadlines associated with a publication of this nature. The final version owes much to the assiduous and thoughtful editing of Anna Fabrizio at ABC-Clio, particularly in the struggle to achieve consistency in style and form.

I am grateful to Ben Kiernan for his writings on 20th-century Cambodia and for his comments on the first draft of the Introduction and Chronology, as well as recommending me as the compiler of this volume to Bob Neville, Editor of the World Bibliographical Series.

Warren Horton, Director-General of the National Library of Australia, and Warwick Cathro, Assistant Director-General, gave permission for me to download the Australian Bibliographic Network records without charge on the understanding that the final database would be given to the National Library of Cambodia as part of the NLA's Regional Cooperation Program.

Some items in the bibliography have annotations gathered from another source, and I would like to extend my thanks for permission to include them. Some fifty entries, mainly works covering Southeast Asia in general, are drawn from the *Vietnam* (1992) volume of the World Bibliographical Series by David G. Marr, with the assistance of Kristine Alilunas-Rodgers, by kind permission of the author. Such items are indicated in the present volume by the following citation, '[David G. Marr with Kristine Alilunas-Rodgers]'. In addition, twenty-three film synopses from various film publications are included. These are acknowledged separately in the relevant entries.

All bibliographers must surely owe a debt to those who have gone before. I am no exception here, and must pay specific homage to Henri Cordier, Paul Boudet, Rémy Bourgeois, Raymond Nunn, Donald Clay Johnson, Mary Fisher, Zaleha Tamby, John Marston and Ronald Thomas as well as to others working in this field today, such as Raoul Jennar, Walter Aschmoneit, Jacques Népote, and Christiane Rageau. Three major bibliographies on the literature of genocide were immensely helpful in identifying items relevant to Cambodia. They were Israel W. Charny's *Holocaust and genocide bibliographic database* (Jerusalem: Institute on the Holocaust and Genocide, 1994. version 2.2), Samuel Totten's *First-person accounts of genocidal acts committed in the twentieth century: a critical annotated bibliography* (q.v.) and the Cambodian Genocide Data Bases (q.v.). A special mention should be made of Raoul Jennar's *Les clés du Cambodge* (The keys to Cambodia) and David Chandler's *History of Cambodia* (qq.v.), which were invaluable reference tools, especially for the Chronology and Introduction.

Introduction

Cambodia – the very name has a resonance, conjuring images either of its ancient artistic wonders or of the horrors it suffered during the 1970s under the Khmer Rouge genocide and the US bombing. In the early 1990s the blue helmets and white vehicles of the United Nations operation there formed a constant staple for Western television news.

The country often described in the 1950s and 1960s as an 'oasis of peace' has gone through eight different changes of government since it gained independence from France in 1953 – most of them associated with violence and trauma. This introduction was written in the aftermath of the events of 5-6 July 1997, in which the streets of Phnom Penh saw scenes of battle as tanks and B-40s were brought in against strongholds of FUNCINPEC, the political party of then First Prime Minister, Prince Norodom Ranariddh.

The area known as Cambodia or Kampuchea (which is just a more literal way of transcribing the same Khmer word into roman script) has been inhabited by human beings since at least the Stone Age. Pebble implements have been found dating back at least 600,000 years, but relatively few prehistoric sites have been found.

The site of Laang Spean .(in present-day Battambang Province) shows habitation from around 6,800 BC, by people who may be termed 'Hoabinhian' (after the province in the north of Vietnam where many such sites have been found). By around 4,290 BC the people at Laang Spean were making pottery with cord markings. From around 3,000 BC the fertile river areas along the Mekong and the Tonle Sap and the Khorat Plateau (in what is now Thailand) were home to hunters and gatherers who practised simple forms of agriculture, and who probably form one of the ancestral lines of modern Khmers. Rice was grown and some animals domesticated, with wild game, fish and shellfish also eaten. It had long been thought that these people may have migrated into the area from southern China or northern Vietnam, bringing agriculture with them, but this is by no means certain. Another view suggests that agriculture and later bronze (by at least 1,500 BC) came rather from the southern, coastal areas, and that these local cultures should be considered to have developed rather more autonomously. Three sites near Melou Prey (in present-day Preah Vihear Province) have revealed surface finds of bronze implements, but their dates are not yet known, and Samrong Sen (in present-day Kompong Thom Province) has shown evidence of habitation by around 1,230 BC, and there is some basis to conclude that the Angkor area may have been occupied around the same time.

In any event, it is clear that by the middle of the last millennium BC a number of separate settlements had developed into substantial social aggregations, viewed as the earliest cities, with major earthworks and moats suggesting defensive formations or water reservoirs, especially around Phimai (in present-day Thailand) and in eastern Cambodia, especially near Mimot (in present-day Kompong Cham Province). These proto-urban settlements of over 1,000 people had a degree of social differentiation and stratification as economic development provided some surplus. This process led to the formation of the earliest states, with officials, soldiers and rulers, and to the emergence of writing.

The next significant phase in Cambodian development is what were termed 'Indianized states' by the French scholar George Coedès. The degree to which these states were influenced by Indian culture or by local indigenous values and patterns is a matter of some debate, as is the question of whether it was a process best described as domination, borrowing, or rather convergence. Whatever the case it is clear that these religious and linguistic influences from India were pervasive in the court culture of a number of city states by the beginning of the Christian era, and that they resulted from trade contacts rather than conquest. Regretfully, historical sources are few and far between, and principally consist of accounts by Chinese travellers from as early as 225 AD – so much so that it is even the Chinese names by which these polities are known!

The first historical sources on Cambodia relate to the entity known by China as Funan, centred in the Mekong Delta. The major site excavated in the early 1940s by Louis Malleret is Oc Eo, nowadays in Vietnam about 25 kilometres from the coast, but presumably on the seaboard at the time of its heyday as the major port of Funan, which may derive from the old Khmer word 'bnam', meaning mountain, giving rise to expectations that the capital may be found around Banam in present-day Prey Veng Province. Another significant site now being excavated by Cambodian and US archaeologists is that of Angkor Borei (Ancient Angkor) in present-day Takeo Province. An important feature of Funan was its extensive irrigation system extending for more than 100 kilometres. The extent of the kingdom is uncertain. The Chinese sources termed it an empire, but there is now growing scholarly opinion that it may have consisted of a series of somewhat autonomous city states. Funan sent tribute missions to the Chinese courts from 243 AD until the 6th century (including live rhinoceros and elephants) by which time increasing numbers of local stone inscriptions start to provide an indigenous historical record, if only of the activities of royalty. Trade missions were despatched throughout Southeast Asia and South Asia as well as to China.

It would seem that around the 6th and 7th centuries Funan declined in power, with its place taken by Chenla (again we have only the Chinese name) somewhat further north, as the centre of gravity moved up the Mekong River into what is today southern Laos. Chinese sources suggest that Chenla split into two states – Water (Lower) Chenla and Land (Upper) Chenla – in the 8th century, but others suggest that, as with Funan, Chenla should be regarded more as a series of rather more independent city states, with those of the delta area by the 9th century falling under attack from what was referred to as 'Java', but which may more likely have been by Malay seafaring powers.

Early in the 9th century Jayavarman II (c.770-c.834) became the first identifiable Khmer king and, although he left no inscriptions himself, was later regarded as the founder of Angkor and was said to have asserted Khmer unity and independence from 'Java' in 802 as he established his capital of Mahendraparvata in the Kulen hills in the north of present-day Siem Reap Province and established the devaraja (so-called god-king) cult.

The glorious period of Angkor lasted for six centuries, during which time the capital moved numerous times, hundreds of temples were constructed and extensive urban settlements with a complex water management system based on reservoirs over 6 kilometres in length were established. In the 12th century the ruler Suryavarman II (1113-c.1150) constructed the magnificent Angkor Wat and extended his kingdom in many directions, imposing his own nominee on the Cham throne to the east in present-day central Vietnam. The Chams retaliated, however, and sacked Angkor in 1177, although they were driven out again in 1183 after several years of fighting led by Jayavarman VII (1181-c.1218), who went on to reign in even grander style than his predecessors and to assert his dominion over the Chams and into present-day Laos, Vietnam, Thailand and even Malaysia. He presided over a massive building programme including the city of Angkor Thom with walls measuring 3 kilometres on each side, and magnificent temples such as the Bayon, Ta Prohm and Preah Khan, a series of hundreds of rest houses and hospitals and a network of roads throughout the kingdom.

Following Jayavarman's death in 1218 Angkor began its decline. Various theories for this decline have been advanced, including: over-extension and reliance on slavery; the emergence of Theravada Buddhism based on austerity and salvation through individual effort in contrast to the great monumental tradition of Mahanya Buddhism; a shift to a related dynasty in Ayudhya (in present-day Thailand); the collapse of the irrigation system and ecological and environmental change; or the need to move to a capital with easier access to the sea to engage in growing external trade. Whatever the cause, Khmer decline gave the opportunity for relative Thai and Lao ascendancy, although even up to the early 15th century reports were made of wealth and pomp, and tributes continued to be sent to China. While 1431 has traditionally been regarded as the 'fall' of Angkor following a Thai siege and conquest, it is now thought more likely that for some reason (as discussed above quite possibly for its sea access) in the early 15th century the Khmer kings decided to relocate their capital down to the Chatomuk (Four Faces) junction of the Tonle Sap and Mekong rivers near present-day Phnom Penh, with a population that included Malays, Chinese and Chams as well as Khmers. With the rise of Theravada Buddhism the practice of building grand religious monuments and temples ceased, and there are far fewer material remains of this time.

Cambodian history from this period of several centuries has been regarded as the country's 'dark ages' because of this relative dearth of both monuments and documentary sources, compared with previous and subsequent historical periods. In recent years scholarly attempts have been made to fill in the blanks, principally on the basis of Chinese and Thai accounts, but also of folklore, such as the tale of the old woman Penh who found a piece of driftwood resembling the Buddha image at the confluence of the Mekong and Tonle Sap rivers, and there constructed a hill (phnom) on which to build a temple – the place becoming known as Phnom Penh (Penh's Hill) and the temple, which still remains at the heart of the city, as Wat Phnom (Hill Temple).

Various accounts are given of successions and disputes between rulers and chieftains of different polities within Cambodia over the next two centuries, with the centre of power around Phnom Penh or Oudong (just upstream along the Tonle Sap). At the end of the 15th century King Chan was deposed by forces from the east (in what is today Vietnam), and then sought refuge and support from the west (in today's Thailand), returning with an army from Ayudhya to defeat his rivals. This marks the beginning of a pattern that persists even today in Cambodian politics, with leaders and political movements seeking assistance and intervention from Thailand or Vietnam in order to improve their weight in the Cambodian political balance of forces.

From 1512-15 Tome Pires wrote his *The suma oriental of Tome Pires: an account of the East, from the Red Sea to Japan, written in Malacca in 1512-1515*, translated and edited by A. Cortesao (London: Hakluyt Society, 1944. 2 vols. Reprinted, Nendeln, Liechtenstein: Kraus Reprint, 1967), which included the first European account of Cambodia, described as 'warlike'. In 1556 the Portuguese missionary Gaspar da Cruz wrote the first European eyewitness account of his year-long stay in Lovek, residence of the king on the Tonle Sap near Oudong, which incidentally makes no reference to Angkor, indicating its relative demise at the time. In *South China in the sixteenth century: being the narratives of Galeote Pereira, Fr. Gaspar Da Cruz, O.P. [and] Fr. Martin De Rada, O.E.S.A. (1550-1575)*, edited by C. R. Boxer (London: Hakluyt Society, 1953. xci, 388p.), he describes the country as having one-third of its able-bodied males belonging to the Buddhist monkhood or sangha, and as being under firm domination from the throne of King Chan. During this period Ayudhya's power weakened, partly in response to attacks from Burma, and Cambodian rulers began to mount forays extending their territory westwards, but attacks from Ayudhya and also from Laos in the north were also mounted into Khmer territory, with Lovek conquered by the Thais in 1594, and the Khmer king appealing to the Spanish government in the Philippines for assistance.

In the 1590s Spanish and other European traders and adventurers came to join the Asian foreign communities in Lovek, Phnom Penh and Oudong and more documentary reports of the period are to be found. The Spanish missionary San Antonio reported all kinds of precious wares – gold, silver, gems, silk, ivory and rare animals like elephant, buffalo and rhinoceros – and described the society reported as being split between the nobility and the slaves. No mention is made of the mass of rural rice farmers or of any artisans. In 1623 King Chey Chetta, who had married a Vietnamese (Nguyen) princess, allowed the Nguyen lords to establish a custom house at Prey Nokor, which later became known as Saigon. The growth of Saigon as a trading port was accompanied by settlement of Vietnamese peasants throughout the Mekong Delta (known still today by many Cambodians as Kampuchea Krom, or Lower Cambodia). By 1749, under military pressure from Nguyen forces, Cambodia ceded the remainder of the lower Mekong Delta, and the Chinese Mac family was appointed to govern this region from the town of Ha Tien.

In the last years of the 18th century Thai pressures on Cambodia intensified, and in 1772 their troops sacked Phnom Penh, burning it to the ground. In 1779 Prince Eng, then a boy only seven years of age, was placed on the throne at Oudong as a Thai protégé. A graphic demonstration of the level to which Cambodia had become subject derives from the fact that he was crowned in Bangkok in 1790, returning to rule from Oudong in 1794.

The tables were turned by his own son Ang Chan who moved allegiance from the Thai to the Vietnamese court in Hue, and in 1807 Vietnam even established a protectorate over Cambodia. Excavation of the Vinh Te canal in the Mekong Delta in 1817 using Cambodian forced labour left a memory of brutal exploitation of Cambodians by Vietnamese overlords, and was one of the precipitating factors behind an anti-Vietnamese uprising in 1820. In 1835 King Ang Chan died, and Vietnamese officials held a Vietnamese ceremony to install his second daughter, Princess Mei, to govern Cambodia as a Vietnamese protectorate. During this period many Vietnamese officials and colonists were brought into the country, creating a time-bomb that exploded in the 1970s.

The first half of the 19th century saw a further escalation of the tussle between Vietnam and Thailand for control of Cambodia, with intrigues and sallies into the western and eastern regions and then the virtual annihilation for some years of Cambodia as a separate state. Vietnam proclaimed direct rule in 1840, taking Princess Mei and her regalia to Saigon. In response Prince Ang Duong was brought back from Thailand and proposed to become king. Subsequently, in 1846 a joint Vietnamese-Thai protectorate over Cambodia was proclaimed. King Ang Duong's coronation in 1848 inaugurated the modern Cambodian dynasty, restoring Theravada Buddhism as the state religion.

Other even stronger external forces were already poised in the wings, however, and in the form of scholars, missionaries and explorers began a concerted penetration of the country. France, which by this stage was finalizing its control over the length and breadth of Vietnam, saw further opportunities in neighbouring Cambodia. In 1850 the French missionary Charles-Emile Bouillevaux visited Cambodia, including Angkor. His account, published in France in 1858, attracted great public attention. In 1853 King Ang Duong sent presents to Emperor Napoleon III offering 'humble homage'. From 1858-60 the French naturalist and explorer Henri Mouhot recorded in words and detailed drawings the temples of Angkor. In 1863 Admiral Bonard visited Angkor, and Prince Norodom signed a treaty with French naval envoys in Oudong, under which protection by a French Resident (Ernest Doudart de Lagrée) was exchanged for timber concessions and mineral exploration rights.

At the same time, in an attempt to secure its own position versus the French colonial power Thailand strengthened its ties to Cambodia's western provinces of Battambang, Sisophon, Siem Reap, Melou Prey, Tonle Repou, Kompong Svay and Pursat, whose rulers at this time gave their allegiance more directly to Bangkok than to the relatively weak Cambodian king in Oudong. At this time of crisis a new king, Norodom, was crowned in 1864, and the following year he took some 10,000 people from Oudong to proclaim a new capital at Phnom Penh. The impending domination by France was not welcomed by all, and anti-French protests led by Achar Sva and Pou Kombo lasted for several years in various parts of the country.

Cambodia felt the full force of the French notion of 'mission civilisatrice' (civilizing mission). The new capital Phnom Penh was to be built in grand style, with boulevards and quays, bridges and public buildings including a Royal Palace combining Thai and European styles. Scholarly endeavours were pursued with some vigour. As early as 1866 the Mekong Exploration Commission was established, with a significant expedition headed by Doudart de Lagrée and Francis Garnier setting off to trace the river's course upstream to its source. Unfortunately it turned out to be far too difficult a path to yield the expected water trade route into China. However, their forays into Siem Reap were particularly fruitful, and the plaster casts and fragments of sculptures from Angkor were shown at the Universal Exhibition in Paris in 1867, before being transferred to a permanent colonial exposition. Ten years later explorer Louis Delaporte took back to France some seventy major sculptures as well as plaster casts, which were exhibited at the Universal Exposition of 1878 at the Trocadéro in Paris, before forming part of the magnificent Guimet Museum collection of Khmer art. French architect Lucien Fournereau visited Angkor in 1887-88, making detailed architectural drawings from which engravings were made, as well as the first photographs, and taking back more sculptures and casts.

In 1867 a *modus vivendi* was reached between France and Thailand with the signature of a treaty under which Thailand renounced suzerainty over Cambodia but retained the seven northwestern provinces.

Anti-French uprisings continued, with the half-brother of the King, Prince Si Votha, mounting a notable rebellion in 1876. In 1884 King Norodom surrendered by treaty many administrative, judiciary, financial and commercial powers to a French Resident-General. Rebellions organized by Si Votha continued until 1887.

By 1887 French administrative control was becoming firmly entrenched. The Indochinese Union was established over Cambodia and the three parts of Vietnam, with Laos incorporated six years later. In 1889 the first French Resident-Superior was appointed to the

Protectorate of Cambodia and the following thirty years saw a series of administrative, social and cultural measures to shore up the basis for France's economic domination of the country. A royal ordinance of 1897 defined and circumscribed the powers of the council of ministers. Slavery was abolished, and royal authority was weakened *vis-à-vis* the French Resident-Superior.

The great French scholarly institution of oriental studies, the École Française d'Extrême-Orient (EFEO – French School of Far Eastern Studies), was founded in 1898 in Hanoi and three years later in Phnom Penh. Mechanical publishing and printing was introduced – firstly for official publications (1890) and later for newspapers (1899) and books (1908). A font of Khmer characters was cast in France (1884), though it was not until several years later that the government printing office was established, and the first Khmer typewriter developed (1909).

From 1902-11 French military officers Étienne Aymonier and Étienne-Edmond Lunet de Lajonquière carried out the first stage of the task of making an inventory of Khmer monuments both in Cambodia and Thailand. Henri Dufour and Charles Carpeaux prepared a detailed monograph on the Bayon, including a photographic record of the bas-reliefs, which required the clearing of undergrowth and fallen masonry. In 1905 the EFEO established an archaeological museum in Phnom Penh to exhibit some of their finds which had not been sent to France.

In 1906 King Sisowath succeeded Norodom, who had died some two years before, and the Sisowath period saw the zenith of colonialism in Cambodia, symbolized by a series of expositions in France and the 1906 highly successful Royal Ballet tour to France, led by the King himself, which captured the imagination of many including Auguste Rodin. In 1907, under great pressure from France, Thailand returned to Cambodia the provinces of Battambang, Sisophon and Siem Reap, and the Angkor complex was placed under the control of the EFEO, which established a permanent archaeological mission and conservation programme. More than 200 European tourists visited the complex that year, marking the beginning of a phenomenon that continues today. A series of schools and other educational and cultural institutions were established, including a School of Administration and a Pali religious school (1914), the latter being part of the French attempt to sever the relationship between the Cambodian and Thai sangha. 1920 saw the foundation of the Albert Sarraut Museum (the future National Museum of Cambodia) and the School of Fine Arts (later to become the Royal University of Fine Arts) under the inspiration of George Groslier, and the following year witnessed the foundation of what was to become the National Library and National Archives of Cambodia.

Recounting the documented achievements of the colonial project masks the fact that French rule was never accepted by many Cambodians and that outright rebellion was an accompanying contrapuntal theme. Notable incidents included those led by Vises Nheou in Battambang and Kampot (1908-09) and by Ouch in the regions of Kompong Svay and Baray (1913-16). Imposition of tax controls and forced labour in 1916 resulted in protests and petitions involving tens of thousands, perhaps 100,000 peasants flocking to Phnom Penh to present their grievances to the king. Abuses by the colonial administration led to the assassination of Félix Louis Bardez, Resident of Kompong Chhnang, renowned for his harshness in enforcing payments of taxes.

The period of grand colonial splendour really started its decline at the end of King Sisowath's reign. His successor, King Monivong, was crowned in 1928 just on the eve of the Great Depression. With the rise of fascism and the Second World War following the Depression, France was never again in a position to play an imperial role, despite an attempt to do so in the early 1950s.

Some important milestones in the development of institutions that had political and cultural ramifications for Cambodia need mentioning here. The Buddhist Institute was established in 1930, and in the same year the Indochinese Communist Party (ICP) was formed. In 1936 the first Khmer-language newspaper *Nagaravatta* (Pali for Angkor Wat) was founded by Son Ngoc Thanh and Pach Chhoeun. It favoured moderate reforms, and was defined by its publishers as 'nationalist-socialist'. The same year saw the opening of Sisowath High School, the first lycée in Cambodia. In 1938 the first Khmer novel, in prose form, *Suphat* by Rim Kin, was published.

The outbreak of war in Europe had immediate repercussions in Cambodia. Under a 1940 Franco-Japanese treaty Indochina was placed under Japanese military control with the French Vichy government retaining responsibility for administration and security. France was forced once again to cede to Thailand the province of Battambang and parts of Siem Reap, Kompong Thom and Stung Treng (though the Angkor complex was left under Cambodian control). In 1941 King Monivong died and a young Prince Norodom Sihanouk was chosen by the French governor-general to succeed to the throne. While nationalist revolts led by Buddhist monks and intellectuals surfaced, Sihanouk defended the position of the Vichy French until 9 March 1945, when a Japanese *coup de force* overturned French administration in Indochina, with locals appointed to replace colonial officials. King Norodom Sihanouk proclaimed the sovereignty of Cambodia as part of the Japanese 'Greater East Asia Co-prosperity Sphere'. On the defeat of

Japan, however, Sihanouk declared the loyalty of Cambodia to France and approved French plans to establish an Indochinese Federation within the French Union. In contrast, Ho Chi Minh proclaimed Vietnam's independence on 2 September.

Nationalist forces, particularly in Vietnam, were too strong for such a neo-colonial plan to succeed, however, and eventually at the end of 1953 France began transferring powers to a fully independent Cambodia. During this transitional period resistance forces fighting for nationalist and communist ideals entrenched themselves in many areas of the country. In 1951 the ICP was dissolved and an independent Khmer Revolutionary People's Party (KPRP) was established in Cambodia.

The strength of the nationalist and communist forces in Vietnam, both against the French and later against the United States, in the First and Second Indochina Wars had, and indeed continue to this day to have, a profound effect on the development of Cambodia's history. In 1954 they forced out the French after the fall of Dien Bien Phu. The Geneva Conference Accords confirmed the independence of Cambodia. Unlike Vietnam and Laos no recognition or territory was given to the Cambodian rebel forces. Over 1,000 Cambodian communists and sympathizers retreated and regrouped in Hanoi.

Within a year of his country's formal independence, in 1955 Sihanouk abdicated in favour of his father Norodom Suramarit in order to play a more direct political role, through the Sangkum Reastr Niyum (Popular Socialist Community). Through a combination of repression against his opponents, attraction of mass support through populist projects of development and playing a role on the world stage as a champion of neutrality and non-alignment, Sihanouk managed to stay on top of a deteriorating political and economic situation. However, he was unable to resist the impact of the war on the country, and in 1962 the South Vietnamese air force began the bombing of Cambodian villages with outright US interventions and bombing to follow.

Resistance forces grew in strength, especially after 1967 with the outbreak of the Samlaut rebellion (in Battambang Province), with those declaring a communist allegiance – termed by Sihanouk 'Khmers Rouges' (Red Khmers) – in the ascendancy. The Communist Party of Kampuchea (CPK – which had developed from the KPRP) fell under the control of Saloth Sar, later known as Pol Pot. He broke the previous close relations with the Vietnamese Communist Party and followed a direction inspired by the Chinese Cultural Revolution. In opposition to Sihanouk's attempts at economic reforms, such as the nationalization of banks and foreign trade, and the renunciation of US military and economic aid, right-wing forces gained the ascendancy in the military and civilian administration. In March 1970 during his absence overseas Sihanouk was ousted in a pro-US military coup led by Lon Nol and Sirik Matak.

Sihanouk and Saloth Sar met almost immediately in Beijing and announced the formation of the FUNK (National United Front of Kampuchea) and the GRUNK (Royal National United Government of Kampuchea). In May US-South Vietnamese forces launched an invasion of Cambodia. The Lon Nol government steadily lost control of the countryside despite (or perhaps in large part because of) the massive US bombing in which over half a million tonnes were dropped, particularly during the B-52 carpet bombing of 1972-73. By early 1975 an estimated two million refugees had fled to Phnom Penh seeking safety from the bombing and the fighting. Much of the countryside was laid to waste and many farm animals had been killed. Rice was not planted and the refugee population was almost entirely dependent on food aid sent in by the United States – up the Mekong from Saigon until that route was cut, leaving only an airbridge to Phnom Penh for the last months.

On 17 April 1975 the Khmer Rouge took Phnom Penh and immediately put into place the policies that were to characterize the three years, eight months and twenty days of their régime. The urban population was driven out of the capital and towns. Within days attacks were mounted on islands under Vietnamese control, and about 250,000 (of 400,000) residents of Vietnamese origin started to flee the country – almost all of those who did not leave in these early days were subsequently killed. All identified members of the Republican government and military chiefs were executed. Sihanouk was confirmed as Chief of State and the GRUNK became nominally the government of Democratic Kampuchea (DK), while in fact policies were determined by the CPK Party Centre, known to the people only as Angkar (the Organization).

In March 1976 Sihanouk was deposed as Chief of State to be replaced by Khieu Samphan. In the one and only meeting of the People's Assembly, Saloth Sar (under the name of Pol Pot) became leader of the government. The S-21 prison and interrogation centre (later known as Tuol Sleng) was established at a Phnom Penh high school, as the central point of a nationwide network of terror. Perhaps 15,000 people were sent to Tuol Sleng but only 7 are known to have survived. Many thousands of the prisoners were meticulously photographed and documented and their 'confessions' extracted before being executed at Choeung Ek (later known as one of the major 'killing fields') on the outskirts of the city.

In 1977 the DK government launched attacks across both its eastern and western borders into Thailand and Vietnam where the earlier raids were escalated into large-scale attack on Vietnamese towns, combined with a campaign to exterminate all Vietnamese in Cambodia, all Khmers speaking Vietnamese and all Khmers having relationships with Vietnamese. In September in a five-hour speech before departing to China, Pol Pot revealed that Angkar was a manifestation of the CPK. Five Vietnamese divisions entered Cambodia in a show of strength, following which diplomatic relations with Vietnam were broken.

In 1978 tensions between Cambodia and Vietnam broke into outright war. DK mounted significant attacks into Vietnamese territory. Pol Pot purged the Eastern Zone, accusing its Secretary So Phim of treason and collusion with Vietnam. Hundreds of thousands of Cambodians in the Eastern Zone fled to Vietnam and testified to atrocities committed by the Khmer Rouge. Radio Hanoi then called on Cambodians to rebel against the Khmer Rouge régime. Persecution reached ever closer into the heart of Angkar with the arrest and execution of the vice-prime minister, and ministers of communications and industry. The United Front for the National Salvation of Kampuchea (Renakse), led by Heng Samrin, was established and was immediately recognized by the governments of Vietnam, Laos and the Soviet Union. On 25 December the Vietnamese army launched a large offensive supported by the Renakse forces sweeping through the eastern part of Cambodia and meeting little resistance.

On 7 January 1979 the last DK train from Phnom Penh pulled out from the station with Ieng Sary on board as the Vietnamese army and Renakse forces entered the city. The People's Republic of Kampuchea (PRK) was formed, with Heng Samrin as President and Hun Sen as Minister for Foreign Affairs, and the Kampuchean People's Revolutionary Party (KPRP) as the governing party.

Hun Sen's government entered upon the huge task of rebuilding the country ostracized and isolated from the West for having come to power with the help of Vietnam. Finally, after the collapse of the Soviet Union and the other Eastern European nations which had been giving financial support, and the withdrawal of Vietnamese forces in 1989, Hun Sen was forced to sign the Paris Peace Agreements in 1991, recognizing the Khmer Rouge as a legitimate political participant in the UN-supervised elections. The United Nations Transitional Authority in Cambodia (UNTAC) was formed, deploying 20,000 personnel and $2.8 billion over the next 19 months and concentrating its scrutiny on the State of Cambodia administration. Despite having signed the Agreements, the Khmer Rouge did not comply with a single one of their conditions, boycotting the elections, and remaining with its armed forces intact.

Elections were held in May 1993 in which FUNCINPEC gained the greatest share of the vote (forty-five per cent), followed by the CPP (thirty-eight per cent). Hundreds of irregularities were reported and the CPP refused to accept UNTAC's declaration of the poll. A breakaway challenge threatened secession of the eastern provinces under CPP control, but was dropped when Sihanouk brokered a coalition government between FUNCINPEC and CPP. The First Prime Minister, Prince Norodom Ranariddh, came from the party winning the majority of votes and Second Prime Minister, Hun Sen, from the party that controlled most of the armed forces, police and civil service. This dual structure was echoed down the line in the ministries, in provincial government and in the armed forces, where generals commanded their own troops almost independently, as before. With the adoption of the new constitution on 23 September 1993 King Norodom Sihanouk was restored to the throne.

This uneasy coalition between Ranariddh and Hun Sen prevailed for nearly four years, but the tensions between the two men and their parties were always close to the surface and rose periodically into open hostility. Very little legislation was passed by the National Assembly, and the Constitutional Commission was not even established. Rifts within FUNCINPEC and the BDLP, some say fanned by the CPP, resulted in the ousting of leading figures Sam Rainsy, Norodom Sirivudh (FUNCINPEC) and Son Sann (BLDP).

Money has flowed into the towns, particularly to the capital city, but what has flourished are enterprises of little social value – hotels and bars, car and mobile-phone dealers – financed in part no doubt by the rape of the country's precious timber and gem resources. In the countryside there has been little improvement, and many of the poorest people have lost the few social and economic supports they were able to rely upon during the 1980s.

Corruption and political violence have continued to provide the constant backdrops to Cambodia's recent history. At least four opposition journalists were assassinated and on 30 March 1997 a grenade attack on an opposition rally led to the deaths of at least twelve people. Skirmishes between personal bodyguards and forces loyal to Ranariddh and Hun Sen erupted briefly several times before breaking into outright warfare in early July 1997 in which First Prime Minister Norodom Ranariddh was ousted.

Two political forces outside the government continued to exert their power over it through the four years past and even to this day. On the one hand stands King Norodom Sihanouk. Despite brokering the Ranariddh-Hun Sen coalition, he has stood back from day-to-day political involvement, in fact spending little time in the country as he receives medical treatment in Beijing. However, he retains what may be seen as rather a reserve power and from time to time he has hinted at using it while giving oblique comments on events as they unfold. He endorsed the delegation to the 1997 United Nations General Assembly of the new Hun Sen-Ung Huot coalition government, but at the same time has said he continues to regard his son Ranariddh as First Prime Minister.[1]

The other outside power is that of the Khmer Rouge. One year after the Ranariddh-Hun Sen government was formed, the National Assembly voted to outlaw the Khmer Rouge and to offer amnesty to those who wished to join the government. Over the next three years many thousands of soldiers, sometimes in whole units, crossed over, mostly being more or less integrated into the Royal Cambodia Armed Forces. At the same time government offensives were mounted and some gains made, although the Khmer Rouge forces continued to control many areas of the country, especially in the north and west, and to mount kidnapping and harassment raids into government-held areas. In late 1996 Ieng Sary, Khmer Rouge senior figure in the west around Pailin, broke with those in the north around Anlong Veng. In June 1997 it was the turn of the Khmer Rouge in Anlong Veng to come into the limelight. Ranariddh announced that Pol Pot was to be handed over for trial and that Khieu Samphan wanted to play a political role in the elections. As perhaps their final joint action, both prime ministers wrote to the UN Secretary General asking for an international tribunal to be established to try Pol Pot.

The July events overtook these moves, at least for the time being, and a new First Prime Minister, Ung Huot, representing FUNCINPEC, was endorsed by the National Assembly on 6 August. The National Assembly also stripped Ranariddh of his parliamentary immunity and Hun Sen has said that if Ranariddh returns to Cambodia he will be jailed and tried for his role in the events leading up to the July fighting.

The new government that emerged on the rout of the FUNCINPEC armed forces has Second Prime Minister Hun Sen of the former socialist Cambodian People's Party playing the dominant role. Although the government still includes FUNCINPEC, it marks a new balance of political forces after the collapse of the problematic coalition that came to government through the Paris Peace Agreements and the 1993 election.

It seems hard to imagine that, nearly twenty years after the overthrow of their genocidal régime, the Khmer Rouge still deals many of the cards in Cambodia. The July 1997 change of government was

[1] For the official justification by the victorious parties for their actions see *White paper: background on the July 1997 crisis – Prince Ranariddh's strategy of provocation* (Ministry of Foreign Affairs and International Cooperation. Phnom Penh: Ministry of Information, 1997. 27p.).

precipitated by manoeuvrings to make military and political gains by winning over Khmer Rouge factions.

First Prime Minister Ranariddh fled the country on the eve of the shoot-out, and afterwards appeared in Washington, New York and Paris, voicing the intention of mounting a resistance in conjunction with various military and political figures who spent the best part of the 1980s in the resistance on the Thai border. But it very soon became evident that Ranariddh's forces were mounting joint military moves in alliance with the remaining Khmer Rouge forces from Anlong Veng in the north of the country making them a significantly more substantial force. Perhaps more significant than the military moves though was the political and economic fallout from the July events. The United States cut its aid to Cambodia in response to what it termed Hun Sen's '*coup d'état*' and it is leading a campaign once again to deny representation in the United Nations General Assembly by the government in control inside Cambodia. In September 1997 the Credentials Committee voted to leave the Cambodian seat vacant, and the International Monetary Fund decided to suspend its assistance.

Are we seeing a return to the isolation of the 1980s, or will the new coalition prove strong enough to cope with the country's economic and social problems; to turn to the tasks of reconstruction and development; and to gain domestic and international credibility?

The new government has to grapple with appalling poverty, perhaps nine million land-mines and with the Khmer Rouge and Ranariddh's forces still fighting in the northwest of the country, as well as a reimposition of international ostracism. Fragile social and economic institutions and continuing warfare, hunger and disease are Cambodia's prevailing characteristics in the late 1990s as in so many centuries past.

Chronology

c.6800 BC	Emergence of 'Hoabinhian' culture in Laang Spean (Battambang).
c.4200 BC	Development of cord-marked pottery at Laang Spean.
c.3000 BC	Settlement along the Mekong and Tonle Sap rivers by people growing dry rice and domesticating animals.
c.1500 BC	Bronze artefacts in use in Melou Prey (Preah Vihear) and Samrong Sen (Kompong Thom).
c.500 BC	Proto-urban settlements, especially around Phimai (now in Thailand) and Mimot (Kompong Cham) which developed into early states, showing social differentiation.
150 AD	Rise of the polity known as Funan, centred in the Mekong Delta region, with canals, brickworks and advanced artefacts discovered at Oc Eo (now in Vietnam), Banam (Prey Veng) and Angkor Borei (Takeo). Rather than a unified kingdom Funan is a collective term for a number of smaller entities.
225 AD	First Chinese accounts of Funan.
243 AD	First tribute missions from Funan to China.
357 AD	Growth of Hindu-Brahman religion and Sanskrit writing system in Funan, two of many indicators of trade and cultural contact with India.
500 AD	Drainage canals developed into irrigation systems in Funan, with probable development of wet rice cultivation.
	A Siva cult thrives, perhaps on the mountain of Ba Phnom (Prey Veng, once considered to be the ritual centre of Funan). By now Buddhism is also practised in Funan alongside localized religious cults, with worship of ancestor spirits (*neak ta*) to whom offerings are still made today.

590 AD	Funan declines, and is thought to have given way to what may be collectively termed two new polities along the Mekong – Upper (Land) Chenla and Lower (Water) Chenla.
611 AD	Earliest dated Khmer-language stone inscription so far found.
613 AD	Earliest dated Sanskrit-language stone inscription so far found.
802 AD	Jayavarman II establishes the kingdom of Angkor (from the Sanskrit word *nagara* meaning 'city' or 'state'), declaring himself a 'universal monarch', and promoting the *devaraja* (often translated as 'god-king') cult.
879 AD	Construction of the Preah Ko brick temple in Roluos, east of Angkor, ushering in the Roluos style of architecture, including the Bakong temple mountain, the first stone temple in Cambodia.
900 AD	Construction of the Bakheng temple mountain marks the founding of the royal city of Sri Yasodharapura, on the site of the Angkor complex.
950 AD	Khmer armies invade Champa on the coast of central Vietnam.
1113-50	Construction of Angkor Wat (dedicated in 1131 by Suryavarman II), now thought to have been built according to specific cosmological measurements representing time and space.
1128	Suryavarman II of Cambodia sends Khmer and Cham armies and ships against Vietnam.
1145	Cambodia invades Champa and occupies its capital until driven out four years later.
1177-78	Cham invasion by land and water in which the fleet, commanded by Jaya Indravarman IV, sails up the Mekong and catches Angkor by surprise, killing the monarch and pillaging the city.
1181	Coronation of Jayavarman VII. He had constructed temples, highways and rest houses throughout a wide area north of the Tonle Sap (Great Lake) into present-day Thailand, Laos and Vietnam. The Bayon was the central point of his city of Angkor Thom, and other fine temples from this time include Preah Khan and Ta Prohm.
1190	Jayavarman VII of Cambodia defeats Cham forces and moves to annex Champa, accomplished in 1203.

1207	Jayavarman VII sends Cambodian troops, with Burmese and Siamese contingents, against Vietnam. Subsequent conversion of his kingdom to Theravada Buddhism following increasing interaction with the Thai and Mon peoples, being one possible cause for the abandonment of practices symbolic of the Angkor period, such as inscriptions, stone temples, a Hindu-oriented royal family and irrigation.
1218	Death of Jayavarman VII.
1220	Khmer forces leave Champa, restoring the throne to the Cham prince Angsaraja.
1296-97	Chou Ta-Kuan, an envoy from China, stays in Angkor and records everyday life and administrative practices.
1431	Traditionally given as the date for the 'fall' of Angkor, with Khmer centre of power moving southwards to the Chatomuk (Four Faces) junction of the Tonle Sap and Mekong rivers near present-day Phnom Penh, with a population that included Malays, Chinese and Chams as well as Khmers. Thai attacks were mounted on Angkor and wars between Thais and Khmers raged until the 19th century, with few documentary sources remaining. Some historians say that Khmer populations also moved west to Ayudhya in modern Thailand.
1512-15	Tome Pires wrote the first European account of Cambodia.
1556	Gaspar da Cruz wrote the first European eyewitness account of his year-long stay in Lovek, then the residence of the king on the Tonle Sap near Oudong, which makes no reference to Angkor.
1560	Dated inscriptions reappear at Angkor, showing some continuity of occupation and reconstruction.
1587	Thai siege of Lovek, with Khmer king appealing to the Spanish government in the Philippines for assistance.
1590s	Spanish and other European traders and adventurers come to join the Asian foreign communities in Lovek, Phnom Penh and Oudong.
1594	Thais capture Lovek.
1623	King Chey Chettha, who had married a Vietnamese (Nguyen) princess, allows Vietnam to establish a custom house at Prey Nokor, which later became known as Saigon.

1640s	The growth of Saigon as a trading port.
	Vietnamese peasants begin to settle and develop irrigated ricefields principally in unoccupied and swampy land throughout the Mekong Delta.
1650-1700	Thai suzerainty outweighs that of the Nguyen over Cambodia.
1749	Under military pressure from Vietnamese (Nguyen) forces, Cambodia cedes the remainder of the lower Mekong Delta though it is still even today known by many Cambodians as Kampuchea Krom (Lower Cambodia). The Chinese Mac family is appointed to govern this region from the town of Ha Tien.
1772	Thai sacking of Phnom Penh.
1779	Prince Eng, only seven years old, placed on the throne at Oudong as a Thai protégé.
1790	King Eng crowned in Bangkok, returning to Oudong in 1794 to restore the monarchy.
1806	Coronation of King Ang Chan, son of Eng, who moved allegiance from the Thai to the Vietnamese court in Hue.
1807	Vietnam establishes a protectorate over Cambodia.
1811-20	Assaults on Cambodian territory from Thai and Vietnamese forces.
	Excavation of the Vinh Te canal in the Mekong Delta in 1817 left a memory of brutal exploitation of Cambodians by Vietnamese overlords, and led to an anti-Vietnamese uprising in 1820.
1835	Death of King Ang Chan and investiture by Vietnamese officials in a Vietnamese ceremony of his second daughter, Princess Mei, to govern Cambodia as a Vietnamese protectorate with the introduction of many Vietnamese officials and colonists.
1836-46	Numerous anti-Vietnamese uprisings and Thai intrigues. The Vietnamese response was to take over direct rule in 1840, taking Princess Mei and her regalia to Saigon. Prince Ang Duong was brought back from Thailand and proposed to become king.
1846	Establishment of a joint Vietnamese-Thai protectorate over Cambodia.
1848	Coronation of King Ang Duong inaugurates the modern Cambodian dynasty.
	Theravada Buddhism restored as the state religion.

1850	French missionary Charles-Emile Bouillevaux visits Cambodia, including Angkor. His account is published in France in 1858.
1853	King Ang Duong sends presents to Emperor Napoleon III offering 'humble homage'.
1858-60	French naturalist and explorer Henri Mouhot records in words and detailed drawings the temples of Angkor.
1860	Death of King Ang Duong.
1862	Franco-Vietnamese treaty signed.
1863	French Admiral Bonard visits Angkor.
	Norodom assumes the throne and signs treaty with French naval envoys in Oudong, under which protection by a French Resident (Ernest Doudart de Lagrée) was exchanged for timber concessions and mineral exploration rights.
	The local rulers of the provinces of Battambang, Sisophon, Siem Reap, Melou Prey, Tonle Repou, Kompong Svay and Pursat at this time gave their allegiance more directly to Bangkok than to the relatively weak Cambodian king in Oudong.
1864	Coronation of King Norodom I.
	Anti-French protests led by Achar Sva and Pou Kombo last for several years in various parts of the country.
1865	The king and about 10,000 people leave Oudong and proclaim new capital at Phnom Penh.
	Construction of the Royal Palace combining Thai and European styles.
1866	Establishment of the Mekong Exploration Commission, with a significant expedition headed by Doudart de Lagrée and Francis Garnier. Their plaster casts and fragments of sculptures from Angkor are shown at the Universal Exhibition in Paris in 1867 and later transferred to a permanent colonial exposition.
1867	Franco-Siamese Treaty: Siam renounces suzerainty over Cambodia but retains the annexed provinces.
1876	Nationalist anti-French uprisings led by half-brother of the king, Prince Si Votha, continue into 1877 when Norodom accepts in principle some reforms, though never implements them.
1877	First round of French administrative changes pressed on Norodom.

	French explorer Louis Delaporte takes back to France some seventy major sculptures as well as plaster casts, which were exhibited at the Universal Exposition of 1878 at the Trocadéro in Paris, before forming part of the great Guimet Museum collection of Khmer art.
1884	King Norodom surrenders by treaty many administrative, judiciary, financial and commercial powers to a French Resident-General. Rebellions organized by Si Votha continue until 1887.
1887	Indochinese Union is established over Cambodia and three parts of Vietnam. Laos is incorporated six years later.
1887-88	French architect Louis Fournereau visited Angkor, making detailed architectural drawings from which engravings were made, as well as the first photographs, and taking back more sculptures and casts.
1889	Resident-Superior appointed over the Protectorate of Cambodia.
1890	First official publication printed in Cambodia, the *Annuaire illustré du Cambodge*.
1897	A royal ordinance defines the powers of the council of ministers and establishes five ministries. Slavery is abolished. Royal authority is weakened *vis-à-vis* the French Resident-Superior.
1898	Establishment of the École Française d'Extrême-Orient (EFEO – French School of Far Eastern Studies) in Hanoi.
1899	First newspaper published in Cambodia, produced by lithograph, *Le Petit Cambodgien*.
1900	A report drafted by Prince Yukanthor, son of King Norodom, describes abuses of French colonial administration and provokes a scandal known as the 'Yukanthor affair'. Yukanthor lives out his life in exile rather than apologise to his father.
1901	Establishment of the EFEO in Phnom Penh.
1902-11	French military officers Étienne Aymonier and Étienne-Edmond Lunet de Lajonquière begin the task of making an inventory of Khmer monuments both in Cambodia and in Thailand. Henri Dufour and Charles Carpeaux prepare a detailed monograph on the Bayon, including a

photographic record of the bas-reliefs, which require clearing of undergrowth and fallen masonry.

1904 Death of King Norodom.

1905 Establishment of an EFEO Archaeological Museum in Phnom Penh.

1906 Coronation of King Sisowath. The same year he leads a highly successful Royal Ballet tour to France, capturing the imagination of many, including Auguste Rodin.

1907 Franco-Siamese Treaty restores to Cambodia the provinces of Battambang, Sisophon and Siem Reap. A bilateral commission delineates for the first time the border between the two countries both on maps and on the ground.

The Angkor complex is placed under the control of the EFEO, establishing a permanent archaeological mission and conservation programme. More than 200 European tourists visit the complex that year.

1908 First printing of a Khmer literary text.

1908-09 Revolts organized by Vises Nheou in Battambang and Kampot.

1909 Publication of a Khmer translation of parts of the Buddhist *Tripitaka* text.

Introduction of the first Khmer typewriter but not widely used.

1912 Adoption of a Penal Code.

Pierre Loti writes the first European fiction set in Angkor in *Un pèlerin d'Angkor* (A pilgrim of Angkor).

1913 Unrest in the regions of Kompong Svay and Baray led by Ouch continue spasmodically until 1916.

1914 Foundation of what was to become the School of Administration. A Pali religious school opens in Phnom Penh.

1916 Imposition of tax controls and forced labour, resulting in protests and petitions, involving tens of thousands, perhaps 100,000 peasants flocking to Phnom Penh to present their grievances to the king.

1917 Opening of the first rice mill in Cambodia.

1920 Adoption of a Civil Code and a Code of Civil Procedure.

Foundation of the Albert Sarraut Museum (the future National Museum of Cambodia) and the

	School of Fine Arts (later to become the Royal University of Fine Arts) under the inspiration of George Groslier.
1921	Foundation of what was to become the National Library and National Archives of Cambodia.
1923	Clara and André Malraux visit Angkor, are arrested and tried for vandalizing and stealing sculptures from the newly revealed Banteay Srei temple, often regarded as the most beautiful of them all.
1924	Development of the Buddhist temple schools as a vehicle for modern education.
1925	Franco-Siamese Treaty of Friendship confirms the frontiers adopted in 1907.
	Abuses by the colonial administration lead to the assassination of Félix Louis Bardez, Resident of Kompong Chhnang, renowned for his harshness in enforcing payments of taxes.
1926	Foundation of the literary journal *Kampuchea Suriya*, dealing mostly with religious subjects though also serving as a vehicle for literature.
1927	Death of King Sisowath.
1928	Coronation of King Sisowath Monivong.
1930	Banteay Srei is totally dismantled and reconstructed – the first in Cambodia to be treated according to the Dutch anastylosis method used in Indonesia.
	Formation of the Indochina Communist Party (ICP).
	Establishment of the Buddhist Institute and laying of the first railway tracks in Cambodia.
1931	The Colonial Exposition at Vincennes, Paris, at which an almost life-size cardboard reproduction of Angkor Wat forms the central attraction.
1936	Popular Front electoral victory in France. Trotskyists and ICP members together mount campaign for an autonomous and representative Indochinese Congress.
	Foundation of the first Khmer-language newspaper *Nagaravatta* (Pali for Angkor Wat) favouring moderate reforms, defined by its publishers as 'nationalist-socialist'.
	Opening of Sisowath high school, the first lycée in Cambodia.
1937	Franco-Siamese Treaty reconfirms the 1925 Treaty.

1938	Publication of the first Khmer novel, in prose form, *Suphat* by Rim Kin.
1939	Proposal for division of administrative responsibilities along the maritime area between Cochinchina and Cambodia put forth by the Governor General of Indochina, expressly reserving the political question of delineation of the border.
1940	Following joint military operations between French and Thai forces, Franco-Japanese treaty places Indochina under Japanese military control with the French Vichy government responsible for administration and security. As a result of Japanese pressure France is forced to cede to Thailand Battambang and parts of Siem Reap, Kompong Thom and Stung Treng (though Angkor was left under Cambodian control).
	Death of King Monivong. Prince Norodom Sihanouk chosen by Admiral Decoux, the Vichy representative, to succeed.
1941	Sihanouk crowned king.
1942 (20 July)	Anti-French demonstration in Phnom Penh led by Buddhist monks and known as the 'umbrella war'.
	The newspaper *Nagaravatta* is shut down.
1943	The French Resident announces plans to romanize the Khmer alphabet. The plans are abandoned in 1945 after strong protests especially from the monkhood.
1944	Envoys representing General de Gaulle and the Free French are parachuted into Indochina by the British.
1945	On 9 March a Japanese *coup de force* overturns French administration in Indochina, with locals appointed to replace colonial officials.
	Norodom Sihanouk proclaims sovereignty of Cambodia as part of the Japanese 'Greater East Asia Co-prosperity Sphere'.
	On 15 August Japan surrenders. Sihanouk declares loyalty of Cambodia to France and approves French plans to establish Indochinese Federation within the French Union.
	Ho Chi Minh proclaims Vietnam's independence on 2 September.
1946	End of protectorate status for Cambodia which is granted limited autonomy but France retains control of defence and foreign affairs.

	Khmer Issarak (Free Khmer) groups lead unrest in the Siem Reap area.
	Constituent Assembly elections (first democratic elections ever held in Cambodia). Democratic Party wins absolute majority on a very moderate anti-colonial and modernizing platform.
	Return to Cambodia of western provinces occupied by Thailand since 1941.
	December bombing of Haiphong by France marks the real beginning of the First Indochina War which spilled over into Cambodia in the 1950s. Vietnamese respond by forming Vietminh guerrilla forces.
1947	Drafting of a constitution with Cambodia becoming a constitutional monarchy.
	Legislative elections result in another absolute majority to Democratic Party.
1949	Franco-Cambodian Treaty establishes Cambodia as an independent state associated with the French Union, described by Sihanouk as 'fifty per cent independence'. Cambodia states that it wishes to maintain as unresolved the question of territories annexed by the French colony of Cochinchina.
1950	US President Harry Truman approves $15 million in military assistance to the French in Indochina. By the end of 1950 Washington has already provided $150 million in military and economic aid.
	On 17 April the first congress of the Khmer resistance forms the Khmer Issarak Association or United Issarak Front, twenty-five years to the day before the Khmer Rouge take Phnom Penh. Assassination of Democratic Party leader Ieu Koeus.
1951	Dissolution of the ICP, but communist movements of Cambodia, Laos and Vietnam publish a common programme.
	Establishment of the Khmer People's Revolutionary Party (KPRP).
	Legislative elections. Democratic Party is still the major party but its support has fallen markedly.
1952	Growing influence of Issarak groups, many of which were close to the Vietminh. Soon half of the

country is unsafe for government troops. In a coup Sihanouk dismisses the Democratic Party government and assumes full powers for three years with political and military support from France.

1953 Sihanouk promulgates a decree declaring the nation in danger and dissolves the National Assembly. Debut of 'Royal Crusade for Independence'. Sihanouk confers the regency upon his father and departs for France.

Gradual transfer of powers from France to Cambodia (August-November).

1954 Fall of Dien Bien Phu.

Geneva Conference Accords confirm the independence of Cambodia. Unlike Vietnam and Laos no recognition or territory is given to the rebel forces led by the Issarak United Front.

Over 1,000 Cambodian communists and sympathizers regroup in Hanoi.

Creation of the National Bank of Cambodia.

Creation of Southeast Asia Treaty Organization (SEATO) in Manila, designed largely to counter communist successes in Indochina.

1955 Norodom Sihanouk abdicates in favour of his father Norodom Suramarit and creates the Sangkum Reastr Niyum (Popular Socialist Community).

Bandung Conference.

American-Cambodian military assistance accord.

Legislative elections in which Sangkum wins every seat and in which opposition newspaper editors are arrested.

Cambodia is admitted to the United Nations. Sihanouk refuses Cambodian membership in SEATO.

1956 Promulgation of a series of important constitutional reforms, including the right to vote for women, and the election of an assembly in each province and in the capital.

Opening of the Royal Administrative School.

Visit of Sihanouk to China, Soviet Union and Czechoslovakia.

Chinese-Cambodian Declaration of Friendship and aid. First official visit of Chou En Lai.

1957	Neutrality of Cambodia proclaimed.
1958	Legislative elections. Women vote for the first time. Electoral campaign slanted against the leftist Pracheachon (People's) Party, after the Democratic Party collapsed under pressure from Sihanouk. The Sangkum retains every seat.
	Establishment of diplomatic relations with the People's Republic of China.
1959	Opening of the international airport at Pochentong, Phnom Penh, with construction financed by France.
	Plot against Sihanouk by Dap Chhuon, governor of Siem Reap, exposed and Chhuon assassinated. The United States, Thailand and South Vietnam were somewhat implicated in this and several other plots.
	Opening of the Phnom Penh-Sihanoukville Highway financed by the United States. Provincial assemblies are suspended and have never been re-established.
1960	South Vietnam claims a number of coastal islands.
	Opening of the port of Sihanoukville constructed with French finance.
	Death of King Suramarit. Sihanouk refuses the Crown and declares a National Assembly with Queen Kossamak representing the Cambodian dynasty.
	Sihanouk is chosen by referendum as Head of State.
	The underground KPRP holds its Second Congress at which it changes its name to the Workers Party of Kampuchea (WPK), and elects Tou Samouth as Party Secretary, followed in rank by Nuon Chea and Pol Pot.
	Sihanouk presents to the United Nations General Assembly a plan to create a neutral zone in Southeast Asia.
1961	Sihanouk launches a plan for village community development. He condemns colonialism, imperialism and racism.
1962	The first, and so far the only, census records a population of 5,740,115.
	Legislative elections. The Sangkum retains every seat and is in fact the only contestant.
	Decision of the International Court of Justice to restore the temple of Preah Vihear (occupied and claimed by Thailand) to Cambodian sovereignty.

Disappearance and assassination of Tou Samouth, leader of WPK.
South Vietnamese air force bombs Cambodian villages.

1963 Congress of the clandestine WPK. Saloth Sar (later known as Pol Pot) assumes the position of Secretary General, and brings his own group into the leadership (Ieng Sary, Nuon Chea, Son Sen, Vorn Veth and Chhit Choeun, also known as Mok), sidelining those more sympathetic to Vietnam. Saloth Sar and Ieng Sary take over underground resistance in Kompong Cham where they are under the protection of Vietnamese communists in an area code-named 'Bureau 100'.
Sihanouk announces economic reforms, such as nationalization of banks and foreign trade, and renounces US military and economic aid.

1964 US Congress passes Gulf of Tonkin resolution, giving President Johnson extensive power to act in Southeast Asia. Government protests against incursions across Cambodian borders by South Vietnamese forces supervised by American officers, using napalm and heavy armaments, and by the US air force. Security Council convenes to discuss Cambodian complaints.
Inauguration of the Khmer-Soviet Technical Institute, built with aid from USSR.
Visit of Sihanouk to Peking results in promise of significant Chinese military aid and an undertaking by China to support Cambodia in the event of external aggression.
Creation of four new universities.
Inauguration of an Olympic stadium and sporting complex in Phnom Penh.

1965 First Conference of the Peoples of Indochina in Phnom Penh.
Breaking of diplomatic relations with the United States.
Saloth Sar, Keo Meas and other leading communists leave 'Bureau 100' for Hanoi, going by foot along the Ho Chi Minh trail. In Hanoi they meet with those who had regrouped there following the 1954 Geneva Accords. Saloth Sar spends two months in Beijing and Pyongyang.

A secret Chinese-Cambodian military treaty is signed by which the government of Cambodia undertakes to welcome and protect Vietnamese communist forces in frontal regions, and allow passage of matériel from China destined for Vietnamese combatants.

Another secret accord between Sihanouk and the Vietnamese communists allows the Cambodian army to retain ten per cent of military aid transitting through the port of Sihanoukville.

US military authorities authorized to attack Cambodian territory. The first US combat troops arrive in South Vietnam.

1966 The Asia Foundation office in Phnom Penh is closed down after denunciation by Sihanouk as being an agent of US imperialism.

Beginning of Soviet military aid.

The WPK changes its name to the Communist Party of Kampuchea (CPK) and moves its headquarters from 'Bureau 100' to the province of Ratanakiri.

Pol Pot determines that his Vietnamese allies are in fact the greatest enemy, and embarks on a policy of secretly disposing of those who had been close to them.

Charles de Gaulle makes a grand tour with Sihanouk, speaking at a mass rally at the Olympic stadium in Phnom Penh, and calling on the United States to withdraw from Vietnam.

Legislative elections. In spite of a violent press campaign, Khieu Samphan, Hou Yuon and Hu Nim are re-elected but the Right still has a large majority with Lon Nol named as President of the Council of Ministers. Sihanouk forms a counter-government and coins the expression 'Khmers Rouges' (Red Khmers) to designate Cambodian communists.

1967 Sihanouk goes to France for two months. In his absence Lon Nol institutes a brutal method of rice collection by the army, paying to the peasants only a third of the price on the open market. Peasant uprisings in the south of the province of Battambang (the Samlaut rebellion) lasting four to five months.

Permanent office of the South Vietnamese Resistance National Liberation Front (NLF) established in Phnom Penh.

Suppression of all newspapers with exception of four dailies under the control of the Ministry of Information.

Khieu Samphan, Hou Yuon and Hu Nim all leave the city to join the resistance after being denounced by Sihanouk for having provoked the Samlaut rebellion.

1968 Peace talks open in Paris between representatives of North Vietnam and the United States.

CPK attack on government post in Battambang province celebrated by the Khmer Rouge as the beginning of armed struggle. Simultaneous rebel attacks in six provinces with tens of thousands of villagers joining the rebels.

Opening of an airport and a university in Battambang.

1969 President Nixon announces the first US troop withdrawals from South Vietnam under the policy of 'Vietnamization' of the war.

Establishment of the Provisional Revolutionary Government of the Republic of South Vietnam (PRG).

First bombardment of Cambodia by American B-52s marks the beginning of a fourteen months' secret bombardment known as 'Operation Menu'.

Diplomatic relations are officially re-established with the United States. US Air Force planes spray defoliants over 85,000 hectares in Kompong Cham.

Cambodia becomes a member of the International Monetary Fund.

Petrol refinery and beer brewery established in Sihanoukville.

1970 On 18 March Sihanouk ousted during his absence overseas in pro-US military coup by Lon Nol and Sirik Matak. National Assembly then votes to strip him of the office of Chief of State.

Sihanouk and Saloth Sar meet in Beijing and announce the formation of FUNK (National United Front of Kampuchea) and the GRUNK (Royal National United Government of Kampuchea).

In May US-South Vietnamese forces launch an invasion of Cambodia, leading to massive demonstrations in the United States and the shooting of

	four students at Kent State University. International conference in Jakarta calls for withdrawal of all foreign troops from Cambodia. South Vietnamese aircraft destroy University of Kompong Cham.
	The United States supplies military equipment to the government of Lon Nol to the value of US$7.5 million.
	On 9 October Lon Nol proclaims the Khmer Republic, and then launches Operation Chenla I military campaign, but the weak government army is routed by the resistance, aided by seasoned Vietminh and North Vietnamese Army forces. FUNK announces increasing control of the country (fifty per cent by October, seventy per cent by December).
1971	CPK commits one of its first-known large-scale massacres in which all of the villagers who had sheltered Vietnamese communist soldiers were killed.
	The Chenla II campaign, the last large-scale military operation of the Khmer Republic, ends with government troops completely routed.
	Civil liberties and political rights are abolished.
	Lon Nol dissolves National Assembly.
1972	Presidential elections in which Lon Nol is elected with fifty-five per cent of the vote. Legislative elections.
	North Vietnamese commandos destroy the Chruy Changvar bridge in Phnom Penh (originally constructed as part of Japanese war reparations to Cambodia, not re-built until 1993 with Japanese aid).
1973	Signing of the Paris Accords on Vietnam (27 January) under which US ground troops are withdrawn, but bombing escalates massively.
	North Vietnamese progressively retire from the interior of Cambodian territory.
	Sihanouk visits zones controlled by FUNK.
	Start of agrarian collectivization in zones controlled by FUNK revealing authoritarian policies later to characterize Khmer Rouge rule of the entire country, including the abolition of money and the elimination of Sihanoukists and communists who had lived in Vietnam.

Beginning of American river and air bridge to bring food for isolated Phnom Penh, swelled with hundreds of thousands of refugees from the devastated countryside.
In August Neak Luong, south of Phnom Penh, is bombed by US B-52s with more than 400 civilians killed and wounded. US bombings are brought to an end – 539,129 tonnes were dropped on Cambodia.
Cambodian civil war continues as Lon Nol régime becomes increasingly isolated in Phnom Penh through Khmer Rouge offensives.

1974 Khmer Rouge gain control of the ancient capital of Oudong, just north of Phnom Penh. In an ominous portent of what was to happen after they gained control of the whole country the population was driven out of the town and all known military and civil administrators, teachers etc. were killed. After three-and-a-half months the Lon Nol forces retake the town.

1975 On 17 April the Khmer Rouge takes Phnom Penh and drives the urban population out of the city. Within days attacks are mounted on islands under Vietnamese control, and about 250,000 (of 400,000) residents of Vietnamese origin start to flee the country. All members of the Republican government and military chiefs are executed.
Sihanouk is confirmed as Chief of State and the GRUNK becomes the government of Democratic Kampuchea (DK).
Hou Yuon is killed, apparently after opposing the brutal evacuation of the cities and other radical measures announced at a May meeting of the CPK Party Centre, known to the people only as 'Angkar' (the Organization).
Queen Kossamak dies in Peking.
Return of Sihanouk to Phnom Penh to preside over a meeting of the Council of Ministers, but he is given no real role and is held under virtual house arrest.
In October French missionary François Ponchaud describes the horrors of the régime on the basis of refugee accounts and radio broadcasts.
Third national congress of CPK held in December.

1976	Promulgation of the Constitution of Democratic Kampuchea, and the second and last Council of Ministers presided over by Sihanouk. Formation of an Assembly of Representatives of the People of Kampuchea in which Pol Pot (Saloth Sar) is 'elected' as representing plantation workers. In March Sihanouk is deposed as Chief of State to be replaced by Khieu Samphan. In May a round of negotiations is held with Vietnam on the question of delineating the border, but the Cambodian side breaks off the talks. Pol Pot is interviewed by the Vietnamese press; relations seem cool but correct. In the one and only meeting of the Assembly, Pol Pot is named leader of the government. For a brief period of two weeks from 27 September Nuon Chea replaces Pol Pot as First Minister, but Pol Pot soon reassumes the leadership role. The S-21 prison and interrogation centre (later known as Tuol Sleng) is established at a Phnom Penh high school, as the central point of a nationwide network of terror. Perhaps 15,000 people enter Tuol Sleng but only 7 are known to survive. Many thousands of the prisoners are meticulously photographed and documented and their 'confessions' extracted before being executed at Choeung Ek (later known as one of the major 'killing fields') on the outskirts of the city.
1977	DK launches attacks against Thai villages, while raids across the Vietnamese border escalate into large-scale attacks on Vietnamese towns, combined with a campaign to exterminate all Vietnamese in Cambodia, all Khmers speaking Vietnamese and all Khmers having relationships with Vietnamese. Arrest and execution of Hu Nim, Minister of Information. DK rebuffs Vietnam's proposal to negotiate and, after a second large-scale attack, Vietnam retaliates, pushing DK troops back 16 kilometres inside Cambodia. Hun Sen attempts to flee to Vietnam but is repelled and with his companions hides for several months in the forest.

In September, in a five-hour speech before departing to China, Pol Pot reveals that Angkar is a manifestation of the CPK.

So Phim forms a dissident organization.

Five Vietnamese divisions enter Cambodia briefly in a show of strength. Diplomatic relations broken with Vietnam.

1978 DK mounts significant attacks into Vietnamese territory. Pol Pot purges the Eastern Zone, accusing its Secretary So Phim of treason and collusion with Vietnam. Hundreds of thousands of Cambodians in the Eastern Zone flee to Vietnam and testify to atrocities committed by the Khmer Rouge. Radio Hanoi calls on Cambodians to rebel against the Khmer Rouge régime. Pol Pot unleashes purges in the Eastern Zone, leading to the suicide of So Phim. Heng Samrin flees to Vietnam. Persecutions reach ever closer into the heart of Angkar with the arrest and execution of the vice-prime minister, and ministers of communications and industry.

Creation of the United Front for the National Salvation of Kampuchea (Renakse) led by Heng Samrin, which is immediately recognized by the governments of Vietnam, Laos and the Soviet Union.

On 25 December the Vietnamese army launches a large offensive supported by the Renakse forces sweeping through the eastern part of Cambodia meeting little resistance.

Assassination of Scottish Professor Malcolm Caldwell on a visit to Phnom Penh together with two US journalists.

1979 Departure of the last DK train from Phnom Penh on 7 January, with Ieng Sary on board as Vietnamese army and Renakse forces enter the city ending the three-year, eight-month and twenty-day régime of the Khmer Rouge.

Formation of the People's Republic of Kampuchea (PRK), with Heng Samrin as President and Hun Sen as Minister for Foreign Affairs, and the Kampuchean People's Revolutionary Party (KPRP) as the governing party. Adoption of a new constitution recognizing three sectors: state, co-operative and family.

Sihanouk sent abroad by Pol Pot and appears before the UN Security Council on behalf of DK condemning the Vietnamese invasion. Ieng Sary arrives in Peking and receives US$5 million to continue the struggle. The Security Council demands retreat of 'foreign troops', recognizing DK as the only legal government of Cambodia. The Vietnamese army reaches the Thai border, and the DK army retreats driving before it more than 100,000 civilians.

In Phnom Penh the Tuol Sleng interrogation centre is transformed into a genocide museum and a People's Revolutionary Tribunal is convened, declaring Pol Pot and Ieng Sary guilty of the crime of genocide, and condemning them to death in absentia.

The Khmer Rouge gains international support, with the UN General Assembly voting ninety-one for, twenty-one against and twenty-nine abstentions, to condemn the Vietnamese intervention, commencing an annual ritual by which for the next fourteen years the government effectively in control of the country was denied recognition and external legitimacy.

There are 650,000 refugees in 13 camps along the frontier of Thailand, sustained by international aid, and an emergency international aid programme brings some food relief inside Cambodia.

1980 The PRK starts the long process of rebuilding the social and economic infrastructure of the country. People return to the towns and new civil servants are recruited. Currency (the riel) is re-established. Re-opening of the Faculty of Medicine in Phnom Penh.

Recognition of the PRK by India – the only country outside the pro-Soviet bloc to do so.

Wind-up of the international humanitarian aid programme inside Cambodia but it continues in the border camps.

Vietnamese forces attack zones controlled by the Khmer Rouge and cross the Thai border.

1981 Sihanouk forms FUNCINPEC as his newest political vehicle within the anti-PRK resistance.

Inside Cambodia a National Assembly is elected, and adopts a new Constitution.

1982 On 22 June the Khmer Rouge, FUNCINPEC and KPNLF form the Coalition Government of Democratic Kampuchea (CGDK) which retains in place all DK diplomats and is accorded the Cambodian seat at the United Nations.

First announced partial withdrawal of Vietnamese troops.

Formation of a 'bamboo curtain' along the Thai border involving the mobilization of tens of thousands of soldiers, many of whom perish from malaria or mines.

Vietnam-Cambodian military pact signed.

1983 Second Vietnamese withdrawal of 10,000 troops.

The National Assembly of PRK receives report from a Research Committee that took testimony in all provinces of the country, indicating that more than three million died under the Pol Pot régime.

1984 On 20 May the first commemoration of the 'Day of Hatred' is held to pay homage to the victims of the Pol Pot genocide.

Hun Sen declares that Sihanouk and Son Sann (KPNLF) may play a political role if they return to Cambodia and recognize the Constitution. Vietnamese offensive against CGDK bases.

1985 Hun Sen named President of the Council of Ministers while retaining the Foreign Affairs portfolio. Hun Sen proposes a formula for the settlement of the conflict.

All CGDK bases within Cambodia wiped out in a Cambodian/Vietnamese offensive. US Congress approves $10 million in military and economic aid to the non-communist factions of the CGDK.

Conference of the ministers of foreign affairs of the three countries of Indochina accept that Jakarta should play an intermediary role in negotiations.

PRK institutes five-year military service.

Fifth Congress of the KPRP elects many non-communist delegates and formally recognizes the private economy.

1986 CGDK poses its conditions for a settlement of the conflict.

	Commercial and economic accord signed between PRK and USSR.
	Australian Minister for Foreign Affairs, Bill Hayden, proposes an international tribunal to try Pol Pot and other Khmer Rouge leaders. Opening in Phnom Penh of the Joint Australian NGO Office.
	The Khmer Rouge and Sihanouk forces announce a common military operation.
1987	Opening of telecommunications station in Phnom Penh, with Soviet aid, re-establishing telephone and telex links cut in 1975.
	PRK adopts a policy of national reconciliation with all except Pol Pot and his close associates.
	PRK announces a new five-point peace plan.
	First meeting between Sihanouk and Hun Sen outside Paris.
1988	The PRK announces that it would accept Sihanouk as head of state.
	Re-establishment of the University of Phnom Penh with eleven faculties.
	First Jakarta Informal Meeting among all Cambodian factions, later joined by ASEAN, Laos and Vietnam.
1989	On 29-30 April the National Assembly adopts a new Constitution. PRK becomes the State of Cambodia with a new flag and national anthem; capital punishment is abolished; Buddhism is declared the state religion; private property and the market economy are re-established; all reference to socialism is removed from the Constitution which declares the country to be neutral and non-aligned.
	Opening of the first Paris Conference on Cambodia presided over by France and Indonesia. After one month it is suspended without reaching agreement, particularly on the future role of the Khmer Rouge and the use of the term genocide to describe the DK period.
	Official withdrawal of the last remaining 26,000 Vietnamese troops.
	Australian Minister of Foreign Affairs, Gareth Evans, presents a new peace plan which proposes the presence of a transitional administration under the authority of the United Nations.

1990 US Secretary of State James Baker announces that Washington will withdraw all support from Cambodian opposition groups that include the Khmer Rouge.

A US Senate hearing reveals that Chinese aid to the Khmer Rouge has reached US$100 million, while US aid to the non-communist resistance has reached US$24 million.

Second Jakarta Informal Meeting. Creation of the Supreme National Council with six members from each side. At its first meeting Sihanouk is named as president and thirteenth member of the SNC, upsetting the parity arrangements.

The Khmer Rouge continue to mount attacks inside Cambodia including two on trains killing many people.

The Cambodian seat at the United Nations is left vacant but the DK delegation remains in New York.

The five permanent members of the Security Council (P5) discuss the Australian plan and draw up principles for negotiations involving a peace-keeping role for the United Nations. Intensive negotiations between all factions and interlocutors.

Informal Meeting on Cambodia in Jakarta discusses a now elaborated Australian plan, but the Cambodian parties stick to their previous positions.

1991 Military *coup d'état* in Thailand with its leader insisting on Khmer Rouge participation in any new government.

Beginning of ceasefire in Cambodia, but soon violated.

In Geneva the UN Commission on Human Rights for the first time recognizes genocide and crimes against humanity were committed in Cambodia.

China announces the cessation of military aid to the Khmer Rouge, but continues economic aid.

The SNC takes over the Cambodian seat at the UNGA and adopts an electoral plan which is proportional within each province.

Cambodia is represented at the World Bank for the first time since 1974.

KPRP changes its name to Cambodian People's Party (CPP), declaring adherence to democratic pluralism, a market economy and human rights.

	On 23 October the Cambodian Peace Agreements are signed in Paris by eighteen governments and members of the SNC.
	UN involvement over the next 19 months eventually deploys 20,000 personnel and $2.8 billion (including repatriation of refugees, but excluding individual country expenditures).
	Khieu Samphan returns to Phnom Penh but, after being violently attacked by a mob, he returns to Bangkok.
1992	US President Bush lifts the US commercial embargo on Cambodia in place since 1975.
	Yasushi Akashi is chosen to head the United Nations Transitional Authority in Cambodia (UNTAC).
	Human rights associations are established in Cambodia.
	Buddhism is officially restored as the state religion.
	The Security Council adopts an operational plan scheduling a total ceasefire by 31 May, demobilization of seventy per cent of armed forces by 30 September and elections before May 1993.
	The Khmer Rouge secretly decides not to implement its obligations under the Peace Accord.
1993	Elections held on 23 May throughout Cambodia except for zones held by Khmer Rouge. UNTAC announces that FUNCINPEC gained the greatest share of the vote (forty-five per cent), followed by the CPP (thirty-eight per cent). Hundreds of irregularities are reported and the CPP refuses to accept UNTAC's declaration of the poll.
	Prince Norodom Chakrapong and Defence Minister Sin Song stage a breakaway challenge announcing secession of the eastern provinces under CPP control.
	The secession is dropped when Sihanouk brokers a coalition government between FUNCINPEC and CPP, with major ministries to be run jointly. Inauguration of the new coalition government on 23 September between FUNCINPEC and the CPP, with Prince Norodom Ranariddh as First Prime Minister and Hun Sen as Second Prime Minister and restoring Norodom Sihanouk as king. The

opposing armies are nominally integrated as the Royal Cambodian Armed Forces (RCAF), but in effect continue to function as separate units under their existing commanders.

1994 In February government troops mount major attacks on Khmer Rouge bases and take Anlong Veng and Pailin, but they are soon lost again.

In April three foreigners are kidnapped on the road from Phnom Penh to Sihanoukville. Months of reports and demands for ransom ensue, but it is later discovered that they were murdered soon after capture.

In July Khmer Rouge forces attack a train travelling from Phnom Penh to Sihanoukville, killing thirteen Cambodians and kidnapping and later murdering three more foreigners.

The National Assembly passes a law declaring the Khmer Rouge to be an illegal organization, but offering a six-month amnesty for members surrendering to the government. The amnesty is in fact never terminated, and thousands of troops move across to join over the next three years mostly being more or less integrated into the RCAF.

The Khmer Rouge announce the formation of a parallel government.

Also in July the government moves against Prince Norodom Chakrapong and Defence Minister Sin Song, said to have been on the brink of attempting a second rebellion.

Chakrapong is allowed to go into exile, while Sin Song is jailed.

In October there is a cabinet shake-up in which Sam Rainsy (from FUNCINPEC) is sacked from his position as Finance Minister, following increasing tensions between himself and the CPP. Foreign Minister Norodom Sirivudh (also from FUNCINPEC) resigns in protest against Rainsy's sacking.

In December government troops mount major attacks on Khmer Rouge bases in four provinces.

1995 The Cambodian Genocide Program is established in January at Yale University to document the crimes of the Khmer Rouge, with principal funding by the

US government, establishing a Documentation Center in Phnom Penh and later making its findings available on the Internet.

In June Sam Rainsy is expelled from FUNCINPEC and then from the National Assembly. In October Sam Rainsy establishes the Khmer Nation Party with strong nationalist, even chauvinist and revanchist, views. Much of the KNP's activity is focused on building trade unions, particularly among the textile workers in Phnom Penh, independent of the government and especially the CPP, which had previously dominated the union movement. The government maintains that this party has no legal standing as the new electoral law has not yet been passed by the National Assembly.

In November former Foreign Minister Prince Norodom Sirivudh is sent into exile following charges arising from a tapped telephone call in which he is alleged to have threatened to kill Hun Sen.

1996 FUNCINPEC have a congress in March in which it is decided to build an independent profile for FUNCINPEC and not to face the 1998 elections in coalition with the CPP.

In May newspaper editor Thun Bunly (member of the KNP) becomes the fourth journalist to be slain since the 1993 elections.

In August Ieng Sary is announced as defecting from the Khmer Rouge with his political and military units intact. He is given an amnesty and retains control of the area around Pailin. The Khmer Rouge is now officially considered to remain intact only in the area around Anlong Veng, with Khieu Samphan and (Ta) Mok the most senior active cadres, but Pol Pot still in the wings. In October Ieng Sary forms a new political organization, the Democratic National Union Movement (DNUM). In November fighting erupts between FUNCINPEC and CPP troops in Battambang town, leading to an agreement that any troop movements would require specific authorization from both chiefs of general staff, and resulting in the withdrawal to Phnom Penh of the deputy governor who is considered to have acted provocatively.

In December an international cultural festival is held at Angkor Wat in which seven countries present dance sequences from their interpretation of the Ramayana.

1997 In February Ranariddh announces that FUNCINPEC will campaign with DNUM against the CPP in the next election, to be held before May 1998 in a new political coalition known as the National United Front (NUF), virtually recreating the old CGDK as an anti-CPP alliance.

In March British deminer Christopher Howes and twenty-six Cambodian deminers are kidnapped in Siem Reap.

On 30 March a grenade attack on a KNP rally outside the National Assembly building results in at least twelve people being killed and many wounded. Sam Rainsy escapes injury and immediately leaves the country, but one of his bodyguards is among those killed.

In June, as perhaps their final joint action, both prime ministers write to the UN Secretary General asking for an international tribunal to be established to try Pol Pot. There are reports that Pol Pot is being detained by some of his erstwhile followers, and will be handed over for trial.

Attempts are made by Ranariddh for Khieu Samphan to be rehabilitated and accepted into the government in exchange for Pol Pot. Ranariddh discusses the programme of the NUF with (Ta) Mok, and meets Khieu Samphan in Thailand. Several incidents of crossfire between FUNCINPEC and CPP troops erupt, particularly between bodyguards of the two prime ministers. Khieu Samphan announces the formation of a new National Solidarity Party which will support a FUNINPEC-NUF coalition. In Paris Sam Rainsy announces that a *coup d'état* is imminent. Ranariddh leaves the country. On 5-6 July Hun Sen mounts a military campaign against key FUNCINPEC offices and military strong points in Phnom Penh, alleging that Ranariddh had been infiltrating illegally imported arms and Khmer Rouge troops in order to strengthen his hand in the lead-up to the elections. FUNCINPEC is soon routed in the capital, with key military leaders retreating to the border area with Thailand around O'Smach and putting up some resistance, before resuming its longstanding but supposedly terminated military alliance with the Khmer Rouge. The Minister of Interior Ho Sok and other senior FUNCINPEC leaders are killed in Phnom Penh – some forty cases of extra-judicial execution are reported. Prince Ranariddh denounces Hun Sen from outside the country, and succeeds in getting some cuts in foreign aid and a delay in Cambodia's admission to ASEAN, which had been expected in late July. Foreign Minister Ung Huot from FUNCINPEC agrees to replace Ranariddh as First Prime Minister. This replacement is endorsed on 6 August by more than two-thirds of the National Assembly, including a majority of FUNCINPEC members. The National Assembly also votes ninety-eight to one to strip Ranariddh of his parliamentary immunity so that he could face prosecution for violations of law relating to the July events, although King Sihanouk presses for Ranariddh's right to participate in the elections.

On 25 July, the remaining Khmer Rouge at Anlong Veng invite US journalist Nate Thayer to witness and film a so-called trial of Pol Pot. After a short hearing, with denunciation by a range of people for recent crimes against the organization (but no mention of genocide), he is found guilty and 'condemned to life imprisonment'. Viewers see the old man saying nothing throughout the hearing, and watch him being led gently away by his captors.

Acronyms and Abbreviations

ADB	Asian Development Bank
ANS	Sihanoukist National Army
ARVN	Army of the Republic of Vietnam
ASEAN	Association of Southeast Asian Nations
CCC	Cooperation Committee for Cambodia
CDRI	Cambodian Development Resource Institute
CEDORECK	Centre for Documentation and Research into Khmer Civilization
CGDK	Coalition Government of Democratic Kampuchea
CIA	Central Intelligence Agency (US)
CICP	Cambodian Institute for Cooperation and Peace
CIDSE	International Cooperation for Development and Economic Solidarity
CNRS	National Centre for Scientific Research (France)
CPK	Communist Party of Kampuchea
CPP	Cambodian People's Party
DK	Democratic Kampuchea
ECAFE	Economic Commission for Asia and the Far East
EFEO	French School of Far Eastern Studies
ESCAP	Economic and Social Commission for Asia and the Pacific
FUNCINPEC	National United Front for an Independent, Neutral, Peaceful and Cooperative Cambodia
FUNK	National United Front of Kampuchea
GDP	Gross Domestic Product
GRUNK	Royal Government of National Union of Kampuchea
ICORC	International Committee on the Reconstruction of Cambodia
ICRC	International Committee of the Red Cross
IRRI	International Rice Research Institute
ISEAS	Institute of Southeast Asian Studies (Singapore)

Acronyms and Abbreviations

KPNLF	Khmer People's National Liberation Front
KPRP	Khmer/Kampuchean People's Revolutionary Party
MIA	Missing in Action
NCR	Non-communist Resistance
NGO	Non-government Organization
PDK	Party of Democratic Kampuchea
PRK	People's Republic of Kampuchea
SANGKUM	Sangkum Reastr Niyum (Popular Socialist Community)
SEARCA	Southeast Asian Regional Centre for Graduate Study and Research in Agriculture
SEAMEO	Southeast Asia Ministers of Education Organization
SIDA	Swedish International Development Cooperation Agency
SIL	Summer Institute of Linguistics
SNC	Supreme National Council
SOC	State of Cambodia
UNBRO	United Nations Border Relief Operation
UNDP	United Nations Development Programme
UNESCO	United Nations Educational, Scientific and Cultural Organization
UNFPA	United Nations Fund for Population Activities
UNHCR	United Nations High Commission on Refugees
UNICEF	United Nations International Children's Emergency Fund
UNIFEM	United Nations Development Fund for Women
UNRISD	United Nations Research Institute for Social Development
UNTAC	United Nations Transitional Authority in Cambodia
USAID	United States Agency for International Development
WHO	World Health Organization

The Country and Its People

1 **Area handbook for the Khmer Republic (Cambodia).**
Donald P. Whitaker, Judith M. Heimann, John E. MacDonald, Kenneth W. Martindale, Rinn-Sup Shinn, Charles Townsend. Washington, DC: U.S. Government Printing Office, 1973. xiv, 389p. bibliog. (DA Pam 550-50).

One of a series of handbooks prepared by Foreign Area Studies (FAS) of the American University, Washington, DC, first issued in 1956 under the title *U.S. Army area handbook for Cambodia*. The handbook was designed for use by 'military and other personnel', and seeks to provide a compilation of basic information on social, economic, political and military institutions and practices. Finished in 1972, in many areas its information has been superseded by later studies, especially considering the drastic changes in population, the military, and society which have occurred in Cambodia since then. However, it has continuing utility for comparative research. The outline and assessment of dissenting political and military formations is especially interesting. A three-page 'Country Summary' provides standard information on topography, population numbers, religion, imports and exports, and railways etc., while in-depth sections are devoted to social, political, economic, and national security information. The index indicates the broad range of details featured in the study, including the National Youth Association, restaurants, leftists, and Brahmanism, and the thirty-five-page bibliography, divided according to the chapter headings, is most useful.

2 **Beyond the nine dragons: discover the exotic cultures of the Mekong River.**
Allen W. Hopkins, photographs; John Hoskin, text; J. R. Nelson, the voice; Guy Viuya, scanning; Wendy Hiraoka, packaging design; and Bill Creighton, video on demand. Hong Kong: The Black Box Inc., [1995]. 1 CD-ROM disk for Windows or Macintosh. (Documentaries on Disc).

In this departure from the usual companion piece, The Black Box Inc. have taken some of the images and text from *The Mekong: a river and its people* (q.v.) to make something quite different. With voice, music and twenty minutes of video footage as well as additional textual material such as maps and historical prints, we are presented with a professional, attractive and easy-to-use CD introduction to the region, with fair coverage of Cambodia in the section entitled 'Great Water'. It is sold separately or bundled with the book (q.v.).

3 **Cambodge I & II.**

ASEMI, no. 13 (1982). 525p.; no. 15 (1984). 497p. special issues.

In an attempt to provide a new all-encompassing review of Cambodian scholarship, anthropologist Marie Martin commissioned articles from a wide range of French and (unusually) Cambodian specialists. Martin was part of the research group Langues et Civilisations de l'Asie du Sud-Est et du Monde Insulindien (Languages and Civilizations of Southeast Asia and the Indian Archipelagic World) led by Georges Condominas, which was responsible for publishing the *ASEMI* series. The quality varied considerably and the volumes were not widely circulated, but the effort is worth revisiting.

4 **Le Cambodge.** (Cambodia.)

Jean Delvert. Paris: Presses Universitaires de France, 1983. 127p. bibliog. (Que sais-je?, 2080).

Published as a volume in the popular 'Que sais-je?' (What do I know?) series, this book deserves notice for it is circulated widely. Jean Delvert, author of *Le paysan cambodgien* (q.v.), the definitive work on the Cambodian peasantry, covers a broad range of topics in this little tome including nature, history, rural life before 1970, society and recent history, providing a concise, yet valuable overview of Cambodia for the general reader. It is also a product of its times, and of the bitter political debate surrounding Cambodia, so that this general account of the country contains a strident attack on the People's Republic of Kampuchea – the government of the day. Delvert's introduction speaks of a scandal: 'The Khmer people risk biological disappearance. "Democratic Kampuchea" has been occupied since 7 January 1979 by the Vietnamese army and is led by a government installed by Hanoi . . .', a polemic pursued again in the final chapter.

5 **Cambodge.** (Cambodia.)

Photographs by Information Khmère, Claude Guioneaud, Raymond Cauchetier, Charles Meyer, SUN. Phnom Penh: Ministère de l'Information du Gouvernement Royal du Cambodge, 1962. 307p. bibliog.

Distributed throughout the world via Cambodian embassies in the 1960s, this coffee-table book may still be found in many public libraries, and so still may be a good port of call for a general reader wanting an impression of the country during the early 1960s. Brief entries on government, education, economy and so on are elucidated by tables, maps and copious black-and-white photographs.

6 **Cambodgien.** (Cambodian.)

G. H. Monod. Paris: Centre de Documentation et de Recherche sur la Civilisation Khmère, 1983. 95p. Originally published as *Le Cambodgien* (The Cambodian), Paris: Larose, 1931.

This is an eclectic attempt to describe the personality of 'the Cambodian' by a former French Resident, a Cambodian provincial governor. He discusses the mythical origins of the Khmer people, then provides a chapter on structures of the world as perceived in the framework of popular beliefs. In this basically Indic framework Hell has sixteen floors under our feet. The first floor is the best, for punishment there lasts only nine million years. The author then describes several families and life histories. Women's clothing, which we see now as traditional, is branded by him (writing in 1930) as a recent fashion imported from neighbouring Siam. He also explains how to dig a canoe from a tree trunk and enlarge it with the careful use of fire.

7 **Cambodia 1990.**
Cultural Survival Quarterly, vol. 14, no. 3 (1990). 88p. special issue.

This special issue of *Cultural Survival Quarterly* takes on considerable significance as a rare record of achievements in the cultural rebuilding of Cambodia after 1979. A number of recognized researchers (Chandler, Kiernan, Vickery, Ebihara), experts and NGO workers inside Cambodia and the refugee camps in Thailand, observe and document Cambodian culture in the broader sense of the word – from traditional ballet, music and literature to agriculture, religion and the traditional 'krama' scarf and even to politics, sociology and justice. The interviews with Prime Minister Hun Sen, Minister for Information and Culture Chheng Phon, and Mayor of Phnom Penh Thong Khon, are particularly valuable primary sources.

8 **Cambodia: a country profile.**
Grant Curtis. Stockholm: Swedish International Development Authority, 1989. [12], 194p. bibliog.

A report prepared for the Swedish International Development Authority with a foreword by Börje Ljunggren, Assistant Director General SIDA, Head of Department for Asia and Latin America. Although prepared in 1989, and containing a considerable amount of dynamic, and therefore superseded, data, this slim volume is still useful for a variety of people engaging in business or research in Cambodia. Grant Curtis was one of the handful of foreigners to spend a substantial amount of time in Cambodia – over two years before he produced this profile and then some years afterwards, in different positions with UN agencies and NGOs. Curtis is an acute observer and a careful researcher and his data is valuable both for the fact that it was compiled at a time when so little was available and also, in some ways all the more so, now that the accomplishments of the PRK period are downgraded or ignored to such an extent, as the myth of Cambodia's salvation and rebuilding by UNTAC becomes inscribed as the truth. The profile consists of clearly written chapters on history, politics and government, the economy, trade and finance, agriculture, rubber, forestry, fisheries, industry, transportation and communications, tourism, education, health, women, refugees, and international development assistance. Clear tables, with basic data on socio-economic conditions of 1989, a bibliography and several appendices complete the work.

9 **Cambodia: a portrait.**
Photography by Tim Hall, text by John Hoskin. Bangkok: Asia Books, 1992. 200p. map. bibliog.

Published in 1992, this 'portrait' was perfectly timed for Cambodia's international 'coming out', a point not lost on companies such as Shell, Pepsi, and Heineken, which helped fund its creation. Aptly titled, this book is indeed a portrait – emphasizing certain characteristics – within an accurate informative framework. Chiefly consisting of illustration, Hoskins' chapters on the historical setting, the land, people, Angkor, Phnom Penh, and traditions, each have a few pages of succinct explanation to accompany the photographs, all of which are good and clear, many also beautiful. Old French photographs and engravings are included, as well as a bibliography and brief chronology. The coffee-table format, atmospheric pictures and factual yet highly readable text would make it a good introduction to Cambodia for somebody considering travelling there. A French edition, translated by Denis-Armand Canal was published in 1995 (Phnom Penh?: Quatre Fleuves).

10 **Cambodia: its people, its society, its culture.**
David J. Steinberg, in collaboration with Chester A. Bain, Lloyd Burlingham, Russell G. Duff, Bernard B. Fall, Ralph Greenhouse, Lucy Kramer, Robert S. McLellan. New Haven, Connecticut: HRAF Press, 1959. 350p. maps. bibliog. (Survey of World Cultures, no. 5).

Prepared as a 'collation and synthesis of the best and most authoritative contemporary materials' to be used as a handbook by the United States government, from materials collected in the Human Relations Area Files (HRAF), set up in each of sixteen supporting universities by a non-profit research organization of the same name, established in 1949 and affiliated to Yale University. The Cambodia volume was developed from a monograph prepared at the University of Chicago by Norton Ginsburg and Frederick Eggan entitled *Area handbook on Cambodia* (Chicago: University of Chicago for the HRAF, 1955). Like the others in this series, the book does not claim to represent original work, and it contains no footnotes to support the data presented. An index and a bibliography do, however, assist greatly. Previous volumes in the series dealt with Poland, Jordan, Iraq and Saudi Arabia, and this selection reveals much about both Cambodia and the United States of the 1950s. The work provides a thorough and concise study of Cambodia, its people, customs, history, religion, politics, geography, economy and foreign relations. Useful information on population, ethnic groups, economic and social indicators and the Buddhist calendar is included in sixteen tables at the end of the main text. A section dealing with information dissemination will prove of special interest for students of US intervention in Cambodia.

11 **Cambodia.**
Claudia Canesso. New York: Chelsea House, 1989. 96p. (Places and Peoples of the World).

Suitable for use by school students, this small hardback book has a map, many pictures, clear simple text, and a basic glossary and index. Published in 1989, it is already out of date, because of the many recent political changes in the country, but remains useful for the other areas it covers such as the land, early and modern history, Angkor, culture and ethnicity, government, and economy. Four pages of fact and history 'at a glance' add to the book's appearance of being an objective reference tool, but it definitely carries a pro-Western perspective, with Cambodia in 1988 described as being 'once again a puppet of Vietnam, which is in turn influenced by the Soviet Union'.

12 **Eternal Phnom Penh: contemporary portrait of a timeless city.**
Photography by Thomas Renaut, text by Richard Werly, foreword by Jean Lacouture. Hong Kong: Fortune Image Ltd for Les Éditions d'Indochine, [1995]. 96p. (City Heritage).

Another volume in this series of books on Saigon, Vientiane, Hanoi and Rangoon – the 'panoply of charming cities' as introduced by Jean Lacouture. These are cities which for the next few years at least, may be termed 'eternal', presumably because of their recent relative isolation from the West. The foreword by Lacouture unintentionally identifies some of the problems for foreigners attempting to 'freeze the soul of Phnom Penh, to show what lasts'. He reminisces, 'This was a world of . . . budding potential, a world that the challenge of colonialism worked to reshape and awaken'. Some of the images are memorable and subtle, but many are clichés reproduced with garish colours. While each picture has a paragraph devoted to it, the captions, frustratingly, do not give details of locations of the sites, and are appallingly translated into English with such unfortunate phrases as 'the fish sauce adorned by all Khmer'. An alternative title for the book could be 'Pastiche of Phnom Penh'.

13 **Khmers: l'éternel et l'éphémère.** (Khmers: the eternal and the ephemeral.)
Dunnara Meas, text by James Burnet, preface by Marc Riboud. Paris; Pondicherry, India: Kailash, 1995. 173p. bibliog.

There are many pretty picture-books on Cambodia these days. While also beautiful, this book has a discernable aesthetic difference. Comprising composed, clear pictures, the collection seems to stem more from a compulsive urge to document life, to provide a visual, eyewitness record, than to resort to the postcard cliché so often seen. In black-and-white, some semi-abstract, these images have an arresting quality, some bearing a sense of reference to world art history. Marc Riboud's preface speaks accurately of Meas as a photographer returning to the country from which the barbarians drove him with a perspective, not of exoticism or dispossession, but with the tenderness of retrieval. Angkor, Phnom Penh and the countryside and faces and shadows of the people going about their daily life are the subject of over 100 photographs taken in the 1990s, accompanied by Burnet's text of reverie.

14 **The Khmers.**
Ian Mabbett and David P.Chandler. Oxford: Blackwell, 1995. 289p. bibliog. (The Peoples of South-East Asia & the Pacific).

With abundant natural resources for rice-based agriculture, Cambodia was once regarded as an especially favoured and wealthy place. Today it is one of the poorest countries in the world. This stark contrast provides the backdrop to an account of the Khmer people, probably the most readable introduction to Cambodian civilization and ancient history available, written by Mabbett and Chandler, both from Monash University, Melbourne. The main part of the book, based mainly on already published accounts, is the fifteen chapters written by Ian Mabbett, covering the period from antiquity to the fall of Angkor in 1432. David Chandler's final two chapters cover the whole period since then. The authors describe the organization of the ancient empire and tell of the daily life of the kings, priests, farmers, artists and craftspeople who all created modern Cambodia. Those looking for a more complete account of the latter period could turn to Chandler's other well-known histories. Appendices contain a 'Chronological survey of Angkor's rulers' and 'The periodization of religious art and architecture'.

15 **The land and people of Cambodia.**
David P. Chandler. New York: Harper Collins Publishers, 1991. ix, 210p. bibliog. Originally published, Philadelphia: Lippincott, [1972]. (Portraits of the Nations).

Chandler examines the development of the Khmer empire which, shaped by internal tensions, conflict and subjugation, evolved into a nation still marred by wars. As

Cambodia is typified as a poor country, the life and role of the peasant is emphasized in this history, as are historical modes of social organization and relationships with the environment. Whilst of limited extent, and essentially prepared for high school students and the general reader, this work manages to explore a broad range of aspects of Cambodian life, many in considerable depth. A succinct survey of politics in the Sihanouk era (1953-70) and a virtually anthropological profile of a Cambodian farmer are particular highlights of both the first edition, and of the 1991 revision, which adds several new chapters dealing with the overthrow of Sihanouk in 1970, the Lon Nol and DK regimes, and the post-1979 reconstruction. The latter edition ends on a cautious note of hope for foreign economic aid and for the installation of a new polity that would enable 'the ancient country of Cambodia to rejoin the world'. The book contains a filmography and discography as well as a bibliography.

16 **The living Mekong.**

Charles Burleigh. Sydney; London: Angus & Robertson, 1971. 137p. maps.

Although published over twenty-five years ago, this book is included because it is readily available in public libraries, and still provides a good, basic introduction to the people and landscape of the Mekong. Burleigh, educated in Holland and Australia, combined science with a love of travel and of Asia. This book is a product of 'many Mekong journeys, always by local trading boats . . . sleeping with just a mat on the floor, washing in the Mekong every evening, and eating rice and sparse meat dishes with fingers from communal bowls. Inevitably, my interest was the daily family life and work of the river people when growing their food, plying their boats, building houses and practising their hundred and one necessary trades'. The photographs afford a good account of techniques such as pottery making in Kompong Chhnang and the use of fish traps in Kratie.

17 **The Mekong: a river and its people.**

John Hoskin, text; Allen W. Hopkins, photographs. Bangkok: Post Publishing Co., 1991. 303p. maps. bibliog.

In claiming to be 'the first book to take the challenge of exploring the world's twelfth longest river', scant recognition is made of the arduous efforts of explorers in days of yesteryear. Nevertheless, it was a major undertaking to travel along and record in photographic and textual form the 4,200 kilometres of the river's course through six countries from Tibet to the South China Sea. Following two introductory chapters, the book is divided into 'Turbulent river' (China), 'Mother of waters' (Laos, Thailand, Burma), 'Great water' (Cambodia), and 'The nine dragons' (Vietnam). Hopkins' photographs depict the river's range of moods and activities along its banks, while Hoskins writes his usual perceptive, elegant and informative prose, drawing on a background of historical and artistic understanding that distinguish his work from that of most travel writers. Valuable reproductions of engravings, stamps and architectural drawings add to the original contributions of the book's authors, but no individual credits are given, and some of the photographs are reproduced in somewhat garish tones. This has been used as the basis for the CD-ROM publication, *Beyond the nine dragons: discover the exotic cultures of the Mekong River* (q.v.).

18 **Monographie du Cambodge.** (Monograph on Cambodia.)
René Morizon. Hanoi: Imprimerie d'Extrême-Orient, 1931. 284p. (Inventaire Général de l'Indochine [Société de Géographie, Hanoi], fasc. 6).

A thorough handbook on Cambodia prepared for the 1931 Colonial Exposition in Paris, and published also as part of the 'General Inventory of Indochina' series. Morizon, who was Deputy Administrator of the Indochina Civil Service, divided his study into four parts: Cambodian history prior to its colonization by France and its administrative organization; the country and its inhabitants; agriculture, forestry, fisheries, mines and commerce; and French 'works' in the intellectual and educational fields, in health, civil service and the economy. Morizon views Cambodia from the perspective of a colonialist, and praises the contributions made by France. 'If they do not always understand our intentions, at least they give an absolute confidence to those France has assigned to represent her, and who have the mandate to educate and improve them. Thanks to us, Cambodia, eternal victim of belligerent and avid neighbours, of oppressive mandarins, fatalist and apathetic Cambodians who nostalgically regret the past and disdain the present, now aspire to other than the meagre satisfactions of a vegetative life.' Plates and a bibliography contribute to the utility of this overview of the situation in Cambodia at the height of the colonial period.

19 **National Geographic.**
Washington, DC: National Geographic Society, 1888- . monthly.

Readily available at many public libraries this periodical is not to be neglected if one is seeking striking photographs and well-crafted text. The May 1982 issue (vol. 161, no. 5), for example, carries two major articles by Peter T. White, Wilbur E. Garrett and David Alan Harvey – 'The temples of Angkor: ancient glory in stone' and 'Kampuchea wakens from a nightmare' – while occasional articles have appeared in subsequent years, especially on the preservation of Angkor (1989 and 1992) and on the Mekong (1993). To search the archive of *National Geographic*, see its Internet site – http://wvoyag.nationalgeographic.com – where articles on Cambodia are listed as far back as 1912, mostly with predictable titles such as 'Forgotten ruins of Indo-China' or 'The mystery of Angkor'.

Anthropologie des Cambodgiens. (Anthropology of Cambodians.)
See item no. 346.

Cambodia: a country study.
See item no. 873.

Les clés du Cambodge. (The keys to Cambodia.)
See item no. 875.

Encyclopedia of Asian history.
See item no. 877.

The people of the rice fields.
See item no. 939.

The land in between [braille]: the Cambodian dilemma.
See item no. 968.

Geography, Maps and Atlases

20 **Atlas of physical, economic, and social resources of the Lower Mekong Basin.**
Prepared under the direction of the U.S. Agency for International Development, Bureau for East Asia, by the Engineer Agency for Resources Inventories and the Tennessee Valley Authority for the Committee for Coordination of Investigations of the Lower Mekong Basin (Cambodia, Laos, Republic of Viet-Nam, and Thailand), United Nations Economic Commission for Asia and the Far East. [New York: United Nations?], 1968. 1 vol. (loose-leaf). maps. bibliog. Scale – 1:2,000,000.

The developmental purpose of this atlas, produced by the UN Economic Commission for Asia and the Far East, ECAFE (now ESCAP), is alluded to in the preface – 'The impressive fact about the Mekong River as a natural resource is not its great length, its vast drainage basin, or the volume of its flow, but the negligible extent to which it and its tributaries have been developed'. However, the material included in the atlas is diverse and extensive, making it useful to a variety of readers. Although it was published over twenty-five years ago, studies of geography, climate, and soil fertility in the 'Physical Resources' section are valid today, while much of the 'Human Resources' and 'Social and Economic Infrastructure' sections could be extremely useful for comparative research. Considering the lack of development in Cambodia since 1968, the material frequently reflects today's situation, covering subjects such as urban areas, fish catch, location and language of ethnic groups, in detail as precise as the number of beds in hospitals. Each topic is illustrated by an extremely detailed map (with a transparent overlay), tables and a passage of text in both English and French.

21 **Atlas of thematic maps of the Lower Mekong Basin: prepared on the basis of satellite imagery (Landsat I and II).**
Information note by the Secretariat, United Nations, Economic and Social Commission for Asia and the Pacific, Committee for Co-ordination of Investigations of the Lower Mekong Basin. [Bangkok?]: The Committee, 1977. iv, 72, 4p. maps. bibliog. Limited; MKG/49 Rev. 1.

Three maps (Land Use, Pedo-Geomorphologic and Land Capability) in two parts each have been prepared on the basis of satellite images recorded in 1972-73, as well as a range of existing maps, documents and aerial photographs. Coverage is 600,000 square kilometres – the catchment areas of the lower Mekong, including all of Cambodia except the southwest area in which water drains into the Gulf of Thailand. The scale is 1:1,000,000 with each map piece measuring roughly 1 square metre. Vital to a reading of the maps is the explanatory note which supplements the impressive colour-formed images. The maps' valuable findings are interpreted in concise language accompanied by annexes on zones of rainfall, dynamics of vegetation succession, a table of soil comparison and other such interpretative graphs. Two additional studies (outlines of sedimentation in the Mekong delta, and the Nam Mun and Nam Chi Basin in northeast Thailand) may be particularly important given the current controversy over resource management in those areas.

22 **Cambodge, Laos, Viêt Nam.** (Cambodia, Laos, Vietnam.)
Cartographers, Katalin Eckschmidt, Kartográfiai Vállalat. Budapest: Cartographia, 1990. map. 620604-01.

With text in French, English, German, and Hungarian, this colour map shows administrative borders, major roads, border and river crossing points, airports, rail and shipping routes and some archaeological sites. Four insets are included. Features include text on the verso, indexes to place-names, regions and some features; title panels, and coverage and location maps. Relief is shown by shading, gradient tints, and spot heights; depths are shown by contours and gradient tints. The scales used are as follows: country maps – 1:2,000,000; Ha Noi – 1:17,000; Vientiane – 1:14,000; Ho Chi Minh City – 1:15,000; city map and administrative map – 1:7,900,000.

23 **Cambodge-Viet-nam.** (Cambodia-Vietnam [map].)
[Saigon: Shell, 1960]. map. K. D. So 288 – Ngay 19/1960.

A colour map of Cambodia and south Vietnam showing transportation, forests, places of interest and populated places. On the reverse side in English, Khmer, Vietnamese and French are distances in kilometres and a list of Shell service stations – while many of these are no longer operating some, such as in Phnom Penh, are being renovated and reopened, even some with 24-hour supermarkets attached!

24 **Cambodge: carte administrative et routière.** (Cambodia: administrative and road map.)
[Phnom Penh]: Service Géographique des FANK, 1973. map. SG-3/73 1000-C00 1264. Scale – 1:1,000,000.

This colour map shows major towns in the provinces, waterways, railways, national routes, and islands, etc. Most of the Mekong delta region in Vietnam is included, interestingly with Khmer as well as Vietnamese names for the major towns (even

Saigon), reflecting the revanchist perspective of the Lon Nol government. While no land use or topography is indicated, major mountains and ranges are identified, as are smaller rivers. A distance table is included. Twenty years later, this map is still readily available in Phnom Penh markets, or sold by children making the rounds of the city's expatriate cafes.

25 **Cambodge: carte scolaire.** (Cambodia: school map.)
Revised, designed and published by the Geographic Service of FANK. Phnom Penh: Service Géographique des FANK, 1971. map. SG-10/71-1000-117 C001188.

An excellent colour map, providing both Khmer, and romanized, names of provinces, towns, rivers and islands. National routes – with distances – are shown, as well as railway lines and airports. Much of Vietnam's delta area is included, with Khmer transliteration of Vietnamese names, Cambodian names and roman transliteration, constituting a minor linguistic study. Relief is indicated by shading and spot heights, and monsoon wind directions are also shown. Each place-name is identified as either provincial capital, district capital or village, and accompanied by an additional table of road distances.

26 **Cambodge: carte touristique.** (Cambodia: tourist map.)
[Phnom Penh: Royaume du Cambodge, Service Géographique, 1968]. map. SG-9/68-124-1000-C000214.

An amusing, illustrated, colour tourist map which, along with provinces, towns and major roads, shows what delights may await the traveller in various places across the country. Quaint pictures of hill people, tigers, gems, temples and ants' nests appear amid rivers, railways and roads. Distances between major towns are given. Many of the attractions remain intact, if difficult to get to, even though the map is pre-1970 and is a souvenir in itself.

27 **Cambodge: carte.** (Cambodia: map.)
[Hanoi?: GGIC, 1911?]. map.

Prepared for the Resident Superior, Paul Luce (1905-11). The map appears in four sections, measuring about 1 square metre when combined, with minimal topographical shading. Rivers and smaller tributaries are shown, as are areas of swamp and ponds. Despite its age, this map maintains its relevance and, as it details even the most tiny settlements, is literally covered with the names of villages.

28 **Cambodge.** (Cambodia [map].)
Phnom Penh: Service Géographique des FANK, 1970. map.

Within 1 square metre an enormous amount of information is represented. Provinces are shaded in different colours, while district boundaries and towns are also shown. Infrastructure such as roads, transport and settlements are recorded in good detail. Terrain is more lightly indicated, but spot heights and rivers are clearly marked. Along with a basic legend, tables provide road distances between major towns and a numbered key for additional place-names.

29 **Cambodia travel map.**

[Hong Kong]: Periplus Editions, [1994?]. map. (Travel Map).

A colour map of Cambodia (scale – 1:1,100,000), including a location map in the margin, which shows relief by hill shading and spot heights. On the verso are maps of Phnom Penh (scale – 1:17,000), with index, and Angkor temples (scale – 1:95,000), as well as some tourist information.

30 **Cambodia [map].**

Cartographic Mapping Institute. Vancouver, Canada: International Travel Maps, 1995. map. Scale – 1:800,000.

A basic geographical and political map, showing province boundaries and capitals as well as topography and natural features. Suitable for tourists, it provides a brief country profile by Jack Joyce, an inset showing Cambodia's location in the region, and indications of some historical sites and places of interest. More detailed maps of Angkor and Phnom Penh are inset.

31 **East Asia road map.**

Prepared under the direction of CINCUSARPAC by the U.S. Army Map Service, Far East. [Washington, DC: U.S. Army Map Service?], 1964- . maps. (Series 1306).

These colour maps (79 x 75cm or smaller Lambert conformal conic projection – coverage complete in four sheets) were produced in 1963 by photographic methods. Despite a qualifier that the map has not been field-checked, its detail is remarkable, showing schools, bridges, canals, villages etc., on a shaded topographical background, with a contour interval of only 20 metres. Each map in the series, which also covers Laos and Vietnam, represents about 30 square kilometres. Water-depth curves are indicated as well as vegetation type and density on land. A complete aerial picture of the geography and infrastructure of Cambodia at the time is thus assembled – obviously serving a military purpose. Place-names are provided in Khmer and English, and there is a small glossary of place-terms with transliterated Khmer, Khmer script and English. The map would be entirely suitable today for use by small-time pilots.

32 **Les frontières du Viêtnam: histoire des frontières de la péninsule.**

(The frontiers of Vietnam: history of the frontiers of the peninsula.) Edited by Pierre-Bernard Lafont. Paris: L'Harmattan, 1989. 268p. bibliog.

The first in a series on the history of the borders of the Indochinese peninsula, this book includes four essays on the southern frontier, two of which are of more general interest: Nguyen The Anh looks at Vietnamese texts, and Po Dharma at the frontiers of Champa. Of most relevance to Cambodia are Mak Phoeun's study of the frontier between Cambodia and Vietnam from the 17th century to the establishment of the French Protectorate as presented in Royal Khmer chronicles, and Pierre-Lucien Lamant's work on the period from the middle of the 19th century to the present. Mak Phoeun traces the southern movement of the Vietnamese and the relentless retreat of the Khmer frontier from the middle of the 17th century. The court at Hue saw the frontier as an administrative matter, to be altered as it pleased. He includes a map showing Vietnamese expansion during the period. Lamant continues by documenting the history of the steady pressure on Cambodian territory. He points out that up until the time of French colonization the records as to the borders are scarce and it is impossible to draw a clear line. The French attempted to do so but Cambodia has never accepted their ruling as final, periodically asserting instead that all areas occupied by Khmers are Cambodian.

33 **Frontiers of Asia and Southeast Asia.**
J. R. V. Prescott, H. J. Collier. Melbourne: Melbourne University Press, 1977. 106p. 45 maps.

A study of the history of the boundaries between countries in Asia and Southeast Asia. Sections on Thailand's eastern border, the boundaries of Laos with Cambodia and Vietnam, and the Cambodia-Vietnam boundary, each offer a one-page description of the major geographical qualities of the border regions and how they were determined. In general this was done to suit the needs of the French colonialists at Cambodia's expense. Each section is accompanied by a map of the relevant areas. The first four maps in the work provide general information on the physical and colonial history of the whole region. Only proclaimed maritime borders are considered. This is a good background summary for an understanding of current disputes.

34 **Géographie du Cambodge, de l'Asie des moussons et des principales puissances.** (Geography of Cambodia, of monsoon Asia and the principal powers.)
Tan-Kim-Houn. Phnom Penh: [Imprimerie Henry], 1963. 3rd ed. 1 vol. maps.

Part one of this volume is a general school-level introduction to geography, on seasons, eclipses, days and nights, the earth and the universe. The second part, on Cambodia, contains extensive facts and figures on the land, human settlement, and economy of Cambodia, such as: soil composition, hydrography, coastline, population and ethnic composition, political and administrative organization, a summary of data from each province, natural resources, industry and trade, transport and communication. Part three is a collection of brief country summaries (major exports, populations, seasons, etc.) for the rest of Asia. The maps contained in the volume are very basic, single colour and of rather poor quality.

35 **Le Phnom Kulen et sa région: carte et commentaire.** (Phnom Kulen and its region: map and commentary.)
Jean Boulbet. Paris: École Française d'Extrême-Orient, 1979. 136p. maps. bibliog. (Collection de Textes et Documents sur l'Indochine, 12).

A map and detailed text on the region of Phnom Kulen (Mount Kulen), the most notable formation close to the temples of Angkor, and indeed the source of much of the stone used in their construction, transported down by the Siem Reap River. It forms a unique bio-geographical environment, with a rich cultural history. Boulbet studied the area from 1967-75, and continued his work outside Cambodia after the Khmer Rouge took power. In 1973 Boulbet and Bruno Dagens published an inventory of archaeological sites in the region, in a special issue of *Arts Asiatiques* (Asiatic Arts), vol. 27. The earlier maps were enhanced with the assistance of aerial photography to produce this geographic and archaeological map. The text describes the climate, ecology and social and cultural life of the people of this region.

36 **Phnom Penh Cambodia '96: first 3D city map.**
Phnom Penh: Quess Ltd., 1996. 1 folded sheet.

The '3D' map shows central Phnom Penh, lacking the western or far northern districts of the growing city. Obviously commercially funded, occasionally a small advertisement for a hotel or business obliterates a block or street. Restaurants and private companies are highlighted, but travellers will have to look harder to find other attractions. However, on the back of the map is a thorough chart for finding such services as Japanese food or vehicle accessories, and an index of markets, temples, places of interest, etc. A 1996 calendar, with seasonal fruits shown, a brief profile of the country, and a small but useful map of Angkor and Siem Reap are also included.

37 **Phnom Penh [map].**
Drawn and reproduced by 110 Map Production Coy. R. E. [London]: 110 Production Coy. R. E., 1945. map. Scale – 1:5,000. HIND 1069 Phnom Penh.

This is an excellent colour map which, without being cluttered, manages to present information about the city, on land use, geography, infrastructure and culture. Water is shown at March (dry season) levels. Urban density is indicated, and important buildings are darkened. Numbered locations refer to services (port, military, administrative, commercial, ecclesiastic, miscellaneous, medical, hotels etc., school and industrial) from yacht clubs to churches, experimental farms to factories. Inset is a map of the northern suburbs. The map was prepared for the assault on Japanese-held Cambodia.

38 **Phnom Penh: water mains.**
[London]: Published by the War Office, 1945. map. 1,110/12/45/ S.P.C. (Geographical Section, General Staff, no. 4593A).

A town plan of Phnom Penh's water mains transposed onto a base map showing transportation, water features, built-up areas and buildings. Relief is shown by the hachures. The base was compiled and drawn by ACIU and the War Office in 1945. Since the upgrading of the water supply and sewerage pipes in Phnom Penh began in the mid-1990s this map is mercifully finally becoming outmoded, but nevertheless remains interesting. The waterworks at Chroy Chongvar, water-pipe dimensions, settlement patterns as well as roads and rail networks near the rivers are shown.

39 **Rand McNally official map of Vietnam, Laos and Cambodia.**
[Chicago?]: Rand McNally and Co., [between 1965 and 1967]. 1 map.

This full-colour wall map is on a scale of 1:1,250,000. It includes indexes to major place-names and geographical features, a glossary of foreign terms and populations of major towns, as well as short descriptions of each country. The heights of significant mountains are shown in metres, but otherwise physical relief is not shown. Roads are indicated, coded as to their surface material and breadth, as well as their route numbers.

40 **UBD Cambodia, Laos and Vietnam: including city maps of Ho Chi Minh, Ha Noi and Viangchan (Vientiane).**
Macquarie Park, New South Wales: Universal Press Pty Ltd., 1994. map. (International Map Series, Map 175).

A map of Cambodia, Laos and Vietnam showing international and province boundaries, transportation, water features, forests, rice fields, places of interest and populated places.

Relief is shown by shading and spot heights. The legend is in French, English and German. Ancillary maps are included of Viangchan (Vientiane) [scale c.1:13,300], Thanh Pho Ho Chi Minh [scale c.1:14,800], and Ha Noi [scale c.1:16,600].

41 **Vietnam, Laos, Kampuchea 1:1,500,000 [map].**
Nelles Verlag. Munich: Nelles Verlag, [1990?]. map. (Nelles Map Series).

A colour map showing relief by shading and spot heights. Large towns and villages are indicated as well as main road and rail routes, airfields and some places of interest. It is not very detailed but provides a good first introduction to the geographical features of the country.

Altérations biologiques des grès cambodgiens et recherche de moyens de protection: essai de synthèse. (Biological changes to Cambodian sandstone and the search for means of protection: summary of tests.)
See item no. 121.

Carte archéologique de la région d'Angkor. (Archaeological map of the region of Angkor.)
See item no. 128.

Lovea, village des environs d'Angkor: aspects démographiques, économiques et sociologiques du monde rural cambodgien dans la province de Siem-Réap. (Lovea, village in the neighbourhood of Angkor: demographic, economic and sociological aspects of the rural Cambodian world in the province of Siem Reap.)
See item no. 415.

Cambodia, rice-growing areas and population.
See item no. 611.

Cambodia land cover atlas 1985/87-1992/93 (including national and provincial statistics).
See item no. 655.

Centre urbain de [Siemreap, Battambang et Pursat]. (Urban centre of [Siem Reap, Battambang and Pursat].)
See item no. 656.

Tâ Kèo: étude architecturale du temple. (Ta Keo: architectural study of the temple.)
See item no. 820.

Gazetteer of Cambodia.
See item no. 878.

Tourism and Travel Guides

42 **Angkor: an introduction to the temples.**
Dawn F. Rooney, photography by Michael Freeman. Bangkok: Asia Books; Hong Kong: Odyssey, 1994. 240p.

A thorough background section introduces the geography, history, religion and architecture of Angkor to the potential temple-wanderer. Rooney's introductory writing is extremely informative and useful in itself, even without the temple guide, which is also thorough. Forty monuments are treated individually – their location, access points, building dates, ruling monarch, religion and art style are provided in point form, then their background and layout are discussed in more detail. Many of the individual entries on the monuments are accompanied by plans or Freeman's lovely photographs. Helpful tips and evocative or amusing quotations are included, to make this excellent guide not only practical but also inspiring. The book is an essential edition for the tourists who consider themselves travellers. See also Michael Freeman's *A guide to Khmer temples in Thailand and Laos* (Bangkok: River Books, 199?. 315p.).

43 **Angkor: heart of an Asian empire.**
Bruno Dagens, translated by Ruth Sharman. London: Thames & Hudson, 1995. 191p. (New Horizons); New York: Henry N. Abrams, 1995. A translation of *Angkor: le forêt de pierre* (Angkor: the forest of stone), Paris: Gallimard, 1989.

A superb little scrapbook containing a *mélange* of newspaper clippings, photographs and excerpts from scholarly and literary accounts of Angkor since Chou Ta-Kuan's visit in 1296. Dagens, who worked for the Angkor Conservation for seven years from 1965, shows the sensationalism that developed in the West at the supposed discovery of the lost civilization of the Khmers. He tracks down primary source material, such as the beautiful 1889 architectural drawings by Lucien Fournereau, travel posters, advertisements, fiction and music with an Angkor theme, and the models created for the Colonial Exposition of 1931. Eclectic as it is, this work is provided with the scholarly apparatus of index, footnotes and bibliography and, now appearing in

English translation as well as its original French text, provides travellers to Cambodia with the most convenient and easy-to-read compendium of background interpretation of Angkor and its representation. Dagens has done extensive academic and conservation work in India and Laos, as well as Cambodia.

44 **Angkor: temples en péril.** (Angkor: temples in peril.)
Albert Le Bonheur. Paris: Herscher, 1989. 263p.

A combination of stunning photographs and extensive text on the state of the temples and the need for restoration makes this one of the new coffee-table books which has something to say as well as to display, but it is an expensive item.

45 **Cambodia/Laos.**
Publisher, Günter Nelles; project editor, Annaliese Wulf; editor, J-Martina Schneider; picture editor, Heinz Vestner; translation and English editor, Angus McGeoch. Munich: Nelles Verlag, 1994. 256p. maps. (Nelles Guides).

Wonderful photographs and detailed maps from the Nelles cartographers together with Annaliese Wulf's readable and informative text make this a most welcome addition to recent guides to Cambodia. The historical section is rich with colour, containing historic photographs and plates as well as data, and the political commentary provides a succinct but accurate picture of the country up to October 1993. Within a relatively small amount of space the section on Cambodia (p. 1-157) manages to include quite extensive sections on architecture and art, with commentary on various styles and periods, and detailed guidebook information on the National Museum in Phnom Penh, and all the major temples in Angkor. The concluding 'Guidelines' section contains up-to-date necessary tourist information, which is quite adequate despite the absurd introductory sentence,'As everywhere else in South-East Asia, tourism in Cambodia started in the 1960s'. No vocabulary or phrase lists are included. A 100-page section on Laos and a 5-page index complete the volume which, although bearing the name of an English translator and editor, offers no evidence of previous publication (presumably in German).

46 **The Cambodia less travelled.**
Ray Zepp. Phnom Penh: Bert's Books, 1996. 182p. maps.

At last, a travel guide written by someone who is not scared to address the trouble tourists may get into, providing information rather than opinion about security risks. The author maintains that Phnom Penh is the most dangerous place in the country, but advises against, and includes no information about, travel to much of the northwest. Instead he details fifteen journeys from Phnom Penh (the city he proclaims as only ten minutes from Cambodia!), as brief as a half-day across the river and as lengthy as seven days (minimum) in Mondulkiri. Each of the fifteen descriptions includes a simple map of the place concerned, but a thorough country map showing the national routes would help readers make the most of the book. Zepp is a traveller who likes to wander off the beaten track, and enjoy a peaceful place to the full. In his informal writing style, he shares many of his pleasant experiences and knowledge in a manner rare for a travel guide – neither gung-ho and boastful nor supercilious, but thoughtful and very positive. Anecdotes about special little places, Cambodian names, religion, mannerisms, the birdlife and so on are intermingled with practical information and even some philosophy to make this much more than a how-to book. Suggestive rather than prescriptive, this is a sensible, easy-to-use guide, perfect for flexible travellers who love to find their own entertainment and to move at their own pace. Zepp has updated this invaluable guidebook with more detailed information on the remoter parts of the country in two supplements, *The Cambodia less travelled: Northwest supplement (Ratanikiri [sic], Mondulkiri)* (Phnom Penh: Bert's Books, June 1997. 35p. maps) and *The Cambodia less travelled: Northeast supplement (Pursat, Battambang, Sisophon, Poipet)* (Phnom Penh: Bert's Books, June 1997. 42p. maps). The northwestern provinces were considered somewhat safer than they had been, but they have been racked by fighting since these supplements were published, and so Zepp's cautionary remarks that the region remains 'politically and militarily volatile' are all the more to be heeded. The political upheaval of July 1997 means these supplements will probably remain fairly hard to obtain – I bought my copies in the clearing sale of Bert's Books as he left Cambodia, declaring publicly that he did not want to live in an authoritarian state, closing down his bookshop, hostel and recently launched publishing house. Zepp turns his hand from providing general tourist information to a more considered attempt to understand and explain in popular terms the art of the temples, described by the author as 'wat-watching [which] is very like bird-watching' in *A field guide to Cambodia's pagodas* (Phnom Penh: Bert's Books, June 1997. 70p. bibliog.). The introductory section discusses pagoda etiquette and the history and practice of Buddhism in Cambodia, in which Zepp points out that most words inscribed in temples are in Pali or Old Khmer which can be understood by very few monks. Further, most of the monkhood were killed under the Khmer Rouge and today's monks 'often have only vague ideas of the stories, if they recognize them at all. A young monk may invent details for the visitor in order to make the story sound plausible'. Zepp goes on to describe motifs and stories under the following headings: animals, gods and other creatures; the Buddha's life; the Jataka tales; and then to give more detail on some twenty-two temples in Phnom Penh. Although not a scholarly work, and without annotation, it is a careful and eminently readable book that would make an enormous difference to the ability of the visitor to appreciate the content and styles of Cambodia's temple art.

47 **Cambodia: a lonely planet travel survival kit.**

Chris Taylor, Tony Wheeler and Daniel Robinson. Hawthorn, Victoria: Lonely Planet Publications, 1996. 2nd ed. 170p. maps. (Lonely Planet Travel Survival Kit).

Following the well-known and successful Lonely Planet formula, this volume provides 'Facts about the country' with the necessary 'Facts for the visitor', 'Getting there and away', 'Getting around' and then some more details of Phnom Penh, Angkor and brief notes on other parts of the country. So much has changed since the first edition of this guide was written in the midst of UNTAC's descent upon Cambodia, and yet the descriptions of the continuing civil war, the hardships and dislocation of the population, the continuing dangers of minefields, and the difficulties of travel (particularly bans on foreigners using buses and trains) remain valid observations today. Tony Wheeler visited Cambodia in 1992, gathering data to update Daniel Robinson's Cambodia chapter of the 1991 *Vietnam, Laos & Cambodia: a travel survival kit* (q.v.), and the second edition has been updated to mid-1995. This aside, the historical overview is clear, concise and fair. Basic geographic, cultural and touristic information is of Lonely Planet's usual high standard, making it the most practical traveller's guide to have with you on the journey, even if others may have better photographs and more extensive historical and cultural notes. Unfortunately, advice on the best time of year to visit the Bokor Hill Station with its 'pleasant climate, rushing streams, forested vistas and stunning panoramas of the sea' remain tragically unrealizable in today's Cambodia, and a more cautionary tone is taken in this second edition which reported that seven foreigners had been murdered in Cambodia since 1994. This slim volume is not cheap, compared to the marginally more expensive three-country guide, but it does have the advantage of slipping easily into a bag or even a pocket. A French version also appeared in 1992.

48 **Fielding's guide to the world's most dangerous places.**
Rodondo Beach, California: Fielding Worldwide, 1995. maps.

Cambodia is given the dubious status of a five-star rating in the danger stakes – along with Algeria, Chechnya, Colombia and Libya. This is the opposite of other guidebooks that presume all danger has gone, and entice the foreigner to presently inaccessible destinations. But the book's approach is over the top considering the thousands of foreigners who visit the Angkor temples each week, or who live comfortable expatriate lives in Phnom Penh where, despite genuine concerns for personal security against robbery, their principal worries relate to interruptions in electricity supply and telecommunications services rather than kidnappings and terrorist attacks, which sadly do still prevail in some parts of the country. Cambodia was edged out of the top five danger spots in the 1997 edition, but this was published before the July 1997 events. Also available on the Internet at http://www.fieldingtravel/com/dp/index.html[.]

49 **Guide archéologique aux temples d'Angkor: Angkor Vat, Angkor Thom et les monuments du petit et du grand circuit.** (An archaeological guide to the temples of Angkor: Angkor Wat, Angkor Thom and the monuments of the little and grand circuits.)
Henri Marchal. Paris: G. van Oest, 1928. vii, 217p. maps. bibliog.
Later published, Saigon: Société des Éditions d'Extrême-Asie, [1930].

An extensive description of, and tourist guide to, the major monuments and temples on what are still known as the little (or small) and grand circuits. The work includes explanations of the bas-reliefs of Angkor Wat and the Bayon, floor plans of Angkor Wat, the Bayon, Preah Khan, Ta Keo, and Ta Prohm and a map of the centre of Angkor Thom city. Some very good plates depict details from the bas-reliefs and sculptures. The book finishes with a plea for tourists to show respect for religious traditions and to refrain from taking parts of the monuments away with them. It includes an index of names of places and monuments, and a map of Cochinchina (Saigon and Cambodia). A loose addendum revises some dates and old hypotheses. Despite its age, this remains a useful guidebook by Angkor's curator of the time, and it still circulates in photocopied form in the markets of Phnom Penh and Siem Reap.

50 **Guide to Phnom Penh.**
Phnom Penh: Women's International Group, 1995. 67p. map. bibliog.

One of the many guidebooks now being produced, this one has a certain advantage in that it includes homilies and useful pieces of information gathered by expatriates actually living in the city these days, and contains advice on services and merchandise (providing a range of information from where to go for beauty treatments – including waxing – to key cutting and medical treatment). The back page contains a fold-out map of Phnom Penh. Some information is offered on tourist attractions and destinations, but for anyone travelling beyond Phnom Penh there is little material. All proceeds from the sale are donated to Cambodian charities, but though the book certainly meets the traveller's needs, it is unfortunately readily available only in Phnom Penh itself.

51 **A guide to Phnom Penh.**
Robert Philpotts. London: Blackwater Books, 1992. 3rd ed. 140p. maps.

A slight book, with a homespun image set in courier typeface with hand-drawn maps. However, Philpotts' guide deserves mention, as it is already into its third edition, and is widely distributed in Thailand and Cambodia by Asia Books. The sixteen pen-and-ink sketches by the author are quite engaging, and although the touristic information is delivered in a chatty, informal manner, the book is useful and reasonably accurate.

52 **A guide to the Angkor monuments.**
[Siem Reap, Cambodia]: Angkor Conservation Office, [1994]. leaflet.

A handy B4 sheet folded as a slim brochure, with a map of 'Archaeological sites in the Angkor region', a brief introduction and a paragraph on each of thirty-seven sites, arranged into five chronological groups with comments on the main features of each site, its time of construction, under whose rule it was built and the best time of day to see it. Produced with the help of (the British) Volunteers Service Overseas on the basis of research by EFEO, it is sold widely in Siem Reap and Phnom Penh for US$1, with all proceeds going to the Angkor Conservation Office.

53 **Henri Parmentier's guide to Angkor.**
Henri Parmentier. Phnom Penh: EKLIP, 19-?. 220p. maps.

A classic text by the 1930s' head of the archaeological service. Two introductory chapters give a thorough background in religion, including Hindu and Buddhist beliefs, and architecture, including descriptions of historical building styles and materials. Tens of temples and monuments are treated individually and supported by over forty black-and-white photographs. However, since it was written much statuary has disappeared from some temples, while others have been restored. Parmentier actually worked on many of the sites he describes, and so makes informed assessments of the temple-builders' construction techniques as well as of the symbolism of the temples' artistic decoration. His guide is both scholarly and personal with notes such as 'The paths, not always being maintained, it is good to take a coolie furnished with a machete'. A photocopied edition is readily available in Cambodia, and would suit a traveller with an academic or romantic interest in Angkor.

54 **Indochine: un guide Artou.** (Indochina: an Artou guide.)
Jacques Népote. Geneva: Éditions Olizane, 1989. 396p. maps. bibliog. (Les Guides Artou).

A guidebook with unusual depth. Népote brings his scholarship to bear and, rather than providing specific travel information, offers historical, archaeological and cultural background, including flora and such perspectives as the historical interpretation of the layout of Phnom Penh. Thirty-three colour photographs by J.-P. Grandjean complement engravings, special maps and literary sources to give delight and a good introduction to the French reading tourist. Although devoted to Indochina as a whole, Cambodia is not treated as an appendage of Vietnam, but takes up a quarter of the volume as well as being covered in the Indochina overview. An index and glossary are provided.

55 **Maverick guide to Vietnam, Laos and Cambodia.**
Len Rutledge. Gretna, Louisiana: Pelican Publishing Co., 1994. 382p. maps. (Maverick Guide Series).

Despite the cover photograph of the Bayon temple, Cambodia occupies less than fifty pages of this book and, although bearing a 1994 imprint, the text was written in 1992, and contains much information (both political and tourist) left over from pre-UNTAC days.

56 **Les monuments du groupe d'Angkor.** (Monuments of the Angkor group.)
Maurice Glaize, photographs from l'École Française d'Extrême-Orient. Paris: Adrien-Maisonneuve, 1963. 3rd ed. xiii, 280p.

'Glaize' is the classic guidebook. For those who need a straight technical description, it is still useful and has been reprinted many times, as recently as 1993. It is more fashionable nowadays to have guidebooks with lavish photographs and romantic dissertations, but a short precise factual description is still what many travellers require. Back home, you'll enjoy beautiful coffee-table books. But when walking and sweating, climbing and descending the temple's stairs, you need dry hard facts in a compact form. This is what Glaize provides.

57 **Nouveau guide d'Angkor.** (New guide to Angkor.)
Henri Marchal. Phnom Penh: Henry, 1961. 245p. bibliog. maps.
Originally published in English as *Guide to Angkor: Angkor Vat, Angkor Thom and monuments of great circuit and little circuit* (Saigon: Société des Éditions d'Extrême-Asie, 1930). A translation of *Guide archéologique aux temples d'Angkor: Angkor Vat, Angkor Thom et les monuments du petit et du grand circuit* (Paris: Van Oest, 1928).

Modestly presented as a simple and clear guide, with no pretence at erudition, the former curator of Angkor monuments, Henri Marchal, here passes on the benefits of his long and deep appreciation of Angkor to the general public. Over sixty individual temples are individually described and many are also given some interpretation, with particular attention paid to the bas-reliefs of Angkor Wat, Bayon and Baphuon which, in Marchal's view, 'present an anecdotal character, sometimes amusing, that may make the visit more agreeable'. The individual descriptions are preceded by some forty pages of introductory text. This volume, once again circulating in photocopy reprint with colour cover in Phnom Penh, remains a valuable companion for a journey to Angkor.

58 **Le palais d'Angkor Vat: ancienne résidence des rois khmers.** (The palace of Angkor Wat: former residence of the Khmer kings.)
Général de Beylié, preface by Georges Maspéro. Hanoi: F.-H. Schneider, 1904. [37]p. bibliog.

Contains simple floor plans with some sketches of the temple windows.

59 **Phnom Penh & Cambodia.**
Roland Neveu. Bangkok: Great Little Guide Ltd., 1993. 131p. maps. bibliog.

The first page states 'This book is the result of research undertaken by a number of friends and relations'. Accordingly its style is informal and chatty. The guide attempts to cover hotels, restaurants, and places of interest in Siem Reap, Battambang and Sihanoukville as well as Phnom Penh. A thorough and diverse index leads the reader to information on topics such as banks, travel agents, modes of transport, NGOs and political parties. A background history of the country is presented like a 'briefing'. However, little cultural information, such as polite behaviour or useful Khmer phrases, is provided. Mostly directed towards press people and other professionals, it is unfortunately fairly specific to the UNTAC period, and the security situations and services described may be quite different from those available today.

60 **A Shell guide to Cambodia.**
Phnom Penh: Société Shell du Cambodge in co-operation with the Cambodian National Office of Tourism, 1966. 55p. maps.

Comprises brief entries on the main tourist attractions and destinations of the time, with some historical and geographical interest.

61 **Vietnam, Laos & Cambodia: a travel survival kit.**
Daniel Robinson, Joe Cummings. Hawthorn, Victoria: Lonely Planet, 1991. 563p. maps. (Lonely Planet Travel Survival Kit).

While superseded by the 1992 *Cambodia: a lonely planet travel survival kit* (q.v.), many travellers may decide to acquire the combined Vietnam, Laos and Cambodia edition in the interest of convenience, so it is also included here. With nearly 100 pages devoted to Cambodia, and containing plates of illustrations, plans and an index, it is a useful guide. See the remarks on the later Cambodia volume for more detail of its contents, which have, of course, been updated and somewhat expanded in the latter.

62 **Vietnam, Laos and Cambodia handbook 1995.**
Editors, Joshua Eliot, John Colet, Jonathan Miller and Georgina Matthews; cartographer, Sebastian Ballard. Bath, England: Trade & Travel Publications; Chicago: Passport Books, 1994. 527p.

Ninety pages of information on Cambodia are to be found in this easy-to-carry, compact hardbound book which, in addition to the three countries mentioned in the title, also has sixty pages on Bangkok. Although presented as a 1995 edition, political events mentioned stop at September 1993, with the exception of the April 1994 kidnapping of foreign tourists. Handy boxes and sidebars provide facts and figures and cover interesting issues such as the two sides in the debate about the role of irrigation under the Angkor kings, as well as biographical data on Pol Pot and Norodom Sihanouk. The book contains a limited word-list and few maps, but an unusual one of national parks is included.

Le Cambodge et ses monuments: la province de Ba Phnom. (Cambodia and its monuments: the province of Ba Phnom.)
See item no. 156.

Vietnam, Laos & Cambodia [braille]: a travel survival kit.
See item no. 971.

city.net Cambodia.
See item no. 980.

Lonely Planet Destinations: Cambodia.
See item no. 986.

Travellers' Accounts and Exploration

63 **Angkor and the Khmers.**
Malcolm MacDonald, with 112 photographs by Loke Wan Tho and the author. Singapore: Oxford University Press, 1987. 158p. Originally published as *Angkor,* London: Jonathan Cape, 1958.

Sir Malcolm MacDonald was British Commissioner-General for Southeast Asia in the 1950s and in that role made frequent visits to Cambodia. This book, first published in 1958, is one product of his work, written in a style that might be expected of a colonial administrator of his time. It is principally an account of the founding of the temple city of Angkor Wat and the Cambodian kings that built it. While it is a useful contemporary document, with an assessment of the young King Norodom Sihanouk, the book suffers from the all too familiar mistaken idea that French explorers rediscovered the abandoned temple complex as they stumbled across it in the Cambodian jungle, and that except for this it would have disappeared. The volume includes reproductions of ninety-one photographs taken by Loke Wan Tho (otherwise unidentified) and twenty-one by MacDonald himself.

64 **L'Annam et le Cambodge: voyages et notices historiques, accompagnés d'une carte géographique.** (Annam and Cambodia: historical travels and reports, accompanied by a geographic map.)
C.-E. Bouillevaux. Paris: Victor Palmé, 1874. 544p. map.

Bouillevaux was one of the earliest French people to spend any length of time in Cambodia. He was a Christian priest who stayed for two years in southern Vietnam before seeking refuge in Cambodia in 1850. He spent two days at Angkor in December of that same year, and then, after a time in Laos, he settled in Battambang in 1855. In 1858 in Paris his *Voyage en Indochine 1848-1856* was published. After he returned to France, this later book was published, in which he embellished his earlier description and added to it a polemic against the extravagant claims that Mouhot had 'discovered' the site, which Bouillevaux pointed out was, of course, never actually lost by the Cambodians themselves, and which he himself had visited, and published his descriptions of, some five years prior to Mouhot's first reports.

65 **Bali and Angkor: a 1930s pleasure trip looking at life and death.**
Geoffrey Gorer. Singapore; Oxford; New York: Oxford University Press, 1986. 240p. maps. Originally published, [London]: Michael Joseph Ltd., 1936.

Gorer travelled for three months through Sumatra, Java, Bali, Thailand and Cambodia. His stated purpose was to try to work out the role of 'those illogical manifestations, art and religion in the life of the community'. As his travels were brief he admits he saw many of his sights from hotel and car windows. He reveals considerable knowledge of European art but sadly does not restrain the strength of his opinions on areas he knows little about. Chiefly focusing on aesthetics, Gorer presents his strong opinions in lively, sometimes judgemental, language, for example, calling the hill of Phnom Penh a 'nasty little wart'. Although the work is not terribly informative it is interesting and often amusing, especially for readers who have knowledge of the places he discusses. It includes a detailed and appreciative chapter on Angkor Wat.

66 **Bibliographie des voyages dans l'Indochine française du IXe au XIXe siècle.** (Bibliography of travels in French Indochina from the 9th to the 19th centuries.)
Antoine Brébion. New York: Burt Franklin, 1970. 299p. (Bibliography and Reference Series, 395). Originally published, Saigon, 1910. (Geography and Discovery, 8).

Most of the book comprises a chronologically ordered list of the main authors on their travels to Indochina, including a short biography, and a bibliography of their writings with quotations of the most important passages. Later sections give chronological lists of the missionaries (by order) and general adventurers. A now quite outdated bibliography of scholarly studies follows, and then indexes which separately list anonymously authored works by title and other works by author. An appendix subsequently published in Saigon in 1911 does not appear to have been included in the Burt Franklin republication.[David G. Marr with Kristine Alilunas-Rodgers]

67 **Bitter victory.**
Robert Shaplen. New York: Harper & Row, 1986. 309p. maps.

Robert Shaplen, a writer who had spent much time in Indochina during the years of the US-Vietnam war, returned to Vietnam in 1984, curious to re-acquaint himself with, and understand, that country's nature. He questions why a country which sought peace for so very long would involve itself in the Cambodian conflict, to which he devotes one chapter. Over the course of a week he interviews many Cambodians, about surviving the Pol Pot years and rebuilding their country. He is particularly interested in the dynamics of the relationship between Cambodians and the Vietnamese advisers and military forces. Much of the chapter explains the complex origins of the situation in Cambodia, the moral issues of international involvement in the conflict and as such is an accessible modern history, with opinion gently included. Interviews with Sihanouk are recorded, as are conversations with leading political and press people of the 1960s and 1970s. It is a positive and hopeful book, with a strong sense of the social and historical responsibility of all nations of, and all nations involved in, Indochina. An index is included.

68 **Cambodian glory: the mystery of the deserted Khmer cities and their vanished splendour: and a description of life in Cambodia today.**

H. W. Ponder. London: Thornton Butterworth, 1936. xii, 320p. maps.

Indebted to the renowned art historians George Groslier and Philippe Stern, Ponder has presented what is basically an historical and social study of Cambodia in an informal, accessible form. Ranging from reflection on the personalities of the authors of ancient inscriptions to outlining Cambodia's main agricultural products, Ponder writes in an informal style, never failing to acquaint the reader with both important historical matters and trivial gossip about his fellow hotel guests. Visits to villages, dance performances, museums and many temples, major and minor, are intelligently recounted.

69 **Derailed in Uncle Ho's victory garden: return to Vietnam and Cambodia.**

Tim Page. London: Touchstone, 1996. 258p.

Renowned photographer Tim Page, whose images include the most memorable of the American war in Vietnam, here describes his rail and road journeys through Vietnam in 1985 and again in the 1990s, mingled with nostalgic sentimental recollections of the exploits of the foreign journalists during the war. Page devotes three chapters to his return to Cambodia in the 1990s to search for information surrounding the 1970 disappearance of his friend and fellow photographer, Sean Flynn, and several press colleagues. They were abducted in Svay Rieng by Vietnamese soldiers, but apparently were handed over to the Khmer Rouge and taken to Kompong Cham on the eastern bank of the Mekong where they were held for some months before being executed. Page arranged for the planting of a sacred bodhi tree in Vietnam's former DMZ (demilitarized zone) as a monument to all the journalists who died, like Flynn, in the Vietnam War. The intensity of emotion in this section of the book contrasts strongly with the raucous and irreverent tone of the rest of the text, in which the local people seem to function only as backdrop and constant threat to foreigners' fun and games.

70 **Down Highway One: journeys through Vietnam and Cambodia.**

Sue Downie, illustrated by Venn Savat. St. Leonards, New South Wales: Allen & Unwin, 1993. xviii, 234p. map; Hong Kong: Asia 2000, 1993.

Sue Downie is an Australian journalist (principally working in radio) who lived in Cambodia from 1990 to 1995, covering this period's many changes in régime before becoming adviser to the Ministry of Information in the new Royal Government of Cambodia. This book is an account of a journey she took in 1988 along the famous Highway One, part of which had earlier been known as the Mandarin Way. Downie relates meetings with various people along the way, along the 2,100 kilometres from Lang Son on the China-Vietnam border to Phnom Penh, describing the atmosphere and daily rhythms of their lives, while including broader observations and reminiscences from several later trips along the highway, and from her experiences covering both countries as a journalist.

71 **A dragon apparent: travels in Cambodia, Laos and Vietnam.**
Norman Lewis. London: Eland, 1982. 317p. map. Originally published, London: Cape, 1951. Republished as part of *The Norman Lewis Omnibus*.

Permeated by a dismissive or condescending tone, which would be rare to find in academic or travel writing today, which tends to respect 'otherness', rather than be appalled and yet fascinated by it. The Khmer and Cham civilizations are described as 'brilliant and neurotic'; the Cambodians and Laotians today as people '. . . in monastic retirement, non-participants . . . in the march of progress . . . listless and degenerate'. Lewis does not introduce himself, or the purpose of his travels, the record of which was published in January 1951, as the Vietminh were wresting their country from the French. The author reaches Cambodia from Saigon, driving through disputed territory. Four chapters deal with Cambodia and, despite his strong notions about how one measures progress or cultural superiority, Lewis provides a philosophical, entertaining depiction of the country and its people. The political situation was turbulent during his trip, and asides are made about Khmer Issarak attacks and 'piracy'. That he was travelling just before the countries became independent, and emphasized the potential of Indochina uniting to form a barrier against communist China is one of the most interesting aspects of the book, as he discusses the suitability of communism to Cambodians with various local and French officials along the way. Lewis holds an interview with His Majesty, King Sihanouk, about Cambodia's desire for the French to leave. The neon-noise of the Chinese contribution to Phnom Penh, Madame Shum's 'salon de desintoxication', nightclubs, the French troops, and the compulsory pilgrimage to Angkor make a long-distant trip by a stranger tangible today.

72 **Eaux et lumières: journal de route sur le Mékong Cambodgien.**
(Water and light: travel diary on the Cambodian Mekong.)
George Groslier. Paris: Société d'Éditions Géographiques Maritimes et Coloniales, 1929. 105p.

A fascinating account of Cambodian village and temple life along the four major rivers in the high water months of 1929 and the low water months of 1930. Not written by any ordinary traveller, but by George Groslier, the man in charge of temples and monuments throughout the Protectorate, who brought the experience of fifteen years' residence in Cambodia as well as his academic knowledge to the task of writing the journal of the journeys to as many temples as he could visit from the river road. Here he sets aside the scholarly recording of the temples to tell us of the details of the journey itself and the sights he saw – from the dramatic fish trapping forays of the Tonle Sap to conversations with village elders. Interspersed are the stories of the explorers who went before – such as the first French envoy, one M. de Montigny, sent by Napoleon III, who arrived in Kampot in 1855 and found it was too hot and Phnom Penh was too far away, so he returned to France without meeting the King who was awaiting his visit! Throughout the book are references to the penetration of Chinese business and culture all over the country. Twenty-four black-and-white photographs accompany the text.

73 **Elvin's rides.**
Harold Elvin. [London]: Longmans, [1963]. 1 vol. maps. Also published in large print edition, Leicester, England: Ulverscrift, 1963. 203p. maps.

These are a traveller's tales with a difference, as Elvin records a motorcycle ride in 1963 from Bangkok to Siem Reap via Aranyaprathet, together with Ramesh Desai. The account switches between description of the journey itself – the heat, dryness, 'inedible' food, the terror of bandits, and the elusive jungle that was found only at Siem Reap – and Elvin's impressions of the temples, with a particular wry and idiosyncratic turn of phrase that lift them above the myriad run-of-the-mill descriptions. 'A word describes Angkor Wat. Strong. . . . It looked so established: as the earth, the sea, the rain and the wind are established . . . all the buildings are a riot of carving that has the crimp of scalloped butter about it . . . Angkor, you give all who love creation the sublime shot in the arm.' Several photographs show the motorcycle and the ruins, including one at the Door of the Dead where Philippe Lavoisier was murdered by bandits 'on this spot' in 1926. The book also contains chapters on 'Ride to Chieng Mai' and 'Ride to Hell' (in Lapland).

74 **Escape with me!: an Oriental sketch-book.**
Osbert Sitwell. Hong Kong: Oxford University Press, 1986, xv, 339p. bibliog. (Oxford Paperbacks). Originally published, London: Macmillan, 1939.

Intended for amusement, as a descriptive record and not for instruction, this 'Oriental sketchbook' is admittedly escapist. Sitwell aims to describe, with the traveller and art-lover's eye, rather than to analyse the social conditions and history of what he sees, despite being known as somewhat of a political campaigner. Divided into two parts, book one, 'Exotic vistas', deals with Indochina, while book two focuses entirely on China. Sitwell sailed from Marseilles to Saigon, then travelled overland to Phnom Penh and subsequently Angkor. A chapter each is devoted to Phnom Penh, Angkor, the annals of Chinese emissary Chou Ta-Kuan, and the town of Siem Reap. Romantically and thoughtfully described, Sitwell calls upon archaeologists and poets to enrich his depiction of Cambodia. He is grateful to Dr. Marchal, Dr. Quatrich Wales and Monsieur Goloubew, whose investigations he refers to frequently. Despite its age and pervading orientalism this is a fairly informed and entertaining read. It includes an index.

75 **L'exploitation du Mékong: la mission Ernest Doudart de Lagrée – Francis Garnier (1866-1868).** (The exploitation of the Mekong: the mission of Ernest Doudart de Lagrée – Francis Garnier, 1866-68.)
Jean-Pierre Gomane. Paris: L'Harmattan, 1994. 287p. maps. bibliog. (Recherches Asiatiques).

A recent French re-examination of the historic exploration of the Mekong in 1866-68. Gomane, who was an officer in the French marines in Indochina, here describes the mission to determine the possibility of opening a navigable route from China to Saigon. While it demonstrated the impracticality of such a project, it nevertheless provided considerable scientific information about a region previously uncharted by Westerners, and stands as a monument to the heroic efforts of the explorers, with the leader Doudart de Lagrée dying en route and his deputy Garnier completing the mission. Gomane makes good use of the documents of the mission itself, adding substantial annexes on the members of the expedition and ancillary documentation surrounding their mission. The bibliography is of particular importance, organized into archival sources, documents by members of the mission and secondary sources. An index is also contained.

76 **Explorers of South-East Asia: six lives.**

Edited and introduced by Victor T. King. Oxford: Oxford University Press, 1995. 280p. (Oxford in Asia Paperbacks).

King states that his aim is to provide the 'more human', personal dimension to the study of European expansion and exploration in Southeast Asia to 'the broad conceptual terms' generally employed by social scientists. Six of the most notable explorers (two French, two Scottish, one Dutch and one Norwegian) were selected, and experts on their time and place were invited to devote approximately fifty pages to each to explore their 'successes and failures, their trials and tribulations'. Cambodia features, if not centrally, in two of the stories – those of the French explorers Henri Mouhot, written by Michael Smithies, and Francis Garnier, written by Milton Osborne. Mouhot's journey to Angkor in 1859-60 occupies only eleven pages, as the emphasis is on the more exploratory journeys he made in Thailand/Laos. As Smithies points out Angkor was certainly not 'lost', and Mouhot himself never claimed to have 'rediscovered' it, as others have so often proclaimed. Cambodia likewise receives only some ten pages in Osborne's account of Garnier's life, and his participation and brief leadership of the renowned Lagrée-Garnier Mekong Expedition, which took two years and twenty-four days from Saigon through territories controlled by various authorities of Cambodia, Laos and Burma into southern China. While it failed in its attempt to establish the Mekong River as a commercial route for trade with China, Osborne concludes that it 'still remains as one of the greatest journeys of the nineteenth century'. The book sadly lacks an index.

77 **An eyewitness account of the Cambodian expedition.**

Diego de Aduarte, translated by Alfonso Felix Jnr. Manila: Historical Conservation Society, 1988. 45p. (General History of the Philippines, pt. 1, vol. 31). (Historical Conservation Society, no. 47).

A transcript of the 46th-48th chapters of volume one of Fr. Diego de Aduarte's 'Historia de la Provincia del Santo Rosario de la Order de Predicadores en Filipinas, Japon y China' (History of the Province of Santo Rosario of the Order of the Preachers in the Philippines, Japan and China), describing his journey from Manila to Cambodia in 1595. It has been translated into English by Alfonso Felix Jnr, President of the Historical Conservation Society, as part of a project to write a general history of the Philippines. De Aduartes claims the journey followed the visit to Manila by a Portuguese and a Spanish ambassador from the King of Cambodia. It is a lively and richly informative account and, despite probable inaccuracies or exaggeration, reveals much about the nature of trade, navigation, battles, power struggles, and customs of the Cambodian region, and about the attitudes of the Spanish missionaries.

78 **Four faces of Siva: the detective story of a vanished race.**

Robert J. Casey. Indianapolis, Indiana: Bobbs-Merrill, 1929. xi, 373p. maps.

A classic orientalist work filled with tales of tigers, jungles, naked natives, buried cities and moonlight dances. Although a romanticized record of the 'shrines of the vasty distance', Angkor is examined in a fairly empirical way and despite the obvious taint of the times the author is very sympathetic to his guide's beliefs, oral legends and 'superstitions'. The book is a mélange of novel, travelogue and scholarship, all wrapped in the so-called mystery of 'who built Angkor?'. Casey quotes from Aymonier, S. Marchal, Mouhot, and Chou Ta-Kuan and refers to Pavie's documentation of local stories. The photographs are also useful for comparisons to Phnom Penh and Angkor today.

79 **The French in Indo-China: with a narrative of Garnier's explorations in Cochin-China, Annam and Tonquin.**
Preface by Dean Meyers. Bangkok: White Lotus, 1994. 142p.

First published by T. Nelson and Sons, Paternoster Row, Edinburgh, in 1884, this little book provides a useful selection from the first-hand accounts of the major early French exploratory voyages. The first three chapters represent a reworking by an unknown hand of the journal kept by Francis Garnier of the 1866-68 Garnier/Doudart de Lagrée expedition up the Mekong to China. Then follow chapters on 'Dr Morice and the Mekong', describing Cochinchina in 1872, and 'Mr Mouhot in Cambodia' on his journeys between 1858 and 1861. This was the form in which the book was published in 1879, but an expanded edition followed in 1884 with two chapters offering some analytical interpretation of the French presence by the unnamed presenter and presumed translator of the travellers' tales, who concludes thus: '. . . it has become plain, even to the French, that a good deal of troublesome work is cut out for the pioneers before they can enjoy their hearts' desire – an Empire in the Far East'. White Lotus here presents another affordable reprint, complete with thirty-two period engravings and a somewhat undistinguished new preface, which sadly does not speculate on the identity of the original compiler and editor.

80 **Gecko tails: a journey through Cambodia.**
Carol Livingston. London: Weidenfeld and Nicolson, 1996. 262p.

An eminently readable travel account of UNTAC and post-UNTAC Cambodia. Although concentrating too heavily on the banalities and inanities of the naive traveller becoming worldly-wise journalist, which it does very well nevertheless, it certainly brings out the flavour of the town and of today's expatriate lifestyle. Also, somehow or other the experiences of Cambodia and Cambodians do filter through and leave their impression on the reader as well as on Livingston herself. It is perhaps the best book one could hand to one's family or friends when they ask with incredulity, 'are you off to Cambodia again?'.

81 **The gentleman in the parlour: a record of a journey from Rangoon to Haiphong.**
W. Somerset Maugham. London: Pan Books in association with Heinemann, 1986. 175p. Originally published, London: William Heinemann Ltd., 1930.

'. . . if you like language for its own sake, if it amuses you to string words together in the order that most pleases you, so as to produce an effect of beauty, the essay or the book of travel gives you an opportunity. . . . Your style can flow like a broad placid river and the reader is borne along on its bosom with security; he need fear no shoals, no adverse currents, rapids or rock-strewn gorges.' So Somerset Maugham introduced his delightful record of travel, whose title is taken from the essayist Hazlitt who spoke of the joys of travel, being able to shake off the trammels of the world and public opinion and be known only as 'The Gentleman in the Parlour'. Only fifteen pages of this slim book relate to Cambodia, but they are worthy of attention by virtue of their colour and the reputation of the author, who arrived by boat at the port of Kep and travelled by car up to Phnom Penh, and thence by boat to Siem Reap. He speaks of the statue of Harihara in the Museum in Phnom Penh thus – 'here, unexpectedly, he has come across something that will for the rest of his life enrich his soul' – and on Angkor – 'I have never seen anything in the world more wonderful . . . but I do not know how on earth I am going to set down in black and white such an account of them as will give even the most sensitive reader more than a confused and shadowy impression of their grandeur'.

82 **Hard travel to sacred places.**
Rudolph Wurlitzer. Boston, Massachusetts: Shambhala, 1994. 161p.

This cathartic work is more coincidentally than consciously to do with Cambodia. Scriptwriter of the film *Little Buddha* and novelist, Wurlitzer, and his wife, photographer Lynn Davis, travel to Thailand, Burma and Cambodia, nominally for her to photograph sacred Buddhist sites, but really in an attempt to cope with the recent death of her son, as 'Western seekers looking for redemption in the East'. The three countries provide backdrops and props for personal drama, and interior journeying. Alternately poetic and banal, the narrative ranges over diverse territory to include travel details, Buddhist precepts, newspaper reports and extracts from spiritual and academic works. The reader is transported rapidly from musings on the spiritual impact of Angkor Wat to the broken tap back in the hotel room. In the work, Wurlitzer notes 'Lynn and I . . . are ripping off images and drama experiences and bringing them back to the reductive shredder of our own culture. It is up to us to assimilate and transform these experiences, not to exploit or showcase them' but unfortunately much of the book does just that.

83 **Henri Mouhot's diary: travels in the central part of Siam, Cambodia and Laos during the years, 1858-61.**
Abridged and edited by Christopher Pym. Kuala Lumpur: Oxford University Press, 1966. maps. bibliog.

Until the republication in 1992 of Mouhot's full account of his *Travels in Siam, Cambodia, and Laos, 1858-1860* (q.v.), this abridged version was the only easily accessible edition of this naturalist's carefully documented and beautifully illustrated account of his journeys, which offer a wealth of detailed observations that he made as he walked 800 leagues over three years.

84 **Un hiver au Cambodge: chasses au tigre à l'éléphant et au buffle sauvage, souvenirs d'une mission officielle remplie en 1880-1881.**
(A winter in Cambodia: hunting for tiger, elephant and wild buffalo: memories of an official mission, mounted in 1880-81.)
Edgar Boulangier. Tours, France: Mame, 1887.

This is the typical colonial view of a trip to Cambodia. From Paris to Saigon, the trip is short – only one month. All the usual cliches are here, in particular, musing over how the people who built Angkor came to fall to such a low situation. He attributes to an ancient Chinese visitor the idea that the Angkor armies had millions of soldiers. He relishes in a sadistic description of corporal punishments of which he obviously approves (when applied to 'natives', of course). An interesting part of the trip comes when the group goes north of Kompong Thom, 'through uncultivated savannahs', after 20 kilometres crossing the then Siamese border, into the land of the Kuys. They then reach the 'capital', a village called Kietruer, with monks and a pagoda, not far from the main smelting works at the foot of the Iron Mountain (Phnom Dek), which was the traditional source of iron for ancient Cambodia whose production he estimates at 3 tonnes a year. As a culmination of these colonialist views, he advocates the development of poppy cultivation: 2,000 hectares would suffice to provide for the consumption of the 30,000 opium smokers of Cochinchina. He also advocates the creation of a native military force, a railway system and a colonial bank, all of which were indeed to come to pass in the ensuing years.

85 **King cobra: an autobiography of travel in French Indochina.**
Harry Hervey. New York: Cosmopolitan Book Corp., 1927. 301p.

Like many travellers, Hervey first encountered Angkor in a book as a child and was mesmerized. Years later he travelled there from Saigon in a French motor car, to experience a 'sense of exquisite fulfilment' upon a night-time excursion through Angkor Wat. Writing in a florid style, Hervey briefly describes the major temples and their political and cultural history as it was then known, but devotes most of his words to romantic pondering about the ancient past. However, the chapter on Phnom Penh is more lively and contains interesting observations, especially about the 'good life' to be had by the French colonials and the royal family. He also colourfully recounts the voyage he took up the Mekong. It is a classic work, often verging on the erotic, always aesthetic in its description of the East.

86 **The land in between: the Cambodian dilemma.**
Maslyn Williams. Sydney; London: Collins, [1969]. 255p.; New York: Morrow, 1970. bibliog.

An easy-to-read and thoughtful account of the author's visit to Cambodia in the late 1960s. Williams depicts a country standing still, not daring to cross the brink of modernization, where all public political life was carefully stage-managed. He alludes to the then extremely divided and not highly visible guerrilla rebellions in various parts of the country where the government ruled by day and the guerrillas by night. His travels throughout the country afford glimpses of rural life and the workings of local bureaucrats. Traditional ceremonies, provincial capitals and newly built health and educational institutions – Sihanouk's proudest achievements – are counterpoised against the lifestyles of the Cambodian élite, glamorous social events, fast cars, spoilt young people and intense gossip. Rivalry between the French and Americans for political influence was evident.

87 **Land of the white parasol and the million elephants: a journey through the jungles of Indo-China.**
Sidney J. Legendre, illustrated from photographs by Gertrude Legendre. New York: Dodd, Mead & Company, 1936. 315p. Reprinted, microfilm/xerography, Ann Arbor, Michigan; London: University Microfilms International, 1982.

An entertaining account of an expedition for the American Museum of Natural History, which Legendre's wife Gertrude had instigated. 'It had been her urge to push through uninhabited jungles . . . she proved to be the only member of the expedition who never cried quits.' Partly a practical guide and partly a personal narrative, it is also an honest attempt at describing unfamiliar culture. Legendre offers such advice as that 'bacon cannot be purchased in Hanoi', reflection that he 'cannot imagine anything more pleasant than a life spent with a bottle and a gecko', and wry observations about the natives and the French. Amid hunting and being entertained, the party manages to have amusing encounters with local officials and characters, as well as exploring magnificent landscape. Their travels take them primarily through Vietnam and Laos; only one chapter is devoted to Cambodia, which includes descriptions of a night at the Metropole in Kompong Thom, and hunting with a special rifle for a large, rare ibis around Angkor.

88 **Little vehicle: Cambodia & Laos.**

Alan Houghton Brodrick. London: Hutchinson, [1949?]. vi, 266p.

Written in 1947, the book records the author's travels in Cambodia in 1939, when, as he explains, 'the European grip upon most of south-eastern Asia was still secure', a grip that was broken first by the Japanese army and later at the hands of independence movements. He paints a serene picture of Cambodia and of its capital Phnom Penh, where there are 'no grubby suburbs' and 'no ring of misery encircles the place'. The author explains the title: 'But to-day, Hinayana Buddhism is so all-pervasive in Cambodia, that I can think of no better name to give this book than "Little Vehicle". The State religion and the Established Church still link Cambodia with the India to which the Khmers owed their civilization. If, however, Cambodia owes much to India, the land of the Khmers is not a "Little India" . . . The creations of Khmer art are creations, not copies'. This is an interesting snapshot of the period which provides some detail of ceremonial life and of provincial centres.

89 **Mekong upstream: a visit to Laos and Cambodia.**

Wilfred G. Burchett. Berlin: Seven Seas, 1959. 289p. maps.

Previously published, Hanoi: Red River Publishing House, 1957.

An account from the radical reporter and writer who was renowned for political commitment to the underdog of any situation he was covering. With great integrity, he never sought to disguise his allegiance, telling stories from the 'other side', and discrediting US foreign policy around the world. Although Burchett lived in Cambodia for four years and knew the country well, he was at first loath to acknowledge the truth of reports by refugees fleeing the Khmer Rouge régime. However, he later broke a long relationship with the *New York Guardian*, which refused to adopt an anti-Pol Pot position, despite Burchett's 1978 reports from the Kampuchea-Vietnam border. *Mekong upstream* was one of the first books ever published about 20th-century Cambodian politics, and Burchett was the first (and for many years the only) Western writer to analyse the early history of communism in Cambodia. It is a richly descriptive book, capturing street life in Phnom Penh and the rural cycles of subsistence. While his attention is given to the Khmers, rather than the expatriate circuit, they do not avoid being romanticized to some extent. State farm systems, gem mining, a tiger hunt and the temples at Angkor are described, but the book is predominantly a political analysis of Cambodian factions' roles and histories, religion's role in the nationalist movement, and the nature of Sihanouk's 'neutrality'. Two parts of the book are each devoted to Laos and Cambodia. While his avowedly pro-Asian bias leads him to exaggerate some phenomena and neglect others, his assessments and sources are generally far better informed than any other journalist's or even than intelligence reports of the time.

90 **Mission Pavie Indo-Chine 1879-1895.** (The Pavie Indochina Mission 1879-95.)

Auguste Pavie. Paris: Leroux, 1898. 3 vols. SOM D.278.

This multi-volume work contains the detailed reports of a number of Indochinese missions directed by Auguste Pavie over sixteen years. In addition it contains a single volume on the literature of Cambodia, Laos and Siam, containing an introduction and French translations of the folk tales: 'Neang Roum Say Sock'; 'Les douze jeunes filles' (Twelve young girls); 'Vorvong et Saurivong' and 'Neang Kakey'. This is followed by original Khmer, Lao and Thai texts and plates. Its introduction describes how Pavie sent thirteen young Cambodian men to Paris for study in 1885, to form l'École Cambodgienne (the Cambodian School) – later transformed into l'École Coloniale (the Colonial School) – and how eleven of them joined him in 1888 for his expedition to pacify the Black River, but that four of these died on the expedition (two from fever, one from wounds and one in captivity). This book testifies to their heroic deeds 'in the territories that they assisted to make French'.

91 **Mistapim in Cambodia.**

Christopher Pym, photographs by the author. London: Hodder & Stoughton, [1960]. 192p.

The author of *The road to Angkor: journey from Champa, Viet-Nam to Angkor, Cambodia* (q.v.) returned in 1956 to immerse himself in Cambodia for nearly two years. 'I had two objectives – travel and study. Besides visiting remote Khmer ruins in the forests of Cambodia, I wanted to meet the modern Khmers (Cambodians) and penetrate their way of life. Too often in the past the ruins of Angkor had overshadowed the descendants of its builders, and whatever interest I had in the ancient Khmers, I was determined not to let it overshadow the modern Khmers.' Pym vividly describes city life (especially the Chinese in Phnom Penh, with whom he lived), opium smoking with the French, the Royal Ballet and even audiences with King Norodom Suramarit and with Prime Minister and former King, Prince Norodom Sihanouk. Festivals punctuating the Buddhist year, the visit to Cambodia by Chinese Premier Chou En Lai, and a triumphant return of Sihanouk from one of his many overseas trips are all recounted. The book contains no footnotes but includes quaint dialogues and personal anecdotes, and a wealth of observations on Cambodian life and customs and their intersection with Western modernity.

92 **A pilgrimage to Angkor.**

Pierre Loti, based on a translation by W. P. Baines, edited and introduced by Michael Smithies, illustrations by Euayporn Kerchouay. Bangkok: Silkworm Books, 1996. 107p.

Loti (Julien Viaud), a French naval officer, eccentric, socialite, exotic novelist and travel writer, travelled to Angkor in 1901. He visited a mausoleum built by King Norodom and was received at the Royal Palace in Phnom Penh along the way from Saigon to Angkor, where he spent only two days. Previously published as *Siam,* which was edited to appear quite archaic, this edition is introduced and footnoted by Michael Smithies, who also revised the translation, making it more faithful to Loti's original work. His writing style is evocative and romantic, favouring artistic form over historical content. It offers an inspirational, sometimes fanciful impression of Angkor Wat and the Bayon, and could be used as an accompaniment to a drier guide.

93 **River road to China: the Mekong River Expedition 1866-73.**
Milton Osborne. London; Sydney: George Allen & Unwin, 1997. 2nd ed. 249p. map. Originally published, London: Allen & Unwin; New York: Liveright, 1975.

This is a well-timed new edition given the recent resurgence of interest – economic, cultural and scientific – in the Mekong River. In 1866 French explorers made a difficult and dangerous two-year journey up the Mekong, from the delta to the mountains of southwest China. Led by Francis Garnier and Ernest Doudart de Lagrée, who died *en route*, they were seeking possibly to lay claim to the area, find abundant resources, map and document the river and its inhabitants and find a trade route with China. The journey has renewed relevance in the context of today's international and regional involvement in the Mekong's development. Osborne writes beautifully and objectively, exploring not only the characters of the French explorers but the character of their time and place in history. The work is extremely well informed and well researched, and at the same time engagingly presented. The second edition is enhanced with colour reproductions of illustrations by the expedition's artist, Delaporte. An index and author's note make this fascinating story easy to use as a history. This second edition was first published in 1996 (Singapore: Didier Millet) with a different cover.

94 **The road to Angkor: journey from Champa, Viet-Nam to Angkor, Cambodia.**
Christopher Pym. London: Hale; London: Travel Book Club, 1959. 185p.

A classic traveller's tale, filled with astute and sensitive observation of local life. Pym travelled for seven weeks in 1957, through what was a newly-independent Cambodia, seeking to find the remnants of an ancient road linking Angkor to the coast. As he travelled on foot, covering 450 miles, his view of the country is sympathetic to the village-level experience. He recounts details about animal life, various tribal groupings, the importance of the king, spiritual beliefs, food and architecture, as well as his own joys and difficulties along the journey. Both entertaining and informative, it can be read purely for pleasure or as a guide to change and continuity in some of the remoter parts of Cambodia.

95 **Les ruines d'Angkor de Duong-Duong et de My-son – Cambodge et Annam.** (The ruins of Angkor, Duong-Duong, My-son – Cambodia and Annam.)
Charles Carpeaux. Paris: Augustin Challamel, Librairie Coloniale, 1908. 259p.

This volume comprises the letters, travel diary and photographic plates made by Charles Carpeaux, Chief of Practical Works for the EFEO. They were collected by his mother on his death at only thirty-four years of age in Saigon in 1904. It contains reports of his four 'missions', two in Cambodia (1901-02 and 1904) and two in Annam (1902 and 1903-04) and a note on the significance of two bas-reliefs taken from Angkor. The text is interspersed with 66 of the more than 2,000 photographs he took during his work in Indochina, and they reveal valuable information on the state of the monuments, the work involved in their restoration, and on daily life, revealing Carpeaux as a sensitive and acute observer.

96 **The Straits of Malacca, Siam and Indo-China: travels and adventures of a nineteenth-century photographer.**
John Thomson, with an introduction by Judith Balmer. Oxford: Oxford University Press, 1993. 178p. (Oxford in Asia Hardback Reprints). Originally published as *The Straits of Malacca, Indo-China and China or Ten years' travels, adventures and residence abroad*, London: Marston, Loward Searle, 1875.

A valuable reprint of the first six chapters of Thomson's original work with its engravings, supplemented by sixteen of Thomson's Southeast Asian photographs (only two of Cambodia) and a twenty-four-page introduction by Judith Balmer outlining Thomson's life and his travel photography. John Thomson lived in Southeast Asia from 1861 to 1868, and visited Cambodia for several months in 1865, during which time he took the first photographs of Angkor Wat. This journey is described in a fifty-page chapter with six engravings from his photographs (at that time the process of mechanically reproducing photographs for publication was not yet developed). Thomson travelled from Bangkok by boat, on foot, and by elephant and pony through to Sisophon and across the Tonle Sap lake to Siem Reap, where the Siamese governor warmly received the party. After spending several days photographing the principal monuments (Angkor Wat and Bayon in particular), they first attempted to return to Bangkok westward over the mountains but, finding this route impenetrable, they turned back and followed the Tonle Sap down to Phnom Penh and then travelled overland to Kampot and by boat back to Bangkok. Thomson's masterful photographs were made under extremely difficult conditions, which Balmer describes in the introduction. The photographic process was laborious and required carrying heavy equipment, fragile glass plates and chemicals, and establishing a dark tent at every site. Some of his Cambodian photographs appeared in Thomson's 'small (and now rare) edition' of *The Antiquities of Cambodia*, in 1867, and it is a delight to see them here, though so few in number. Can we soon see a reproduction of the complete set?

97 **Thoughtful traveller's Thailand, Burma, Cambodia and China.**
Rachel Wheatcroft. s.l.: Allborough Publishing, 1992. new ed. [330]p. Originally published as *Siam and Cambodia in pen and pastel*, London: Constable, 1928.

On the journey described here, Wheatcroft visited many countries including Burma and Vietnam. Two chapters are devoted to Cambodia, the first on the basis of her own observations and the second referring to those by Chinese diplomat Chou Ta-Kuan in 1296-97, and by French scholar George Groslier in the 20th century. Her writing style is conversational and anecdotal, reflecting her desire to travel affordably and to meet people. She hopes that, in 'some slight degree sketches replace a common tongue . . .' in her meeting with other cultures. Fresh and simple line-drawings perhaps do this more effectively than the pastels, which are very small and slightly fuzzy. This is a quaint travel journal, recommended more for interest than information.

98 **Tiger balm: travels in Laos, Vietnam & Cambodia.**
Lucretia Stewart. London: Chatto & Windus, 1992. vi, 267p. map.

A journalist who spent many of her formative years in Asia, Stewart offers a personal and sympathetic portrait of the people and places she encountered on her solo travels through Laos, Vietnam and Cambodia. It contains accounts of experiences and stories relayed to her by locals, and of observations on landscape and culture, with much about culture shock, and some quotations from reputed historians. Stewart recounts both the joys and frustrations of a white woman's travel in foreign cultures, and for this reason alone it stands out from the large body of mostly mediocre travel writing on Cambodia.

99 **Travels in Siam, Cambodia, and Laos, 1858-1860.**
Henri Mouhot, with an introduction by Michael Smithies. Singapore: Oxford, 1992. 2 vols. in 1. maps. bibliog. (Oxford in Asia Hardback Reprints). Also published, Bangkok: White Lotus, 1986. Originally published, London: John Murray, 1864.

This beautifully bound volume contains, in addition to Mouhot's text and Smithies' introduction, a preface by the author's brother, a memoir giving details of Mouhot's life by the naturalist Belinfante, appendices listing new species Mouhot had 'discovered', atmospherical observations, seven tales translated from Chinese, an impressive Cambodian vocabulary, and a small collection of personal letters to, from, and about, Henri Mouhot. The body of the text is based on his travel journals, taken by his loyal servants from the jungle in Laos where he died in 1861, and arranged by his brother Charles. His extensive travels, skillfully recounted, are accompanied by engravings from many of his own sketches. It is a fitting tributary edition to the renowned adventurer, professor, naturalist and artist. See also the abridged edition published under the title, *Henri Mouhot's diary: travels in the central part of Siam, Cambodia and Laos during the years, 1858-61* (q.v.).

100 **Travels on the Mekong.**
Louis de Carné. Bangkok: White Lotus, 1994. 320p.

A report on the most famous expedition in Indochina – the 1866-73 exploration of the Mekong River as a trade route and as a way to build French political influence in the area.

101 **Voyage au Cambodge: l'architecture khmer.** (Journey to Cambodia: Khmer architecture.)
L. Delaporte. Paris: Delagrave, 1880. 462p. map. bibliog.

Delaporte participated in the 1866-68 mission exploring the Mekong River and Indochina and then led the 1873 mission sent to explore Khmer monuments. He subsequently went on to found the Musée Khmer (Khmer Museum), Paris. As well as recounting the architectural discoveries, this huge tome is graced with 175 engravings and a map.

102 **Voyage d'exploration en Indochine.** (Voyage of exploration in Indochina.)
Francis Garnier, revised and annotated by Léon Garnier. Paris: Hachette, 1885. 1 vol. Originally published in 2 vols., Paris: Hachette, 1873. maps.

The original report of the major exploratory mission 4,000 miles up the Mekong from its mouth in Saigon through Vietnam, Cambodia, Thailand, Laos, Burma and China. The leader, Ernest Doudart de Lagrée, died *en route*, and his deputy Francis Garnier completed the mission and published this account. Milton Osborne's rendition, *River road to China: the Mekong River Expedition 1866-73* (q.v.) makes the tale accessible to the general English-speaking reader, but Garnier's own words still stand as the definitive account of their trials and tribulations.

The living Mekong.
See item no. 16.

Des français au Cambodge: anthologie. (By the French in Cambodia: anthology.)
See item no. 202.

Down highway one [sound recording]: journeys through Vietnam and Cambodia.
See item no. 965.

Flora and Fauna

103 **Bats from Thailand and Cambodia.**
John Edwards Hill and Kitti Thonglongya. *Bulletins of the British Museum (Natural History): Zoology*, vol. 22, no. 6 (1972), p. 171-96. bibliog.

The majority of specimens documented originate from Thailand, with the Cambodian specimens mostly having been obtained by J. M. Klein from the Muséum National d'Histoire Naturelle (National Museum of Natural History) in Paris. The text consists of an account of species, by name, providing location, and matched to previous records or reports. Figures show: length of skull and rostrum in Cynopterus sphinx, comparison between Asian regions; and length of forearm and ear in Cynopterus sphinx and C. brachyotis in Burma, Tenasserim, Thailand, Indochina, Malaya and Sumatera, Java and Ceylon. Tables provide measurements of Rhinolophus shameli, R. coelophyllus, and Myotis annectans. The occurrence of each species, notes on their previous documentation by naturalists, and the implications for classification of the finds are included in the species list. Only seven species from this list are noted as occurring in Cambodia. This paper includes illustrations.

104 **Bibliographie botanique de l'Indochine.** (Botanical bibliography of Indochina.)
Alfred Pételot. Saigon: Centre National de Recherches Scientifiques et Techniques. Archives des Recherches Agronomiques et Pastorales au Cambodge Laos Vietnam, 1955. 102p. (Archives de la Recherche Agronomique, 24).

Having researched plants in Indochina from the 1920s, and also spent time in Europe checking specialized libraries, Pételot was well qualified to compile this bibliography. Books, periodical articles, and other reports are listed within the subdivisions of botanical branches: phanerogams, pteridophytes, bryophytes, fungi, algae, and lichens. Each section is structured alphabetically by author, with a veritable explosion of publications in the 1920s and 1930s, and relatively few after 1944. This work is more comprehensive than Pételot's 1929 bibliography entitled *La botanique en Indochine,* incorporating the new material published and the extensive fieldwork carried out since then. No index is provided. [David G. Marr with Kristine Alilunas-Rodgers]

105 **Bibliographie botanique indochinoise de 1970 à 1985: documents pour 'La flore du Cambodge, du Laos et du Viêtnam'.** (Indochinese botanical bibliography: documents for 'The flora of Cambodia, Laos and Vietnam'.)

J. E. Vidal, Y. Vidal and Pham Hoang Ho. Paris: Muséum National d'Histoire Naturelle, Laboratoire de Phanérogamie, 1988. 132p.

A later version of an article published in *Bulletin de la Société des Études Indochinoises* (Bulletin of the Society of Indochinese Studies), New Series, vol. 47, no. 4 (1972), p. 657-748. The work was prepared as a continuation to Pételot's *Bibliographie botanique de l'Indochine* (q.v.) on the basis of a number of more general bibliographies of Southeast Asia, and on the author's study tour in 1971 in which local works with limited circulation were also identified. Jules Vidal, a researcher from the French CNRS, reports the results (primarily French- and English-language items) in various indexes: author-title, subject, taxonomic, and publications searched. There are no annotations.

106 **Bibliography to floras of Southeast Asia: Burma, Laos, Thailand (Siam), Cambodia, Viet Nam (Tonkin, Annam, Cochinchina), Malay Peninsula, and Singapore.**

Clyde F. Reed. Baltimore, Maryland: [s.n.], 1969. 191p.

The author was, at the time of publication of this stencilled typescript, a research botanist and plant explorer for the United States Department of Agriculture, and collaborator in the Department of Botany of the Smithsonian Institution, Washington, DC. The bibliography reports 3,800 works, almost entirely in French. It covers floristic works and taxonomic and monographic treatments of both vascular and non-vascular plants, including cultivated, agricultural and medicinal plants, forestry, and fossil flora, and related publications in climatic and edaphic phenomena. Presented here in a single list, alphabetized by author, it is not clear how many items relate to Cambodia. There are no indexes or annotations.

107 **Bois-bambou: aspect végétal de l'univers jörai.** (Bamboo: vegetal aspect of the Jorai universe.)

Jacques Dournes. Paris: Éditions de Centre National de la Recherche Scientifique, 1969. 196p. (Atlas Ethno-linguistique, Second Series, Monographies, 2). Previously published as nos. 4-5-6 and 9-10-11 of the *Journal d'Agriculture Tropicale et de Botanique Appliquée* (1968).

The author lived among the Jorai of southern Vietnam from 1955 to 1968. The Jorai people are considered to be related to the Cham and Malay minorities and at that time numbered some 200,000 people, living in an area stretching from the plateau of southern Vietnam to the Ratanakiri province of Cambodia. Dournes here describes the universe of the Jorai, which he sees as the key to their social structure, the object of his research. Twenty-six plates of photographs supplement the text, and indexes to botanical and vernacular names are provided.

108 **Bryogéographie du Mont Bokor (Cambodge).** (Bryogeography of Mount Bokor, Cambodia.)
P. Tixier. Vaduz, Liechtenstein: J. Cramer, 1979. 121p. bibliog. (Bryophytorum Bibliotheca, no. 18). (Bryophyta Indosinica, no. 24).

On the basis of studies carried out between 1967 and 1970, the author provides 'a bird's eye view' of the physiography and vegetal formation of Mount Bokor in southern Cambodia. His main purpose is to present information on the bryophytes (mosses) of this environment from the taxonomical, ecological, sociological and biogeographical points of view. Tables, drawings and seven photographs complement the text.

109 **Contributions to a revision of the orchid flora of Cambodia, Laos and Vietnam.**
Gunnar Seidenfaden. Fredensborg, Denmark: Kai Olsen, 1975. 1 vol. bibliog.

This item provides the English and Latin names for the wealth of orchid flora of Cambodia, and contains illustrations. Descriptions are given in English, with a summary in French.

110 **Éléments de botanique indochinoise.** (Botanical elements of Indochina.)
P. A. Pételot, M. Magalon. Hanoi: Imprimerie d'Extrême-Orient, 1929. 205, xiip.

The authors present material used in their lectures at the University of Indochina, Hanoi, as a guide and supplement for the students' own observation. Elementary introductory chapters on cells and tissues are followed by discussions and examples of each part of the plant, and then detailed classification. Some 41 plates with 278 line-drawings illustrate the work.

111 **La faune sauvage du Cambodge: moeurs et chasse.** (The wildlife of Cambodia: habits and the hunt.)
Charles Dumas. Phnom Penh: Aymonier, [1944]. 280p. bibliog.

Divided into sections on bovides, elephants, great cats, gibier large and medium, and then diverse animals and birds, followed by a table of principal species with their French, Cambodian, Vietnamese and scientific names. This work combines a general description of hunting experiences and techniques with more detailed descriptions of each of the major animals. Previous works on hunting in Indochina had not covered Cambodia, with its distinctive geology, climate and animals, especially the kouprey. Supplemented with twenty-eight photographs and fourteen drawings from the pen of Jean Camus, unfortunately the engravings of proud beasts contrast horribly with the photographs of their corpses alongside smiling hunter and gun. Only fifty copies of this work were printed.

112 **A field guide to the birds of South-east Asia: covering Burma, Malaya, Thailand, Cambodia, Vietnam, Laos, and Hong Kong.**
Ben F. King and Edward C. Dickinson, illustrated by Martin W. Woodcock in collaboration with John Darnell, Ian C. T. Nisbet [and] David Wells. London: Collins, 1975. 480p. maps. bibliog.

This book covers all of the 1,198 species known to have been encountered prior to 31 May 1971 in the area covered. An attempt has been made to systematize 'suitable, distinct and brief' English names for the birds listed together with their scientific names, identification data, variation, measurements, voice, range, habitat and family accounts, and each species has been given a number. Copious black-and-white illustrations and sixty-four plates supplement the text. Indochina is divided into nine areas according to Delacour (1931), but the distribution table is not included, as it was intended to be published separately. This compact and easy-to-use volume contains an index and a useful, partially annotated bibliography.

113 **Flore du Cambodge, du Laos et du Viêtnam.** (Flora of Cambodia, Laos and Vietnam.)
Published under the direction of A. Aubréville; principal editor, Mme Tardieu-Blot. Paris: Laboratoire de Phanérogamie, Muséum National d'Histoire Naturelle, 1960-92. 27 vols. bibliog.

Comprises volumes 1-12, Supplément à la Flore générale de l'Indo-Chine (Supplement to the general flora of Indochina), and volumes 13-26, Révision de la Flore générale de l'Indochine (Revision of the general flora of Indochina).

114 **Flore et végétation orophiles de l'Asie tropicale: les épiphytes du flanc méridional du Massif Sud Annamitique.** (Flora and mountain vegetation of tropical Asia: orchids on the southern flank of the South Annamite Massif.)
P. Tixier. Paris: SEDES, 1966. 240p. bibliog.

Although limited to a study of the Dalat region of southern Vietnam, the results are of interest to anyone studying the Cambodian equivalents. It provides details of some 450 epiphytes (orchids, ferns, algaes, lichens etc.) found, and discusses their distribution and contribution to the ecology of the region. A significant bibliography of nearly 400 items published between 1854 and 1965 is included.

115 **Flore générale de l'Indo-Chine.** (General flora of Indochina.)
H. Lecomte, H. Humbert. Paris: Masson (later Laboratoire de Phanérogamie, Muséum National d'Histoire Naturelle), 1907-51. 7 vols. and *Tome préliminaire* and *Supplément*.

Two specialists provide a comprehensive descriptive flora of vascular plants, with keys to genera and species, full synonymy, references and citations, and vernacular names, etc. In the *Tome préliminaire* (1944) there are chapters on physical features, climate, geology, vegetation and forest, and botanical exploration. The *Supplément* comprises additions and corrections to the original work, but it does not cover all the families. The Muséum's collections continue to be examined and described in a multi-volume work entitled *Flore du Cambodge, du Laos et du Viêtnam* under the direction of A. Aubréville (q.v.).

116 **Le gisement de vertébrés du Phnom Loang (province de Kampot, Cambodge): faune pléistocène moyen terminal (Loangien).** (Vertebrae deposit from Phnom Loang, province of Kampot, Cambodia: middle late pleistocene fauna (Loangien).)
M. Beden and C. Guérin, with a foreword by J. P. Carbonnel. [Paris: ORSTOM, 1973]. 97p. bibliog. (Travaux et Documents de l'ORSTOM, no. 27).

J. P. Carbonnel was the researcher from the CNRS on the joint CNRS-ORSTOM geological mission to Cambodia in 1966 and 1967. He discovered a significant prehistoric deposit in the limestone caves of Kampot in southern Cambodia, which was analysed in the Poitiers Laboratory for Paleontology of Vertebrates. Only one cave, C57 of Phnom Loang, has delivered, in a pleistocene level, many remains of vertebrates, and is the first discovery of Pre-Neolithic fauna in the south of Indochina. 'Its essential interest lies in the association between well-known species from terminal middle Pleistocene layers of North Indochina and a Rhinoceros sondaicus guthi animal characterized by a relatively large size and premolars of high evolution degree. The faunal unit, named Loangien, would be parallelized with the upper Yenchingkuaonian, from the terminal middle Pleistocene.' Guérin analysed the Rhinoceros, while Beden studied the other remains.

117 **Introduction à l'ethnobotanique du Cambodge.** (Introduction to the ethnobotany of Cambodia.)
Marie A. Martin. Paris: Éditions du Centre National de la Recherche Scientifique, 1971. 257p. bibliog. (Atlas Ethno-Linguistique. 2. sér.: Monographies).

Based on research carried out in 1965-66, Martin presents principally the taxonomic results in over 200 pages of description and classification. She complements this with forty photographs and fifty pages of narrative text setting the context and discussing plants as used by humans in Cambodia. After reviewing epigraphic sources, then examining taxonomies of the 18th and 19th centuries through to more modern studies, Martin moved on to her own extensive observation and research of over 450 of the 500 plants here recorded. A bibliography and indexes to botanical and vernacular names are provided.

118 **Inventaire général de l'Indochine: la faune de l'Indochine – vertébrés.** (General inventory of Indochina: the fauna of Indochina – vertebrates.)
Réné Bourret. Hanoi: Société de Géographie, 1927. 453p. bibliogs.

Bourret provides a classified listing of vertebrates, with as many examples as could be located. There are brief physical descriptions of each order, suborder, family, and species, with some names in Vietnamese or other vernacular languages. Bibliographies are placed at the beginning of each chapter. Indexes are by French name and by family and species. [David G. Marr with Kristine Alilunas-Rodgers]

119 **Les oiseaux de l'Indochine française.** (The birds of French Indochina.)
J. Delacour, P. Jabouille. Aurillac, France: Imprimerie du Cantal Républicain, 1931. 4 vols. bibliog. At head of title: Exposition coloniale internationale, Paris, 1931.

The only comprehensive work on birds of Indochina, the result of five expeditions by Delacour over an eight-year period. It offers a descriptive and annotated list of around 1,000 species and subspecies. The bibliography contains entries on about 200 general and specialized books and 80 periodical articles. An appendix at the end of Volume 4 lists a few additional species or subspecies. [David G. Marr with Kristine Alilunas-Rodgers]

120 **Les serpents de l'Indochine.** (The snakes of Indochina.)
René Bourret. Toulouse, France: Henri Basuyau, 1936. 2 vols. bibliog.

The first volume of this work is a study of the fauna and the second is a systematic descriptive catalogue. Detailed descriptions, line-drawings, bibliographical references, and information on species distribution make this a scholarly work that is essential for an understanding of this topic even sixty years after its publication. Bourret was Professor at the University of Hanoi and held a doctorate in natural science.

Les plantes médicinales du Cambodge, du Laos et du Vietnam. (Medicinal plants of Cambodia, Laos and Vietnam.)
See item no. 446.

Archaeology

121 **Altérations biologiques des grès cambodgiens et recherche de moyens de protection: essai de synthèse.** (Biological changes to Cambodian sandstone and the search for means of protection: summary of tests.)
Pierre Fusey. Paris: École Française d'Extrême-Orient, 1991. viii, 91p. bibliog. (Publications Hors Série de l'École Française d'Extrême-Orient).

From observations made in 1961, 1963 and 1966 in Siem Reap, Fusey discusses the processes of organic degradation of stone, due to climatic and botanical attack, and suggests ways of combating their effects.

122 **Annales: Université Royale des Beaux-arts.** (Annals: Royal University of Fine Arts.)
Phnom Penh: Editions de la Faculté d'Archéologie, Institut de Recherches et de Documentation, 1967- . irregular. Title also appears in Cambodian.

Gives an indication of the type of research being carried out in the Royal University of Fine Arts, Phnom Penh, prior to its destruction and closure for many years. Some of the projects have been picked up again, while others need to be rescued from oblivion. The text is chiefly in French with some Cambodian.

123 **The archaeology of mainland Southeast Asia from 10,000 B.C. to the fall of Angkor.**
C. F. Higham. Cambridge, England: Cambridge University Press, 1989. 387p. bibliog.

Higham's book reviews comprehensively the archaeology of Thailand and Indochina back to 12,000 years ago, and develops a synthetic framework based largely on environmental change over time and space. As one of the leading figures in the surge of modern archaeological work that has occurred in Thailand since the 1960s, Higham attempts to generalize the 'Thailand perspective' to apply to Indochina too, especially northern Vietnam, which has been the other main focus of archaeological studies in mainland Southeast Asia. Higham's review of the Hoabinhian and related cultures notes that the practice of polishing the edges of stone tools appeared around 10,000 years ago, cord-marked pottery was abundant after 8,000 years ago, and remains of rice have now been recovered in a Hoabinhian context. Polished stone materials and pottery are the main artefacts, supplemented by bronze metallurgy, after 4,000 years ago. In north-central Vietnam, much larger mound sites, associated with the Dongson culture, accumulated after 500 BC. The culture is most famous for the proliferation of bronze artefacts, notably the Dongson drums, but other developments included iron metallurgy, probable double-cropping of wet rice, and the establishment of societies run by hereditary chiefs. At around the same time the Cham appear to have colonized coastal central Vietnam from island Southeast Asia, as indicated by a spate of urnfields containing cremated human remains and grave-goods of bronze, iron, glass, precious and semi-precious stone. The book also contains 175 illustrations. [David G. Marr with Kristine Alilunas-Rodgers]

124 **L'archéologie du delta du Mékong.** (Archaeology of the Mekong delta.)
Louis Malleret. Paris: École Française d'Extrême-Orient, 1959-63. 4 vols. maps. bibliog. (Publications de l'École Française d'Extrême-Orient, vol. 43).

An enormous work describing the findings of Malleret's 1940s' excavations of the site of Oc Eo, located southwest of the entrance of the Bassac River into the sea as part of the Mekong delta. Oc Eo was clearly a major city, probably the port city of the polity called Funan in Chinese sources from 225 AD. Malleret's work was cut short by political turmoil in 1948 and not resumed, and some ten years later Malleret began the process of publication in four volumes: Volume one, 'L'exploration archéologique et les fouilles d'Oc Eo' (The archaeological exploration and excavations of Oc Eo), includes extensive reports of the statuary; Volume two, 'La civilisation matérielle d'Oc Eo' (The material culture of Oc Eo), discusses stoneware, pottery and metallic objects found; Volume three, 'La culture de Founan' (The culture of Funan), examines coinage, jewellery and glassware from the site and from elsewhere in Vietnam; and Volume four,'Le Cisbassac' (The Cisbassac), reports possibly related sites east of the Bassac River and in the Dong Nai delta. Comparison is made also with Indian materials and Roman coinage. An index is provided to the four volumes, together with plans, extensive tables, chemical analysis of soils and artefacts and 248 plates.

125 **Atlas archéologique de l'Indo-Chine: monuments du Champa et du Cambodge.** (Archaeological atlas of Indochina: monuments of Champa and Cambodia.)
E. Lunet de Lajonquière. Paris: Imprimerie Nationale, 1901. 24p. maps. (Publications de l'École Française d'Extrême-Orient).

Includes five maps, one of Indochina and four of Cambodia and Annam, each divided into northern and southern areas. Archaeological sites and ancient roads and bridges are clearly differentiated from contemporary settlements, which are also shown to enable easy access. Topography is indicated by subtle shading, creeks and rivers are shown in detail, and mountain ranges are named. Province and residence boundaries are marked. As the maps are on a scale of 1:500,000 and cover the whole of

Cambodia, those seeking a more detailed picture of the sites at Angkor should use the *Carte archéologique de la région d'Angkor* (q.v.) or other more recent publications. Two tables provide lists of the mapped monuments by region and alphabetically, providing origin, location and notes.

126 **Le Cambodge.** (Cambodia.)
J. Boisselier. Paris: A. et J. Picard et Cie, 1966. xvi, 480p. bibliog. (Manuel d'Archéologie d'Extrême-Orient. 1 ptie, Asie du Sud-Est, 1).

A manual of archaeology for Asia was planned as long ago as 1930 by French archaeologists, but this first volume on Cambodia did not appear until the mid-1960s, with volumes for Vietnam, Thailand-Laos, Champa-Burma and Indonesia to follow. Boisselier, lecturer in Indian and Southeast Asian archaeology at the Paris Faculty of Arts was certainly an appropriate choice, and the Southeast Asian sub-series was directed by the old master George Coedès himself, the author of the preface to this volume. An introduction to the geographical and historical setting is followed by part one on prehistory, protohistory and early history up to the mid-6th century. The principal focus of the work is the historical periods covered in part two, where the material is presented according to form: architecture, decor, deposits for items of worship, statuary, metalwork, ceramics and other techniques.

127 **Une campagne archéologique au Cambodge.** (An archaeological campaign in Cambodia.)
Adhemard Leclère. Hanoi: F.-H. Schneider, 1904. 13p. map. bibliog. Extract from *Bulletin de l'École Française d'Extrême-Orient*, July-September 1904.

This campaign took place in the province of Kratie in the early 1900s. Several interesting artefacts were found, such as the charter of the foundation of the well-known Sambok monastery, the statues of *neak ta* spirits, like Ci-Tep (so powerful and feared, said the Khmer governor, that it has to be kept inside a closed temple). The ruins of Sambaur, a frontier town visited and described by Van Wustoff in 1642, were identified and objects collected.

128 **Carte archéologique de la région d'Angkor.** (Archaeological map of the region of Angkor.)
Based on the work of the EFEO, of the Aviation Militaire (Military Aviation) and the Service Géographique (Geographic Service). [s.l.]: Service Géographique de l'Indochine, 1939. map.

A colour map of the archaeological sites of Angkor showing transportation, water features, vegetation, cultivation, built-up areas and buildings. Relief is shown by contours and spot heights. Published in June 1939, this is a beautiful and extremely informative document which broadly maps the archaeological area around Angkor Wat. It extends as far east as to include Wat Trach and Phnom Baux, south to Phnom Krom, and west to Phra Ta Moni and Ta Tok. The legend is extensive, with symbols indicating current land use, ponds, vestiges of dykes, bridges, foundations of buildings, ruins, and paved and unpaved roads both ancient and modern. As such it provides a picture both of the ancient city and its surrounds as well as the overlaid civilization as of the 1930s.

129 **Disciplines croisées: hommage à Bernard Philippe Groslier.** (Interwoven disciplines: homage to Bernard Philippe Groslier.)
Under the direction of Georges Condominas, with collaboration by Denise Bernot, Marie Alexandrine Martin, Monique Zaini-Lajoubert. Paris: Éditions de l'École des Hautes Études en Sciences Sociales, 1992. 377p. maps. bibliog. (Atelier Asemi, no. 2).

A memorial volume for the renowned archaeologist and scholar who died in 1986, aged only sixty. Born in Phnom Penh, son of the likewise renowned George Groslier (q.v.), and grandson of an administrator of Cambodia, Bernard Philippe went on to fulfil family expectations and devoted his life to the study and understanding of ancient Cambodia through the employment of modern scientific archaeological techniques in the Angkor Conservation, which he directed from 1960 until it was forced to close by the encroaching war. Fourteen international scholars write here in homage, with articles on a range of subjects, to illustrate the breadth of Groslier's interests and expertise (including history, archaeology, linguistics, architecture, ethnology, literature and ecology), while three write about Groslier himself. The volume also contains illustrations, a bibliography of his writings from 1949, and an obituary he wrote for his father.

130 **Documents graphiques de la conservation d'Angkor: 1963-1973.** (Graphic documents of the conservation of Angkor.)
Jacques Dumarçay. Paris: École Française d'Extrême-Orient, 1988. 58p. bibliog. (Publications de l'École Française d'Extrême-Orient. Mémoires Archéologiques, no. 18).

This volume provides a valuable overview of the work of EFEO in its principal undertaking, the Angkor Conservation, in the period before its temporary abandonment in 1973 due to the encroaching war. Dumarçay's essay is complemented by sixteen plates. The volume also contains a separate study, 'La fouille du Sras-Srang' (The excavation of Sras-Srang) by Paul Courbin.

131 **Documents topographiques de la conservation des monuments d'Angkor.** (Topographic documents of the conservation of the Angkor monuments.)
Edited by Christophe Pottier. Paris: École Française d'Extrême-Orient, 1993. v. (Publications de l'École Française d'Extrême-Orient. Mémoires Archéologiques, no. 21).

A valuable collection of seventy-two topographic maps made between 1960 and 1970 under the direction of Bernard Philippe Groslier, with the exception of plate 1, made in 1934-35 by Trouvé and Marchal (which, although containing several errors, continued to be used until 1965!). Dumarçay provides an introduction explaining the context of these maps' creation and application.

132 **Polish conservators of monuments in Asia.**
Editor-in-chief Lech Krzyanowski. Warsaw: Wydawnictwa PKZ (The State Enterprise the Ateliers for Conservation of Cultural Property), 1994. 39p.

This publication was issued on the occasion of the exhibition, 'Polish Conservators of Monuments in Asia', held at the Asia Pacific Museum in Warsaw (28 April-5 June

1994). Only eight pages are devoted to Cambodia and that includes illustrations. The work covers the years 1980-93 in which the Polish conservators were working chiefly on restoring the Reamker frescoes in the Silver Pagoda, Phnom Penh.

133 **Recherches préhistoriques dans la région de Mlu Prei: accompagnées de comparaisons archéologiques et suivies d'un vocabulaire Français-Kuy.** (Prehistoric research in the Mlu Prei region: together with archaeological comparisons and followed by a French-Kuy vocabulary.)
Paul Lévy. Hanoi: Imprimerie d'Extrême-Orient, 1943. 122p. map. bibliog. (Publications de l'École Française d'Extrême-Orient no. 30).

The results of surface digging of the Mlu Prei (Melou Prey) archaeological site, north of Kompong Thom, in 1937-38, are reported here. The nearest Khmer village is 30 kilometres away. Further north, the villages are ethnically Kui (Kuy), though these people are not identified as a minority in today's Cambodia. Many stone axes and adzes were found. Lévy follows the ideas of Heine-Geldern on diffusionism, and makes a lot of comparison with equivalent material retrieved in Europe. No attempt has been made at dating, with the finds classed as simply Central Indochinese Neolithic. Insecurity has prevented prehistoric research in Cambodia for the last generation, so this report is still of considerable importance.

134 **Restoration of a Khmer temple in Thailand: July-October 1972.**
P. Pichard. Paris: UNESCO, 1972. 57p. maps. Serial No.: 2807/RMO.RD/CLP.

An archaeological report on the restoration of Phnom Rung, one of the former Khmer empire's centres in what is now northeast Thailand. The author studied the issues involved with the restoration during 1972, in collaboration with senior staff from Thailand's Fine Arts Department, to write this UNESCO report. Focusing on the priorities of the now-completed restoration project, the report assesses the condition of the temple in great detail, and includes accompanying plans and photographs. It is most useful for students of archaeology, or as a record of the processes involved in turning a 'ruin' into a hugely popular, accessible, 'cultural site'. The temple was later at the centre of an international debate in 1988, over the return from the United States of a 'stolen' lintel.

135 **Safeguarding and development of Angkor.**
Prepared by UNESCO for the Inter-governmental Conference on the Safeguarding and Development of the Historical Area of Angkor, Tokyo, 12-13 October 1993. [Tokyo: UNESCO, 1993]. 90p.

A brief history of the ancient capital and its rulers, European explorations and excavation serves as an introduction to a broad overview of past and present efforts to preserve and protect the important Angkor site. Accompanied by historical and contemporary photographs of the temples are summaries of non-governmental, Cambodian and international government initiatives and financial commitments, and various relevant resolutions and conventions. Future 'concerns' regarding the conservation of monuments, archaeology, regional development and site development are presented in detail. Technical datasheets on twenty monuments include individual plans with notes on previous restoration work, state of conservation and recommendations for urgent actions. These datasheets would be of interest to archaeologists and interested visitors alike, while the document itself is a user-friendly reference source for organizations or scholars. The report was prepared by the Angkor Unit of the Division of Cultural Heritage, UNESCO with printing financed by the governments of France and Japan. Unfortunately no proper introduction identifying the players or the process involved in its compilation is provided; neither is there an index, and the bibliography is extremely scant, including only reports produced since 1989, although earlier French material is referred to in the datasheets.

136 **Stations préhistoriques de Somron-Seng et de Longprao, Cambodge.** (Prehistoric sites of Somron-Seng and Longprao, Cambodia.)
H. Mansuy. Hanoi: F.-H. Schneider, 1902. 29p.

This is the study of a 'kjokkenmoedding', a shell mound area, exploited by local peasants, which was discovered by Roques in 1876, and was one of the first formal archaeological digs in the country. Stone tools, archaic pottery and some bronze artefacts were recovered from the Kompong Thom site, now usually transliterated as Samrong Sen and dated at c.1500 BC.

137 **Study and preservation of historic cities of Southeast Asia.**
Yoshiaki Ishizawa. Tokyo: Institute of Asian Cultures, Sophia University, 1990. [4], 198p. (Cultural Heritage in Asia, Manual no. 4).

A record of the papers discussed, a film screened, and the Sophia Appeal, which were presented at the International Symposium on the Preservation of the Angkor Complex, held following the International Symposium on the Study and Preservation of Historic Cities of Southeast Asia, in Tokyo, 1985. Professor Yoshiaki Ishizawa, who was one of the first foreign specialists to visit Angkor after the Khmer Rouge period, noted damage and deterioration of the temples, and advised the Conservation of Angkor committee. His resulting report is an evocative and distressing paper, followed by an account on the 'Technical problems of the restoration of the Angkor monuments', by Professor Dr. Daigoro Chihara. A discussion on UNESCO's efforts towards the preservation of Angkor follows, and finally a copy of the Sophia Appeal for the safeguarding of the Angkor Complex, which was adopted at the symposium, is reproduced. The text is in Japanese, English, Thai, Cambodian, Indonesian, Malay and Burmese.

Archaeologia mundi: Indochina.
See item no. 138.

Articles sur le pays khmer. (Articles on the country of the Khmers.)
See item no. 147.

Nouvelles inscriptions du Cambodge. (New inscriptions from Cambodia.)
See item no. 167.

Angkor Vat: description graphique du temple. (Angkor Wat: graphic description of the temple.)
See item no. 753.

Le Bayon d'Angkor Thom: bas-reliefs. (The Bayon of Angkor Thom: bas-reliefs.)
See item no. 765.

Le Bayon. (The Bayon.)
See item no. 766.

Charpentes et tuiles khmères. (Khmer framework and roof-tiles.)
See item no. 769.

Cultural sites of Burma, Thailand, and Cambodia.
See item no. 774.

Le cinquantenaire de l'ÉFEO: compte rendu des fêtes et cérémonies. (The fiftieth anniversary of the EFEO: report of the festivals and ceremonies.)
See item no. 839.

History

Southeast Asia and Indochina

138 **Archaeologia mundi: Indochina.**
Bernard Philippe Groslier, translated from the French by James Hogarth. Cleveland, Ohio; New York: The World Publishing Co.; London: Muller; Geneva: Nagel, 1966. 283p. bibliog.

In this volume the French scholar George Groslier attempts to present to the general reader a picture of the whole Indochina region from the beginnings of human civilization up to colonial times. He brings his erudition to the task and presents a number of good photographs.

139 **Brahmin and Mandarin: a comparison of the Cambodian and Vietnamese revolutions.**
Robert S. Newman. [Melbourne: Centre of Southeast Asian Studies, Monash University], 1978. 27, 2p. bibliog. (Working Papers/Centre of Southeast Asian Studies, no. 15).

Prepared in 1976, although not published until two years later, this paper compares the Vietnamese Confucian tradition, stressing social obligations, with the otherworldly concerns of Indianized Cambodia. Newman sees this contrast as the root of differences in the revolutionary behaviour of the two victorious communist movements, concluding: 'Traditional ideology, world view, and myths, patterns of social organization and political administration in China and Vietnam have led to a smoother process of adjustment to revolutionary change. Cambodia, and the rest of the Indic world, in order to change itself, may decide to look to Western or Chinese forms as well as substance. This process will necessarily be more difficult and of a more drastic and radical nature than in Vietnam'.

140 **The Cambridge history of Southeast Asia.**

Edited by N. Tarling. Cambridge, England: Cambridge University Press, 1992. 2 vols. maps. bibliog.

Nicholas Tarling, leading New Zealand historian, has edited this encyclopaedic effort, which includes contributions by most of the best-known and well regarded historians of the region who write in English, with particularly strong representation from Australia. Among the historians represented are John Legge and Ian Mabbett (Monash University), Anthony Reid (Australian National University), Barbara Watson Andaya (University of Auckland), Paul Kratoska (Singapore), and C. M. Turnbull (formerly of Hong Kong University). The approach is chronological, with volume one covering 'From early times to c.1800' and volume two going up to '1975: the Communist victories in Indochina'. Within broad periods, themes and issues are studied, such as political economy, religion and popular beliefs, interactions with the outside world and adaptation, the state and society, anti-colonial movements, nationalism and modernist reforms. Maps, both geographical and historical, and an extremely thorough index complement the text, along with an extensive bibliographical effort, covering regions, country groupings and some individual countries, as well as special topics compiled by Paul Kratoska.

141 **A history of South-East Asia.**

Daniel George Edward Hall. Basingstoke, England: MacMillan, 1981. 4th ed. Reprinted 1993. 1,070p. bibliog. Originally published, 1955.

For forty years now this text has served as the introduction to Southeast Asian history for generations of students, and indeed can itself be said to have helped create the subject in its own right – not just as the study of an area where Indian and Chinese influences crossed over. Hall was the first head of a department of Southeast Asian studies (Professor of the History of South-East Asia, School of Oriental and African Studies, University of London) and long remained the doyen of the field, notwithstanding the criticism that his approach over-emphasized the importance of the mere five centuries since Europe appeared on the scene, at the expense of the millennia that went before – a criticism that he took on board, progressively modifying the text in subsequent editions. Even apart from its historiographical value, the text remains important as a reference tool alone with its lists of the dynasties of each régime, its illustrations and maps, its thorough index and its fifty-page bibliography (revised in each edition). Cambodia features in each of the parts.

142 **The Indianized states of Southeast Asia.**

Georges Coedès, edited by Walter F. Vella, translated by Susan Brown Cowing. Canberra: Australian National University Press, 1975. [410]p. English translation first published, Honolulu: East-West Center Press, 1968. Originally published as *Les états hindouisés d'Extrême-Orient* (The Hinduized states of the Far East), Hanoi, 1944 and then revised and expanded in 2nd and 3rd editions in 1947 and 1964.

This is the work of Coedès that has undoubtedly had the greatest circulation and impact, and in either the original French edition or in English translation has been set as a basic university text in many countries around the world. Here Coedès lays out his thesis: 'culturally speaking, Farther India today is characterized by more or less deep traces of the Indianization that occurred long ago as seen in vocabulary and script, law and administration, religion and arts and architecture . . . To reduce these facts to a rather crude formula, it can be said that the Cambodian is an Indianized Pnong'. Coedès presents his work in chronological sequence, dealing with the region as a whole, rather than in geographic subregions or today's nation-states. In it he presents and summarizes the work of others – whether historians or epigraphers – as well as his own rich scholarship on Sukothai, Srivijaya and Cambodia. Intended not only for the general public but also for scholars, Coedès provides over 100 pages of notes, 5 maps and 2 genealogies. Although his emphasis has been challenged, and one could even say superseded, by other research showing the persistence of more indigenous traditions than he gives credit to, there is no doubt that this is the fundamental source on the past 2,000 years of the region's history.

143 **Malcolm Caldwell's South East Asia.**

Edited by Bob Hering and Ernst Utrecht. Townsville, Queensland: Committee of South-East Asian Studies, James Cook University of North Queensland, 1979. 137p. bibliog. (South East Asian Monograph Series, no. 5).

A memorial volume dedicated to the memory of Malcolm Caldwell, the Scottish scholar who took a left-wing perspective on his analyses of Southeast Asia, and who was killed during a visit to Cambodia in December 1978, following a private meeting with Pol Pot. While some have alleged that he may have conveyed criticisms of the régime to Pol Pot, resulting in his death, there is no supporting evidence for such an interpretation, and the cause of his death remains obscure. Here fellow scholars review his contributions to Southeast Asian studies and to the tradition of engaged scholarship and political activism.

144 **The roots of French imperialism in Eastern Asia.**

John Frank Cady. Ithaca, New York: Cornell University Press; London: Oxford University Press, 1954. 322p. maps. bibliog.

This book remains the best study in English of French attitudes and behaviour in relation to East and Southeast Asia during the important 1840-61 period. Cady links French government actions to three lobby groups: Catholic missionaries of French nationality; merchants eager to penetrate new markets in competition with Great Britain; and the Navy. He concludes that 'The taproot of French imperialism in the Far East from first to last was national pride – pride in culture, reputation, prestige, and influence' (p. 294). A final chapter discusses the period 1861-85, particularly in relation to Tonkin, Annam and Cochinchina, but without the confidence and grasp of detail characteristic of earlier chapters. [David G. Marr with Kristine Alilunas-Rodgers]

145 **SEADAG Seminar on Communist movements and regimes in Indochina.**

Proceedings of a seminar held at Asia House, New York, 30 September – 2 October 1974. 1 vol. variously paginated.

Four papers contributed to this Southeast Asia Development Advisory Group (SEADAG) of the Asia Society seminar relate to Cambodia, and they provide a valuable record of perspectives some six months before the Khmer Rouge finally toppled the Lon Nol régime. Contents include: 'The Khmer Rouge: revolutionaries or terrorists?' by Donald Kirk; 'The Khmer resistance: an internal perspective' by Peter

A. Poole; 'The Khmer resistance: external relations' by Sheldon W. Simon; and 'Norodom Sihanouk: a leader of the left?' by Milton Osborne.

146 **Southeast Asia: an introductory history.**
Milton Osborne. Sydney: George Allen & Unwin, 1995. Fully revised and updated 6th ed. 288p.

The author designed this volume for readers with little or no prior knowledge of the region. Concentrating mainly on the past three centuries, he is anxious to explore common themes, for example 'The European advance and challenge', 'Asian immigrants in Southeast Asia', 'The Second World War', and 'Revolution and revolt', rather than to describe particular events in any given society. Country experts will blanch at some of Osborne's generalizations, although his own professional background leads him to be more proficient and thoughtful in relation to Cambodia and Vietnam. There is an unannotated list of suggested reading and a very simplified time chart.

The Second Indochina War: Cambodia and Laos today.
See item no. 235.

Vietnam or Indochina?: contesting concepts of space in Vietnamese nationalism, 1887-1954.
See item no. 563.

Southeast Asian Affairs.
See item no. 870.

General history of Cambodia

147 **Articles sur le pays khmer.** (Articles on the country of the Khmers.)
George Coedès, compiled by Claude Jacques. Paris: École Française d'Extrême-Orient, 1989. 2 vols.

A most valuable collection, reprinting the articles on Cambodia by this famous scholar in two volumes. The first contains some forty articles published in *Études Cambodgiènnes* (Cambodian Studies) between 1911 and 1956; and the second contains a further collection of twelve articles from the *Bulletin de l'EFEO* (Bulletin of the EFEO) and ten from the *Cahiers de l'EFEO* (Notebooks of the EFEO) together with four comprehensive indexes of inscriptions, proper names, Sanskrit and Khmer words and words in other languages. The collection was compiled by Claude Jacques, who also compiled the indexes together with Elisabeth Kolhatkar. The breadth and depth of the scholarship of Coedès is revealed strikingly in this collection (the first article of which was written in 1904 when he was only eighteen years old), spanning the fields of archaeology, philology, history and sociology in the style of the consummate scholar of his day.

148 **Cambodia will never disappear.**

Anthony Barnett. *New Left Review*, no. 180 (March/April 1990).

Cambodia's imminent disappearance as a nation is a persistent theme in the country's scholarship and politics alike and yet, Barnett contends, it is essentially the invention of the French colonial administration. Their interpretation of the ruins of Angkor was imparted to the Khmer élite who had been left with few historical records from which to draw their own conclusions. French orientalism stressed past greatness in contrast to modern degeneration and thus reinforced the idea of the necessity for European intervention. Norodom Sihanouk, himself appointed by the colonial régime, has consistently emphasized the alarming possibility when, in fact, the only likely demise was his own. Although a relatively short piece, this deserves mention as a counter to the dominant paradigm's claims of thorough-going Vietnamization and its ongoing support to the Khmer Rouge at the time this article was written. Barnett considers Cambodia's survival to be assured 'thanks to the tenacity of the Khmer villagers'.

149 **Cambodia, past and present.**

O. P. Paliwal. New Delhi: Lancer International, 1991. xiv, 109p. maps. bibliog.

Combining an Indian perspective and a clear sympathy with socialist ideals, Paliwal sees the origins of Pol Potism in Stalinism, and contrasts this with the 'one glorious decade of the People's Republic of Kampuchea', leading up to the 1989 Paris Peace Agreement. Jawaharlal Nehru, writes Paliwal, attributed the origins of the name Cambodia to the well-known town in ancient India called Kamboja, situated in the region of Kandahar in present-day Afghanistan. Hindi and Khmer consonants and vowels have almost the same number and the same pronunciation, he argues. From its origins in the Indian tradition, Cambodia suffered colonial domination by the French and later the interference of US imperialism, which then ruler Prince Sihanouk claimed was behind the coup that deposed him. Paliwal's text is accompanied by black-and-white photographs and an index.

150 **Facing the Cambodian past: selected essays 1971-1994.**

David Chandler. Chiang Mai, Thailand: Silkworm Books; Sydney: Allen & Unwin, 1996. 331p. bibliog.

A collection of twenty-three essays written over a period of thirty-four years. The book is organized in five parts: 'Angkor and memories of Angkor'; the period covered by Chandler's own PhD thesis, 'Cambodia before the French'; 'The colonial era'; and 'Cambodia since 1975'. There are two concluding essays on 'History and tragedy' – the first was written in 1979 and the other revisited the same theme in 1994. Many of these essays were presented as conference papers and then developed into articles in a wide range of publications, some of which are quite difficult to track down these days, making it most useful to have them assembled into one volume. While the themes and indeed much of the content of these essays will be familiar to those who have had the benefit of reading Chandler's major histories, these shorter studies have the advantages of revealing the scope of his scholarly attention and allowing room for musings of a quieter and more reflective nature than possible in the more directed works. As he moves into retirement Chandler looks back and sees the persistence of the weight of the past in Cambodian history, and the cautious optimism he expressed several years ago has now shifted back to a more pessimistic prognosis.

151 **Histoire du Cambodge depuis le 1er siècle de notre ère, d'après les inscriptions lapidaires, les annales chinoises et annamites et les documents européens des six derniers siècles.** (History of Cambodia from the 1st century AD, according to stone inscriptions, Chinese and Annamite annals and European documents of the last six centuries.) Adhemard Leclère. Paris: P. Geuthner, 1914. Reprinted, New York: AMS Press, 1975. xii, 547p. bibliog.

The prodigious Leclère concluded his scholarly work on Cambodia with this publication. He had spent twenty-five years in Cambodia, fifteen of which were devoted to recording its laws, before he moved on to customs, religion and government. His history is divided into the Cambodia of legends and inscriptions and the Cambodia of chronicles and historical documents. A wealth of material is provided with copious notes but unfortunately even in reprint it has no bibliography or index, and lacks the illustrations and maps of some later studies. Nevertheless it is a key example of French scholarly fascination with, and study of, the history, art and culture of this exotic colonial possession and remains a major source.

152 **A history of Cambodia.** David P. Chandler. St. Leonards, New South Wales: Allen & Unwin, 1993. 2nd ed. xv, 287p. maps. bibliog.

This is a thoroughly revised and updated edition of a text originally published in 1983, covering roughly 2,000 years of Cambodian history. Regarded as one of the foremost historians on Cambodia, Chandler includes in this edition new material on post-independence Cambodia, but the period after 1945 is more fully treated in his subsequent work, *The tragedy of Cambodian history: politics, war and revolution since 1945* (q.v.). This book records the beginnings of Cambodian history in the first millennium, the influence of the Angkor kings and the fall of the Angkor civilization, the crisis of the 19th century and the imposition of French rule, and the gaining of independence. The new material focuses on the unstable but influential career of Prince Norodom Sihanouk, the bloody reign of Pol Pot's Khmer Rouge, and the relative calm that followed Pol Pot's defeat by Vietnam. This is a very readable book and a basic text on the history of Cambodia, and is one of very few attempts to cover this broad sweep. An Asian edition (Chiang Mai, Thailand: Silkworm Books, 1993) and a US edition (Boulder, Colorado: Westview Press, 1992) of this work have also been published.

153 **The Khmers of Cambodia: the story of a mysterious people.** I. G. Edmonds, photographs by the author. Indianapolis, Indiana: Bobbs-Merrill, [1970]. 160p. map. bibliog.

A typical, though rather late, example of the 'mysterious Khmers' genre. Edmonds writes that the Khmers were 'a strange race who came from no one knows where, built a mysterious empire, and then saw that great civilization collapse for reasons as unknown as the race's origin . . . Suddenly all this changed. Cambodia is regularly in the headlines, diplomats accord it a serious attention, and the United States Pentagon has more than a passing interest in it . . .'. The book covers geography, society and history from Angkor up to the Sihanouk period in a readable and easy style, if one can get through the romantic overlay.

154 **Les Khmers.** (The Khmers.)
Solange Thierry. Paris: Editions du Seuil, 1964. 189p. bibliog. (Le Temps qui Court).

Although not presenting the results of original research this little book is included because of its wide circulation in France in the Sihanouk era of the 1960s and now again in the markets of Phnom Penh in a photocopied reproduction with colour binding. Thierry gives an overview of Cambodian history with some discussion of geography, art and culture, concluding with the country's place in the Third World.

155 **Recherches nouvelles sur le Cambodge.** (Recent research on Cambodia.)
Edited by François Bizot. Paris: EFEO, 1994. 366p. (Études Thématiques, no. 1).

First in a series conceived by Denys Lombard, the new Director of EFEO, this contains eighteen papers on various topics arranged in three parts: 'Language and religious texts'; 'History'; and 'Space and architecture'. It is edited by François Bizot, who has gathered together an impressive collection of principally European scholars, and who has provided an introduction placing their work into a historical context, noting that the last twenty years have seen an influx of enthusiasm from the fields of anthropology, ethnology and sociology without leaving behind the terrain established by their predecessors in philology and archaeology, as exemplified by Coedès. It is not, as the name may imply, a review of recent research, but rather a selection from this growing body of work.

Les frontières du Viêtnam: histoire des frontières de la péninsule. (The frontiers of Vietnam: history of the frontiers of the peninsula.)
See item no. 32.

The royal family of Cambodia.
See item no. 328.

Le paysan cambodgien. (The Cambodian peasant.)
See item no. 419.

Angkor.
See item no. 759.

Vie quotidienne dans la péninsule indochinoise à l'époque d'Angkor (800-1300). (Everyday life in the Indochinese peninsula in the Angkor period, 800-1300.)
See item no. 835.

Dictionary of the modern politics of South-East Asia.
See item no. 876.

Major political events in Indo-China 1945-1990.
See item no. 880.

Pre-Angkor and general inscriptions

156 **Le Cambodge et ses monuments: la province de Ba Phnom.**
(Cambodia and its monuments: the province of Ba Phnom.)
Étienne Aymonier. Paris: Imprimerie Nationale, 1897. 47p. bibliog.
Extract from *Asiatique*.

The hill complex known as Ba Phnom, like other enormous rocks soaring from the Mekong alluvial delta plain – like the Black Lady Mountain, near Tay Ninh, Phnom Chiso, south of Phnom Penh, the Nui Ba The near the site of Oc Eo, and many others – has a political and religious role in the history of Lower Cambodia, probably from the early so-called Funan period. The author describes the mountain as it was a century ago, with all the pagodas ruined and abandoned. He mentions several statues of *neak ta* spirits, the most feared being Me Sa Ba Phnom, the White Lady of the Sacred Mount (he says the word Ba is a corruption of Brah, meaning 'sacred'), who has *neak ta* ministers to rule over her realm. He also mentions a village nearby, inhabited by descendants of Laotian prisoners of war, who had retained their language – a testimony to the fact that mass deportations was a longstanding tradition in this area. He does not mention the royal cult of the Me Sa, nor the reported tradition of human sacrifices, recently replaced by the yearly sacrifice of a buffalo. A complete analysis of these cults has not yet been attempted.

157 **A chrestomathy of pre-Angkorian Khmer.**
Philip N. Jenner. [Honolulu, Hawaii]: University of Hawaii, 1980-88.
4 vols. maps. bibliog. (Southeast Asia Paper, no. 20).

A fundamental text appearing in four volumes. Volume one, 'Dated inscriptions from the 7th and 8th centuries', accounts for nearly all dated Old Khmer epigraphy. Jenner has converted transliteration of thirty-four Khmer inscriptions into Khmer characters, arranging the texts to highlight their structure. He identifies a few lexical items not previously understood and provides notes to help readers develop a grasp of pre-Angkor Khmer. Each inscription is given a date, name, source of previous publication and provenance as well as an introduction including information about the stone block it was inscribed on, where it was found, and what the salient features of its text are. The Khmer transcripts are then followed by explanatory notes which provide analysis of some words, grammar, usage and corresponding modern terms where applicable. Volume two, 'Lexicon of the dated inscriptions', presents the vocabulary of the inscriptions contained in volume one. The effective word count is 2,365, with the word bases divided into bound forms, primary and secondary derivatives, and bound and free compounds. Each entry is cited in modern Khmer, Anglo-American transliteration, phonemic transcription and followed by etymological information. Volume three, 'Undated inscriptions from the 6th-8th centuries' follows a similar arrangement to volume one. It contains 22 of the 114 found, but as yet undated, inscriptions which are best suited to illustrating the value of pre-Angkor epigraphy and language. They are arranged by the centuries they are presumed to belong to, and then by an inventory number. Jenner is anxious to inform readers that the smaller number of undated inscriptions he has presented reflects their inferior legibility, not their unimportance relative to the dated ones, as fifty per cent of the total vocabulary of the pre-Angkor corpus is found only in the undated inscriptions. Volume four, 'Lexicon of the undated inscriptions', contains 3,470 items from 94 published inscriptions, adding 1,000 items to the lexicon of the dated inscriptions. It contains a table which analyses the items fractionally, breaking them down into dated and undated, and then into loans, word bases, free and bound; derivatives, free and bound; and the totals. Table two analyses the distribution of the items in the inscriptions, both dated and undated. This volume also contains a small summary of the meaning and method of the extensive work Jenner undertook. He believes texts can be regarded as linguistic archaeology, and the purpose of his work as being to recover and describe as much of the ancient lexicon as possible. All four volumes have been arranged with students' needs in mind, offering encouragement for those who seek to utilize this elemental work. Jenner stresses that much of the results are provisional.

158 **Chronological inventory of the inscriptions of Cambodia.**
Philip N. Jenner. [Honolulu, Hawaii]: Southeast Asian Studies, Center for Asian and Pacific Studies, University of Hawaii, 1982. 2nd rev. ed. vii, 54p. (Southeast Asia Paper, no. 19).

This work meets the need for a systematic approach to Cambodian epigraphy, which is commonly listed according to what are now archaic inventory numbers. Coedès' *Listes générales des inscriptions et des monuments du Champa et du Cambodge* (General lists of inscriptions and monuments of Champa and Cambodia) (q.v.), which is the main reference for any cataloguing of inscriptions, is basically ordered according to accession. With this inventory Jenner does not seek to replace it but simply to order its items in a more coherent format. All inscriptions are ordered by date (Christian calendar) – with undated entries arranged according to century or century range – distinguished according to language, and traced to previous published texts. The appendix lists the items numerically, not chronologically, and provides their plate numbers so that they may be easily traced to where they apppeared in publication.

159 **Le Founan.** (Funan.)
M. É. Aymonier. Paris: Imprimerie Nationale, 1903. 47p. bibliog. Extract from *Journal Asiatique*, January-February 1903.

The then director of the École coloniale (Colonial School) attempts to synthesize the discussion on the localization of Funan, using whatever information may be culled from the Chinese sources. This is another example of how geographical names have travelled up and down the whole of Southeast Asia. Reflecting on the possible inhabitants of Funan, he mentions, among a 'diversity of races', the 'Khmer Doem', the 'primitive Khmers'. This was the name Pol Pot used, almost fifty years later, to sign one of his very first articles. Aymonier uses mostly the work of Ma Tuan Lin in *Ethnographie des peuples étrangers à la Chine* (Geneva: H. Georg, 1876-83), for which a good annotated modern translation is very much wanted. The best comprehensive study of this material was published one year later by Paul Pelliot in the *Bulletin de l'École Française d'Extrême-Orient* (q.v.). Advancement throughout a further century of research is not impressive.

160 **Histoire de l'ancien Cambodge.** (History of ancient Cambodia.)
Étienne Aymonier. Strasbourg, France: Imprimerie du Nouveau Journal de Strasbourg, [191?]. 198p. bibliog.

This is explicitly a book aiming at popularizing knowledge on Cambodia. Aymonier believed that after Alexander the Great's inroad into India, a tide of Indian emigrants crossed the black water (the Indian Ocean) to settle in Indochina, a theory which was subsequently rejected. He believed that Khmers came from the northeast and displaced

Chams. He gave the meaning of Funan as 'mountain', long before Coedès to whom this invention is usually attributed. He said the story of the mythical couple given as the ancestors of the Khmers is confirmed by Chinese sources. Aymonier had many qualities but he was a poor and gullible historian, basing his views on too many suppositions. There is an interesting description of Angkor Borei, which he identified with Vyadhapura, the City of the Hunter, believed to be the main centre of Funan, still to be confirmed or denied. He believed in a period of Javanese hegemony in which we do not believe anymore. It seems that all the major conceptual misunderstandings which are so acute in Coedès' work were already argued by Aymonier. For instance, 'it is pointless', he said, 'to mention the existence of these tiny kingdoms (roitelets) in establishing our list of Khmer kings, because we have not enough information on them and mostly because they did not rule over a unified kingdom'. But this unified kingdom was itself a myth created by the historians, blinding themselves to the realities visible in the inscriptions and even in the Chinese sources, a myth that has unfortunately been passed on to the present-day Cambodians.

161 **Indian cultural influence in Cambodia.**
B. R. Chatterjee. Calcutta, India: U. P., 1964. 2nd ed. xv, 288p. maps.

This work was submitted as a doctoral thesis at the University of London in 1926 by Chatterjee. who was once head of the South-East Asia Department at the Indian School of International Studies, New Delhi. This second edition, 1964, remains largely unchanged, but has had appendices added on archaeological finds from the intervening years. Although old, this book represents an important stage in Khmer studies, including the contentious issue of cultural influence in the 'Hinduized states' of Southeast Asia. Chatterjee's thesis is laid out in chapters on: early legends and traditions; Funan; early kings of Kambiya; anarchy and foreign domination; Jayavarman II and successors; Yasovarman and Angkor Thom; the rise of Buddhism; Suryavarman II and Angkor Vat; and the last monarchs of Kambiya. He explains in great depth, not only the links between Indian and Cambodian law, culture, religion, literature, and architecture, but also the context of the Indian influence's origins.

162 **Inscriptions du Cambodge.** (Inscriptions of Cambodia.)
Edited and translated by G. Coedès. Hanoi, Paris: École d'Extrême-Orient, 1937-66. 8 vols. bibliog. Vols. 3-5 have imprint, Paris: Boccard. Vols. 6-8 have imprint, Paris: École Française d'Extrême-Orient. (Collection de Textes et Documents sur l'Indochine, no. 3).

Coedès' magnum opus (but by no means representing most of his intellectual output), these eight volumes contain reference to over 1,000 inscriptions, the overwhelming majority of which are transcribed and translated herein. It also provides information on the place where the inscriptions were found, their current location, a rough description, the language in which it is couched, the probable period of carving, a number identifying the rubbing and the bibliographical reference to its translation. This work forms the basis for most subsequent historical work carried out on the ancient Cambodian kingdoms. Amazingly Coedès carried out this painstaking work in his spare time while serving as Principal of the Lycée Descartes in Phnom Penh.

163 **Inscriptions of Kambuja.**
R. C. Majumdar. Calcutta, India: Asiatic Society, 1953. xxvii, 641p. map. bibliog. (Asiatic Society Monograph Series, no. 8).

Majumdar has sought to make Khmer inscriptions accessible to Indian scholars of Sanskrit by casting them into Devanagari. The 300 inscriptions, dating from the 5th to the 14th centuries, are printed in Nagari characters. Khmer versions of the texts are not included. Around 500 pages of the inscriptions' text with summaries of their content in English are supplemented by additional 'new' inscriptions and additions to the text, notes, an alphabetical list according to where the inscriptions were found and an index of proper names. A brief introduction outlines a basic history of the Cambodian country, people, and royalty. Majumdar believes that, through a study of the Khmer usage of Sanskrit, the collection aids in tracing the migration of scholars between India and Cambodia.

164 **Inscriptions sanscrites du Campa et du Cambodge.** (Sanskrit inscriptions of Champa and Cambodia.)
Institut National de France (National Institute of France). Paris: Imprimerie Nationale, 1885. 632p. bibliog. (Notices et Extraits des Manuscrits de la Bibliothèque Nationale et d'Autres Bibliothèques, vol. 27, nos. 1 and 2).

At the time this work was published around 300 rubbings of Cambodia's inscriptions had been sent to Europe, mostly by Aymonier. The first to translate some of them was Hendrik Kern, a Dutch scholar. M. A. Barth, a student of Abel Bergaigne, started to work on them but died in a mountain accident. Bergaigne, and other students, Senart and Sylvain Lévy, carried out the first translations of the Sanskrit inscriptions, saying the understanding of the Old Khmer inscriptions was 'not yet much advanced'. And, one may note that it has been sidetracked ever since in the academic world. Barth says in his preface: there is no easy inscription. 'All of them confront us with unknown facts, of which the consequences are obscure; they are like fragments without a context.' This is the beginning of an ongoing effort to understand what the ancient people had in mind when they had these texts carved in stone. The main contribution was made, of course, by George Coedès. Will a new generation of epigraphists further the work of these early scholars?

165 **Kambuja-Desa or, An ancient Hindu colony in Cambodia.**
R. C. Majumdar. Philadelphia: Institute for the Study of Human Issues, 1980. viii, 165p. bibliog. Reprint of the 1944 ed. (University of Madras, India), issued as the Sir William Meyer lectures, 1942-43.

The text is a series of lectures delivered for the Sir William Meyer Lectures in 1942-43 but also includes footnotes and a list of inscriptions on which the study is mostly based. Over six chapters Majumdar attempts to cover the history of Kambuja-Desa: the aspects of Hindu culture which were introduced; the Hindu inspiration for monuments; and how art and institutions based on an Indian model developed and became uniquely Cambodian. Written from an Indian perspective, with theories of a Greater India, and of the decline of the Khmer Empire being largely due to a separation from the 'motherland', this interpretation has been somewhat superseded, but was an important and timely study which remains useful, especially as it helped to delineate the field of Cambodian historiography.

166 **Listes générales des inscriptions et des monuments du Champa et du Cambodge.** (General lists of inscriptions and monuments of Champa and Cambodia.)
George Coedès. Hanoi: Imprimerie d'Extrème-Orient, 1923. 300p.

This information by Coedès on Cambodian inscriptions, but including newly found items and also covering Champa, can also be found in *Inscriptions du Cambodge* (q.v.), published fifteen years later. The 'Monuments' section by Henri Parmentier gives the co-ordinates of each monument to a precision of 10 kilometres.

167 **Nouvelles inscriptions du Cambodge.** (New inscriptions from Cambodia.)
Saveros Pou. Paris: École Française d'Extrême-Orient, 1989. (Collection des Textes et Documents sur l'Indochine, 17).

Saveros Pou here brings up to date the earlier lists of inscriptions (principally that of Coedès) by adding material found in the postwar period.

168 **Le pays khmer avant Angkor.** (The country of the Khmers before Angkor.)
Claude Jacques. *Journal des Savants* (January-September 1986), p. 59-83.

The successor of Coedès, Claude Jacques, is the leading specialist on Khmer epigraphy in France. In this paper he takes a cautious and critical approach to the Chinese sources dealing with Funan and Chenla, the supposed predecessors of Angkor in the area believed to be populated by Khmer-speaking populations. From the pre-Angkor inscriptions, he draws the conclusion that the succession of a king was almost always dramatic and violent. He also notes that genealogies given by the Angkor kings do not really square with names known from inscriptions written at the time of their supposed ancestors. Jacques has been proposing a view of the Khmer political realm as mostly fragmented polities. As a result, history is more complicated than its current version would lead us to believe.

169 **The Sdok Kak Thom inscription.**
Adhir Chakravarti, with a preface by Ramesh Chandra Majumdar. Calcutta, India: Sanskrit College, 1978-80. 2 vols. bibliog. (Calcutta Sanskrit College Research Series, no. 111-12).

Chakravarti provides an extensive scholarly presentation. Volume two (*The Sdok Kak Thom inscription*) contains the text and translation of the inscription, while Volume one (*A study in Indo-Khmer civilization*) gives an analysis of the functioning of the different political, social, economic and religious institutions to which reference is made in the inscription, with considerable discussion and debate with previous interpretations. Particular attention is given to the cult of the Devaraja (the so-called God-King) for this is the sole inscription to be deciphered so far that makes explicit mention of this important feature of the Angkor kingdoms. This exposition is followed by notes, a glossary and separate archaeological, geographical and historical indexes. While recognizing the extent of Indian cultural and spiritual influence over the whole region of Southeast Asia, Chakravarti holds the view that the 'basic structure[s] of the material civilization i.e. the social, economic and political institutions of the country were left comparatively unaffected. Under Indian garb these remained essentially heritages of the earlier Austro-Asiatic culture'.

170 **Studies in Sanskrit inscriptions of ancient Cambodia: on the basis of first three volumes of Dr. R. C. Majumdar's edition.**
Mahesh Kumar Sharan, foreword by C. Sivaramamurti. New Delhi: Abhinav Publications, 1974. xxvii, 372p. map. bibliog.

This volume was originally a thesis approved for the degree of Doctor of Literature, University of Magadh, Bodh Gaya in 1974. From his study of 148 inscriptions and secondary sources Sharan constructs an account of the administration, socio-economic life, religious practices and art and architecture of ancient Cambodia. A brief description of each inscription includes date, location, king to whom it is ascribed, its current condition and the metre in which it is written. Three maps are included, one showing the routes of Indian journeys to Southeast Asia and another the sites of inscriptions. A series of black-and-white plates depicts details of bas-reliefs and figures from, for example, the Bayon, Angkor Wat, the Baphoun and Banteay Srei. Despite the use of many Sanskrit terms this is an accessible study which is particularly valuable for its insights into ancient Khmer society, its religious cults and deities and its Indian influences. A chart of Sanskrit/roman transliteration is included.

171 **Towards Angkor: in the footsteps of the Indian invaders.**
H. G. Quaritch Wales, with a foreword by Francis Younghusband. London: George G. Harrap & Co., 1937. 248p. maps. bibliog.

Although quite outdated, and conveying the now rejected perspective of Cambodian culture as being simply derivative of that of India, this volume may still have value, particularly in its ubiquity in public libraries around the English-speaking world. It includes illustrations and an index.

Recherches préhistoriques dans la région de Mlu Prei: accompagnées de comparaison archéologiques et suivies d'un vocabulaire Français-Kuy. (Prehistoric research in the Mlu Prei region: together with archaeological comparisons and followed by a French-Kuy vocabulary.)
See item no. 133.

Inventaire descriptif des monuments du Cambodge. (Descriptive inventory of Cambodian monuments.)
See item no. 788.

Rapports entre le premier art khmer et l'art indien. (Connections between early Khmer art and Indian art.)
See item no. 809.

Angkor (802-1432)

172 **The ancient Khmer Empire.**

Lawrence Palmer Briggs. Philadelphia: American Philosophical Society, 1974. 295p. maps. bibliog. (American Philosophical Society, Philadelphia. Transactions, n.s., 41 pt. 1). Originally published, 1951.

In an account presented to the American Oriental Society, Middle West Branch meeting on 4-5 April 1951, renowned French scholar George Coedès assessed this work of Briggs 'as marking a significant milestone. For the first time the mass of French erudition relating to the history and archaeology of ancient Cambodia had been brought together and analysed for the benefit of English speakers. Why did the French scientists, and especially the EFEO, leave this to an American consular official to do? Coedès believes that Briggs has managed to meet strict scientific criteria as well as satisfying the needs of a wider public. With clear plans and style, and exhaustive documentation, Coedès says he did not find a single lacuna in the 750-item bibliography, and that perhaps Briggs put too much in, covering even now-abandoned theories. However, this is the only criticism Coedès makes of the composition which, he believed, deserves only eulogies.

173 **Angkor life.**

Stephen O. Murray. San Francisco: Bua Luang Books, 1996. 111p. maps. bibliog. Available from Bua Luang Books, 2215-R Market St, San Francisco, CA 94114 USA.

Based on the 13th-century observations of Chou Ta-Kuan (transliterated by Murray in Pinyin as Zhou Daguan), on 19th-century French archaeology and on his own 'comparativist experiences', Dr. Murray attempts to reconstruct the society that gave rise to the monuments and cities of Angkor. Murray, a sociologist of religion, anthropologist and public-health consultant, visited Cambodia in 1993, after a lifetime's fascination with Khmer art and architecture. The book focuses on daily life, divided into areas such as dress and rank, child-rearing, roads, books and libraries and irrigation. Four small maps, an index, an annotated bibliography and a large glossary, as well as numerous black-and-white photographs and line-drawings, complement the text. While he presents little original research, others' findings are discussed in a lively manner and extensively footnoted. Often written in the first person, the chapters are very brief, and occasionally include Murray's own conjecture and analysis. Simple and approachable, this volume would make a good companion to a guide of the temples or an excellent resource for school projects.

174 **Angkor: an introduction.**

George Coedès, translated and edited by Emily Floyd Gardiner. Singapore: Oxford University Press, [1986]. 4, 118p. bibliog. Originally published, 1963.

A revised translation of *Pour mieux comprendre Angkor* (To better understand Angkor) (Paris: Librairie d'Amérique et d'Orient Adrien Maisonneuve, 1947. 2nd ed. Publications du Musée Guimet. Bibliothèque de Diffusion, no. 55), this is a brief, yet authoritative work, intended to paint the necessary background to provide visitors with an understanding of Angkor in its context. The chapters are based on eight lectures Coedès delivered in Hanoi, and differ from the French version in that they have been slightly abridged and do not include a history of the changing archaeological approaches relating to Angkor. The chapters deal with: the historical and religious setting; theories about Angkor; personal cults; temples or tombs; architectural symbolism; the mystery of the Bayon; Jayavarman II, founder of the royal dynasty of Angkor; and the last great king of Angkor, Jayavarman VII. The author presents the temples and various scholars' opinions on them, skillfully interpreting both to offer his own theories. It is a history in the old-fashioned sense, about great monuments and the great men who built them and, while current historians may approach the subject differently, this work remains, and will continue to remain, fundamental to the study of Angkor.

175 **Angkor: monuments of the god-kings.**
Text by Joan Lebold Cohen, photographs by Bela Kalman. New York: H. N. Abrams, [1973]. 239p. map. bibliog.

A beautifully designed, large-scale book, using photographs of the temples and their details as reference points for discussion of the art, architecture and social purpose of Angkor. Three chapters – on early Angkor, Angkor Wat, and Angkor Thom – each include a thorough introduction and profiles of the major temples of that period. Features such as a map of Southeast Asia with good, clear detail of Cambodia, a plan of the central part of the Angkor site, a chronology of ancient rulers, monuments and historical events, a glossary, and a bibliography, amply supplement the informative text. Bela Kalman's photographs play an equal part beside Cohen's words in presenting an atmospheric and academic introduction to the Angkor complex.

176 **L'armement et l'organisation de l'armée khmère: aux XIIe et XIIIe siècles: d'après les bas-reliefs d'Angkor Vat, du Bàyon et de Banteay Chmar.** (Armament and organization of the Khmer army in the 12th and 13th centuries: according to the bas-reliefs of Angkor Wat, the Bayon, and Banteay Chmar.)
Michel Jacq-Hergoualc'h, preface by Jean Boisselier. Paris: Presses Universitaires de France, 1979. 240p. bibliog. (Publications du Musée Guimet. Recherches et Documents d'Art et d'Archéologie, no. 12).

A fascinating and detailed study of military organization under Suryavarman II (c.1113-50) and Jayavarman VII (c.1181-1218) as gleaned from the bas-reliefs of monuments attributed to their reigns – Angkor Wat, the Bayon and Banteay Chmar. Numerous illustrations and photographs depict details of the bas-reliefs. The commentary examines the roles of different types of chariots, the cavalry, elephants, the infantry, ships of war, the use of allied armies and mercenaries, and, of course, the enemies. Jacq-Hergoualc'h also studies the crowds of people who travelled with the armies, their military music and the standard bearers (*les porteurs d'insignées honorifiques*). Compulsory reading for anyone contemplating a detailed study of the monuments, this work is also suitable for generalists who seek an insight into Angkor's society.

177 **Les dieux d'Angkor.** (Gods of Angkor.)
Translated and edited by Kong Phirun. Phnom Penh: Tevoda, 1993. 170p. Originally published in Khmer, Phnom Penh: Tevoda, 1973.

One of the few examples of Cambodian scholarly writing in print today. Thach Van Phat and Keo Sophun wrote their explanation of the decadence and downfall of the great Angkor civilization just as the newly independent Cambodia was wracked with war and strife and was on the eve of its greatest shock, the Khmer Rouge period. They summarize the historical developments and various theories advanced by scholars, and conclude by ascribing Angkor's demise to three factors: policies of China that advanced independence and threats from Cambodia's neighbours (such as Siam); the drain on the economic infrastructure and population base from constant wars against the Chams and Siamese, and from massive temple construction, both leading to the collapse of the irrigation system; and lack of unity among the Khmers, with the demise of the god-king and the split between support for royal Brahmanism and popular embrace of Theravada Buddhism. The work concludes with a passionate assertion that the Khmers did not disappear and are the rightful inheritors of the grand civilization of their past. Kong Phirun, with assistance from AIK/Cedoreck, has taken the initiative to bring this work back into circulation, publishing both French and Khmer editions.

178 **L'empire Khmèr: histoire et documents.** (The Khmer Empire: history and documents.)
Georges Maspéro. Phnom Penh: Imprimerie du Protectorat, 1904. 115, x, viip. bibliog.

Member of a brilliant dynasty of scholars, Georges Maspéro held the position of Resident of Kompong Speu. Contrary to the approach taken by Aymonier, he starts by reviewing the sources, exhibiting a healthy sense of scepticism about their value. He makes a courageous attempt to establish a complete chronology. The second part of the book deals with 'Foreigners and the establishment of the French Protectorate'. His interpretation sometimes includes wild statements like this: 'Whatever the primitive religion of the Khmers and their cult, it was forgotten after Hindu civilization entered Indochina'. It was up to his daughter, Evelyne Porée-Maspéro, later to prove this kind of statement entirely wrong.

179 **Histoire d'Angkor.** (History of Angkor.)
Madeleine Giteau. Paris: Presses Universitaires de France, 1974. 128p. bibliog. (Que sais-je?, no. 1580).

Madeleine Giteau may be the only survivor of the old generation of those who started to work in Angkor before or around the time of the Second World War. She was for a long time the curator of the former Albert Sarraut Museum (now the National Museum of Cambodia), where so many well-known Khmer works of art are conserved. She is the living memory of all the museums where Khmer collections are stored because she has catalogued and studied more Khmer artefacts than anybody else. She accepted the challenge to write a history of Angkor in a very popular collection (Que sais-je? – What do I know?) of booklets always limited to 125 pages. It is a miracle of scholarship and conciseness, compressing that six-century-long history into six chapters, adding a chapter on what we believe we know about Angkor society and one chapter on Cambodia after Angkor. Many books tell less in considerably more pages.

180 **The Khmèr temple of Práh Vihar.**
Charles Nelson Spinks. Canberra: Australian National University, 1959. 29p. bibliog. (George Ernest Morrison Lecture in Ethnology, 21).

An excellent introduction to this temple complex on the border of Cambodia and Thailand, which has served as a symbolic point of tension as the two countries have wrested control back and forth. Although accessible for all intents and purposes only from Thailand due to its location on the edge of a precipice, it was legally declared part of Cambodia in 1962 by the International Court of Justice, but it is still fought over between the government and the rebel Khmer Rouge troops. This work is an important piece of historical research setting the temples in relationship to their time and to other sites.

181 **Les ruines d'Angkor: étude artistique et historique sur les monuments khmers de Cambodge Siamois.** (The ruins of Angkor: artistic and historic study of Khmer monuments of Siamese Cambodia.)

Lucien Fournereau and Jacques Porcher. Paris: Ernest Leroux, 1890. 2 vols.

This book is valuable mostly because of the very good quality photographs it contains. They are probably among the best ever published before the work of restoration began. The second volume of pictures principally shows surface decoration, bas-relief and sculpture. The text is the classic colonial chitchat, with many silly ideas about history, like the notion that some Roman traders visited the country and 'maybe exercised some influence on Khmer architecture'! Its only merit is to remind us that the text of the famous 12th-century visit of Chinese ambassador Chou Ta-Kuan, describing Angkor as a rich and powerful city-state, was first translated into French by Abel Rémusat in *Nouvelles annales des voyages* (1819-25), half a century before Angkor was heralded by Mouhot. This could explain the preconceived ideas which the French historians later tried to impress on the epigraphic and archaeological evidence.

182 **Select Cambodi[a]n inscriptions: the Mebon and Pre Rup inscriptions of Rajendra Varman II.**

Mahesh Kumar Sharan, foreword by Upendra Thakur. Delhi: S. N. Publications, 1981. xiv, 265p. bibliog.

Includes the Sanskrit text, translations and transliterations of the Mebon and Pre Rup inscriptions of Rajendravarman II who reigned in Angkor from 944-68 AD. Sharan claims, 'These rare documents lucidly analyse the events in a chronological sequence with historical objectivity'. Sharan, in 1987, was head of the Department of Ancient Indian and Asian Studies at Gaya College, Bhar, and consequently highlights Indian influence, but also the Cambodian contribution to Sanskrit literature, which includes some inscriptions that 'excel even the best compositions at home'. In conjunction with the excellent introductions to the inscriptions, the texts reveal much about ancient Cambodian literature, religion, politics, economics and cultural history. The volume also includes Sanskrit texts of inscriptions (Devanagari and Roman) and English translation.

183 **La stèle de Ta-Prohm.** (The stele of Ta-Prohm.)

George Coedès. [Hanoi: s.n., 190?]. 42p. bibliog.

Discovered in 1882, this inscription by King Jayavarman VII is widely known as the inscription of the hospitals. It has been used to depict the Angkor kings as devout Buddhists, burning with compassion for their subjects. Nothing can be more misleading.

Angkor and the Khmers.
See item no. 63.

An eyewitness account of the Cambodian expedition.
See item no. 77.

A pilgrimage to Angkor.
See item no. 92.

Documents graphiques de la conservation d'Angkor: 1963-1973. (Graphic documents of the conservation of Angkor.)
See item no. 130.

Inscriptions du Cambodge. (Inscriptions of Cambodia.)
See item no. 162.

Kambuja-Desa or, An ancient Hindu colony in Cambodia.
See item no. 165.

Listes générales des inscriptions et des monuments du Champa et du Cambodge. (General lists of inscriptions and monuments of Champa and Cambodia.)
See item no. 166.

Towards Angkor: in the footsteps of the Indian invaders.
See item no. 171.

Le Cambodge. (Cambodia.)
See item no. 197.

Recherches sur le vocabulaire des inscriptions sanscrites du Cambodge. (Research on the vocabulary of Sanskrit inscriptions in Cambodia.)
See item no. 396.

Ancient Cambodia.
See item no. 750.

Angkor Vat: description graphique du temple. (Angkor Wat: graphic description of the temple.)
See item no. 753.

Angkor: art and civilization.
See item no. 756.

Angkor.
See item no. 758.

Le Bayon. (The Bayon.)
See item no. 766.

Cambodia: restoration and revival.
See item no. 767.

The cultural history of Angkor.
See item no. 773.

Earth in flower: an historical and descriptive study of the classical dance drama of Cambodia.
See item no. 781.

A golden souvenir of Angkor.
See item no. 783.

Iconographie du Cambodge post-Angkorien. (Iconography of post-Angkor Cambodia.)
See item no. 786.

Inventaire descriptif des monuments du Cambodge. (Descriptive inventory of Cambodian monuments.)
See item no. 788.

Palaces of the gods: Khmer art & architecture in Thailand.
See item no. 805.

Phnom Bakheng: étude architecturale du temple. (Phnom Bakheng: architectural study of the temple.)
See item no. 808.

Tâ Kèo: étude architecturale du temple. (Ta Keo: architectural study of the temple.)
See item no. 820.

Le Temple d'Içvarapura (Banteay Srei, Cambodge). (The temple of Içvarapura – Banteay Srei, Cambodia.)
See item no. 821.

The temples of Angkor: monuments to a vanished empire.
See item no. 822.

Cambodia: the Angkor mystery.
See item no. 916.

Post-Angkor (1433-1863)

184 **Angkor et le Cambodge au XVIe siècle: d'après les sources portugaises et espagnoles.** (Angkor and Cambodia in the 16th century: according to Portuguese and Spanish sources.)
Bernard Philippe Groslier with collaboration from C. R. Boxer. Paris: Presses Universitaires de France, 1958. 194p. map. bibliog. (Annales du Musée Guimet. Bibliothèque d'Ẹtudes, t. 63).

Bernard Philippe Groslier was the son of a great Angkor curator and director of the Fine Arts School in Cambodia, and was therefore born into things Khmer. He received a rounded education in history, archaeology, and the arts. He was the best qualified man in the best place, right on the spot in Siem Reap, leading the Conservation which he left in 1972, only after he had been wounded and stabbed in a mad attack. His early death in 1986 left a deep void in Khmer studies that has not yet been filled. His thesis on the Portuguese and Spanish sources on Cambodia in the 16th century is a model of scholarship. It has been widely used by later historians but the original is well worth considering. As in his other writings, future scholars will discover gems that will help them to dig deeper and deeper into Cambodia's still obscure history, because Groslier, with his extraordinary familiarity with the field and the people, had, besides his cautiously established scholarly work, also thundering intuitions which will serve to feed new research for several generations.

185 **Cambodia after Angkor: the chronicular evidence for the fourteenth to sixteenth centuries.**

Michael Theodore Vickery. PhD thesis, Yale University, New Haven, Connecticut, 1977. 2 vols. bibliog. Also available in microform, Ann Arbor, Michigan: University Microfilms International, 1977.

Vickery, whose writings have spanned Cambodian history from precolonial to post-UNTAC times, presented this dissertation for a Yale doctorate in 1977. Previous histories of the 14th to 16th centuries had been based on Cambodian and Ayutthyan chronicles, which in this study Vickery aims to show refer to and derive from each other, and include faulty dating and parts that are entirely fictitious. After analysing each chronicle in parts one and two, he compares them in part three to provide a new synthesis of chronicular history and to suggest a new basis for further post-Angkor history. He maintains that Angkor did not 'fall', but was supplanted through changes in power and economics in the region. He provides excellent introductions and commentaries for the chronicles as well as an appendix on the transliteration, transcription and script. The thesis is conveniently summarized in 'The composition and transmission of the Ayudhya and Cambodia chronicles' in *Perceptions of the past in Southeast Asia*, edited by Anthony J. Reid and David G. Marr (q.v.).

186 **Cambodia before the French: politics in a tributary kingdom, 1794-1848.**

David Porter Chandler. PhD thesis, University of Michigan, Ann Arbor, Michigan, 1973. vi, 212 leaves. bibliog. Also available in microform, Ann Arbor, Michigan: University Microfilms International.

Chandler's doctoral thesis covers a period that is still often neglected – the first half of the 19th century – an era still often presented as a time of darkness in which Cambodia was in danger of being swallowed up by Vietnam and/or Thailand. Chandler examines the foreign policy of the time and the reigns of Eng, Chan, Queen Mei and Duang. His overview of everyday life and the structure of Cambodian society is important to an understanding of contemporary Cambodia. Those Western, and possible Vietnamese, observers who equated a lack of strongly centralized bureaucratic institutions with anarchy disregarded the significance of the system of personal superordination and subordination which held the society together. By playing one power against another, the nation's leaders ensured its survival but, in Chandler's view, their policies exacted a heavy toll on the population as a whole, with numbers declining sharply during the period.

187 **Chroniques royales du Cambodge.** (Royal chronicles of Cambodia.) French translation by Mak Phoeun and Khin Sok, with comparison of the different versions and an introduction by Mak Phoeun. Paris: École Française d'Extrême-Orient, 1981-88. 3 vols. bibliog. (Collection de Textes et Documents sur l'Indochine).

The volume contains the following three texts: 'Des origines légendaires jusqu'à Paramaja 1er' (From the legendary origins up to Paramaja I) translated by Mak Phoeun, 1984; 'De Bana Yat à la prise de Langvaek' (From Bana Yat to the seizure of Langvek) translated by Khin Sok, 1988; and 'De 1594 à 1677' (From 1594 to 1677) translated by Mak Phoeun, 1981. Westerners have regrouped under the word 'chronicles' a vast array of written documents which were found, mostly in the 19th century, in the royal palaces, in monasteries and also in big family homes all over Southeast Asia. The documents themselves were not very old, as the material on which they are written does not generally last more than two or three centuries. Some of course are copies of lost originals. The conditions in which they were written, and the identity of the scribes or of the sponsors are generally unknown. These documents seem in most cases to have been part of a system of power. They were not distributed to a general public but kept like 'treasures' in the recesses of palaces occupied by powerful figures. The writers must have been religious figures because no one else had a good command of writing. The style and conventions of writing all point to the role of legitimization that the chronicles had at some points. Their rewriting and manipulations also testify to the fact that they were useful to the rulers. Western scholars discovered these chronicles and treated them as historical documents. This is not astonishing since they did the same with the early European documents that they unearthed at the time. A number of legends were thus coldly treated as facts. The critical work of evaluating the chronicles, in this case the Cambodian chronicles, written in the 19th century, although initiated by Michael Vickery, is not complete and not even unanimously accepted in the scholarly community. The real importance of the chronicles may be more sociological than historical. As sources for dated facts, they should always be confirmed from other external sources. Mak Phoeun and Khin Sok have the enormous merit of having attempted to create a single version (from the several known incomplete manuscripts) and to translate it into a European language, together with a great number of learned footnotes. This was a formidable task and they should be thanked for having achieved it. In the process, they have become, each in his own right, two of the first Khmer scholars to write in an erudite way on the history of their country.

188 **The composition and transmission of the Ayudhya and Cambodian chronicles.**
Michael Vickery. In: *Perceptions of the past in Southeast Asia.* Edited by Anthony Reid and David Marr. Singapore: Heinemann for the Asian Studies Association of Australia, 1979, p. 130-54.

In this summary of his doctoral thesis *Cambodia after Angkor: the chronicular evidence for the fourteenth to sixteenth centuries* (q.v.) Vickery illuminates this period of Cambodian history that has long lain in the trough between glorious Angkor and colonial splendour.

189 **La deuxième intervention militaire vietnamienne au Cambodge (1673-1679).** (The second Vietnamese military intervention in Cambodia, 1673-79.)
Mak Phoeun, Po Dharma. *Bulletin de l'École Française d'Extrême-Orient*, vol. 77 (1988), p. 229-62.

Utilizing Khmer, Vietnamese and French sources, the authors describe efforts by the Nguyen lords to intervene forcibly on behalf of one group of Cambodian princes against another. There are detailed discussions of Cambodian court politics and various armed encounters. Eventually successful, the Nguyen obtained control of the territory around present-day Ho Chi Minh City. Mak Phoeun and Po Dharma published an article in the same journal earlier (1984) on the first Vietnamese intervention, 1658-59. [David G. Marr with Kristine Alilunas-Rodgers]

190 **Histoire de Cambodge de la fin du XVIème siècle au début du XVIIIème.** (History of Cambodia from the end of the 16th to the beginning of the 18th century.)
Mak Phoeun. Paris: École Française d'Extrême-Orient, 1995. 508p. bibliog. (Monographies, 176).

Mak Phoeun is well equipped to undertake the description and discussion of this under-documented period of Cambodian history as the author of three volumes of the Cambodian royal chronicles, which represent his principal source, *Chroniques royales du Cambodge* (q.v.). In addition, he draws on inscriptions and on other recent histories (particular reference is made to Tran Nghia, Vickery and Chandler). This work covers the period generally regarded as one of Cambodia's decline, from the capture of its capital Longvek by the Siamese in 1594 to the settlement of the Mekong delta (Kampuchea Krom) by the Vietnamese from 1700-01. A comprehensive bibliography and index complement this 176th work in the venerable ÉFEO monograph series.

191 **Societal organization in sixteenth and seventeenth century Cambodia.**
May Ebihara. *Journal of Southeast Asian Studies,* vol. 15 (1984), p. 280-95.

In a sociological analysis Ebihara shows patterns of behaviour from a long-ago historical period that can be seen as persisting until today. 'There was constant tension between the power of the king and local lords and officials. . . . In such struggles, entourages of patrons and clients were critically important as supports for various actors. . . . Common folk . . . needed patrons for protection and aid in coping with the pressures that impinged upon their lives.'

Le Cambodge entre le Siam et le Viêtnam (de 1775 à 1860). (Cambodia between Siam and Vietnam, from 1775 to 1860.)
See item no. 526.

Iconographie du Cambodge post-Angkorien. (Iconography of post-Angkor Cambodia.)
See item no. 786.

Colonial period (1863-1953)

192 **L'affaire Yukanthor: autopsie d'un scandale colonial.** (The Yukanthor affair: autopsy of a colonial scandal.)
Pierre L. Lamant. Paris: Société Française d'Histoire d'Outre-Mer, 1989. 243p. bibliog. Originally presented as the author's doctoral thesis, University of Paris-III, 1979. (Bibliothèque d'Histoire d'Outre-Mer. Nouvelle Série. Travaux, no. 6).

The near-forgotten Yukanthor affair was a scandal in Paris in 1900. A son of King Norodom, Yukanthor, was sent to Paris by his father, in an unofficial mission in order to protest the colonial policy, which Norodom thought was depriving him of his independence and ability to rule. As the king could not directly confront the high-ranking colonial administrators, who had extracted the 1884 vassal treaty from him at gunpoint, he chose this indirect way to speak his mind. As he received scant attention in Paris, the prince, with the help of some journalists, started a press campaign. The colonial lobby reacted swiftly and the prince was sent packing. He fled to Brussels and later to Singapore and Bangkok, and never returned to Cambodia. For Lamant, who has been teaching the colonial history of Cambodia for some time, digging in the archives unearthed some unpalatable truths. By making good use of a number of contemporary newspapers as well as official documents, he provides us with a well-told and revealing story of the arrogance of the colonial masters.

193 **André Malraux: the Indochina adventure.**
Walter G. Langlois. London: Pall Mall Press, 1966. 259p.

Documents and discusses the writer and activist Malraux's formative two-year stay in Indochina, which has been largely neglected by scholars. Langlois recounts how a young writer of literary fantasies returned to France a committed social reformer. A novelist, travel writer and philosopher of art, Malraux was a Parisian who studied Sanskrit, became President of the World Committee against War and Fascism, fought for the Republicans in the Spanish Civil War, was a resistance leader in France, Minister of Information for the first De Gaulle government, and a guest of the Kennedys at the White House. He became infamous in 1924 when he and his party were tried and imprisoned in Phnom Penh for stealing from an Angkor temple. On a later trip he became a co-organizer of the 'Young Annam' movement and launched the short-lived newspaper, *L'Indochine* (Indochina) which reappeared as *L'Indochine Enchainée* (Indochina in chains). Langlois seeks to justify Malraux's early escapades. The author, who had corresponded with Malraux himself regarding this book, uses a number of primary printed sources and information supplied by eyewitnesses in his effort to lay to rest rumours regarding Malraux's conduct in Indochina and contribute a more positive image to the body of criticism and history of this enigmatic figure. For a different perspective, and one that brings into focus the role of his wife Clara, who travelled with him but who is generally ignored in most biographies of the famous André, see Isabelle de Courtivron's 'The other Malraux in Indochina', in *Biography,* vol. 12, no. 1 (Winter 1989), p. 29-42.

194 **Battambang during the time of the Lord Governor.**
Tauch Chhuong; translated by Hin Sathin, Carol Mortland and Judy Ledgerwood. Phnom Penh: Cedoreck, 1994. 143p. maps. bibliog. Originally published in Khmer in 1974.

The author is now director of Books and Reading in the Ministry of Culture and Fine Arts, but at the time he wrote this book was a school teacher in Battambang. His intention was 'to research the history of Battambang, my native town, so that it could be compiled for the youth of later generations, as is done for the youth of the developed countries'. In so doing, Tauch Chhuong has performed a valuable service, for it is perhaps the only such document written by a Cambodian, and stands beside only a handful of other ethnographies by foreign observers. His work is all the more precious because many of his twenty-one informants, the youngest of whom was born in 1894, are almost certainly no longer alive. Described on the cover as 'a social history of Battambang Province under Siamese occupation (1795-1907)' the book contains three chapters of history, followed by chapters on: the land and people before 1907; administration; the economy; artistic life; cultural life; Lok Machas (the Lord Governor); Kamphaeng (the fort); the wives and children of the Lord Governor; the return of Battambang Province to Cambodia; and after the Lord Governor's move to Baschim. The translation and publication was funded by the East West Center in Honolulu, Hawaii.

195 **Le Cambodge et la colonisation française: histoire d'une colonisation sans heurts (1897-1920).** (Cambodia and French colonization: history of a trouble-free colonization, 1897-1920.)
Alain Forest. Paris: L'Harmattan, 1980. xii, 542p. maps. bibliog.

Based principally on documents in the Archives d'Outre-Mer (Overseas Archives) in Aix-en-Provence, France, this book grew out of Forest's 1979 thesis, which itself developed from his 1973 'Mémoire de Maîtrise' thesis at the University of Paris VII, and it represents one of the key studies of the French colonial occupation of Cambodia, complementing the work of Milton Osborne. Like Osborne, Forest concentrates more on the political, administrative and cultural aspects, though he also gives attention to the economy. Forest states that he adopts the perspective of a documentalist rather than a theorist, hoping to understand and to make understandable what has occurred. The principal questions addressed are: how did colonialism contribute to Cambodian society, and what were the motor forces of that colonialism?; and how did Cambodian society receive and react to that colonialism, and what did it put in place or adjust to account for the foreign presence, actions and discourse. Published with the support of CNRS, this forms the first book in a series from the Centre de documentation et recherche sur l'Asie du sud-est et le monde insulindien (Centre for Documentation and Research on Southeast Asia and the Archipelagic World).

196 **Le Cambodge et la décolonisation de l'Indochine: le caractère particulier du nationalisme khmer de 1936 à 1945.** (Cambodia and the decolonization of Indochina: the particular character of Khmer nationalism from 1936 to 1945.)
Pierre L. Lamant. In: *Les chemins de la décolonisation de l'empire colonial français*. (Paths to the decolonization of the French empire.) Under the direction of Charles-Robert Ageron. Paris: Institut d'Histoire du Temps Présent. Editions du Centre National de la Recherche Scientifique, 1986.

An interesting study of the role of leaders such as Monireth, Sihanouk, Son Ngoc Thanh, Pach Chhoeun and others in the early independence movement. Lamant provides some interesting material on Sihanouk's attitude at this time. Compared with their Vietnamese counterparts, these early actors are depicted as relatively unconcerned with ideology. Lamant studies the influence of the Indochinese Communist Party from its formation in 1930, and the role of the Buddhist clergy. Lamant finds it difficult to judge the real importance of some of the early anti-French movements. The relative low level of mass involvement did not necessarily indicate lack of support for independence.

197 **Le Cambodge.** (Cambodia.)
Étienne Aymonier. Paris: Ernest Leroux, 1900-04. 3 vols. maps. bibliog.

A three-volume compendium on Cambodia by one of France's archetypal 'colonial scholar bureaucrats', this monumental work still stands today as a touchstone for the Cambodia of yesteryear.

198 **Cambodia under the tricolour: King Sisowath and the 'mission civilisatrice' (civilizing mission) 1904-1927.**
John Tully. Clayton, Victoria: Monash Asia Institute, 1996. 352p. bibliog.

Tully sets out to examine what he calls the Faustian contradictions of colonialism in Cambodia as both a blessing and a curse. His exposition dwells more on the blessings, conceding that the country had been saved from probable dismemberment and had gained some benefits of Western civilization, especially in public works, communications, economic development and public health. On the other hand France's democratic values of 1789 were not for export and Cambodia's age-old traditions of absolutism were never challenged. The Sisowath period was the zenith of French colonialism, celebrated at colonial expositions and with the memorable 1906 tour to France of the king and his Royal Ballet, but was to begin its demise after only another fifteen years. The work is based almost exclusively on French archival documents, using only two indigenous sources (both in translation), the Sisowath chronicles and Tauch Chhuong's history of Battambang. Tully attributes this lack to the Khmer 'preliteracy' of the time, but other perspectives could well have emerged had he pursued his research in Cambodia itself.

199 **Des français au Cambodge: anthologie. Vol. 1. Les beaux jours du Protectorat.** (By the French in Cambodia: anthology. Vol. 1. The beautiful days of the Protectorate.)

Dominique Bérard. Phnom Penh: Espace Bayon, [1995?]. 99p.

A selection of the work of seventeen French authors, from Bouillevaux in 1850 to de Portales in 1931. The compiler states that it is 'neither complete nor definitive' but 'limited by the availability of the texts and by personal choice for anecdotal interest and literary value'. She describes her authors as initially missionaries and explorers, and the second generation as tourists or government functionaries, but with constant themes: the poverty of the country, prevarication and hopes; the idea of race; the Chinese as the enemy; the Khmer psychology; and the strangeness of the monuments. This is a modest publication, likely to have limited distribution outside Cambodia, but it is a useful compilation of some elusive items, with unfortunately scanty bibliographical descriptions.

200 **The emancipation of French Indochina.**

Donald Lancaster. New York: Octagon, 1974. 445p. map. bibliog. Originally published, Oxford: Oxford University Press, 1961.

Much of the information in Lancaster's account of the French intervention in Indochina and of events leading up to the fall of Dien Bien Phu in May 1954 is based on his discussions with Vietnamese nationalists while working in the British legation in Saigon from 1950-54. Although the main focus is Vietnam, Cambodia is specifically mentioned in most sections. The book gives an overview of European conquest and describes the French administration as well as the emergence and struggles of the Vietminh and other nationalist forces.

201 **Un empire colonial français: l'Indochine.** (A French colonial empire: Indochina.)

Work published under the direction of Georges Maspéro. Paris: Les Éditions G. van Oest, 1929-30. 2 vols. maps.

This collective book was published in preparation for the 1931 Colonial Exhibition in Paris, more or less commemorating the second colonial French empire, started with the conquest of Algiers in 1830 (the first empire, including India and Canada, having been lost to the British in the 18th century, for want of naval power). This period, on the eve of the 1929 world crisis, stands now as the apex of this French empire. After 1931, with the Nghe Tinh Soviet rebellion in Vietnam, the collapse had started. This book, says Albert Sarraut, several times Minister of Colonies, is a 'testimony of grandeur and glory of the French genius' in the self-congratulatory tone that permeates the articles, written by the best scholars of the time. It contains a number of photographs, some of which are particularly interesting, such as one of an isolated massive vaulted brick gate, called the Gate of Annam, which for several centuries was the border post between Dai Viet (Vietnam) and Champa, and that of a Jarai tomb with remarkable wood carvings of ancestors, which are probably not even to be seen in any museum. Some Jarai groups live in Cambodia, but their tombs disappeared long ago, so this may be the only remaining trace.

202 **French Indo-China.**
Virginia Thompson. London: George Allen & Unwin, 1937. 517p. map. bibliog.

Thompson lays out for the first time in English and with an American political scientist's approach the details of the French administration, and its economic foundations, on the basis of a sound investigation of the major French sources, mentioned in a useful bibliography. Some colour from the period is given in her discussion of the impact of colonists and colonials, with, for once, the women in these categories gaining a mention. As usual with almost all books on Indochina, it is heavily dominated by a concern for things Vietnamese (in this case seen as 'Annamite') and Cambodia and Laos are presented under the dubious rubric, 'Peoples of Indian Culture'. Despite this inauspicious heading, the treatment is sympathetic and gives details of intellectual and artistic developments as well as some attention to ethnic minorities.

203 **The French presence in Cochinchina and Cambodia: rule and response (1859-1905).**
Milton E. Osborne. Bangkok: White Lotus, 1996. 379p. maps. bibliog. Originally published, Ithaca, New York; London: Cornell University Press, 1969. 397p. maps. bibliog.

For both southern Vietnam and Cambodia, trends set in the first five years of French rule – the withdrawal of the authority of the Mandarin class in Cochinchina and the unwilling submission of Norodom to French demands in Cambodia – set patterns that were to continue into the 20th century. Osborne argues that, although strategic considerations may have motivated the original annexations, the French were guided by their perceived 'mission civilisatrice' (civilizing mission). France's interest in Cambodia was subsidiary to the more pressing claims for involvement in Cochinchina. Osborne traces the rising tension between Norodom and the French administrators whose attempted reforms threatened his power. The culmination was the 1884-86 revolt, resulting in a temporary brake on the development of French power, but Norodom was soon after eclipsed. Osborne stresses the continuing different character of the two regions, and the contrasting effects on each of the French presence. By the early 20th century Cambodia was more quiescent than it had been for decades, whereas the substantial changes wrought in Cochinchina contributed to a search by many Vietnamese for a new philosophical framework to replace that which had been irrevocably damaged by the colonial experience. Osborne's work is based principally on French sources, and concentrates on those locals who worked with them, and on the areas of colonial activity. The bibliography is valuable, containing notes on archive sources and unpublished material as well as monographs and articles.

204 **La geste française en Indochine: histoire par les textes de la France en Indochine des origines à 1914.** (French exploits in Indochina: textual history of France in Indochina from its origins to 1914.)
Georges Taboulet. Paris: Adrien Maisonneuve, 1955-56. 2 vols. (Librairie d'Amérique et d'Orient).

A starting-point for any student of France's involvement in Indochina, although by no means the place to stop, given its vigorous support of the colonial project. Within the two volumes are reproduced over 200 documents and reports regarding the French administration and domination of Indochina. Volume one deals with early, mainly missionary, activities from the 17th to mid-19th centuries, and focuses on Tonkin and Cochinchina. The first mention of Cambodia is the 1767 establishment of an official outpost. Volume two starts with the establishment of the French presence in southern Indochina (meridionale) from 1358-1884. Chapters on Cambodia include documents of the 'discoverers' of Angkor, the 1863 placement of Cambodia under French protection, the return of Battambang to Cambodia by Thailand in 1907, and many more. This volume contains an extensive index of names as well as fifty-three illustrations. David Marr (in the 1992 *Vietnam* volume in the World Bibliographical Series, co-authored by Kristine Alilunas-Rodgers) sees this work as 'one of the most impressive defences of French colonialism', with Taboulet trying 'to convey a picture of idealism, self-sacrifice, intellectual curiosity, stubbornness and dedication to the motherland'.

205 **A history of the Cambodian independence movement, 1863-1955.**
V. M. Reddi. Tirupati, India: Sri Venkateswara University, [1970]. iv, ii, 228, 10, viip. bibliog.

Based on a PhD thesis presented to the Indian School of International Studies, New Delhi. Reddi gives a positive assessment of the role played by Sihanouk in 'winning freedom' for Cambodia, concluding 'it was largely due to his stewardship of the movement that Cambodia escaped the heavy loss of human and material resources which has marred the course of similar movements in Asia and Africa in recent times'. Tragically this optimistic conclusion was not to be sustained in the following years.

206 **Iconographie historique de l'Indochine française: documents sur l'histoire de l'intervention française en Indochine.** (Historical iconography of French Indochina: documents on the history of French intervention in Indochina.)
Paul Boudet and André Masson. Paris: G. van Oest, 1931. 62p. At head of title: Direction des Archives et des Bibliothèques de l'Indochine.

Published for the Colonial Exhibition held in Paris in 1931, this is a collection of documents and plates on the early colonial figures and martyrs of French Indochina, mainly sourced from the archives of Indochina. The publication states that the authors were inspired to compile the collection in order to 'conserve the memory of this pious manifestation and to resuscitate through images the physiognomy of the men who have given Indochina to France and the setting into which it was received'.

207 **Indochine, la colonisation ambiguë.** (Indochina, the ambiguous colonization.)
Pierre Brocheux and Daniel Hémery. Paris: Éditions la Découverte, 1995. 427p. maps. bibliog. (Textes à l'Appui: Serie Histoire Contemporaine).

As signalled in the title, the authors bring a new approach to the study of the Indochinese colony – neither glorifying the empire, nor adopting the anti-colonialist paradigm. They rather see the colonial project as combining external force and an internal process that led to 'a partnership, if fragile, between the old and new dominant classes and colonized elites'. So they seek to chart the variations and evolution of relationships. Regrettably this work carries on the old tradition of

Indochina being seen almost entirely in Vietnamese terms so Cambodia and Laos received little individual attention, though the observations on the colonial edifices have relevance of course to developments in those countries also. Economic analysis is the strong suit here, with research in the archives and summaries of recent theses providing consolidation of a considerable amount of new material. The annotations to each chapter contain a wealth of bibliographical references, only some of which are repeated in the final bibliography. The lack of an index is another disappointment.

208 **La première guerre d'Indochine (1945-1954): bibliographie.** (The First Indochina War, 1945-54: bibliography.)
Alain Ruscio. Paris: L'Harmattan, 1985. bibliog.

This volume contains more than fifty entries specifically on Cambodia. As well as historical works, and publications on current affairs and testimonies, it includes items of literature and films.

209 **La présence militaire française en Indochine 1940-1945.** (The French military presence in Indochina 1940-45.)
Claude Hesse d'Alzon. Vincennes, France: Publications du Service Historique de l'Armée de Terre, 1988. 375p. maps. bibliog.

Designed in part to rehabilitate historically the armed forces who obeyed the collaborator Vichy régime during the Second World War, this study also demonstrates how poorly prepared France was to offer any opposition to Japanese intervention. Of particular interest is the chapter on the 1940-41 Franco-Thai confrontation. Later efforts of the French 'resistance' within Indochina are greatly overstated by the author. There are several appendices which provide a chronology of events, a list of legislative texts and regulations, lists of military organizations, and details of regiments and insignia. [David G. Marr with Kristine Alilunas-Rodgers]

210 **Le royaume du Cambodge.** (The Kingdom of Cambodia.)
Jean Moura. Paris: Leroux, 1883. 2 vols. map.

This is a masterful book. Before there was a colonial administration, Indochina was under the government 'of the admirals'. Jean Moura was a naval officer who was despatched early on to be the representative of the French government in its capacity as protecting power, accredited to King Norodom. This two-volume book is an attempt to write an encyclopaedia of Cambodia covering topics including geography, plants, minerals, religions, festivals, government, coronation, civil servants, law, prisons, literature, astronomy, marriage and divorce, funerals, 'savages', Chinese, etc. The second volume is the first translation of a long fragment of a Khmer chronicle, followed by a description of Angkor and some considerations on Khmer arts. As a whole, it must be noted that Moura was the source of much of what was written after him. It is the best of what the colonial administrator could do, while of course exhibiting all the prejudices of the time, but as such it is a historical document. It has never been reprinted but 115 years later it still makes fascinating reading.

211 **La vie quotidienne des Français en Indochine 1860-1910.** (Everyday life of the French in Indochina 1860-1910.)
Charles Meyer. Paris: Hachette, 1985. 298p.

Describes an Indochina that exists no longer, and the daily lives of the adventurers, administrators, missionaries and others who made up the French population of her exotic colonies in the East. The book recounts the construction of the French cities – Saigon, Phnom Penh, Hanoi and Vientiane. 'Au Cambodge de Norodom' (In the Cambodia of Norodom) new arrivals disembarked in Phnom Penh, laden with their European and Chinese treasures, and ice made in Saigon (the colonialists established ice factories), amidst an atmosphere of amiable disorder. Relations between colonizers and colonized were different from those in Cochinchina. Eventually most administrators adjusted to a people who accepted their presence with neither hostility nor servility, providing their beliefs and traditions were respected. Meyer recounts the exploits of some of the 'characters' of the expatriate scene. For those who steered clear of traps such as the magic of opium and the charm of the 'little wives', it was a place of many opportunities.

Monographie du Cambodge. (Monograph on Cambodia.)
See item no. 18.

Mission Pavie Indo-Chine 1879-1895. (The Pavie Indochina Mission 1879-95.)
See item no. 90.

River road to China: the Mekong River Expedition 1866-73.
See item no. 93.

Post-1940

General

212 **Cambodge: histoire et enjeux: 1945-1985.** (Cambodia: history and stakes: 1945-85.)
Camille Scalabrino, Ben Kiernan, Steve Heder, Michael Vickery, Pierre Brocheux, Joel Luguern, Marie-Claire Orieux, Alain Rustenholz, Serge Thion. Paris: L'Harmattan, 1985. 237p. bibliog. (Asie-débat, 2).

As its title indicates, this is a contribution to the debate on Kampuchea, the nature of the Pol Pot régime and the People's Republic of Kampuchea. While the authors differ in their attitude to Vietnam and its intervention, most are concerned to develop an understanding that goes beyond the shallow anti-communism of some other contemporary analysts.

213 **Cambodge 1940-1991, ou, La politique sans les Cambodgiens.** (Cambodia 1940-91, or, Politics without the Cambodians.)
Vandy Kaonn. Paris: L'Harmattan, 1993. 157p.

An unusual perspective is presented here by Vandy Kaonn, one of a handful of intellectuals who stayed to help rebuild his country after the overthrow of Pol Pot. Kaonn studied sociology in Paris, returning to Cambodia to teach philosophy and work as a journalist under the Sihanouk régime. After enduring the hardships and horrors of the Khmer Rouge, he was elected member of the National Assembly for Battambang in the elections of 1981, and established the Institute of Sociology in Phnom Penh. Falling out of favour with the government over a move to establish a new political party, in 1989 Vandy Kaonn decided to leave and apply for political asylum in France. This essay represents his reflections on Cambodian history over five decades, in large part based on his own recollections and experiences. It is a depressing work, concluding with pessimistic words about the country having become ungovernable: 'The corruption and incompetence of officials, nepotism of the prince, lack of professional training for the youth, make Cambodia an ideal prey for "exotic predators"'.

214 **Cambodge: la révolution de la forêt.** (Cambodia: revolution of the forest.)

François Debré. [Paris]: Flammarion, 1976. 261, [8]p. map. bibliog.

Debré writes during the time that Cambodia was under the oppressive rule of the Khmer Rouge. He looks beyond the refugee reports that provided the sole basis for most other writings at the time, to look at the historical evolution of the rebels then holding power. The forest/jungle is the focus of his analysis – the forest then covered two-thirds of the country, and had since time immemorial served as the refuge and wellspring for those rejecting the authority of the palace. A notable feature is the first-hand testimony of the resistance fighter Ouk Samith.

215 **Cambodia, a shattered society.**

Marie Alexandrine Martin, translated by Mark W. McLeod. Berkeley, California: University of California Press, 1994. xxi, 398p. bibliog. A translation of *Le mal cambodgien* (The Cambodian sickness), Paris: Hachette, 1989.

'Despite historical vicissitudes, Khmer society seems to be unchanged by the centuries.' This is one of the themes that Martin investigates in this history of Cambodia, which examines predominantly the period since independence. There are also chapters on ancient Cambodia ('A conservative society') and the colonial heritage. The anti-communist perspective of the book should not be very difficult to find for the average reader. Nor should be the sympathy for Sihanouk and for the legacy of French rule. 'The negligence of the Khmer monarchs had brought the country to the brink of ultimate catastrophe: the disappearance of Cambodia as a political and territorial entity. The first attempt at a Franco-Cambodian rapprochement was undertaken by a Khmer king who sought to save his kingdom from disaster.' Other authors treat such material more critically. Nevertheless 'Shattered society' takes a much more sociological approach to the subject matter than most works and therefore fills in many blanks left by other texts. For this reason alone it is a very useful volume. Written between 1965 and 1975 – when Martin was travelling through remote regions working on her ethnobotanical research (q.v.) – and updated for the English edition from 1991 to 1993 (with the benefit of research she conducted, interviewing refugees in Thailand in the early 1980s), the book includes a useful chronology and a number of appended documents.

216 **The Chinese rulers' crimes against Kampuchea.**
[Phnom Penh]: Ministry of Foreign Affairs, People's Republic of Kampuchea, 1984. 132p.

The topic of Chinese policy towards Kampuchea is examined in five periods: in the 1950s; in the 1960s; from 1970 to 1975; from April 1975 to 1977; and from 1978 until 1984. This is the official viewpoint of the PRK government and is interesting as a document of that time. It expresses a view that was also held in Hanoi – 'without Chinese support the genocidal Pol Pot clique would not have been able to carry out such horrendous offenses against the Kampuchean people, just as without the support of the American imperialists, Israel would not be able to perpetrate such towering crimes against the Arab and Palestinian peoples'. The view is put forward that solidarity between the three countries of Indochina is essential: 'separation from Vietnam and Laos means death; solidarity between them means revival'.

217 **Conflict neutralization in the Cambodia War.**
Sorpong Peou. Kuala Lumpur: Oxford University Press, 1996. 304p. (South-East Asian Social Science Monographs).

The author believes that the world does not fully understand domestic conflicts in Third-World countries in general, and the Cambodian conflict in particular. He holds that the Cambodian conflict cannot stand on its own feet unless everyone involved clearly understands its intractable problems.

218 **Des courtisans aux partisans: essai sur la crise cambodgienne.**
(From courtiers to partisans: essay on the Cambodian crisis.)
Jean-Claude Pomonti and Serge Thion. [Paris]: Gallimard, 1971. 374p. map. bibliog. (Collection Idées, no. 230).

A valuable contemporary analysis of the crisis in Cambodia surrounding the overthrow of Sihanouk in 1970, the installation of the pro-US Lon Nol régime, and the ensuing civil war and massive pogrom against Vietnamese settlers. Thion and Pomonti, two left-wing observers, in contrast to many other commentators of that time, did not glorify the *ancien régime* (old order) of Sihanouk, and put the blame wholly on outside forces, but instead look back into its character, seeking to uncover the internal, as well as the external, reasons for its downfall. They sum up the situation thus – 'Cambodia is in labour. Many will want to perform a caesarian section' – and they declare their hope that the revolutionary forces will prevail in the class struggle unfolding with the anticipated withdrawal of US forces from the region removing the false shoring up of the tiny bourgeoisie. The volume contains an important collection of eight documents as appendices, ranging from 1886 (proclamations of the king and the French Resident General tightening French control over Cambodia), through to examples of the discourse of the Sihanouk era to statements issued around the 1970 coup.

219 **Explaining Cambodia: a review essay.**
Serge Thion. Canberra: Department of Political and Social Change, Division of Politics and International Relations, Research School of Pacific and Asian Studies, Australian National University, 1994. 54p. bibliog. (Working Paper Series/Political and Social Change, no. 11).

A think-piece presented in the discursive style of the detached French academic. Thion visited Australia in 1993 and gave several lectures along the lines revealed in this review of the literature on Cambodia of the past five years. In Thion's view: 'Although the Khmer Rouge's rule projected itself as a complete break-away from the past, and thus an isolated atypical period, it is nevertheless difficult to abstract it from its two breeding grounds, the convoluted history of Cambodia and the strait jacketed history of the Communist movement'. Some seventeen books are selected for analysis, but the really interesting part is less the analysis than the flights of thought taken by Thion in his commentary. The books reviewed provide the runway for his own eloquent and idiosyncratic views on history and on the unfolding political events involving Cambodia.

220 **How Pol Pot came to power: a history of communism in Kampuchea, 1930-1975.**
Ben Kiernan. London: Verso, 1985. xvii, 430p. maps. bibliog.

A masterly piece of historical research based on archival sources in France and Cambodia, and on interviews with over 500 Cambodians. It is based on Ben Kiernan's 1983 PhD thesis for Monash University, Melbourne and was published two years later. Although out of print, it remains the essential study of the development of communism in Cambodia up to the Khmer Rouge period. The dramatic title and cover images of a map of Cambodia turning into a skull in six steps may mislead the potential reader into thinking this is a popular read. Not so. The introduction, in just fourteen pages, sets the material and intellectual social context for what follows. Kiernan goes on to explain how 'the movement's initial leadership was primarily Buddhist and rural in background, while the Pol Pot group was primarily urban and French-educated. The story of how the latter took the place of the former, and how each in turn managed to mobilize a substantial following, is the subject of this book'. Kiernan, now Associate Professor of History at Yale University, New Haven, Connecticut, in 1996 published the sequel on Pol Pot in power, *The Pol Pot regime: race, power, and genocide in Cambodia under the Khmer Rouge, 1975-79* (q.v.).

221 **Peasants and politics in Kampuchea, 1942-1981.**
[Edited by] Ben Kiernan and Chantou Boua. London: Zed Press, 1982. viii, 401p. map. bibliog.

A collection of key documents and commentary on political and economic developments in Cambodia over the forty years from the Umbrella War of 1942, known as 'the first demonstration to awaken Khmer consciousness'. Excerpts from the doctoral theses by Hu Nim and Hou Yuon and a 1964 study on co-operatives by the latter form some of the most detailed studies of their society carried out by Cambodians and are extremely valuable documents. The book also includes: 'Looking back at Cambodia, 1942-76' by Michael Vickery; 'The Umbrella War of 1942' by Bunchan Mul; a series of first-hand testimonies of life under the Khmer Rouge, and four separate chapters by Ben Kiernan outlining different phases of the development of Cambodia's revolutionary movement. The contributions are in English, some of which have been translated from the Khmer (by Chantou Boua) and from French (by Ben Kiernan).

222 **Réalités Cambodgiennes.** (Cambodian Realities.)
[Phnom Penh: EKLIP, 1956-75. weekly]. Available on microfilm from Library of Congress Photoduplication Service, Washington, DC on 35mm reels. Supplements accompany some numbers.

Founded in 1956 by Trinh Hoanh, and later edited by Lee Eng, this weekly magazine aimed at the French-speaking Cambodian general public included cultural, social and historical reports on aspects of Cambodia. It survived the shift from reporting on Sihanouk and his political organization the Sangkum to covering the war and the resistance forces from the perspective of the Khmer Republic.

223 **The struggle for Indochina 1940-1955.**
Ellen Hammer. Stanford, California: Stanford University Press, 1966. 373p.

This book was written, the author declares, in an attempt to depict a segment of living history without the benefit of the historian's hindsight. The first twelve chapters of the book were completed in 1954 when the nations of French Indochina were engaged in struggling for independence from colonial rule. Chapter thirteen, completed in 1955, evaluated US policy as seen from the vantage point of the Geneva Conference.

224 **The tragedy of Cambodian history: politics, war and revolution since 1945.**
David P. Chandler. New Haven, Connecticut; London: Yale University Press, 1993. new ed. [408]p. First published, 1991.

An important work by one of the foremost historians on Cambodia, this book covers the period since the Second World War. Chandler draws on his experience as a United States foreign service officer in Phnom Penh in the 1960s, as well as on interviews and archival material. The greatest tragedy was, of course, the brutal period of Khmer Rouge rule after 1975, but the emphasis of the book is the Sihanouk period, which is shown to contain the roots of the ensuing tragedy as the prince sought to destroy all opposition and to concentrate power in his own hands. The narrative ends with Vietnam's defeat of the Khmer Rouge in 1979. This history is based on an account of the activities of the country's main political leaders and is not a social history. Chandler believes that the Pol Potist Communist Party of Kampuchea was a Marxist-Leninist party which differed from similar parties (in Vietnam and elsewhere) in the level of violence and utopianism and in the absence of discussion of policies inside the group. This book is a companion volume to Chandler's *A history of Cambodia* (q.v.), covering the period since Angkor.

225 **Watching Cambodia: ten paths to enter the Cambodia tangle.**
Serge Thion. Bangkok: White Lotus, 1993. xxv, 290p. bibliog.

A stunning photograph graces the cover of this book – it shows a Buddhist monk in saffron robes walking down a dirt road. Close behind him plods an official, clad in dark safari suit and rubber thongs, a briefcase under his arm, sunglasses and a blue UNTAC cap on his head. Further back is a row of gleaming white UNTAC armoured cars under the quintessential natural symbol of Cambodia – the sugar palm tree (*thnaot*). Somehow the photograph captures much of what Serge Thion addresses in his 'ten paths', essays written over twenty years of observing Cambodia: the persistence of traditional symbols and manners of behaviour; conflicting and competing agents of power and change; and the damage caused by outside intervention (most notably of course the US bombing, but more recently the activities of the UN). Most of the material in the book has been published elsewhere, but it is refreshing to read it anew, alongside Thion's interpretation of the unfolding UNTAC operation, which he names 'United Nations Traditional Apathy in Cambodia'. The contents include: 'Within the Khmer Rouge' (1972); 'The agrarian question in Indochina' (1973); 'The ingratitude of the crocodiles' (1980); 'The Cambodian idea of revolution' (1981); 'Cambodia: background and issues' (with Michael Vickery, 1981); 'The pattern of Cambodian politics' (1982); 'Time for talk' (1987); 'Indochinese refugees in France' (1987); 'Genocide as a political commodity' (1992); and 'Cambodia 1992'; and four appendices.

First and Second Indochina Wars (1945-54 and 1954-75)

226 **America and the Indochina Wars, 1945-1990: a bibliographical guide.**

Lester H. Brune and Richard Dean Burns. Claremont, California: Regina Books, 1991. 286p. map. bibliog. (New War/Peace Bibliographical Series, no. 1).

Prepared as a supplement to *The Vietnam conflict: its geographical dimensions, political traumas and military developments* (Santa Barbara, 1973), and *The wars in Vietnam, Cambodia and Laos, 1945-1982: a bibliographic guide* (q.v.), this work carries the study of the literature on this subject forward a further eight years, and gives a more accurate representation of the scope of its coverage by reference to 'America and . . .', since it is the US perspective that prevails in this as in so many other materials published about the wars. The works cited are all in English and are widely available in the United States. Some sixty-six items on Cambodia are listed.

227 **Cambodia: the widening war in Indochina.**

Edited by Jonathan S. Grant, Laurence A. G. Moss, Jonathan Unger. New York: Washington Square Press, 1971. vii, 355p. map. bibliog.

In mid-1970 demonstrations and university strikes broke out across the United States in opposition to Nixon's extension of the Vietnam War into Cambodian territory. This collection of essays was put together in order to meet the demand from protesting students, teachers and others for more information about the expanded conflict. As they did with this edition, the Committee of Concerned Asian Scholars continues to compile and present analyses on Asia which diverge from those readily available in mainstream media. The Committee was formed in 1968 by scholars and students who believed academic endeavour should be combined with political and ethical concerns, and were opposed to the US role in Asia. Contributors include Noam Chomsky and Robert Shaplen. With the common theme that immediate withdrawal by the United States was the only solution, the essays are divided into sections on the extension of the war, the conditions in Cambodia which preceded the 1970 coup, the coup and its implications, ecocide as an instrument of war, and the repercussions of involvement for the United States. Appendices include: President Nixon's address to the nation about Cambodia, on 30 April 1970; the Proclamation of the Royal Government of National Union under the leadership of the National United Front of Kampuchea; Mao Tse-tung's Statement on the Cambodian invasion; a chronology, biographical sketches and list of groups and organizations of Cambodia. The essays are introduced by an excellent summary of the events and political dynamics of the time, as viewed by the editors (all members of the Committee of Concerned Asian Scholars, University of California, Berkeley), and make a good historical resource.

228 **Conflict in Indo-China: a reader on the widening war in Laos and Cambodia.**

Edited by Marvin and Susan Gettleman, and Lawrence and Carol Kaplan. New York: Random House, [1970]. xiii, 461p. bibliog.

This book brings together articles and primary sources analysing the spread of the US war against Vietnam into Cambodia and Laos. Divided into three sections it covers: the early heritage and colonialism; independence and the Geneva Accords of 1954; the struggle for neutrality; and the spread of the war. Well-known contributors on Cambodia include Wilfred Burchett, Paul Sweezy and Harry Magdoff. Primary sources and statements by Richard Nixon, Lon Nol and Sihanouk are included, and the work remains a valuable source.

229 **End of a war: Indochina 1954.**

Philippe Devillers, Jean Lacouture. New York: Frederick A. Praeger, 1969. 412p. bibliog.

This is the English translation of a work written in 1959 and published in French as *La fin d'une guerre: Indochine 1954* (Paris: Éditions de Seuil, 1960). In the light of subsequent events – namely the US involvement in the Second Indochina War – the English version was revised. A section dealing with the situation in Cambodia, Laos and the two zones of Vietnam between 1954 and 1960 was replaced with a section by Devillers on how 'France's Asian responsibilities were transferred to the United States'. The book subsequently focuses very much on Vietnam but is useful background reading, especially section two which deals with the 1954 Geneva Peace Conference.

230 **The history of the Vietnam war.**

Compiled by Douglas Pike and the Indochina Archive. Ann Arbor, Michigan: University Microfilms International, 1988- . 365,000p. on microfilm.

This massive microfiche edition contains 365,000 pages of material on the war, about twelve per cent of the total accumulation of documents at the Indochina Archive, University of California, Berkeley. Some eighty per cent of the material is in English, the remaining twenty per cent in Vietnamese, Khmer, Lao, French and Russian. Many entries include an English translation or synopsis. The collection is divided into ten 'units': grand strategy and general assessment; general military history; topical history; political settlement efforts; National Front for the Liberation of South Vietnam (NLF); Democratic Republic of Vietnam (DRV); Republic of Vietnam (RVN); Cambodia and Laos; Asian region; and chronology. Despite its size and promotional claims, this microfiche edition is neither comprehensive nor organized according to detached scholarly criteria. The structure of the collection reflects the priorities of the US units which originally acquired and processed many of the data, as well as the particular conceptual preferences of the compiler. [David G. Marr with Kristine Alilunas-Rodgers]

231 **Incursion: from America's chokehold on the NVA lifelines to the sacking of the Cambodian sanctuaries.**
J. D. Coleman. New York: St. Martin's Press, 1991. xviii, 294p.

A defence of the 1970 US invasion of Cambodian territory, dubbed by Richard Nixon an 'incursion' whose main objective was to capture the fabled Central Office for South Vietnam (COSVN) of the North Vietnamese Army. Coleman's perspective is of the US Army, particularly its 1st Cavalry Division, with which he served as information officer and lieutenant colonel. Fiercely critical of the anti-war movement and of the CIA alike as having sowed seeds of doubt in the US capacity to prevail, he asserts that, in its interdiction of supplies, 'the Cambodian incursion had bought the Thieu government twenty-three months'. Even though written some twenty years afterwards, he does not discuss either the impact of this operation, nor the secret bombing campaign that preceded it, on the people who lived in this eastern part of Cambodia.

232 **Indochina in conflict: a political assessment.**
[Edited by] Joseph J. Zasloff [and] Allan E. Goodman. Lexington, Massachusetts: Lexington Books, [1972]. xv, 227p. bibliog.

A collection of essays which examine the politics of the conflict in Indochina as it stood in 1972, from the viewpoint of the establishment. Themes covered in the essays include the communist challenge to existing régimes, the nature of those régimes and the international dimensions of the conflict. The twelve contributors include professors, State Department staff members and journalists. Seeking to present a regional picture of political forces, the factions and groupings of Vietnam, Laos and Cambodia are all discussed, with particular sensitivity to their interrelationship and the influence of international forces. Communist victory in the three countries was assessed as a possible but unlikely outcome by many of the contributors. Earlier versions of the papers were presented at a seminar of the Vietnam, Laos and Cambodia panel of the Southeast Asia Development Advisory Group (SEADAG) of the Asia Society at Asia House in New York on 7-8 May 1971.

233 **Into Cambodia: spring campaign, summer offensive, 1970.**
Keith William Nolan. Novato, California: Presidio Press, 1990. xvii, 468p. map. bibliog.

The fourth book in Nolan's chronicle of what he saw as 'this misunderstood war, fought the wrong way but for noble goals', this volume looks at one of the most significant events of the Second Indochina War as it affected Cambodia. Nolan's is a history of the war as seen and fought by US soldiers and is full of evocative descriptions of camaraderie and shared tragedy. Containing detailed descriptions of the battles fought, this is a useful source for students of the United States war in Vietnam and Cambodia, and of United States social history.

234 **Pawns of war: Cambodia and Laos.**
Arnold R. Isaacs, Gordon Hardy, MacAlister Brown, and the editors of the Boston Publishing Company. Boston, Massachusetts: Boston Publishing Company, 1987. 192p. bibliog. (The Vietnam Experience).

Published and written largely by US war correspondents in the region some ten years earlier, this book is yet another salvo in the Vietnam War. It takes the view that in Laos in 1975 and in Cambodia in 1978 the Vietnamese had gained hegemony. 'Cambodia and Laos had often suffered at the hand of Vietnam, their far more populous and powerful neighbour.' The particular value of this work is its photographic record from agencies such as SYGMA, Magnum, and Time-LIFE, unfortunately credited only in a listing at the back of the book and not alongside the photographs themselves.

235 **The Second Indochina War: Cambodia and Laos today.**
Wilfred Burchett. London: Lorrimer Publishing Ltd.; New York: International Publishers, 1970. 160p. bibliog. (Third World Series).

Burchett offers his interpretation of the unfolding war 'to show that what is happening in Cambodia and Laos today has nothing to do with "Sihanouk Trail" or "Ho Chi Minh Trails", "Vietcong sanctuaries" or "bases", but represents a logical extension of policies followed by the United States in the area from 1954 onwards – policies deliberately planned in the name of "filling the power vacuum" created by the collapse of French colonialism in Indochina. . . . the end-result is gunboats up the Mekong and a second Indochina war. It is typical of the development of neo-colonialism that they are puppet gunboats. It is also typical that Thailand and South Vietnamese Asiatics are co-operating with Cambodian sub-puppets to tear Cambodia to bits and transform it into a sub-colony'. The book is the product of Burchett's fifteen years' first-hand experience, and bears his inimitable polemical stamp. Passion combined with facts and personal observation makes this book remain an important source in understanding the period.

236 **The Second Indochina War: a short political and military history, 1954-1975.**
William S. Turley. Boulder, Colorado: Westview Press, 1986. 238p. bibliog.

Succinct and to the point, this work covers a huge amount of history in relatively few words, and has a refreshingly broad perspective, which (in contrast to most US versions of the war) takes into account the actions and policies of the other actors and those acted upon. The widening of the war and the bombing of Cambodia is dealt with briefly from the point of view of US strategic policy. Perhaps a useful introduction or counterpoint to Shawcross's *Sideshow: Kissinger, Nixon and the destruction of Cambodia* (q.v.), this is most appropriate to the classroom setting.

237 **Sideshow: Kissinger, Nixon and the destruction of Cambodia.**
William Shawcross. London: Hogarth, 1991. 457p. map. bibliog. Originally published, London: Deutsch, 1979. New edition with additional material published, London: Hogarth, 1986.

More than any other work, Shawcross's most important and best piece of political writing exposed to Western readers the cynicism and corruption behind the Nixon administration's policy towards Cambodia, a pawn in the manoeuvrings aimed at ending the war in Vietnam but in a way that would force the Vietnamese to pay for generations to come. The bombing and invasion of Cambodia were merely tactical moves in that broader strategy. Under the pretext of seeking out the 'hub of North Vietnamese activity' peaceful towns were invaded, bombarded and burnt. Strategic rather than tactical bombing was the order of the day because it boosted the air force's independence from the army. This episode ranks amongst the most barbaric of the 20th century, and tragedy in Cambodia was the collateral damage. This is a book to read and return to many times as a study of power and an insight into the personalities of US leaders at the time.

238 **The wars in Vietnam, Cambodia and Laos, 1945-1982: a bibliographic guide.**

Richard Dean Burns, Milton Leitenberg. Santa Barbara, California; Oxford: ABC-Clio Information Services, 1984. xxxii, 290p. maps. (War/Peace Bibliography Series, 18).

This is the most carefully organized, easy-to-use publication of its kind, with nine subject chapters, each further subdivided, and entries alphabetized by author. Chapters and many subchapters are provided with useful introductions. Entries (totalling 6,202) are annotated only if a title fails to convey the content, or the author represents a very specific position. Publications in languages other than English are generally ignored, with the exception of French accounts of the First Indochina War. There is a definite tilt towards the American experience, with separate chapters on the policies of the executive branch, on 'Congress, international law and negotiations', and on 'The War at home'. Although the title of the bibliography suggests extensive attention to the 'Third Indochina War' (1978-), only seventy-three entries are provided. There is an author index. [David G. Marr with Kristine Alilunas-Rodgers]

The war in Cambodia, 1970-75.
See item no. 258.

L'Armée au Cambodge et dans les pays en voie de développement du Sud-Est asiatique. (The army in Cambodia and in the developing countries of South-East Asia.)
See item no. 451.

Indian foreign policy in Cambodia, Laos, and Vietnam, 1947-1964.
See item no. 546.

Sihanouk (1953-70)

239 **Before Kampuchea: preludes to tragedy.**

Milton Osborne. Sydney: George Allen & Unwin, 1979. 197p. maps.

On the basis of journal observations made during his doctoral fieldwork in Cambodia in 1966, Milton Osborne set out in 1979 to find some of the origins of Pol Pot's Kampuchea in the conditions that preceded it. 1966 was an election year in which Prince Sihanouk for the first time announced he would not personally preselect the candidates. A conservative National Assembly was returned, and was followed by the rightist coup of 1970. Osborne argues that the events of 1966, in which Sihanouk's control of the Cambodian state became less certain, was fundamental to later events. Ominous too was the cross-border attack on a Cambodian village close to Vietnam by United States helicopters. Along with his analytical and cogitative reflections on political events, Osborne sketches delicate and incisive pen pictures of places and people he knew during his stay informed by his more than two years' assignment as a diplomat in Phnom Penh in the late 1950s. A former analyst for the Australian intelligence services and an authority on Cambodia, Milton Osborne is the author of a number of other books on the country, including a recent controversial biography of Norodom Sihanouk, *Sihanouk: prince of light, prince of darkness* (q.v.).

240 **Cambodia in the Southeast Asian War.**
Malcolm Caldwell and Lek Hor Tan. New York; London: Monthly Review Press, 1973. xiii, 446, [4]p.

An important document of its time, placing the Cambodian situation in a wider political framework than just as a 'sideshow' to the conflict in Vietnam. Caldwell and Tan bring a clear left-wing perspective to bear as they seek an understanding of the Sihanouk–Communist coalition against the United States-based Lon Nol Khmer Republic. Particularly significant in that it was drafted before the release of the Pentagon Papers brought these events to the attention of a wider public, it looks at the effects of the 'Nixon Doctrine in its purest form', as Nixon himself referred to Cambodia, with the displacement of one-third of the population between May 1970 and November 1971. The chapter headings reveal the unusual methodology, comparing the French and American impact on Cambodia: 'The first "Protectorate": France and Cambodia'; 'Into the quagmire: America and Indochina before Geneva'; 'The pursuit of neutrality: Cambodia and the powers (1954-1966)'; 'The erosion of neutrality: America and the rise of the Cambodian right (1966-1969)'; 'A gamble that failed: Sihanouk and the Cambodian right (1969-March 1970)'; 'From nationalism to revolution: the coup and its aftermath (March-May 1970)'; and 'Cambodia resurgent: Sihanouk and the people's liberation struggle'. Some thirteen appendices contain the text of a number of important communiqués and statements, but regrettably the book has neither index nor bibliography, although each chapter has a number of bibliographical references.

241 **Cambodia: the search for security.**
Michael Leifer. London: Praeger, 1967. ix, 209p. bibliog.

Leifer examines Cambodia's problems of external security and the relevant domestic political background of what was regarded as a 'peaceful oasis in the inferno of Southeast Asia'. He traces the origins of Sihanouk's policy of neutrality, developed largely due to the alignment of powerful neighbours with different superpowers, and to Sihanouk's desire for recognition by the eventual victors in Vietnam. Domestic factors were also important. Sihanouk endeavoured to play off the Left against the Right, particularly before 1955 and the formation of the Sangkum. Ironically, in the light of later events, Leifer thought domestic stability had been ensured. The book is particularly useful for detail regarding Sihanouk's diplomatic relations with the United States and Britain.

242 **Derrière le sourire khmer.** (Behind the Khmer smile.)
Charles Meyer. [Paris]: Plon, [1971]. 406p. map. bibliog.

Meyer's affection for the Cambodian people, developed during his many years in the country, is reflected in this history of the Kingdom of Cambodia from 1953 to the immediate aftermath of the March 1970 coup. He maintains that the particular nature of the country and its people allowed for a unique relationship, more of cohabitation than of domination, between the French colonizers and their colonized subjects. Sihanouk's fifteen years of guided democracy failed to raise the living standards of the ordinary people, allowing a wealthy and corrupt élite to prosper, while those labelled 'communist' could be arrested and imprisoned after a mockery of a trial. Meyer concludes that ultimately the economy was the Achilles heel of the Sangkum period. In foreign policy, however, despite mistakes of the later years, Sihanouk's exceptional intuition, his ignorance of the classical rules of diplomacy, and above all his refusal to indulge in secret diplomacy, delivered fifteen years of peace and a chance of survival to his country. Led by the General, the Prince and the Mandarin, the 1970 coup once more placed Cambodia's survival at risk. The Lon Nol régime was totally submissive to the South Vietnamese, the United States bombing was causing devastation and North Vietnamese troops were also present in large numbers. However, Meyer cautions those expecting the destruction of this small country not to forget the strong national sentiment of many young Cambodians. An interesting map shows which areas of the country were currently under the control of various armed groups.

243 **My war with the CIA: Cambodia's fight for survival.**
Norodom Sihanouk, as related to Wilfred Burchett. Harmondsworth, England: Penguin Books, 1973. 271p.; London: Allen Lane, 1973; New York: Pantheon, 1973.

The account by the one overthrown, of the sixteen years leading up to Lon Nol's coup of 18 March 1970. Sihanouk's stated intention was to 'set the record straight', seeing events through the optic of 'the struggle to maintain peace and independence; the sovereignty and neutrality of our country'. The scribe and translator, Wilfred Burchett, the Australian journalist with thirty years' experience in Asia, is unashamedly sympathetic to the narrator. Burchett's introduction begins, 'For sixteen years, Cambodia lived under the shadow of that which happened on 30 April 1970, when United States tanks rolled across her frontiers and United States bombers started the systematic process of reducing Cambodian towns and villages to rubble and ashes', and concludes, 'The present work is viewed by the author as a weapon in the struggle to regain his country's independence, and as a warning to other countries marked down as future victims'. To underscore this point, Andreas Papandreou was invited to write the introduction, drawing parallels with his experience of being toppled in 1967, and seeing the text as 'a revealing account of the tactics used by the ruthless imperialist power of the West, the United States of America, to infiltrate, corrupt, subvert, colonize and subjugate an independent, neutral and peace-loving nation'. Reading this passionate account some twenty-five years later, after all the horror that Cambodia has endured in the interim, is a heart-wrenching and sobering experience. One asks, 'what if? . . . what if?' and wonders, 'if only . . . if only . . .', but these questions and wondering must relate also to Sihanouk himself, and to the story that is not told here of his domestic repression, intolerance and myopia.

244 **Politics and power in Cambodia: the Sihanouk years.**
Milton Osborne. Camberwell, Victoria: Longman Australia, 1973. viii, 120p. map. bibliog. (Studies in Contemporary Southeast Asia).

Written in the light of the 1970 coup that overthrew Sihanouk, this book is an attempt to analyse his domestic policies and to redress the imbalance caused by overwhelming interest by foreign observers in his foreign policy. Osborne traces Sihanouk's evolution from a young man who was unsure of himself and willing to rely on advisers, to a seasoned operator whose decision to abdicate the throne so he could stand for parliament in 1955 was a 'stroke of political genius'. Osborne also touches on the strong backing Sihanouk received from other members of the élite, including Sirik Matak and Lon Nol, in consolidating his power after independence. It was Prince Sihanouk's political strategy that allowed him to maintain control of the country as successfully as he did but, by the end of his reign, with the Left having fled or been crushed, he had no more room to manoeuvre. By 1968 the country and the régime were beset by a sea of troubles. The Prince's ability to control his relatives, including his wife Monique, diminished, and accusations of gross corruption abounded. The Vietnamese communists were increasing their use of Cambodian territory as a transit route. By 1968 governance of the country had largely slipped from Sihanouk's hands but it is not clear how well the Prince, surrounded by people who would not air their grievances in public, understood the situation. While in many ways superseded by Osborne's 1994 biography of Norodom Sihanouk, *Sihanouk: prince of light, prince of darkness* (q.v.), this work is still valuable for students of the period.

245 **The Samlaut rebellion and its aftermath, 1967-70: the origins of Cambodia's liberation movement.**
Ben Kiernan. Melbourne: Centre of Southeast Asian Studies, Monash University, Melbourne, [1975?]. 2 vols. bibliog. (Working Papers, no. 4-5).

Samlaut represented the first wave, the 'baptism of fire for the small but steadily growing Kampuchean revolutionary movement', as peasants rebelled against oppressive and arbitrary actions of soldiers and officials taking land in resettlement schemes. It has a symbolic resonance, and in the 1990s is still an area of contest between government and resistance forces, though sadly even poorer today than in the 1960s, and with the added scourge of the minefields laid by all sides. These two papers were later published as a chapter in *Peasants and politics in Kampuchea, 1942-1981* (q.v.).

246 **Sangkum Reastr Niyum: le développement général du Cambodge (années 1960).** (Sangkum Reastr Niyum: the development of Cambodia in the 1960s.)
Norodom Sihanouk. [s.l.: s.n.], 1991. 1,187p. maps.

Sihanouk's version of the achievements of his (and Cambodia's) 'golden age'. Dedicated to the 'Khmer People of the Sangkum' the collection includes official government publications of the time and excerpts from commentaries favourable to Sihanouk. The material is presented in chapters on: the press and books; education; agriculture; irrigation and water reservoirs; industry, water and electricity; medico-social progress; tourism and hotels; and urbanization and the general development of the cities. A shorter section entitled 'Witnesses of the 1970s' contains testimonies to the ongoing support for Sihanouk after the 1970 coup against him. The 1980s are dealt with similarly. Mainly in French but with some English commentary, the work includes numerous photographs of factories, hospitals and hotels built during the Sangkum period. Unfortunately, the publisher is not cited, but the work was printed in Thailand by Rama Printing, and can be found in major research libraries.

247 **Sihanouk speaks.**
John P. Armstrong. New York: Walker, 1964. 161p. maps. bibliog.

Intrigued by the 'playboy Prince' image of a ruler who also appeared to be ruling a country successfully, Armstrong set out to reveal the energetic and enigmatic Sihanouk. Intended for an American audience, this work seeks to understand and present Sihanouk's ideas sympathetically, in an effort to increase American respect for Cambodian policy. Armstrong stayed in Cambodia for six months and was one of the guests included on a tour of the country which Sihanouk conducted personally, enabling him to question the Prince at some length. The book examines Sihanouk as prince in history, on independence, at the United Nations and in relation to the communists and to the West, and it includes a basic index. This is an explanatory work which relies heavily on Sihanouk's own words.

Personalités du Cambodge. (Cambodian personalities.)
See item no. 325.

Sihanouk: prince of light, prince of darkness.
See item no. 331.

L'Armée au Cambodge et dans les pays en voie de développement du Sud-Est asiatique. (The army in Cambodia and in the developing countries of South-East Asia.)
See item no. 451.

Confidential U.S. State Department special files.
See item no. 535.

Foreign relations of the United States.
See item no. 540.

The sources of economic grievance in Sihanouk's Cambodia.
See item no. 606.

Lon Nol (1970-75)

248 **'Certain and inevitable misfortune': war and politics in Lon Nol's Cambodia, March 1970-December 1971.**
John A. Tully. MA thesis, Institute for Contemporary Asian Studies, Monash University, Clayton, Victoria, 1990. vi, 155 leaves. maps. bibliog.

An analytical commentary on the first two years of the Lon Nol régime from the March 1970 coup to the time of the Chenla II military campaign. Tully covers: the decline of Sihanouk; the coup and the invasion; the downhill road as the effect of the war and United States invasion were felt; and the twilight – Lon Nol's stroke, the growing corruption and the débâcle that was Chenla II. Although only a minor thesis at master's level, this work helps document a period that has received relatively less scholarly attention than those preceding and succeeding it, and presents a very different, and much more negative, perspective from that of Justin Corfield – *Khmers stand up!: a history of the Cambodian government 1970-1975* (q.v.).

249 **Fighting Cambodia.**
Reports of the delegation of Chinese journalists to Cambodia.
Peking: Foreign Languages Press, 1975. 60p.

Written by the first delegation from their primary backer who visited the Khmer Rouge liberated zones in March 1975, it is not surprising that this booklet presents a panegyric for the new society supposedly being constructed in Cambodia. The chapter headings tell the story: 'A new Cambodia after five years of people's war'; 'Visit to the Phnom Penh front'; 'Song of victory on the Mekong River'; 'Angkor's sons and daughters love their homeland'; 'Self-reliance works wonders'; 'New look in Cambodia's countryside'; 'Opening a new chapter in history'; and 'The Chinese and Cambodian people are like brothers'. The reports are in the form of snatches or fragments of experience, from a number of regions – from Stung Treng and Kompong Cham in the north, to Takeo and Kampot in the south, Siem Reap in the northwest, and to the outskirts of Phnom Penh itself, where the journalists drove in captured American jeeps.

250 **The impact of revolution on Cambodian peasants: 1970-1975.**
Kate G. Frieson. PhD in Politics, Department of Politics, Monash University. 273 leaves. maps. bibliog. Available on microfiche, Clayton, Victoria: Monash University.

Frieson takes issue with the notion that the 'Red Khmer' enjoyed widespread support among the peasantry during the period from 1970 to 1975. The preconditions for widespread support for the revolutionary movement were lacking in Cambodia where landlessness and exploitation by landlords was not a big problem. Frieson's research is based largely on oral histories given by 111 Cambodian women and men from mainly semi-literate rural backgrounds. She argues that for most peasants the decision to support the revolutionaries was motivated by the desire for 'safety for their families, security from troop harassment, [and the] ability to grow rice and meet basic subsistence needs'. The peasants' distrust and dislike of the Khmer Rouge were the major causes of the revolution's eventual failure. This study will be particularly interesting for those concerned with the concept and history of peasant revolutions and the role of Cambodia's peasantry in the history and politics of their country.

251 **The Indochinese peoples will win.**
Edited by Foreign Languages Publishing House. Hanoi: Foreign Languages Publishing House, 1970. 150p. map.

With the 18 March 1970 overthrow of Norodom Sihanouk by General Lon Nol and the 14 April ARVN (Army of the Republic of Vietnam) attacks into Cambodia, the war took an ominous new turn. One reaction was for the anti-imperialist parties to convene an emergency meeting in southern China, with Beijing's assistance, to hammer out a counter-strategy. The public dimensions of this 24-25 April 'Indochinese People's Summit Conference' are exhibited in this publication, including a quadrilateral 'Joint declaration' and opening and closing speeches by Prince Sihanouk, Prince Souphanouvong (Lao Patriotic Front), Nguyen Huu Tho (NLF – National Front for the Liberation of South Vietnam), and Pham Van Dong (DRV – Democratic Republic of Vietnam). Several days after this meeting, President Nixon sent large American troop formations into Cambodia. Also included in this volume are a fold-out map of Indochina, a chronology for the events of 5 March-15 May 1970, a 1 May Hanoi declaration of support for the 'Joint declaration' and the 3 May Political Program of the National United Front of Kampuchea (NUFK), released in Beijing. In retrospect, the 24-25 April conference marked the highpoint of anti-imperialist co-operation: within a year China was negotiating separately with the US, and by 1973 relations between the NUFK and the DRV/PRG had become strained. [David G. Marr with Kristine Alilunas-Rodgers]

252 **Khmers stand up!: a history of the Cambodian government 1970-1975.**
Justin J. Corfield. Clayton, Victoria: Centre of Southeast Asian Studies, Monash University, 1994. xvii, 253p. map. bibliog. (Monash Papers on Southeast Asia, no. 32). Originally published, Melbourne: Khmer Language Culture Centre, 1994.

Based on Corfield's doctoral thesis, this is one of the few available histories of the Lon Nol period (Khmer Republic, 1970-75) and includes brief accounts of the period of French colonial rule and the Sihanouk years following independence. The book unusually presents as an account of how a valiant experiment in democracy failed. For its documentation of the period alone it is valuable reading as it collects much original material and is extensively documented. Corfield believes that, despite official denials, 'The evidence that the United States and her allies were involved in the plot (to overthrow Sihanouk) is now overwhelming'. He says the urban middle class were quickly buoyed up with a new sense of patriotism and national identity with Sihanouk's demise. But the new régime faced innumerable problems and was itself deeply divided with at least eleven different governments during the period of the régime. Corfield believes that as a result of corruption and incompetence the opportunity for a democratic republic was lost. The cost of this failure – which was partly the result of the contemporary secret US carpet bombing of Cambodia – was high; its failure opened the way for the entry of the Khmer Rouge into Phnom Penh. Corfield believes that the attempt to establish republican government with US support might have been more successful had it been tried earlier.

253 **Political change in wartime: the Khmer Krahom revolution in Southern Cambodia, 1970-1974.**
Kenneth Michael Quinn. *US Naval War College Review*, no. 28 (Spring 1976), p. 2-31.

Quinn, an official of the US State Department who had served in Cambodia (and who returned as Ambassador in 1995) interviewed refugees who fled to southern Vietnam in 1973-74 from southeastern Cambodian zones under control of the Khmer Rouge (*krahom* is the Cambodian word for 'red'). In this shortened version of his internal report, Quinn draws from the refugee accounts a pattern of behaviour of draconian authoritarianism, harshness and even the use of torture and execution as instruments of policy that unfortunately was to engulf the whole country.

254 **La République khmère: 1970-1975.** (The Khmer Republic: 1970-75.)
Ros Chantrabot. Paris: L'Harmattan, 1993. 216p. bibliog.

The author was a teacher and a journalist until the coup which toppled King Sihanouk in 1970. He then participated in power, being among those surrounding Lon Non, Lon Nol's brother, and editing a daily newspaper. In fact, he witnessed the beginning of the Republic and was later discarded. He presents a good description of the scramble for power of the diverse political clans who tried to grab Sihanouk's legacy, although his own affiliation makes him a bit shortsighted as far as royals (Queen Kossomak and Prince Sirik Matak) are concerned. Political memoirs written by Khmers are rare. This one is of good quality.

255 **The Senate's war powers: debate on Cambodia from the Congressional Record.**
Edited by Eugene P. Dvorin. Chicago: Markham Publishing Company, [1971]. x, 244p. (Markham Political Science Series).

By a teacher of American government who had become disillusioned with the ability of the legislature to maintain democracy and perform an educative function, despite its constitutional role and renowned quality of debate. As the nature of US government had changed to become more concerned with foreign policy, so too had the nature of congressional debate, with an undeclared war being fought in Vietnam and Nixon using constitutional powers to order troops into Cambodia without congressional consultation. Using excerpts from the Congressional Record, reduced and selected to be accessible to the lay reader, Dvorin presents the two-month debate on Cambodia which took place in the US Senate in 1970. The material is arranged chronologically. Editorial comment is kept to a minimum, and largely reserved for the introduction.

256 **Two essays on Cambodia.**
Noam Chomsky. Nottingham, England: Bertrand Russell Peace Foundation for *The Spokesman*, 1970. [1], 57p. bibliog.

Includes 'On Cambodia' and 'Postscript on Cambodia', reprinted from the *New York Review of Books* (1970). These two essays were later included as the Cambodia chapter in the book *At war with Asia* (London: Fontana/Collins, 1971. Spokesman Pamphlet no. 5). Penned in response to the US and South Vietnamese invasion of Cambodia just one month after the coup that brought Lon Nol to power, these two essays denounce and ridicule US actions to support the Lon Nol régime, which, in Chomsky's view, were aimed at preventing the emergence of a mass leftist movement for national liberation. Sihanouk's alliance with the Khmer Rouge, following the coup, created for the first time the possibility of widespread support among the peasantry. The corrupt élite behind the coup had manufactured their own doom. This invasion, ostensibly to save Cambodia from the North Vietnamese, failed to produce a single Vietnamese casualty – instead peasants were being strafed and ARVN forces were raping and pillaging. Chomsky's strident condemnation of US imperialism, and support for the revolutionary forces, backed by considerable reference to contemporary sources, provides essential reading for students of the period.

257 **War and politics in Cambodia: a communications analysis.**
Sheldon W. Simon. Durham, North Carolina: Duke, 1974. 178p. bibliog.

An analysis in the strict political science tradition, somehow reducing the pain of the war to percentages and to cyphers. Nevertheless, it presents an interesting view of the roles of the various players in the overthrow of Sihanouk and the formation of the Lon Nol government and its civil war, written on the eve of the victory of the Khmer Rouge.

258 **The war in Cambodia, 1970-75.**
Text by Kenneth Conboy and Kenneth Bowra, colour plates by Mike Chappell. London: Osprey, 1989. 48p. map. (Men-at-Arms Series, no. 209).

Although published in 1989, and containing some descriptions of uniforms in the early 1980s, this book concentrates on the Lon Nol period, as indicated in the title. The authors present a brief historical overview of the war, with details of the development of different parts of the armed forces, of US military assistance and of the resistance, complemented by photographs and colour plates illustrating all aspects of uniform and armory, and detailed 'Order of Battle' lists of the FANK (Forces Armées Nationales Khmere) for 1970, and of the NVA/VC (North Vietnam Army/Viet Cong), the latter lists 'based on FANK and allied intelligence sources through early 1973'.

Cambodge: la révolution de la forêt. (Cambodia: revolution of the forest.)
See item no. 214.

How Pol Pot came to power: a history of communism in Kampuchea, 1930-1975.
See item no. 220.

Before Kampuchea: preludes to tragedy.
See item no. 239.

The Samlaut rebellion and its aftermath, 1967-70: the origins of Cambodia's liberation movement.
See item no. 245.

Selected, annotated, English-language bibliography of the Kampuchean revolution.
See item no. 280.

Demographic materials on the Khmer Republic, Laos, and Vietnam.
See item no. 339.

A wilderness called peace.
See item no. 711.

Crisis Cambodia.
See item no. 921.

Front line.
See item no. 927.

Khmer! Khmer!: Cambodia in conflict.
See item no. 930.

Democratic Kampuchea (1975-79)

259 **Asian holocaust: coverage of the Khmer Rouge by three US news organizations 1974-1979.**
Edward A. De Marco Jr. Masters thesis, University of Georgia, Athens, Georgia, 1988. Order no. AAC 1334337.

Discusses the Khmer Rouge period in Cambodia's history as reported by CBS News, *Time*, and the *New York Times*.

260 **Cambodia, 1975-1978: rendezvous with death.**
Edited by Karl D. Jackson. Princeton, New Jersey: Princeton University Press, 1989. 333p. bibliog.

Karl Jackson – Professor of Political Science at the University of California, Berkeley, United States Deputy Assistant Secretary of Defense for East Asia and the Pacific from 1986 to 1988, and then Special Adviser to the President for East Asia and Pacific Affairs – edited this volume, seeking 'to design a book that would illuminate the most salient dimensions of revolutionary Cambodia: how the revolutionaries came to power, what they believed in, their organizational structure, the economic system, social and religious life, and the pattern and origins of the violence of their rule'. The contents are: 'The Khmer Rouge in context' by Karl D. Jackson; 'The unexpected victory' by Timothy Carney; 'The ideology of total revolution' by Karl D. Jackson; 'The organization of power' by Timothy Carney; 'The economy' by Charles H. Twining; 'Social change in the vortex of revolution' by François Ponchaud; 'The pattern and scope of violence' by Kenneth M. Quinn; 'The photographic record' by David Hawk; 'Explaining the terror' by Kenneth M. Quinn; 'Intellectual origins of the Khmer Rouge' by Karl D. Jackson; and four appendices containing Party documents, translated by Carney. All but two of the authors are long-serving officers in the US State Department, including Twining and Quinn, the two US ambassadors to Cambodia since the Paris Peace Accords were signed in 1991, and Carney, who took leave from the State Department to serve as UNTAC's Director of Education and Information. A tremendous amount of valuable material has been synthesized in this volume, which remains a most important source for studying the Pol Pot period. The befores and afters of that period are not pursued. Jackson dismisses the impact of US bombing on the rise to power of Pol Pot and on the murderous policies his régime implemented, and that topic has only a single reference in the index. And the authors do not conclude that the government trying to rebuild the shattered Cambodia should have been recognized and assisted – at the time the book was published, the US State Department was supporting the coalition that included the Khmer Rouge itself, and only in 1994 did the US Congress vote to investigate the genocide that this book so definitively demonstrates occurred in Cambodia from 1975 to 1978.

261 **Cambodia, 1975-1982.**

Michael Vickery. Sydney: George Allen & Unwin in association with South End Press, 1984. xiii, 361p. 3 maps. bibliog. Originally published, Boston, Massachusetts: South End Press, 1984.

The first serious scholarly attempt to come to terms with the nature of the Pol Pot régime, by Michael Vickery, an American historian who worked in Cambodia in the late 1960s, and in the early 1970s went to work in the border camps in Thailand with Cambodian refugees. He polemicizes against what he terms the Standard Total View (STV) of Pol Pot terror, presenting instead an account of widely varying, if generally severe and sometimes brutal, hardships experienced by city people sent out to fend for themselves in the countryside. He interprets the revolution as one with the peasantry as the motor force, 'pulling' along the ideologues, rather than as the work of a vanguard Marxist-Leninist party.

262 **Cambodia: starvation and revolution.**

George C. Hildebrand, Gareth Porter. New York: Monthly Review Press, 1976. 124p. maps. bibliog.

Published in 1976 by two supporters of the liberation forces in Indochina, this was an attempt to defend the actions taken by the Khmer Rouge against the first critical reports, which the authors dismiss as propaganda by media hostile to the revolution. Cambodia is seen as only the latest victim of an ideology that demands negative portrayal of social revolution. In their eyes, by 1975 only the revolutionary Left had the will and capacity to resolve the food problem. They contrast the Lon Nol government's failure to stave off starvation in Phnom Penh, even though it was underwritten by US aid, with the FUNK, which not only fed its own forces, but also the three million people living in its enclaves. They report that the Khmer Rouge had 'begun one of the most thoroughgoing agricultural revolutions in history, rebuilt much of the basic infrastructure necessary to a developing economy and quickly resumed industrial production'. The evacuation of the cities is seen as a 'rationally conceived strategy for dealing with urgent problems that faced postwar Cambodia', which indeed had some basis in truth, but the authors give no attention to the repressive treatment meted out to the people in the implementation of any of these policies.

263 **Cambodia: the Eastern Zone massacres: a report on social conditions and human rights violations in the Eastern Zone of Democratic Kampuchea under the role of Pol Pot's (Khmer Rouge) Communist Party of Kampuchea.**
Ben Kiernan. [New York]: Columbia University, Center for the Study of Human Rights, [1987?]. iv, 101p. map. bibliog. (Documentation Series/Columbia University, Center for the Study of Human Rights, no. 1).

Kiernan bases this detailed account of the 1978 persecution in the Eastern Zone on interviews with eighty-seven witnesses. The report is significant in showing the extent of organized violence wrought by the Khmer Rouge: they engaged in group retaliation; and people from the Eastern Zone were deported, marked by being forced to wear blue scarves, and then eliminated.

264 **Cambodia: year zero.**
François Ponchaud, translated from the French by Nancy Amphoux. London: Allen Lane; New York: Holt, Rinehart & Winston; Harmondsworth, England: Penguin, 1978. xvi, 212p. maps. A translation of *Cambodge année zéro*, Paris: Julliard, 1977.

When it appeared in French in 1977, this was one of the very first published accounts of what was taking place inside Cambodia after the Khmer Rouge took power and expelled almost all foreigners. Ponchaud, a French priest who had lived in Cambodia for over ten years, and who had knowledge of the Khmer language, was able to monitor radio broadcasts and interview refugees in Thailand, who came mainly from Battambang and Siem Reap provinces. The horrors they related were initially denied and dismissed as propaganda by many who had political hopes for what the new régime would bring. Regrettably, later accounts confirmed the worst.

265 **The Cambodian agony.**
Edited by David A. Ablin and Marlowe Hood. Armonk, New York: M. E. Sharpe, 1990. lxi, 434p. maps. bibliog.

Although not published until five years later, these papers emanated from an international conference, 'Kampuchea in the 1980s: prospects and problems', organized by the editors and held in November 1982 at the Woodrow Wilson School of Public and International Affairs, Princeton University, Princeton, New Jersey. Contents include: 'Revolution in full spate: Communist party policy in Democratic Kampuchea' by David Chandler; 'Revolution and reformation of Cambodian village culture' by May Ebihara; 'International human rights norms and Democratic Kampuchea' by David Hawk; 'Patterns of Cambodian politics' by Serge Thion; 'Refugee politics: the Khmer camp system in Thailand' by Michael Vickery; and others, including an incisive look at agriculture in 'Kampuchea's ecology and resource base: natural limits on food production strategies' by John V. Dennis, arguing that the Green Revolution's high-yield rice strains are not suitable for Cambodia. Although some of these essays have later been republished elsewhere, this collection retains its significance as a reflection of a range of political analyses at a time relatively soon after the ousting of Pol Pot from control over Cambodia. Chandler's paper, which analyses a December 1976 Party document is of particular note.

266 **De sang et de larmes: la grande déportation du Cambodge.** (With blood and tears: Cambodia's great deportation.)
Bernard Hamel. Paris: A. Michel, 1977. 277p. maps.

Bernard Hamel, who had lived in Phnom Penh during the Sihanouk era, interviewed a large number of Cambodian refugees in camps in Thailand, combining their stories to present this account of the expulsion of the population of Phnom Penh as the Khmer Rouge took power. Published in 1977, this was one of the early accounts of the Khmer Rouge atrocities and, as such, its veracity was challenged by those who did not want to believe what was happening.

267 **Discours: prononcé par le camarade Pol Pot, secrétaire du Comité central du Parti communiste du Kampuchea au meeting commemorant le 17è anniversaire de la fondation du Parti communiste du Kampuchea et à l'occasion de la proclamation solennelle de l'existence officielle du Parti communiste du Kampuchea, Phnom Penh, le 27 septembre 1977.** (Discourse: pronounced by Comrade Pol Pot, Secretary of the Central Committee of the Communist Party of Kampuchea on the occasion of the seventeenth anniversary of the foundation of the Communist Party of Kampuchea and the solemn proclamation of the existence of the Communist Party of Kampuchea, 27 September 1977.)
Gentilly, France: Diffusé par Comité des Patriotes du Kampuchea démocratique en France, [1977 or 1978]. 68p.

This is perhaps the most important speech Pol Pot ever delivered. Here he reveals that the *Angkar* (Organization) ruling Cambodia was in fact what had become of the Communist Party of Kampuchea, of which he was Secretary-General. The speech was tape-recorded and broadcast at the time when Pol Pot himself was on his way to China to seek recognition, in the same way that Cambodian rulers of ancient times sought legitimacy from the Chinese emperors. The BBC recorded and translated it, and that original version differs somewhat from the edited version released by the DK government in French and English, circulated by supporters in various parts of the world, as in this publication.

268 **Interview of Comrade Pol Pot, Secretary of the Central Committee of the Communist Party of Kampuchea, Prime Minister of the Government of Democratic Kampuchea to the Delegation of Yugoslav Journalists in visit to Democratic Kampuchea, March 17, 1978.**
Phnom Penh: Department of Press and Information, Ministry of Foreign Affairs, Democratic Kampuchea, 1978.

As one of the very few items published by the Khmer Rouge government, this pamphlet has a significance beyond its content. Pol Pot here reveals that he was a student in Paris and that he visited Yugoslavia for some weeks as part of an 'international work brigade', indicating that the Cambodian students in France may not have been completely orthodox members of the Communist Party.

269 **Kampuchea dossier.**
Hanoi: Vietnam Courier, 1978-79. 3 vols.

This three-volume collection provides the position advanced by the Vietnamese government in the lead-up to, and aftermath of, its intervention in Cambodia. The Vietnamese government invaded Cambodia in January 1979, overthrowing Pol Pot's government of Democratic Kampuchea and installing the People's Republic of Kampuchea. Volume one contains a series of first-hand reports of life under Pol Pot, as well as a chronology on the breakdown of relations between Cambodia and Vietnam, and an appendix with a number of official government statements from both sides. Volume two contains articles by Vietnamese writers and concentrates on Chinese-Vietnamese relations. Volume three, which appeared shortly after the August 1979 trial of Pol Pot and Ieng Sary, was subtitled 'The dark years', and contains some documents presented at the trial. It includes forty-two photographs.

270 **Kampuchea.**
Antonin Kubes. Prague: Orbis Press Agency, 1982. 207p.

Chiefly comprising illustration, this book has particular value as a photographic record of the early years of the PRK and for its inclusion of rare photographs from the DK period itself, such as: pictures of Pol Pot and other leaders; Chinese experts assisting DK; and Malcolm Caldwell, a Scottish professor sympathetic to the revolutionary undertaking of the Khmer Rouge, and Elizabeth Becker at Angkor Thom in December 1978, just days before Caldwell's murder. Alongside the images runs the text, consisting of commentary by Czech journalist Antonin Kubes interspersed with the personal story of Professor Nuon Sarit then working at the National Museum of Cambodia. He had been a university lecturer in philosophy before Pol Pot came to power. He survived the Khmer Rouge rule and fled across the border to Vietnam in late 1978, joining the National United Front for the Salvation of Kampuchea and entering Phnom Penh on 10 January 1979, only days after Pol Pot had been driven from the city.

271 **The Khmer Rouge gulag: 17 April 1975 – 7 January 1979.**
Henri Locard. Paris, Canberra, Phnom Penh: [The author], 1995. 30p.

Locard's essay demonstrates that prisons and torture were widespread under the Khmer Rouge régime of Democratic Kampuchea in the years 1975-79. The infamous Tuol Sleng prison (called S-21 in Pol Pot's days), at which over 15,000 people were held and tortured before being executed, was only the tip of the iceberg. Factories, hospitals and re-education camps all formed a part of the gulag, says Locard, in addition to a closely interconnected three-tier prison network that criss-crossed and enmeshed the entire country. The number of deaths in this prison system might have exceeded 400,000. Copies of the pamphlet may perhaps be found at the Tuol Sleng Genocide Museum, or ordered from the author: Henri Locard, 86, rue Pasteur, 69365 Lyon, France.

272 **Khmers Rouges!: matériaux pour l'histoire du communisme au Cambodge.** (Khmer Rouge!: materials for the history of communism in Cambodia.)
Serge Thion, Ben Kiernan. Paris: J.-E. Hallier – Albin Michel, 1981. 396p. bibliog.

Published in 1981, in this work two Western scholars who had expressed their support for the liberation movement as it came to power in April 1975 begin to come to terms with what actually happened under the Pol Pot régime, constructing what they call 'materials for the history of communism in Cambodia'. Thion, a French scholar who had lived in Cambodia during the Lon Nol period, contributed the majority of the book, reproducing his 1972 article on visiting a Khmer Rouge zone, his 1980 piece on the Khmer Rouge's attack on Vietnam, a chronology of the Khmer communist movement, and another 1980 piece on the bias of press coverage of Cambodia. Kiernan republished his 1976 work on the Samlaut rebellion, and presents his 1979 paper on Pol Pot and the Cambodian communist movement. Although all these items have appeared in other publications, some in English – see *Peasants and politics in Kampuchea, 1942-1981* and *Watching Cambodia: ten paths to enter the Cambodian Tangle* (qq.v.) – it seems appropriate to include this text for its contemporary significance as a genuine and sympathetic attempt to understand what went so terribly wrong.

273 News From Kampuchea: Journal of the Committee of Patriots of Democratic Kampuchea.

Kensington, New South Wales: The Committee, 1977-79. irregular.

Produced by a collective of Cambodian Australian and Australian supporters of the Khmer Rouge régime, at least in its initial stages. Like many left-wing activists and sympathizers, the editors saw the liberation of Phnom Penh as a victory, and they had great hopes for the establishment of an egalitarian society. In an attempt to balance the anti-communist coverage in the mainstream press, the magazine aimed to tell Kampuchea's side of the story, and reprinted reports by Khmer Rouge leaders, including Khieu Samphan and Ieng Sary, as well as original writings by members of the group, including the report on 'Our experiences during the liberation of Phnom Penh, April 1975' by Chou Meng Tarr and Shane Tarr (volume one: numbers one and two). In 1977 Chantou Boua and Ben Kiernan were expelled from the collective for opposing repressive actions of the Khmer Rouge government and the publication became more stridently Maoist in tone, carrying critiques of Soviet revisionism and Vietnamese hegemonism.

274 Peace with horror: the untold story of communist genocide in Cambodia.

John Barron and Anthony Paul; research associates, Katherine Clark and Ursula Naccache. London: Hodder and Stoughton, 1977. [21], 234p. bibliog. Originally published as *Murder of a gentle land*, New York: Reader's Digest Press, 1977.

Basing their accounts mainly on testimony from refugees on the Thai-Cambodian border, the majority of whom came from Battambang and Siem Reap provinces, including Ponchaud's interviews, Barron and Paul compiled the first English-language book on the situation in Cambodia after the Khmer Rouge took control. In direct contrast to Hildebrand and Porter's defence of Khmer Rouge action (q.v.), they saw what was happening as 'cataclysmic'. On the evacuation of the cities they quote Fernand Scheller, UNDP chief in Phnom Penh: 'What the KR are doing is pure genocide. They will kill more people this way than if there had been fighting in the city. There is no food outside'. Barron and Paul estimate that 10 per cent of those evacuated died in the process, with a further 12 per cent dying of starvation and disease during 1975, and 8 per cent more in 1976. With estimates of 100,000 executions and 20,000 people dying while trying to flee the country, they place the number of deaths from 17 April 1975 to 1 January 1977 at a minimum of 1,200,000.

275 **Pol Pot and Khieu Samphan.**
Stephen Heder. Clayton, Victoria: Monash University, Centre of Southeast Asian Studies, 1991. 28p. bibliog. (Working Papers/Centre of Southeast Asian Studies, Monash University, no. 70).

A rare piece of biographical work on two of the Khmer Rouge's top leaders.

276 **Pol Pot plans the future: confidential leadership documents from Democratic Kampuchea, 1976-1977.**
Translated and edited by David P. Chandler, Ben Kiernan and Chantou Boua, with a preface by David P. Chandler and Ben Kiernan. New Haven, Connecticut: Yale Center for International and Area Studies, 1988. xviii, 346p. bibliog. Translated from Khmer. (Monograph Series/Yale University Southeast Asia Studies, no. 33).

An exceptional collection of eight primary-source documents from the DK, provided to the authors in 1979-80. Except for DK Minister of Information Hu Nim's 1977 confession (one of those from the Tuol Sleng Museum, Phnom Penh) these documents appear to have been prepared before or after meetings of the leaders of the CPK, the 'Party Centre', in 1976, except for one that is undated. Some are attributed to Pol Pot himself. The major text is the eighty-page document, 'The Party's four-year plan to build socialism in all fields, 1977-1980'. The authors have variously translated and introduced each document, only one of which was ever published by the Khmer Rouge, and that in a journal restricted to the party cadre. They also provide an introduction that places the documents in context, and trace a shift in attitude over the fourteen months of the documents' composition – becoming 'darker, less hopeful and more vindictive', teeming with references to enemies, compared to microbes that 'would destroy the revolution, unless destroyed themselves', '. . . while the leaders of the régime blamed what was happening on foreigners, class enemies and traitors, most others probably had little difficulty in placing the blame on the men and women who had agreed in 1976 to transform Kampuchea in a particular way by taking a super great leap forward . . . into the dark'. As the authors say, one value of the collection is that it provides a rare account from within, and rare also in being written, as most of the history of this period has been developed from 'oral and overwhelmingly hostile recollections'.

277 **The Pol Pot regime: race, power, and genocide in Cambodia under the Khmer Rouge, 1975-79.**
Ben Kiernan. New Haven, Connecticut: Yale University Press, 1996. 477p. bibliog.

A masterful account of the three years, eight months and twenty days of the Pol Pot régime. On the basis of interviews with over 500 refugees, and examination of the scant primary documentary evidence remaining from the régime (particularly the prison records and a newly uncovered cache of Commerce Ministry archives), as well as the more extensive secondary literature, Kiernan displays his familiar grasp of both incisive detail and broad and analytical interpretation, giving us the first really considered understanding of what really went on in Democratic Kampuchea. Zone by zone he chronicles the descent into ever greater destruction, as the carnage drew ever closer to the centre itself. A new aspect examined is the extent to which resistance was mounted – albeit unsuccessfully – before the formation in late 1978 of the front that swept Pol Pot aside with Vietnamese assistance. Kiernan here revises his earlier view, shared with Vickery (q.v.), of the peasant basis for the Pol Pot régime, concluding now that race and power were the two explosive elements that came together, detonated by the social destruction of the war, to create the bomb that was Pol Pot's genocide.

278 **Résistances au Vietnam, Cambodge et Laos, 1975-1980.** (Resistance in Vietnam, Cambodia and Laos, 1975-80.)
Bernard Hamel. Paris: L'Harmattan, 1994. 268, [3]p. map. bibliog.

The author was a long-time Reuter's correspondent in Phnom Penh. He has often been used by Sihanouk who likes to manipulate journalists to his own ends. This is a typical product of the rabid anti-communist literature genre. All the rumours were collected on the Thai-Khmer border to show that the post-1975 régimes in Indochina, in Cambodia, in Laos and Vietnam, were facing armed resistance guerrillas. The level of speculation on what was happening inside these régimes is just astonishing. If, for Laos, there were indeed armed activities (which have persisted until now) stemming from some factions of the Hmong who had sided with the Americans during the war, for the two other countries, such wishful thinking was given as fact. The credibility of the book was weak at the time of publication. It was further eroded when we learned more about what was really taking place.

279 **Revolution and its aftermath in Kampuchea: eight essays.**
Edited by David P. Chandler and Ben Kiernan, [with contributions by] Anthony Barnett, Chantou Boua, William Shawcross, Serge Thion, Michael Vickery, Gareth Porter. New Haven, Connecticut: Yale University Southeast Asia Studies, 1983. x, 319p. maps. bibliog. (Monograph Series/Yale University Southeast Asia Studies, no. 25).

This publication was sponsored by the Joint Committee on Southeast Asia of the Social Science Research Council and the American Council of Learned Societies. Five of the nine papers, by Chantou Boua, Ben Kiernan, William Shawcross, Serge Thion and Michael Vickery, are from a seminar held in Chiang Mai, Thailand, from 11-13 August 1981. These have been complemented by papers from David Chandler, Gareth Porter and Anthony Barnett, and Serge Thion provides a 'Chronology of Khmer communism, 1940-1982'. The authors present differing perspectives, with Thion and Vickery presenting pictures of Pol Pot's Democratic Kampuchea with less centralized control than that shown by Barnett and Kiernan. Porter brings in the Vietnamese perspective, and Boua gives some encouraging views on reconstruction after 1979. Although most of the authors have gone on to refine and develop their views and, in most cases, to publish more substantial studies of the DK régime, this book retains its significance as representing a range of interpretations and perspectives from the period soon after Pol Pot's overthrow. The lack of an index for such valuable and disparate data is most regrettable, and seems to be a consistent shortcoming in Yale's 'Monograph Series'.

280 **Selected, annotated, English-language bibliography of the Kampuchean revolution.**
Ines Rodriguez. *Southeast Asian Research Materials Group Newsletter*, no. 18 (May 1981), p. 1-23.

Compiled by a member of staff of the National Library of Australia, this contains eighty-eight items in English, including both books and articles. Although mainly on the revolutionary war (1975-79) and the Khmer Rouge period (1975-79), it also contains earlier background materials. Items are arranged within periods and then carefully further divided into categories representing the dominant themes. The bibliography is well annotated.

281 **The situation in Cambodia, 1975-1982.**

Kathleen Gough. *Contemporary Marxism*, no. 6 (1983), p. 209-26.

The extreme measures taken to transform Cambodia into a 'purely agricultural society' between 1975 and 1979 are explained in terms of a complex of factors: prior urban-based destruction of the countryside; the desire to recapture the ancient Khmer empire; ancient traditions of torture and cruelty; a crude interpretation of Maoist doctrines; misanthropy among the régime's leaders; and fear of rebellion by factions of the Communist Party.

282 **The slogans of Angkar: the thoughts of Pol Pot.**

Henri Locard. Phnom Penh; Lyons, France: [The author], 1995. 193p.

Locard here provides some 300 slogans reported as being from the DK, some of which perhaps more closely resemble the reworking of traditional proverbs, or oft-repeated sayings. Each slogan is given in Khmer script, transliteration, and in English and French translation. Many are also accompanied by some commentary. The slogans are organized into seven groups: slogans of triumph to the glory of the régime; slogans of inspiration, directly Maoist; *Angkar* and its methods; the hunt for 'the enemy' and for superfluous classes; work; collective life; and the death of the individual. A ten-page introduction sets the scene. Regrettably, Locard provides neither sources nor context for the slogans. The list includes official, unofficial and even 'counter' slogans, with the latter identified by an underlining of their number.

283 **War crimes of the Pol Pot and Chinese troops in Vietnam.**

Commission of Inquiry Into the Chinese Expansionists' and Hegemonists' Crime of War of Aggression. Hanoi: The Commission, 1979. 66p.

In September 1979 the Vietnamese government published this booklet containing two formal communiqués: 'On the crime of war of aggression of the Pol Pot-Ieng Sary clique, henchmen of the Chinese expansionists and hegemonists in the eight southwestern border provinces of Vietnam', 25 August 1979; and 'On the crime of war of aggression of the Chinese expansionists and hegemonists', 15 May 1979. Evidence is presented of violations of the Cambodian-Vietnamese border on the ground (as early as three days after the end of the war in Vietnam, on 3 May 1975), and in maps published by the DK government (August 1977), and testimony is reported from Cambodian prisoners of war on the intentions behind their assaults. Details are given particularly of massive cross-border attacks in 1978, causing over 400,000 Vietnamese to flee their homes, abandoning over 100,000 hectares of arable land. At the same time, Vietnam had to cope with 180,000 Cambodians and 20,000 Chinese from Cambodia who crossed the border to seek refuge. Reference is made to the violations of international law involved in this aggression, in the genocidal massacres of Vietnamese civilians, and in war crimes. The Chinese government is named as the 'co-culprit' who masterminded the aggression. The verdict of the PRT (People's Revolutionary Tribunal) trial of Pol Pot and Ieng Sary (see item no. 509) is upheld.

284 **When the war was over: the voices of Cambodia's revolution and its people.**

Elizabeth Becker. New York: Touchstone, 1986. 502p. bibliog.

Elizabeth Becker's much-quoted book is described on its cover as 'the definitive book on the Cambodian revolution'. Becker covered the Cambodian war for the *Washington Post* in the 1970s, and is a graduate in Asian Studies from the University of Washington, Seattle. From the rise of the Cambodian Communist Party, through the collapse of the Lon Nol régime, Pol Pot's accession to power, and Vietnam's defeat of the Khmer Rouge, the book presents a detailed sketch of the most tragic period in Cambodian history. Illustrating her account with numerous anecdotal episodes, Becker sets out to paint the Khmer Rouge experiment in agricultural barbarism as the ultimate communist revolution, writing also that Vietnam in 1979 became the military lord over Cambodia, occupying a country it had coveted for decades. This book has been used as a principal source by those who hold the view that Vietnamese communism and its Cambodian counterpart have been the catalyst for the region's historical and political agonies.

Malcolm Caldwell's South East Asia.
See item no. 143.

Fighting Cambodia.
See item no. 249.

Political change in wartime: the Khmer Krahom revolution in Southern Cambodia, 1970-1974.
See item no. 253.

Brother enemy: the war after the war.
See item no. 286.

Choses vues au Cambodge. (Things seen in Cambodia.)
See item no. 292.

Kampuchea, from tragedy to rebirth.
See item no. 297.

Postwar Indochina: old enemies and new allies.
See item no. 300.

Beyond the horizon: five years with the Khmer Rouge.
See item no. 312.

Cambodian-American Women's Oral History Project.
See item no. 317.

The death and life of Dith Pran.
See item no. 318.

The early phases of liberation in northwestern Cambodia: conversations with Peang Sophi.
See item no. 320.

Prisonnier de l'Angkar ou 'Angkar a les yeux de l'ananas'. (Prisoner of the Angkar or 'Angkar has the eyes of a pineapple'.)
See item no. 326.

Surviving the killing fields: the Cambodian odyssey of Haing S. Ngor.
See item no. 335.

To destroy you is no loss: the odyssey of a Cambodian family.
See item no. 337.

Le génocide Khmer Rouge: une analyse démographique. (The Khmer Rouge genocide: a demographic analysis.)
See item no. 340.

Kampuchea: a country adrift.
See item no. 341.

Kampuchea: a demographic catastrophe: a research paper.
See item no. 342.

Language reform in Democratic Kampuchea.
See item no. 390.

Communist party power in Kampuchea (Cambodia): documents and discussion.
See item no. 459.

The bureaucracy of death.
See item no. 476.

Centralized terror in Democratic Kampuchea: scope and span of control.
See item no. 484.

Collection of first-person accounts of the Cambodian genocide.
See item no. 486.

Facing death.
See item no. 491.

Genocidal Center at Choeung Ek.
See item no. 495.

Genocide and democracy in Cambodia: the Khmer Rouge, the U.N., and the international community.
See item no. 496.

Journey to Cambodia: investigation into massacre by Pol Pot regime.
See item no. 501.

Kampuchea: decade of the genocide: report of a Finnish inquiry commission.
See item no. 503.

The killing fields.
See item no. 505.

People's Revolutionary Tribunal held in Phnom Penh for the trial of the genocide crime of the Pol Pot-Ieng Sary clique (August-1979): documents.
See item no. 509.

Pol Pot's Cambodia: was it genocide?
See item no. 510.

Tuol Sleng.
See item no. 520.

Black paper: facts and evidences of the acts of aggression and annexation of Vietnam against Kampuchea.
See item no. 524.

The four days of Mayaguez.
See item no. 541.

Great victory of the Cambodian people: warmly congratulating the patriotic Cambodian armed forces and people on the liberation of Phnom Penh and all Cambodia.
See item no. 544.

Red brotherhood at war: Vietnam, Cambodia, and Laos since 1975.
See item no. 557.

Vietnam's intervention in Cambodia in international law.
See item no. 564.

The killing fields.
See item no. 931.

The secrets of S-21.
See item no. 949.

Surviving the killing fields [sound recording].
See item no. 970.

People's Republic of Kampuchea and State of Cambodia (1979-93)

285 **Affaires cambodgiennes 1979-1989.** (Cambodian affairs 1979-89.) Camille Scalabrino, François Grunewald, Bui Xuân Quang, Joël Luguern, Chantou Boua, Ong Thong Hoeung, Michael Vickery, Esméralda Luciolli, Frédéric Salignac, Serge Thion, Yang Baoyun, Marie-Claire Orieux. Paris: L'Harmattan, 1989. 256p. (Asie-débat, 5).

The second in the 'Asie-débat' (Asia Debate) series to be devoted to Cambodia, this volume examines to Cambodia's reconstruction after the devastation of the Pol Pot years. Contributions range across anthropology, politics, demography, language and law, all written by people (mostly established scholars) with a close relationship with Cambodia. The result is a valuable record of links with Cambodia and opinions on its course during these years of reconstruction.

286 **Brother enemy: the war after the war.**
Nayan Chanda. San Diego, California: Harcourt Brace Jovanovich, 1986. 479p. 4 maps.

Nayan Chanda was on the ground in Indochina as the correspondent for the *Far Eastern Economic Review* for most of the period covered in his compelling record of the geopolitical circumstances that followed Vietnam's victory in 1975. As an account of the conditions that gave rise to armed conflict between the nominally socialist countries of Southeast Asia – culminating in Vietnam's incursion into Cambodia and the 'lesson' China dealt Vietnam as a result, invading across Vietnam's northern border – this volume is unsurpassed. The error US planners had made, arguing that a communist Vietnam would be the cutting edge of Chinese expansion in Asia, was based on their failure to understand that nationalism, not ideology, was fundamental to shaping politics in the region. The significance of United States President Carter's decision to back away from normalizing relations with Vietnam after 1975 and Vietnam's friendship treaty with the Soviet Union are both examined in Chanda's revealing account of the complex and complicated political conditions of the time. Containing a useful chronology and annotations, but without a bibliography, this first-hand account sheds valuable light on an otherwise clouded period.

287 **Le Cambodge à deux voix.** (Cambodia in two voices.)
Françoise Corrèze and Alain Forest, with the collaboration of Vu Can. Paris: L'Harmattan, 1984. 206p.

The authors offer an unusual perspective – both having spent some years in Cambodia during the late 1960s, teaching and carrying out research (Corrèze, whose real name was Juliette Baccot, for her thesis on ethnology in O'Russey on the outskirts of Phnom Penh; and Forest, in a village 60 kilometres away down the Mekong) and both demonstrating a left-wing, activist point of view, but from different eras (Corrèze as a partisan in the French resistance and member of the Communist Party, and Forest as a militant in the 1960s, advocating a 'third force' in Indochina). They return to Phnom Penh shortly after Pol Pot was driven out, commenting on what has befallen Cambodia since they left, and appealing for the recognition and reconstruction of the country. The book was edited by the Vietnamese journalist and commentator on Cambodia, Vu Can, who has contributed two essays as an annex, together with an interview with the Minister for Planning, Chea Soth.

288 **Le Cambodge de Sihanouk: espoir, désillusions et amertume 1982-1993.** (Sihanouk's Cambodia: hope, disillusions and bitterness 1982-93.)
Richard Sola. Paris: Sudest Asie, 1994. 340p.

Sola adopts a scholarly approach in these articles on the unfolding Cambodian diplomatic and political developments written between 1982 and 1993, principally for the *Journal de Genève* (Geneva Journal). The author of four previous books with a doctorate in Asian Studies for a thesis on Chinese diplomacy in Indochina, Sola is now a professor at the Institute for the Study of International Relations in Paris. In this collection he conveys his somewhat cynical views on Sihanouk's 'political somersaults' and his strong opposition to the inclusion of the Khmer Rouge in the Paris Peace Agreement, indeed advancing his proposition that this was a violation by all signatories of their obligations under the Genocide Convention and Convention on Crimes Against Humanity. His pen was scathing also throughout the UNTAC period at the lack of action taken against the Khmer Rouge as it continuously violated the conditions it had signed and agreed to. Benefiting from the freshness of contemporary commentary, the collection does however suffer from the lack of an overall framework and from the decision to rearrange the articles from a chronological sequence into 'themes'. The somewhat eclectic annexes serve to cloud further the author's principal intent.

289 **Cambodia watching down under.**

Geoffrey C. Gunn, Jefferson Lee. Bangkok: Institute of Asian Studies, Chulalongkorn University, 1991. xxx, 328p. bibliog. (IAS Monographs, no. 047).

A critical view of Western scholarship and journalism on Cambodia since 1975. Gunn and Lee seek to situate their work in the tradition of Edward S. Herman and Noam Chomsky's *The political economy of human rights* (Montreal: Black Rose Books; Boston, Massachusetts: South End Press, 1979; Sydney: Hale & Iremonger, 1980. 2 vols.) but rather serve up an odd mixture of a copious collection of data on events and their reporting together with tendentious, sometimes bombastic assertions, throw-away lines and cheap shots. Identifying the real problem of Cambodia as 'Vietnam's invasion and occupation of Cambodia in Jan 1979', Gunn and Lee downplay if not deny the genocide by the Khmer Rouge, merely alluding in passing to the 'internal developments of Cambodia between 1975 and 1979 including the human loss stemming from either disease, famine, purge or conflict'. Somehow this reality has eluded Gunn and Lee, as did the establishment of the PRK on 7 January 1979, which is missed from their chronology of events that meticulously records the visit of one of the authors to Siem Reap in 1988. The book has no index and suffers from very sloppy proofreading, but it does gather together a valuable collection of media statements on Cambodia in the Australian press in recent years, as well as being itself a part of the polemic.

290 **Cambodia, Vietnam, and the problems of the construction of socialism.**

J. Posadas. London: Fourth International Publications, 1979. [3], 28p. (A European Marxist Review Publication).

An attempt to interpret the war between Vietnam and Cambodia from a socialist angle in this somewhat esoteric pamphlet by Juan Posadas, Argentinian leader of one of the Trotskyist currents. Writing in January 1979, he begins his thesis with the following words: 'The events in Cambodia are not a struggle between Socialist countries or an invasion by Vietnam. It is a popular uprising against a bureaucratic camarilla and a Stalinist dictatorship'. He refutes seeing 'intervention' as the issue, and goes on to concentrate on the counter-revolutionary role of China and the progressive role of Vietnam as 'an instrument of progess'. Despite some interesting perspectives, Posadas never really moves from the plane of theoretical abstraction and presents a cardboard-cutout analysis with little basis in the concrete realities of events unfolding far away across the world.

291 **Cambodia.**

John Pilger. In: *Heroes.* London: Pan, 1990; London: Vintage, 1994. rev. eds., p. 383-459. bibliog. Originally published, London: Jonathan Cape, 1986.

The Cambodian section of this book by John Pilger is divided into four chapters: 'Year Zero'; 'Is there no pity?'; 'Year One'; and 'Year Ten' (added in 1989). In these chapters the noted Australian print and film journalist brings together his impressions, conclusions and, above all, emotions, on visiting Cambodia in 1979 and 1980 and on the 'political football' of international aid to Cambodia. Like the rest of this book, which ranges across the globe, these chapters provide committed and passionate reflection formed on the basis of documented interviews and personal observations.

292 **Choses vues au Cambodge.** (Things seen in Cambodia.)

Françoise Corrèze. Paris: Éditeurs Français Réunis, 1980. 21p. map.

Returning to Cambodia in December 1979 as a member of a team delivering medical supplies, Françoise Corrèze records her impressions and fragments of conversations as she revisits the country in which she spent five years teaching. She pays particular attention to the Cham village of O'Russei, some 80 kilometres from Phnom Penh on the road to Kompong Chhnang, where she had done her anthropological fieldwork (under her real name, Juliette Baccot) some ten years earlier, whose population had been severely affected by Pol Pot's genocide against the Chams. Included as annexes to the work are interviews with various aid workers and with Nguyen Khac Vien in Hanoi, as well as excerpts from the press and other contemporary documents. A passionate and emotional personal response to the desperate circumstances of the day this book rises above most of this genre because of the additional angle given by the author's long experience in Cambodia.

293 **Democratic Kampuchea: waging people's war.**

New York: Coalition in Support of Democratic Kampuchea, 1979. 34p.

A fervent defence of the Khmer Rouge against what it calls the Vietnamese invasion conducted with the full backing of the Soviet Union. The volume contains five items: a political statement of the coalition in support of Democratic Kampuchea; a list of coalition members (twenty organizations including the Communist Party Marxist-Leninist); a brief history of the Vietnamese aggression; a statement of the government of Democratic Kampuchea, 11 January 1979; and a speech by Prince Norodom Sihanouk to the UN Security Council, 11 January 1979. As such, it is an important document of its time.

294 **Distant voices.**

John Pilger. London: Vintage, 1994. 625p. bibliog. Originally published, London: Vintage Books, 1992.

The distant voices Pilger seeks to evoke here are those he sees as being suppressed by the new world order, particularly by the monopolistic global control of the media, as exemplified in the 'mythmakers' coverage of the Gulf War, which was the stimulus for this book. Pilger gathers together in this volume essays written for the *New Statesman, Society, The Guardian* and the *Independent*. The 1994 edition includes five chapters on Cambodia (p. 401-94) that go up to the dismantling of the PRK by UNTAC. '. . . I have described the synthesis between Nixon and Kissinger on the one hand and Pol Pot and his gang on the other. What the former began from afar, the latter completed. Only the method varied. To understand that is to begin to understand the true nature of the crime perpetuated in Cambodia and where the responsibility for it lies.'

295 **A history of the Cambodian non-communist resistance 1975-1983.**
Justin Corfield. Clayton, Victoria: Centre of Southeast Asian Studies, Monash University, 1991. 33, [1]p. bibliog. (Working Papers/Centre of Southeast Asian Studies, Monash University, no. 72).

Corfield here provides valuable details of the evolution of the so-called 'non-communist resistance', although it would appear that it did very little actual resisting save in alliance with the Khmer Rouge, with whom a formal alliance was proclaimed in July 1982. He demonstrates that this alliance resulted from outside pressure and the NCR's desire for political and military backing. Given the paucity of scholarly sources on this topic, Corfield's work is of particular documentary significance, based largely on primary sources, such as interviews and ephemeral articles and pamphlets.

296 **Kampuchea, a question of survival.**
Joseph J. Zasloff. Hanover, New Hampshire: American Universities Field Staff, 1980. 2 vols. bibliog. (Reports/American Universities Field Staff, 1980, no. 46-47, Asia).

A slim but historically important report with the following section headings: Khmer refugee camps; the Pol Pot supporters and internal security in Kampuchea; feeding the hungry: the politics of assistance; Kampuchea and the outside world; and future political prospects. The author has been a professor of Political Science, consultant to the US State Department, member of the Peace Corps and he holds a doctorate in International Studies. In the report he summarizes some of the events and issues surrounding the massive refugee exodus from Cambodia after the Khmer Rouge defeat, and the ensuing humanitarian aid operations. Although the work is composed mostly of reportage and contains valuable documentation and figures about the camps and aid bodies, some readers may find his political perspective somewhat heavy. Nevertheless, information to do with the human suffering amid the loaded political situation in the region at the time is readily available in this booklet.

297 **Kampuchea, from tragedy to rebirth.**
[Compiled by E. V. Kobelev]. Moscow: Progress Publishers, 1979. 183p. A translation of *Kampuchiia, ot tragedii k vozrozhdeniiu.*

A collection of translated Russian essays in two parts: the first functioning as a testimony to the tragedy perpetrated against Cambodians under Pol Pot; and the second a presentation of the KPRP's efforts to rebuild a nation after 1979. It includes: the ambitious declaration of the Khmer United Front for National Reconciliation reconstruction mission, pledging repatriation, freedom of movement and increased literacy; a report from the People's Revolutionary Tribunal examination of the crimes of Pol Pot and Ieng Sary; the Manifesto of the Kampuchean People's Revolutionary Council; and a short biography of Heng Samrin (General Secretary of the KPRP Central Committee) and his speech at the Victory Meeting in Phnom Penh. Most of the essays are clearly written, using testimonies and interviews with Cambodian survivors. The writing styles reflect the politics of the editors, with phrases such as 'denunciation of imperialist and reactionary obscurantists' and only a few essays supplement reportage with deeper political analysis. However, the collection is an important contribution to the documentation of Cambodia's genocide and early years of reconstruction.

298 **Kampuchean diary, 1983-1986.**

Selected articles by Jacques Bekaert. Bangkok: DD Books, 1987. [163]p. maps. Reprint of articles originally published 1983-86.

'Published in the *Bangkok Post* . . . as a regular column [it] is an attempt to cover the war in Cambodia with the benefit of the geographical proximity and the frustration of unequal access to the protagonists of the drama. . . . Access to Cambodia [was] made of patience, rare trips into the interior, glimpses of reality and endless visa requests. Long hours spent reading translations of official material published in Phnom Penh only partly compensate the impossibility of "being there . . .". The same could be said of the party of Democratic Kampuchea, better known as the "Khmer Rouge". Even more than the PRK it is a secretive organization, and its contacts with the press even more limited.' Bekaert visited Cambodia only once in this period – to report on the Vietnamese withdrawal in 1983, but his regular column reported, albeit in a somewhat cynical way tinged with a strong dose of anti-communism and suspicion of the Vietnamese, developments on the ground inside Cambodia and in the various opposition forces on the border with Thailand, as well as the view from ASEAN. This compilation is a valuable resource for anyone going back over this period of Cambodia's history. The final reports from 1986 reported on the demise of Pol Pot, then 'retiring' due to ill health (a decade before recent 1996 reports of his supposed death and 1997 video footage of a staged trial by his erstwhile Khmer Rouge subordinates). Bekaert's final words anticipated the post-1993 coalition in saying, 'it looks increasingly like the Sihanoukists of the ANS (Sihanoukist National Army) plus some of the KPNLF (Khmer People's National Liberation Front) soldiers and the draftees of the Heng Samrin army have more in common than anyone else'.

299 **Kampuchean occupation and resistance.**

Steve Heder. [Bangkok]: Institute of Asian Studies, Chulalongkorn University, Bangkok, 1980. 121p. (Asian Studies Monographs, no. 027).

Heder's study of the political situation inside Kampuchea in the ten-month period from January to October 1979, examines the local level form and structure of, and the popular reaction to, the National Salvation Front régime and the Vietnamese troops that were supporting it. His information is drawn mainly from interviews with 250 people in refugee camps, transit centres, squatter settlements and resistance bases along the Thai-Kampuchean border. Heder chooses to perpetuate the Khmer Rouge classification of the population as 'New' and 'Old' people, differentiating those who joined the revolution in the liberated zones prior to the official formation of Democratic Kampuchea in April 1975 from those who came later under Khmer Rouge control. New people and a large section of the old people at first welcomed the Vietnamese but quickly grew disillusioned with their presence in the country and the failure of the Front to restore urban life, capitalism and rural production. Heder claims the Vietnamese and Front members assured themselves large rice rations while the majority of the population went without. In Heder's view, for the old or base people in the resistance the 'Vietnamese invasion' was the worst thing that could have happened. Among the resistance forces there were: the Khmer Sereikar – a collection of various petty warlord movements operating militarily in small areas along the Thai-Cambodian border – who had been revitalized by the 'invasion' but were too divided to capitalize on the new opportunities; Democratic Kampuchea (the Khmer Rouge), decimated by their defeat; and Sihanouk, still enjoying popular support but with no detectable organized presence.

300 **Postwar Indochina: old enemies and new allies.**

Edited by Joseph J. Zasloff. Arlington, Virginia: Center for the Study of Foreign Affairs, 1988. 290p. map. (Study of Foreign Affairs Series).

The Center for the Study of Foreign Affairs was established in 1982 as part of the Foreign Service Institute of the US Department of State to keep government staff in various agencies informed of emerging foreign policy concepts, through conferences, research, exercises and publications such as this. The essays collected in the volume were presented as papers at a 1987 conference at the centre by various specialists including Nayan Chanda (q.v.). Zasloff introduces the papers with a summary of events in Indochina since US withdrawal, and the fluctuation of both public and government interest in the region. The book is a reflection of the renewed American interest which followed almost a decade of 'amnesia'. It examines the relationships to have emerged between Indochinese states and their interaction with external powers, twelve years after the communist victories of 1975. Well over half of the eleven papers devote specific attention to Cambodia.

301 **Report from Vietnam & Kampuchea: lessons for the fight against Washington's new Vietnam war in Central America and the Caribbean.**

Diane Wang, Steve Clark. New York: Pathfinder Press, 1984. 70p.

Produced by the socialist publisher, Pathfinder, this pamphlet offers a pro-Vietnamese perspective on nation-building following the end of the Indochinese wars of the 1970s. In Kampuchea in 1984 the authors visited Phnom Penh, Kompong Chhnang and some villages in Kandal, meeting people and interviewing government leaders. They deplore the US and Western blockades of Vietnam and Kampuchea, and UN recognition of Khmer Rouge leaders and support for Khmer Rouge camps on the Thai border. Articles on surviving Pol Pot's holocaust, on rebuilding the economy, on a farm and fishing solidarity group, and on how health care is being revived, combine polemic with detailed observation, descriptions of community projects, and records of personal stories – potentially very useful to researchers. The articles in this pamphlet appeared initially in the weekly socialist newspaper the *Militant* and the bi-weekly news magazine *Intercontinental Press*.

302 **The Third Indochina conflict.**

Edited by David W. P. Elliott. Boulder, Colorado: Westview Press, 1981. xii, 247p. bibliog. (A Westview Replica Edition).

An early attempt by a group of scholars to analyse the roots of the conflict between the Khmer Rouge régime and the People's Republic of Vietnam and to posit what they call the 'Vietnamese invasion' within the context of evolving international relations. Elliott concludes that the essential ingredients of an explosive compound were: Vietnam-Kampuchea, China-Vietnam and the US/China/USSR triangle. Most contributors take as given the Vietnamese régime's desire to dominate Indochina politically but their conclusions as to the immediate motivations for the 1978 intervention differ. The book does not attempt to analyse the Khmer Rouge's domestic policies. Contributors include David W. P. Elliott, Stephen P. Heder, Gareth Porter, Charles Benoit, Robert G. Sutter and Banning Garrett. Many of the chapters evolved from papers presented to the annual meeting of the Association for Asian Studies, March 1979 and a Conference on the Third Indochina Conflict held at Pomona College, Claremont, California in April 1979.

303 **Time on whose side in Cambodia?**

Jonathan Stromseth. Bangkok: Institute of Security and International Studies, Chulalongkorn University, Bangkok, 1988. 58p. bibliog. (ISIS Paper, no. 2).

Most of this booklet was prepared during Stromseth's period as a Fulbright scholar in 1985-86 at the National University of Singapore, before he went on to study at Columbia University, New York. Stromseth puts forward the view that the success of the Vietnamese dry season military offensive in 1984-85 has called into question the military dimension of ASEAN's strategy in Cambodia. He assesses the state of the resistance and proposes a change in ASEAN's policy, to cut its support for the Khmer Rouge and to support some negotiations between the 'non-communist resistance' and the PRK government in Cambodia.

304 **Vietnam, Kampuchea, Laos: an eye witness report.**

Women's International Democratic Federation. [Berlin]: The Federation, 1979. 31p.

A group of women sympathetic to the socialist cause and to the PRK visited Cambodia in 1979. Their report serves to document the crimes of the Khmer Rouge whose residue and traces they witnessed as well as the beginnings of the reconstruction. Their words also form part of the polemic for international aid and recognition of the PRK, and for denial of the same to the Khmer Rouge.

305 **Vietnam, Thailand, Kampuchea: a first hand account.**

Helen Ester. Canberra: Australian Council for Overseas Aid, 1980. iv, 50, ivp. map.

An early report of the reconstruction of Cambodia by the PRK written by an Australian journalist, representing part of the campaign to secure development assistance for, and recognition of, the new government. It contains an interview with Foreign Minister Hun Sen, and a biography of President Heng Samrin.

306 **The Vietnamisation of Cambodia.**

J. R. Pouvatchy. [Kuala Lumpur]: Institute of Strategic and International Studies, 1986. 14p.

Pouvatchy, who had previously studied the Vietnamese ethnic group in Cambodia, depicts Cambodia in the mid-1980s as consisting of the following bleak elements: a Vietnamese military presence disproportionate to the Khmer Rouge threat; the encouragement of Vietnamese civilian settlement and intermarriage; encroachments on the border; the domination of Vietnamese personnel in the distribution of food; and the education of orphans in schools staffed by Vietnamese. In his view, which shared little resemblance with what others saw on the ground in Cambodia at the time, the process of Vietnamization would soon be complete.

307 **A visit to Banteay Chhmar: reaching the Khmer soul.**

M. H. Lao. [Thailand?]: Khmer Buddhist Association (K. P. N.L. F.), 1989. [56p.]. maps.

This impassioned tract reports the emotions of M. H. Lao following the KPNLF seizure (or liberation) of Banteay Chhmar from Cambodian government forces in

October 1989. He reports that 212 troops defected, and that 3 tanks were captured. The Secretary-General of KPNLF, Ieng Mouly, also came to make a two-day visit on behalf of the President, Son Sann, who was then in New York at the United Nations, where the opposition coalition continued to hold Cambodia's seat. The party of ten rode five motorbikes for several hours to the ruined fort. After an overnight stay, emergency aid was distributed and speeches made. This book and a video film of this, Ieng Mouly's third venture inside Cambodia with resistance forces, was to be used by the KPNLF as part of their propaganda effort. M. H. Lao concludes: 'The state of Banteay Chhmar Castle which has almost all fallen apart is not different from that of Cambodia under Communism and Vietnamese rule. Both that monument and the nation have fallen almost to pieces. I am optimistic, though . . . Who knows if Banteay Chhmar will not be recorded in our history as our "Liberty Bell"?' M. H. Lao is better known as Lao Mong Hay, who became Director of the Khmer Institute of Democracy in Phnom Penh from 1995.

308 **War and hope: the case for Cambodia.**
Prince Norodom Sihanouk, translated from the French by Mary Feeney; with introductions by Gérard Brissé, and William Shawcross. London: Sidgwick and Jackson, 1980. xl, 166p. Originally published, New York: Pantheon Books, 1980. A translation of *Chroniques de guerre* (Chronicles of war), Paris: Hachette, 1979.

Published in French soon after Pol Pot's overthrow, and in English translation the following year, this book reveals the contradictory reasoning that has characterized Sihanouk, permitting him to denounce the Khmer Rouge for its crimes against the Cambodian people, against himself and his own family, while still being prepared to work with them; denouncing the People's Republic of Kampuchea as 'the Yuons' [Vietnamese] lackeys', and yet in the very same book stating that 'the current Vietnamese presence in our country . . . is the people's only protection against being massacred by the Khmer Rouge', and the plan to ally Sihanouk with the Khmer Rouge and the KPNLF 'would be tantamount to putting a starving and bloodthirsty wolf in with a lamb'. Here he proposes a new Geneva Conference on Indochina, to form an International Control Commission (as in 1954), a ceasefire, and an internationally supervised election – a scenario similar to that which was indeed played out some twelve years later, but not before Sihanouk had spent nearly a decade throwing in his lot once again with the Khmer Rouge in coalition with the KPNLF. This is a fascinating presentation of 'the mercurial Sihanouk'. Sihanouk attributes the origins of the reconciliation policy to US President Jimmy Carter and contrasts this with the bellicose approach of the Nixon administration. Introductions by both Gérard Brissé, on the background to the events of the 1970s, and by William Shawcross, author of *Sideshow: Kissinger, Nixon and the destruction of Cambodia* (q.v.), are included.

Cambodia, 1975-1982.
See item no. 261.

Kampuchea.
See item no. 270.

Résistances au Vietnam, Cambodge et Laos, 1975-1980. (Resistance in Vietnam, Cambodia and Laos, 1975-80.)
See item no. 278.

Revolution and its aftermath in Kampuchea: eight essays.
See item no. 279.

The survivors, Kampuchea, 1984.
See item no. 336.

Vulnerable in the village.
See item no. 436.

Cambodia: a political and military overview.
See item no. 454.

The Cambodian People's Party and Sihanouk.
See item no. 456.

Kampuchea: politics, economics and society.
See item no. 466.

Les 'nouveaux' Khmers rouges: enquête, 1979-1990: reconstruction du mouvement et reconquête des villages. (The 'new' Khmer Rouge: enquiry, 1979-90: reconstruction of the movement and reconquest of the villages.)
See item no. 467.

Pol Pot, peasants, and peace: continuity and change in Khmer Rouge political thinking, 1985-1991.
See item no. 469.

The return of the Khmer Rouge.
See item no. 471.

Aftermath: the struggle of Cambodia & Vietnam.
See item no. 523.

Le Cambodge dans la tourmente: le troisième conflit indochinois, 1978-1991. (Cambodia in torment: the third Indochinese conflict, 1978-91.)
See item no. 525.

The causes and implications of the Vietnamese invasion and occupation of Kampuchea.
See item no. 533.

The China-Cambodia-Vietnam triangle.
See item no. 534.

Kampuchea between China and Vietnam.
See item no. 549.

Red brotherhood at war: Vietnam, Cambodia, and Laos since 1975.
See item no. 557.

Report of the International Conference on Kampuchea: New York (13-17 July 1981).
See item no. 558.

The third Indochina war: the conflicts between China, Vietnam, and Cambodia.
See item no. 560.

The Third International Conference on Kampuchea, 25-26 July 1987, Bangkok, Thailand.
See item no. 561.

Vietnam's intervention in Cambodia in international law.
See item no. 564.

Vietnam's withdrawal from Cambodia: regional issues and realignments.
See item no. 566.

A further look at UNTAC's performance and dilemmas: a review article.
See item no. 576.

UN peacekeeping missions: the lessons from Cambodia.
See item no. 581.

The challenge of reform in Indochina.
See item no. 591.

Punishing the poor: the international isolation of Kampuchea.
See item no. 641.

Australian Cambodian Quarterly.
See item no. 848.

Indochina Chronology.
See item no. 859.

Back to Kampuchea.
See item no. 910.

Cambodia – Kampuchea.
See item no. 911.

Cambodia – the betrayal.
See item no. 912.

Cambodia year ten: a special report by John Pilger.
See item no. 914.

Cambodia: the struggle for peace.
See item no. 918.

Cambodia: year one.
See item no. 919.

Cambodia.
See item no. 920.

The eagle, the dragon, the bear and Kampuchea.
See item no. 923.

Kampuchea after Pol Pot.
See item no. 929.

The Mekong.
See item no. 935.

The ninth circle.
See item no. 936.

Peter Jennings from the killing fields.
See item no. 940.

The prospects for peace.
See item no. 942.

Return to year zero: a special report by John Pilger.
See item no. 945.

Return to Year Zero?
See item no. 946.

Roving Report.
See item no. 947.

The tenth dancer.
See item no. 953.

World in action.
See item no. 956.

Kingdom of Cambodia (1993-)

309 **Cambodia's New Deal: a report.**
William Shawcross. Washington, DC: Carnegie Endowment for International Peace, 1994. 106p. (Contemporary Issues Paper, no. 1).

The striking photograph by Tim Page on the cover sits at odds with the message in the more than 100 pages of text that follow. The photograph shows a United Nations helicopter carrying FUNCINPEC leader Prince Norodom Ranariddh hovering above a crowd of supporters. While the United Nations flag flies proudly, the people are huddled on the ground desperately seeking protection from each other against UNTAC's mighty whirlwind, and hanging on to colourful *kramas* (Cambodian scarves) and electioneering placards, T-shirts and caps. Shawcross sees it differently: 'What can be said for certain is that Cambodia has been given the best chance for peace it ever had – thanks to the overall success of UNTAC'. Not that he sees the Cambodia of 1994 as without very serious problems. His view is that it is 'still a semi-feudal country, a place of bargaining, survival, and lawlessness', with its success depending on: 'the health and good stewardship of King Norodom Sihanouk; the effectiveness and honesty of the coalition government; the power of the Khmer Rouge and the conduct of their Thai supporters; and the continuous intervention and assistance of the international community'. Shawcross gives a great deal of support in this volume to Sam Rainsy, then Minister of Finance, who was later dismissed and expelled from FUNCINPEC, and has since established his own political party. This volume calls for continuing international financial and technical assistance, but also for the Cambodian government 'to fulfill the promises of the historic election that the world brought to Cambodia'.

310 **Cambodia: from UNTAC to Royal Government.**
Frank Frost. *Southeast Asian Affairs* (1994), p. 79-101.

Frost is a parliamentary researcher on issues relating to the Australian government departments of Foreign Affairs, Defence and Trade and has written a number of papers on the political situation in Cambodia since 1980. He followed closely the unfolding of the international negotiations, especially in his monograph *The peace process in Cambodia: issues and prospects* (Mt. Gravatt, Queensland: Centre for the Study of Australia-Asia Relations, Griffith University, 1993). His task in this personal paper (not an official document) is to summarize the political and economic situation at the time of the 1993 UN-sponsored elections. He believes UNTAC's efforts to maintain a ceasefire were blocked by the Khmer Rouge, and its attempts to promote human rights were limited by resistance from elements in the Cambodian People's Party. Nonetheless, UNTAC 'held firmly to its peace-keeping mandate'. The elections were successful, but 'naturally did not stop the process of political conflict in Cambodia' in which the CPP used events like the threatened secession of eastern provinces to pressure FUNCINPEC into a power-sharing arrangement. Frost notes the difficulties created by the refusal of opponents of the CPP to allow promised foreign aid to be delivered during the UNTAC period. He concludes that Cambodia had grounds for optimism, balanced with caution about the scale of the problems faced by the country. His 1996 paper *Cambodia's troubled path to recovery* (Canberra: Parliamentary Research Service, 1996) struck an even more sober tone.

311 **Whither Cambodia?: beyond the election.**
Timothy Carney, Tan Lian Choo. Singapore: Indochina Unit, Institute of Southeast Asian Studies, 1993. 51p.

The newly formed Indochina Unit of ISEAS in Singapore was established 'to meet the increasing need for information and scholastic assessment on the fast-changing situation'. This slim volume certainly addressed the fast-changing situation, being contemporary commentary on the May 1993 elections from two people who were on the spot. The scholastic nature of the publication is less clear. It was evidently produced from transcripts of a meeting, presumably at ISEAS, presumably in mid-July 1993. However, no such information is provided to the reader. Nor is the 'Chairman' of the twenty-three-page discussion on the two papers identified, save in passing as 'Heng Chee', from which we can deduce it was the new ISEAS Director, Chan Heng Chee. Timothy Carney, then director of UNTAC's Division of Information and Education, reveals clearly the perspective he brought to that job, with his principal criticisms directed at the Cambodian People's Party and the assessment that the Khmer Rouge, having failed in its 'Plan A', to disrupt the elections, was now moving onto 'Plan B', to participate in political life, a strategy from which Carney does not demur. Tan Lian Choo, Bangkok correspondent for the *Straits Times* provides more of a mood-piece on the atmosphere surrounding the elections, and she looks into the future, asking: whether Ranaridhh will succeed as a 'modern leader' introducing a new generation; whether the CPP 'stalwarts . . . are planning a sinister underground alternative chain of command'; and whether the army will back the new government or 'will it be playing its own games?'.

Le Cambodge de Sihanouk: espoir, désillusions et amertume 1982-1993.
(Sihanouk's Cambodia: hope, disillusions and bitterness 1982-93.)
See item no. 288.

The struggle for rice, fish and water.
See item no. 435.

Kingdom of Cambodia: diminishing respect for human rights.
See item no. 506.

Cambodia after the cold war: the search for security continues.
See item no. 527.

Cambodia.
See item no. 588.

Cambodia.
See item no. 589.

The CICP Newsletter.
See item no. 856.

Our children didn't come home.
See item no. 938.

Personal Accounts, Biographies and Autobiographies

312 **Beyond the horizon: five years with the Khmer Rouge.**
Laurence Picq, translated by Patricia Norland. New York: St. Martin's Press, 1989. 218p. map. (A Thomas Dunne Book).

This is an extraordinary account by one of the only foreigners to have survived the Khmer Rouge régime. It also represents one of the very few records of the functioning of a Democratic Kampuchea ministry between 1975 and 1979. Picq, a Frenchwoman, was married to Suong Sikoeun, a member of the Cambodian resistance who became a middle-ranking Khmer Rouge cadre. As a *de facto* member of the Cambodian community in exile in China in the early 1970s, Picq learned Chinese, supported the achievements of the Cultural Revolution and was honoured to have met Chou En-lai. Picq left Peking in October 1975 with her two small children, in order to join her husband who had been fighting to liberate Kampuchea. She hoped she would be able to contribute to the building of a more beautiful and brotherly society. Picq's physical and psychological strength through the trials that were to follow are a testimony to human heroism. She worked in kitchens, child-care centres and as a translator in Ieng Sary's foreign ministry, experiencing both the satisfaction of living and working communally, and terror as cadres and old friends were purged in deadly cycles. Used alternately as symbol of unforgivable imperialism or the international importance of the Kampuchean revolution, Picq was never allowed to forget her bourgeois origins, and was a constant source of shame to her dogmatic husband, who remained loyal to the Ieng Sary section of the Khmer Rouge until at least late 1996. A postscript to this book appeared in the pages of the *Phnom Penh Post* at that time, when Picq wrote in horror, opposing the amnesty given to Ieng Sary, and Sikoeun responded, attacking her as soft and ungrateful.

313 **Beyond the killing fields: voices of nine Cambodian survivors in America.**
Usha Welaratna. Stanford, California: Stanford University Press, 1993. xxi, 285p. bibliog. (Asian America).

An account of the Cambodian refugee experience in which nine Cambodians tell their stories of life in Cambodia before Pol Pot's régime in a largely non-Western,

Indianized, Theravada Buddhist culture. They tell of their traumatic survival of the Khmer Rouge holocaust, and of their escapes and their experiences in a new society, the United States. Like the Cambodians, Usha Welaratna is also Buddhist, an immigrant to the United States from Sri Lanka who met her Cambodian subjects in a temple in northern California in 1987. Her project began as a masters degree thesis at the San José State University, San José, California. The stories of the nine are interspersed with chapters on history, society, the Khmer Rouge revolution, arrival in the United States, and interpretations of the killing fields. About 150,000 Cambodians reached the United States in the wake of the Pol Pot years, and the community is now substantially larger.

314 **Borany's story.**
Borany Kanal and Adrienne Jansen. Wellington, New Zealand: Learning Media, Ministry of Education, 1991. 96p. map.

Produced by the New Zealand Ministry of Education for use in high schools, Borany's story would be useful to others wanting to learn about the Cambodian 'holocaust'. It makes no attempt to analyse or explain the political and social forces behind recent Cambodian history, but is rather a brief autobiography of a survivor. Borany's story is simply told, from growing up in a wealthy family in Phnom Penh, the Khmer Rouge takeover when she was seven, and her family's exodus and experiences under the régime, to their eventual resettlement in New Zealand. Importantly, she looks at some of the issues involved in being a refugee – her own emotions and expectations and those of the people in her new country. Although brief, it manages to provide valuable insights into many major issues such as grief, change, loss, cultural differences, Khmer superstitions and beliefs, and national identity. The text is also available with an accompanying booklet of teacher's notes.

315 **Brother number one: a political biography of Pol Pot.**
David P. Chandler. St. Leonards, New South Wales: Allen & Unwin, 1993. xiv, 254p. map. bibliog. Originally published in 1992, Boulder, Colorado: Westview Press.

Pol Pot is the name indelibly associated with the Khmer Rouge genocide of 1975-79. Although officially removed from formal positions of power, he remained at the head of the Khmer Rouge until at least mid-1997, when he was supposedly condemned to life imprisonment by his followers. David Chandler, one of the most established historians of Cambodia, turns his hand at a new genre in this biographical portrait, based largely on secondary sources and not on a personal interview with the subject himself. Originally named Saloth Sar, Pol Pot has lived in secrecy hidden behind numerous aliases of which Pol Pot is the best known, and Brother Number One was for some time used internally within the Khmer Rouge. This is an eminently readable volume in which Chandler evocatively recreates the atmosphere of the various chapters in Pol Pot's life, seeking the explanation for his genocidal acts in his psychology and personality rather than in political terms.

316 **Cambodian witness: the autobiography of Someth May.**
Edited and with an introduction by James Fenton. London: Faber, 1988. 287p. Originally published, 1986.

This is another autobiographical account of life under the Khmer Rouge. May, son of a Phnom Penh doctor, had begun a medical course at university when he and the thirteen other members of his family were forced to flee the city when the Khmer Rouge came to power in 1975. For four years they attempted to survive by posing as uneducated peasant farmers. Only four of the family, including the author, lived through the overthrow of the Khmer Rouge régime, subsequently emigrating to the United States as refugees. May opens with an account of his life as a child and student in Phnom Penh, describing the corruption and collapse of Lon Nol's republic. The book's centre-piece is a distressingly almost repetitious account of his own episodes of hard labour, starvation, disease and people being 'taken away' under the Khmer Rouge. But May and his sisters also receive assistance from one of the Khmer Rouge, which was essential to their survival. Towards the end of his account, May makes a few generalizations from his own experience, and also begins to describe the disintegration of the rule of the Khmer Rouge. The work's greatest value is perhaps in the way it conveys a sense of what life was like under Pol Pot as one of the 'New People' (those who had come from the town in 1975).

317 **Cambodian-American Women's Oral History Project.**
Contact The Cambodian Women's Project, The American Friends Service Committee, 15 Rutherford Place, New York, NY 10003, USA.

The Oral History Project currently houses extensive oral histories (all are between ten and sixteen hours in length and are in the Khmer language) of ten women survivors of the Cambodian genocide. A bibliography of related materials was published in 1984.

318 **The death and life of Dith Pran.**
Sydney H. Schanberg. Harmondsworth, England; New York: Penguin Viking, 1985. 78p. (Elisabeth Sifton Books).

This book contains the text of Schanberg's essay that appeared originally in the 20 January 1980 issue of *The New York Times* Sunday magazine. Dith Pran's story itself is better known than any other Cambodian story through its depiction in the movie *The killing fields* (q.v.), but the original essay is still worth reading for the intensity and contemporaneity of the personal rendition. Schanberg explains his purpose in the foreword: 'The story of Cambodia is a universal one – it is not a new thing that small countries and vulnerable countries get abused by the large and powerful. But the awfulness of what happened in Cambodia should not be allowed to blur into a historical generality . . . It appears here as it was written, in 1980. Events since then have altered the details of Cambodia's existence, but the basic fact of life for these people has remained unchanged. The Cambodians are still everyone's pawns and are still suffering terribly. It is my hope that this chronicle of the relationship and experiences of the two of us – an American and a Cambodian brought together by a war – will help provide a glimpse of this history'.

319 **The demigods: charismatic leadership in the Third World.**
Jean Lacouture, translated from the French by Patricia Wolf. London: Secker & Warburg, 1971. [10], 300, vip. bibliog. This translation originally published, New York: Knopf, 1970. Originally published as *Quatre hommes et leurs peuples* (Four men and their people), Paris: Éditions du Seuil, 1969.

Written by well-known French journalist and writer Jean Lacouture, and presented as a doctoral thesis, this unusual book blends anecdote with analysis. Extremely readable, it paints the portraits of four 'Rain Makers', leaders of Third-World nations

– Nasser, Bouguiba, Nkrumah and Sihanouk – who are analysed according to the author's theories about power and its personal manifestations in poor countries. He views Sihanouk's 'direct monarchy' of the 1950s and 1960s in terms of concepts such as the incarnation and assumption of leadership, the Asian ability to grasp form and design more readily than concepts, and 'government by laughter'. The author consistently chooses to discuss his leadership in personal and cultural terms, rather than as any aspect of international politics or as a result of any domestic machinations, and even presents the Lon Nol régime as the caretaker for Sihanouk while he repairs his health in France. Approaching Sihanouk from such an uncommon angle provides much food for thought.

320 **The early phases of liberation in northwestern Cambodia: conversations with Peang Sophi.**

David P. Chandler with Ben Kiernan and Muy Hong Lim. [Melbourne: Centre of Southeast Asian Studies, Monash University, 1977]. 16p. bibliog. (Working Papers/Centre of Southeast Asian Studies, no. 10).

Although only a slight work, and followed by more substantive pieces on the revolution by both Kiernan and Chandler (qq.v.), this work deserves attention as one of the earliest direct accounts of the behaviour on the ground of the Khmer Rouge. Drawn by Chandler from nine hours of recorded conversation between Muy Hong Lim, a graduate student at Monash University, and Peang Sophi, a thirty-two-year-old Cambodian, who describes his experience during 1975 in Battambang province. The digest of, and commentary on, his views is followed by the text of six revolutionary songs from Democratic Kampuchea.

321 **Indochina's refugees: oral histories from Laos, Cambodia and Vietnam.**

Joanna C. Scott. Jefferson, North Carolina: McFarland & Co., 1989. xiii, 312p. map.

A collection of personal accounts by refugees from Vietnam, Cambodia and Laos. Joanna Scott visited the Philippine Refugee Processing Centre and, with the help of community leaders, recorded the stories over eight months. The stories from Vietnam are told by those who emigrated both legally and illegally and with varying backgrounds – they include a monk, a soldier, a housewife, and others. The Cambodian stories are almost exclusively accounts of serving under Pol Pot. Scott acknowledges that the stories from Laos are the least consistent as a body, due to the separation of elements of its society after 1975. They are moving stories, united by the expression of a common desire for freedom, and excellently translated. An index and photographs are included.

322 **The killing fields.**

Christopher Hudson. London; Sydney; Auckland: Pan Books, 1984. 249p.

Based on articles by Sydney Schanberg and screenplays for the film of the same name, Christopher Hudson retells the story of Dith Pran and Sydney Schanberg from August 1973 as they cover the war in Cambodia as journalists for *The New York Times*, through the liberation of Phnom Penh by Khmer Rouge troops, Schanberg's departure with Pran left behind, and Pran's horrific personal experiences under Pol Pot rule and subsequent flight from Cambodia, until October 1979 when they meet again in a refugee camp on the border between Thailand and Cambodia. All the anguish and tension of the film is preserved in this riveting account of the relationship between two men as well as of the world disintegrating around them.

323 **The murderous revolution: life & death in Pol Pot's Kampuchea.** Martin Stuart-Fox, based on the personal experiences of Bunheang Ung. Chippendale, New South Wales: APCOL, 1985. viii, 203p. maps. bibliog. Later published, Bangkok: The Tamarind Press, 1986, and to be republished in 1997 by White Lotus.

Bunheang Ung, a former student of fine arts and cartoonist for *Nokor Thom* (Great Country) newspaper, tells the story of his family's experiences in Pol Pot's Cambodia through the intermediary of Australian academic Martin Stuart-Fox. The distance of the third-person narrator shields the reader from the pain and anguish that characterize other accounts, and Stuart-Fox provides considerable additional material in the text and in the bibliographical footnotes. It is Bunheang's drawings that are really the most memorable aspect of this work, in over fifty elaborately crafted cartoons showing the oppressive, horrific and intrusive nature of the régime.

324 **One crowded hour: Neil Davis combat cameraman.** Tim Bowden. Sydney: Collins Australia, 1987. 436p.

A biography of the famous Tasmanian cameraman-photographer who made his home in Phnom Penh before its fall to the Khmer Rouge in 1975. Renowned for his great skill, bravery and luck with shooting and surviving combat, he made a point of travelling with local military corps rather than foreign troops. Davis is considered somewhat of a hero, and a memorial collection of his papers and work diaries is held in the Australian War Memorial. This work, by long-time friend and colleague, Bowden, relies on Davis' diaries, correspondence and friends' recollections, and is a warm, upfront account of his career and personal life. His compassion, womanizing, humour, humility and dignity are simply and accessibly presented. Davis' career began with the Tasmanian Government Film Unit, and spanned most of Southeast Asia, from Borneo to Vietnam, encompassing many conflicts, recording war with a feel for the common people, regardless of their political alliances, although Davis never really questioned the role of the United States and its allies (including Australia) in sending in troops to 'stem the tide against communism'.

325 **Personalités du Cambodge.** (Cambodian personalities.) Phnom Penh: Réalités Cambodgiennes, 1963. 303p.

Contains some 350 brief biographies with many portraits of Cambodians prominent during the 1950s and early 1960s.

326 **Prisonnier de l'Angkar ou 'Angkar a les yeux de l'ananas'.** (Prisoner of the Angkar or 'Angkar has the eyes of a pineapple'.) Henri Locard and Moeung Sonn. [France]: Fayard, 1993. 381p. (Les Enfants du Fleuve).

Of the many testimonies of personal tragedies and suffering under the Khmer Rouge, this volume stands out as an exception in that it gives details of prison life. Prepared from interviews in French between 1990 and 1992, this book tells the story of Moeung

Sonn, an engineer working in Sihanoukville when the Khmer Rouge came to power. He ignored his wife Phally's pleas to escape in a boat, certain that his technical skills would be utilized in building the new Cambodia. As the family was driven out of the city, he decided not to reveal his background, and initially joined the fate of many others as a virtual slave in the countryside, but soon was made chief of a small group of fifteen families. This was not to last and, by December 1975, having been denounced for favouritism, he was taken off to a prison and placed in the dreaded *knaoh* (shackles). Somehow he survived, as few others did, some three periods of imprisonment, and was used in the prison as a designer of crude machines. During the Khmer Rouge rule, he lost six children, his mother and father and many other relatives. Having survived Pol Pot, Moeung Sonn and Phally, who had been separated, each decided to escape to Thailand when their ordeal ended, fearful of what lay ahead under yet another régime. They made their way across the dangerous Cardamon mountains, evading mines and soldiers, and to Thailand. By mid-1981 both were in France, where they have had three more children. The series 'Les enfants du fleuve' (Children of the river) is designed to bring the realities of life in other countries to young people in France, and to encourage their support for aid activities. It is endorsed by the NGO 'Enfants de Mekong' (Children of the Mekong). Henri Locard is a professor of English at the Université Lumière-Lyon 2, and is continuing his studies into the prison system of the Khmer Rouge régime.

327 **Retour à Phnom Penh: le Cambodge du génocide à la colonisation.** (Return to Phnom Penh: Cambodia from the genocide to colonization.) Y Phandara, presented by Jean Lacouture. Paris: A.-M. Métailié, 1982. 276p.

A rare account of the Khmer Rouge period by a supporter who willingly returned to help rebuild his country after the overthrow of Lon Nol in 1975. He was imprisoned, as were some hundreds of other returnees, at the Boeung Trabek school in Phnom Penh, but unlike most of his colleagues, Phandara survived.

328 **The royal family of Cambodia.** Justin J. Corfield. Melbourne: Khmer Language and Culture Centre, 1993. 2nd ed. 135p. bibliog.

This second edition includes new information on the Cambodian royal family made available since the book first appeared in 1990. It is not a narrative but a recent lineage based on the system employed by 'Burke's royal families of the world', and includes biographical information and forty-eight photographs. The book grew out of Corfield's doctoral research on the history of the Khmer Republic 1970-75, published as *Khmers stand up!: a history of the Cambodian government 1970-1975* (q.v.) in 1994, supplemented with additional interviews. It covers the period from King Ang Eng 1779-96 to the present-day King Norodom Sihanouk, and includes a useful index of people for easy reference. It is available from the Khmer Language and Culture Centre, (Publications) 77, Rosanna, Victoria, 3084, Australia.

329 **Sihanouk et le drame cambodgien.** (Sihanouk and the Cambodian drama.) Bernard Hamel. Paris: L'Harmattan, 1993. 275p.

This book deals with the 1965-70 period, at the close of the Sihanoukist régime. The author was a journalist who was considered to be influential at the time, a kind of right-wing balance to the role of left-wing adviser played by Charles Meyer. Each of them actually wrote a book on the same period, both warning they would use damning evidence drawn from their own private archives. In both cases the result has been somewhat less than was promised. Either there was no damning evidence on Sihanouk's handling of the political issues, or they did not dare to use it, out of fear for themselves. The first possibility is more likely. Thus Hamel's book is just a short history of Sihanouk's last years as an ever less effective head of state. Its merit is that it puts into perspective the obvious responsibilities of the prince himself in the weakening of his régime.

330 **Sihanouk reminisces: world leaders I have known.**
Prince Norodom Sihanouk with Bernard Krisher. Bangkok: Duang Kamol, 1990. 191p. Previously published as *Charisma and leadership: the human side of great leaders of the twentieth century*, Tokyo: Yohan, 1990.

The selection of the thirteen world leaders (none of whom was still in power) about whom Sihanouk wished to write in 1990, and indeed the decision at that time to write a book of this nature, says a lot about the political judgements and inclinations of the author. The subjects were: De Gaulle; Nehru; Sukarno; Nasser; Chou En-lai; Mao Tse-tung; Tito; Khrushchev; Haile Selassie; Enver Hodja; Ceausescu; Boumédienne; and Sékou Touré. An appendix listing Sihanouk's meetings with these people, and essays on 'Charisma and leadership' by Sihanouk, and on Sihanouk by Bernard Krisher, complement the sketches. Krisher, an American journalist and publisher based in Tokyo, had been introduced to Sihanouk by Sukarno in 1963, and had visited Cambodia several times, writing about Sihanouk and his rule there before his 1970 overthrow, and had at one stage been banned for his comments about the Queen Mother's economic activities. He worked with Sihanouk in Beijing for a week in 1988, taping the reminiscences, which were to be complemented by handwritten anecdotes of events and conversations, the whole designed as a 'light tribute to friends who had passed away'. The most pervasive topics (in both Krisher and Sihanouk's chapters) are food, wine and women, and while Sihanouk admits that Ceausescu was a megalomaniac, his crimes were not as bad as those of Hitler and Pol Pot (with whom Sihanouk was in coalition at the time the book was written!) and it was the mysterious and evil power of his wife Elena that turned his absolutism 'progressively more despotic'. In this and in an assessment that 'Mao's fatal flaw must surely have been his questionable judgement . . . in women' the book says more about Sihanouk than the subjects.

331 **Sihanouk: prince of light, prince of darkness.**
Milton Osborne. St. Leonards, New South Wales: Allen & Unwin, 1994. 283p. bibliog.

'This book is a critical unauthorised biography of Norodom Sihanouk of Cambodia', intended to provide an account of Sihanouk's life, presented chronologically. Osborne portrays Sihanouk's extraordinary political survival from his coronation by the colonial régime in 1941 until late 1993 as King of Cambodia for a second time. Osborne concludes that Sihanouk's greatest weakness has been that 'he has shown an inability to recognise that views and decisions other than his own were worthy of attention and that what he has cited as his positive achievements were often flawed or, worse, little more than fantasy'. It is a fascinating account, written in Osborne's inimitable fluid style that has general appeal and, while individual footnotes are not given, each chapter is followed by extensive notes with sources for most points of significance.

332 **Souverains et notabilités d'Indochine.** (Sovereigns and notables of Indochina.)
Paris: Editions du Gouvernement Général de l'Indochine, 1943. xix, 112p.

An attempt to produce a 'Who's Who' of Indochina from the perspective of the colonial administrators of the day. Each entry contains a photograph and brief biographical data. In line with the French policy of using Vietnamese people in the administration of Cambodia, most of the people listed are of Vietnamese origin. However, some Cambodians (and Laos), including members of the royal family, officials from the colonial administration and monks are covered. Among portraits of the region's sovereigns is a picture of a very young King Norodom Sihanouk.

333 **Stay alive, my son.**
Pin Yathay with John Man. New York: Free Press, 1987. xiii, 240p.

Before April 1975, Pin Yathay was a French-speaking engineer living in Phnom Penh. In the years following the Khmer Rouge victory he was one of the 'New People', forced to labour incessantly, and he suffered the loss of seventeen family members. He and his wife survived with their young son until they attempted to flee to Thailand. The book's title comes from Yathay and his wife's difficult decision to leave their sick child behind in a Khmer Rouge hospital when they fled. Along with harrowing personal recollections, the book includes observations about changes in the political climate, cadre leadership and living conditions, which contribute to the historical documentation of a nation's darkest years. This volume is an adaptation of *L'utopie meurtrière* (The murderous utopia) (Paris: R. Laffont, c.1980).

334 **The stones cry out: a Cambodian childhood 1975-1980.**
Molyda Szymusiak, translated by Linda Coverdale. London: Sphere, 1987. 307p. map. A translation of *Les pierres crieront*, Paris: La Découverte, 1984.

Molyda's story opens with the shelling of Phnom Penh, the day before it fell to the Khmer Rouge in 1975, when she was twelve years old. What follows is a harrowing account of her family's attempts to survive the Pol Pot years, experiences unfortunately typical for so many Cambodians during those dark years. With a gentle and even written style she recounts the exodus from her home, relocation near Battambang, back-breaking work, killings and torture, her own illness, the death of several family members, her perception of the Khmer Rouge organizational system and the changes it underwent, the eventual arrival of Vietnamese forces, and her eventual escape to Thailand and then migration to France. Of a family of eighteen persons, only she and three others survived. Tragically, in the early days of Khmer Rouge control, a young 'Sihanouk Khmer Rouge' soldier warned the family that the new régime would not look kindly upon their bourgeois background and volunteered to take them to the Vietnamese border, but they declined his offer.

335 **Surviving the killing fields: the Cambodian odyssey of Haing S. Ngor.**

With Roger Warner. London: Pan Books, 1989. 478p. Published in the United States under the title *A Cambodian odyssey,* New York: Macmillan, 1987; New York: Warner, 1989. First published in Great Britain, London: Chatto & Windus, 1988.

'I have been many things in life: a trader walking barefoot on paths through the jungles, a medical doctor, driving to his clinic in a shiny Mercedes, and in the past few years, to the surprise of many people, and above all to myself, I have been a Hollywood actor. But nothing has shaped my life as much as surviving the Pol Pot régime. I am a survivor of the Cambodian holocaust. That's who I am.' So Haing Ngor opens the story of his life and the terrible suffering he and his family endured. He lost both parents, and his wife and their unborn child died in his arms. He left Cambodia in 1979 and now lives in the United States, where he became best known as the actor who played Dith Pran in *The killing fields* (q.v.). Despite his criticism of the PRK government for its Vietnamese character, Ngor played a public role opposing the return of the Khmer Rouge, and its continued recognition as a valid participant in the Cambodian polity until his tragic death – he was shot outside his house in Los Angeles in 1996.

336 **The survivors, Kampuchea, 1984.**

Photographed by Prashant Panjiar, written by Arindam Sen Gupta. New Delhi: Patriot Publishers, on behalf of Indian Centre for Studies on Indo-China, 1984. 132p.

A passionate plea for recognition of the PRK, with striking photographs of Cambodia in the early days of reconstruction. The text tells the personal story of Men Saman, driven by the Khmer Rouge from Phnom Penh to Battambang and held with a thousand others in jail, but mercifully escaping execution, when Pol Pot was overthrown in 1979.

337 **To destroy you is no loss: the odyssey of a Cambodian family.**

JoAn D. Criddle and Teeda Butt Mam. New York: Atlantic Monthly Press, 1987. 289p. map.

The title of the book comes from a slogan used by the Khmer Rouge as part of their psychological tactics to control communities, 'To keep you is no benefit, to destroy you is no loss'. A harrowing record of life under the Khmer Rouge and early days of Vietnam's occupation, it is indeed an odyssey. Criddle writes as if Mam is telling her story in the first person. A story representative of the experience of tens or even hundreds of thousands of Cambodians it begins with the fall of Phnom Penh and ends with a 109-day trek to escape to Thailand. The final chapter tells of her and her family's new lives in the United States as self-affirming and life-affirming.

Explorers of South-East Asia: six lives.
See item no. 76.

War and hope: the case for Cambodia.
See item no. 308.

Kampuchean refugees 'between the tiger and the crocodile': international law and the overall scope of one refugee situation.
See item no. 363.

Collection of first-person accounts of the Cambodian genocide.
See item no. 486.

Khmer! Khmer!: Cambodia in conflict.
See item no. 930.

The killing fields.
See item no. 931.

The last God-King: the lives and times of Cambodia's Sihanouk.
See item no. 932.

Our children didn't come home.
See item no. 938.

Public enemy number one.
See item no. 943.

Borany's story [sound recording].
See item no. 963.

Cambodian witness [sound recording]: the autobiography of Someth May.
See item no. 964.

Stay alive my son [braille].
See item no. 969.

Surviving the killing fields [sound recording].
See item no. 970.

Population and Demography

338 **Cambodge: faits et problèmes de population.** (Cambodia: facts and problems of population.)
Jacques Migozzi. Paris: Éditions du Centre National de la Recherche Scientifique, 1973. 303p. bibliog. (Atlas Ethno-linguistique. 2. sér. Monographies).

In the old-fashioned style of population studies, Migozzi places a lot of emphasis on marriage customs in his survey of Cambodian population up to 1973. He does, however, provide very interesting background on the social and cultural context in which these activities take place, which is the main point of the study. The book is the result of research carried out during a long stay in Cambodia beginning in 1963 when Migozzi was teaching geography at the Faculty of Arts and Human Sciences in Phnom Penh. It includes extremely useful information on causes of mortality, emphasizing hygiene, malnutrition and malaria. It is sad to realize conditions have changed little even today, except for the recent tragic advent of HIV/AIDS. The statistical information is taken mainly from the 1960s, when more was collected than it is today. Nonetheless, like current demographers, Migozzi was somewhat limited by the lack of complete statistical data. Migozzi also investigates the qualitative elements of demography under the headings of history, economy and sociocultural factors. This is perhaps the most useful part of the book, which draws on Migozzi's doctoral studies at the Sorbonne under Professor Jean Delvert completed in 1967, and expanded and updated for this edition. Examined in the study are aspects of urbanization, Cambodia's ethnic minorities, the forms and processes of marriage, polygamous practices and concubinage, the influence of socio-economic changes on births and fertility rates, and factors contributing to mortality.

339 **Demographic materials on the Khmer Republic, Laos, and Vietnam.**
Compiled by Ng Shui Meng. Singapore: Institute of Southeast Asian Studies, 1974. viii, 54p. (Library Bulletin, no. 8).

The Institute of Southeast Asian Studies, established in Singapore in 1968 as a regional research centre for scholars concerned with modern Southeast Asia, particularly focused on the problems associated with modernization and social change. At the time of publication in 1974, few demographic studies of the region had been made. The author notes the difficulty of gathering information because of political turbulence, and the unreliability of official figures at a time when competing governments would like to show they have control over the majority of a population. This is rather a compilation of existing materials than a result of collecting primary data, and she selects those that give some explanation of general population patterns. The materials deal with demographic analysis, ethnography, geographical distribution, density and economic activities of the population, as well as various sources of statistics. The book includes mostly articles and monographs, official documents and previously unpublished sources, which are unannotated and presented under the categories: General; Demographic materials and analyses; Rural/urban population; and Refugees. The texts are predominantly English and French, with a few Vietnamese and Chinese items. Material from the French period and (then) more recent period is the most frequent, with a fair number on Cambodia. Ng continued her work with a synthesis of much of the material reported here, published as *The population of Indochina: some preliminary observations* (q.v.).

340 **Le génocide Khmer Rouge: une analyse démographique.** (The Khmer Rouge genocide: a demographic analysis.)
Marek Sliwinski. Paris: L'Harmattan, 1995. 175p. (Collection Recherches Asiatiques).

Polish psychologist Marek Sliwinski presents a demographic analysis of the Khmer Rouge period, with comparative data for preceding and succeeding periods. Details of family members alive in 1970, and subsequent births and deaths, were collected between 1989 and 1991 from three samples: a pilot study of 63 Cambodian families living in France; some 589 families in Site B camp in Thailand; and a survey of 1,296 people within 150 kilometres of Phnom Penh. His findings confirm the shocking statistics that almost a quarter of Cambodians died of unnatural causes between 1975 and 1979. Deaths are segmented by sex, age, occupation, religion, ethnic group, province of origin and education as well as by the time, place and manner in which they occurred. One might question whether the data from these samples can be extrapolated for the whole country, and it is likely to under-represent the rural population, but Sliwinski has attempted to relate his data to 1970 estimates of population distribution. Undoubtedly this small book will be a lightning rod for the continuing debate, but no matter what, it represents an important study for all seeking a greater understanding of what actually happened in Cambodia under the Khmer Rouge rule.

341 **Kampuchea: a country adrift.**
Ea Méng-Try. *Population and Development Review*, vol. 7, no. 2 (June 1981), p. 209-28.

Without the assistance of a population census since 1962, estimating the size of Cambodia's population and the extent of losses under the Khmer Rouge has been a task for demographic detectives. Ea Méng-Try estimates the 1979 population at 5 or 6 million, and compares this figure to a 1970 projection of 9.5 million for 1979 under normal circumstances. Deaths from violence would have numbered about 120,000, according to CIA estimates for 1975-77 and Méng-Try's estimates for 1978. The total loss of life is estimated to be between 1 and 1.2 million. Excessive mortality also occurred from: loss of food supply; evacuation and forced emigration; collectivization; and overwork and stress among women. In addition, excessive male mortality caused a dramatic decline in fertility. This is a serious attempt to estimate the demographic effects of the Khmer Rouge régime.

342 **Kampuchea: a demographic catastrophe: a research paper.**
National Foreign Assessment Center. Washington, DC: The Center, 1980. iii, 14p. bibliog. GC 80-10019U.

Research for this report was completed on 17 January 1980, and it was published in May 1980. One of the key documents in the debate about Cambodia's population and the extent of the Khmer Rouge killings, it was criticized sharply by Michael Vickery in his article, 'Democratic Kampuchea: CIA to the rescue', in the *Bulletin of Concerned Asian Scholars*, vol. 14, no. 4 (Oct.-Dec. 1982), p. 45-54, for simply repeating Barron and Paul's 1977 figures (q.v.). Vickery said that 'The purpose of this hasty CIA report is to put the pro-Vietnamese Heng Samrin regime in its worst possible light'. For further discussion on the demographic aspects of the debate on genocide, see also: Ben Kiernan, 'Orphans of genocide: the Cham Muslims of Kampuchea under Pol Pot', *Bulletin of Concerned Asian Scholars*, vol. 20, no. 4 (Oct.-Dec. 1988), p. 2-33; Michael Vickery, 'Comments on Cham population figures', *Bulletin of Concerned Asian Scholars*, vol. 22, no. 1 (Jan.-Mar. 1990), p. 31-33; and Judith Banister and E. Paige Johnson, 'After the nightmare: the population of Cambodia', in *Genocide and democracy in Cambodia: the Khmer Rouge, the U.N., and the international community* (q.v.).

343 **The population of Indochina: some preliminary observations.**
Ng Shui Meng. Singapore: Institute of Southeast Asian Studies, 1974. 126p. map. bibliog. (Field Report Series, no. 7).

Although severely out of date, this volume retains its usefulness as one of the few attempts to grapple seriously with the demography of Indochina, and so of Cambodia. The author carried out the research as the practical component of her MA in Sociology, of which this study is an outgrowth. She begins by noting the paucity of materials, with no official census having been carried out in either Laos or Vietnam, and with only one census in Cambodia, in 1962 which, while giving population counts for each province, lacked more refined data on the vital statistics of the population. Additional data has come from various United Nations and ECAFE sources and from the studies of French colonial geographers such as Gourou and Robequain. Some background is given of the geographical setting and the history of ancient kingdoms before more detailed summaries are attempted of the colonial and post-independence periods, showing population size, density, growth and distribution. Some comment is made on patterns of growth, age-sex structures and urbanization, as well as on the issue of refugees. It is estimated that fifteen to twenty per cent of the total population have fallen into the latter category at one time or another due to the wars.

344 **Prolific survivors: population change in Cambodia 1975-1993.** Jacqueline Desbarats. Tempe, Arizona: Arizona State University, Program for South East Asian Studies, 199?. 236p.

The recent history of war and devastation in Cambodia and the resulting emigration by hundreds of thousands of refugees has led to widespread images of a country deep in throes of economic and demographic stagnation. Recently, however, the country has been experiencing a social, economic and demographic resurgence. This book examines the current population situation and its recent evolution and sketches out the implications of salient demographic trends on the prospects for both social and economic change and development.

345 **Résultats préliminaires du recensement général de la population, 1962.** (Preliminary results of the general census of population, 1962.) [Phnom Penh: s.n., 1963]. [iv], 93p.

A vital primary source as the only census ever to be conducted in Cambodia, undertaken before the massive population upheavals of the 1970s. As well as having intrinsic value, it is a crucial piece of information for those trying to assess the extent of loss during those upheavals, and the proportion of the population involved.

Ethnic Groups and Physical Anthropology

346 **Anthropologie des Cambodgiens.** (Anthropology of Cambodians.) Georges Olivier, with the collaboration of Jean Moullec. Paris: École Française d'Extrême-Orient, 1968. 430p. maps. bibliog. (Publications Hors Série de l'École Française d'Extrême-Orient).

A revision of Olivier's 1965 Doctor of Science thesis, published as *Les populations du Cambodge* (The populations of Cambodia). Olivier later revealed a change of mind, not only as to his findings on Cambodia, but also 'on how one should study a population'. The volume still retains its physical anthropological approach, if no longer the now unpopular endeavour to establish racial characteristics and stereotypes, with detail of cranial measurements and photographs of 'typical' Khmers, Chams and other Cambodians. Moullec's contribution is to do the same kind of differential analysis of blood types.

347 **Au pays des superstitions et des rites: chez les möis et les chams.** (In the land of superstitions and rites: among the Möis and the Chams.) Commandant Baudesson, drawings by Paule and Mona Baudesson. Paris: Plon, 1932. 276p. maps. bibliog.

Commandant Baudesson, formerly of the Missions d'Études du Transindochinois (Study Missions of the Transindochina [railway project]) reports from his own observations and those of others on the teams. Details are given of each ethnic group's physical appearance, and their economic, social and intellectual life. Thirty-six photographs and four drawings provide valuable supplement to this documentation of these communities on the eve of their disruption by outside pressures.

348 **Bibliography of the peoples and cultures of mainland Southeast Asia.**

John Fee Embree, Lillian Ota Dotson. New Haven, Connecticut: Yale University, Southeast Asia Studies, 1950. 821p.

Because this volume has yet to be revised or superseded, it retains value as a reference survey of the materials published in Western languages up to 1950, particularly in the realms of anthropology, ethnology, religion, literature and language. Entries are arranged according to broad subject headings, with no index. This bibliography should be employed in combination with the later descriptive compendium, *Ethnic groups of mainland Southeast Asia* (q.v.). [David G. Marr with Kristine Alilunas-Rodgers]

349 **The Chinese in Cambodia.**

William E. Willmott. Vancouver: Publications Centre, University of British Columbia, 1967. xiv, 132p. bibliog.

As social disruption to the Chinese community in Cambodia was extreme under the Khmer Rouge, this 1967 study may serve to provide historians with a comparative source, and to be a record of memory for surviving members of the community. Willmott, an anthropologist from the University of British Columbia, is concerned with the nature of the Chinese community in its relation to Cambodian society. He spent a year in Cambodia, travelling to major centres of Chinese population and conducting statistical, historical and legal research on the community. Demographic features and the ethnic status, economic position, legal status, and social organization of the Chinese community are discussed, with much historical detail, as are emerging and merging élites in Cambodian society as a whole. Two appendices explain the process of estimating the size of the Chinese population and using the 1962 census for studying ethnicity.

350 **Ethnic groups of mainland Southeast Asia.**

Frank M. Lebar, Gerald C. Hickey and John K. Musgrave. New Haven, Connecticut: Human Relations Area Files, 1964. 288p. map.

Deals with the area from north Malaysia to southern Szechwan in latitude and in longitude from Tibetan-Burman-speaking Assam to Hainan Island and eastern Kwangsi in South China. The cultural summaries record synonyms for groups and language names; an index of variant spellings, locally restricted names etc., is also included. The study of each group is presented in segments on: orientation; settlement pattern and housing; economy; kin groups; sociopolitical organization; and religion. The Mon-Khmer are classed as Austroasiatic. The seven-page section on the Khmer was written by May Ebihara, and based on fieldwork in an unidentified village 30 kilometres southwest of Phnom Penh which she conducted in 1959 and 1960. She believes the study's findings to be largely applicable to Khmer peasant culture as it occurs over a large area. She also refers briefly to urbanization and Westernization. Topics discussed include the sexual division of labour, kinship terms, marriage traditions and regional bureaucratic structures, amongst many more classically anthropomorphological subjects. The work is useful mainly for comparative studies and to record past customs and behaviour, as so much has changed due to the tremendous social upheavals undergone by the Khmer peasants in the thirty-five years since the research was carried out. Small sections are also included on minority ethnic groups, described as upland groups related linguistically to the Chams. Inside the back cover are two colour fold-out maps showing distribution.

351 **L'hemoglobine E au Cambodge.** (Haemoglobin E in Cambodia.) Sok Heangsun. Paris: École Française d'Extrême-Orient, 1958. 76p. bibliog. (Publications Hors Série de l'École Française d'Extrême-Orient).

Although published nearly forty years ago, and bearing the somewhat dated spirit of racialist analysis and differentiation, this small publication presents a rare compendium of data on the blood types of various Cambodian peoples. On the basis of the presence of Haemoglobin E in the blood of Khmers, Chams and especially in the tribal minorities then termed 'Phnong' (savage), and its absence in the blood of Chinese, Vietnamese, Laotians and Malays in Cambodia, Heangsun believes he confirms Coedès's position that 'the Cambodian is a hinduized Phnong'.

352 **Minorities in Cambodia.** [London?]: Minority Rights Group, 1995. bibliog.

Published with support from CIDSE and other organizations and individuals, this is a most useful handbook updating information after the massive population devastations and shifts during the war and the Khmer Rouge periods. It contains chapters on: the Cham and the Vietnamese (both drafted by Baldas Goshal); indigenous 'hill tribes' and the Chinese (drafted by Jae H. Ku); and ethnic policies under the new Cambodian government. Containing a bibliography, glossary, conclusion, and recommendations, this is an essential tool for understanding modern Cambodia beyond that of the Khmers. The research for the report was carried out during 1992-93 by the International Centre for Ethnic Studies (a Sri Lankan non-governmental organization), under the overall supervision of its director, Radhika Coomaraswamy. The draft report was revised and updated by David Hawk.

353 **The political structure of the Chinese community in Cambodia.** W. E. Willmott. [London]: University of London, Athlone Press, 1970. viii, 211p. bibliog. (London School of Economics. Monographs on Social Anthropology, no. 42).

Based on research conducted in 1962-63, principally in Phnom Penh, this work concentrates on the internal political organization of the Chinese communities, rather than on an analysis of the relationship of the Chinese to the larger Cambodian community, which formed the subject of Willmott's *The Chinese in Cambodia* (q.v.). Interviews with 250 elderly men born in China complement demographic data on the major Chinese communities, and library and newspaper research. At that time the population of Phnom Penh was estimated to be one-third Chinese. Their relations with the Khmers was viewed as 'relatively cordial', ascribed by Willmott to the fact that the Chinese were concentrated in commerce, while Khmers and Vietnamese competed in the areas of rice-growing and fishing, overlaying historical hostility between the two nations. Willmott demonstrates that the Chinese were the middlemen even before the French colonized Cambodia, and that the French administration perpetuated this role as economic intermediary, with ethnic and class divisions coinciding. The community structure survived up until the Second World War, and returned in a weakened form to independent Cambodia, until officially phased out between 1954 and 1958, as Chinese born in Cambodia were entitled to assume Cambodian citizenship, had to pay taxes directly to the government, and as Cambodia developed relations with the People's Republic of China, while many of the old congregations had been Kuomintang-controlled. Willmott compares this system with the plethora of associations (economic, cultural, religious and political) usually found in overseas Chinese communities and in China itself, and he concludes his study with an analysis of their emergence in the new post-1958 situation, when there were five daily Chinese newspapers in Phnom Penh (until all private newspapers were closed in 1967), and fifty Chinese schools throughout the country.

354 **Les Samre ou Pear: population primitive de l'ouest du Cambodge.** (The Samre or Pear: primitive people of the west of Cambodia.) R. Baradat. [Hanoi: s.n., 1941?]. 148p. map. bibliog.

This is the classic source on the main cluster of non-Khmer population which is not considered as no longer part of the 'national minorities' (using the Russian style of denomination). These people are not noted nowadays, as every one of them would officially be called a Khmer. They lived on the periphery of the great plain, either in the Cardamon mountains or the forests north of the Tonle Sap Lake. The word Samre means 'the tattooed ones' and comes from the word *sre*, meaning ricefield, because the tattooes resemble their dams in the ricefields. The first Chinese travellers in southern Indochina mentioned the fact that the population was dark, tattooed and naked. Pear means 'colour' and refers to the supposed darkness of the skin. There have certainly been melanodermic populations in Southeast Asia in the very distant past, related to Melanesians and Australians, and probably also to Africans. Some photographs by Baradat show individuals who may exhibit this kind of ancestry. He scans the previous literature and describes religious rites, complete with trances, that one can see in any Khmer pagoda, with a little bit of luck. Interestingly, the regions inhabited by these 'savages' or 'primitives', as the colonial parlance would have it, formed the main fortresses of Pol Potist influence after they were driven from the plain by the Vietnamese army in 1979, and they remain so even today.

355 **Un village en forêt: l'essartage chez les Brou du Cambodge.** (A village in the forest: shifting cultivation among the Brus.) Jacqueline Matras-Troubetzkoy, preface by Georges Condominas. Paris: SELAF, 1983. 429p. bibliog. (Langues et Civilisations de l'Asie du Sud-Est et du Monde Insulindien, ASEMI, no. 7).

The author lived among the Bru people in this montagnard village in the then newly established province of Ratanakiri, recording one full cycle of shifting cultivation from February to December 1967. The book was not completed until 1975, and then not published for a further eight years, but it retains its significance as one of the few in-depth studies of this fast disappearing mode of agriculture.

The Vietnamisation of Cambodia.
See item no. 306.

La thalassémie au Cambodge. (Thalasemy in Cambodia.)
See item no. 449.

Vietnam's war in Cambodia: historical experience, settler politics, and prospects for the future.
See item no. 565.

Florilege jörai. (Jorai anthology of verse.)
See item no. 729.

Ethnologue Database: Cambodia.
See item no. 985.

Overseas Populations and Refugees

356 **An annotated bibliography of Cambodia and Cambodian refugees.**
Compiled by John Marston. Minneapolis, Minnesota: Southeast Asian Refugee Studies Project, Center for Urban and Regional Affairs, University of Minnesota, 1987. 121p. (Southeast Asian Refugee Studies Occasional Papers, no. 5).

This bibliography was compiled as a reference tool for people working with Cambodian refugees in the United States. It includes 578 entries, all in English, based on the collection of the University of Minnesota library system and the Southeast Asian Refugee Studies Project, and was compiled during 1984-85, although not published until 1987. A single listing is given for each item, in one of seventeen broad subject categories, but a subject index gives multiple access points. Call numbers are given for those items held in the University of Minnesota. The selection of items and the annotations provided reveal the background knowledge of the author, who is himself a scholar of Cambodian politics and language.

357 **Bamboo & butterflies: from refugee to citizen.**
JoAn D. Criddle. Dixon, California: East/West Bridge Publishing House, 1992. 2nd ed. 220p.

An extended family's story of migration from refugee camps in Thailand and from Cambodia to the United States told through interviews with, and first-hand accounts of, different members of the family of Teeda Mam in a sequel to the book, *To destroy you is no loss: the odyssey of a Cambodian family* (q.v.). This is a North American success story but does not gloss over all the difficulties of cultural alienation, generational differences and intercultural communication. The book also offers some insight into various aspects of Cambodian culture and the scars left by the Khmer Rouge experience.

358 **Beyond the killing fields.**

Photographs by Kari René Hall; text by Josh Getlin, Kari René Hall; edited by Marshall Lumsden. New York: Aperture in association with California State University, Long Beach and Asia 2000 Ltd., Hong Kong, 1992. 216p.

Site 2 (refugee camp) in Thailand with some 200,000 residents was, until the repatriation of the refugees in 1992-93, the largest Cambodian city in the world outside of Phnom Penh. In early 1988 Kari René Hall took the magnificent photographs that make this heart-wrenchingly beautiful record of the broken lives and bodies of the people trapped there, many having lived their whole lives within that barbed wire fence, relying on the daily shipment of food, water and medicines from the United Nations. The war haunted the place daily, as shells fell nearby and sometimes within the camp, and as soldiers slipped away to join the opposition armies fighting the Cambodian government – sometimes under pressure, sometimes from conviction, but often just to escape from the boredom of living in a cage. Getlin and Hall's text reveals the stories that lie behind the images on the page – the ambitions and dreams for tomorrow as well as the frustrations of today and the nightmares of yesterday.

359 **Cambodian humanitarian assistance and the United Nations (1979-1991).**

Bangkok: OSRSG United Nations, 1992. 106p.

The disjunction between the rather grand sounding title and the topics actually covered in this book parallel the disjunction in reality between the enormous humanitarian needs of the country called Cambodia and the UN decision to deny recognition to its government, and to restrict its humanitarian assistance almost entirely to the 350,000 refugees on the Thai border rather than to the 7 million people inside the country itself. Nevertheless, this publication does provide a record of the work of the various UN agencies, and also makes reference to the work of many NGOs both within and outside Cambodia. The appendix contains tables listing the status of contributions of United Nations member countries as at 31 December 1991. Perhaps the most interesting part of the volume are the profiles written by refugees who, after surviving the killing fields, found themselves in another 'detention' in Thailand. Striking photographs by Timothy Carney and Michael Flamm are included.

360 **Community profiles, 1991 census, Cambodia born.**

Bureau of Immigration and Population Research. Canberra: Australian Government Publishing Service, 1995. 49p. bibliog. AGPS Cat. no. 94 21568. (Community Profiles/ Bureau of Immigration and Population Research).

An extremely valuable close examination of the 17,555 people recorded in the 1991 Australian census as being 'Cambodia-born', and some brief data on the 4,053 people recorded as being born in Australia, with one or both parents born in Cambodia. Chiefly containing tables, the book gives details of this community as to: geographic distribution (43.3 per cent in Sydney and 37.3 per cent in Melbourne), age (median 30.0), sex (50.1 per cent male), family composition (84.5 per cent with offspring, 15.2 per cent with only one parent, 3.3 per cent of persons living in single-person households, 25.7 per cent as adult couples involving a non-Cambodian partner), year of arrival in Australia (95.7 per cent since 1975), citizenship (79 per cent Australian), education (17.2 per cent with no schooling at all, compared to 0.9 per cent for the Australian population overall), employment (39.6 per cent unemployed – three times the Australian rate), languages spoken (2.4 per cent speaking English at home, and a further 49.8 per cent reporting that they spoke English well, compared to 21.8 per cent and 58.3 per cent for the wider Non-English Speaking communities in Australia) and religion (59.9 per cent Buddhist, 5 per cent Baptist and 4.2 per cent Catholic). Sixteen tables and twenty figures were prepared by the Bureau of Immigration and Population Research, to amplify a text written by James Coughlan of James Cook University.

361 **Displaced lives: stories of life and culture from the Khmer in Site 2, Thailand.**

[Bangkok?]: International Refugee Committee, [198?].

This book deals with life and social structure in Site 2, the biggest of the six camps for displaced persons along the Thai-Cambodian border in the 1980s. The focus is on story-telling and the transmission of traditional cultural values through it. Folk-tales and stories and individual reflections on life both before, and during, the Site 2 experience are included. They were recorded through oral history interviews and edited minimally so as to retain the differences in language as well as outlook. Stories are presented in both English and Khmer.

362 **Kampuchea, balance of survival.**

Timothy Carney. Bangkok: Distributed in Asia by DD Books, 1983. rev. ed. 104p. map. Originally published, 1981.

The book does not make clear who the publisher is, and it includes a note stating: 'Neither the photographs nor the text should be taken as United States government policy or analysis. Profits are for Khmer relief'. Taken while working for the United States Embassy along the Thai-Cambodian border and on trips to Phnom Penh between May 1979 and December 1981, Carney's black-and-white photographs show his perspective on the refugee crisis, and on the situation in Phnom Penh, and his introduction and commentary convey his strong opposition to the Vietnamese presence in Cambodia and to the new government in Phnom Penh. He divides the refugees into two categories: those peasants and city dwellers who fell under the Khmer Rouge régime's harsh control when it took power in 1975; and the peasants, troops and cadres who still believed in the 'Khmer Rouge vision of Cambodia's future' or who were subject to the discipline of that régime. Carney captured some graphic shots of refugees, their exodus, their daily lives and the international aid effort. Other interesting pictures include a traditional New Year celebration at the Khmer Rouge-controlled Kamput camp along with a commentary on the tension created by the return of Buddhism to the Khmer Rouge-controlled holding centres. The work includes a chronology of events from January 1979 to February 1981.

363 **Kampuchean refugees 'between the tiger and the crocodile': international law and the overall scope of one refugee situation.**

Hanne Sophie Greve. [New York]: Hanne Sophie Greve, [198?]. 2 vols. (687p.) maps. bibliog.

Deals with the situation of Cambodian refugees in Thailand. The title of the book refers to a Cambodian proverb meaning being on the horns of a dilemma, usually applied to the destiny of Cambodia between Thailand and Vietnam.

364 **Khmer culture in the Mekong Delta.**
Dinh Van Lien, Thach Voi (et al.). *Vietnamese Studies*, no. 97 (1990), p. 7-85.

Nine authors, mostly of Vietnamese origin, offer brief essays on the origins of the 800,000 Khmer residents in southern Vietnam, and their folk literature, plastic arts, pagoda decorations, theatre, Buddhist calendar, and New Year's festival. While several contributors are anxious to assert that Khmers in Vietnam are different from those in adjacent Cambodia, due to separate historical experiences, other writers simply offer ethnographic descriptions. [David G. Marr with Kristine Alilunas-Rodgers]

365 **Khmer Rouge abuses along the Thai-Cambodian border.**
Asia Watch Committee. [Washington, DC]: Asia Watch Committee, 1989. 42p. bibliog. (Asia Watch Report).

A consultant's report by Mary Kay Magistad, with the assistance of David Hawk, based on interviews with refugees and various officials in November 1988. Between June and November 1988 the Khmer Rouge attempted to move up to 15,000 Cambodian refugees from camps under their control in Thailand to combat zones close to, or inside, Cambodia in order to prepare for military operations against the PRK as Vietnamese troops withdrew from the country. Based largely on interviews with refugees on the border, the work summarizes what is known of these forced removals and of ongoing human rights abuses within the Khmer Rouge-controlled camps.

366 **Political pawns: refugees on the Thai-Kampuchean border.**
Josephine Reynell. Oxford: Refugee Studies Programme, 1989. xi, 201p. maps. bibliog. (An RSP Study).

Originally conducted for the World Food Programme, this is a detailed case-study of socio-economic life in three of the eight refugee camps on the Thai-Cambodian border that received assistance from the United Nations Border Relief Operation. Material was gathered during visits to the camps – Site 2, Greenhill, and Site 8 – in 1986. Reynell provides valuable information for those interested in refugee issues and those who wish to understand the process by which the camps and their inhabitants came to be used as political pawns in international politics. A most useful bibliography of material published by Cambodians in the camps is included.

367 **The quality of mercy: Cambodia, holocaust, and modern conscience.**
William Shawcross. New York: Simon & Schuster, 1984. 464p. map. bibliog.

William Shawcross is best known for his book *Sideshow: Kissinger, Nixon and the destruction of Cambodia* (q.v.). This is his account of the international relief effort that followed the 1979 overthrow of Pol Pot by the Vietnamese army and its Cambodian counterparts. The main part of the relief effort terminated in 1981 as a political protest against the continuing Vietnamese presence in Cambodia. Opening with a recollection of his father's account of the Jewish holocaust, Shawcross endeavours to scrutinize the role of conscience in international affairs, and the way compassion can be subverted for political gains. Shawcross himself mixes compassion with a distinct anti-Vietnamese and anti-communist attitude, in his sharp criticism of the Cambodian government and his focus on the many 'border relief' efforts that – while they may often have reflected humanitarian intentions – unquestionably helped to rejuvenate the defeated Khmer Rouge. Yet the book is a valuable account of the international mission that addressed one part of the Cambodian famine that emerged in Pol Pot's wake, recording especially the work of UNICEF and the ICRC.

368 **Refugee Abstracts.**
Geneva: International Refugee Resource Centre, 1982-December 1984; Refugee Documentation Centre (UN), March 1985-December 1986; Centre for Documentation on Refugees (UN), 1987-93. quarterly.

Publishes abstracts summarizing literature on refugees in various parts of the world. The abstracts are in English or French.

369 **Rice, rivalry, and politics: managing Cambodian relief.**
Linda Mason and Roger Brown, with a foreword by Rudy von Bernuth. Notre Dame, [Indiana]: University of Notre Dame Press, 1983. xv, 218p. map. bibliog.

A discussion of the madness that permeated the camps along the Thai-Cambodian border, where refugees from the Khmer Rouge and people herded across the border by the Khmer Rouge mingled with Khmer Rouge officials and soldiers who used them as bargaining chips in their (successful) claims still to be in control of enough people and territory to justify retaining Cambodia's seat in the United Nations and access to international assistance. The role played by various governments and NGOs in this sorry tale is recorded.

370 **Voices, stories, hopes: Cambodia and Vietnam: refugees and volunteers.**
Members and friends of the Jesuit Refugee Service, edited by Adrian Lyons. Melbourne: Collins Dove, 1993. xiii, 173p.

Reports what it was like for the Cambodians and Vietnamese who were compelled to leave their countries following years of conflict. The stories were gathered between 1980 and 1992 and compiled by members and friends of the Jesuit Refugee Service, a well-reputed NGO which has been working in the region for many years and continues to do so. Refugee workers supplement the personal stories with their own tributes to the courage of refugees they have known, and brief essays about broader social aspects of beginning life in a new country such as: counselling victims of violence; why people flee; and Australian lawyers in Hong Kong camps. The stories and essays are grouped by theme: voices from Cambodia; from the Khmer camps; the Vietnamese at sea; from the Vietnamese camps; and voices of refugee workers. This book is both touching and informative, presenting both the human side to the figures and news items, and an outline of the legal, political and social context of the stories.

Indochina's refugees: oral histories from Laos, Cambodia and Vietnam.
See item no. 321.

From rice truck to paddy field: a study of the repatriation and reintegration needs of vulnerable female heads of household and other vulnerable individuals living in the Cambodia refugee and di[s]placed persons camps along the Thai-Cambodian border.
See item no. 428.

Hope for a new life: Cambodia special report.
See item no. 430.

Cambodia: doughnut dreams.
See item no. 915.

House of the spirit: perspectives on Cambodian health care.
See item no. 928.

Which way home.
See item no. 954.

Languages and Linguistics, Dictionaries and Grammars

371 **American national standard system for the romanization of Lao, Khmer, and Pali: approved July 18, 1978.**
American National Standards Institute, Inc. and Secretariat, Council of National Library and Information Associations. New York: American National Standards Institute, 1979. 14p. Prepared jointly with the Orientalia Processing Committee of the Library of Congress. (ANSI, Z39.35-1979).

Although difficult to comprehend, for English and Khmer speakers alike, this standard has formed the basis for most transliterations into roman script of Cambodian materials as they have been catalogued in Western libraries. Its difficulty stems from the fact that it was designed to permit reverse transliteration (conversion back into Khmer script) and therefore each of the thirty-three consonants and twenty-three vowels had to be uniquely identified, clearly impossible within the twenty-six letters of the English alphabet, necessitating the use of unfamiliar combinations and diacritic signs.

372 **Bibliography and index of mainland Southeast Asian languages and linguistics.**
Franklin E. Huffman. New Haven, Connecticut; London: Yale University Press, 1986. 640p. (Yale Language Series).

This is an attempted exhaustive listing of 'anything ever written in any language about any language of Mainland South East Asia'. While including some relevant items from the previous bibliographies, its main purpose is to list items which appeared after *Bibliographies of Mon-Khmer and Tai linguistics* (1963) and *Bibliography of Sino-Tibetan languages* (1957 and 1963). Huffman expands his coverage to five fairly accepted divisions: Austroasiatic (including Khmer); Tibeto-Burman; Tai-Kadai; Miao-Yao; and Mainland Austronesian (including Chamic). It excludes Sino-Tibetan and Malay. The items listed (some of which are unpublished) are monographs, articles, theses, dissertations, conference papers, including pedagogical materials, epigraphical studies, translated texts, and, for rare languages, ethnographic and demographic information. The works are listed alphabetically by author. The approximately 10,000 entries are also indexed by language and subject, forming a *de-facto* compendium of 2,500 to 3,000 language and dialect names.

373 **Cahiers d'Études Franco-Cambodgiens.** (Franco-Cambodian Studies.)
[Phnom Penh]: Centre Culturel et de Coopération Linguistique, Service de l'Ambassade de France, 1993- . irregular.

Published to disseminate papers fom meetings held in conjunction with Cambodian-French co-operation, especially those from the Khmer-French Centre of Linguistics at the University of Phnom Penh. All of the publications are in French. Issue number one (1993) is an introduction to a grammar for Cambodia by Sylvain Vogel and Michel Igout; number two (1993) contains studies of toponymy in ancient Khmer by Long Seam; number three (1994) has an examination of linguistics by Vogel and de Bernon; and number four (1995) is an introduction to a study of Old Khmer by Savaros Pou and Sylvain Vogel.

374 **The Cambodian alphabet: how to write the Khmer language.**
Derek Tonkin, edited by Chau Seng. Bangkok: Trasvin Publications, 1991. 62, [5]p. Originally published as *Modern Cambodian writing*, Phnom Penh, 1962.

A small textbook in a handy format enjoying a comeback in its reprint edition. Whilst warning that his presentation of the genius of the Cambodian writing system may appear dogmatic, his book is simple and approachable. Seeing writing as the key to mastering Khmer language, Tonkin provides a brief background and general remarks about the alphabet before introducing the various parts of writing. Usefully, specimens of differing styles and format of Cambodian printing and handwriting are included, although unfortunately the type font used throughout the book is small and rather difficult for beginners to identify and copy.

375 **Cambodian linguistics, literature and history: collected articles.**
Judith M. Jacob, edited by David Smyth. London: School of Oriental and African Studies, 1993. [viii, 318]p.

A collection of articles – twelve on linguistics, four on literature and two on history – penned by Jacob, a foremost British authority on Cambodia, and published between 1960 and 1992. In 1952 Jacob established the School of Oriental and African Studies programme in Cambodian language and literature, still the only full lectureship on Cambodian in a British university, a post she held until her retirement in 1988. Many people, including Franklin Huffman (q.v.) who introduces this volume, have been among her students, and her textbooks and dictionaries (q.v.) are widely known. Her considered views on matters linguistic, literary and historical have not been so accessible, published as they were in a range of international journals and books over more than thirty years, so it is timely to have them brought together as a testimony to her work and as a tool for further study and research.

376 **Cambodian literary reader and glossary.**

Franklin E. Huffman and Im Proum. New Haven, Connecticut: Yale University Press, 1977. vi, 325, 152p. bibliog. (Yale Linguistic Series).

The third and final volume of Cambodian readers in the 'Yale Linguistic Series' (qq.v.), this work can be used by advanced readers of Khmer without the preceding volumes as it includes a cumulative glossary. It consists of thirty-two extracts from the main genres of Cambodian literature, spanning thirteen centuries. Despite the tendency of Cambodian literature to integrate apparently disparate genres, the authors have arranged the texts into sections: political criticism; the modern novel; historical prose; miscellaneous short poems and songs; didactic literature; romantic epic; mythological epic; religious epic; and Ream-Kei (Ramayana). The English introduction briefly provides a context for the works included, additional to the preface and glossary accompanying each extract, which are all in Khmer. Part two is a Khmer-English glossary which sometimes gives a phonetic representation as well as translation.

377 **Cambodian system of writing and beginning reader with drills and glossary.**

Franklin E. Huffman, with the assistance of Chhom-Rak Thong Lambert and Im Proum. New Haven, Connecticut: Yale University Press, 1970. xii, 365p. bibliog. Added title in Cambodian. (Yale Linguistic Series).

Huffman presents this work on the Cambodian writing system and grammar followed by short written pieces moving from simple accounts of daily life and customs to more formal reports of government and religion. Estimated to require seventy-five classroom hours, although students may require considerably more, the course is recommended to be taken in conjunction with *Modern spoken Cambodian* (q.v.), and only to be commenced after a basic familiarity has been achieved with the spoken language.

378 **Cambodian-English dictionary.**

Robert K. Headley, Jr., Kylin Chor, Lang Khem Lim, Lim Hak Kheang and Chen Chun. Washington, DC: Catholic University of American Press, 1977. 2 vols. (xxvii, 1,495p.). bibliog. (Publications in the Languages of Asia, no. 3).

Probably the most authoritative, and definitely the most comprehensive, English-Khmer dictionary, this was produced by a team of four Cambodians (Kylin Chor, Lang Khem Lim, Lim Hak Kheang and Chen Chun) and one American scholar, Robert Headley. Prepared for English speakers, it gives a transliterated form according to a chart in the introduction, which also contains a brief explanation of the Khmer language, together with a select bibliography. Although some twenty years out of date, it is still widely used, and circulates freely in the Phnom Penh markets in a good photocopied reproduction.

379 **Cambodian-English, English-Cambodian dictionary.**
Kem Sos, Lim Hak Kheang, Madeline E. Ehrman. New York: Hippocrene Books, 1990. 355p. Parallel title in Cambodian.

The glossary of words utilized in the 1995 US State Department's *Contemporary Cambodian* course by the same authors (q.v.) forms this dictionary of 7,500 entries. It is for those adept in both English and Khmer scripts, as it uses no transliteration. Some usage is indicated, such as whether a word is informal, used to refer to animals or people, etc. While useful, it has been rather thoughtlessly arranged and packaged, and comes without an introduction of any depth. In fact the book is the facsimile reprint of the glossary, and its one-page introduction referring to the seven modules is quite meaningless in the context of the dictionary.

380 **Colloquial Cambodian: a complete language course.**
David Smyth. London: Routledge, 1995. 241p. Two accompanying cassettes available for separate purchase. (Colloquial Series).

A twenty-lesson introduction to the basics of spoken Cambodian and to the script. A very clear and easy-to-follow course for those who wish to learn to speak basic Cambodian. The book and accompanying cassettes are designed also to allow the student the choice to learn to read and write the language. The tapes are very clear and dialogue is spoken at a sensible pace. Translations are provided in easy-to-follow phonetics as well as very legible Khmer script. For those English speakers not used to international phonetics, who may find Franklin Huffman's system (q.v.) frustratingly difficult, this course may provide an easier approach to the problem of learning Cambodian.

381 **A concise Cambodian-English dictionary.**
Judith M. Jacob. London; New York: Oxford University Press, 1974. xxxiv, 242p.

A most useful dictionary for students who may not be able to afford, and may be intimidated by, weightier tomes.

382 **Contemporary Cambodian.**
Kem Sos, Madeline E. Ehrman, Lim Hak Kheang. Washington, DC: Foreign Service Institute, Department of State, for sale by the Superintendent of Documents, US Government Printing Office, 1974-75. 7 vols. (Foreign Service Institute Basic Course Series). Prepared and published with the support of the Defense Language Institute, Department of the Army. Political institutions joint project of Foreign Service Institute and Defense Language Institute. Item 872-A. S/N 4400-01527.

A seven-volume collection intended to enable a student to learn Cambodian according to their field of interest or profession. These topic-oriented modules are: the land and economy; the political institutions; the social institutions; and the individual in society. They are supported by three fundamental volumes (Glossary, Introductory lessons and a Grammatical sketch) which act as a companion to the four modules or as a brief description of the Khmer language. The collection was produced with the support of the Defense Language Institute, US Department of the Army. It uses both

Khmer script and transliteration, which, although appearing simpler, is not of the same standard as the phonetic system used in Jacob's *Introduction to Cambodian* (q.v.) or later, more user-friendly publications.

383 **Dictionnaire cambodgien-français.** (Cambodian-French dictionary.)
Joseph Guesdon. Paris: Plon, 1930. 2 vols. At head of title: Ministère de l'Instruction Publique et des Beaux-Arts, Commission Archéologique de l'Indochine.

Although now over sixty-five years old, and clearly lacking a huge number of contemporary terms, this dictionary continues to be consulted because of its thoroughness (containing over 20,000 words) and scholarly treatment. The author, Abbot Joseph Guesdon, is noted for his design of Khmer type and for having published a number of literary texts, as well as for his missionary works.

384 **Dictionnaire vieux khmer-français-anglais.** (Old Khmer-French-English dictionary.)
Saveros Pou. Paris: Centre de Documentation et de Recherche sur la Civilisation Khmère, 1992. xxv, 555p. Title also appears in Old Khmer. (Bibliothèque Khmère. Série B, Travaux et Recherches, v. 3).

This is a remarkable achievement. Saveros Pou has scanned inscriptions to collect the words used on stones (7th-13th century) and attempts to elucidate their meaning. Others have also ventured onto this ground, for example Bernard Philippe Groslier had such a dictionary in his unpublished papers; and Long Seam, a remarkable Cambodian linguist, has deposited a 2,000-page Old Khmer-French-Russian dictionary at the Library of the Academy of Sciences in Moscow where he worked for many years, and which should be published in the near future. However, so far Pou's monumental work is the only one on the market, and it is extremely useful.

385 **English-Khmer dictionary.**
Franklin E. Huffman and Im Proum. New Haven, Connecticut: Yale University Press, 1978. xix, 690p. bibliog. Parallel title in Khmer script. (Yale Language Series).

The authoritative English-Khmer dictionary to serve as a counterpart to the Headley *Cambodian-English dictionary* (q.v.). It circulates widely inside Cambodia in a photocopied edition.

386 **English-Khmer phrase book.**
Prepared by Robert K. Headley, Jr. and Kassie S. Neou for Field Operations Division, Office of General Services, United Nations. New York: United Nations, 1991. 126p.

Produced for the vast majority of the 22,000 UNTAC soldiers and officials who were not Khmer speakers, this useful book is still circulating in Cambodia, sold at a reasonable price in the markets in a photocopied edition. The authors are both well known, with Robert Headley, an American scholar, having written one of the authoritative Cambodian-English dictionaries (q.v.), and Kassie S. Neou active in the human rights area in Cambodia, after living for some years in the United States. The romanization system they have chosen to use is quite distinct from international phonetics and also from the Huffman system, which is more widespread in Cambodia. The major part of the book is 'Words and phrases', listed under topics such as: useful phrases; going places and getting around; communications – making a phone call; and work – hiring an employee. Brief grammar notes, a phonetic key, an index to English words and a list of the Khmer alphabet give some support to the lists, together with two schematic UN maps of the country's provinces and of Phnom Penh city. The book's chief advantage is that, unlike most of the language-learning books written before 1970, it uses contemporary words and situations, with video recorders, telephones and air transport taken for granted.

387 **Intermediate Cambodian reader.**
Edited by Franklin E. Huffman, with the assistance of Im Proum. New Haven, Connecticut: Yale University Press, 1972. viii, 502p. bibliog. Added title in Cambodian. (Yale Linguistic Series).

The second in the Huffman series of three Cambodian readers, taking the student from short passages into a variety of different reading experiences.

388 **Introduction to Cambodian.**
Judith M. Jacob. Oxford: Oxford University Press, 1990. xii, 341p. bibliog.

Eminently reputed, Judith Jacob was formerly Senior Lecturer in Cambodian at the School of Oriental and African Studies at the University of London. This book was mostly prepared in Cambodia during 1965, and initially made up a course curriculum. It is a thorough, if older-style textbook, designed for use with a Cambodian teacher, or with tapes for solo study, and arranged so that the course can be followed entirely in transcription or with exercises in Khmer script. It introduces the student to both spoken and written language format and vocabulary. The phonetic transcription and analysis of syllable structure are based on those devised by Professor E. Henderson. Native speakers also aided Jacob with some of the exercises and fidelity. An index gives the locations in the exercises of various grammatical features. A concise transliterated Cambodian-English and English-Cambodian dictionary is also included.

389 **Khmer-English pocket dictionary = Vacanukrom haopae.**
Preap Sok. Phnom Penh: [s.n.], 1973. 614p.

Although over twenty years old, this dictionary is still sold widely in photocopied form in Cambodia. Although the typeface is not terribly clear, it is in a convenient small format, listing 'the 10,000 most frequently used words'. It is intended principally for Khmer readers, and gives the Khmer pronunciation of the English words.

390 **Language reform in Democratic Kampuchea.**
John Marston. MA thesis, University of Minnesota, Minneapolis, Minnesota, 1985. 59p.+ appendices.

In this study Marston documents some key changes in vocabulary introduced by the Khmer Rouge. In particular he highlights the flattening of hierarchy as revealed in the elimination of the complexity in Khmer language, especially the range of status-oriented pronouns and alternative verbs, exemplified by 'to eat', which was reduced from the eleven forms listed by Headley (q.v.) to one simple form (*hoop*). Although based on only seven informants, all of whom were 'new people' originating from the urban areas, and all of whom had left Cambodia as refugees and were then settled in the United States, the findings are helpful in understanding the social dynamics of the Khmer Rouge period from a perspective that is all too seldom examined and recorded.

391 **Lectures cambodgiennes.** (Cambodian readings.)
Saveros Pou. Paris: Cedoreck, 1991. rev. ed. 109p. Originally published, Paris: Maisonneuve, 1968.

Twenty-five passages in modern Cambodian progress from simple words and letters to extended dialogue and prose. A single glossary organized in the order of the Cambodian alphabet, provides French translations. The typography is clear and sharp and it is sturdily bound. This volume is a valuable reprint from Cedoreck of material developed by the noted Cambodian linguist, Saveros Pou, for teaching in 1967. The intention is gradually to introduce the student to various aspects of Cambodian pronunciation and syntax, thereby developing not only the ability to comprehend texts, but also to acquire a sufficient base vocabulary for further study.

392 **A lexicon of Khmer morphology.**
Philip N. Jenner, Saveros Pou, edited by Philip N. Jenner. [Honolulu, Hawaii]: University Press of Hawaii, 1982. lxiv, 524p. bibliog. (Mon-Khmer Studies, no. IX-X).

Although published as a special double issue of the journal *Mon-Khmer Studies: a Journal of Southeast Asian Languages* (q.v.), this work is substantial enough to deserve a separate entry in this bibliography. The authors see their work as 'a first attempt to organize the native lexicon of Khmer into derivational sets . . . which should have historical and comparative as well as synchronic relevance'. It contains 5,645 items (1,702 wordbases and 3,943 derivatives, generally formed through the addition of affixes to the wordbase). The work comprises a 50-page introduction, followed by nearly 450 pages of the lexicon itself (with words shown in the Khmer script and the transliterated form as well as in English translation). It includes a bibliography and indexes of Thai forms, Old and Middle Khmer forms, and Modern Khmer forms.

393 **Modern spoken Cambodian.**
Franklin E. Huffman, with the assistance of Charan Promchan and Chhom-Rak Thong Lambert. New Haven, Connecticut: Yale University Press, 1970. xiv, 451p. Added title in Cambodian. (Yale Linguistic Series). Also available accompanied by 14 audio cassettes, [Ithaca, New York]: Spoken Language Services, [1970]. Reprinted, Ithaca, New York: Cornell University, 1984 and 1987.

Although produced twenty-five years ago, this book and its accompanying set of tapes remains one of the best available introductory paths for English speakers into the complexities of speaking and understanding the Cambodian language. Huffman guides the student through thirty-one lessons involving dialogue, grammar and drills, comprehension and conversation, estimated to require 225 classroom hours. Beginning with daily situations, the coverage moves on to more complex topics such as agriculture, industry, and government which obviously suffer more from being outdated. The course is based on the 'audio-oral' method of language teaching developed at Yale University, which retains copyright, and adopted at Cornell University, which reprinted the work in 1984 and again in 1987, though cheap reprints of the original abound in the markets and bookshops in Phnom Penh. Huffman acknowledges the roles played by Chanan Promchan, Chhom-Rak Thong Lambert, and Im Proum, whose voice features on the accompanying tapes. While Huffman's transliteration system is relatively easy to grasp, and certainly preserves most of the distinguishing sounds of spoken Cambodian, it is idiosyncratic, according neither to standard international phonetic symbols nor to normal English pronunciation.

394 **Mon-Khmer Studies: a Journal of Southeast Asian Languages.**
Nakhorn Pathom, Thailand: Summer Institute of Linguistics and Mahidol University, 1964- . bibliog.

The first issue appeared in 1964 as a publication of the Linguistic Circle of Saigon with joint sponsorship from the Summer Institute of Linguistics, which had helped found the Circle in 1959. Its initial emphasis was on languages in Vietnam, but it later extended its focus to cover Southeast Asian languages as a whole, especially those of the Mon-Khmer family. Amazingly enough, the publication has survived through all the vicissitudes of war and changes of régime. From 1964 to 1969 it was published in Saigon; a single issue appeared from Southern Illinois University in 1973; another single issue was produced in 1976 by SIL in Manila; from 1977 the title was published by the University of Hawaii; and in 1992 the journal moved to Mahidol University in Thailand. The current editorial board is complemented by an extensive international list of Consulting Editors.

395 **The new Oxford picture dictionary.**
E. C. Parnwell, translated by Im and Sivone Proum, illustrations by Ray Burns. Oxford: Oxford University Press, 1991. 152p. maps. Includes index. English and Cambodian text.

This English-Cambodian edition is useful for beginners in both languages, and especially for Cambodian children in English-speaking countries.

396 **Recherches sur le vocabulaire des inscriptions sanscrites du Cambodge.** (Research on the vocabulary of Sanskrit inscriptions in Cambodia.)
Kamaleswar Bhattacharya. Paris: École Française d'Extrême-Orient, 1991. 89p. bibliog. (Publications de l'École Française d'Extrême-Orient, no. 167).

Bhattacharya is the authority on Sanskrit as used in ancient Cambodia, and in this study he discusses the vocabulary from the only surviving sources – the inscriptions.

397 **Selected bibliography on Cambodia in Western languages: (August 1981), and, First supplement (November 1984).**
Franklin E. Huffman. Ithaca, New York: Distributed by Southeast Asia Program, 1985. rev. ed. 29p.

Both the first text and the supplement are divided into two parts, covering widely available and more specialized material. The first text contains a general bibliography (p. 1-17), which lists around 140 titles readily available in large public libraries, and a selected bibliography on language and literature (p. 18-22), containing around 45 items of more specialized research material. The entries are not annotated. They include journals, dictionaries, theses and art books. The supplement, compiled in November 1984 (p. 23-29), contains a further 99 items encompassing both general, and language and literature themes.

398 **La toponymie khmère.** (Khmer toponomy.)
Saveros Lewitz (Pou). *Bulletin de l'École Française d'Extrême-Orient,* vol. 52 (1967), fasc. 2, p. [375]-450. bibliog. Doctoral thesis, Faculty of Arts and Human Sciences, University of Paris, 1966.

A technical analysis dealing with population and language, old voiced occlusives being devoiced, accentuation, alternating consonants, the problems of sibilants and, finally, containing a section on toponymy. She says that a systematic comparative study of Khmer dialects should be undertaken. Almost thirty years later, this remains to be accomplished, and linguists still complain about its absence.

399 **Vacanunakram Khmer = Dictionnaire cambodgienne.** (Cambodian dictionary.)
Phnom Penh: Japan Committee for Republication and Relief of Cambodian Buddhist Books, 1983. 5th ed. 2 vols.

The authoritative Cambodian-language dictionary prepared by the Buddhist Institute over nearly thirty years of work under the leadership of Superior Chuon Nath of Wat Ounalom, and is known as the 'Chuon Nath dictionary'. The first edition was published in 1938, and the fifth appeared in 1967 and 1968. It is still relied upon widely in Cambodia and is considered one of the most significant publications in Khmer letters. This fifth edition was republished in 2,000 copies in 1983 by the Japan Committee for Republication and Relief of Cambodian Buddhist Books. A further 2,000 were reprinted in 1989, and it is now widely available in the markets in photocopied form.

Recherches préhistoriques dans la région de Mlu Prei: accompagnées de comparaison archéologiques et suivies d'un vocabulaire français-kuy. (Prehistoric research in the Mlu Prei region: together with archaeological comparisons and followed by a French-Kuy vocabulary.)
See item no. 133.

Recherches nouvelles sur le Cambodge. (Recent research on Cambodia.)
See item no. 155.

A chrestomathy of pre-Angkorian Khmer.
See item no. 157.

The slogans of Angkar: the thoughts of Pol Pot.
See item no. 282.

Medical dictionary Vichananukrum vichearas.
See item no. 444.

English-Khmer law dictionary = Vacananukram chbab anglais-khmer.
See item no. 490.

South-East Asia languages and literatures: a select guide.
See item no. 746.

Ethnologue Database: Cambodia.
See item no. 985.

Religion

400 **Buddhism and the future of Cambodia.**
Rithisen, Thailand: Khmer Buddhist Research Center, 1986. 165p. bibliog.

Partly a religious and philosophical treatise on Cambodian culture and history, this brief work is also a politically loaded polemic against Vietnamese involvement in Cambodia by members of the opposition 'government' in exile. It includes chapters by: KPNLF president Son Soubert, discussing the 'Historical dimensions of present conflict' in terms of Buddhist karma; Ieng Mouly, executive assistant to the prime minister of the Coalition Government of Democratic Kampuchea, outlining the 'Causes of suffering and the options of a strategy to rebuild Khmer society'; Dr. Sombon Suksamran, exploring the 'Buddhist concept of political authority'; and Sonn Sann on 'Buddhism and the future of Cambodia'; and other contributors. Although it may be difficult to find, it provides an important source for students and scholars.

401 **Le buddhisme au Cambodge.** (Buddhism in Cambodia.)
Adhémard Leclère. New York: AMS Press, 1975. xxxi, 535p. bibliog. Reprint of the 1899 edition published by E. Leroux, Paris.

The prodigious Leclère here turns his eye to the religious beliefs and practices of the majority of Cambodians, his preface (written in Kratie, Cambodia in 1898) defending his choice to write of the daily reality rather than a theoretical text-based exposition. After a preliminary chapter on the introduction of Buddhism to Cambodia prior to 665 AD (the date first mentioned in inscription), he goes on in ten parts to describe Cambodian views on cosmogony, the inhabitants of the universe, ontology, the Buddha and his disciples, forms of worship, the doctrine, art and architecture, and ethics. Despite its erudition, few references are made to sources of information, save to the few written sources that are used in the preliminary chapter.

402 **Buddhism, political authority, and legitimacy in Thailand and Cambodia.**
Somboon Suksamran. In: *Buddhist trends in Southeast Asia.* Edited by Trevor Ling. Singapore: Institute of Southeast Asian Studies, 1993, p. 101-53. bibliog. (Social Issues in Southeast Asia).

The introduction to this chapter examines Buddhism as one of the main socializing, acculturizing and unifying forces in the formation of community and concepts of political authority. The Cambodian section analyses Buddhism in Khmer politics, Sihanouk and Buddhist socialism, Lon Nol and the political mobilization of Buddhism, Buddhism under the Khmer Rouge, Buddhism and the Heng Samrin government, and the preservation of Buddhism, providing an overview of the relationship between Buddhism and sociopolitical changes in Cambodia over the second half of the 20th century. Somboon bases his analysis on government slogans and public statements, legal edicts and extensive references in this brief but focused essay.

403 **The calling of the souls: a study of the Khmer ritual Hau Bralin.**
Ashley Thompson. Clayton, Victoria: Monash Asia Institute, 1996. 24p. (Working Papers. Monash University, Centre of Southeast Asian Studies, no. 98).

Like Adhémard Leclère (q.v.) as early as 1899, Thompson rejects the claim that Cambodian Buddhism lacks a concept of the soul and cites the notion of the Sanskrit *viññan* as the equivalent of the Western concept. Thompson here sheds light on the Khmer 'soul' by reference to the notion of *bralin* – multiple material and independent entities which animate not only humans but also certain objects, plants and animals. These entities pass between the internal and the external and, in so doing, are susceptible to corruption and loss, and therefore at critical moments, particularly in rites of passage, need to be called back to restore the individual. She discusses this calling of the souls or *hau bralin* ritual, both as it has been recorded in research over the past century, and in contemporary observation inside Cambodia and in Cambodian refugee communities, where it survives in abbreviated form at times of homecoming, shock or illness. The ritual clearly stems from Animism but both integrates, and has been integrated, into both Brahmanic and Buddhist practices. In this essay of just over twenty pages, Thompson eloquently expostulates the main theme of her Masters thesis, supervised by Savaros Pou, from the University of Paris, where she is currently completing her doctoral dissertation. She also teaches Khmer civilization in Cambodia at the University of Fine Arts.

404 **Cambodge: la crémation et les rites funéraires.** (Cambodia: cremation and funerary rites.)
Adhémard Leclère. Hanoi: F. H. Schneider, 1906. 154p. bibliog.

Leclère describes the funeral of the Buddha, as reported in the canonical texts, and the ritual for ordinary people. The ceremonies are organized by the *achars*, people who have a knowledge of religion and rituals. They are not monks, although they have been in the past. The third chapter is a description of the ritual used for King Norodom in April 1904, probably the last one conducted according to the ancient rules. The dead body was placed in a squatting position inside an urn (1.2m high, 60cm wide at the neck), with 4 kg of gold jewels. Every three to four days, the body liquids were tapped and taken to the river. This lasted two years. (There is a graphic description in the novel by Roland Meyer, *Saramani, danseuse khmère* (Saramani: Khmer dancer) (q.v.). Before describing cremation, Leclère mentions what he says is a fading tradition. Some very religious people wanted to have their body decarnated. Special knives were used to cut out the flesh, on which wild birds would prey. The author says he has never seen anything more revolting. There is no better or more detailed description of this kind of ceremony.

405 **The cathedral of the rice paddy: 450 years of history of the church in Cambodia.**
François Ponchaud. Paris: Le Sarment; Fayard, 1990.

Ponchaud, who was sent to Cambodia by the Paris Foreign Missions Society in 1965 and has remained there since, except when deported by the Khmer Rouge in 1975, looks back at the 450 years of church history in Cambodia. Despite limited success, except among the resident Vietnamese population, there were apparently numerous attempts to evangelize Cambodians, as documented here by Ponchaud. Since his sources are limited to the diaries and letters of the foreign missionaries one gets to know little about the lives of those Cambodians who did convert. The major theme of the book is the trials and tribulations faced by missionaries and converts alike as they pressed on with their project despite great setbacks. Of more general interest are the two appendices: one giving insight into Khmer religion and superstition, showing the difficulties of explaining God to them; the second is an attempt by Ponchaud to draw on this background to explain or analyse the Khmer Rouge philosophy.

406 **Le chemin de Lanka.** (The way of Lanka.)
F. Bizot. Paris: École Française D'Extrême-Orient, 1992. 352p. bibliog. (Textes Bouddhiques du Cambodge).

For a long time, Western scholars who wrote on Buddhism in Cambodia referred to the known and published corpus of Buddhist texts in Pali. Their translation into Khmer was a late ploy invented by the French to cut the links between Khmer and Siamese monks, accused of indoctrinating their Cambodian brethren in anti-French propaganda. Finot, Leclère (qq.v.) and others described official ceremonies and commented on the canonical texts and the 'lives' of the Buddha (*Jataka*) which had a central place in popular literature. Bizot chose another approach: he went to the wats, and observed, listened, and carefully read the Khmer manuscripts that could sometimes be found in monasteries if the superior liked you. He has published several very interesting books which aim to show Khmer Buddhism from inside. The Pali origins are of course fundamental, but Bizot was also interested in the process by which religious knowledge is transmitted and he demonstrated that the direct ancestor is Mon Buddhism. (Mons were the inhabitants of Thailand, before the Thais arrived from the north by the 10th century.) In this book, Bizot publishes, translates and footnotes a Khmer text describing steps to be taken on the way to immortality – a very beautiful and moving human experiment in the control of the soul and the body, in a rather Tantric way. Bizot is thus unveiling new dimensions of a religion not seen by scholars immersed in libraries. Bizot had to consult with many old people over twenty years in order slowly to understand this difficult text.

407 **Le culte des génies protecteurs au Cambodge: analyse et traduction d'un corpus de textes sur les 'neak ta'.** (The cult of the guardian spirits in Cambodia: analysis and translation of a corpus of texts on the *neak ta*.)

Alain Forest. Paris: L'Harmattan, 1992. 254p. bibliog. (Recherches Asiatiques).

The first part of the book is an analysis rich in views and ideas which lead to an interesting and open field for further research. One question, for instance, is whether the *neak ta* local cults are observed since the Khmer Rouge period. No observations have been reported so far, although the cults most certainly survive. The second part of the book consists of the translation of twenty-seven texts gathered by the Commission of Mores and Customs published in Khmer as *Brajum rioeng breng* (Phnom Penh: Institute Bouddhique, 1962. Reprinted, Paris: Institut d'Asie du Sud-Est, 1982). These stories pertain to the protective spirits called *neak ta* which can be construed as meaning the 'Old People', or the 'Ancestors' or the 'Genii'. Alain Forest, who has written a history of part of the colonial period, is on familiar ground as, at one point, he had wanted to be a missionary. He in fact wants to uncover the reason behind the successive failures of the missionaries' attempts to convert Khmers. It may lie in the persistence of popular beliefs.

408 **The devaraja cult.**

Hermann Kulke, translated from the German by I. W. Mabbett. Ithaca, New York: Southeast Asia Program, Department of Asian Studies, Cornell University, 1978. xx, 48p. bibliog. (Data Paper. Southeast Asia Program, Cornell University, no. 108). Original German version published in *Saeculum*, vol. 25, no. 1 (1974).

A study of the 'god-king' cult in Cambodia by the Indologist Kulke, provoking some re-examination of accepted understandings of the cult's significance. As well as adding detailed research into the Cambodian context of this Indian-derived concept, the study contributes to an understanding of the nature of royal power in other Indianized kingdoms of ancient Southeast Asia. Kulke maintains that many previously proposed theories by experts such as Coedès (q.v.) are inconsistent or unsatisfactory. Through an analysis of epigraphic and archaeological material, particularly the Sdok Kak Thom inscription, he suggests that epigraphic mention of the devaraja cult and the monuments which housed *lingas* (centres of royal cults) do not refer to the same thing. Rather, royal cults are possibly derivations of prehistoric folk religion, while the 'god king' could well have been Siva, who was worshipped as king of the gods. Breaking with the accepted scholarly tradition in this field, Kulke concludes, 'the Sdok Kak Thom inscription offers no warrant at all for the theory that the kings of Angkor were "god kings"'. Judith Jacob contributes notes on certain Old Khmer terms, which she helped translate into English for this work. Despite the monumentality and age of the subject, Kulke's study is readable, concise and refreshing.

409 **Le don de soi-même: recherches sur le bouddhisme khmer III.** (The gift of oneself: research on Khmer Buddhism III.)
François Bizot. Paris: École Française d'Extrême-Orient, 1981. 206p. bibliog. (Publications de l'École Française d'Extrême-Orient, no. 130).

French scholar, François Bizot, here examines the *pansukul* rite in which a piece of cloth is donated to a Buddhist monk. The first part of the work discusses the practice of this rite in Cambodia, Thailand and Laos, in both official clerical circles, particularly as part of funerary ceremonies, and among the non-reformed Mahanikay, where it is also used in healing ceremonies. Particular attention is devoted to the Chak Mahapansukul ceremony. Photographs from 1967-79 complement the text. The second part goes on to study the evidence for the Chak Mahapansukul in Khmer texts. Additional notes point to its practice in Burma, and appendices provide transliterations of the texts previously discussed and facsimile reproductions of the palm-leaf manuscripts themselves.

410 **Les êtres surnaturels dans la religion populaire khmère.** (Supernatural beings in popular Khmer religion.)
Ang Chouléan. Paris: Cedoreck, 1986. 349p.

This book's appearance was good news for at least two reasons. First, it was breaking new ground in the field of Khmer anthropology, where almost nothing had been done for decades; second, it was written by a Khmer scholar, heralding a new generation of Khmer scholars, trained to master all the traditional sources, both local and foreign, on Khmer society and its past, and yet proficient with social sciences methods. It is usually believed that the religion of the Khmers is Buddhism. For a century, most scholars, both Khmers and foreigners, would have been reluctant to accept the notion of a 'Khmer popular religion'. They would only accept the idea that there is an archaic stratum which is embedded inside a larger and more important body of Buddhist beliefs. But most people in Cambodia would respect a statue of the Buddha, not so much because of the Buddha, but because it is the location of a powerful 'spirit of the statue of the Buddha'. Does this represent Buddhism thinly covering animist beliefs, or traditional religion using a thin make-up of Buddhism? Ang Chouléan would probably dodge this issue, as it is a sensitive one, related to the image of the country, its appeal to foreign donors and tourists, and so on. Buddhism is a better cover as far as markets are concerned. He talked to a great number of people and comes up with a description of the supernatural beings, which almost all Khmers (as well as Thais, Vietnamese and other Southeast Asians) believe surround us in an invisible way. Most of these beings are very nasty and quite dangerous. They are full of jealousy; they often want to harm human beings. That explains a lot about why we are sick, have accidents or suffer miseries in our life. All those who have some use for an anthropological approach to Khmer studies hope that Ang Chouléan, who is back in Cambodia, and is well equipped, will concentrate on furthering his research which is extremely promising. What he has done so far, in this book and other articles, is excellent.

411 **Le figuier à cinq branches: recherche sur le bouddhisme khmer.** (The fig tree with five branches: research on Khmer Buddhism.) François Bizot. Paris: École Française d'Extrême-Orient, 1976. iv, 164p. bibliog. (Publications de l'École Française d'Extrême-Orient, no. 107).

With its foreword written on 16 April 1975, this was truly one of the last works to be penned in pre-Khmer Rouge Cambodia. Bizot began his work in the early 1970s in Siem Reap (Srah Srang) but, due to the war, soon had to leave his chosen area for the relative security of the Phnom Penh area (Pochentong). He concentrated on recording the holdings of Buddhist temples in Phnom Penh and surrounding Kandal province, registering some 455 manuscripts, most of which were photocopied or (if in too poor condition) re-transcribed. This work constitutes the first volume in the series, 'Recherches sur le Bouddhisme Khmer' (Research on Khmer Buddhism). It consists of an introduction on Buddhism and Buddhist studies in Cambodia, and then moves on to the text selected for transcription, translation and analysis from Wat Kambol, Phnom Penh. The text is in French and romanized Khmer. Bizot has continued his work on the manuscripts he took with him from Cambodia from his new base in Thailand, from where he directs the continuing output of the series as well as the new programme of the EFEO in Cambodia, in which texts are registered and microfilmed.

412 **Khmer Buddhism and politics from 1954 to 1984.** Yang Sam. Newington, Connecticut: Khmer Studies Institute, 1987. v, 97p. bibliog.

Published by the Khmer Studies Institute, Connecticut, this work attempts to examine how the political changes which have occurred since liberation from French colonization have affected Khmer religion and society. Seeing Buddhism as the core of Khmer culture the author believes an understanding of history must first include a study of Buddhism's significance. Differences between classical Buddhism and the Cambodian form are explored. Sihanouk's policy of 'Buddhist socialism', the use of monks by warring factions, the Khmer Rouge strategy for eliminating Buddhism, and the restoration of Buddhism since 1979 are analysed. Based also on fieldwork and interviews with refugees, the study includes a broad bibliography.

413 **Les religions brahmaniques dans l'ancien Cambodge d'après l'épigraphie et l'iconographie.** (Brahman religions in ancient Cambodia according to epigraphy and iconography.) Kamaleswar Bhattacharya. Paris: École Française d'Extrême-Orient, 1961. 197p. bibliog. (Publications de l'École Françaisé d'Extrême-Orient, no. 49).

Considered by the author to be the most important element of the Indo-Khmer civilization, the Brahmanic religions have been taken as the starting-point for research that will later also extend to Buddhism. The study covers the period from the 1st to the 14th centuries, through the so-called Indianized period of Cambodian history, in three periods (Funan, Chenla and Angkor), in the geographic area covered by ancient Cambodian kingdoms, extending into the present territories of Laos, Thailand and Vietnam. In addition to the indigenous epigraphical and iconographical sources, Bhattacharya has also turned to Chinese annals and travellers' accounts, as well as to original Indian works. Epigraphical sources are considered to be well documented in published works, but not so for iconography, for which the photographic collection of the Guimet Museum was used. The study deals with Sivaism, Vishnuism, minor cults, the cult of fire and residues of Vedism, and syncretism of Sivaism and Vishnuism. Bhattacharya notes the extent of Indian influence during this period as well as the persistence of autochthonous traditions, and the Cambodian tendency to syncretism, as symbolized in Harihara, in which Siva and Vishnu are united in a single body, and as shown in many temples devoted to one god but showing themes relating to another.

La guirlande de joyaux. (The garland of jewels.)
See item no. 732.

Ramaker ou l'amour symbolique de Ram et Seta. (Ramaker, or the symbolic love of Ram and Seta.)
See item no. 740.

House of the spirit: perspectives on Cambodian health care.
See item no. 928.

Samsara.
See item no. 948.

Social Structure and Social Anthropology

414 **Changing Khmer conceptions of gender: women, stories, and the social order.**

Judy Ledgerwood. PhD thesis, Cornell University, Ithaca, New York, 1990. 365p. bibliog. Available on microfilm from University of Michigan, Ann Arbor, Michigan.

Ledgerwood is an American anthropologist who speaks Khmer fluently. The field research work for her dissertation was conducted in 1987-88, through interviewing some 200 people in 6 Cambodian communities in the United States. The concerns of the work, in which she related views of her informants to the literature and to observations of Khmer communities in Cambodia and in other countries, are shown in the chapter headings: 'Khmer religion as an engendered system'; 'Khmer literature'; 'Remembered lives, observed lives: images of women in Cambodia. 1930-1970'; 'Democratic Kampuchea 1975-1979'; 'The refugee camps 1979-1989'; 'Khmer conceptions of social order'; and 'Khmer in America'. The project was borne of her observation of Khmer culture changing in the United States and an understanding of the deep need most Khmer people feel to preserve their culture and thus identity. In this context she examines the importance of gender roles to the question of identity, and the role stories play in describing various female roles within Khmer ethnic identity.

415 **Lovea, village des environs d'Angkor: aspects démographiques, économiques et sociologiques du monde rural cambodgien dans la province de Siem-Réap.** (Lovea, village in the neighbourhood of Angkor: demographic, economic and sociological aspects of the rural Cambodian world in the province of Siem Reap.)

Gabrielle Martel. Paris: École Française d'Extrême-Orient, 1975. 359, [18]p. maps. bibliog. (Publications de l'École Française d'Extrême-Orient, no. 98).

Martel observed this village, 17 kilometres west of Siem Reap, over a period of fifteen months in 1961-62, and completed the manuscript in 1967, although it was not published until some years later, when the environment she described had already been obliterated by the war and the Khmer Rouge. Lovea, at that time, was a rice-growing community of 130 households. Martel describes its ecological and demographic dimensions as well as its economic and social aspects, and her appendix of the year's calendar of village activities rounds out this valuable document from 'former times'.

416 **Nagara and commandery.**
Paul Wheatley. Chicago: Department of Geography, University of Chicago, 1983. xv, 472p. (Research Papers/University of Chicago, Department of Geography, no. 207-288).

A tentative study of the main factors involved in the transformation of tribe to state, and village to city. Not for the lay reader, it has been written for urbanists, with a view to comparative studies, but necessarily includes background information on the cultural context of the social, political and economic processes of relevance. This section functions as the notes and references to the argument of the text. Accordingly, it forms a two-way bridge between ancient Southeast Asian history and analysis of the nature of urban phenomena. Touching on no less than five distinct cultural traditions, the study incorporates opinion on Khmer and pre-Khmer settlement and social structure. Angkor Borei, Oc Eo, Vyadhapura, Wat Phu and Angkor, all receive Wheatley's scholarly attention as he explores, among other aspects, concepts of urbanism, chiefs and chiefdoms, urban genesis, and the role of hydrology.

417 **Notes sur la culture et la religion en péninsule indochinoise: en hommage à Pierre-Bernard Lafont.** (Notes on culture and religion in the Indochinese peninsula: in homage to Pierre-Bernard Lafont.)
Edited by Nguyên Thê Anh and Alain Forest. Paris: L'Harmattan, 1995. 252p. bibliog. (Recherches Asiatiques).

Members of the National Centre for Scientific Research (CNRS) research group 1075, of which Lafont was the founder, prepared this Festschrift for him. An introductory essay placed Lafont's work in perspective, highlighting his contribution to the study of minority ethnic groups, particularly the Tay and the Cham, and to having revivified Cham studies. The volume contains a list of Lafont's publications from 1951 to 1994, including ten books. Among the fifteen articles, three relate specifically to Cambodia: Khing Hoc Dy on 'The cat in Khmer literature and culture'; Alain Forest and Mak Phoeun on 'The Angkor period in Khmer royal chronicles'; and Pierre-L. Lamant on 'The royalty and monarchy in Cambodia'. Another two articles relate to Cham communities throughout Southeast Asia.

418 **Parenté et organization sociale dans le Cambodge moderne et contemporain: quelques aspects et quelques applications du modèle le régissant.** (Kinship and social organization in modern and contemporary Cambodia, some aspects and applications of the prevailing model.)
Jacques Népote. Geneva: Olizane (Études Orientales); Cedoreck (Bibliothèque Khmère), 1992. 255p. bibliog.

A fascinating and complex study of Cambodian kinship relations. The author spent almost twenty-five years pursuing this area of study, by observation in Cambodia itself, in discussion with Cambodians resident in France, and in examining written records – both Khmer records (in the form of customary law, histories and tales) and those written by earlier European observers. On the basis of linguistic, ethnographic and historical analysis, Népote, who reports a predominance of matrilineal ties in Cambodia, constructs a model with eight types of familial relations: families, residential units, the royal family, the country of the Khmers, acquired relatives or allies, buddhist relatives, clients, and people with whom one comes in contact. He then plots these eight relations in time, space and logic in a two-dimensional model, but states that they would be better represented as a cube.

419 **Le paysan cambodgien.** (The Cambodian peasant.)
Jean Delvert. Paris: École Pratique des Hautes Études – Sorbonne and Mouton & Co., 1961. 740p. maps. (Le Monde d'Outre-Mer Passé et Présent: Études, no. 10).

Noting that much had been written about Angkor and the past, art, architecture, royalty etc. but very little about the lives of people, the author set out to redress the imbalance with what still must be termed the definitive study of the Cambodian peasantry. The five sections of the book deal with: natural conditions in Cambodia; agrarian civilization; population and economy; rural society; and regional life. The work includes twenty-five maps, architectural illustrations, illustrations of implements and modes of transport as well as photographic depictions of daily life. Delvert found great diversity, but noted that unifying factors such as the rhythm of the seasons and Buddhism create major common characteristics. Concerned by the rate of population growth a shift towards urbanization caused by pressure on the land, Delvert argued for a method of modernization of agriculture that would allow the peasants to keep their land and their culture while also catering to the growing population. Appendices list: provinces and *sroks* (districts) studied; places where cotton and silk were produced; areas of different sorts of riziculture; yields of paddy per hectare; and average land holdings, income and expenses.

420 **La paysannerie du Cambodge: et ses projets de modernisation.**
(The peasantry of Cambodia: and their projects of modernization.)
Hou Yuon. Doctoral thesis in Sciences Economiques, Faculté de Droit, Paris, 1955. 285p.

Of the theses written in France by Cambodian students in the 1950s, (as Serge Thion has pointed out) Hou Yuon's was the only one not dedicated to King Norodom Sihanouk but instead is dedicated to the 'peasants and workers of Cambodia'. Hou Yuon explained that he chose his topic because of the weight of the peasantry in the Cambodian economy, and because modernization of the countryside was the necessary basis for transformation of Cambodia from an economically semi-feudal and semi-colonial country into an independent and prosperous national economy to meet the needs of the people. His intention was to determine the fundamental character of the economy by examining the mode of production and the social relations of production, and then to analyse the material and social conditions of the different classes of peasants. Essential measures included the abolition of usury and the development of agricultural co-operatives. 'Cambodia is rich but the Cambodians are poor' was the main conclusion of the study, with 'all to gain in peace, all to lose in war'. Key parts of the thesis were translated by Ben Kiernan as chapter one of *Peasants and politics in Kampuchea, 1942-1981* (q.v.). Hou Yuon returned home after writing this thesis, joined Sihanouk's Sangkum and was elected to the National Assembly in 1958, being appointed to the Cabinet from 1962-63. He was driven out of public life by Sihanouk in 1967, accused of instigating the Samlaut rebellion, and joined the resistance; being named Minister of Interior, Communal Reforms and Co-operatives and member of the Central Committee of the CPK. However, he was not mentioned after the Khmer Rouge came to power in 1975 and was alleged in Hu Nim's 'confession' to have opposed the evacuation of the cities and abolition of money, and to have advocated stronger ties with Vietnam and the Soviet Union. He is believed to have been executed by the régime.

421 **Sisters of hope: a monograph on women, work and entrepreneurship in Cambodia.**
Nandini Azad. Phnom Penh: UNDP/ILO, Small Enterprise and Informal Sector Project, March 1994.

Following the greater destruction of males during the Pol Pot period, it was estimated that women made up sixty-five per cent of the population in the early 1980s, many taking the major responsibility for their family. This book presents twenty case-studies based on interviews with women entrepreneurs in the small enterprise and informal sector. The aim is to portray the reality of life and work in urban settings, and the factors that have influenced the women in becoming entrepreneurs. These studies have been used to develop training materials and for planning small and micro-business projects at the grassroots level, and to 'highlight the various survival strategies that the Cambodian women entrepreneurs have adopted in the last two decades'.

422 **Svay: a Khmer village in Cambodia.**
May Mayko Ebihara. [New York]: Columbia University, 1968. 2 vols. Available from University Microfilms, no. 71-17,577.

Presented as a doctoral thesis in 1968, this provides a comprehensive anthropological study of village life prior to the extensive turbulence beginning in 1970. Ebihara records and analyses the village (given the fictional name of Svay) – its setting and social structure, economic organization, religion, life cycle, political organization, and relations with the surrounding world – as well as providing a background picture of Cambodia and concluding thoughts on Southeast Asian cultures and the concept of peasantry. It was the first detailed study of Khmer peasant culture, based on fieldwork between 1959 and 1960, and remains one of the very few, if not the only, such study of a Khmer village. Family and kinship structure, social status and sense of community are discussed in detail, as are crafts, cultivation and household finances. Religious practices and socialization, the relation of the village to national politics and conceptions of outside communities are also addressed in this landmark work. A comparison of the same village under the Khmer Rouge and then under the PRK is provided in her chapter in the Ablin and Hood book, *The Cambodian agony* (q.v.).

423 **When every household is an island: social organization and power structures in rural Cambodia.**
Jan Ovesen, Ing-Britt Trankell, Joakim Ojendal. Uppsala, Sweden: Department of Cultural Anthropology, [199?]. 99p. bibliog. (Uppsala Research Reports in Cultural Anthropology, no. 15).

This study has the character of an anthropological survey of the social situation in the Cambodian countryside. Very little social science research has been carried out on location in rural Cambodia and, as part of its planning of a country strategy, the Swedish International Development Cooperation Agency (SIDA) commissioned a study of social organization and power structures in rural Cambodia. The book is based primarily on studies of the existing literature, supplemented by brief fieldwork in a rural environment. It is meant as a first inventory of problems and prospects that may be of some use for development planners as well as for academic researchers. The authors are two anthropologists and one development researcher.

424 **Women in Kampuchea.**
Chantou Boua. Bangkok: UNICEF, 1981. 28p.

Chantou Boua, a Cambodian who was studying in Australia when the Khmer Rouge took over the country, returned in 1981 to document the status and conditions of Cambodian women, a topic she has continued to study and to write about. She is one of the few authors to continue to give credit to the efforts of reconstruction undertaken during the PRK period. See particularly her series of articles in the *Phnom Penh Post* (q.v.) in 1995.

425 **Women: key to national reconstruction.**
[Phnom Penh]: Secretariat of State for Women's Affairs, March 1995. 78p.

This volume is Cambodia's Country Report for the Fourth World Conference on Women held in Beijing in September 1995. The Secretariat of State for Women's Affairs was established following the formation of the new Royal Government in November 1993, placing the issue of women's affairs in a newly prominent position. The report provides a general assessment of women's status in Cambodia between 1980 and 1995, focusing on eight areas of 'disparities between men and women': inequality in the sharing of power and decision-making at all levels; mechanisms to promote the advancement of women; lack of awareness of, and commitment to, women's rights; poverty; women's access and participation in the definition of economic structures and policies, and in the productive process itself; access to education, health and employment; violence against women; and effects on women of continuing national and international armed and other kinds of conflict. Support to the Secretariat was provided by CDRI, CIDSE and Oxfam UK and International, with particular input from Chantou Boua.

Peasants and politics in Kampuchea, 1942-1981.
See item no. 221.

The impact of revolution on Cambodian peasants: 1970-1975.
See item no. 250.

Souverains et notabilités d'Indochine. (Sovereigns and notables of Indochina.)
See item no. 332.

Comprehensive paper on Cambodia.
See item no. 633.

Report of the economic and demographic statistical assessment mission to Cambodia.
See item no. 651.

Cambodian culture since 1975: homeland and exile.
See item no. 768.

Social Issues, Mines, and Returning and Internal Refugees

426 **Aftermath of war: humanitarian problems of Southeast Asia.**
Dale S. De Haan, Jerry M. Tinker. Washington, DC: US Government Printing Office, May 1976. 589p.

This is a report prepared by staff of the US Senate Subcommittee to Investigate Problems Connected with Refugees and Escapees, chaired by Senator Edward Kennedy. It is divided into three parts: relief and rehabilitation inside Indochina; refugee problems in Thailand: and refugee resettlement in the United States. The bulk of the volume is taken up by supporting documents. Particularly noteworthy is a ninety-three-page report of a UN mission to Vietnam in March 1976 which canvassed problems of postwar reconstruction. [David G. Marr with Kristine Alilunas-Rodgers]

427 **Culture and society in posttraumatic stress disorder: implications for psychotherapy.**
James K. Boehnlein. *American Journal of Psychotherapy*, October 1987, vol. 41, no. 4, p. 519-30.

Contains case-studies of two Cambodian women, aged twenty-four and forty-seven years, who exhibited post-traumatic symptoms following their experiences of imprisonment during Pol Pot's régime. These symptoms were exacerbated by a number of factors resulting from their emigration to North America, including separation from past traditions and change in social status. In addition to the specific cases, different approaches to cross-cultural psychotherapy are discussed. See also *American Journal of Psychiatry*, 1985, 142(8), p. 956-59 for Boehnlein's details of treatment given to a specific group of twelve Cambodians.

428 **From rice truck to paddy field: a study of the repatriation and reintegration needs of vulnerable female heads of household and other vulnerable individuals living in the Cambodia refugee and di[s]placed persons camps along the Thai-Cambodian border.**

Lynda Thorn. [Phnom Penh]: UNHCR, [1991]. xi, 111p. map. bibliog.

Commissioned and published by the United Nations High Commission on Refugees, this report was compiled to assess the needs of the 350,000 Cambodian refugees from camps in Thailand, providing an unusually deep look into the composition of the refugee population and devoting particular attention to the social needs of its vulnerable members: female-headed households, the elderly, the physically and mentally disabled and the chronically sick. Samples of the questionnaires used are given, along with recommendations for action, which were unfortunately not implemented in reality. The operation carried out by the UNHCR in 1992-93 was proclaimed successful, more as a 'people mover' meeting the repatriation aims, rather than one fulfilling its long-term reintegration and survival aims. See *Hope for a new life: Cambodia special report* and *Between hope and insecurity: the social consequences of the Cambodian peace process* (qq.v.) for the balance sheet on those two aims and the film *The Tan family* (q.v.) for a personal and rather depressing account.

429 **Getting the message about mines: towards a national public information strategy and program on mines and mine safety: a discussion paper on the priorities for the production of mine-awareness material commissioned by the Cambodia [i.e. Cambodian] Mine Action Centre.**

Susan Aitkin. Phnom Penh: UNESCO, 1993. 1 vol. map. bibliog.

One of the most acute social problems in Cambodia is the danger posed by mines to humans (and animals too) in huge areas of the country. Awareness of the extent of the minefields, the appearance of the mines themselves and appropriate local action and responses are the focus of this timely report.

430 **Hope for a new life: Cambodia special report.**

[Phnom Penh?]: Public Information Section, UNHCR, September 1993.

An excellent resource on the implementation of the repatriation of 350,000 Cambodian refugees from Thailand between March 1992 and April 1993. Maps on the initial destinations of returnees, graphs showing monthly and cumulative totals, and delightful photographs show the 'upside' of this operation which, with the elections, was the major success story of the United Nations Peace Plan. The many difficulties faced by the returnees and their situation after the short-term assistance packages expired, are not recorded here in this promotional and congratulatory publication.

431 **Internally displaced persons in Cambodia: needs assessment report.**

Phnom Penh: Cambodian Displaced Persons Working Group, 1991. 10p. map.

This is an extremely detailed report on the situation of displaced persons within Cambodia at the beginning of 1991 and proposals for action by international aid agencies. At this time government funds were largely exhausted. Chapters cover the historical background, the government response, external assistance, population movement, health and sanitation, food aid, water, shelter, agriculture, material assistance, education, transport and logistics, and improvements in the local Red Cross, and are accompanied by numerous tables. Costings for each proposal are listed, as are the contents of the various kits to be distributed. An executive summary is provided. The tone of the writing is dry, although it is clear from the content that the assessment is often based on close observations by the authors.

432 **Land mines in Cambodia: the coward's war, September 1991.**
Eric Storer, Rae McGrath for Asia Watch, Physicians for Human Rights. New York: Human Rights Watch and Physicians for Human Rights, 1991. [4], iii, 129p.

Written by Eric Stover, freelance writer and consultant to Human Rights Watch and Physicians for Human Rights, and Rae McGrath, director of Mines Advisory Group, this was a pioneering report on the devastation caused by land-mines in Cambodia and continues to be one of the major sources of information on that topic. The authors present: a thorough study of the background to mine warfare dating back to the Vietnam War; a technical explanation as to the types of mines used, and their medical, social and psychological effects; and the problems posed by the approaching repatriation of more than 300,000 refugees from the Thai border. All four factions had used mines and failed to keep systematic records of where they were laid. All had received training in warfare from foreign forces and, in the case of the KPNLF and FUNCINPEC, at least some of this came from the British Special Air Services (SAS). The authors propose a programme of eradication and warn that the costs of failure will be very high. Two useful appendices contain the text of the 'United Nations convention on prohibitions or restrictions on the use of certain conventional weapons which may be deemed to be excessively injurious or to have indiscriminate effects' and a brief description of the major refugee camps in Thailand. Maps show positions of UNBRO-assisted border camps from 1985-91 and provinces of birth and of intended return of refugees from Sites 2, 8 and B.

433 **Relief and rehabilitation of war victims in Indochina: hearings.**
Subcommittee to Investigate Problems Connected with Refugees and Escapees, US Senate. Washington, DC: US Government Printing Office, 1973. 4 vols.

Chaired by Senator Edward Kennedy, the Refugee Subcommittee conducted Indochina hearings on four occasions between April and August 1973, the results being reproduced in the 573 pages of these 4 volumes, entitled: 'Crisis in Cambodia'; 'Orphans and child welfare'; 'North Vietnam and Laos'; and 'South Vietnam and regional problems'. Besides the verbal testimony of various experts, a large number of written statements, memoranda and press reports are provided in appendices. Further background is available in *Problems of war victims in Indochina* (Washington, DC: US Government Printing Office, 1972. 4 vols). [David G. Marr with Kristine Alilunas-Rodgers]

434 **Relief and rehabilitation of war victims in Indochina: one year after the ceasefire.**

Nevin S. Scrimshaw, Dale S. De Haan, Jerry W. Tinker (et al.). Washington, DC: US Government Printing Office, Jan. 1974. 399p.

The US Senate Subcommittee to Investigate Problems Connected with Refugees and Escapees, chaired by Senator Edward Kennedy, commissioned this report by specialists in various fields, who travelled to North and South Vietnam, Laos and Cambodia, then consulted with experts in Geneva, Rome, Tokyo and New York. Although the investigations took place soon after the signing of the Paris Agreement in January 1973, it was already becoming clear that fundamental issues remained unresolved. Useful information is provided here on social problems which continued to plague Indochina after 1975, including refugee resettlement, defusing unexploded ordnance, the physical rehabilitation of war victims, and the care of orphans. There are six appendices, notably Appendix VI (p. 219-395), which contains photo-reproductions of the various ceasefire documents signed between January and June 1973. A subject index facilitates access to an otherwise confusing text organization. [David G. Marr with Kristine Alilunas-Rodgers]

435 **The struggle for rice, fish and water.**

Phnom Penh: Cooperation Committee for Cambodia, 1995. 36p.

A document prepared for distribution at the 1995 World Summit on Social Development in Copenhagen by the Working Group on Aid Coordination representing non-government organizations working in Cambodia. Supported by the Cooperation Committee for Cambodia with the assistance of the Cambodian Development Resource Institute and other NGOs, it puts the NGO case for development in Cambodia, covering the context of the Social Summit, poverty and deprivation in Cambodia, the needs for national reconstruction and the case for a people-centred development strategy. This is an important contribution to the discussion about Cambodia's current development needs.

436 **Vulnerable in the village.**

Paul Davenport, Sr. Joan Healy and Kevin Malone. Melbourne: Overseas Services Bureau and World Vision Australia, 1995. 123p.

As a result of the political settlement in Cambodia, thousands of former refugees were moved after 1993 from camps on the Thai border to locations inside Cambodia, with the assistance of the UNHCR. Some of the younger refugees had spent their whole lives in the camps, and most joined the repatriation without having farm land to return to. This is the report of a significant study by the local NGO Akphiwat Khum, with the support of the Overseas Services Bureau and World Vision, of the plight of many of these returnees and landless farmers in Battambang province. The report calls for a shift of emphasis in development assistance to food security issues, to optimum land use, and to the investigation of 'coping strategies' among the rural poor and returnees. It is an absolutely invaluable resource for the study of poverty and social conditions in today's Cambodia.

437 **War of the mines: Cambodia, landmines and the impoverishment of a nation.**

Paul Davies and Nic Dunlop. London: Pluto Press, 1994. 172p. maps. bibliog.

Following an all-too-brief chronology, this book launches into a detailed discussion of the effect on Cambodian society of its nearly thirty-year-long history of often indiscriminate and profligate mine-laying. Three of the book's eight chapters and two of its four appendices concentrate on the Rattanak Mondul district in Battambang province, giving details of injuries and deaths, effects on life and mine-clearing operations. Other chapters and appendices are concerned with prosthetics, the use and abuse of land-mines globally (by Rae McGrath), and land-mines and international humanitarian assistance. A feature of the book is its lavish illustration with black-and-white photographs by Nic Dunlop.

438 **The warrior heritage: a psychological perspective of Cambodian trauma.**

Seanglim Bit. El Cerrito, California: S. Bit, 1991. 233p. bibliog. Later republished, Bangkok: White Lotus.

The cover notes say this is the first scholarly effort to examine, from the Cambodian perspective, the psychological dimensions of the profound trauma referred to as the 'Cambodian genocide'. A native-born Cambodian, who was an official in the Ministry of Finance before leaving for the United States in 1975, Seanglim Bit gained a Doctorate in Education with emphasis on Social Psychology from the University of San Francisco and he practises in the area of mental health, specializing in post-traumatic stress. As the title indicates, he believes the heritage of violence and conflict is deep in Cambodian culture. The divorce between the pacifist beliefs of Buddhist ideology and the often violent reality of Cambodian life and history form the basis of his psychological interpretation of the genocide and its traumatic effects. The origins of these contradictions are traced back to the days of Angkor. According to the author, Cambodia desperately needs to enlist a new generation of Angkor creators, not as warriors but as builders. The current generation is the first, he says, that has not been brutalized and can therefore begin these weighty tasks with a clean slate. The text is not footnoted, and is followed by a fairly scant bibliography and several appendices that bear little relevance to the argument being presented, leaving some question as to the academic substance of the work. Nevertheless it presents some incisive points of observation and analysis, as for instance 'Cambodian culture places great importance on upholding rigorously determined standards of behavior for members of society, yet simultaneously tolerates deviant behavior by those who violate the social norms without serious consequences'.

439 **The will to live.**

Text and photographs by Jacques Danois. [s.l.]: UNICEF, [1980?]. 117p.

From October 1979 to late 1980 Jacques Danois visited, wrote about, and photographed, Kampuchea and its people as they emerged from the horrors of the Pol Pot years. The result is a collection of articles presenting snapshots of the rebirth of Cambodia, depicting: education and health systems rebuilt from scratch; agriculture restarted with the help of donations of food and seeds; the difficulty of travel on ruined roads; the emotional and spiritual devastation which so many had to overcome in order to continue with their lives; a generation of teenagers who could not read or write – or who had forgotten how; and young boys more experienced in the killing fields than the paddy fields. While sometimes too romantic in its portrayal of peasant life and the Cambodian people, this easy-to-read book and its many photographs illustrate the enormity of the reconstruction tasks undertaken during the 1980s and the spirit and will to live that brought out the best in so many people in those early years. While not belaboured, the positive contribution of Vietnam is also acknowledged.

440 **World summit for social development: country report.**
Phnom Penh: Royal Government of Cambodia, March 1995. 29p.

Against the background of the destruction caused by the Khmer Rouge régime and the developments following the Paris Peace Agreements of 23 October 1991, this small pamphlet is a statement by the Royal Government of Cambodia outlining its social and economic development priorities. The role of the government, it believes, is to 'create an enabling economic, political, cultural and legal environment that will enable people to achieve social development'. The statement is followed by a list of key social indicators.

Sangkum Reastr Niyum: le développement général du Cambodge (années 1960). (Sangkum Reastr Niyum: the development of Cambodia in the 1960s.)
See item no. 246.

National health development plan 1994-96.
See item no. 445.

Food for people: family food production in Cambodia.
See item no. 617.

Towards restoring life.
See item no. 646.

Report on the socio-economic survey of Cambodia 1993/94.
See item no. 652.

Indochina Issues.
See item no. 860.

Silent sentinels: coward's war.
See item no. 950.

The Tan Family, March – April 1995.
See item no. 952.

Public Health and Medicine

441 **Contribution à l'étude des plantes médicinales du Cambodge: en particulier de divers Garcinia et du Vitex Pubescens Vahl.** (Contribution to the study of medicinal plants of Cambodia: in particular Garcinia varieties and Vitex Pubescens Vahl.)
Phana Douk. Paris: Imprimerie Ménez, 1966. 264p. bibliog.

This is the doctoral thesis of Phana Douk, Doctor in Pharmacy, Diploma in Serology, from the Faculty of Pharmacy, Paris. Dedicated 'to my country, Cambodia', it commences with a catalogue of 459 species of medicinal plants in Cambodia, and then moves on to a more detailed study of particular plants: Garcinia; Holarrhena; Vitex Pubescens Vahl; followed by concordances and an alphabetical table of scientific names. The author acknowledges use of Menaut's *Matière médical du Cambodge* (Medical material dealing with Cambodia) (Hanoi: Imprimerie d'Extrême-Orient, 1930) and Pételot's works on plants and their use (q.v.). Where possible Phana Douk has given the plant's chemical composition and bibliographical references, especially during the previous ten years. The work includes thirty-one figures (of which six are colour photographs pasted in).

442 **Grossesse et accouchement en milieu réfugié khmer du Cambodge à la France.** (Pregnancy and childbirth in the Khmer refugee environment from Cambodia to France.)
Meas Saran. Aulnay-sous-Bois, France: École d'Infirmières, Centre Hospitalier Intercommunal, 1987. 41p.

A discussion of traditional Cambodian approaches to pregnancy and childbirth and how these have evolved under the influence of political changes in Cambodia and the French medical environment in which this refugee community now finds itself.

443 **Kantha Bopha: a children's doctor in Cambodia.**
Beat Richner – Beatocello. Zurich, Switzerland: Verlag Neue Zurcher Zeitung, 1996. 119p.

The book describes, from a personal point of view, the work of Dr. Beat Richner at the Kantha Bopha Children's Hospital in Phnom Penh. A controversial figure, Richner was an assistant doctor at the hospital in 1974-75, until the Khmer Rouge forced it to close. He returned to Cambodia from Switzerland in 1991, and was asked to rebuild Kantha Bopha, which he now directs. He is also heard as a cellist under the stage name 'Beatocello' in fund-raising musical performances. Known especially for his outspoken criticism of the World Health Organisation and other international agencies, Richner rejected the idea of low-cost universal primary health care as 'poor medicine for poor people in poor countries' and instead has turned Kantha Bopha into a modern, relatively high-tech hospital of a standard the rest of the Cambodian health service simply could not afford. He raises the funds for this himself, from private sources. In this book he takes on the WHO and other aid agencies, making his particular criticisms of international assistance.

444 **Medical dictionary/Vichananukrum Vichearas.**
Thai Hoa, Maurice Bauhahn. Bangkok: Cama Services, 1991. 2 vols. (1,617p.).

An ambitious project to document medical terminology at a time of extreme needs in the area of health.

445 **National health development plan 1994-96.**
Phnom Penh: Ministry of Health, Kingdom of Cambodia, 1994. 251p. map.

A detailed and comprehensive plan for the development of health services in Cambodia. The 'over-riding concern is to reach the majority of our people . . . through a primary health care approach based on the District Health System', according to the Minister's introduction. It presents the health situation (morbidity and mortality) and health policy, and defines a national system of improved district health care as the basis for development of health services. Including an informative discussion of health-care financing and identifying the large funding gap that must be filled by foreign assistance, this is an impressive report, which is complete with comprehensive statistical information. It contains four annexes, including a population density map.

446 **Les plantes médicinales du Cambodge, du Laos et du Vietnam.**
(Medicinal plants of Cambodia, Laos and Vietnam.)
Alfred Pételot. Saigon: Centre National de Recherches Scientifiques et Techniques, 1952-54. 4 vols. (Archives des Recherches Agronomiques au Cambodge, au Laos et au Vietnam, nos. 14, 18, 22, 23).

In this major compendium by an acknowledged specialist, relevant plants are introduced according to botanical family, with descriptions including scientific name, vernacular name (including Chinese characters, if known), locality, and physical description, but with no illustration. Volume 4 is mostly devoted to indexes according to therapeutic properties and names of plants, divided by language. With the growing international interest in medicinal plants, these volumes continue to attract chemists, pharmacists, physicians and practitioners of alternative medicine. [David G. Marr with Kristine Alilunas-Rodgers]

447 **The ritual space of patients and traditional healers.**
Maurice Eisenbruch. *Bulletin de l'École Française d'Extrême-Orient*, vol. 79, no. 2 (1992), p. 282-316.

Eisenbruch, formerly a senior associate in anthropology at the University of Melbourne and now working in France with CNRS, has worked extensively in Cambodia and with Cambodian refugees in Australia. Drawing on previous work by Condominas, he develops a spatial map at three levels – patient, village and universe – with which to discuss Cambodian society's concept of the body.

448 **La santé publique au Cambodge.** (Public health in Cambodia.)
Phnom Penh: Ministère de l'Information, 1962. 58p.

Although dated, this work gives an overview of the public health system during the Sihanouk period. A description is provided of the principal institutions, such as hospitals and centres of medical education, and of the plans for public health and campaigns against tuberculosis and malaria.

449 **La thalassémie au Cambodge.** (Thalasemy in Cambodia.)
Thor Peng Thong. Paris: École Française d'Extrême-Orient, 1958. 65p. bibliog. (Publications Hors Série de l'École Française d'Extrême-Orient).

Closely related to the research of Sok Heangsun (q.v.), this study looks at the occurrence of thalasemy in Cambodia, particularly dangerous when the subject has Haemoglobin E in the blood.

L'hemoglobine E au Cambodge. (Haemoglobin E in Cambodia.)
See item no. 351.

House of the spirit: perspectives on Cambodian health care.
See item no. 928.

Politics, Administration, Government and Defence

450 **Allied and equal: the Kampuchean People's Revolutionary Party's historiography and its relations with Vietnam (1979-1991).**
K. Viviane Frings. Clayton, Victoria: Centre of Southeast Asian Studies, Monash University, 1994. 40p. bibliog. (Working Papers/Monash University Centre of Southeast Asian Studies, no. 90).

Based on an analysis of five Kampuchean People's Revolutionary Party histories published during the 1980s, this paper studies factors such as the dates given for the formation of the party, references to 'Kampuchea-Vietnam Solidarity', the account of the anti-colonial struggle, attitudes towards Sihanouk, the demonization of Pol Pot and the obliteration of his early relations with Vietnam, in an attempt to discover the real attitudes of party leaders towards their Vietnamese comrades. The KPRP set out to prove that its history of revolutionary struggle was as long as that of the Vietnamese. As well as legitimizing its rule, this was part of the effort to make it clear that Cambodia was an equal partner with, not the little brother of, Vietnam. An epilogue deals with the 1992 history which skates over the party's communist past and refers to the newly named Cambodian People's Party as the little brother of Sihanouk's Sangkum Reastr Niyum. Appendices include a list of the published KPRP histories and a chronology of the party's history from 1930 to 1991.

451 **L'Armée au Cambodge et dans les pays en voie de développement du Sud-Est asiatique.** (The army in Cambodia and in the developing countries of Southeast Asia.)
Maurice Laurent. Paris: Presses Universitaires de France, 1968. 318p. bibliog. (Travaux et Mémoires de la Faculté de Droit et des Sciences Économiques d'Aix-en-Provence).

Published only two years before the coup and before Cambodia was engulfed in a military conflict that lasted more than twenty years, one reads this volume with a sense of regret at the positive expectations laid out by the author, and a bitter taste of wondering what might have been had a different course been followed. Laurent concluded that Cambodia had resolved the problem of establishing an equilibrium between the army, the state and the nation, by involving the army in national development, after 1955 following a different course from the Western democratic model. China and Burma are seen as having some parallels, but the overwhelming attention of this work is on Cambodia itself. The study commences only with the French colonial forces and does not examine Cambodian traditional military structures. It looks in great detail at the role of the military in the First Indochina War and in Sihanouk's 'Crusade for Independence', and also at the Geneva Accords and the development of the Sangkum. The third and final part discusses the lessons of the Khmer experience and the evolution of the role of the army. Laurent was a colonel in the French army, who served for many years as an expert attached to the Cambodian Ministry of National Defence, before submitting his doctoral thesis in law, which gave rise to this publication.

452 **Bulletin Administratif au Cambodge.** (Administrative Bulletin of Cambodia.)
Phnom Penh: Résident Superieur, 1902-49. irregular.

Published in French from 1902 and in Khmer also from 1911, this journal was divided into two parts: official – containing acts, ordinances and circulars; and non-official – containing reports and statements by officials relating to administrative matters. Chronological and subject indexes were provided.

453 **Le Cambodge administratif.** (The Cambodian administration.)
A. Silvestre. [Phnom Penh]: Imprimerie Nouvelle Albert Portail, 1924. 638p.

The classic description of the administrative structure of colonial Cambodia – an essential tool for those studying its history.

454 **Cambodia: a political and military overview.**
Bertil Lintner. *Jane's Intelligence Weekly*, vol. 6, no. 10 (Oct. 1994), p. 467-73.

Freelance journalist Bertil Lintner provides for this renowned intelligence review a survey of the biggest, most ambitious and most expensive peace effort in the United Nations' history, the supervision of elections in Cambodia in 1993 at a cost in excess of US$2 billion. Writing a year after the elections, Lintner concludes that 'what at first appeared to be an astute compromise soon proved to be little more than conservation of the old CPP regime' despite the outcome of the election in which the royalist FUNCINPEC won the biggest vote. Lintner sees the main long-term beneficiaries of the deteriorating situation in Phnom Penh as the Khmer Rouge. The review includes background on Khmer Rouge leaders, the state of Cambodia's armed forces, foreign involvement, the Khmer Rouge Provisional Government of National Union and National Salvation, and possible successors to King Norodom Sihanouk.

455 **Cambodia in the zero years.**
Rosemary H. T. O'Kane. *Third World Quarterly*, vol. 14, no. 4 (Nov. 1993), p. 735-48.

O'Kane attempts to classify the political nature of the Khmer Rouge régime that ruled Cambodia between April 1975 and January 1979, but in the end fails to be completely convincing. Applying a definition taken from Arendt and rejecting the views of

Friedrich and Brzezinski, O'Kane concludes that the Khmer Rouge imposed a 'rudimentary totalitarian system'. In this she finds both the causes and the downfall of the zero years, citing war as the central concern. This theoretical discussion seems not able to reveal much at all about the specific underlying nature or causes of the Khmer Rouge régime, but it could be a useful starting-point for further critical examination of the issue.

456 **The Cambodian People's Party and Sihanouk.**
K. Viviane Frings. *Journal of Contemporary Asia*, vol. 25, no. 3 (1994), p. 356-65.

A valuable commentary on the political transformation of the Kampuchean People's Revolutionary Party into the Cambodian People's Party in 1991. Frings claims the KPRP 'renounced its history of revolutionary struggle' in order to come to agreement with former ruler Prince Norodom Sihanouk and his son Ranariddh to end the post-1979 civil war. Frings argues CPP leaders now trace the origins of their party to the defeat of Pol Pot in 1979 rather than to the Indochinese Communist Party of the 1930s, as they had previously done, a point developed further in her monograph *Allied and equal* (q.v.).

457 **The Cambodian People's Party: where has it come from, where is it going?**
Michael Vickery. *Southeast Asian Affairs,* 1994, p. 102-17.

A thoughtful essay, linking observations on the CPP's line-up in the 1993 elections and subsequent coalition government with a longer and deeper analysis of the party's ideological and structural evolution, through all its congresses and governments since its founding congress of 1951. Vickery refutes the conclusions reached by others (such as Steve Heder and David Chandler) that the old guard has strengthened its position, or that nothing had changed, to develop a thesis that the CPP had never held a strong 'Marxist-Leninist' ideology or structure, and that what elements of these had existed were progressively dismantled from 1987, so that CPP policies advanced during the 1993 elections differed from FUNCINPEC only 'with respect to the Khmer Rouge, Hun Sen calling for their defeat and Ranariddh advocating reconciliation'. Vickery concludes by suggesting 'it would not be surprising to see a realignment opposing a group of technocrats and intellectuals, mostly of the younger generation from all three parties, and in general non-royalist, to old CPP party stalwarts, royalists and opportunists'.

458 **Communism in Indochina: new perspectives.**
Edited by Joseph J. Zasloff, MacAlister Brown. Lexington, Massachusetts: D. C. Heath & Co., 1975. 299p.

Earlier versions of the twelve papers in this collection were presented at a seminar on Communist Movements and Regimes of Indochina at the University of Pittsburgh for the Southeast Asia Development Advisory Group (SEADAG) of the Asia Society, 30 September-2 October 1974. The Society was formed in 1956 as an educational institution to foster American understanding of Asia. SEADAG's aims were to facilitate collaboration and communication between American and Asian scholars and policy makers, and it enjoyed close relations with Washington. Four chapters are devoted to Cambodia: 'External relations of the Khmer resistance' by Sheldon Simon, which examines the dependence and independence of the Khmer Rouge and possibilities for a diplomatic settlement up until the end of 1974; 'Revolution and political violence 1970-74' by correspondent Donald Kirk, which presents evidence about the leadership and operational tactics of the Khmer Rouge; 'Norodom Sihanouk: a leader of the left?' by Milton Osborne; and 'Communism and ethnic conflict 1960-75' by the chair of the Laos-Cambodia council of the Asia Society, Peter Poole. The introduction by Zasloff provides a summary of the regional and international context of the papers' studies, and updates the rapid changes that had taken place between the papers' drafting and the book's publication after April 1975. Many of the predictions made by the authors were lived out, while others indicate just how unknown the nature of the Khmer Rouge was to Western analysts.

459 **Communist party power in Kampuchea (Cambodia): documents and discussion.**

Compiled and edited with an introduction by Timothy Michael Carney. Ithaca, New York: Southeast Asia Program, Department of Asian Studies, Cornell University, 1977. 68p. bibliog. (Data Paper, no. 106).

Perhaps the first serious assessment of the origins and character of the political leadership of the 1975-78 Khmer Rouge régime, this short monograph contains: a historical background to the communist party, later the Party of Democratic Kampuchea, by Carney; documents from the PDK; and accounts of the Khmer Rouge régime by Ith Sarin, a former Cambodian education official and 'defector' (with translations by Carney). Carney was a US foreign service official at the embassy in Phnom Penh and completed this work during a Department of State assignment to Cornell. He outlines the origins of Cambodian communism in the Vietminh-oriented wing of the anti-French Issarak independence movement and its sudden emergence as a national force during the collapse of the US-backed Lon Nol régime in the 1970s. He documents the pro-Chinese and increasingly anti-Vietnamese sentiments of the leadership under Soloth Sar (Pol Pot), and considers the reasons for peasant support of the communist party and for its success in 1975 in the shadow of the secret US bombing of Cambodia. The study is essential reading for students of Cambodian history.

460 **De l'évolution et du développement des institutions annamites et cambodgiennes sous l'influence française.** (The evolution and development of Annamite and Cambodian institutions under French influence.)

Jean Leclerc. Rennes, France: Edoneur & Ruesch, 1923. 174p. Doctoral thesis in economics.

On the establishment of French rule and its beneficial effects, with details of its administrative basis and on the division of powers between the French and Cambodian authorities. There is a revealing chapter on education, described as 'One of the most practical ways of assuring our conquest'. Leclerc provides information the three levels of 'franco-indigène' (run by French and Cambodian authorities) schools (preparatory, primary and colleges – in Cambodia there is only one of the latter, the Sisowath College in Phnom Penh), and the establishment of the University of Indochina in Hanoi in 1918.

461 **The eyes of the pineapple: revolutionary intellectuals and terror in Democratic Kampuchea.**

R. A. Burgler. Saarbrücken, Germany: Verlag Breitenbach, 1990. viii, 438p. maps. bibliog. (Nijmegen Studies in Development and Cultural Change, no. 3).

In his capacity as editor of the left-wing Dutch *Vietnam Bulletin* Roel Burgler resisted accepting the mounting evidence of terror inside newly liberated Cambodia. Later his sympathies lay with the 'underdog' Cambodia in the face of Vietnamese arrogance. But eventually he came to acknowledge that mass killings had indeed occurred, and he went on to pursue this study from the 'humanistic ideals of the Left'. He examines what happened in the DK period, looking at the Cambodian historical context and the ideology of the Khmer Rouge, and he compares this with other communist revolutionary régimes, particularly the Soviet Union, China and Vietnam. Burgler views the specific Cambodia causes as including: isolation and betrayal, the God-Prince Sihanouk, a weak peasantry, traditional fear of the Vietnamese, a brutal war and the traumatic American bombing, factional strife and extreme suspicion. He concludes with these words: 'Democratic Kampuchea was not an attempt at auto-genocide by a group of lunatics. It was a conscious and rational, albeit very radical, attempt to create a classless and contradiction-free, modern and independent society . . . by any means possible'. A Dutch summary is included at the end of the book. The lack of an index frustrates the reader.

462 **The Indochinese Communist Party's division into three parties.**

Motoo Furuta. In: *Indochina in the 1940s and 1950s*. Edited by Takashi Shiraishi and Motoo Furuta. Ithaca, New York: Cornell University, 1992, p. 143-63. (Translations of Contemporary Japanese Scholarship on Southeast Asia).

Using extensive Vietnamese archival documentation, Furuta refines his earlier view that the formation of the Indochinese Communist Party (a change of name for the Vietnamese Communist Party founded in the same year) in the 1930s was a product of the 'class struggle' policy of the ICP, while its division in the early 1950s into three national parties reflected the switch to the line of a 'revolution for national liberation'. But why did this change occur precisely in 1951? According to Furuta, until 1949 the Vietnamese communists appear to have hoped for good relations with popular (bourgeois) régimes in Cambodia and Laos. However, following France's signing of agreements with the Bao Dai government in Vietnam and the monarchies in Cambodia and Laos, the Vietnamese party began a campaign for mass organization in the neighbouring countries. And, by adopting a strategy of people's democratic revolution at home along the lines of the successful Chinese revolution, the Vietnamese party acknowledged differences in the slower pace of political development in Cambodia and Laos. This is a thoughtful paper that deserves consideration by scholars of Indochinese communism and political history.

463 **Les institutions politiques et l'organisation administrative du Cambodge ancien, VIe-XIIIe siècles.** (Political institutions and administrative organization of ancient Cambodia, 6th-13th centuries.)
Sachchidanand Sahai. Paris: École Française d'Extrême-Orient, 1970. 184p. bibliog. (Publications de l'École Française d'Extrême-Orient, no. 75).

Although considerable work has been done on the cultural and religious aspects of ancient Cambodia, this is one of the rare attempts to come to grips with the political institutions. Basing his work on the inscriptions of the period, especially those recorded by Coedès (q.v.), Sachchidanand Sahai deals with his subject under the following topics: the influence of political treaties with ancient India; the royalty; the central administration; the territorial administration; the judiciary; the fiscal régime; external policies; and feudal elements in the administration.

464 **Journal Officiel de l'Indo-Chine Française.** (Official Journal of French Indochina.)
Hanoi, Saigon: Gouvernement-Général de l'Indochine Française, 1899-1950. twice weekly. Available on microfilm, Paris: L'Association pour la Conservation et Réproduction Photographique de la Presse, 1965.

The official government gazette for French Indochina overall, carrying laws, regulations, policies, reports, and appointments. Issued in two parts: the first part, published in Saigon, covers Cochinchina and Cambodia; the second section, published in Hanoi, covers Annam and Tonkin.

465 **Journal Officiel du Cambodge.** (Official Journal of Cambodia.)
Phnom Penh: Secrétariat Général du Conseil des Ministres, Bureaux des Publications Officielles, 1945-73, 1985-93. mainly irregular but semiweekly, 1965-70; weekly, 1952-57. Also available on microfilm, Wooster, Ohio: Micro Photo Division, Bell & Howell, [1979]. 12 reels.

Began publication on 22 March 1945, issued by the new government established by the Japanese occupation forces. The *JOC* took over the task of publishing acts and orders from the *Bulletin Administratif au Cambodge* (q.v.), which continued to publish notices and circulars until 1949 when the *JOC* took over publication of all official acts and notices related to Cambodia. It was published in both French and Khmer, as *Reach Kech* up to 1973, with the name changed to reflect the official status of the government as a republic from 1970. It reappeared in Khmer as *Reach Kech* in 1985. An index, *Répertoire analytique des actes du Gouvernement royal: années: aout 1950-décembre 1960* was published for the years 1950-60 (q.v.).

466 **Kampuchea: politics, economics and society.**
Michael Vickery. London: Pinter, 1986. xviii, 211p. map. bibliog. (Marxist Regimes Series); Sydney: Allen & Unwin; Boulder, Colorado: Lynne Rienner, 1986.

In a relatively brief historical section Vickery surveys the views on a number of controversies. His main concern, however, is a discussion of the political system of the People's Republic of Kampuchea. He considers the constitution and the structure and personnel of the party and the government. This discussion is very detailed, with tables of the membership, including the political origins, of leading party and state bodies. Vickery also looks at the economy, and the domestic and foreign policies, of the PRK, although here the discussion is briefer. The book is directed towards university students of Cambodian politics, and is an eminently readable text.

467 **Les 'nouveaux' Khmers rouges: enquête, 1979-1990: reconstruction du mouvement et reconquête des villages.** (The 'new' Khmer Rouge: enquiry, 1979-90: reconstruction of the movement and reconquest of the villages.)
Christophe Peschoux. Paris: L'Harmattan, 1992. 303p. maps. bibliog.

What is to be made of the rhetoric of the Khmer Rouge since 1979 and especially after 1985? Have they, as claimed, made fundamental shifts in their vision, values, concepts and political ideas? Peschoux examines the Khmer Rouge's history and strategies throughout the 1980s starting with the process of rebuilding after the 1979 defeat. Based on over seventy interviews with deserters and refugees from Khmer Rouge zones, two internal documents probably written by Pol Pot or Noun Chea and interviews with various observers and participants in the Cambodian conflict of the 1980s, it is a well-argued case that little has changed. It is a must for anyone wishing to understand the true nature of this organization and of the problems that beset the United Nations-brokered peace process as a result of the Khmer Rouge's inclusion.

468 **The origins and development of radical Cambodian communism.**
Kenneth Michael Quinn. PhD thesis, Graduate School of the University of Maryland, 1982. ix, 262p. Available in microform from University of Michigan, Ann Arbor, Michigan, order no.: 83-23577.

On the basis of field research conducted on southwest Cambodia from 1972-74, Quinn (appointed US ambassador to Cambodia in 1995) seeks to explain how Pol Pot and his followers gained power, their goal for a new social and economic order, and the ideological positions which allowed violence to be used so widely. Materials used include original party documents, statements by DK leaders, interviews with refugees, and assessments by other scholars. Quinn concludes that: the Khmer Rouge were so alienated by what they saw as an unjust society that they believed only a paroxysm of violence would allow an egalitarian society to be established in place of the old; this revolution had as its model the Great Leap Forward, but modified the Chinese approach to use a far greater degree of violence and fear; methods were learned from Stalinists in Eastern Europe; and impoverished rural youth became the Cambodian equivalent of the Red Guard, who, with early harsh training became capable of carrying out brutal policies, as hardened cadre. As a step-by-step account of how they rose to power, and an analysis of the roots of their political philosophy, it is more a technical rise-and-fall analysis, rather than a broad socio-politico-cultural study of how and why it occurred.

469 **Pol Pot, peasants, and peace: continuity and change in Khmer Rouge political thinking, 1985-1991.**
D. W. Ashley. [Bangkok]: Indochinese Refugee Information Center, Institute of Asian Studies, Chulalongkorn University, 1992. 79p. bibliog. (Institute of Asian Studies. Chulalongkorn University. Paper Series, no. 004).

Attempts to explain how the Khmer Rouge leadership, primarily being Pol Pot and Nuon Chea, have 'maintained the faith' in their ideology, despite their horrific record. To understand how they have done so, Ashley examines their conception of events, their understanding of the struggle after 1979, and their strategy for the post-peace settlement era. As gathering such data is very difficult, Ashley's findings can only be tentative. His sources include translations of leaked internal party documents, interviews with Cambodian refugees and NGO/UN workers from the border camps, radio broadcasts and others' studies. He deals with the material in the following order: the ideology of Angkor 1975-78, examining secrecy, concepts of the nation, results of voluntarism, and the Vietnamese enemy; rationalizing the 'killing fields', analysing DK morality, popularity, and explanations of 1975-78; and post-1985 Khmer Rouge political thinking, outlining the 'ceaseless' struggle, society, ranks, popular support and post-liberation politics and economics. Ashley believes that, albeit a simplification, the events of the Pol Pot time can be traced to the aims and assumptions of the Party leadership, which he documents and analyses here. The main elements of the new orientation of the Khmer Rouge are seen to include a stress on politics rather than military struggle, the preservation of the Khmer Rouge ranks, the adoption of a bourgeois liberal, rather than crudely voluntaristic, economic and political policy, and the identification of Vietnam (rather than the bourgeoisie) as the main enemy.

470 **Répertoire analytique des actes du Gouvernement royal: années: aout 1950 – décembre 1960.** (Analytical listing of acts issued by the Royal Government: August 1950 – December 1960.)
Phnom Penh: Centre Royal de Documentation et d'Édition, 1962. 180p.

An analytical index of the *Journal Officiel du Cambodge* (q.v.) from August 1950 to December 1960.

471 **The return of the Khmer Rouge.**
Jacques Bekaert. *Southeast Asian Affairs*, (1993), p. 130-46.

Bekaert is a Bangkok-based Belgian journalist who specializes in Indochinese affairs. In this paper he concludes that in 1992 the Party of Democratic Kampuchea (Khmer Rouge) 'appears to have gained support . . . at least for the main themes of its propaganda: denunciation of the Vietnamese presence, corruption of the Phnom Penh regime . . . and the need to . . . reinforce the power of the SNC [Supreme National Council]', and that growing numbers of Cambodians seemed to believe a Khmer Rouge presence in parliament or government would be in the country's basic interests. Bekaert has provided a useful summary of the strategy of the Khmer Rouge in the years after 1979 and especially during the UNTAC episode.

472 **The rise and demise of Democratic Kampuchea.**
Craig Etcheson. Boulder, Colorado: Westview, 1984. xvi, 284p. maps. bibliog. (Westview Special Studies on South and Southeast Asia).

A detailed and valuable analysis from a political scientist's perspective that brings its readers closer to a comprehension of the seemingly incomprehensible – the Cambodian tragedy of 1975-78. Etcheson deals with Khmer Rouge history in stages: gestation (1930-60); the early revolutionary stage (1960-67); the late revolutionary stage (1968-75); consolidation and society building (1975-78); and utopia and pandemonium. The contrast between the goals of the revolution as a whole, and the methods employed by the tiny clique of leaders who eventually dominated Cambodian politics, on the other hand, could not be more striking and Etcheson helps his readers to understand why. Revolution entails both the overthrow of the old order and the construction of the new. The Khmer Rouge were masters at the first but totally failed in the second. The book contains a wealth of useful information for students of the period and the movement. Two appendices include the constitution of Democratic Kampuchea and a chronological history of Kampuchea. The author is manager of the Cambodian Genocide Program (q.v.).

Cambodia will never disappear.
See item no. 148.

L'armement et l'organisation de l'armée khmère: aux XIIe et XIIIe siècles: d'après les bas-reliefs d'Angkor Vat, du Bàyon et de Banteay Chmar. (Armament and organization of the Khmer army in the 12th and 13th centuries: according to the bas-reliefs of Angkor Wat, Bayon, and Banteay Chmar.)
See item no. 176.

The foreign politics of the Communist Party of Vietnam: a study of communist tactics.
See item no. 539.

Indochina Issues.
See item no. 860.

Kampuchea Démocratique Bulletin d'Information. (Democratic Kampuchea News Bulletin.)
See item no. 862.

Human Rights, Genocide, Constitution and Legal System

473 **2,035,000 murdered: the hell state, Cambodia under the Khmer Rouge.**

R. J. Rummel. In: *Death by government.* R. J. Rummel, with a foreword by Irving Louis Horowitz. New Brunswick, New Jersey: Transactions Publishers, 1994, p. 159-208. bibliog.

The contents page of *Death by government* reads somewhat like a video-game scoreboard. Only certain régimes make it into part two, as 'Dekamegamurderers', while this chapter on Cambodia under the Khmer Rouge appears in part three, with 'The lesser megamurderers'. Other chapters receive titles such as 'The Pakistani cutthroat state' and 'Tito's slaughterhouse'. One almost feels as if the author is trying to sell us something with this shock-horror marketing of information. Bizarrely, the foreword suggests that the 'measurement of life-taking propensities of states, societies and communities' may be the only universally relevant field of social science. Despite the insensitive, if not obscene, presentation of the material, Rummel's studies contribute to the historical documentation of crimes against humanity. He attempts to make the study of killing an exact science, to 'determine its nature and scope in order to test the theory that democracies are inherently nonviolent'. In Cambodia he estimates that close to 2,400,000 people were murdered by the Khmer Rouge. He provides a simplistic political analysis of the régimes which led to, and followed, that of Pol Pot as well as documenting their role in causing unnatural deaths. It is an extensive study, including tables showing Cambodian democide rates compared to that of others, Cambodian democide by perpetrator, living conditions under the Khmer Rouge, estimated versus predicted Cambodian population and so on. Numerous annotations indicate the sources for his conclusions.

474 **Blue scarves and yellow stars: classification and symbolization in the Cambodian genocide.**

Gregory H. Stanton. Montreal: Montreal Institute for Genocide Studies, Concordia University, 1989.

International lawyer Greg Stanton here draws an analogy between the blue scarves allocated by the Khmer Rouge to condemned deportees from the Eastern Zone after an uprising there in 1977 and the yellow stars allocated to condemned Jews by the Nazis. In both cases the groups were marked out for special discriminatory treatment, even death, by the oppressor.

475 **Boudhiba Report concerning human rights violations including Cambodia.**

New York: United Nations, 1979. E/CN.4/1335/1979 (Boudhiba).

Comprises reports and testimony submitted by member states to the Sub-Commission on the Prevention of Discrimination and the Protection of Minorities of the UN Commission on Human Rights (UNCHR). Boudhiba, the Chairman of the Sub-Commission, examined the reports and analysed the violations of the Universal Declaration of Human Rights. He concluded that this was the worst case since Nazism, and that the Khmer Rouge carried out 'auto-genocide'. Although it had commissioned this report, the UNCHR has so far never considered its findings. Many other related documents can be found among the official papers of the UNCHR (E/CN.4/Sub.2/414/1978 in the UN documentation series).

476 **The bureaucracy of death.**

Anthony Barnett, Chantou Boua and Ben Kiernan. *New Statesman*, 1980, vol. 2, no. 5, p. 669-76.

An early account of the S-21 (Tuol Sleng) prison in Phnom Penh, a former high school used by the Khmer Rouge as a detention and interrogation centre. They left documentary and photographic records that are now being studied and made publicly available. This article includes significant extracts from the confession of Hu Nim (DK Minister of Information) and indeed this was the first time such a document was published, indicating the internal purges of high-ranking Khmer Rouge cadre.

477 **Cambodia at war.**

Human Rights Watch/Asia; Human Rights Watch Arms Project. New York: Human Rights Watch, 1995. 166p.

Cambodia today is far from realizing the Paris Peace Accords' promise of a country at peace where human rights are ensured and respected. This report, based on three missions to Cambodia between March 1994 and February 1995, documents cases of murder, rape, hostage-taking, and the use of famine as a weapon by the Khmer Rouge in their new 'scorched earth' tactics. The report also examines severe abuses by government soldiers against civilians, including secret detention, extortion and murder, and the failure of the government in most cases to prosecute its own officials responsible, and even documents government retaliation against institutions and individuals critical of those abuses. Human Rights Watch analyses foreign support for both the Khmer Rouge and government forces, and calls for an end to the provision of arms and military equipment to the warring parties, as well as for an abolition of the use, acquisition and stockpiling of antipersonnel landmines. It also calls on international donors to insist that the Cambodian government hold its officials, civilian and military, accountable for gross violations of human rights.

478 **Cambodia, the justice system and violations of human rights.**
New York: Lawyers Committee for Human Rights, 1992. iv, 74p. bibliog.

Since 1978 the Lawyers Committee for Human Rights has worked to promote international human rights and refugee law and legal procedures in the United States and abroad. For two weeks in September 1991 a delegation headed by James Ross visited Phnom Penh, Kandal and Kompong Speu and met with judges, prosecutors and government officials. The report, written by Ross, outlines aspects of the State of Cambodia (SOC) legal system, its evolution since 1979 and its operation at the time of the study, concluding that the system functioned to guard the interests of the state and the ruling party at the expense of fundamental human rights. Recommendations include: amendments to laws to conform with standards on international human rights law; an independent judiciary and autonomous bar; measures to safeguard against torture and ill treatment of prisoners; adequate defence representation in court; a genuine criminal code excluding counter-revolutionary activities and like offences; and laws to permit formal legal redress for abuses. The work is an interesting summary of aspects of the SOC legal system and its history during the 1980s.

479 **Cambodia: human rights before and after the elections.**
Sidney Jones and Dinah PoKempner. *Asia Watch*, vol. 5, no. 10 (1993). 41p.

This report concludes that 'Cambodia will go to the polls on May 23 in an atmosphere of political and ethnic violence and renewed civil war'. In an attempt to determine 'how, or perhaps whether, human rights of Cambodians can be protected under whatever government comes to power', the authors study UNTAC's record of protecting human rights. Their findings, concentrating only on political and legal rights, are critical of all four factions and of UNTAC itself. While most emphasis and publicity is given to abuses condoned or conducted by the State of Cambodia, it is clear that those in zones controlled by FUNCINPEC and the KPNLF were probably as bad or worse, in proportion to the size of the populations covered. Khmer Rouge atrocities are also mentioned. UNTAC personnel themselves sometimes failed to set a desirable example and bungled attempts to see that justice was administered impartially.

480 **Cambodia: revolution, genocide, intervention.**
Barbara Harff. In: *Revolutions of the late twentieth century.* Edited by Jack A. Goldstone, Ted Robert Gurr, Farrokh Moshiri. Boulder, Colorado: Westview Press, 1991, p. 218-34.

Harff analyses the Cambodian case against Goldstone's model of 'declining state resources relative to expenses and the resources of adversaries, increasing elite alienation and disunity, and growing popular grievances and autonomy'. She finds that the model does not really fit, and that in Cambodia's case it was rather the Vietnam war that brought genocidal consequences as peasants retaliated against the urban people.

481 **The Cambodian genocide.**

David Hawk. In: *Genocide: critical bibliographic review*, Vol. 1. Edited by Israel W. Charny. London: Mansell; New York: Facts on File, 1988, p. 137-54.

Hawk has written the Cambodian chapter of this work which contains twelve other examples, each of which provides a critical review of the literature followed by an annotated bibliography.

482 **Cambodia.**

Ben Kiernan. In: *Genocide in the twentieth century: an anthology of oral histories*. New York: Garland Publishing, 1993, p. 429-81. Republished in paperback as *Century of Genocide*, New York: Garland, 1995. 488p.

This volume contains critical essays and oral testimony on genocidal acts in various countries including Cambodia in this chapter by Ben Kiernan. The introductory essay is by Samuel Totten, Israel Charny, and William Parsons (qq.v.). See also *Genocide in the twentieth century: critical essays and eyewitness accounts*, edited by Samuel Totten, William S. Parsons and Israel W. Charny (New York: Garland, 1995. lvi, 570p.).

483 **The Carter administration, human rights, and the agony of Cambodia.**

Sheldon Neuringer. Lewiston, New York: E. Mellen Press, 1993. ii, 98p. bibliog.

Neuringer sets out to compare the US reaction to the Nazi holocaust with its attitude to this later example of genocide. Slow to react to reports of atrocities, the Carter administration finally designated the Khmer Rouge régime 'the worst violator of human rights in the world today' but emerging rapprochement with China set the scene for little talk and less action. Three weeks before losing the 1980 election to Ronald Reagan, the Carter administration plumbed the depths of *realpolitik* when it voted to accept the credentials of Democratic Kampuchea for entry to the United Nations. The volume includes an afterword on the years from 1981 to 1993 and a bibliographical essay, providing a useful analysis of US policy towards Cambodia from 1977 to 1993.

484 **Centralized terror in Democratic Kampuchea: scope and span of control.**

Craig Etcheson. New Haven, Connecticut: Cambodian Genocide Program, Center for International and Area Studies, Yale University, 1997. 10p. + 8 maps + 3p. of tables. bibliog.

Prepared for the Association of Asian Studies 49th Annual Meeting, held in Chicago, 14-16 March 1997. Etcheson, Manager of the Cambodian Genocide Program (CGP), reports on the findings of the first two years' work. He reports Documentary Evidence, particularly from the *Santebal* (Khmer Rouge secret police) establishing the relationship between S-21, the Tuol Sleng prison and a network of zone and regional centres throughout the country; and Mass Grave Evidence from 68 sites in 9 provinces, with a total of some 5,120 mass grave pits (estimated to be perhaps one-quarter of the total in the country).

485 **Les codes cambodgiens.** (Cambodian laws.)
Adhémard Leclère. Paris: Ernest Leroux, 1898. 2 vols.

After his *Recherches sur la législation cambodgienne: droit privé* (Research on Cambodian legislation: private law) (q.v.) with three volumes totalling 1,200 pages of texts and analysis, Leclère went on to publish this translation of a body of 54 laws, which, he says, most people ignored and nobody enforced. These texts, which probably do not really deserve the name of 'laws', were written between the 17th and 19th centuries. This work is a motley arrangement of heterogeneous pieces of writing, elaborated in unspecified circumstances. But as testimonies of vanished periods, they are extraordinarily important because they are the only surviving Khmer views on Khmer society of that time. The royal chronicles were written or rewritten after 1820 and are of much less sociological value.

486 **Collection of first-person accounts of the Cambodian genocide.**
Interviewed by David Hawk, John Marston and Sotheary Doung. [s.l.: s.n.], 1979.

Tapes and transcripts of first-person accounts about the Cambodian genocide recorded by David Hawk (over 125), John Marston (over 60) and Sotheary Doung, and others. They are held in the Library of Congress after having been catalogued by the Social Science Research Council. Marston (q.v.) and Sotheary Doung gathered data concerning language change under the Khmer Rouge.

487 **Comprehending the Cambodian genocide: an application of Robert Jay Lifton's model of genocidal killing.**
Eric Markusen. *Psychohistory Review*, 1992, vol. 20, no. 2, p. 145-69.

This article summarizes Lifton's work on genocidal killing and applies his emerging theoretical model to the Cambodian genocide. Markusen finds that Lifton's model – which features a sequence from psychohistorical dislocation (severe social and cultural disruption) to totalistic ideological response to violent victimization (of a group alleged to be responsible for the collective trauma) – is consistent with events before and during the Cambodian genocide.

488 **Les constitutions du Cambodge 1953-1993.** (The constitutions of Cambodia 1953-93.)
Texts compiled and presented by Raoul M. Jennar. Paris: La Documentation Française, 1994. 118p. bibliog.

A fine addition to basic reference books on Cambodia, of which there are all too few. Jennar has searched widely for authoritative texts of the six constitutions Cambodia has been subject to in the past forty years alone! They are presented here in full with a page or two of introductory comment on the context in which each was adopted. Jennar adds to these important basic texts a short essay on 'Cambodian revolutions' and a substantial bibliography. In the essay Jennar advances the proposition – previously made by Serge Thion (q.v.) – that the repeated revolutions Cambodia has traversed have made sudden changes, but these have neither prevented continuity nor a return to the point of departure. Jennar identifies certain features shared by all: concern for territorial integrity and unity; proclamation of neutrality and non-alignment (except for the pro-US Khmer Republic); and the persistence of an omnipresent state, little inclined to recognize and respect autonomous sectors of society, to the extent (in the present constitution) of projecting a law to control the free market. Liberties proclaimed in all the constitutions are conceded, and always subject to the discretion of the authorities who may suspend them, in the name of public order and national security. The Cambodian people are always regarded as passive subjects, even as children, slaves or comrades, but never as citizens and responsible actors, and certainly not as the sole source of legitimacy of power. Jennar adds a bibliography of over 500 items, which is especially useful to students of modern Cambodian politics and history.

489 **Démocratie cambodgienne: la constitution du 24 septembre 1993.**
(Cambodian democracy: the constitution of 24 September 1993.)
Maurice Gaillard. Paris: L'Harmattan, 1994. 186p. (Collection Points sur l'Asie).

An unusual approach, applying textual analysis to the 1993 Constitution, and interpreting it in terms of 'the affirmation of national identity' and 'the quest for stability'. The full text of the Constitution is translated into French from the Khmer text that was adopted by the National Assembly, and indexes are given to 'favourite words' and 'favourite themes'. Maurice Gaillard, of the Faculty of Juridical Sciences at the University of Lumière-Lyon 2, France, is critical of the text in constitutional terms, repeating Raoul Jennar's assessment of it as containing 'naive formulas' and 'vague terms' and, in comparison with the pre-1970 and 1972 constitutions, as 'very much regressed in terms of public law and juridical rigour', and Gaillard's final chapter is entitled 'Tomorrow democracy' indicating its absence from the present constitutional arrangements.

490 **English-Khmer law dictionary = Vacananukram chbab anglais-khmer.**
Phnom Penh: The Asia Foundation, 1994. draft ed. 317p.

In 1992 this book began to be developed as a simple law glossary or lexicon, but it was soon found that the need to provide definitions of legal terminology was as pressing as the mere translated term, and so the project was expanded. The Dictionary Project Team was headed by Mr. Koy Neam, and the work was carried out in consultation with a wide range of Cambodian and foreign law experts, and based on many existing legal texts and dictionaries. The project was funded by USAID, The Asia Foundation and the Catholic Office for Emergency Relief and Refugees. While still in draft form, it is already a valuable tool, but it could certainly benefit from a Khmer index, as it is at present accessible only via the English terms.

491 **Facing death.**
Special issue of *Photographers International*, no. 19 (April 1995). 107p.

An astonishing selection of 100 photographs from the more than 6,000 restored and printed by Chris Riley and David Niven and the staff of Tuol Sleng as a project of the Photo Archive Group. These are images of the prisoners, in the main photographed as they were admitted to the prison, not knowing exactly what fate awaited them. Here we see in stark reality the fear, confusion and puzzlement of individuals when faced with the bureaucracy of death. Women holding their babies in arms, and young children fix your eyes as they stare from the page along with men – soldiers with their uniforms on, or ripped off – and then the awful few photographs of the bodies lying bloodied on the floor at the end of their ordeal. The last photograph is of one of the

7 survivors of the 15,000-or-so who passed through Tuol Sleng. A sculptor, Im Chhan, sits with the image of himself as prisoner taken seventeen years earlier. The images are the most powerful indictment of what went on in Cambodia between 1975 and 1979 and they speak for themselves. Nevertheless the short textual pieces accompanying the pictures have their own part to play. Editorial by Juan I-Jong describes 'some of these portraits [as] undoubtedly among the most powerful in the history of photography'. David Chandler's introduction sets the context in which the photographs were taken and in which the Genocidal Museum was constructed, and the issue also contains an interview with Riley and Niven by Juan I-Jong on the work of restoration. These 100 images were mounted as an exhibition in Cambodia, and internationally in 1995 as the basis of the 'Facing death' exhibition, and a full set of photographs from Tuol Sleng (including a number not restored by the Photo Archive Group) have now been scanned by the Cambodian Genocide Program (q.v.) to be made available on the Internet for identification.

492 **Facing history and ourselves – holocaust behavior: an annotated bibliography.**
Margaret A. Drew. New York: Walker, 1988. 124p.

A bibliography of material for educators on the holocaust and also on the genocides in Armenia and Cambodia. Extensive annotations provide both historical and literary commentary. The work would also be suitable for secondary-school and tertiary students.

493 **First-person accounts of genocidal acts committed in the twentieth century: a critical annotated bibliography.**
Samuel Totten. New York; Westport, Connecticut; London: Greenwood Press, 1991. 350p. bibliog. (Bibliographies and Indexes in World History; no. 21).

Totten provides bibliographical details and annotations of a wide variety of primary accounts (memoirs, diaries, oral histories, autobiographies, interviews, court testimony and eyewitness statements) of survivors and other witnesses (including journalists, liberators, relief workers, bystanders, diplomats, etc.) of the following genocidal acts: the Armenian genocide; the Soviet man-made famine in Ukraine; the Soviet deportations of whole nations; the holocaust; the fate of the Gypsies during the Holocaust years; the Khmer Rouge slaughter of the Cambodian people; and many recent occurrences.

494 **Les frontières du Cambodge.** (The frontiers of Cambodia.)
Sarin Chhak. Paris: Dalloz, 1966. 1 vol. bibliog. (Centre d'Étude des Pays d'Extrême-Orient, Asie du Sud-Est, 1).

A doctoral thesis presented at the Faculty of Law and Economic Sciences of the University of Paris and welcomed as a major contribution to an obscure yet vital area of inquiry in a preface by Norodom Sihanouk. Sarin here presents his findings on the Cambodian borders with Vietnam and Laos, with the intention of publishing a second volume on the Thai-Cambodian border. Each section of the border is examined physically and represented in maps as well as being thoroughly researched in written documents and treaties, the most significant of which are presented as annexes to the work. He concludes that there is considerable evidence of the loss of territory by Cambodia during the French occupation, particularly to Vietnam, but that this was carried out simply through administrative measures, and not on the basis of international treaties. He calls for resolution of this matter as a key issue for Cambodia's independence and sovereignty and appeals for Vietnam to participate in a peaceful approach to its solution. Sarin, who played an important part in expatriate politics in France in the 1960s, was Ambassador to Cairo in 1966 and joined the opposition to the Lon Nol government and went on to work with the Khmer Rouge government, but tragically he disappeared in the turmoil surrounding the overthrow of Pol Pot.

495 **Genocidal Center at Choeung Ek.**
Phnom Penh: Information and Culture Service, 1989. 1 brochure folded into 14 leaves of illustrations. maps.

Thousands of visitors to Choeung Ek, widely known as the 'killing fields' on the outskirts of Phnom Penh, will have been handed this simple black-and-white brochure with its chilling photographic evidence of the executions and burials there. Some 86 out of 129 mass graves were exhumed in 1979-80, and it is estimated that 15,000 people, mainly from the Tuol Sleng prison, met their end at Choeung Ek between 1975 and 1979. In 1989, to commemorate the tenth anniversary of the overthrow of Pol Pot, the remains were removed from wooden shelters into a stupa to be more appropriately honoured and there they remain to this day, with the exception of the 'European' skulls which were apparently taken away by the MIA investigation teams from the United States – it seems these victims cannot rest with their fellows in this strangely serene and holy place.

496 **Genocide and democracy in Cambodia: the Khmer Rouge, the U.N., and the international community.**
Edited by Ben Kiernan. New Haven, Connecticut: Yale University, Southeast Asia Studies, 1993. 335p.

A collection of papers presented at a conference under the same name held at the Yale Law School in February 1992, consisting of substantial essays by a range of leading scholars on various aspects of Cambodian society between, during, and after the Khmer Rouge period. The genocide (with Serge Thion debating the use of the term genocide) is viewed from a demographic perspective (Judith Banister and E. Paige Johnston), and in terms of the impact of this period on rural Cambodia (Chantou Boua, Kate Frieson and May Ebihara). The book also contains major articles on the genocide and international law (Gregory Stanton) and on the inclusion of the Khmer Rouge in the peace process (Ben Kiernan), and its appendices contain some unusual input from Cambodian political actors themselves – Khieu Kanharith (Secretary of State for Information in the post-1993 government) and Douc Rasy (former Dean of the Law School at the University of Phnom Penh and now president of the Licadho human rights group in Cambodia), and an outline of the UN Peace Plan by Heidi Annebi, director of Peace Keeping Operations for the United Nations. Ben Kiernan's introduction firmly places this book in its context as part of the campaign to oppose the return of the Khmer Rouge and to bring its leaders to trial under the Genocide Convention of 1948.

497 **Genocide: conceptual and historical dimensions.**
Edited by George J. Andreopoulos. Philadelphia: University of Pennsylvania Press, 1994. x, 265p. bibliog. (Pennsylvania Studies in Human Rights).

Raphael Lemkin, who coined the term genocide, described a key component as 'the criminal intent to destroy or to cripple permanently a human group. The acts are directed against groups, as such, and individuals are selected for destruction only because they belong to these groups'. His definition contributed much to the 1948 UN Genocide Convention. Since that time, genocide as a social process has developed into a field of study. The papers in this collection were presented at a 1991 conference at the Yale Law School under the auspices of the Orville H. Schell Jr. Center for International Human Rights. Written very much in contemporary academic language are four essays outlining the conceptual dimensions of genocide. Part two, 'The reality of genocide', presents case-studies, which include 'The Cambodian genocide: issues and responses', by Ben Kiernan. He maintains that the record of Pol Pot's 1975-79 régime is a clear case of genocide against four Cambodian groups – monks, ethnic Vietnamese, Chinese and Chams. He also raises the possibility of the persecution of Eastern-Zone Khmers being seen as 'auto-genocide'. He points out that despite irrefutable evidence against the Khmer Rouge, no government has been willing to take a case against them to the International Court of Justice. Appendices contain the text of the 1948 UN Genocide Convention and chronologies of the case-studies presented in part two.

498 **How to avoid (legally) conviction for crimes of genocide: a one act reading.**
Israel W. Charny. *Social Science Record*, September 1987, vol. 24, no. 2, p. 89-93.

An imaginary discussion between Talaat, Hitler, Stalin, Idi Amin, and Pol Pot with their lawyers, 'Satan, Conformist, and Whore'. It explores some of the limitations of the UN Genocide Convention and suggests that its definition of genocide should be revised and expanded.

499 **Introduction bibliographique à l'histoire du droit et à l'ethnologie juridique.** (Bibliographical introduction to the history of law and juridical ethnology: E/11, Indochina.)
Yvonne Bongert, published under the direction of John Gilissen. Brussells: Éditions de l'Institut de Sociologie, Université Libre de Bruxelles, 1967. 102p. map. (Centre d'Histoire et d'Ethnologie Juridiques).

This bibliography contains a listing of 1,173 items on French Indochina as a whole and its constituent parts including Cambodia, followed by material from the three independent countries (Cambodia, Laos and Vietnam) and on their ethnic minorities. Works are arranged according to legal and ethnological categories. Bongert was Professor in the Faculty of Law and Economic Sciences at the University of Paris.

500 **ITNetwork.**

ITNetwork (International Network on Holocaust and Genocide). Ryde, New South Wales: Macquarie University, Centre for Comparative Genocide Studies [1995]- . Former title, *Internet on Holocaust and Genocide*, Jerusalem: Institute on the Holocaust and Genocide, [1986?-].

Contains regular articles on the Cambodian genocide. Volume 12, no. 1-2, for example, has a number of crucial papers, some from the conference, 'Cambodia: power, myth and memory' held at Monash University, Clayton, Victoria in December 1996 including: 'From theory to facts in the Cambodian genocide' by Craig Etcheson; 'Obedience, culture & the Cambodian genocide' by Alex Hinton; 'Samey Pol Pot: the Pol Pot era – an eyewitness account' by Thida B. Mam; and 'The myth always wins: Cambodia in the UNTAC era' by John Weeks.

501 **Journey to Cambodia: investigation into massacre by Pol Pot regime.**

Honda Katuiti. Tokyo: Committee of Movement for Publishing English Version of 'Journey to Cambodia', 1981. 191p.

A translation of a series of articles published in the Japanese newspaper *Asahi Shimbun* in which Honda reports on interviews with over 100 village leaders concerning deaths in their own families during the Khmer Rouge period. He concludes that the 216 families studied suffered a mortality rate of 44 per cent.

502 **Kampuchea: after the worst.**

Floyd Abrams and Diane Orentlicher in close consultation with Steve Heder. New York: Lawyers Committee for Human Rights, 1990. xi, 161p. bibliog.

Interviews conducted with refugees on both sides of the Thai/Cambodian border in late 1984 and early 1985 are used to analyse the human rights situation in the PRK and areas under the control of the Khmer Rouge (DK) and the KPNLF. The bulk of the report deals with the PRK although the authors were not granted access to the country by the Phnom Penh government. While acknowledging improvements since the ousting of the Khmer Rouge, and the 'modest' success of the régime in re-establishing basic government services, the report concludes that arbitrary arrest, detention and torture are common and that political repression was widely practised. The authors acknowledge the difficulty of assessing the degree of political repression from an analysis of refugee flows during the course of a civil war and on the basis of the testimony of refugees. A second section of the work looks at the history of the Pol Pot régime, the administrative and command structures of Khmer Rouge forces, arrest and detention, and physical integrity. Section three examines: the background to the KPNLF and its early years of operation; current conditions, including physical integrity; adjudicatory procedures and the situation in three camps – Prey Chan, Ampil Banteay and Rithisen. First published in 1985, the 1990 reprint does not update the information in the original report but corrects some typographical errors.

503 **Kampuchea: decade of the genocide: report of a Finnish inquiry commission.**

Edited by Kimmo Kiljunen. London: Zed Books, 1984. xii, 126p. maps. bibliog. (Third World Studies).

A revised version of *Kampuchea in the seventies* (1982), this is a report of the Kampuchea Inquiry Commission established in Helsinki in October 1980 to 'study the political, social and economic development of Kampuchea and the subsequent legal implications and repercussions on international politics, especially in light of the events of the 1970's'. This work provides a good summary of the results of the Khmer Rouge régime and the early years of the PRK, studies the ramifications under international law and human rights conventions of the actions of governments both domestic and foreign, and analyses Finnish policy towards the country.

504 **Kampuchea: political imprisonment and torture.**

London: Amnesty International Publications, 1987. ii, 84, [5]p. map. Amnesty International index ASA/23/05/87.

Published at a time of mounting pressure for a political settlement and an end to the Western embargo on Cambodia, this report, widely known to have been written by Steve Heder (q.v.), was used as a major argument against recognition of the PRK. Subtitled *Torture and political imprisonment in the People's Republic of Kampuchea (Cambodia)*, this is a report of alleged human rights abuses by the PRK régime. Without access to the country, information was gathered over several years from Cambodian refugees on the Thai border and supplemented by media commentaries and information from non-governmental sources. Alleged abuses by members of the coalition government in exile are also briefly covered but with far less emphasis. Limitations on access to FUNCINPEC-controlled areas were advanced as the reason. Appendices include: summaries of 24, from among more than 100, reported cases of political prisoners held without charge or trial in the PRK; and a history of Amnesty's actions regarding human rights abuses during the Khmer Rouge régime. Also included are a map of the country, a floor plan of T-3 prison and sketches illustrating two torture methods reported to have been used on political suspects.

505 **The killing fields.**

Edited by Chris Riley and Doug Niven. Santa Fe, New Mexico: Twin Palms, 1996. 112p. bibliog.

Contains 100 photographs, selected from the 6,000 of those recently restored and printed by the Photo Archive Group. These 100 images form the basis of the 'Facing death' exhibition, which has been shown in a number of countries. Some 15,000 people were incarcerated in Tuol Sleng, and only 7 survived. The pictures have a jolting impact, and reveal the breadth of people caught up in the net of terror – soldiers, sailors, bureaucrats, farmers, men, women, children and even babies. The details and incidental things caught by the photographer's lens show even more – hands grasping each other tightly, fellow prisoners lying on the floor, a baby's hand reaching up to its mother, a French police photographic apparatus, two hearts pierced by an arrow in graffiti on the wall. This reproduction of the photographs in the form of an art book is, as David Chandler has remarked, disquietingly 'luscious'. Fortunately, some context is given to the images through the memoirs of Vann Nath, one of the seven survivors, who was interviewed by Sara Colm, who also translated and edited his words, and Chandler's essay on 'The pathology of terror in Pol Pot's Cambodia'.

This first edition was limited to 3,000 case-bound copies and is available from Twin Palms, Santa Fe, New Mexico, 87501, USA.

506 **Kingdom of Cambodia: diminishing respect for human rights.**
London: Amnesty International, 1996. 63p. Amnesty International index ASA 23/02/96.

Since the 1987 publication of *Kampuchea: political imprisonment and torture* (q.v.), Amnesty International has issued at least six reports on the general state of human rights in Cambodia: *State of Cambodia, human rights developments, October 1, 1991 to January 31, 1992* (1992); *State of Cambodia, update on human rights concerns* (October 1992); *Human rights concerns July – December 1992* (1993); *Kingdom of Cambodia, human rights and the new government* (1994); *Human rights and the new government* (1995); and this 1996 report. Problems covered include political prisoners and their treatment, extra-judicial killings, freedom of expression and the rights of ethnic minorities. Abuses by the Party of Democratic Kampuchea (PDK – Khmer Rouge) are also listed. Numerous shorter reports and 'Action Alerts' take up single issues such as the country's press laws or constitution, the arrest or harassment of political opposition figures and the murders of several media critics. Available from local Amnesty International offices, the material provides useful information on those aspects of political human rights that fall within Amnesty's mandate. This 1996 report contains a summary and an appendix on the Status of Cases of Human Rights Violations reported by Amnesty International.

507 **Mekong Law Report: Cambodia.**
Dirksen Flipse Doran & Le, Legal Advisers. Phnom Penh: Dirksen Flipse Doran and Le, April 1996. 44p.

Part of a series of three reports, the other two covering Laos and Vietnam. The Cambodia publication describes the economic and legal systems and efforts by the Royal Cambodian government to design and implement economic policy. The report highlights investment opportunities, which differ considerably from those in Laos and Vietnam because Cambodia has steered towards the path of a minimally restricted free market economy. Nine tables are included, and charts throughout the book show trends in growth sectors and the structure of institutions such as the Cambodian Development Council and Cambodian Investment Bank. Topics covered are investment procedures, investment structures, taxation, banking and finance, in addition to the laws pertaining to contracts, property and land. Attention to issues of workplace safety and workers' rights is minimal. This law company also produces a regular column on the Cambodian legal system in the *Phnom Penh Post* (q.v.).

508 **The nature of genocide in Cambodia (Kampuchea).**
Ben Kiernan. In: 'Teaching about genocide'. Edited by Samuel Totten and William S. Parsons. Special issue of *Social Education*, 55(2), Feb. 1991, p. 84-133.

Social Education is the official journal of the National Council for Social Studies and, as such, has the possibility of influencing the curriculum and providing resources for teaching throughout the United States. In addition to Cambodia, other cases include Australia, Burundi, the holocaust, the Gypsies and the 'Vanished Americans', as well as several theoretical papers.

509 **People's Revolutionary Tribunal held in Phnom Penh for the trial of the genocide crime of the Pol Pot – Ieng Sary clique (August-1979): documents.**
A group of lawyers of Cambodia. Phnom Penh: Foreign Languages Publishing House, 1990. xii, 311p.

A selection of the principal testimonies and other judicial documents presented at the August 1979 trial in which Pol Pot and Ieng Sary were condemned to death in absentia.

510 **Pol Pot's Cambodia: was it genocide?**
David Hawk. In: *Toward the understanding and prevention of genocide: proceedings of the International Conference on the Holocaust and Genocide.* Edited by Israel W. Charny. Boulder, Colorado: Westview Press, 1984, p. 51-59.

Hawk, a former executive director of Amnesty International, who has devoted considerable effort to documenting the Cambodian genocide, discusses Khmer Rouge violations, including genocidal actions against Buddhist monks and the Islamic Cham minority. He concludes that even under the restricted definition of genocide as usually inferred from the Genocide Convention, the mass murders in Cambodia qualify as such, since there were target groups such as the Cham (an Islamic minority) and the Buddhist monks. He ascribes the lack of action in this case as stemming from political cynicism and indifference.

511 **Rebuilding Cambodia: human resources, human rights, and law: three essays.**
Dolores A. Donovan, Sidney Jones and Dinah PoKempner, Robert J. Muscat, edited and with an introduction by Frederick Z. Brown. Washington, DC: Foreign Policy Institute, Paul H. Nitze School of Advanced International Studies, Johns Hopkins University, 1993. vi, 116p. bibliog.

An attempt to analyse 'the Cambodian problem' in terms of human resources, human rights, and the legal framework, this collection of three essays provides thoughtful insights by well-informed experts. Their starting-point is how UNTAC could best have prepared Cambodia for its transition to a liberal democracy and market economy. Unlike several other contemporary commentaries on the legal and human rights situation, Dolores A. Donovan's overview of the legal system under the PRK is assisted by a knowledge of comparative law and socialist legal theory. Sidney Jones and Dinah PoKempner assert that human rights is something unknown in Cambodian history. Their protection will therefore be a matter of 'putting in place what was not there before'.

512 **Recherches sur la législation cambodgienne: droit privé.** (Research on Cambodian legislation: private law.)
Adhémard Leclère. Paris: Augustin Challamel, 1890. xiv, 328p.

This is part of an attempt by a high-ranking colonial administrator and scholar to gather Khmer written documents pertaining to legal problems and organize them into a body of laws, along the lines inherited from Latin and Greek Codes. This was easily done in Vietnam (as in translation by Philastre) where such a codified body of texts existed since the reforms of Gia Long at the beginning of the 19th century. But no such a thing existed in Cambodia and Leclère single-handedly tried to establish such a corpus – see his *Codes cambodgiens* (q.v.). Three other volumes were written to expand the concept. Under the Protectorate, the courts were run by Cambodian judges. In the present volume, Leclère says the texts are rare and difficult to discover. 'They are almost never consulted; but they live deep inside the conscience of the Khmers and they dominate the whole administrative organization.' Perhaps this was wishful thinking. He analysed the eight classes of free men, resulting in a short treatise on Khmer political sociology, including patronage, whose political role he says is almost finished. He compares the situation of the non-Khmer 'savages' with the indigenous tribes of the United States. He writes: 'For the Khmer, the savage is a not-yet captured slave, an inferior man, a talking ape, as they sometimes put it'. The author then studies the family, and the slave system. The majority of the population was in one or the other of many categories that we roughly translate as 'slave'. Twins, for example, were taken away and made state slaves. The book ends with an interesting part on land ownership, running against the common view in insisting that private property was already established in Cambodia before colonization.

513 **Recherches sur la législation criminelle et la procédure des Cambodgiens.**
Adhémard Leclère. Paris: Challamel, 1894.

Another collection of texts and laws, dealing with criminal procedures. In the preface, Leclère complains that some laws are unknown or even kept secret. 'It is obvious to me', he says, 'that the king and some other concerned persons do not want to communicate these laws to the French out of fear that they would make them known to the Cambodians.' He says a study of Laos would aid an understanding of Cambodia because, under a thin Siamese veneer, Laos is endowed with the same ancient organizational pattern as Cambodia. The first part of this work deals with justice regulations (procedure), investigation, courts, and the use of ordeals. Sometimes, he adds elements he has heard of but without any written document to support them. The second part deals with the penal code, punishments (many of them quite harsh), crimes and offences against the state, including an interesting law on loans. Leclère's aim is in fact to rationalize a legal system, which by its nature was not systematic, because French colonial administrators were supposed to keep an eye on the Khmer courts, which acted in ways that were probably impossible to understand for people educated in the spirit of the Roman law.

514 **Recherches sur le droit public des Cambodgiens.** (Research on the public law of the Cambodians.)
Adhémard Leclère. Paris: Augustin Challamel, 1894. 328p.

The author entertains some strong ideas about Khmer history that would not be shared by many today. But this book is mostly a study of government, including the high-ranking dignitaries, the 'means of government' (law, census, patronage, oath, army, clergy), the territorial organization, the ill-fated appanages, and, most interestingly, the income of the king. This coverage makes a fascinating book, which ranges well beyond merely describing public law.

515 **Reexamining the doctrine of humanitarian intervention in light of the atrocities in Kampuchea and Ethiopia.**
Michael Bazyler. *Stanford Journal of International Law*, 1987, vol. 23, no. 2, p. 547-619.

Part one provides specific details of the deaths of 'over a million' people in Cambodia and in Ethiopia; Part two discusses the humanitarian intervention as a doctrine of international law, both historically and in today's context; Part three proposes criteria by which to measure such intervention; and Part four returns to apply these criteria to the two cases of Cambodia and Ethiopia.

516 **Report of the fact-finding mission to Cambodia.**
Hong Kong: Asian Human Rights Commission, 1994. 52p.

From 28 March to 1 April 1994 a mission of three members (Toshiro Ueyanagi, lawyer from Japan; Ms. Ubonrat Siriyuvasak, lecturer from Thailand; and Mr. Lakshman Gunasekera, journalist from Sri Lanka) and two staff members of the Asian Human Rights Commission (Ms. Aida Jean Manipon, general secretary; and Mr. Wong Kai Shing, programme officer) visited Cambodia. During their five days in the country they met with a number of Cambodian human rights activists, officials, Buddhist monks and international representatives. They attended a court in session, a prison, an ethnic Vietnamese village, the Tuol Kork red-light district, the Tuol Sleng Genocidal Museum, and the Choeung Ek killing field. The five headings of the report indicate the breadth of their concerns: building a democratic society; law and justice; women in Cambodia; minorities and ethnic groups; and land-mines and demining. A series of recommendations were made for each area examined, including such specific ones as urging the participation of women in the decision-making process, suggestions concerning HIV education and care, and amendment of the Constitution to ensure equal rights for non-Khmers.

517 **Systematic torture, extra-judicial executions and acts of genocide in Cambodia under Khmer Rouge rule.**
Photographs and text [by] David Hawk; typescript and photographs, accompanied by Khmer Rouge prison documents from the S-21 (Tuol Sleng) extermination centre in Phnom Penh, [1982]. [bound photocopies].

This collection formed the basis of a 1982 exhibition entitled 'Cambodian witness'. The photographs were taken by Hawk on two trips to Cambodia in March and April 1982.

518 **Tuol Sleng confessions.**
Microfilmed by Cornell University, Ithaca, New York.

Some 4,187 confessions of the 14,000 prisoners held in the Tuol Sleng prison during the Pol Pot period, microfilmed and boxed by Cornell University. A database, created on Filemaker II, is available for consultation and is also on the Internet on The Cambodian Genocide Program site (q.v.).

519 **Tuol Sleng photographs.**
Phnom Penh: Tuol Sleng, 1994.

This collection consists of almost 6,000 photographs of prisoners taken during the Pol Pot period. The negatives were copied and restored by the Tuol Sleng staff under the direction of American photographers Douglas Niven and Chris Riley of the Photo Archive Group with support from Cornell University, Ithaca, New York. They have now been scanned by the Cambodian Genocide Program and are available on the CGP site on the Internet (q.v.).

520 **Tuol Sleng.**
Phnom Penh: [Information and Culture Service?], 198?. 40p.

Handed out to every foreign visitor to Tuol Sleng, this little brochure covers all the key aspects of the shocking events that took place in this former high school within the city of Phnom Penh, converted into a prison and torture centre under the Khmer Rouge. During 1993 Sihanouk proposed its conversion back into a school, but thousands of petitions opposed this as long as the perpetrators of the crimes remained unpunished, and so it remains as a Genocidal Museum. The brochure contains photographs taken by the Khmer Rouge of their victims as admitted to the prison and as they were undergoing torture as well as paintings depicting the various tortures administered.

521 **The war against free speech: letter from Human Rights Watch and the new Cambodian Press Law.**
New York: Human Rights Watch, 1995. 15p.

This volume states: 'Over the last year, the Royal Cambodian Government has waged a campaign to silence its critics, targeting independent newspapers and political figures for prosecution and harassment. On more than a dozen occasions, it has suspended, shut or confiscated newspapers or brought criminal complaints against journalists. A controversial new press law is unlikely to halt these abuses as it allows confiscations, closures and criminal prosecutions to continue'.

The Chinese rulers' crimes against Kampuchea.
See item no. 216.

Cambodia: the Eastern Zone massacres: a report on social conditions and human rights violations in the Eastern Zone of Democratic Kampuchea under the role of Pol Pot's (Khmer Rouge) Communist Party of Kampuchea.
See item no. 263.

De sang et de larmes: la grande déportation du Cambodge. (With blood and tears: Cambodia's great deportation.)
See item no. 266.

Kampuchea dossier.
See item no. 269.

Peace with horror: the untold story of Communist genocide in Cambodia.
See item no. 274.

Kampuchean refugees 'between the tiger and the crocodile': international law and the overall scope of one refugee situation.
See item no. 363.

Genocide by proxy: Cambodian pawn on a superpower chessboard.
See item no. 543.

Undeclared war against the People's Republic of Kampuchea.
See item no. 562.

Vietnam's war in Cambodia: historical experience, settler politics, and prospects for the future.
See item no. 565.

Guirlande de cpap. (Garland of cpap.)
See item no. 731.

The secrets of S-21.
See item no. 949.

The Cambodian Genocide Program.
See item no. 977.

The digital archive of Cambodian holocaust survivors.
See item no. 984.

The Documentation Center of Cambodia.
See item no. 985.

Foreign Relations

522 **A l'école des diplomates: la perte et le retour d'Angkor.** (Learning from the diplomats: the loss and the return of Angkor.)
Colonel F. Bernard. Paris: Les Oeuvres Représentatives, [1933]. 238p. map. bibliog.

As an officer in the French army, the author was president of the Delimitation Commission of the Franco-Siamese Border, which established the border on the ground, horse-riding all along its length, in 1904-07. He was writing in 1933, presumably as a retired officer, free to vent his feelings. Starting with the 1685 de Chaumont embassy to King Narai he moves on to the Montigny mission in 1856, which started the process by which the French protectorate was imposed on Cambodia. The origin of the move was more circumstantial than planned: 'Going through Singapore, Mr de Montigny learned from our [French] consul some very odd details. He acquired the conviction that in fact a small state called Cambodia existed, which was located in-between Cochinchina and Siam'. He says diplomats had only the vaguest ideas about the realities in the field and could not figure out proper maps to which, he says, they added strange names 'for the sake of verisimilitude'. Speaking of a high-ranking colonial civil servant, he says: 'The Cambodians of today are of no interest to him but he was full of solicitude for the Cambodians of the past' (a not uncommon phenomenon even today). The title must be understood as an irony: the diplomats, in fact, should learn from the people who really know the place.

523 **Aftermath: the struggle of Cambodia & Vietnam.**
Anthony Barnett, John Pilger. London: New Statesman, 1982. 151p. maps. (NS Report, no. 5).

This slim book contains twenty essays previously published in the *New Statesman* from 1978-81. The essays are grouped in six parts: Vietnam; Kissinger and the historical record; Cambodia; The bureaucracy of death; The United Nations; and From Vietnam to El Salvador. It is a strong polemic, whose approach is laid out by Pilger in the introduction, 'Indochina is where a superpower intervened with all its might, short of nuclear weapons (and these were contemplated), in order to subdue and subvert and to control nations considered to be of importance to its dominance of world politics. It was beaten; and that had never happened before; and the object of American policy today is to redress this to gain a "better result" than that which was declared, ignominiously, on the rooftops of Saigon in April 1975'.

524 **Black paper: facts and evidences of the acts of aggression and annexation of Vietnam against Kampuchea.**
[Phnom Penh]: Department of Press and Information, Ministry of Foreign Affairs, Democratic Kampuchea, September 1978. 89p. maps.
A translation of *Livre noir: faits et preuves des actes d'aggression et d'annexation du Vietnam contre le Kampuchea.*

The basic position of the DK (Khmer Rouge) published (in French and English) in the last months of their rule in Cambodia. The perspective given is one of struggle since 1954: the issue of the party's political direction from 1954 to 1970; Vietnamese attempts at smashing the independent political line from 1970 to 1975; the Paris negotiations and the Vietnamese attempts at destroying Kampuchea's revolution; and the activities of Vietnam towards its objective of annexing and swallowing Kampuchea from 1975 to 1978. Laurence Picq, who typed and retyped the text as it was being written and edited, has said that it came directly from Pol Pot's office. The greater part of this book was later reprinted by Editions Centenaire, Paris and in two parts by Red Flag in Canada in 1979.

525 **Le Cambodge dans la tourmente: le troisième conflit indochinois, 1978-1991.** (Cambodia in torment: the third Indochinese conflict, 1978-91.)
Nicolas Regaud, [preface by Pierre Dabezies]. Paris: Fondation Pour les Études de Défense Nationale, 1992. 438p. maps. bibliog. (Peuples & Stratégies).

Presented as a thesis for a Doctorate in Political Science at the Université Paris I – Panthéon-Sorbonne, 1990. Regaud explains the choice of the subtitle over the more common 'Cambodian conflict' as reflecting its heritage in the two previous conflicts, and also in its recognition of the conflict as having more than local dimensions. Regaud points to three different levels of conflict: local (with Vietnam and its protégé in Phnom Penh, the PRK government, against the three factions of the Cambodian resistance - the DK [Khmer Rouge], FUNCINPEC and KPNLF); regional (the three Indochina countries – Cambodia, Laos and Vietnam – against ASEAN – Indonesia, Malaysia, Philippines, Singapore and Thailand – and China); and global (with China and the United States against Soviet ambitions in Southeast Asia). The conflict is also studied in three different periods: 1978-86, mainly by military means; from Gorbachev's 1986 Vladivostok speech and the Vietnamese Communist Party's Sixth Congress to the First Paris Conference on Cambodia in August 1989; and from the withdrawal of Vietnamese forces from Cambodia in September 1989 until the Paris Peace Conference in October 1991. The text is complemented by a chronological summary 1975-91.

526 **Le Cambodge entre le Siam et le Viêtnam (de 1775 à 1860).**
(Cambodia between Siam and Vietnam, from 1775 to 1860.)
Khin Sok. Paris: École Française d'Extrême-Orient, 1991. 350p. (Collection de Textes et Documents sur l'Indochine, 18).

The author deals with the century before Cambodia became part of the French imperial sphere – a very dark period. Already the Khmer kings were so weak that they could not benefit from the fall of Ayutthaya, the Siamese capital, at the hands of the Burmese in 1767. In 100 pages, Khin Sok writes the history of the kings. The sources are mainly the writings of the first French administrators (Aymonier and Moura) who collected a lot of information from their Cambodian counterparts, and also the Chronicles, *Chroniques royales du Cambodge* (q.v.). The central focus of course is the position of Cambodia cornered between the rival ambitions of its two neighbours, Siam and Vietnam. Siam was the overlord for most of the time, while Vietnam, reunified under the Nguyen Dynasty, was repeatedly invited into the country by ambitious Khmer princes, fighting for power. The second part of the book is probably the most interesting. It deals with the institutions or the high-ranking groups in the kingdom: the king, the royal wives, princes, the brahmins, the nomination of the 'mandarins' and the oath. The 'people' are dealt with in a mere thirteen pages. This treatise on political sociology which is, in fact, a hidden tribute to Aymonier, Leclère and other colonial observers who wrote down everything they saw. This book has already triggered some interesting discussions and one can expect it will continue to do so.

527 **Cambodia after the cold war: the search for security continues.**
Sorpong Peou. Clayton, Victoria: Monash University, Centre for Southeast Asian Studies, 1995. 13p. (Monash Working Papers, 96).

The driving forces of Cambodia's foreign policy are both domestic and geopolitical rather than ideological, argues Sorpong Peou. Cambodian leaders have always tended towards international alliances that give them strength against domestic opponents, and this explains the post-1993 strategy of attracting international support to defeat the Khmer Rouge. For geopolitical reasons (as well as the personal motivations of King Sihanouk), Cambodia now seeks special friendships with China, Laos and North Korea as well as good relations with ASEAN (especially with Malaysia and Indonesia) as a counterweight to the perceived dangers from neighbouring Thailand and Vietnam. Sorpong Peou predicts a continuing close relationship with China and ASEAN as well as an ongoing friendly attitude to the West.

528 **Cambodia in Asean.**
Edited by Kao Kim Hourn. Phnom Penh: Cambodian Institute for Cooperation and Peace, [1995]. 229p.

The proceedings of the Conference on the Treaty of Amity and Cooperation in Southeast Asia (TACSEA): Cambodia's Contribution to Peace and Stability in the Region, held in Phnom Penh, 26-27 June 1995. Acceding to TACSEA is the first condition for membership in ASEAN, and Cambodia officially signed the treaty at the July 1995 meeting of ASEAN in Brunei Darussalam. This conference was held in the lead-up to that ASEAN meeting, and it brought to Phnom Penh ministers of foreign affairs, other senior government officials and scholars from all the ASEAN countries to discuss the issues with a wide range of senior Cambodian politicians and officials. It was sponsored by CICP (Cambodian Institute for Cooperation and Peace), 'an independent, non-partisan and non-government institution' founded in 1994, which at the time of the conference was chaired by former Foreign Minister Prince Norodom Sirivudh (subsequently exiled from Cambodia). The volume was edited by CICP's Executive Director, Kao Kim Hourn. It contains papers presented at the conference, the conference programme and a list of participants, as well as the text of the treaty itself and an unsigned conclusion which remarked that 'there was never any doubt that the consensus reached at the CICP conference was that the . . . decision to become an observer by acceding to the TACSEA was the correct one. But the whole issue of whether Cambodia should be a full member of ASEAN was not fully discussed'.

529 **Cambodia's foreign policy.**
Roger M. Smith. Ithaca, New York: Cornell University Press, [1965]. x, 273p. bibliog. Available in microform from Ann Arbor, Michigan: University Microfilms.

Smith interviewed Prince Sihanouk, was given access to members of his government, and also spoke extensively with HE Mr. Nong Kimny, former Ambassador of Cambodia to the United States, in researching this book. It examines the concept, and policy, of non-alignment as then practised by Cambodia. Smith attempts to reveal to an American public the considerations that had led Cambodia to a policy of non-alignment in the cold war. He does this by outlining the country's history, particularly the decline of the Khmer Empire, the temporary loss of national identity under foreign domination by various powers, and by documenting the independence struggle, relations with major powers and neighbours, concluding with an evaluation of Cambodia's success in achieving non-alignment.

530 **Cambodia's past, present and future.**
Gary Klintworth. Canberra: Strategic and Defence Studies Centre, Australian National University, 1993. 25p. map. bibliog. (Working Paper. Strategic and Defence Studies Centre, no. 268).

Written in March 1993, in the midst of the UNTAC period and the electoral campaign, this paper presents a stark and dramatic picture from a strategic analyst: 'What the country needs is not a fractious democratic government but a strong, charismatic leader with a vision for a new Cambodia. The candidates that meet this requirement are Hun Sen, Pol Pot and Prince Sihanouk, but in Cambodia there is only room for one of them. In these circumstances, and depending on the outcome of the May elections, the UN intervention in Cambodia can be seen as an interlude before the likely resumption of Cambodia's civil conflict'.

531 **Cambodia, Pol Pot, and the United States: the Faustian pact.**
Michael Haas. New York: Praeger, 1991. xv, 163p. bibliog.

Haas went to Cambodia first in 1988 on an Indochina Reconciliation delegation. He became convinced of the errors and dangers of US policy in Cambodia, and sought funding to develop computerized modelling of decision-making in the unfolding international negotiations. His computer analyses provide damning evidence against US policy, which he maintains had been instrumental in sustaining and rebuilding the Khmer Rouge before switching in 1990 to become more critical, and even to call for Pol Pot to be brought to trial. This is an expansion of the first chapter of *Genocide by proxy: Cambodian pawn on a superpower chessboard* (q.v.). It certainly brings a new approach to this topic, but relying on often inaccurate, mutually contradictory and fleeting newspaper stories as sources for analysis leads to many problems, not the least of which is that quantitative not qualitative measures apply, distorting the real meaning and significance of events and policies.

532 **The Cambodian crisis and U.S. policy dilemmas.**
Robert G. Sutter. Boulder, Colorado: Westview Press, 1991. vi, 135p. map. bibliog. (Westview Special Studies on South and Southeast Asia).

Sutter operates within the framework of support for the US government's basic approach to the conflict. He enumerates the United States' political-strategic interests as being centred on assuring a settlement in Cambodia that would: restore stability to Southeast Asia; secure the interests of Thailand and the other members of ASEAN; and check the expansion of Soviet influence – through Vietnam or other means – in Southeast Asia. He analyses changes in Vietnamese policy that led to their withdrawal and detects a subsequent decision by the United States to become more involved with the resistance to the PRK régime. US foreign policy experts are shown as being divided over policy towards Vietnam. Appendices comprise: Guide to key leaders and organizations in Cambodia; Procedural and jurisdictional questions regarding possible normalization of US diplomatic and economic relations with Vietnam; Status of military-political groups active in Cambodia; Contending groups and their stance on a peace agreement; and Key country indicators on Cambodia and Vietnam. Also included is a chronology of events from April 1975 to September 1990.

533 **The causes and implications of the Vietnamese invasion and occupation of Kampuchea.**
Stephen P. Armstrong. Long Beach, California: California State University, 1985. 209p.

Armstrong presents the view that the Vietnamese action in Cambodia was not the realization of federationalist ambitions, but the result of a complex of domestic and international factors. His chapters address: the domestic environment (in Vietnam); foreign policy; the prelude to invasion; and war. Armstrong seeks to contextualize the Vietnamese leadership's apparent abandonment of postwar goals by engaging in wars with Cambodia and China. Concluding that the United Nations holds some responsibility for ignoring the suffering of Cambodians under Pol Pot, he hopes that this work may contribute to greater understanding of the challenges faced by Third-World nations which attempt to act independently of superpower involvement.

534 **The China-Cambodia-Vietnam triangle.**
Wilfred Burchett. Chicago: Vanguard Books, 1981. 235p. bibliog.

In this study Burchett makes a strident case for recognition of the PRK government and for an end to the military and political support extended to the resistance forces opposing it, with the backing of China and the United States. He outlines the history of the communist and nationalist struggle in Cambodia, with some detail given to the rise of the Khmer Rouge. A chapter then describes life under Khmer Rouge rule from 1975 to 1979 on the basis of the survivors' testimonies. Burchett's particular expertise and perspective is brought to bear in the chapter entitled 'Triangular relations', in which he presents personal accounts of meetings with the key players in all three countries through his long period of residence and reporting on the war. The book concludes with an account of the 'survival miracle' of the reconstruction of Cambodia, which Burchett believes should be supported by all progressive people.

535 **Confidential U.S. State Department special files.**
US Department of State. Frederick, Maryland: University Publications of America, 1987- . microfilms.

The first set of documents, on ten microfilm reels, covers the period 1945-49. The second, on forty-four reels, deals with the years 1950-54. The third, on fifty-two reels, continues the story to 1955-59, with the subtitle being expanded to 'Internal and foreign affairs'. Coverage is expected to continue to 1975. Each unit comes with a printed guide. Reports from diplomats in Indochina are mixed with dispatches from posts in London, Paris, Nanjing, Rangoon, Geneva, Moscow and Hong Kong, as well as analyses from relevant State Department offices, the Department of Defense, the Joint Chiefs of Staff, and the White House. [David G. Marr with Kristine Alilunas-Rodgers]

536 **Conflict resolution in Kampuchea: proceedings of the Third International Conference on Indochina.**
Edited by Donald H. McMillen. Brisbane, Queensland: Centre for the Study of Australia-Asia Relations, 1989. 151p. bibliog.

The proceedings of the third of a series of international conferences, held from 24-28 January 1989, commissioned by the Australian Department of Foreign Affairs and Trade, meant to place special emphasis on the four main protagonists (on the one hand the PRK and on the other hand the three coalition parties - FUNCINPEC, KPNLF and the Khmer Rouge). However, the Khmer Rouge, like the People's Republic of China, did not participate. Material presented includes the three major papers: 'National reconciliation and reconstruction in Kampuchea: the road ahead', by Nayan Chanda with remarks by Khieu Kanharith and Troung Mealy; 'Obtaining and securing peace within Kampuchea: the next phase (withdrawal/neutralization)' by Carlyle Thayer with comments by Kusuma Snitwongse and Bui Xuan Ninh; and 'The question of the form of self-determination for Kampuchea and its international guarantees; and the reference paper Kampuchea: one way forward' by Noordin Sopiee with remarks by Victor Ivanov and Sabam Siagian. Also included are summaries of the first and second meetings, and Nayan Chanda's article analysing the 'Sticking points' for the Second Joint Informal Meeting (JIM 2), and the JIM 2 Consensus Statement, providing accessible material for those wishing to understand this phase of the long process of negotiation leading to the 1991 international settlement.

537 **Documents on the Kampuchean problem, 1979-1985.**
Bangkok: Department of Political Affairs, Ministry of Foreign Affairs, [1985]. ix, 189p.

A most useful compilation of primary source material and interpretation from one perspective, that of a key player in the dispute – the Thai government. This volume consists of two parts: part one is a comparison between the ASEAN and 'Indochinese' proposals; part two contains the texts of relevant documents from ASEAN, the Coalition Government of Democratic Kampuchea, the United Nations and 'Indochinese documents'. The use of the term 'Indochinese' with which to lump together the positions advanced by the People's Republic of Kampuchea and the Vietnamese government reflects the position of Thailand and itself illustrates the problem being discussed.

538 **Falling out of touch: a study on Vietnamese communist policy towards an emerging Cambodian communist movement, 1930-1975.**

Thomas Engelbert, Christopher E. Goscha. Clayton, Victoria: Centre of Southeast Asian Studies, Monash University, 1995. 165p. bibliog. (Monash Papers on Southeast Asia, no. 35).

Engelbert and Goscha rely chiefly on Vietnamese documentary sources and on interviews as well as Vietnamese and French archives, and in so doing are able to shed new light on the problematic relationship between Vietnam and Cambodia as it deteriorated into military conflict. They describe the Vietnamese 'losing touch' with their comrades during the vital period between the Geneva and Paris peace conferences (1954-73). Of particular interest is the visit of Saloth Sar (Pol Pot) to Hanoi in 1965, where his policy of self-reliant armed struggle met with a cool response from Le Duan, who counselled a more cautious line, including a united front with Sihanouk against US imperialism and, of course, support for the Vietnamese struggle. Sar was reported to have left the meeting 'without saying anything at all. He did not say one word'. But it appears that China's attitude was different, urging him along the path of armed struggle, and an increasingly anti-Vietnamese perspective. It now seems that there were nearly 200 armed clashes between Vietnamese and Cambodian communist forces between 1970 and 1975 when this book concludes as, for the first time in nearly a century, the four countries of the peninsula (Vietnam, Cambodia, Laos and Thailand) were to deal with each other without the presence of colonial powers.

539 **The foreign politics of the Communist Party of Vietnam: a study of communist tactics.**

Ton That Thien. New York: Crane Russak, 1989. 255p. maps. bibliog.

Published under the auspices of the Information and Resource Centre, Singapore, this work is an attempt to address a neglected field of Vietnamese studies. The author maintains that the 'failure' of the Communist Party of Vietnam (CPV) must be measured against its aims, which have been global, and that understanding the party's foreign politics is vital to a study of Vietnamese communism. The chapter on Cambodia and Laos, backed up by in-depth chapters on the setting for, founding of, and basic thinking of, the CPV, looks at Vietnam's historical 'southward march' into those countries. The Comintern and Vietnamese creation of, and influence on, communist movements in Cambodia is briefly laid out, from its beginning up to the 1980s. As Marr notes in *Vietnam* (q.v.), Thien 'concludes that Vietnamese communists enjoyed great success in serving the interests of their party and international communism, but failed the Vietnamese people badly'.

540 **Foreign relations of the United States.**

US Department of State, Office of the Historian, Bureau of Public Affairs. Washington, DC: United States Government Printing Office, various dates. (Department of State Publications).

As the official record of the foreign policy of the United States, certain *Foreign relations of the United States (FRUS)* volumes relating to events since 1945 are of obvious importance when researching the wars in Vietnam and Cambodia. For the years 1951 and earlier, Indochina is treated within the annual East Asian volumes. For years 1951 and earlier, Indochina is treated within the annual East Asian volumes. For the period 1952-54, see *FRUS* volume 13, entitled *Indochina* and bound in two parts (Washington, DC, 1982). Additional information of relevance for 1952-54 can be found in volume 2 on national security policy, volume 16 relating to the Geneva Conference (April-July 1954), and other volumes dealing with Asia and France. From 1955 the countries were treated individually. Each *FRUS* volume is blessed with an extensive index. [David G. Marr with Kristine Alilunas-Rodgers]

541 **The four days of Mayaguez.**
Roy Rowan. New York: Norton, 1975. 224p.

The author became a passenger on the commercial ship the *Mayaguez* in order to interview at length the crew who survived being captured by the Khmer Rouge in the Gulf of Siam and taken to Kompong Som in May 1975. Written in an informal style, the narrative charts the crew's experiences and touches on the individuals' personal lives. Conflict between the crew over how to react to the capture, the response from the Oval Office to the battle for the crew's rescue, and particulars of the adventure, are the focus of the book, rather than the political significance of the incident. However, the mechanisms of the US government's resolution and action are presented. Part of the royalties from the book have been donated to a fund for the families of the Americans killed during those four days.

542 **From Phnom Penh to Kabul: on January 31, 1980.**
Singapore: Ministry of Foreign Affairs, [1980]. 52p. September 1980.

A strong polemic from Singapore outlining the 1980 ASEAN public position in support of the continued seating of Democratic Kampuchea in the United Nations, and calling for the immediate withdrawal of Vietnamese troops. It presents the situations in Cambodia and Afghanistan as two sides of the same coin – a new Soviet doctrine – and maintains that 'issues of greater consequences than Mr Pol Pot's genocidal past are involved in the Vietnamese request for the unseating of Democratic Kampuchea and its replacement by a puppet regime'. The work includes illustrations.

543 **Genocide by proxy: Cambodian pawn on a superpower chessboard.**
Michael Haas. New York: Praeger, 1991. xiii, 385p. bibliog.

Based on confidential interviews with over a hundred diplomats and others in fifteen countries, Haas argues that Cambodia was sacrificed to power politics. He concludes with a plea that such practices be abandoned in favour of world pluralism in which pawns are not exploited. The volume contains an index.

544 **Great victory of the Cambodian people: warmly congratulating the patriotic Cambodian armed forces and people on the liberation of Phnom Penh and all Cambodia.**
Peking: Foreign Languages Press, 1975. 36p.

A translation of *Chien-pu-chai jen min ti wei ta sheng li*, this is a collection of speeches and messages of congratulation on the overthrow of the Lon Nol government by the Khmer Rouge from leaders of the Chinese government and press, and a speech by Penn Nouth, Prime Minister of the Royal Government of National Union of Cambodia, on the occasion of the 'Cambodian people's liberation of Phnom Penh' in April 1975.

545 **Hope for Cambodia: preventing the return of the Khmer Rouge and aiding the refugees: hearing and markup before the Subcommittee on Asian and Pacific Affairs of the Committee on Foreign Affairs, House of Representatives, One Hundredth Congress, second session, on H. J. Res. 602, June 30 and July 28, 1988.**
Washington, DC: US Government Printing Office, 1989. iii, 98p. Distributed to some depository libraries in microfiche. Shipping list no.: 89-130-P. Item 1017-A, 1017-B (microfiche).

The proceedings of the Subcommittee on Asian and Pacific Affairs of the House of Representatives of the US Congress in the light of the imminent withdrawal of Vietnamese troops. Witnesses appearing before the committee included Dith Pran, Haing Ngor, Kitty Dukakis, David Hawk, David Lambertson and Karl Jackson. Appendices give the text of the House Joint Resolution 602, and letters to the UN Secretary General and President Ronald Reagan from Dith Pran and others. This is only one of many hearings by this and other committees of the US Congress that bear on the Cambodian question particularly from the perspective of examining US foreign policy, and on issues relating to the resettlement of refugees.

546 **Indian foreign policy in Cambodia, Laos, and Vietnam, 1947-1964.**
D. R. SarDesai. Berkeley, California: University of California Press, 1968. viii, 336p. bibliog.

Sino-Indian rivalry and the 1962 border war between China and India provide a backdrop for this study which focuses on India's diplomacy and its role as the chair of the International Control Commission charged by the Geneva Conference with supervision of a truce in Indochina. Chapter five deals with relations between India and Cambodia. The author sees parallels between Sihanouk's attitude towards communism – neutrality that allowed for friendly relations between countries accompanied by hostility to communism at home – and that of the Indian government. Increasing ties between Cambodia and China did not lead to a break in the friendly relations between Cambodia and India. This is a useful text for those wishing to gain an insight into the international relations and diplomacy of the time.

547 **Indochina and problems of security and stability in Southeast Asia: papers and discussion of the conference held at Chulalongkorn University, Bangkok, 18-21 June 1980.**
Edited by Khien Theeravit and MacAlister Brown, sponsored by the Institute of Asian Studies, Chulalongkorn University in association with Institute of Southeast Asian Studies, Singapore, and Institut für Asienkunde, Federal Republic of Germany. Bangkok: Chulalongkorn University Press, 1981. ix, 228p. bibliog.

This volume consists of papers from the Conference on Indochina and Problems of Security and Stability in Southeast Asia, 18-21 June 1980. Of particular interest is the paper by Steve Heder, 'From Pol Pot to Pen Sovan to the villages'.

548 **Indochina in North Vietnamese strategy.**
Melvin Gurtov. Santa Monica, California: Rand Corporation, 1971. 28p. bibliog. (Rand Paper, P4605).

In an attempt to assess Hanoi's policies in Indochina in 1971, Gurtov looks back over the policies of the Vietnamese communists in the previous four decades, from the founding of the Indochinese Communist Party in 1930. [David G. Marr with Kristine Alilunas-Rodgers]

549 **Kampuchea between China and Vietnam.**
Chang Pao-min. Singapore: Singapore University Press, National University of Singapore, 1985. xi, 204p. bibliog.

Although published in 1985 and having therefore been superseded by events since, this book has value for its particular focus, and especially for the forty pages of appendices containing the various treaties between: Cambodia and the People's Republic of China (1960); Vietnam and Laos (1977); Vietnam and the USSR (1978); Vietnam and Cambodia (1979); and Laos and Cambodia (1979). Chang Pao-min was, at the time of publication, a Senior Lecturer in Political Science at the National University of Singapore, and had written two previous books on Sino-Vietnamese relations. He takes a perspective of sympathy towards the 'anti-Vietnamese' resistance forces against what he viewed as Hanoi's ambition for a 'thoroughly united entity in the form of a greater Vietnam', having already gone further than the original French concept of an Indochina federation, and he projected the outcome as dependent upon the military success of either Vietnam or the resistance forces, not forseeing the Vietnamese unilateral withdrawal and the peaceful settlement between the PRK and two of the three resistance forces, leaving only the Khmer Rouge in opposition.

550 **Kampuchea without delusion.**
Sukhumbhand Paribatra. Kuala Lumpur: Institute of Strategic and International Studies (ISIS) Malaysia, 1986. 27p. (ISIS Asean Series).

An argument for a revision of ASEAN policy towards Cambodia on the grounds that a prolongation of the conflict could harm relations among the ASEAN countries and that achievement of ASEAN's policy objectives using current tactics is not likely. A new policy framework should be based on: the assumption that the Vietnamese presence is likely to continue; a phased reduction of support for the Khmer Rouge; the need to build up trust through a process of negotiation with less emphasis on the end-goal; and an increased role for the United States particularly to influence China to lessen its support for the Khmer Rouge. The work is useful for those interested in ASEAN's role in the 'Kampuchea problem' during the 1980s, and it includes extensive footnotes referring to original and hard-to-find documents.

551 **The Kampuchean problem in Thai perspective: positions and viewpoints held by Foreign Ministry officials and Thai academics.**
Compiled by Indochina Studies Program, Institute of Asian Studies, Chulalongkorn University, Thailand. Bangkok: Institute of Asian Studies, Chulalongkorn University, 1985. viii, 103p. (Asian Studies Monographs, no. 032).

On 6 April 1985, some thirty-three Thai Foreign Ministry officials and academics met in a closed-door seminar to discuss 'the Kampuchean problem' defined as arising 'when 200,000 Vietnamese troops invaded Kampuchea on 25 December, 1978'. A sanitized version of the discussion is presented here with 'certain issues which the Ministry of Foreign Affairs and the Institute of Asian Studies believe that, for the time being, should not be disclosed . . . deleted'. Names of individual contributors have also been withheld from the points being made (although they are listed in an appendix, and the questions discussed at the seminar have been supplemented with fifteen more, answered by the Foreign Ministry). In addition, this slim volume contains a series of twenty-five questions put to Professor Khien Theeravit, Department of International Relations of Chulalongkorn University. His answers show strong support for the Thai government policy of opposition to the PRK, through supporting the resistance forces and the CGDK's (Coalition Government of Democratic Kampuchea) holding of the Cambodian seat in the United Nations. The volume includes illustrations.

552 **Khmer-Viet relations and the third Indochina conflict.**
Thu-Huong Nguyen-Vo. Jefferson, North Carolina: McFarland, 1992. x, 22p. bibliog.

This thoughtful but sometimes contradictory work analyses the Vietnamese presence in Cambodia in the 1980s in the light of historical relations between the two countries. The author provides an overview of relations from before the 17th century onwards. Vietnamese opinions were moulded by traditional security considerations based on threats from China and later from Thailand. The international communist movement encouraged the treatment of Indochina as a single bloc. During the 1980s it is highly likely that the Vietnamese government saw Indochinese unity as necessary for the survival of the three countries. But Vietnam was also out to reclaim its 'place in the sun'. For Cambodians there were the memories of some brutality and humiliations meted out by Vietnam in the past and resentment against the current Vietnamese tendency to consider themselves as more developed communists than their Cambodian and Lao comrades. As memories of the Khmer Rouge régime faded 'despite Vietnam's efforts to keep them immortal', the Hun Sen régime gradually began to assert its independence.

553 **The making of Australia's Indochina policies under the Labor government (1983-1986): the politics of circumspection?**
Philip G. O'Brien. Nathan, Queensland: Griffith University, 1987. 31p. (Australia-Asia Papers, 39).

Although really a working paper, and well superseded by events, this item has interest particularly because of its use of primary source material, notably speeches, to highlight a period in which a different course could have been taken. Foreign Minister Bill Hayden's 1983-84 attempts to move towards dialogue with the People's Republic of Kampuchea were soon thwarted (some say by Prime Minister Bob Hawke). O'Brien concludes that Australia would be unlikely to play a leading role again, but this was to be belied when Gareth Evans picked up Stephen Solarz's proposal, which eventually became the basis for the Paris Agreements.

554 **Obstacles to recovery in Vietnam and Kampuchea: U.S. embargo of humanitarian aid.**
Joel Charny, John Spragens with a preface by Laurence R. Simon. Boston, Massachusetts: Oxfam America, 1984. iv, 150p. map. bibliog. (Impact Audit Series, no. 3).

Chapter three concentrates on Cambodia, dealing with problems of delivering famine relief and assistance in the years immediately following Pol Pot's overthrow in the face of official barriers. Written from the perspective of those who supported recognition of the PRK and criticized the policies of the US government. Illustrations are included.

555 **On Kampuchea.**
Truong Chinh. Hanoi: Foreign Languages Publishing House, 1980. 39p. A translation of *Vê vân de Cam-pu-chia.*

Published in response to the continuing United Nations opposition to the newly established PRK government, this pamphlet puts forward the official Vietnamese position. Written by Truong Chinh, member of the Political Department of the Executive Committee of the Central Committee of the Communist Party of Vietnam it optimistically charts the imminent success of the united struggle of the peoples of Vietnam, Laos and Cambodia. 'The Pol Pot corpse is decaying. The wizards in Beijing and Washington cannot revive it.' Regretfully even fifteen years later Pol Pot still seems to be alive and continuing to threaten the country, and a very different country it is from the Kampuchea being so passionately defended in these pages. Greg Lockhart has written an analysis on Democratic Kampuchea's attacks on Vietnam based chiefly on this pamphlet, entitled *'Strike in the south, clear the north': the 'problem of Kampuchea' and the roots of Vietnamese strategy there* (q.v.).

556 **The poverty of diplomacy: Kampuchea and the outside world.**
David Bull. Oxford: Oxfam, 1983. 32p. map. bibliog.

Oxfam was one of the first agencies to provide relief to Cambodia following the defeat of Pol Pot in 1979. This is an account of the relief effort, which after four years had returned some sense of normality to the country. Oxfam and other NGOs continued their work in Cambodia after official Western development and relief assistance was terminated. Oxfam presented an alternative to British diplomacy which then simply worked 'to perpetuate fear and prevent development', demanded Britain vote to leave Cambodia's UN seat vacant, and argued for the immediate resumption of development aid. The report remains a useful historical record and contains illustrations.

557 **Red brotherhood at war: Vietnam, Cambodia, and Laos since 1975.**
Grant Evans and Kelvin Rowley. London: Verso, 1990. rev. ed. xxii, 322p. maps. bibliog.

A carefully reasoned exposition and analysis, this book is essential reading for those wanting a better understanding of the geopolitical circumstances that shaped Indochina in the years after Vietnam's victory in 1975. In writing the book the authors ask 'what happened to socialist internationalism in the paddyfields and forests of Indochina' where 'the hopes of the fathers were buried with the bodies of their sons'. They find the answer not in theories of 'Vietnamese expansionism', for example, but in the concrete realities of Indochina in the 1970s and see the differences between the Indochinese states as emanating from developments in each of the nationalist revolutions in the region since the Second World War. The work contains valuable analysis on: Laos in the period prior to 1975; ASEAN's role as an anti-communist bloc; and the international legalities of Vietnam's overthrow of Pol Pot. This is a revised, updated and expanded edition of the work that first appeared in 1984. The authors reaffirm their previous analysis, while condensing some chapters and adding new material, including two new chapters on US-Soviet-Chinese relations and on more recent developments (up to October 1989) on the Indochinese Peninsula.

558 **Report of the International Conference on Kampuchea: New York (13-17 July 1981).**

New York: United Nations, 1981. iii, 12p. United Nations publication sales no. E.81.I.20–. /A/CONF.109/5.

Called in response to the presence of Vietnamese troops in Cambodia, this conference aimed to find ways to achieve: a total withdrawal of all foreign troops; respect for the sovereignty of Cambodia; and peaceful elections. While not particularly informative as to what was said at the conference – the official record merely lists the names of participating countries, procedural motions adopted and those nations taking part in the debates – it does include the text of the Declaration on Kampuchea adopted by the United Nations and the decision to establish an *ad hoc* committee to search for ways to achieve the UN's aims.

559 **'Strike in the south, clear the north': the 'problem of Kampuchea' and the roots of Vietnamese strategy there.**

Greg Lockhart. [Clayton, Victoria: Centre of Southeast Asian Studies, Monash University, 1985]. 18p. bibliog. (Working Paper. Centre of Southeast Asian Studies, Monash University, no. 36).

A fascinating perspective on Democratic Kampuchea's attacks on Vietnam, which are seen by the author as essentially 'on instruction from Beijing'. Lockhart bases his analysis chiefly on the pamphlet, *On Kampuchea* (q.v.). Lockhart relates this to a strong Vietnamese tradition of seeing Chinese attacks from the north as being paralleled by attacks from the south, a pattern repeated frequently since the 11th century. While this view ignores domestic Cambodian concerns, and downplays specifically Vietnamese-Cambodian issues it provides a useful counterbalance to the 'inexorable hostility' between the two countries that pervades much commentary.

560 **The third Indochina war: the conflicts between China, Vietnam, and Cambodia.**

Jaap van Ginneken, [English translation, David Smith]. Amsterdam: J. van Ginneken, [1983]. 322p. bibliog. A translation of *De derde Indochinese oorlog*.

Ginneken places the Vietnamese intervention in Cambodia in the context of the outbreak of enmity between fraternal communist countries. His is a detailed analysis of the divergence between the Vietnamese and Cambodian communist parties. Policy differences could be attributed partly to different sociological and economic factors within each country. Vietnam's relationship with China is important to Ginneken's understanding of the situation. He acknowledges that the Khmer Rouge committed great atrocities while in power and had a 'hyper-sensitive' attitude towards Vietnam but does not condone Vietnam's role in their overthrow or its military support for the PRK.

561 **The Third International Conference on Kampuchea, 25-26 July 1987, Bangkok, Thailand.**
[Bangkok: s.n., 1988]. 82p. bibliog.

The official record of what is described as the third 'international forum of scholars, academics, journalists, political personalities and representatives of mass organizations from various countries who support the Kampuchean people and the CGDK'. The first conference was held in 1979 in Stockholm and the second in 1981 in Tokyo. Khmer Rouge leader and Vice President of Democratic Kampuchea, Khieu Samphan, warns that, despite its stated intentions, Vietnam will never withdraw its troops but will, instead, try to split the coalition of resistance forces. A message from HRH Norodom Sihanouk, President of FUNCINPEC and of Democratic Kampuchea, delivered by Prince Norodom Ranariddh, stresses that as soon as Vietnamese troops are withdrawn there should be a process of national reconciliation and steps to establish peaceful and neighbourly relations with Vietnam. Other papers and messages come from representatives of the KPNLF, the Governments of Thailand and China, delegations from Japan, the UK, Sweden, Denmark and Nepal and individual academics and journalists: Jan Myrdal, Steve Orlov, Thai Quang Trung, Masanori Kikuchi, Bilveer Sinh, Samir Amin and Khien Theeravit. The conference resolution calls for heightened international pressure for the withdrawal of Vietnamese troops from Cambodia. It was at the concluding press conference that the compiler of this bibliography heard Khieu Samphan utter the unforgettable words that the Khmer Rouge's only mistake during its period of rule over Cambodia was not to have gone far or fast enough in its programme of social change.

562 **Undeclared war against the People's Republic of Kampuchea.**
Phnom Penh: Ministry of Foreign Affairs of the People's Republic of Kampuchea, Press Department, 1985. 71p.

This was a protest, aimed at the international community, against the ongoing armed resistance to the PRK and the foreign assistance which sustained it. As well as supporting the opposition, Thailand is accused of numerous incursions across air space, land and sea frontiers. The PRK is said to have won major military victories and, since the spring of 1985, to have secured the frontier against 'penetration by subversive groups of Khmer émigrés'. The PRK's armed forces have matured and are said to be ready, if necessary, to face the threat alone after Vietnamese troops are withdrawn. However, the PRK remains committed to a peaceful settlement of the conflict. Pol Pot's announced resignation as head of the Khmer Rouge is judged to be neither real nor significant. The text is accompanied by eight pages of illustrated plates.

563 **Vietnam or Indochina?: contesting concepts of space in Vietnamese nationalism, 1887-1954.**
Christopher E. Goscha. Copenhagen: NIAS, 1995. 154p. bibliog. (NIAS Reports, no. 28).

A valuable, thoughtful essay on a vexed question in the politics of Cambodia. Goscha, an American scholar, here looks at chiefly French and Vietnamese sources to shed new light on the debates concerning the physical dimensions of what the Vietnamese nationalist movement was to struggle for. He begins by asking how it was that the Indonesian nationalists succeeded in forging a nation from the various ethnic polities that were grouped together as part of the colonial state, while the Vietnamese eventually refrained from doing the same. In part one Goscha focuses on 'how the mechanics of the French colonial project and the international communist movement converged around 1930 to pull Vietnamese nationalists in Indochinese directions and how this westerly flowing current simultaneously hit up against a nationalist resurgence limited to the eastern part of the peninsula'. In part two he concentrates 'on how Vietnamese communists continued moving in unequivocal Indochinese directions long after declaring a "Vietnamese" nation in 1945 . . . [on] the Communist Party's political plans for an Indochinese state structure and on how full-scale war against the French led Vietnamese communists to construct an Indochinese military, economic and bureaucratic space that linked Laos, Cambodia – and even Thailand – to Vietnam'.

564 **Vietnam's intervention in Cambodia in international law.**
Gary Klintworth. Canberra: AGPS Press, 1989. xviii, 193p. maps. bibliog.

Based on the author's 1988 thesis for the Master of International Law at the Australian National University, Canberra. Klintworth had been concerned with Cambodia since 1967 when he was assigned to cover it for the Australian Army Intelligence Corps. He examines the 1979 intervention, finding that it satisfied criteria under international law both in terms of self-defence and for humanitarian motives, particularly in the light of the lack of action by the United Nations. This is an important work, challenging with scholarly research the prevailing view that condemned Vietnam and ostracized the PRK.

565 **Vietnam's war in Cambodia: historical experience, settler politics, and prospects for the future.**
Milton Takei. PhD thesis, University of Oregon, 1992. 196p. bibliog. Available from Ann Arbor, Michigan: UMI Dissertation Services, 1992.

Takei argues that Cambodia has been the victim of settler politics by Vietnam and that this is the most important factor in determining the opinions of the Cambodian people, in particular the peasantry. In his view the real genocide took place before 1975 and after 1978, stating that it does not make sense 'for a xenophobic organization like the CPK to commit genocide, though it make (sic) complete sense for it to execute those it considers traitors'. Given a neutral political environment he estimates the PDK (Khmer Rouge) would gain around forty per cent support in an election. The reported military strength of the PDK indicates a substantial support base because 'guerrilla warfare requires support among the people to be successful'. Starting from the framework of anti-racism, opposition to the 'civilizing mission' of settler politics and the need to see history from the point of view of its victims, Takei seems to conclude that strong anti-Vietnamese sentiment among ordinary Cambodians is inevitable (and even justified?). Unfortunately his research did not include a visit to Cambodia to talk to ordinary Cambodians. He also does not deal with the use made of anti-Vietnamese traditions by those opposed to the PRK, including the West with its own 'civilizing mission'.

566 **Vietnam's withdrawal from Cambodia: regional issues and realignments.**
Gary Klintworth, editor. Canberra: Strategic and Defence Studies Centre, Research School of Pacific Studies, Australian National University, 1990. 140p. bibliog. (Canberra Papers on Strategy and Defence, no. 64).

The significance of Vietnam's withdrawal from Cambodia in 1989 was the subject of a symposium held at the Australian National University's Department of Political Science in October 1989. This book contains nine papers from the symposium by an interesting range of specialists on Cambodia, Indochina and Southeast Asia, reflecting a variety of perspectives, particularly international relations and strategic studies – Michael Leifer, Bernard Gordon, Leszek Buszynski, Gary Klintworth (also the editor), David Chandler, David Marr, Nayan Chanda, Khieu Kanharith and Douglas Sturkey. The volume's cover summarizes the discussion thus: 'Generally, there was a strong view that the governments of Vietnam and Cambodia would eventually experience a less hostile attitude from China, the US and from several of the key ASEAN states as the fact of the Vietnamese withdrawal was accepted. The Hun Sen government in Phnom Penh, or some variant of it, would also probably be recognised, provided it could survive renewed attacks by an increasingly isolated Khmer Rouge and if a suitably graceful exit was found for China. An alternative more pessimistic view was that most governments would continue to defer to Beijing, that the Khmer Rouge were a potent and ruthless force and that the Hun Sen government would be fighting for its life'.

567 **The Vietnam-Kampuchea conflict: a historical record.**
Hoang Nguyen. Hanoi: Foreign Languages Publishing House, 1979. 54p. map.

This slim booklet consists of a thirty-page essay signed by Hoang Nguyen, discussing the background of the conflict from the Vietnamese viewpoint. Not surprisingly, emphasis is given to the régime's 'exacerbated chauvinism' and, in this, provides important contemporary documentation of the DK attacks into Vietnam and to Vietnam's responses, including proposals for ceasefire, demilitarized zones and peace negotiations made on 5 February and 6 June 1978. Appendices contain a list of thirteen members of the Central Committee of the National United Front for the Salvation of Kampuchea and the text of its inaugural declaration made on 2 December 1978 in a 'Kampuchean liberated zone'. Significant photographs add to the documentation.

Conflict neutralization in the Cambodia War.
See item no. 217.

America and the Indochina wars, 1945-1990: a bibliographical guide.
See item no. 226.

Cambodia: the widening war in Indochina.
See item no. 227.

Cambodia: the search for security.
See item no. 241.

My war with the CIA: Cambodia's fight for survival.
See item no. 243.

The Senate's war powers: debate on Cambodia from the Congressional record.
See item no. 255.

Kampuchea dossier.
See item no. 269.

Cambodia, Vietnam, and the problems of the construction of socialism.
See item no. 290.

Time on whose side in Cambodia?
See item no. 303.

Vietnam, Kampuchea, Laos: an eye witness report.
See item no. 304.

Sihanouk reminisces: world leaders I have known.
See item no. 330.

The Indochinese Communist Party's division into three parties.
See item no. 462.

Cambodia: an Australian peace proposal: working papers prepared for the Informal Meeting on Cambodia, Jakarta, 26-28 February 1990.
See item no. 571.

Punishing the poor: the international isolation of Kampuchea.
See item no. 641.

The eagle, the dragon, the bear and Kampuchea.
See item no. 923.

UNTAC and the Peace Process

568 **Agreements on a comprehensive political settlement of the Cambodia conflict: Paris, 23 October 1991.**
[New York]: United Nations Department of Information, 1991. viii, 49p.

A slim volume containing the four texts that emerged from so many years of wrangling, dealing and fighting to introduce a new chapter in Cambodia's history, signed into international law by Cambodia and eighteen other nations on 23 October 1991. A background note presents the official UN view of the intervening years since Pol Pot was overthrown in 1979 (years in which the United Nations refused to recognize the government that held power inside the country). This is followed by: Final act of the Paris Conference on Cambodia; Agreement on a comprehensive political settlement of the Cambodia conflict, with five annexes (UNTAC mandate; Withdrawal, cease-fire and related measures; Elections; Repatriation of Cambodian refugees and displaced persons; and Principles for a new constitution for Cambodia); Agreement concerning the sovereignty, independence, territorial integrity and inviolability, neutrality and national unity of Cambodia; and the Declaration on the rehabilitation and reconstruction of Cambodia.

569 **Between hope and insecurity: the social consequences of the Cambodian peace process.**
Edited by Peter Utting. Geneva: UNRISD, 1994. English ed. viii, 240p. (UNRISD Report, no. 94.1).

Much is still to be written on the UNTAC (United Nations Transitional Authority in Cambodia) period, which had a major impact on Cambodian society. This book is good preliminary reading; it is the product of a workshop of the same title held in Geneva by UNRISD (United Nations Research Institute for Social Development) at the end of UNTAC's first year in Cambodia, focusing on the impact on the Cambodian economy and society of the large-scale United Nations peace-keeping operation and the dramatic influx of international agencies and personnel that began in 1992. The collection of six essays is introduced by Peter Utting who is research co-ordinator for

UNRISD. Grant Curtis answers the question, 'Transition To What?', arguing that the peace process saw the emergence of new social problems, including a rise in social violence, increased incidence of HIV/AIDS, and a further deterioration in the situation of 'vulnerable groups', and concludes that UNTAC may have in some respects retarded Cambodia's social development. E. V. K. Fitzgerald from Oxford University considers the economic dimensions of the peace process, and argues economic distortions were the product of the UNTAC presence, especially due to the scale of the expenditure (US$ 2.8 billion) relative to the size of the Cambodian economy. A paper on NGOs in transition in Cambodia by Eva Mysliwiec, Director of the Cambodian Development Resource Institute, is included together with a discerning paper based on research into the social consequences of UNTAC on women, children and returnees by Eva Arnvig, who works with the UNDP in Denmark. Finally, an account of returnees by Vance Geiger, a PhD candidate from the University of Florida completes the volume.

570 **Cambodia – the 1989 Paris Peace Conference: background analysis and documents.**

Compiled and edited by Amitav Acharya, Pierre Lizée, and Sorpong Peou. Millwood, New York: Kraus International Publications, 1991. xlviii, 592p. bibliog.

Presents valuable documentary material from the 1989 conference, including the full text of speeches, communiqués and resolutions of the main session and five committees. Supplementary material up to April 1990 takes in the early proposals for an interim UN administration. The authors conclude that neither China nor Vietnam were ready to push their respective clients, and that the Cambodian factions each saw the elimination of their opposition as the road to national reconciliation. As a result, the external need for settlement outstripped the internal, so the high hopes that the conference would achieve peace proved to be grossly misconceived. Others may not share this view, and may see the conflict as being exacerbated by outside powers who expected the Cambodian government to collapse in the wake of the Vietnamese troop withdrawal.

571 **Cambodia: an Australian peace proposal: working papers prepared for the Informal Meeting on Cambodia, Jakarta, 26-28 February 1990.**

Canberra: Published for the Department of Foreign Affairs and Trade by the Australian Government Publishing Service, 1990. vii, 155p.

The Red Book or Australian Plan – a more developed form of Foreign Minister Gareth Evans' November 1989 statement to Parliament – spelling out the basis of a 'comprehensive settlement' involving a major United Nations role in Cambodia in the transitional period towards the staging of elections, and recognizing all parties (including the Khmer Rouge) as legitimate participants in the peace process. Although really an algebraic formula with various options presented at this stage, it was one variant of this Red Book that eventually did prevail in the form of UNTAC. Gareth Evans acknowledges the contribution made by others, particularly Prince Norodom Sihanouk and US Congressman Stephen Solarz.

572 **The Cambodia conflict: search for a settlement, 1979-1991: an analytical chronology.**
Patrick Raszelenberg, Peter Schier in co-operation with Jeffry G. Wong. Hamburg, Germany: Institute of Asian Affairs, 1995. 605p. (Mitteilungen des Instituts für Asienkunde Hamburg, no. 241).

An invaluable and very detailed chronology of the 'Third Indochinese War' and efforts to achieve a settlement. This work is usefully cross-referenced and traces developments over eleven vital years, at times on a daily basis. It provides information such as contents of radio broadcasts which are difficult to find elsewhere. Documents reproduced include: Statement of the five permanent members of the Security Council of the United Nations on Cambodia, New York, 28 August 1990 – with annex; Framework for a comprehensive political settlement of the Cambodia conflict; Joint statement of the Jakarta informal meeting on Cambodia, September 1990; Communiqué of the meeting of the five permanent members of the United Nations Security Council on Cambodia, November 1990 – with proposed structure for the agreements on a comprehensive political settlement of the Cambodia conflict; Explanatory Note, December 1990; Communiqué on Pattaya Meeting, June 1991; Final communiqué of the Supreme National Council of Cambodia, August 1991; and Text of the agreements signed in Paris on October 23 1991 by the states participating in the Paris Conference on Cambodia. Peter Schier, the initiator and co-ordinator of the project, is the permanent representative in Cambodia of the politically conservative Konrad Adenauer Foundation. Most of the information and commentary is drawn from sources collected and selected by Schier.

573 **The Cambodia Settlement Agreements.**
Steven Ratner. *American Journal of International Law*, vol. 87, no. 1 (Jan. 1993), p. 1-41.

A detailed, scholarly analysis (with 238 footnotes) of the Cambodia Settlement Agreements, signed in Paris by nineteen states on 23 October 1991. Ratner explicates the texts, providing the historical and negotiating background; he interprets the legal obligations in the agreements; he analyses the relationship of these agreements to the corpus of similar legal agreements; and he discusses those aspects of the agreements whose legal bases transcend traditional conceptions in international law, or involve innovative undertakings by the signatory states. Ratner's style is clear and he reveals the breadth of understanding he developed as a member of the US delegation to the Paris Peace Conference on Cambodia and the negotiations on Cambodia among the permanent members of the Security Council. He has since gone on to write (with Jason Abrams) a legal opinion for the US State Department (not publicly available) on the options available to prosecute Khmer Rouge leaders for genocide or violation of other human rights. Written at the end of 1992, right in the middle of the UNTAC experience and some six months before the elections, he concluded: 'they embody Cambodia's only hope . . . they do merit the active support of the world community now and in the future, lest they become, like their predecessors in 1954, 1962 and 1973, just another failed attempt to bring peace to Indochina'.

574 **Cambodia: the legacy and lessons of UNTAC.**
Trevor Findlay. Oxford: Oxford University Press, 1994. 170p. bibliog. (SIPRI Research Report, no. 9).

UNTAC failed to bring peace to Cambodia but it did isolate the Khmer Rouge. The operation was most successful where the United Nations was not reliant on the full co-operation of the factions. Findlay has made a thorough study of the technicalities of the operation, lessons for future such projects, and the view of successes and problems of those UN employees who participated in and led it. The views of Cambodians who lived with UNTAC and its aftermath are not so well represented. In Findlay's view, lessons of the exercise include: the need for prompt deployment; the indispensability of advance planning; the need for measured implementation; the appropriate level of reaction in response to non-compliance of the parties – UNTAC's low key administrative approach is assessed as being correct; and the necessity for more effective supervision and control of the civil administration. Problems involved with commanding a multinational military force were: the activities of one notorious Bulgarian division; the parking of UNTAC vehicles outside brothels and bars; and the tendency for individual brigades to operate in their own national interests. Findlay explains that some of the less well-equipped and trained troops established a better rapport with the Cambodian population than their better trained and equipped counterparts from the first world. He also writes that human rights should be a priority for future operations. Appendices include: Documents on Cambodia, 1991-93; and Chronology from 1970-94.

575 **Cambodian chronicles 1–13.**

Raoul M. Jennar. Jodoigne, Belgium: EFERC, 1991-94. 13 parts.

Following the signing of the Paris Peace Agreements in October 1991, EFERC (European Far Eastern Research Centre) was commissioned by the NGO Forum on Cambodia to undertake a project to analyse developments as they unfolded. Over the course of the next two-and-a-half years, Raoul Jennar, Director of EFERC, who had played the same role in the previous two years in sixteen separate reports on the peace process, produced thirteen chronicles. The originals were in French but he also issued his own English translations. The early chronicles assess the chance of success, and highlight the failure, of UNTAC to achieve major objectives, such as the disarmament and cantonment of forces as the Khmer Rouge blatantly refused to comply with any of the agreements. Jennar becomes increasingly critical of UNTAC's 'blunders, weakness and indecisiveness' and speaks frankly and critically of the various Cambodian players. In impassioned language, he calls for a better deal for Cambodia, and he concludes the series on a note of regret for what might have been better done, but with a guarded optimism for the future as the new coalition government began to operate. The French versions were published as a book in 1995 as *Chroniques cambodgiennes* (Paris: L'Harmattan, 1995), and an edition of the English versions with some needed improvements is planned.

576 **A further look at UNTAC's performance and dilemmas: a review article.**

Sorpong Peou. *Contemporary Southeast Asia*, vol. 17, no. 2 (Sept. 1995), p. 207-23. bibliog.

A review of three recent works on UNTAC: *UN peacekeeping in Cambodia: UNTAC's civil mandate* (q.v.) by Michael W. Doyle; *The peace process in Cambodia: issues and prospects* (Nathan, Queensland: Faculty of Asian and International Studies, Griffith University, 1993. 63p., a development of a paper originally published, Canberra: Department of the Parliamentary Library, 1992. 26p.) by Frank Frost; and *International peace keeping: building on the Cambodian experience* (q.v.) edited by Hugh Smith. Sorpong Peou, a Research Fellow at the Institute of Southeast Asian Studies in Singapore, argues that the most critical issue confronting UNTAC was whether it did, or otherwise could have, made a difference in the outcome of the Cambodian conflict. The article concentrates on an institutional assessment of UNTAC but includes political material too. Sorpong Peou maintains that none of the three authors 'has dealt effectively with the burning issue of why the Khmer Rouge was the only party that called it quits just before the elections took place', and goes on to add that they 'overlooked the P-5 (Permanent Five members of the Security Council)'s foreign policy objectives and their impact on the Cambodian peace process'.

577 **The General Assembly and the Kampuchean issues: intervention, regime recognition, and the world community, 1979 to 1987.**
Ramses Amer. Uppsala, Sweden: Department of Peace and Conflict Research, Uppsala University, 1989. 110p. bibliog. (Report, no. 31).

Amer provides detailed data on the voting patterns at the Credentials Committee of the General Assembly, revealing the failure of the Western countries to recognize the régime that overthrew Pol Pot, despite the rhetoric about rejecting his policies.

578 **International peacekeeping: building on the Cambodian experience.**
Edited by Hugh Smith. Canberra: Australian Defence Studies Centre, 1994. xiii, 252p.

Comprises some nineteen papers and a summary of discussion at an International Peacekeeping Seminar held in Canberra from 2-4 May 1994, together with an introduction by Lt. Gen. John Sanderson, the Australian commander of the UNTAC military forces. The papers are presented in three sections: the Cambodian experience; Australian and regional perspectives; and United Nations perspectives. A number of senior Australian officials in all aspects of UNTAC – military, civil, electoral, police and judicial – offer their accounts, as does Foreign Minister Gareth Evans, who was himself closely involved in the process. The overall impression is one of achievement, although some criticisms of UNTAC are made, for instance Lyndall McLean's view that the mandate for the civil component was 'unrealistic, overly ambitious and some aspects were clearly unachievable', and her admission that 'in practice there was no equal application of control over the Cambodian parties. The State of Cambodia became the focus of our attention and any guise of impartiality was lost', and Mark Plunkett's criticism of the paucity of resources given to establishing the rule of law. The volume includes illustrations and an index.

579 **Propaganda, politics and violence in Cambodia: democratic transition under United Nations peace-keeping.**
Edited by Steve Heder, Judy Ledgerwood, with a foreword by David P. Chandler; contributions also by David Ashley, Penny Edwards, Kate G. Frieson, Jay Jordens and John Marston. Armonk, New York; London: M. E. Sharpe, 1996. 277p. bibliog. (An East Gate Book).

Seven former officials with UNTAC Information/Education Division present individual papers, first given at the 1994 meeting of the Association of Asian Studies, the publication of which was supported by the East West Center in Hawaii. All had a background in academic work on Cambodia, and Chandler compares their role to the scholar-bureaucrats of the colonial powers. The chapters cover: politics of violence

(Heder and Ledgerwood); imaging of the other in Cambodian nationalist discourse before and after UNTAC (Edwards); the resumption of armed struggle by the Party of Democratic Kampuchea (Heder); patterns of CPP political repression and violence during UNTAC (Ledgerwood); persecution of Cambodia's ethnic Vietnamese communities during and since UNTAC (Jordens); the nature and causes of human rights violations in Battambang (Ashley); the politics of getting the vote in Cambodia (Frieson); and Cambodian news media in UNTAC and after (Marston). Two appendices contain the text of the 1991 Paris Agreements, and a chronology ranging from the signing of the agreements to the proclamation of the new constitution. As Heder and Ledgerwood say, the contributions 'taken together . . . paint a horrifying picture of a widespread tendency on the part of those [Cambodians] with guns or command over guns to use them to resolve whatever problems might arise'. The United Nations is presented as a neutral umpire of superior moral calibre.

580 **UN peacekeeping in Cambodia: UNTAC's civilian mandate.**
Michael W. Doyle. Boulder, Colorado: Lynne Rienner, 1994. 117p. map. (International Peace Academy Occasional Papers).

The author, Professor of Politics and International Affairs at Princeton University, presents a view of the UNTAC process that is very close to the official analysis of the governments of the United States and Australia. UNTAC's achievements are depicted thus: it was successful in most areas but failed to disarm the factions and fully control the civil administration; it brought an end to full-scale civil war; it organized a successful election thus giving the Cambodian people their first taste of real democracy; it introduced human rights and freedom from foreign domination; it was most successful where it did not require the positive co-operation of the four factions; it was correct not to intervene militarily when the Khmer Rouge refused to respect the Peace Agreement; and it directly contributed to interstate peace in Southeast Asia, a coalition government, the freest press in the region and the beginnings of economic rehabilitation. For future peace-keeping operations the author suggests institutions more democratic than exist in any Western democracy (e.g. an extended Supreme National Council including a chamber for civil society) and he argues that the United Nations should seek more independence in implementation than they had in Cambodia. This work is easy to read and is a good starting-point for an understanding of what is in danger of becoming received wisdom about the UNTAC operation.

581 **UN peacekeeping missions: the lessons from Cambodia.**
Judy L. Ledgerwood. Honolulu, Hawaii: East-West Center, March 1994. 10p. (Asia Pacific Issues: Analysis from the East-West Center, no. 11).

Ledgerwood is a Cambodia specialist at the East-West Center and was previously a fieldworker for the Information Section of UNTAC in Cambodia. Fluent in Khmer, she travelled extensively in Cambodia during the 1993 election period. Ledgerwood concludes the UN mission in Cambodia was an overall success that helped to rebuild a country shattered by a brutal dictatorship and a dozen years of civil war, though hampered by UN bureaucracy and an undisciplined civilian police force.

582 **UNTAC in Cambodia: the impact on human rights.**
Caroline Hughes. Singapore: ISEAS, 1996. 92p.

This study critiques UNTAC's mission from a human rights perspective. It evaluates UNTAC's response to the tensions between continuity and change inherent in the peace-keeping mandate and considers the impact of the choices made during the transition on the long-term future of human rights in Cambodia.

Cambodia's New Deal: a report.
See item no. 309.

Cambodia: from UNTAC to Royal Government.
See item no. 310.

Whither Cambodia?: beyond the election.
See item no. 311.

Radio UNTAC of Cambodia: winning ears, hearts and minds.
See item no. 846.

Economy, Commerce, Industry and Finance

583 **Bulletin Économique de l'Indochine.** (Economic Bulletin of Indochina.)
Gouvernement Général de l'Indochine (1930-37), Service de la Statistique Générale (1947-). Saigon, Hanoi: Imprimerie d'Extrême-Orient, 1898-1952. monthly.

The *Bulletin Économique de l'Indochine* (Saigon/Hanoi) is a prime reference for colonial statistical and economic information on agriculture, forestry, industry, commerce, mining, prices, and demography. It appeared monthly, with occasional special supplements. The issuing body varied over the years; the two most recent are given above. The title varied as well. Available in microfilm from Association pour la Conservation et la Reproduction de la Presse, Paris, and Photo Services, Cornell University, Ithaca, New York. Available in microfiche from Inter Documentation Company, Zug, Switzerland. [David G. Marr with Kristine Alilunas-Rodgers]

584 **Cambodge, laboratoire d'une crise: bilan économique et prospective.** (Cambodia, laboratory of a crisis: the current and prospective economic balance sheet.)
Jacques Népote and Marie-Sybille de Vienne. Paris: Centre des Hautes Études sur l'Afrique et l'Asie Modernes, 1993. 195p.

The poverty of hard economic analysis of Cambodia makes this volume particularly useful. The authors are scholars of some note, with de Vienne having worked previously on overseas Chinese and Thailand, while Népote has written extensively on Cambodian history and society. Here they turn their attention to the economy, placing it in a historical perspective and seeing the economic crisis as having arisen from sociocultural rupture. The book is arranged in three parts: 'Before the war (1950-1970)'; 'More than two decades of ruptures (1970-199?)'; and over half of the text is devoted to the third part, 'The situation since 1979 – the ambiguities of the "peace" boom'. The authors predict that the economic 'boom' and the electoral approach of the peace plan cannot resolve the basic problems which will continue as long as a fundamental social reorganization is not carried out. They prescribe returning Phnom

Penh to its 1950s' urban form, rejecting consumerism and corruption, and returning all peasants to their provinces of origin (strangely reminiscent of the Khmer Rouge evacuation of 1975!), and with restored powers and symbols of the monarchy. While many may find these medicines impractical or unpalatable (or both), this book provides a fascinating view point and a wealth of detail and statistics not easily found elsewhere.

585 **Cambodia's economic development 1945-1995: economic transition and the role of the private sector.**

Peter Annear. *Development Bulletin* (Australian Development Studies Network. Australian National University), vol. 38 (July 1996), p. 19-23; vol. 40 (Jan. 1997), p. 42-46.

This article on the role of the private sector in Cambodia's economic transition includes background on periods and models of development in each political period since independence (Sihanouk, Lon Nol, Khmer Rouge, People's Republic, Royal Government), a discussion of macroeconomic policy in the 1990s, and recent monetary and fiscal reforms. It concludes that, despite the rhetoric, a 'Tiger'-style development (like South Korea or Singapore) is unlikely to be achieved in Cambodia. Volumes 38 (July 1996), and 40 (January 1997) carry other articles by Peter Annear on the themes of economic development, transition and poverty in Cambodia. In volume 40, for example, Annear discusses 'Poverty, development and economic transition in Cambodia', and concludes that disparities of income are wider than is normally found in the least developed countries. He argues that policy changes will be necessary to address the long-term causes of poverty. 'Recent experiences in Cambodia's economic transition' is the theme of an article to be published in volume 42, based on a visit to Cambodia in January 1997. It covers the significance of strikes in the garment industry, recent economic performance and the results of donor support to date. With very little in print about Cambodia's development experience, these articles are particularly valuable, and one can look forward to Annear's PhD thesis, now being written at Deakin University in Melbourne.

586 **Cambodia's economy and industrial development.**

Khieu Samphan, translated by Laura Summers. Ithaca, New York: Southeast Asia Program, Department of Asian Studies, Cornell University, 1979. vii, 122, 9p. bibliog. (Data Paper. Southeast Asia Program, Department of Asian Studies, Cornell University, no. 111).

Despite his later role with the brutal Khmer Rouge, Khieu Samphan's 1959 doctoral thesis remains the best critical account of the French colonial impact on the Cambodian economy and should be read with the work of other Cambodian social analysts of the time including Hou Yuon and Hu Nim. Written in Paris in 1959, the English translation from the French was completed by Laura Summers from the Department of Asian Studies, Cornell University, New York, in 1979. Summers' introduction to the document is in itself an important contribution to the analysis of Cambodia's post-colonial history. France's control of Cambodian trade and its stifling of the indigenous economy were at the root, said Khieu Samphan, of Cambodia's later underdevelopment, leading to the economy's 'vertical disintegration'. So great was the isolation of the distorted industrial sector from agriculture that the national economy could not cohere except by mediation of the international market. 'Contact with France diverted development onto its current semi-colonial and semi-feudal path by integrating the transitional economy into the international market where the most developed country leads.'

587 **Cambodia, the reemergence of new opportunities: business and investment handbook.**

Phnom Penh: Ministry of Commerce, Kingdom of Cambodia, 1996. 531p.

A broad-ranging handbook providing an overview of the current situation and opportunities from the government's perspective, including regulations and procedures. Chapters cover: the country background; the political and administrative structure; macroeconomic development and banking; the legal system; foreign trade; international assistance; travel and tourism; industry, mines and energy; the agricultural sector; forestry and fisheries; telecommunications; the transport infrastructure; the labour force; taxation; and investing in Cambodia.

588 **Cambodia.**

Asian Development Bank Staff. In: *Asian development outlook 1994.* Hong Kong: Oxford University Press, 1994.

The transition to a market economy is the theme of the Asian Development Bank's two-page 1994 report on Cambodia, which notes the satisfactory growth of GDP and gross domestic investment despite adverse conditions, and reports on recent economic reforms. The publication also includes a comparison of growth rates in Cambodia and other Asian economies as well as statistical tables on the state of the world economy, selected indicators for developing Asian countries, savings, investment and growth figures, foreign investment, and more.

589 **Cambodia.**

Laura Summers. In: *Far East and Australasia 1996.* London: Europa, 1995, p. 176-85 (History), 185-91 (Economy). bibliog.

Summers provides concise but comprehensive entries covering pre-colonial, colonial, and independent, Cambodia. She notes the importance of slave labour to the building of Angkor, the strengthening by the French of Cambodians' near-sacred regard for the monarchy, and the erosion of the powers of the National Assembly under Sihanouk. She reserves most attention for the period from the post-1979 establishment of the People's Republic of Kampuchea to the 1989 signing of the Paris Agreements, the UNTAC episode and the recently formed Royal Government of Cambodia. The economy suffered badly up to 1979 as a result of agricultural stagnation and declining growth under Sihanouk, followed by the material destruction and human displacement of the Khmer Rouge. First collectivization and then economic liberalization under the PRK led eventually to the changes in the post-1993 period and the return of international aid and investment. Summers neatly summarizes Cambodia's complex development history. The entry also contains a directory to government ministers and ministries, the press, political parties, banks, etc. In addition, tables report statistical data for the latest three years as reported to the International Monetary Fund and various UN agencies.

590 **Cambodia.**
Prepared by an IMF staff team comprising Owen Evans, Ydahlia Metsgen, Elie Canetti, Ulhas Gunjal, Nancy Happe, Reza Vaez-Zadeh and Yutaka Yokoyama. New York: International Monetary Fund, August 1994. 79p. (IMF Economic Reviews, no. 8, 1994).

Devoted to Cambodia, this is one of a series of IMF reviews on recent economic developments and policies in developing countries. The report is a crisp and precise overview of Cambodia's economy immediately following the 1993 UN-sponsored elections, which paved the way for the return of international organizations to Cambodia, including the IMF. This report – which covers the country's economic history, recent economic developments, fiscal reform, inflation and the liberalization of trade – was written to provide the background necessary for committing Cambodia to structural adjustment policies necessary to gain IMF assistance. While the report concentrates, as would be expected, on inflation and other monetary measures, it provides essential background on the current functioning of the economy and on Cambodia's transition to a market economy. Numerous charts and vital statistics on economic conditions in Cambodia are included.

591 **The challenge of reform in Indochina.**
Edited by Börje Ljunggren. Cambridge, Massachusetts: Harvard University Press, 1993.

A collection of writings on the transition from planned to market economies in the countries of Indochina, covering Vietnam, Laos and Cambodia. The book includes May Ebihara's update of her 1971 anthropological study of a Cambodian village. While most of the other articles focus heavily on Vietnam, two are of particular interest to the understanding of recent economic reforms in Cambodia. The first is Nayan Chanda's account of 'Indochina beyond the Cold War', which details the geopolitical circumstances that prevailed in Indochina following the 1989 demise of socialist planning in Eastern Europe. The second is Ljunggren's own account of the economic reforms in Vietnam, Laos and Cambodia. This is a detailed and comprehensive overview of major importance to the understanding of recent events in the region.

592 **Country Economic Brief: Cambodia.**
Canberra: Department of Foreign Affairs and Trade, June 1993- . semi-annual.

Provided to Australian companies for their internal use, these are less detailed than the Economist Intelligence Unit's briefings – *Country Profiles* and *Country Reports* (qq.v.) – providing specific information concerning Australian business involvement, such as Australian export statistics, political situation, economy, economic reforms, public finance, and challenges (identification of economic problem areas). Sectoral reviews are given of agricultural production, mining, manufacturing, banking, foreign investment, foreign trade, and Australian business involvement. A statistical annex on Cambodia, and on Australian trade statistics, is included.

593 **Country Profile: Indochina.**
Economist Intelligence Unit. London: Economist Intelligence Unit, 1986- . annual.

Published as an annual supplement to the Economist Intelligence Unit's *Country Report: Indochina – Vietnam, Laos, Cambodia* (q.v.), the profiles cover 180 countries in greater depth and scope than do the latter. They are designed for use by companies undertaking international operations, governments and international organizations, with briefings on business developments, political and economic trends, government regulations and corporate practice. The profile provides thorough yet concise updates and background information on population and society, currency, the economy, national accounts, employment, wages and prices, agriculture, forestry and fishing, mining, energy, manufacturing, construction, tourism, transport and communications, finance, foreign trade, external payments and debt, exchange and investment regulations.

594 **Country Report: Indochina – Vietnam, Laos, Cambodia.**
Economist Intelligence Unit. London: Economist Intelligence Unit, 1986- . quarterly.

Formerly the *Quarterly Economic Review of Indochina: Vietnam, Laos, Cambodia* (London: Economist Intelligence Unit, 1952-85. quarterly). Clearly laid out, these concise briefings on the countries' political and economic situation are made more accessible by summaries and use of bold text which function as headlines adjacent to the relevant paragraphs. In every issue each country covered is re-introduced with three tables outlining the political and economic structure. The briefing is then divided into outlook, review, the economy and economic policy, agriculture, industry, infrastructure, banking and finance, foreign trade and payments, and aid. Intended to help companies manage international operations, the reports generally provide a two-year economic outlook, and analysis of political developments revolve around their economic rather than social impact. Frequent and consistent, the information is also available as a computer file. Each year a more in-depth supplement is included in the form of the annual *Country Profile* (q.v.).

595 **Des pionniers en Extrême-Orient: histoire de la Banque de l'Indochine, 1875-1975.** (Pioneers in the Far East: a history of the Bank of Indochina, 1875-1975.)
Marc Meuleau. Paris: Fayard, 1990. 647p. maps.

The Bank of Indochina was much more than a private bank in colonial Indochina, being used by the authorities for the issue of currency and other official monetary functions. As a result, other institutions, particularly non-French banks, found it difficult to compete. Given access to the Bank's archives, Meuleau is able to address some historical issues that have puzzled specialists for a long time, yet much of the story remains in the dark. [David G. Marr with Kristine Alilunas-Rodgers]

596 **The development of capitalism in colonial Indochina (1870-1940).**
Martin J. Murray. Berkeley, California: University of California Press, 1980. 685p.

Given the range of source materials and the intrinsic importance of the topic, it is surprising that this remains the only economic history of Indochina to be published in any Western language since the pioneering French efforts of the late 1930s. The author came to his task primarily out of a desire to test the theoretical categories of Karl Marx in a specific colonial setting. This leads him to focus extensively on the rubber plantations, mines and nascent industries, leaving agriculture to only one chapter. His understanding of the village economy, where almost ninety per cent of Vietnamese, Lao and Cambodians continued to live in the colonial period, is very deficient. French archival materials appear to have been consulted in a hasty manner. However, Murray's searching examination of the vital Banque de l'Indochine (Bank of Indochina) shows what can be accomplished with other sectors of the economy by future researchers. [David G. Marr with Kristine Alilunas-Rodgers]

597 **The economic development of French Indochina.**
Charles Robequain. London: Oxford University Press, 1944. 400p. A translation by Isabel A. Ward of *L'évolution économique de l'Indochine française* (1939). An essay, 'Recent developments in Indochina, 1939-1943' by John R. Andrus and Katrine R. C. Greene, was appended to translation of original 1939 French publication.

The original French edition was printed in 1939, and was much in demand by government departments and research organizations. This American edition was published five years later, in order to meet the growing interest in the development of the Indochinese territory. A supplementary chapter attempts to fill in principal economic changes between the French and English editions. The work is intended to show the changes effected in the economy of Indochina as a result of the French occupation. Traditional areas of production are not covered as thoroughly as more recent areas, and the author refers readers to *Land utilization in French Indochina* (q.v.). An introduction presents an outline of the political formations and geographic position of Indochina, including colonial exploration. General factors in Indochina's economic development are looked at in terms of people, communications, economic theories and the circulation of capital. New economic developments are presented as they stem from French colonization, changes in native agriculture, industry and foreign trade. The author concludes that native living standards have improved as a result of French involvement, but points to remaining human problems which need attention: malnutrition and population expansion. Some rather dated economic theories are used, but the Western developed nations' patronizing approach to the region sounds quite contemporary. However, a broad selection of facts, figures, and analyses make it potentially valuable, although the majority of the material is on Vietnam exclusively.

598 **L'économie du Cambodge.** (The economy of Cambodia.)
Rémy Prud'homme. Paris: Presses Universitaires de France, 1969. 300p. bibliog. (Collection Tiers Monde).

This work grew out of Prud'homme's doctorate from the Faculty of Law and Economic Science of the Royal University of Phnom Penh, from 1965-66. The author maintains that Cambodia was (in 1969) not well known, and little studied, particularly from a statistical perspective, and so he prepared this book especially for students but also for diplomats and others who need an overview. The major chapters concern: population; domestic production; foreign trade; and political economy (involving planning, infrastructure, public finance, money and credit, and foreign aid). While Cambodia was in principle a 'parliamentary monarchy', Prud'homme points out that there was at that time no monarch and no political parties. He describes Cambodia as at the same time underpopulated (with two-thirds of the country 'almost empty', in some areas with only 5 people per square kilometre) and overpopulated (in others bearing up to 600 per square kilometre). According to the 1962 census, only ten per cent of the population was urban, agriculture accounting for eighty per cent of the active population and forty per cent of national production. He describes the government monopolies established in 1963, and he reviews economic planning and development from 1954 to 1964, concluding, with ironic optimism: 'The problem of development in Cambodia does not have the acute, urgent, dramatic character it has unfortunately in so many countries of the Third World'. This work is particularly valuable because of the continuing paucity of economic studies of Cambodia.

599 **The failure of agricultural collectivization in the People's Republic of Kampuchea (1979-1989).**
Viviane Frings. Clayton, Victoria: Centre of South East Asian Studies, Monash University, 1993. vii, 72p. (Working Paper. Monash University, Centre of Southeast Asian Studies, no. 80).

Frings, a Belgian scholar, here sets out to analyse the policies implemented in the Cambodian countryside in the 1980s, showing the persistent gap between theory and practice, and between socialism and Cambodian traditions and behaviour. On the basis of a study of official government and party documents, newspaper and journal articles, and interviews in mid-1992 with peasants, local officials, agricultural cadres and senior officials from the Ministry of Agriculture she concludes that the attempts at collectivization failed in the People's Republic of Kampuchea. While in the early 1980s the *krom samakki* solidarity groups (in which land was worked collectively and implements shared) helped the most disadvantaged sectors of society, kept people in the countryside, and helped them to restart normal lives and agricultural production, collectivist policies were not whole-heartedly implemented, and peasants went back to their traditional practices and behaviour, and to individual farming, as soon as they were able to do so.

600 **Fiscal reform in Cambodia.**
David Coady and Meghnad Desai. London: London School of Economics, Nov. 1990. [31]p.

Coady and Desai visited Cambodia in 1990 at the invitation of Deputy Prime Minister Kong Som Ol to advise the Government of Cambodia on ways to increase its revenues. Written at a time of quickening reform in the direction of private ownership and private enterprise, this brief report looks at the situation of domestic taxes, customs duties, non-tax revenues and agriculture, and notes the extremely low level of revenue collection (4 per cent of GNP) compared to many other lesser-developed countries (15-22 per cent of GNP). This is a valuable source of information about government financing at a time of economic transition and helps fill the gaps left by the paucity of information in most areas. This is a mimeographed document, marked as Second Draft.

601 **Fiscal reforms and macroeconomic stabilisation.**
Magnus Cedergren. Lund, Sweden: Department of Economics, University of Lund, 1995. 65p. bibliog. (Minor Field Study Series, 62).

Cedergren's useful, short account of macroeconomic stabilization in Cambodia was written for his masters degree at the University of Lund. He visited Cambodia in 1995 to conduct interviews and to research the transition process, and has produced one of the few theoretical accounts of changes in the country's economic policy from the mid-1980s. The study focuses on government budget (fiscal) policy in the transition process and discusses taxation measures, public expenditure policy, economic reform, budget performance and inflation management. Observations about Cambodia are placed in the context of theories of macroeconomic stability and economic transition in the formerly socialist economies. He concludes that market reforms will be more likely if political consolidation prevails.

602 **Indices Économiques Indochinois.** (Economic Indices for Indochina.) Hanoi: Service de la Statistique Générale, Gouvernement Général de l'Indochine, 1932-48. irregular.

The first and second series of statistical studies, previously published in *Bulletin Économique de l'Indochine* (q.v.) in 1930-32, were updated and published separately ([First series], Hanoi: Inspection Générale des Mines et de l'Industrie, Statistique Générale de l'Indochine, 1932. 103p.; *Second série*, Hanoi: Gouvernement Général de l'Indochine, Statistique Générale, 1937. 179p.). The first series covers the wholesale price index in Saigon (1926-32), cost-of-living indices for Saigon and Hanoi (Europeans, 1919-31), information on wages, monetary circulation (1924-31), the index of Indochinese shares on the Paris stock market, public share issues by Indochinese firms, foreign trade indices, railway receipts (1913-31), state revenue (1913-31), construction activity in major cities (1923-31), and bankruptcies. The second series covers similar ground and introduces data on gold exports, electricity and automobile imports and sales. Series 3 (July 1947) and Series 4 (Sept. 1949) appeared in 'Suppléments' nos. 12 and 19 of *Bulletin Économique de l'Indochine* (q.v.). [David G. Marr with Kristine Alilunas-Rodgers]

603 **Labour conditions in Indo-China.** Jean Goudal. Geneva: International Labour Office, 1938. 331p.

Goudal, employed by the International Labour Office, executed a study mission in late 1934 and early 1935 'under the auspices of the French Ministry of Colonies and the Government of French Indo-China' (p. iii). These were fast-changing times, however, so that Goudal's consultations became more than the expected cover-up, which is reflected in the volume's discussion of such sensitive issues as forced labour, unfair contracts, poor working conditions, low wages and restrictions on forming trade unions. As part of French Popular Front reforms a new Indochina labour code was enacted in December 1936, which causes the author to be excessively optimistic about improvements in the colony. [David G. Marr with Kristine Alilunas-Rodgers]

604 **Land utilization in French Indochina.** Pierre Gourou. New York: Institute of Pacific Relations, 1945. 588p.

First published in French as *L'utilisation du sol en Indochine française* (Paris: Hartmann, 1940. 466p.) and intended as a companion work to Robequain's study, *The economic development of French Indochina* (q.v.), this is a basic secondary source for understanding indigenous land use in the colonial period. The author approaches the topic under three broad headings: physical background; population distribution; and other factors governing exploitation of the land. Because of Gourou's particular interest in heavily populated rural areas, there is much discussion of the Red River delta. [David G. Marr with Kristine Alilunas-Rodgers]

605 **Les services publics économiques au Cambodge.** (Public service economics in Cambodia.)
Hu Nim. Thèse de Doctorat (Droit Public), Université Royale, Faculté de Droit et des Sciences Economiques de Phnom Penh, 1965. 201 leaves.

Hu Nim was a member of the National Assembly for the Sangkum from 1958 (even a Cabinet Minister in 1962) until he was driven underground by Sihanouk in 1967, accused of instigating the Samlaut Rebellion. From 1970 he held the position of Information Minister in the revolutionary government in the resistance, retaining this position under the DK government until 1977, when he was attacked by the régime, incarcerated in Tuol Sleng, forced to write a lengthy 'confession' and finally executed on 6 July 1977. This is his doctoral thesis in public law, major parts of which were translated by Ben Kiernan as chapter two of *Peasants and politics in Kampuchea, 1942-1981* (q.v.). The thesis consists of three sections: the notion of public service and the development of economic public services; the structures of the Cambodian economy; and the organization and orientation of economic public services in Cambodia. He came to the optimistic conclusion that favourable conditions had opened new perspectives for economic and social development in Cambodia, and that success depended on three fundamental conditions: the participation of the masses; national accumulation; and the increase of democracy, in accordance with the Sangkum's programme of action. An elaborate dedication is made to Prince Norodom Sihanouk, said to regret not being born as a proletarian, and whose desire was to give simple service to the people and contribute to the victory of the popular forces.

606 **The sources of economic grievance in Sihanouk's Cambodia.**
Laura Summers. *Southeast Asian Journal of Social Sciences*, vol. 14, no. 1 (1986), p. 16-34. bibliog.

The 'political economy of status' rather than impersonal market or economic considerations was paramount in economic policy under Sihanouk (1953-69), argues Laura Summers. Consequently, economic life was subordinated to the patterns of deference, consumption and largesse in Khmer society, built around the patronage of the monarch. When economic troubles arose in the 1960s, Sihanouk looked for sources of additional revenue (not production) for the patronage economy, a process that led to the break with the United States and the statization of the economy. State enterprises became the preserve of powerful Cambodian patrons who ran them in their own interests. This policy alienated poor peasants, the commercial class and young technocrats, and led eventually to Sihanouk's downfall in 1970. This is a useful analysis based on Weber's notion of 'status situations' in place of the more common characterization of Cambodia as a typical 'patron-client' society.

607 **Strategy for Cambodia's participation in the ASEAN Free Trade Agreement (AFTA) and its implementation of the Agreement on Common Effective Preferential Tariff (CEPT).**
Keat Chhon and Aun Porn Moniroth, translated by Sok Siphana. Phnom Penh: Cambodian Institute for Cooperation and Peace, 1996. 20p. (English) + 25p. (Khmer).

One of a number of publications by the Cambodian Institute for Cooperation and Peace (CICP) on current political and especially foreign policy issues, this essay by Finance Minister Keat Chhon and Dr. Aun Porn Moniroth discusses Cambodia's planned entry into ASEAN in 1997. AFTA and CEPT are preliminary agreements to ASEAN membership requiring tariffs to be reduced to no more than five per cent between 1998 and 2003. Increased trade and investment and greater labour specialization with increased productivity are the hoped-for opportunities that come through ASEAN, while budget revenue reductions, balance of payments problems and the lack of suitable legal institutions present dangers. The authors argue for a substantial and perhaps time-consuming study of the likely impacts before final decisions are made. The publication contains parallel texts in English and Khmer.

Sisters of hope: a monograph on women, work and entrepreneurship in Cambodia.
See item no. 421.

Mekong Law Report: Cambodia.
See item no. 507.

Cambodian forest policy assessment.
See item no. 612.

Cambodia: from rehabilitation to reconstruction.
See item no. 631.

Cambodia: rehabilitation program – implementation and outlook.
See item no. 632.

Comprehensive paper on Cambodia.
See item no. 633.

Development cooperation report (1994/1995).
See item no. 634.

Implementing the National Programme to Rehabilitate and Develop Cambodia.
See item no. 638.

National Programme to Rehabilitate and Develop Cambodia.
See item no. 640.

Rehabilitation and economic reconstruction in Cambodia.
See item no. 642.

Report of the Kampuchea needs assessment study.
See item no. 643.

Report of the economic and demographic statistical assessment mission to Cambodia.
See item no. 650.

Report on the socio-economic survey of Cambodia 1993/94.
See item no. 651.

The catalog and guide book of Southeast Asian coins and currency: Volume I: France.
See item no. 874.

Stanley Gibbons stamp catalogue: Part 21. Southeast Asia.
See item no. 881.

Agriculture, Forests and Fisheries

608 **Agriculture au Cambodge.** (Agriculture in Cambodia.)
L. Tichit. Paris: Agence de Coopération Culturelle et Technique, 1981. 423p. bibliog.

This text, written in 1969 but not published at the time, was presented some twelve years later for publication on the initiative of a number of NGOs, especially the Association for the Development of Relations with Cambodia (ADRAC), due to the absence of any other monograph covering the subject. A comprehensive review of the geographic and socio-economic context is provided, followed by details of the various agricultural crops, animal products, fishing and forestry. A detailed bibliography containing 415 items is included, with indexes to authors, and to plant and pest names.

609 **Annotated list of insects and mites associated with crops in Cambodia.**
John L. Nickel. College, Laguna, Philippines: Southeast Asian Regional Center for Graduate Study and Research in Agriculture (SEARCA), 1979. iv, 75p. bibliog. A SEARCA publication.

One of the early publications from the post-Khmer Rouge era of reconstruction, as the Philippine-based SEARCA scientists carried out their initial research, prior to establishing the IRRI (International Rice Research Institute) Project. This invaluable compendium of the threatening pests of Cambodia is still used today.

610 **Annual Research Report.**
Cambodia-IRRI Rice Project. Phnom Penh: The Project, [1989?]- . annual.

Comprises detailed reports on a range of research projects and experiments in rice breeding, soil and nutrient management and training programmes. Research procedures, results and recommendations are given. The IRRI-Cambodia Project is funded by AusAID, and was one of the early development aid projects, commencing its work in 1988.

611 **Cambodia, rice-growing areas and population.**
[Washington, DC: Central Intelligence Agency, 1968].
map 59741 8-68.

During the 1970s the CIA prepared a number of maps of areas which it considered to be of high interest. Cambodia was (not surprisingly) included. This map, documenting the areas of the country given over to rice growing is still used at the IRRI-Cambodia Project.

612 **Cambodian forest policy assessment.**
Bill McGrath. Washington, DC: The World Bank, 1996.

The future of Cambodia's rapidly diminishing forests is one of the key economic and environmental questions the new government has to face. But it is inextricably linked to foreign policy and to the question of what to do with the Khmer Rouge – both those who have officially defected to one or other side in the coalition government, and those who are still resisting. Control of the forests is a trump card all sides want to play.

613 **The diminished flood: a baseline survey of deepwater rice cultivation in Cambodia.**
Richard P. Lando and Mak Solieng. [Phnom Penh: IRRI-Cambodia Project], 1990. 117p. maps. bibliog. (Baseline Survey Report, no. 2).

A socio-economic study carried out in Prey Kabass, Takeo and Kompong Trabaek, Prey Veng in 1989-90 by an American anthropologist and a Cambodian agricultural scientist.

614 **Diseases and pests of economic plants of Vietnam, Laos and Cambodia.**
Herbert C. Hanson. Washington, DC: American Institute of Crop Ecology, 1963. 155p.

Contains descriptions of plant (especially rice) diseases and pests and ways to combat them.

615 **Économie agricole de l'Indochine.** (Agricultural economy of Indochina.)
Yves Henry. Hanoi: Imprimerie d'Extrême-Orient, 1932. 696p. maps.

One of the most respected officials in the colony, Henry compiled this massive study to summarize for a metropolitan audience both agricultural accomplishments and remaining problems. In the first section, devoted to native agriculture, the author reveals his worries about the growth of a rural proletariat, the peasants' loss of land to cutthroat money-lenders, and very slow improvements in productivity. The second section concentrates on French-initiated 'grandes cultures', especially plantations devoted to cultivation of rice, tobacco, cotton, rubber, coffee, tea and sugar. He complains that investment levels have not reached those achieved by the Dutch in the Netherlands East Indies or the British in Ceylon and Malaya. The recent debilitating impact of the Great Depression is hardly mentioned. A third and final section describes formal government efforts in Indochina to upgrade agriculture, including expanded hydraulic works, investment incentives, credit institutions, scientific research, and the dissemination of new agricultural techniques. The author includes numerous charts and tables. While the overall presentation is excessively optimistic, much can be learned by readers equipped with the right critical tools. [David G. Marr with Kristine Alilunas-Rodgers]

616 **L'économie commerciale du riz en Indochine.** (The commercial economy of rice in Indochina.)
Nguyen Tan Loi. Paris: Les Éditions Domat-Montchrestien, 1938. 105p.

The author advances arguments in favour of compulsory marketing co-operatives, eliminating the Chinese middlemen, expanding exports to China, improving productivity, and liberalizing credit. Although his proposals were quickly overtaken by the Second World War, many of the variables he discusses remain unchanged today. [David G. Marr with Kristine Alilunas-Rodgers]

617 **Food for people: family food production in Cambodia.**
[Bangkok?]: Unicef, 1992. maps.

A brief but informative booklet on the programmes implemented by UNICEF to aid food production in Cambodia, with particular emphasis on the resettled refugees. It includes all areas of agriculture and covers the social dynamics of the various communities and the programmes, which range from education and training to institution building. Maps and colour photographs clearly and simply outline the programmes and the resettlement of returnees.

618 **Ginger flower and others, traditional rainfed lowland rice varieties, and farmers' decision-making in varietal maintenance in Cambodia.**
Richard P. Lando and Mak Solieng. [Phnom Penh: IRRI-Cambodia Project], 1990. 114p. (Baseline Survey Report, no. 3).

A survey of factors involved in farmers' choices of which varieties of rice to plant. Considerations include eating quality, photoperiod, required inputs, resistance to pests and diseases, and market price. The most popular variety in the market is the Cambodian traditional 'ginger flower' rice.

619 **[Papers on Prek Thnot]: 1. The design of Prek Thnot Dam and power station. 2. Estimation of the design flood for the Prek Thnot Dam. 3. Operation of Prek Thnot Reservoir to obtain optimum benefits from hydro power and irrigation.**
Prepared by Snowy Mountains Hydro-Electric Authority. Cooma, New South Wales: SMEC, 1966. 3 vols. (bound together).

The plan to build the Prek Thnot dam was abandoned due to the political upheavals in Cambodia, but it is now once again under active consideration, and the original detailed plans and descriptions have regained their importance for the environmental and agricultural future of Cambodia as debates rage on the pros and cons of dam construction in the Mekong River Valley.

620 **Les recherches agronomiques en Indochine pendant la première moitié du vingtième siècle: leur impact sur la production rurale: leur évolution ultérieure.** (Agronomic research in Indochina in the first half of the 20th century: its impact on rural production: its subsequent development.)
André Angladette. *Mondes et Cultures* (Paris), vol. 41, no. 2 (1981), p. 189-216. bibliog.

Eager to demonstrate France's colonial achievements, the author takes us through the establishment of a range of institutes and agricultural services, the preparation of scientific inventories of flora and fauna, and the application of research findings to production, for example in rice, corn, sugar, coffee, tea and rubber. Particular attention is given to the Institut de recherches agronomiques (Institute of Agronomic Research), created in 1925 under the leadership of Yves Henry. A concluding section is devoted to research efforts after 1952 in Cambodia, the Republic of Vietnam and the Democratic Republic of Vietnam. [David G. Marr with Kristine Alilunas-Rodgers]

621 **Rice agroecosystems, farmer management, and social organization in Kampuchea: a preliminary assessment and research recommendations.**
S. Fujisaka. Manila, Philippines: International Rice Research Institute, [1988]. 16p. maps. bibliog. (IRRI Research Paper Series, no. 136).

A preliminary study carried out before the IRRI came back to work in Cambodia in 1988. In fact it was largely on the basis of the findings of this report, and of the experiences and contacts established during the research for this study that the decision was made to set up the IRRI-Cambodia project. It contains valuable data from the PRK period.

622 **Rice ecosystem analysis for research priority setting in Cambodia.**
Leng Takseng. Master of Applied Science thesis, Central Luzon State University, Nueva Ecija, Philippines, March 1992.

Leng identified three different wet rice ecosystems and one dry rice ecosystem after studying rice grown in 405 hectares from six villages in the central plain of Cambodia during 1991. He carried out soil and hydrographic analysis and field interviews.

623 **Rice germplasm catalog of Cambodia.**
Vinoy N. Sahai, Ram C. Chaudhary and Sin Savoth. Phnom Penh: IRRI, [1994?]. 103p. bibliog.

In Cambodia during the 1970s and 1980s rice yields did not increase and traditional methods were still practised, in contrast to most other rice-growing societies where new agricultural techniques were applied with initially dramatic results. The International Rice Research Institute (IRRI) with funding from Australia was one of the first international agencies to operate in Cambodia, principally working in introducing high-yield varieties. The inevitable result is a decline in crop germplasm, making it vulnerable to disease and pests. In 1989-90 the IRRI engaged in a systematic collection of rice varieties from thirteen provinces in order to build up the bank for future research. This catalogue provides passport data and morpho-agronomic and physiological traits of Cambodian rice varieties. It includes an index.

624 **Riziculture en Indochine.** (Rice cultivation in Indochina.)
Inspection Générale de l'Agriculture, de l'Élevage et des Forêts. Paris: Exposition Coloniale Internationale, Indochine Française. Section Économique, 1931. 45p. 6 maps.

Characterizing rice fields as seasonally swampy from the local rains, permanently swampy, or seasonally flooded by the major rivers, this study then discusses the rice produced in the major delta areas. Statistical data cover monthly rainfalls, the frequencies and causes of lost harvests, areas under cultivation, production, local consumption and exports during the 1920s. Finally, the study reviews the prospects and progress in irrigation projects, selection of superior strains, and fertilizers. While much has happened in rice-growing since the 1920s, this short essay offers useful background. [David G. Marr with Kristine Alilunas-Rodgers]

625 **Souvenirs d'un monde disparu: les plantations de caoutchouc (Viet-Nam, Cambodge, 1956-1972).** (Souvenirs from a vanished world: the rubber plantations, Vietnam, Cambodia, 1956-72.)
Michel-Maurice Michon. Paris: Pensée Universelle, 1987. 232p.

This is one of a series of books published by the 'vanity press' La Pensée Universelle (Universal Thought) for former colonialists who wanted to make sure their reminiscences were published, but they have only been made available by private distribution and are rarely to be found in a library. Along with Michon's memoirs are those by Raoul Chollet, who directed the carving-out of 7,000 hectares of jungle to become the massive Snuol Plantation in Kampong Cham, and who stayed on through the Japanese occupation, running cars on rice alcohol and trucks on charcoal. The book includes illustrations.

626 **Spey Ampal: a baseline survey of dry season rice in Cambodia.**
Richard P. Lando and Mak Solieng. [Phnom Penh: IRRI-Cambodia Project], 1991. 88p. (Baseline Survey Report, no. 4).

A fascinating and important study of the Spey Ampal area in the Kien Svay District of Kandal, not far from Phnom Penh, marked for its high agricultural output. It is an example of an agronomically successful irrigation system which was introduced at enormous human cost by the Khmer Rouge, but has made the area suitable for mechanized land preparation. The Khmer Rouge also introduced some high-yield rice from China. Since 1979, with assistance from the IRRI-Cambodia Project, a range of high-yield (IR) rice varieties have been used.

627 **Without any real advantage: a baseline survey of rainfed lowland rice culture in Cambodia.**
Richard P. Lando and Mak Solieng. [Phnom Penh: IRRI-Cambodia Project], 1991. 92p. (Baseline Survey Report, no. 1).

A socio-economic study of farmers' knowledge and practices in three provinces (Kandal, Kompong Speu and Takeo). During 1989-90 field interviews and test cuts of rice to measure yield and plants per metre gave valuable baseline data on inputs, outputs and constraints.

Atlas of thematic maps of the Lower Mekong Basin: prepared on the basis of satellite imagery (Landsat I and II).
See item no. 21.

Un village en forêt: l'essartage chez les Brou du Cambodge. (A village in the forest: shifting cultivation among the Brus.)
See item no. 355.

Lovea, village des environs d'Angkor: aspects démographiques, économiques et sociologiques du monde rural cambodgien dans la province de Siem-Réap. (Lovea, village in the neighbourhood of Angkor: demographic, economic and sociological aspects of the rural Cambodian world in the province of Siem Reap.)
See item no. 415.

Le paysan cambodgien. (The Cambodian peasant.)
See item no. 419.

La paysannerie du Cambodge: et ses projets de modernisation. (The peasantry of Cambodia: and their projects of modernization.)
See item no. 420.

Land utilization in French Indochina.
See item no. 604.

Mekong project documentation.
See item no. 639.

The conservation atlas of tropical forests: Asia and the Pacific.
See item no. 657.

Forêts et pays: carte schématique des formations forestières dominantes et de l'occupation humaine. Asie du Sud-Est. (Forests and homelands: a diagrammatic map of dominant forest formations and human occupation. Southeast Asia.)
See item no. 659.

Étude sur les rites agraires des Cambodgiens. (Study into the agrarian rites of Cambodians.)
See item no. 830.

Development Policy and Aid

628 **Aid infusions, aid illusions: bilateral and multilateral emergency assistance in Cambodia 1992-1995.**

John P. McAndrew in collaboration with NGO Working Group on Development Assistance. Phnom Penh: CDRI, 1996. 57p.

The title of this working paper indicates the approach to the subject. Those who have been critical of the politics of aid and development will find this paper absorbing, not to mention realistic. Cambodia itself is an interesting case-study as it has the highest concentration of international organizations in the world. This paper clearly and convincingly exposes the perception that large amounts of aid dollars are pouring into Cambodia, providing statistics and tables that reveal the minimal amount of money that reaches the poor. It breaks down the disbursement of aid by sector, discusses NGO co-operation and links to government, and provides strategies and recommendations towards developing a more effective system. The document has an appendix consisting of sixteen pages, which includes a listing of grant assistance from individual countries and major multilateral donors.

629 **Cambodia, post-settlement reconstruction and development.**

Robert J. Muscat with assistance by Jonathan Stromseth. New York: East Asian Institute, Columbia University, 1989. viii, 143p. bibliog. (Occasional Papers of the East Asian Institute Pacific Basin Studies Program).

From a US and pro-Western perspective, this study looks at anticipated priorities and problems of government and development agencies following a peace settlement in Cambodia. The authors attempt to outline an image of the (then) current conditions which point to future reconstruction and development. They consider political configurations, noting regional power shifts, natural and human resources, traditional Cambodian factional formations, and economic changes. The material utilized ranges from PRK radio broadcasts, journalistic accounts, and interviews with NGO workers. Pre-war comparisons are made using the 1970 World Bank country study. Chapters focus on Cambodia in the 1960s, in 1989, and the management of reconstruction and development, followed by conclusions and recommendations, and a summary of previous US aid to Cambodia. Despite being somewhat overtaken by events, and written without a deep understanding of Cambodia, many of the study's observations and conclusions remain relevant, while it also contributes to an understanding of the settlement and reconstruction process, from conception to its partial implementation.

630 **Cambodia: and still they hope.**
John Nichols. Canberra: Australian Council for Overseas Aid, July 1990. 45p. map. bibliog. (Development Dossier, no. 25).

The Australian Council for Overseas Aid (ACFOA), formed in 1965, is a co-ordinating body for around ninety Australian NGOs working in overseas aid and development, with a strong social justice outlook. One of the series of regular 'Development Dossiers', this slight volume is extremely informative, outlining the recent history of the country and the economic and political situation as of July 1990, and making recommendations regarding the Cambodian seat at the United Nations, the development priorities for overseas organizations, and a call for action by Australian NGOs to the international community to end the conflict and build on the development assistance that had been provided since 1980. It includes 'How the West is helping the return of Pol Pot', a special report by Raoul Jennar (q.v.). Supplementary information includes an index of Australian NGOs working in Cambodia, Gareth Evans' (q.v.) summary of the Peace Plan, and tables on population, women, urbanization, health, education and the economy.

631 **Cambodia: from rehabilitation to reconstruction.**
East Asia and Pacific Region, Country Department I, The World Bank. Washington, DC: The World Bank, February 1994. 190p. map.

Prepared in consultation with the Royal Government of Cambodia, these documents summarize the state of the Cambodian economy in the years immediately following the 1993 UN-sponsored elections and provide information which is not otherwise readily available. ICORC (International Committee on the Reconstruction of Cambodia) is the international conference of donors to Cambodia where an evaluation of Cambodia's economic performance and pledges for further foreign aid have been made. The documents couch policy formulations in the terms of structural adjustment measures, and the transition to a market economy, saying ' . . . the Government needs to foster the expansion of private enterprise and to control the intrusion of the state in market activities'. The 1994 volume includes an analysis of the macroeconomic situation and a sector-by-sector account of the economy, covering the rural sector, transport, energy, water supply, health, education, and natural resources. It includes thirty-three tables and figures in the text, an annex of planned government investments and donors' aid projections, and a comprehensive statistical appendix.

632 **Cambodia: rehabilitation program – implementation and outlook.**
East Asia and Pacific Region, Country Department I, The World Bank. Washington, DC: The World Bank, February 1995. 120p. map. Prepared by Guy Darlan.

This 1995 volume measures progress made against projections in the 1994 report, *Cambodia: from rehabilitation to reconstruction* (q.v.), and outlines in more detail the public investment programme as well as a sectoral accounting of the implementation of development plans, aid disbursements by donors, and an updated statistical appendix. It commends the government for successfully carrying out economic stabilization policies.

633 **Comprehensive paper on Cambodia.**
New York: UNDP, April 1992. 63p. map. bibliog.

With the signing of the 1993 Paris Agreements on a Comprehensive Political Settlement, a Declaration on the Rehabilitation and Reconstruction of Cambodia was also issued. This paper is the UNDP's response to the request by donors to compile a document outlining the work to be carried out and represents one of the first steps by the international donors to move beyond the international blockade of Cambodia in the 1980s. It outlines general economic and social conditions, macro-planning issues, and development needs and priorities. The document focuses on issues of development assistance – such as targeting vulnerable groups – rather than the economic structural adjustment concerns of later reports. It includes a comprehensive list of ongoing infrastructure projects and a consolidated financial summary. Four appendices include development programme profiles and an overview of major donor assistance programmes.

634 **Development Cooperation Report (1994/1995).**
Phnom Penh: Council for the Development of Cambodia, Cambodian Rehabilitation and Development Board, Royal Government of Cambodia, June 1995. 25p.

Prepared with the support of the UNDP, this brief document attempts to summarize the disbursement and impact of aid to Cambodia in 1994 and 1995. This second Development Cooperation Report (the first covered the period 1992/1993) begins with an overview of the economy and an analysis of the external aid situation. The main discussion is over the ways to improve the country's capacity to effectively absorb aid already pledged by foreign donors. Numerous figures and tables detail the sources, uses and regional disbursement of aid in the years 1992 to 1995. It concludes that aid should be continued at present levels, and proposes better management and co-ordination. This report should be read with the *National Programme to Rehabilitate and Develop Cambodia* and *Implementing the National Programme to Rehabilitate and Develop Cambodia* (qq.v.).

635 **Development planning in the State of Cambodia: report of a mission organized by the NGO Forum on Cambodia.**
Phnom Penh, The Hague: NGO Forum on Cambodia, November 1989. 56p.

The purpose of this NGO Forum study was to assist the Cambodian Government to devise a clear development framework at a critical time when little external (Western) technical and financial assistance was available. The document's importance is considerable given the paucity of information available on Cambodia's planning system in the 1980s. The balanced analysis identified two acknowledged weaknesses in central planning methodology: the lack of a method for linking output targets with other variables; and the inability to trace production effects on the balance of payments. It concluded that development planning would inevitably be linked to the effective use of external resources, and it recommended further assistance for technical strengthening of the central planning system.

636 **Directory of humanitarian assistance in Cambodia.**
[Phnom Penh: Cooperation Committee for Cambodia], 1988-95. annual.

A vital role in understanding the diverse range of assistance and, indeed, of organizations participating in Cambodian reconstruction was provided by this directory, produced from 1988 to 1994, with a 1995 update. Cooperation Committee for Cambodia (CCC) is, as its name implies, an organization aimed to achieve co-operation between the various NGOs and international organizations. As well as listing background and current information on 125 organizations and their activities in the 1994 edition, the 1995 listing contains updates for 51, and the usual appendices listing the projects by sector and by province. It is an essential tool, but is from now on to be superseded by output from CCC's projects database and to be read in conjunction with the *Directory of Cambodian NGOs and Associations* (Phnom Penh: PACT, [1996?-]. annual).

637 **I could cry for these people: an Australian Quaker response to the plight of the people of Cambodia, 1979-1993.**
William N. Oats. North Hobart, Tasmania: Quaker Service Australia, 1994. 179p.

An impassioned telling of the story of Australia's major NGO work in Cambodia's reconstruction. The title is taken from a poem written by Valerie Nichols, convenor of Quaker Services Australia (QSA) from 1976-86, on her first visit to Cambodia in 1984, which moved her to recommend QSA support. A modest programme of scholarships for twelve Cambodians to study English in Hanoi in 1985 grew into a major teaching programme at the University of Phnom Penh, which was handed over to a consortium of the University of Canberra and the International Development Program of Australian Universities in June 1993. Overall, the QSA programme saw expenditure of nearly $5 million, but its impact was even greater, being one of the first bridges built to Cambodia from the West, during a period of political isolation of Cambodia. Oats describes clearly the context in which QSA became involved in this ever-expanding programme, and frankly addresses some of the difficulties and vicissitudes faced. His account is enlivened by excerpts from reports and personal diaries of the key QSA personnel as well as illustrations, and it represents a most useful record of the period.

638 **Implementing the National Programme to Rehabilitate and Develop Cambodia.**
Phnom Penh: Royal Government of Cambodia, February 1995.

'Cambodia is resolutely turned towards the future.' These optimistic words open the National Programme to Rehabilitate and Develop Cambodia (NPRD), the Cambodian government's comprehensive programme for rehabilitating and developing the country after years of civil war and international isolation. Written with the assistance of the UNDP, the two volumes were prepared as a guide for government activity and as reports for the 1994 and 1995 ICRC meetings of international donors to Cambodia. The government pledges 'to devote an increasing proportion of its human and financial resources to the support of those activities which facilitate the market process, rather than to those which restrain it' and promises a doubling in GDP by 2004 together with rural and social development. Appendices provide detail on the short-term national programme, on sectoral programmes, and on investment needs, by sector.

639 **Mekong project documentation.**
[Bangkok]: The Committee, 1972. 81p. bibliog. (WRD/MKG/INF/L54 Rev. 23). At head of title: United Nations. Economic Commission for Asia and the Far East.

A bibliography of reports on the Lower Mekong Project. It includes committee sessions, annual and semi-annual reports, executive agent reports, programme reports, seminar and sub-committee reports, and relevant reports by all other UN agencies.

640 **National Programme to Rehabilitate and Develop Cambodia.**
Phnom Penh: Royal Government of Cambodia, February 1994. 42p.

This is a progress report on the NPRD seen in terms of macroeconomic management, the reform of state institutions, the rural economy, social development and key economic sectors. It concludes that tackling any one of Cambodia's many problems would be difficult enough but 'tackling all of them simultaneously is positively daunting'. Four appendices include outlines of development priorities for 1995-96, plans for reform of state institutions, and sectoral projections. The documents are precursors of the later Socio-economic Development Plan 1996-2000.

641 **Punishing the poor: the international isolation of Kampuchea.**
Eva Mysliwiec. Oxford: Oxfam, 1988. xiii, 172p. bibliog.

This publication marks a watershed in the work of international relief agencies (particularly NGOs) working in Cambodia in the years after the overthrow of the Khmer Rouge. Aimed at breaking the Western international blockade on aid to Cambodia and written on behalf of NGOs already active there, the book is both a convincing argument for the changes needed and an indictment of current Western policy. Chapters cover the legacy of the Khmer Rouge, the recovery 1979-87, obstacles to assistance and needs, the role of NGOs, the denial of aid for political reasons, the Thai-Cambodian border situation and the poverty of international diplomacy. In its insistence on pointing out the régime's successes in rebuilding, it does however overlook real problems, such as bureaucratization and human rights violations. With a preface by the UN Under-Secretary General and Senior Advisor, Sir Robert Jackson, a who's who of political organizations and personalities and a chronology of political developments, the book is most useful, and is also illustrated with striking photographs. Appendices include a summary of funds committed to UN-assisted projects by year and by donor country, the UN General Assembly voting record on seating credentials, a summary of NGO projects in the Thai border camps and inside Cambodia, and a matrix on the dimensions of the Cambodian conflict.

642 **Rehabilitation and economic reconstruction in Cambodia.**
Mya Than. *Contemporary Southeast Asia*, vol. 14, no. 3 (December 1992), p. 269-86.

A penetrating analysis by an authority on the economic transition in Southeast Asia. Mya Than argues there was in 1992 a glimmer of hope for a country that had suffered severe economic dislocation as a consequence of continuing war and social and political unrest. The article attempts to analyse the human resources and political conditions needed for Cambodia's development and the pitfalls that may arise. With a profile of socio-economic developments since the mid-1980s, an account of economic reconstruction and of the second (Tokyo) conference of international donors to Cambodia, a survey of the economic system that could emerge following proposed elections, and consideration of priorities for reconstruction, Mya Than finds political and macroeconomic stability to be at the top of the country's priorities for further development, but sees these goals as difficult to achieve. Appendices include the 'Declaration on the Rehabilitation and Reconstruction of Cambodia'; and 'Appeal by the UN Secretary-General for the Immediate Needs and Rehabilitation of Cambodia'.

643 **Report of the Kampuchea needs assessment study.**
Kenneth Watts, Charles Draper, David Elder, John Harrison, Yoichi Higaki and Jean-Claude Salle. [New York]: United Nations Development Programme, 1989. xxvi, 277p. bibliog.

Written by a multi-disciplinary team, the report aimed to review the social and economic situation of the country, assess current programmes of external assistance, identify assistance priorities and their resource requirements, and to recommend preparatory tasks for facilitating aid transfer, as well as a strategy for aid co-ordination following the expected peace settlement. The report is arranged in eight parts, Part one being a country outline which is preceded by an executive summary. Parts two to five, sectoral studies, form the bulk of the report on which Part six, a summary of international responses to Cambodia's crisis, is based. Part seven consists of a number of project profiles which outline the scope of certain sectoral needs. An annotated bibliography of sources used in the course of researching the report forms Part eight. The mission did not visit Cambodia, but collected and reviewed relevant information in order to arrive at its recommendations. While much of the information and many of the conclusions of the report have necessarily been superseded, it is one of the most accurate sources of statistical material on the country's development prior to the UNTAC period. Resource development, manufacturing industries, physical development and infrastructure, social services and culture are assessed in detail, and tables provide such specific information as: precipitation in 145 locations; activities of the Department of Roads and Bridges; and figures for general education enrolment.

644 **Shooting at the moon: Cambodian peaceworkers tell their stories.**
Text by Marje Prior, photography by Heide Smith. Ainslie, Australian Capital Territory: MPA Publishing, 1994. vi, 194p.

Captures the feeling of the time of the resurgence of humanitarian work inside Cambodia, during the recent peace settlement, which Marje Prior touches on in her introduction: 'Cambodia . . . represents a very personal and emotionally challenging experience for westerners and Khmers involved in the rebuilding of this volatile and fascinating country'. The book profiles more than seventy-five peaceworkers, including Cambodian and international NGO staff, UN personnel, expatriate Cambodians who returned to help, business people, electoral officers, refugees returning, politicians and diplomats. The areas of rebuilding they work in include repatriation, education, skills training, mine clearing, health care, election organizing, human rights and legal training, bridge building and cultural revival. Short introductions and chapters provide the background to the history and conditions of the country. Heide Smith's stunning photographs sensitively and aptly accompany the text. The proceeds of the book go to the Australian Media Scholarships Trust, which funds journalists from developing nations to study in Australia.

645 **Subregional economic cooperation: Cambodia, Lao PDR, Myanmar, Thailand, Viet Nam and Yunnan Province of the People's Republic of China.**

[Manila]: Asian Development Bank, 1992- .

The Asian Development Bank (ADB) framework report and related papers from the conferences held in Manila in October 1992 and 1993, and in Hanoi in 1994 to discuss Phase 1 and 2 of the ADB Technical Assistance Initiative for subregional economic co-operation, containing descriptive material on Cambodia, including statistics hard to get elsewhere, overview papers, detailed profiles and strategy reports relating to transport, energy, environmental and human resources, trade and investment, and tourism. The 5th Conference was held in Manila in 1995, and its Proceedings published in 1996 (Manila: Asian Development Bank, 1996. 226p.).

646 **Towards restoring life.**

Meas Nee. Phnom Penh: JSRC, 1995. 79p.

The author concisely and movingly explains the thinking behind the Krom Akphiwat Phum (Village Development Group), which operates in the province of Battambang. Members of the core group work and live in the villages. Meas Nee offers a personalized account of how the experiences of Cambodian villagers destroyed the trust existing among them. The struggle for food dominated life, excluding thought of anything else. He argues the main aim in village development work should now be to strengthen trust among the villagers. Projects implemented without this are likely to fail to give the expected benefits. As trust grows the initiative of the local people will return, generating creative projects attuned to local capacities and needs. This book has insights of general interest, but would be of particular value to development workers.

Polish conservators of monuments in Asia.
See item no. 132.

Political pawns: refugees on the Thai-Kampuchean border.
See item no. 366.

Kantha Bopha: a children's doctor in Cambodia.
See item no. 443.

Your guide to the United Nations in Cambodia.
See item no. 882.

Kampuchea after Pol Pot.
See item no. 929.

Cambodian Human and Natural Resources.
See item no. 978.

CCCNet – Cambodia.
See item no. 980.

USAID assistance for Cambodia.
See item no. 991.

Statistics

647 **Annuaire Statistique de l'Indochine.** (Statistical Yearbook of Indochina.)
Gouvernement Général de l'Indochine, Direction des Affaires Économiques, Service de la Statistique Générale. Hanoi: Imprimerie d'Extrême-Orient, 1927-45; Union Française, Haut-Commissariat de France pour l'Indochine. Saigon: Statistique Générale de l'Indochine, 1948-49. irregular (12 vols. on 4 reels of microfilm available from Cornell University Libraries, Photographic Services, Ithaca, New York).

This yearbook continues the statistical series first published by Henri Brenier in *Essai d'atlas statistique de l'Indochine française* (A tentative statistical atlas of French Indochina) (Hanoi: Imprimerie d'Extrême-Orient, 1914. 256p. 38 maps) up to the fiscal year 1912. The first volume of this official publication covers the years 1913-22 retrospectively, the second deals with 1923-29. After that, coverage is by financial year, e.g. Volume 3 (1930-31), Volume 4 (1931-32), until Second World War disruptions. Some volumes also include retrospective summaries or appendices. With minor modifications over time, data categories include: climate; territory and population; education; health; justice and penal institutions; agriculture, animal husbandry and forests (later including fishing); industry; transport and communications; money and banking; commerce; property and revenues; consumption; army and administrative personnel; public finances; and the territory of Guang Zhou Wan in China (administratively subordinate to French Indochina). Some figures are Indochina aggregates, while others are broken down by region (Annam [central and south], Cambodia, Cochinchina, Laos, Tonkin [and north Annam]) or by province. A detailed table of contents is provided at the end of each volume. Names of issuing authorities present some variations. Material drawn from Volumes 1 and 2 was published separately under the title *Statistique générale de l'Indochine, résumé rétrospectif, 1913-1929* (Hanoi, 1931, 25p.). Material condensed from Volumes 1-9 was published separately under the title *Statistique générale de l'Indochine, résumé statistique relatif aux années 1913 à 1940* (Hanoi, 1941, 48p.), with some revised figures provided, and some previous gaps filled; statistics for the years 1890-1912 are appended. (Available on microfilm from Yale University Microfilming Unit.) [David G. Marr with Kristine Alilunas-Rodgers]

648 **Annuaire Statistique du Cambodge.** (Statistical Annual of Cambodia.)
Royaume du Cambodge, Ministère du Plan. [Phnom Penh]: Direction de la Statistique & des Études Économiques, 1962- . annual. Microfiche edition, Zug, Switzerland: Inter Documentation.

Comprises annual statistics as reported by the government. Neither an introduction nor an index is provided. An English summary was published in some years under the title *Statistical Yearbook*. A retrospective collation of 1937-57 statistics was published in 1961. The last sighted is that for 1971.

649 **Bibliography of statistical sources on Southeast Asia, c. 1750-1990.**
Compiled by Jennifer Brewster, Anne Booth. Canberra: Australian National University, Economic History of Southeast Asia Project, 1990. 120p. (Data Paper Series. Sources for the Economic History of Southeast Asia, 1).

By providing a guide to published primary sources for long statistical time-series, this research tool helps researchers to elucidate Southeast Asia's development process. Entries are grouped by country or group of countries within each category - general; population; agriculture; industry, mining, energy and commerce; transport and communications; trade and balance of payments; money, banking and public finance; national income; wages and the labour force; prices and household expenditure; and social issues. Each entry is arranged chronologically by commencement date of the statistics contained within the publication cited; these are also indicated in square brackets where appropriate. The availability of publications in libraries is supplied - mostly in Australia but also including Yale University and some libraries in Europe and Southeast Asia. [David G. Marr with Kristine Alilunas-Rodgers]

650 **Report of the economic and demographic statistical assessment mission to Cambodia/Report on a gender-specific statistics assessment mission to Phnom Penh, Cambodia.**
Adel Y. Al-Akel, Birgita Hedman. New York: UNDP, 1991. 69p. + 33p.

These two missions were conducted simultaneously in February and March 1991, with both reports, by Al-Akel and Hedman respectively, presented in this volume. The accounts foreshadowed the establishment of the UNTAC mission, charged with organizing the 1993 Cambodian elections, and preparing the way for the re-establishment of international development assistance to Cambodia. Al-Akel provides a brief background section on economic and social planning and statistics and the nature of statistical collection, concluding that by 1991 'The country has reached or approached in many fields the levels of production and services that were known during the 1960s'. Tables and appendices are included. Working for UNIFEM (United Nations Development Fund for Women), Hedman concludes, 'Although a wide range of information is collected, there is a lack of statistics in important fields', including women in development.

651 **Report on the socio-economic survey of Cambodia 1993/94.**
Phnom Penh: Ministry of Planning and the National Institute of Statistics, Royal Government of Cambodia. Sponsored by UNDP, ADB and the National Institute of Statistics, 1994.

Seventy-five per cent of Cambodia's population is in agriculture; twenty-one per cent of households are headed by females; fifty-two per cent of the population is female; the dependent population is ninety-two per cent of the economically active population; the literacy rate is sixty-five per cent; and the wealthiest ten per cent of the population earns forty-seven per cent of income. The only comprehensive such study carried out in recent years, this is an indispensable starting-point for any analysis of the Cambodian economy and social development in the 1990s. The product of a detailed questionnaire and stratified sampling techniques, the report presents consolidated results of the four rounds of the survey carried out through the National Institute of Statistics in 1993 and 1994 with the assistance of the UNDP and the ADB. The survey results give details of household and population characteristics, labour force characteristics, housing characteristics, and household income and expenditure. Numerous statistical tables, figures and appendices are included. Until this report, statistical information on contemporary Cambodia had been very sparse.

652 **Statistical Yearbook for Asia and the Pacific/Annuaire Statistique pour l'Asie et le Pacifique.**
United Nations Economic and Social Commission for Asia and the Pacific. Bangkok: United Nations Economic and Social Commission for Asia and the Pacific, 1974- . annual.

Cambodia is included in this annual bilingual English-French presentation of statistics, usually covering the eleven preceding years. A range of subjects are covered: population; agriculture, forestry and fishing; industrial production; energy; transport and communications; external trade; wages, prices and consumption; finance (including official development assistance); and social statistics (education and medical facilities). Information comes mostly from official national sources, supplemented by data from United Nations agencies (sources are listed in Appendix II). Much of the coverage is uneven, particularly for financial data. [David G. Marr with Kristine Alilunas-Rodgers]

Résultats préliminaires du recensement général de la population, 1962.
(Preliminary results of the general census of population, 1962.)
See item no. 345.

Natural Resources, Environment and Planning

653 **Angkor, a manual for the past.**

Written and compiled by Ang Choulean, Eric Prenowitz, Ashley Thompson, under the supervision of Vann Molyvann. Phnom Penh: Published by the Authority for the Protection and Management of Angkor and the Region of Siem Reap and UNESCO with UNDP and SIDA, 1996. 260p.

This official book deals with the environment of Angkor: the past; the present, including 'Life in Siem Reap province'; the environment today (water demand for the tourist industry, etc.); and the future, dealing with priority projects in cultural heritage and urban planning. The volume goes on to provide a summary of the principal obligations and protective measures taken to date through legal texts. All this bureaucratese is based on concepts developed by the UNESCO special task-force in 1990-92, planning Angkor as a kind of Disneyworld, away from the real Cambodia, for tens of millions of tourists. It was at the time vigorously attacked by Vann Molyvann, an architect with a strong personality and impressive political acumen. Now all this is endorsed by the same Molyvann, who is currently a minister in the Cambodian government, in a book principally aimed at potential international donors.

654 **Bibliography of the geology and mineral resources of Democratic Kampuchea, the Lao People's Democratic Republic, and the Socialist Republic of Viet-Nam, 1951-1975: with supplement 1976-77.**

Committee for Coordination of Investigations of the Lower Mekong Basin (Democratic Kampuchea, Lao PDR, Socialist Republic of Viet-Nam and Thailand). [Bangkok]: The Committee, 1977. 63, iip. MKG/52. 31 August 1977.

Mineral resources play a significant role in the economy of Cambodia, and this bibliography lists the many survey reports and descriptions in the period from the end of the Second World War up until the Khmer Rouge took power. As companies look for sites for future investment, many of these deposits may now be considered for exploitation.

655 **Cambodia land cover atlas 1985/87-1992/93 (including national and provincial statistics).**

Prepared by the Mekong Secretariat. [s.l.: United Nations Development Programme and the Food and Agriculture Organization, 1994].

As Cambodia's forests disappear at an alarming rate, being cut down mainly for export despite official bans, the record of what remains is critical for efforts to protect what is left. This volume consists of 124 leaves of illustrations.

656 **Centre urbain de [Siemreap, Battambang et Pursat].** (Urban centre of [Siem Reap, Battambang and Pursat].)

[Cambodia: Service du Cadastre, 195?]. 3 maps.

Printed in the 1950s, some of the mapping was done during the 1930s. The three maps are a series of simple plans of the three major provincial cities, within administrative limits only. Blocks and their subdivisions are shown, although building type and ownership is not always indicated. Governmental buildings are given priority, and accordingly the maps provide an overview of the French colonial system as evident in architecture and land tenure. Public facilities, military barracks, industrial areas, radio towers, distilleries, prisons etc. are among the features noted. These maps may prove useful for comparative studies, for historians, urban planners or those with romantic attachments to the towns.

657 **The conservation atlas of tropical forests: Asia and the Pacific.**

Edited by N. Mark Collins, Jeffrey A. Sayer, Timothy C. Whitmore. London; Basingstoke, England: Macmillan, 1991. 256p.

Acutely mindful that tropical forests are being destroyed or degraded at a rapid rate, the editors have compiled and interpreted whatever information is available in the hope of contributing to worldwide efforts to grapple with the problem. Part I is a general discussion of the issues, including forest wildlife, the people of the tropical forests, shifting cultivation, agricultural settlement schemes, forest management, the timber trade, government policies, and various plans for the future. Part II contains eighteen country studies; those on Vietnam and Cambodia are less satisfactory than most, due to the lack of up-to-date data in languages accessible to the authors. Nonetheless, they do point up the undeniable deforestation that is under way and offer several good maps. Each chapter contains a list of references. The quality of colour illustrations is excellent and there are two indexes. [David G. Marr with Kristine Alilunas-Rodgers]

658 **Cultural identity and urban change in Southeast Asia: interpretative essays.**

Edited by Marc Askew and William S. Logan. Geelong, Victoria: Deakin University Press, 1994. 252p. maps.

A rare, readable, urban history of Phnom Penh, which focuses on the physical issues of the development of Cambodia's capital city by Parisian planner/architect Christiane Blancot, a teacher in planning history and theory. Blancot has been involved in the preparation of building regulations and planning projects with the City of Phnom Penh. She outlines French colonial efforts to impose European metropolitan methods on a distinctly foreign site. However, she concludes that French solutions to the problems of urban construction interacting with nature did not differ wildly from indigenous Khmer solutions. This brief, yet informative paper includes photographs and maps. Analysis of very recent changes in the city warns of many potential planning disasters in the making.

659 **Forêts et pays: carte schématique des formations forestières dominantes et de l'occupation humaine. Asie du Sud-Est.** (Forests and homelands: a diagrammatic map of dominant forest formations and human occupation. Southeast Asia.)
Jean Boulbet. Paris: École Française d'Extrême-Orient, 1984. 134p. maps. bibliog. (Publications de l'École Française d'Extrême-Orient, 143).

The author began his studies among the Cau Maa' people in the central highlands of South Vietnam, noting how a 'village' for them was not a cluster of houses but a specific set of valleys and hills through which they moved according to certain patterns. Later he expanded his research to other parts of Southeast Asia. This volume develops a typology of interactions between tropical forest and human cultivators, backed up by numerous local examples, diagrams and photographs. The colour fold-out map referred to in the subtitle divides Southeast Asian vegetation into seven categories; unfortunately the green portions representing 'dense forest' have been dramatically diminished in more recent years. No index is provided. [David G. Marr with Kristine Alilunas-Rodgers]

660 **Grand lac du Cambodge: sédimentologie et hydrologie, 1962-63 – rapport de mission.** (Great Lake of Cambodia: sedimentology and hydrology, 1962-63 – mission report.)
J. P. Carbonnel, J. Guiscafré. [Paris]: Ministère des Affaires Étrangères de la République Française; Muséum National d'Histoire Naturelle de Paris, [1965]. viii, 401p. bibliog.

This mission was organized by the French Ministry of Foreign Affairs on behalf of the Mekong Committee and the Royal Cambodian Government with scientific patronage by the National Museum of Natural History in Paris, the Centre of Geodynamic Research and the Office of Overseas Scientific and Technical Research. Carbonnel was the sedimentologist and Guiscafré was the hydrologist for the mission. Data was collected from March 1962 to October 1963, resulting in the setting-up of a rough water-balance for the mean year, and to plot an area-level curve of the Great Lake. Geological and sedimentological analysis was performed, together with a study of the streams' sediment transports. Copious charts and tables and a bibliography of twenty items complement the text, providing crucial benchmark data for any future studies, particularly the effect of deforestation and mining, now reported to be severely affecting this valuable water body. A summary is provided in English.

661 **Mineral resources of the Lower Mekong Basin and adjacent areas of Khmer Republic, Laos, Thailand and Republic of Viet-Nam.**
Prepared by D. R. Workman in collaboration with the Division of Industry and Natural Resources (Mineral Resources Development Section), ECAFE. [New York; Bangkok]: United Nations, Economic Commission for Asia and the Far East, Bangkok, Thailand, 1972. vi, 148p. maps. bibliog. (Mineral Resources Development Series, no. 39).

This work provides an overview of recorded instances of discovery and commercial mining of metallic ore minerals, fuels and industrial minerals in Kampuchea, Laos, Thailand, and Vietnam. Each subsection is accompanied by useful references and, usually, a distribution map, while prospects for future exploitations are also addressed. [David G. Marr with Kristine Alilunas-Rodgers]

662 **Péninsule indochinoise: études urbaines.** (The Indochinese peninsula: urban studies.)
Paris: L'Harmattan, 1991. 222p. maps. bibliog. (Recherches Asiatiques).

A collection by various authors of studies of urban problems in mainland Southeast Asia.

663 **Phnom Penh then and now.**
Michel Igout, photographs by Serge Dubuisson. Bangkok: White Lotus, 1993. x, 179p. maps. bibliog.

This is an important pictorial history of Phnom Penh since its establishment as the capital of Cambodia in 1866. Utilizing maps, plans, sketches and photographs, it documents the colonial period, the heyday of the 1960s and the destruction of the 1970s. Pictures from the 1980s and early 1990s provide a necessary record of the current continuing dramatic changes to the face of the city. Comparative shots of buildings or districts as they have changed are very useful, although occasionally an image appears without a date or location given. Introductory chapters provide an excellent background on the history, geography, demography, and society of the city. The photographer was Serge Dubuisson and the author-geographer, Michel Igout, who in 1993 was the president of the Franco-Cambodian Solidarity Association, and who has brought his architecture students to Phnom Penh for fieldwork and data gathering for their theses.

664 **Review of the geology and mineral resources of Kampuchea, Laos and Vietnam.**
H. Fontaine, D. R. Workman. In: *Proceedings of the Third Regional Conference on Geology and Mineral Resources of Southeast Asia, Bangkok, November 14-18, 1978.* Edited by Prinya Nutalaya. Bangkok: Asian Institute of Technology, 1978 (distributed by Wiley, 1979), p. 539-603. maps. bibliog.

This major review of pre-1978 Indochinese geological studies is divided into five sections. The first gives an overview of geological stratigraphy by era, and the second analyses the tectonic, sedimentary and warping events which underlie the region's geological structure. The main igneous rocks are then briefly considered, followed by a description of the individual mineral deposits (iron, cassiterite, wolframite, molybdenite, chromite, copper, lead and zinc, stibnite, uranium, gold, silver, bauxite, manganese, heavy mineral sands, phosphates, rock salt and gypsums, potash, graphite, limestone, quartz sand, clay minerals, 'pagodite', precious stones, coal, lignite, petroleum and natural gas). The last part includes a bibliography of 214 European-language publications between 1951 and 1977, and a selection of 91 works (all in French) published between 1880 and 1950. [David G. Marr with Kristine Alilunas-Rodgers]

Education

665 **A 1991 State of Cambodia political education text: exposition and analysis.**

Justin Jordens. Clayton, Victoria: Centre of Southeast Asian Studies, Monash University, 1991. 24p. bibliog. (Working Papers. Centre of Southeast Asian Studies, Monash University, no. 71).

Jordens, then a postgraduate student at Monash University, examines one of the key texts used in his thesis. It is the Year 11 'Political education exam paper for secondary school matriculation and university entrance', Phnom Penh, 1990-91. Some contextual background on Cambodia's political and educational system is given in the introduction, and then the text itself is summarized and commented upon. Jordens concludes that the text reveals Cambodia's polity as 'Party-dominated and mass-based (an image which showed cracks under scrutiny)'. It reveals ideological continuity with Cambodia's past régimes, in notions of 'race, fear of external enemies and "construction and defence" as the two-track road to success'. The work represents an unusual approach, perhaps most valuable for its capture of the last moments of a now superseded polity.

666 **Education Handbook – Cambodia: Educam 1993.**

Phnom Penh: Educam, May 1993. 224p.

Extremely useful for its documentation of the situation in Cambodia at the time of the installation of the new government following the UN-supervised elections.

667 **Education in Cambodia notes and suggestions.**

Phnom Penh: Redd Barna – Cambodia, June 1990. 63p.

As well as an overview of the education system, and of its dire need for assistance, this report has particular interest for its coverage of teaching aids, textbooks, and printing capacity and distribution. Institutions visited include the Ministry of Education (Publishing House, Printing Shop, Central Library) and the Ministry of Information and Culture (University of Fine Arts).

668 **National Conference on Education for All (1991 Phnom Penh, Cambodia): Final report.**
[Phnom Penh: s.n., supported by UNESCO, UNICEF, UNDP, 1991]. iii, 210p.

The report of an important conference, addressing the range of educational needs in Cambodia, and documenting the achievements of the PRK government in its rehabilitation of the sector.

669 **Role of the universities in development planning: the Khmer Republic case.**
Tan Kim Huon. Singapore: Regional Institute of Higher Education and Development, 1974. 51p.

Tan Kim Huon, previously Rector of The University of Agronomy, Phnom Penh presented this assessment of the needs, standards, and relationship to economic development of Cambodian universities. Whilst focusing on the tertiary education system, a broad background to the social and economic conditions is also presented. A section of 'Historical background' summarizes basic information on demography, economic policies, the nature and scope of development planning, and section two, 'Development objectives and strategy' looks at relevant constitutional principles, growth and poverty, human resources and investment, and the role of the private sector. Section three, 'Major problem areas', identifies problems of planning, and political and sociocultural constraints, before moving to the more specific analysis of the role of the university in the development picture. This section includes comprehensive information from student enrolment figures to an outline of the extent of university involvement in the formulation and implementation of development plans. Statistical tables for 1960-72 are provided for kindergarten, primary and secondary education, with enrolment figures for the universities given by faculty. Tan Kim Huon makes his assessments and recommendations in a direct manner. This is a bold and far-thinking study, stressing the need for the evolution of a national strategy, and the development of an indigenous education system, which was published, tragically, only the year before the complete elimination of educational institutions across the country.

670 **Le Service de l'Instruction Publique en Indochine en 1930.** (The Public Instruction Service in Indochina in 1930.)
Gouvernement Général de l'Indochine, Direction Générale de l'Instruction Publique. Hanoi: Imprimerie d'Extrême-Orient, 1930. 132p. 3 maps.

This is a wide-ranging explanation and defence of the colonial education system, ten years after the establishment of an Indochina-wide pedagogical apparatus. There are sections on French schools, 'Franco-indigène' private schools, and 'enseignement supérieur' (technical schools plus the University of Hanoi). An extract from Governor General Pierre Pasquier's speech of 15 October 1930, on recent political agitation among Vietnamese students, provides a sobering conclusion. Nine annexes and numerous photographs are also included. [David G. Marr with Kristine Alilunas-Rodgers]

De l'évolution et du développement des institutions annamites et cambodgiennes sous l'influence française. (The evolution and development of Annamite and Cambodian institutions under French influence.)
See item no. 460.

Book sector study of Cambodia: final summary report.
See item no. 837.

Selected resources: people from Cambodia, Laos, Vietnam.
See item no. 900.

Literature

Western literature set in Cambodia

671 **The Angkor massacre.**

Loup Durand, translated by Helen R. Lane. New York: William Morrow & Co., 1983. 476p.

The novel is set primarily between 1969 and 1975 and chronicles the turbulence in Cambodia at this time – the American-inspired riots of Cambodians against the Vietnamese in Phnom Penh, the ousting of Sihanouk by Lon Nol and Sirik Matak, and the gradual rise and consolidation of the Khmer Rouge. The country's unrest is viewed through colonial, white eyes: those of the Corvers, an elderly French couple who have lived most of their lives in Cambodia; Roger Boué, a French architect-turned photographer; Thomas Aquinas O'Malley, the American cultural attaché to Cambodia; and Lisa – an extraordinarily beautiful American. On the Cambodian side are: Kao, a ruthless major in the Royalist army, who discovers a passion for killing; and two opposing Khmer Rouge leaders, Ieng Sary, an educated idealist who rails against the colonization of his land and Hath, a cold-blooded killer. At the pinnacle of the work stands Lara, the enigmatic hero and Kutchai, his native counterpart. Lara the Frenchman, an eighth-generation 'Cambodian', and Kutchai, his Jarai friend since childhood, represent the Cambodia that is to be split apart. Lara marries Lisa and has a son. But that son is destined to leave the country of his father. Lara believes he is Cambodian, and that Cambodia is his identity. However, the horrors that occur in this period eventually convince Lara that he can no longer claim ownership of the country his family colonized, and he leaves. He is 'the last white man' – the last memory of colonization. Kutchai returns to the jungle as leader of part of the disparate Khmer resistance forces.

672 **Blood is a stranger.**

Roland Perry. Richmond, Victoria: Heinemann, 1988. 297p.

Ken Cardinal, a liberal, is determined to locate the killers of his son, Harry, a laser physicist, who, Cardinal discovers, had been working for the United States government and accumulating considerable wealth. Through his search, Cardinal becomes involved in the politics of uranium mining. He allies himself with Aboriginal activists in central Australia, and journeys to Indonesia (Jakarta) where Perdonny, an Australian government official (ASIO), facilitates his assassination of Chan – a breakaway Khmer Rouge leader who has been financing illegal shipments of uranium. Rhonda Mills, an investigative journalist, follows Ken and his quest. Originally motivated by the desire for a 'good story' she eventually succumbs to Cardinal's charms and the two Westerners find an oasis in the midst of Asian corruption. Escaping Indonesia, Cardinal finally journeys to Kampuchea where in the Cardamon mountains he finds both his son and the answers to his questions.

673 **The Cambodia file.**
Jack Anderson and Bill Pronzini. London: Sphere, 1983. 455p. Originally published, New York: Doubleday, 1981.

The stage is set on the eve of the Khmer Rouge victory in April 1975. Six characters are depicted, and they cover the predictable gamut: dissolute Western journalist; 'Quiet American' embassy official/spy; Cambodian young woman in a relationship with the latter; her half-brother, a Khmer Rouge officer with doubts; a hardline extremist Khmer Rouge woman officer and ideologue; and a rich Western liberal concerned with the fate of refugees. Jack Anderson concludes it with an afterword stating that although fictional, the characters 'have their counterparts in real life' and 'the nightmare actually happened'. He states that five weeks after Pol Pot seized power he was ready to write the story, and that it appeared in five consecutive syndicated columns in May 1978. He took the idea of a novel, 'a story that had to be humanized', to Doubleday and the publisher arranged contact with Bill Pronzini. 'We agreed to collaborate on a novel that was to take two years to complete. I supplied the raw facts; he wove them into a human saga'. While critical of the US bombing, the overthrow of Sihanouk in 1970, and even the continued seating in the 1980s of the Khmer Rouge in the United Nations, Anderson attacks the Vietnamese occupiers for corruption and pillage of rice and other supplies, leaving the reader reeling and convinced that there is no way forward save rebirth in the United States.

674 **Cambodia: a book for people who find television too slow.**
Brian Fawcett. London: Penguin, 1989. 207p. Other editions, Vancouver: Talonbooks, 1986; New York: Grove Press, 1988; New York: Collier Books, 1989.

An extraordinary book with two parallel texts – a series of short stories at the top of each page, with as subtext an extended essay on genocide: in Cambodia under the American bombing and under the Khmer Rouge; in the Belgian Congo in the 1890s as reported by Joseph Conrad in *Heart of Darkness*; and, as obliteration of imagination and knowledge in the 'Global Village' of today where technology breeds social and political ignorance. Fawcett, living in Vancouver, Canada, which he sees as 'the periphery of the Imperium', here develops a thesis from Conrad: barbarity comes with technological wealth, and genocide is the twin of bureaucratic authority. The relationship between the stories of contemporary American life and the horrors of Angkor are explained: 'Cambodia may be my subject matter, but the United States and the Global Village is the source of the threat to my existence' and 'Cambodia is the subtext of the Global Village, and the Global Village has its purest apotheosis in Cambodia'. This is thought-provoking in content as well as in its intriguing title.

675 **Cambodian 'incursion'.**

C. B. Christesen. *Overland*, no. 54 (Autumn 1973), p. 30.

In this poem of three four-line stanzas, the writer compares modern war tanks with the juggernauts of the past. The work debunks the assumption that civilization has progressed. The death implicit in these symbols of destruction remains violently constant.

676 **Cambodians.**

David Wilson. *Agenda*, vol. 28 (Autumn 1990), p. 55.

A three-stanza work in free verse, the poem takes the voice of those Cambodians who defiantly rejected the oppression and tortures of the work camps and made their escape through the jungle. The jungle both feeds and feeds off them as the escapees' dreams are invaded by the bloodthirsty Naga, snake king of the Khmers.

677 **Cambodia.**

Anne Edgeworth. In: *Rescuing beached Mondays: collected works performed at Kimbo's from October 1989 to October 1990.* Woden, Australian Capital Territory: Writers at Kimbo's, 1991, p. 131-33.

Consisting of eighteen stanzas of three lines, this poem was written 'after watching a television documentary on the regime there of Pol Pot and the Khmer Rouge'. The poem begins and ends with the territorial markings and battles of the birdlife of the writer's home. Within this framework of the desire for possession the poem speaks of its reaction to the knowledge of the two million slaughtered in Cambodia. Not distanced by time, this indiscriminate genocide overwhelms the writer. It is the number of dead that is most inconceivable – the mountain of two million skulls buried in Cambodian soil and filling the minds of those that know of the massacre. She wonders at the mentality of the killers, of the horrible monotony of their routine work of death: work carried out in the name of territorial control.

678 **Chanthan.**

David Stewart. In: *Burning illusion.* Melbourne: New Humanity Books, 1988, p. 21.

In this haiku verse the poet writes of separation. Away from Cambodia, his lover's heart sickens for her eastern home as did Ruth. But as the poet's loss is lightened by 'our gentle Cambodian moon' so he wishes her longing to be eased by her memories.

679 **Channeary.**

Steve Tolbert. Melbourne: Cheshire, 1991. 154p.

Cheannery, a young Cambodian girl, has her life shattered when the Khmer Rouge attack her small fishing village. With her mother, her baby sister and surviving villagers, they flee across the country, meeting up with Buddhist soldiers who aid their escape. Dysentery, jungle snakes, and land-mines decimate their number and only Cheannery and Mith survive to reach the Thailand border where they take refuge in a Buddhist monastery and refugee camp. In Thailand Cheannery studies languages and tends the sick and injured, eventually being adopted by an Australian nurse. In Australia, she must deal with racist taunts and difficulties of displacement. A fishing holiday with her adopted grandfather gives rise to a crisis in which she both confronts and comes to terms with the nightmare of her past. From page eighty-seven the text is set in Australia (Tasmania).

680 **The clay marble.**

Minfong Ho. New York: Farrar, Straus, Giroux, 1991. ix, 163p.

A story for senior primary school and junior high school students, telling the story of Dara, a twelve-year-old Cambodian girl who flees her country to a refugee camp in Thailand. She loses her family and friends after the camp is shelled.

681 **The cucumber king.**

Edwin Samuel. In: *The cucumber king and other stories.* London: Abelard-Schuman, 1965, p. 11-25.

A celebrated Hollywood film director, Charles Lukatch, and his beautiful young wife, Maria, journey to Cambodia to shoot a musical in the 'Temple of the Cucumber King'. The legend of the Cucumber King concerns a farmer who is instructed by the sovereign to guard his cucumbers against theft. The farmer inadvertently kills his sovereign whose passion for the vegetable prompts him to steal into the garden by night. The farmer is then elected king. Similarly, in the present, the director hires a young Cambodian (known as The Boy) to shoot bats inside the temple. Accidentally, the Cambodian kills Lukatch and claims the now wealthy Maria who has lusted after the youth since their first meeting. This story is to be found in the Royal Chronicles of Cambodia, and indeed is presented as the 'myth of origin' of the present dynasty.

682 **Cut out.**

Christopher G. Moore. Bangkok: White Lotus, 1994. 314p.

Unfortunately the title of this book is all too accurate a summation of its characterizations – cardboard cut-out figures take part in overdramatic crime and sex episodes in the bars of Phnom Penh – a variation from Christopher Moore's usual Bangkok setting. Still, for those who knew the UNTAC period of Cambodia's recent history it provides the thrill of reminiscence and the challenge of recognition of the real people who inspired this somewhat racier and raunchier version of events than many may remember.

683 **The dogs: concerning Cambodia.**

Andrew Lansdown. In: *Counterpoise: poems.* Sydney: Angus & Robertson, 1982, p. 30.

In this poem, the writer compares the ignorance of those in a tin hut who heard 'only the rain' while the dogs killed the bantam hens, with those who were blind and deaf to, and thus ignored, the plight of Cambodians. The final, sixth, stanza poses a question as to the future. The dogs will surely come again, but will we be aware of their destructive power or remain oblivious, hearing only the sounds that comfort?

684 **The downfall of the gods.**

Hugh Clifford. London: Jonathon Murray, 1911. 344p.

This story tells of the building of Angkor Wat and its abandonment. First published in 1911, it is blatantly orientalist in its exoticism of female characters and feminizing of the male, and in its portrayal of the Khmers as an ultimately child-like people, unable to act without instruction, impulsive, and easily transformed into a mob. Recounting the tale of Chun, the 'pretty', 'shapely' and 'delicate' Khmer man who attempts to save his people from the invading Thais, the story details Chun's attempt to rally his people by presenting his lover, Gunda, as The Snake, a goddess figure. The Khmers discover his deception, and while Chun escapes, Gunda is torn to pieces by the women of the temple. The Khmers without divine leadership are unable to defeat the Thais and the nation is enslaved. Although too massive to be destroyed, Angkor Wat is abandoned and overtaken by the jungle. Chun comes to the conclusion that the gods are ephemeral, and only the temples that men raise in their honour will endure.

685 **Du Rififi au Cambodge: opium sur Angkor-vat.**
Auguste Le Breton. Paris: Presses Pocket, 1977. 188p. (Presses Pocket, no. 1480). Reprint of the 1965 edition, Paris: Plon.

A potboiler. The back cover sets the stage: 'Accustomed to danger, with highly trained reflexes, Mike turned around just at the moment when a shadow fell on him; his keen ear having heard the soft sound of something heavy falling on the ground. He didn't reach for his .38; he didn't have time . . .'.

686 **Ecclesiastes: (after the Amnesty report on Kampuchea, 1978).**
Peter Goldsworthy. In: *Dots over lines: recent poetry in South Australia.* Edited by Graham Rowlands. Adelaide: Adelaide University Union Press, 1980, p. 256.

A six-stanza poem, each stanza consisting of three lines, the work is a reaction to the Amnesty International report on Kampuchea, 1978. It speaks of the danger of words. The terms 'nationalism' and 'economics' (like 'the church') now call countries and factions to war, and the lies of history drown out the screams of the dying. The lessons of history, the work claims, are not about lies, or about destroying those words seen by the powerful as subversive – such acts are as ineffectual as an attempt to turn back the tide with a sword. Instead they should focus on the 'pure' truth of the actions of the poor and innocent born into the 'grammar of pain'.

687 **The four faces.**
Han Suyin. London: Jonathan Cape, 1963. 304p.

'A congress of writers; a nymphomaniac; a coup d'état; a murderer; a box of chocolates; an airline called Air-Opium; a Buddhist monk who predicts the past; and some amateur detectives too busy talking to sleuth . . .', so states the publisher's note for this work, which goes on to say 'with these ingredients, in a setting in Southeast Asia, where all tragedy is tinged with comic opera, Han Suyin has composed a satirical novel. In the pleasant, happy little Kingdom of Cambodia, among the ruins of Angkor, a Writers' Congress takes place. As on many such occasions, the participants have ulterior motives. Contrasted with the sanity of the local inhabitants – the Cambodians who only ask to be left in peace – are the machinations of those who try to utilize the occasion to further their own ends. Someone gets killed . . . did sex, drugs, or politics dictate the murder? Living in Southeast Asia, and a spectator of power politics and the intrigues which are played out in the area, Han Suyin has given us much truth concealed as fiction. She will earn the undying hatred of certain writers and certain politicians whose ego she so blithely punctures'.

688 **The gates of ivory.**

Margaret Drabble. London: Penguin Books, 1991. 464p.

This is the third work of a series and revisits the characters of the preceding two novels – *The radiant way* and *A natural curiosity*. Much of the book concerns the character of Liz, focusing on both her attitudes to ageing and to her on-again, off-again marriage to Charles Headleand. Liz receives, in the mail, a package from Cambodia containing the personal effects and mysterious writings of her old friend Stephen. She is determined to find out what has happened to Stephen after he travelled to Cambodia seeking the true story of Pol Pot's revolution, and passed through the 'gates of ivory' (a phrase from Homer's *Odyssey* referring to the passageway of false dreams). Her preparations for a trip to Cambodia and her research into Cambodia's history are interspersed with the narrative of Stephen's trip. Another plot strand concerns Charles Headleand's trip to the Middle East to discover the fate of a colleague who is missing and believed executed by terrorists. Liz eventually travels to Cambodia and the book closes with her conclusion that Stephen is dead, although, for the reader, his fate remains ambiguous. Drabble has each of her characters fail in their search for an absolute truth. Though she reaches for a conclusion about the Khmer Rouge and the atrocities of Pol Pot's régime, her opening quote about the gates of ivory signals to the reader the deceptive nature of all Western understandings of the Orient.

689 **Highways to a war.**

Christopher J. Koch. Melbourne: William Heinemann Australia, 1995. 451p.

The novel opens in April 1976 with photo-journalist Mike Langford announced as having disappeared on an illegal visit inside Cambodia, presumed executed by the Khmer Rouge. The executor of Langford's estate receives his personal effects, principally a series of tapes making up an 'audio diary', and proceeds to Bangkok to find out if he is still alive, and also to discover more about his childhood friend who lived in Asia from 1965, becoming an internationally renowned cameraman during the Vietnam War. Koch weaves Langford's contemporary impressions with reminiscences of friends and colleagues to create a powerful suspense story with yet a deeper and more moving side to it. Based on a *mélange* of Australian cameraman Neil Davis, with Sean Flynn and Tim Page, Koch captures the mood of the times, the atmosphere of the places and the tensions and shifting allegiances of both foreigners and locals as the war ripped apart the social fabric of Vietnam and Cambodia alike. Koch won his second 1996 Miles Franklin Award, Australia's premier fiction prize, for this work.

690 **The history of Cambodia.**

Keath Fraser. In: *Ink lake: Canadian stories selected by Michael Ondaatje*. New York: Viking Penguin, 1990, p. 591-629.

A story about a Canadian journalist kidnapped around Angkor by the Khmer Rouge, raped and forcibly married to the leader Tan Vim. They have a daughter, born in the jungle. After the Khmer Rouge comes to power Tan Vim is denounced for having a Western wife. He flees, and she and the daughter are taken prisoner. The account of her interrogation is interspersed with her recollections of the five years in the jungle with Tan Vim and of her youth in Vancouver. As well as her personal struggle, the story explores purges within the Khmer Rouge and the complex morality of torture.

691 **Jim Tully.**

Anthony Aikman. Bangkok: Three Pagoda Press, 1995. 261p.

An artless fiction which utilizes fact with varying degrees of fidelity. Characters pass like two-dimensional figures through a pastiche of Southeast Asian scenes and scenery, from the jungles of Burma to the Mekong flats of Stung Treng. The protagonist, Jim Tully, is a jaded adventurer/writer searching for a cause, whom the narrator first meets in the rebellious days of Europe in 1968, and then haphazardly follows through Southeast Asia. The final chapter is located in Cambodia at the time of the 1993 elections. Despite the potential for a fascinating blend of plot and travel writing, the book is riddled with generalities and inaccuracies. Cambodia contributes much to the story-line but the book makes no great contribution to literature dealing with Cambodia.

692 **Kampuchea.**

Wendy Poussard. In: *Ground truth.* Kew, Victoria: Pariah Press, 1987, p. 27.

The first stanza speaks of the massive destruction of ordinary things – the water pipes, the cooking pots – often taken for granted. It also speaks of the destruction of human life. The author visits the violent memorabilia of terror displayed at Tuol Sleng and voices her feelings of intrusion and horror. The second stanza is set in Phnom Penh – a city that, while scarred with the reminders of war, is regenerating itself. Fuller regeneration and hope is focused on in the third verse. Here, the schools of the country are without walls or roofs. This openness promises a new attitude towards learning and the salvation of a nation through its children.

693 **The Khmer hit.**

Doug Armstrong. Rochester, England: 22, 1994. 280p. (Soldier of Fortune, no. 6).

The book proclaims its genre in every way – from the title, to the series statement, the name of the publisher, and the cover showing a white man aiming a large weapon, with a black rectangle blocking out his eyes to preserve his identity – so one is in no doubt from the start that one is in the land of the mercenary. Terry 'Dojo' Williams, an ex-British army weapons specialist and unarmed combat instructor trains an élite Cambodian army unit to face the Khmer Rouge on the border with Thailand. 'Already responsible for the deaths of over a million of their own countrymen, the Khmer Rouge knew that time was no longer on their side and they must push their campaign to an altogether new level of ferocity . . .'.

694 **The killing fields, nominated.**

Gig Ryan. In: *Australian satirical verse: the sting in the wattle.* Edited by Philip Neilsen. St. Lucia, Queensland University Press, 1993, p. 263.

This free-verse poem satirizes the American journalist who visits the killing fields to search for and report on war atrocities. Back home, he revels in his heroism and spouts clichés of the horrors of the Khmer Rouge, believing his words give humanity back to the Cambodian people. But Cambodians are not human to this writer. They are stick parents with broods, not children. His artistic sensibility is detached and his heart aches not with compassion for the war victims but for glory and monetary reward.

695 **Little brother.**

Allan Baillie. New York: Viking, 1992. 1st American ed. 144p.

A book for children. In Cambodia after the Vietnamese War, Vithy learns to overcome social upheaval, a hostile jungle, and his own inability to trust, in order to rescue his older brother.

696 **Looking down on Cambodia.**

Chris Wallace-Crabbe. In: *Rungs of time*. Melbourne: Oxford University Press, 1991, p. 44.

Using a chain of images that emphasize the exoticism of Cambodia, this five-stanza poem describes the view of Cambodia from an aeroplane. From the air the blood, the dying and the mass graves are invisible. The country and its islands are swathed in the Thai silk of the sea which covers and softens the brutal facts of the war. From this perspective, the writer wishes a great thumb could obliterate the killing Khmer Rouge; that they could be erased from time and mind. If erased from the mind, then the country below could return to the symbolic place it holds for many – as food – specifically 'duck and bean-shoots' eaten with a silver fork. This image is laced with irony as the author wishes that another fork could disturb the comfortable assumptions held by those at a distance, and reveal the chaos beneath the surface tranquility.

697 **The noble path.**

Peter May. New York: St. Martin's Press, 1993. 340p.

The notes on this book's inside cover proclaim: 'Innocence is a force more potent, sometimes than evil. For it has no concept of its power to destroy. *The noble path* is the story of two people who become its victims. Jack Elliot is a man without a soul. A discredited British Army officer, he kills now for money. For him life is cheap – even his own. Only death comes expensive. And when Ang Yuon, a wealthy Cambodian refugee, asks him to cross from Thailand to rescue his wife and children from the Khmer Rouge, Elliot demands an extravagant fee. For this time he expects, perhaps hopes, to die. But even Elliot is unprepared for the scale of suffering inflicted on an innocent Cambodian people, or for the curse it brings him – a reason to live. Lisa is Elliot's teenage daughter, stepping into the unknown in search of the father she has never met. Following him as far as Bangkok, she falls foul of his ruthless Thai associates. In her innocence she sees the obsequious Tuk Than as no more than a concerned friend of her father, and the beautiful, bewitching Grace as his talented protégé. She does not realise that Tuk's business interests encompass girls as well as guns, and that Grace is a cunning procuress who can find any number of buyers for an innocent English girl. . . . In the fetid jungles of Cambodia or on the storm-tossed South China Sea, in the opulent mansions of Bangkok or its seamy back streets, Elliot and Lisa tread the hard path of enlightenment, and head inexorably towards a final, unexpected, and devastating encounter'.

698 **River of time.**

Jon Swain. London: Heinemann, 1995; London: Minerva, 1996; New York: A Thomas Dune Book, 1997. 281p.

A disappointing piece of work showing that award-winning journalists do not necessarily make great novelists. Swain alternates between mawkish sentimentality in describing his own personal life and love, and rather wooden descriptions of the historical events he lived through, particularly the days in Phnom Penh after the

Khmer Rouge seized the city. Nevertheless, it is valuable for its documentation of events and individuals of 'the Vietnam war', especially the war correspondents. Swain represented Agence France Presse in Vietnam, Laos and Cambodia from 1970 to 1976.

699 **The royal way.**

André Malraux, translated by Stuart Gilbert. New York: Harrison Smith and Robert Haas, 1935. 290p. A translation of *La voie royale*, Paris, 1930.

André Malraux's seventy-five years of life included an extraordinary variety of political, personal and artistic pursuits – see *André Malraux: the Indochina adventure* (q.v.). This is one of his early novels – about an addict and student of oriental studies, Claude, who journeys to the 'dead cities' of Cambodia, aided by Perken, an adventurer who 'had lived amongst the natives, ruled over them in districts where many of his predecessors had been killed'. Claude's aim is to retrieve statues and reliefs from temples along the ancient Royal Way, in order to make himself a fortune, an episode clearly derived from Malraux's own experience in 1924, when he was tried and imprisoned on charge of temple theft. Milton Osborne describes *The royal way* as a minor classic which, as well as being a semi-biographical adventure story, is notable for its political critique of 'the repressive worlds of colonialism in Saigon and Phnom Penh' and as a philosophical reflection on the colonialists' obsession with death and the threatening unknown of the Cambodian jungle ('Fear and fascination in the tropics: a reader's guide to French fiction on Indo-China' in *Asia in Western fiction*, edited by Robin W. Winks and James R. Rush, Honolulu, Hawaii: University of Hawaii Press, 1990, p. 159-74).

700 **Saramani: danseuse khmère.** (Saramani: Khmer dancer.)

Roland Meyer. Paris: Kailash, 1994. 113p. (Sèrie de Culture et Civilisation Khmères; no. 10). Previously published, Saigon, 1919; [Phnom Penh]: Institut Bouddhique, 1972.

An otherwise unremarkable romantic novel contains an interesting description of the royal funeral rites, practised for the last time in 1904 on the death of King Norodom.

701 **Saret.**

Maureen McCarthy. Melbourne: McPhee Gribble and Penguin, 1987. 70p.

Saret is the second book based on the television mini-series *In between*, produced by Trout Films and Open Channel for SBS TV, and tells the story of two illegal immigrants, Saret and his sister Kanya, from Cambodia. Predominately set in Melbourne, the main theme of the text is Saret's struggle to overcome racism and the ignorance of his Australian friends. Though Saret's attempts to explain the Cambodian situation provide a continual undercurrent to the novel, the chief references to Cambodia occur in two flashback sequences.

702 **Saving the boat people.**

Joe David Bellamy. In: *Atomic love: a novella and eight stories.* Fayetteville, Arkansas: University of Arkansas Press, 1993.

Set primarily in Ohio, the work concerns the cultural differences and misunderstandings that arise when a Western woman sponsors a family of Cambodian refugees. The story alternates between the difficulties faced by both groups in their own lives. Eventually Leslie leaves her husband and seeks refuge with the Cambodian family.

703 **The smiling Buddha.**

Margaret Jones. London: Hamish Hamilton, 1985. 304p.

Well-known Australian journalist and former correspondent from Beijing for *The Sydney Morning Herald*, Jones set her second novel in the mythical country of Khamla, seemingly a hybrid of Cambodia and Laos. While many of the names, including Prince Soumidath, have a Laotian ring to them, the political circumstances and physical descriptions are more firmly resonant of Cambodia in the 1970s. The story centres on an Australian woman, wife of an ineffectual English academic who is writing a biography of Soumidath. She leaves her husband to work for a news agency in Bangkok, and becomes caught up in all kinds of intrigue, particularly related to an Irish journalist who is Soumidath's political adviser. The climaxes of the story relate to the Khams (Khmer Rouge) as they manoeuvre for power and then take over the country, imposing draconian egalitarian rule. While the characterization is a bit weak, and the sex and romance scenes laid on with a trowel, the book makes a good read and effectively evokes the atmosphere of Indochina.

704 **Spy at Angkor Wat.**

William S. Ballinger. New York: New American Library, 1966. 128p.

This spy thriller is concerned with CIA agent Joaquin Hawks's mission to rescue the heir to the throne of Cambodia from a group of sinister communists. The Prince is the only person who holds knowledge of the nexus of communist influence in Southeast Asia and is thus of vital importance to cold-war America. Hawks, a multilingual native American, can pass for a number of Asian nationalities. Working alone (his only contact is murdered and he is unable to implicate his government in the machinations of the rescue), Hawks assumes a variety of identities and travels from Phnom Penh to the exotic Stung Srei where he finds the Prince under house arrest. With the help of the beautiful Shara Dar (the Prince's guardian), Hawks escapes with both his friend, Asram, and the Prince, to Angkor Wat. Here, in traditional spy fashion, Hawks and Shara Dar engage in steamy sex while Asram searches for the Prince's plane, their vehicle of escape. After an air battle, all eventually ends well. The troupe lands safely in Saigon where the Prince, Shara Dar and Asram are given refuge in the US Embassy and the injured Hawks disappears with his anonymity and heroism intact. In this vision of the world the communists are murderous and sinister, and the Cambodian natives are simple, trusting and inhabit a world of nature run wild – violent and dangerous to all civilization. The great civilizing force of democracy is seen as a vital necessity for Southeast Asia's future yet it is implicitly fragile and demands constant vigilance against the 'diabolical red plot'.

705 **Swimming to Cambodia: the collected works of Spalding Gray.**
London: Pan, 1987. 304p. (Picador).

This is a collection of seven reworked transcripts of monologue performances by Gray, performed between 1979 and 1985. The collection is named after one monologue (in two parts) that centres on his small part in Roland Joffé's film *The killing fields* (1984) (q.v.). Gray – an actor, performance artist and monolinguist – roams freely from discoursing on events on set and in his spare time on the beaches and in the brothels and bars of Thailand, to imagining events in Cambodia that lie behind the film. Gray states, 'All of my stories are a reporting of actual events, sometimes slightly embellished, a memory of the memory'.

706 **The terrible but unfinished story of Norodom Sihanouk, King of Cambodia.**
Hélène Cixous, translated by Juliet Flower MacCannell, Judith Pike, and Lollie Groth. Lincoln, Nebraska: University of Nebraska Press, 1994. xxvii, 233p. (European Women Writers Series).

Contemporary French feminist writer and critic, Hélène Cixous, wrote this epic play in French. First published in 1985 and performed over two nights in Ariane Mnouchkine's famous Théâtre du Soleil (Theatre of the Sun) in the same year, it was published again in abridged form in 1987, and was translated into English in 1988 for Cixous' visit to lecture in the Women's Studies programme at the University of California, Irvine. The play begins with Sihanouk's abdication in 1955 and ends with his release from house arrest as Vietnamese troops approach Phnom Penh to overthrow Pol Pot. The destiny of the country unfolds through the fifty characters who appear on stage, ranging from the major figures of Cambodian history, those who affected it from outside, such as Henry Kissinger, Pham Van Dong and Chou En-lai, the ghosts of Sihanouk's parents and imaginary characters who personify Cambodia's people. 'I don't want to compare myself with Shakespeare, I just want to follow his path', says Cixous on her work.

707 **Tigers.**
Catherine Browder. In: *The clay that breathes.* [s.l.]: Milkweed, 1991, p. 11-29.

Told from the perspective of Dara, a young Cambodian refugee, the story is set primarily in Kansas. The lives of the Cambodian community, particularly the relationships between the Cambodian women and their new 'foreign' husbands/lovers are chronicled. While on a visit to see tigers at the zoo, Dara spots Nhouk, the head of her village during the Khmer Rouge period. She attacks him as the man who betrayed her family to 'the tigers with two legs'. Nhouk then reveals his own torture and suffering when his son was executed.

708 **Tuol Sleng: Pol Pot's prison [and four other poems on Cambodia].**
Karen Swenson. In: *The landlady in Bangkok.* Port Townsend, Washington: Copper Canyon Press, 1994, p. 81-88.

The five poems on Cambodia are prefaced with two quotes, one from Erich Fromm that points to the human quality of evil and the other from Graham Greene that speaks of the excitement of danger. *Tuol Sleng: Pol Pot's prison* is written in free verse and divided into three stanzas, describing the inadequacy evoked when viewing the pictures that cover the walls of Tuol Sleng. The photograph of Pol Pot is innocuous, without evil. Those of the dead give rise to an obsessive need to contact the terror they express. The purpose of such contact leaves the writer, whose only tools are words, speechless. *The Cambodian box*, again written in free verse and divided into three stanzas, describes a silver betel box seen in a shop window in Bangkok. The beautiful, displaced box evokes the poverty of Cambodia, and the contemplation of its craftsmanship is compared to the deathly craft of the Khmer Rouge. The two nestling geese that form the box represent, in their union, the seeming paradox of the skilled artisan turned skilled killer. *Survivors*, written in the context of cultural imperialism, of the disintegration of the supposed integrity of place, speaks of how the passage of time – ten years – has not been sufficient to ease the memories of horror that curse the Cambodian people. *One at play in the fields*, written in three stanzas, tells first of the homecoming of an imprisoned Cambodian: of how the happy memories of the past lead him to a familiar picnic field which is now a charnel ground. It then focuses on the poet's reaction to the deaths of those deemed 'others' and of her own, European kind. Yet the bones of the dead, without flesh or race, obliterate such distinctions. They evoke a sense of universality, a shared humanity with both the dead and the killers. It is this 'oneness' that will overcome the graveyard horror of the deathly fields and eventually rejuvenate, in the future, the lost joys of the past. Lastly, *Bayon, Angkor Thom* is set amidst the ruins of the temple statues, the writer likening the lust for god-like power of the king who ordered his features to be carved as the Buddha's with that of the guerrilla soldiers who fight among the wreckage. Nature mocks such goals. The tree roots and lichens defile the soldier kings' pretensions of glory and parrots fly in the face of their arrogance.

709 **What really happened in Cambodia.**

Richard Grayson. In: *With Hitler in New York and other stories.* New York: Taplinger, 1979, p. 162-68.

This sinister story is divided into twelve numbered and titled sections that alternate between incidents concerning Pol Pot and a visiting Western journalist and those surrounding a group of Australian and New Zealand tourists in Cambodia. Pol Pot tells the journalist that he wants to eliminate misfits, seen in terms of contradictions. Yet contradictions are shown as being intrinsic in Cambodia – in the abundant existence of semi-animals (gryphons, sphinxes and satyrs) and in language (palindromes such as Lon Nol, mis-spellings, rhymes and puns that disturb conventional meaning and mock assumptions). Finally all contradictions are indeed eliminated, even the semi-animals and the sign-writers, killed by Pol Pot and his Minister of Culture. Back in her Western home the journalist has no words left to express her feelings about Cambodia – 'not much' is all she can utter.

710 **When God slept.**

Peter Bourne. London: Hutchinson, 1956. 336p.

Set in the 12th century, this story follows the adventures of a young Norman-English squire, Michael de Bernay, and his servant, Will. Michael trains under and fights for Sir William of Shepdale with whom he embarks on a Crusade. In the Holy Land both Michael and Will are captured by Arab traders and enslaved in a galley. The ship sails to Kambuja (Cambodia) where they are sold to 'The Lord of the Universe' – an Eastern potentate. Here they become embroiled in the wars between the Khmers and Chams. Overawed by the 'civilization' and riches of Kambuja but sickened by the excesses of cruelty to which he and the other captives are subjected, Michael attempts to come to terms with the startling difference between this land and the one with which he is familiar, eventually seeing similarities between the two. Predominately, however, he is horrified by the extraordinary beauty of the Hindu temples: a beauty built on the pain and death of slaves. Such horror serves only to make Michael cling to the tenets of knighthood with as much passion as he clings to his virginity.

711 **A wilderness called peace.**

Edmund Keeley. New York: Simon & Schuster, 1985. 315p.

A novel, simulating a diary by Sameth, a woman of mixed Khmer, Chinese and European descent. She tells of her own life and the difficulty of deciding whether to flee the country or to stay. An excerpt, entitled 'Cambodian diary', was published in *Best of the small presses, 1984-85*, edited by Bill Henderson (New York: Pushcart Press, 1984, p. 355-404).

712 **The woman on the treadmill: a recollective pastiche on Cambodia, 1964.**

George Woodcock. *Canadian Literature*, vol. 140 (Spring 1994), p. 62-70.

As explained in the 'Introductory note' this piece contains interspersed excerpts from a variety of genres, including journal entries, poems, articles published in American and Canadian magazines, and a chapter of a travel book (*Asia, gods and cities: Aden to Tokyo*). Although all were written during 1964, the writer found his material had relevance to the war and social upheaval that followed. The first poem describes the town of Kompong Chhnang. In the first stanza the colour blue predominates – the blue of the sky and lagoon set against meadows and marshes. The second stanza provides a glimpse of a Cambodian woman on a treadmill: the memory of her toil forming a lasting image of the land itself. The second poem *Ta Prohm* describes the confluence of the life of the jungle and the temple ruins. Exotic trees, insects, and animal life surround a broken tower and Buddha, the spirit of which is as alive as the jungle, evidenced by the signs of worship left in a 'rusty tin'. The search for this 'last hermit' is unsuccessful. The final poem *The diamond bowler of the Khmer kings, Phnom Penh, 1964* serves as an epilogue to the article. The work focuses on the lavish riches of royalty. The first stanza describes the sound of the rehearsing Royal Dancers, banned from sight. The second describes the royal jewels, the throne, the bed of state, the funeral chariot, and the 'diamond bowler' of the title. This black English bowler hat, embellished with rubies and diamonds by the palace jeweller, symbolizes the syncretic joining of East and West.

The gentleman in the parlour: a record of a journey from Rangoon to Haiphong.

See item no. 81.

Cambodia (Kampuchea).

See item no. 717.

Cambodian literature - traditional and contemporary

713 **Astronomie cambodgienne.** (Cambodian astronomy.)
F. G. Faraut. Saigon: F. H. Schneider, 1910. 283p.

Published with the patronage of King Sisowath, Resident Superior Luce and the Indochinese Studies Society (Société des études indochinoises). The author gives a historical introduction to Cambodian astronomy, a science known since ancient times, then goes into great detail of observations and calculations, some translated from the ancient texts with commentary. Faraut studied under the noted Royal Hora (astronomer) Daung, Chang Vang, during 1880 and 1881. Sadly his research results were lost on a visit to France in 1884, and had to be redone completely from 1886, when he returned to Cambodia. The missing notes were subsequently found again, and are here published together with the later work.

714 **Bibliographie des traductions françaises des littératures du Viêt-Nam et du Cambodge.** (Bibliography of French translations of the literature of Vietnam and Cambodia.)
Jacques Baruch. Brussels: Editions Thanh-Long, 1968. 63p. (Études Orientales, no. 3).

Contains thirty-six items in the Cambodian section, primarily literary works, but also including relevant historical, scientific and political items. No annotations are provided, but the book contains indexes to authors, translators etc.

715 **Le Cambodge des contes.** (Cambodia of the stories.)
Solange Thierry. Paris: L'Harmattan, [1986]. 295p. bibliog. (Recherches Asiatiques).

Solange Thierry at one time served as the conservator of the National Museum of Cambodia. This book is a revised version of her doctoral thesis presented in 1976 to the Université René-Descartes. It is a scholarly work which analyses the structure and role of Cambodian folk-tales starting with brief descriptions of the historical and social contexts for Cambodian culture and the role of folk stories within that setting. Thierry relates and analyses tales in themes: birth stories, stories of the invisible, stories of windfalls and stories of quest. The final section of the book discusses narrative techniques and systems of representation. A useful bibliography lists publications then available in Cambodia from which the texts of the stories were drawn, along with many other, mainly French, texts on Cambodian culture and folklore.

716 **Cambodge: contes et légendes.** (Cambodia: tales and legends.)
Collected and published in French by Adhémard Leclère, with an introduction by Léon Feer. Paris: Librairie Émile Bouillon, 1895. 306p.

During the course of travelling throughout the country preparing his masterful three-volume collection of Cambodian laws, the French Resident in Cambodia, Adhémard Leclère, managed to find the time to collect *satra* (manuscripts) found in the temples and monasteries he visited. In his introduction he describes the danger which these texts were facing – in not a single temple or monastery is to be found anything resembling a library, and often the texts are incomplete and the parts scattered across the country. Some stories were told to him for which not even a fragment of the text could be found. Originals were crumbling away due to the ravages of insects and the task of recopying not being done as assiduously as in the past. He therefore undertook the task of collecting manuscripts and taking them to France, to be deposited in the Bibliothèque Nationale (National Library) to ensure their preservation, with no misgivings as to the impact of their removal from their religious or cultural location. The collection presented here in French translation is in six parts: tales of the Buddha; local history; folk-tales; legalistic tales; Jataka stories; and Malay tales. Notes and an introduction are provided by Léon Feer on the relationship of these Cambodian tales to Indian literature. Feer considered all of them to have originated in India, but rewritten in an original way and set into a Khmer context. The collection includes a Khmer version of Cinderella.

717 **Cambodia (Kampuchea).**
Compiled by Judith M. Jacob. In: *South-East Asia*. Edited by Alistair Dingwall. Lincolnwood, Illinois: Passport Books, 1995, p. 154-175. (Traveller's Literary Companion).

This Cambodian chapter is compiled by Judith Jacob, a renowned specialist in Cambodian language and traditional literature, who formerly lectured at the School of Oriental and African Studies, University of London, and the excerpts selected reflect her interests, which may not be those of the run-of-the-mill 'traveller' for whom the 'Traveller's literary companion' series is intended. The other countries seem to be represented by selections including more contemporary works.

718 **Cambodian folk stories from the Gatiloke.**
Retold by Muriel Paskin Carrison, from a translation by Kong Chhean. Rutland, Victoria: C. E. Tuttle Co., 1987. 139p. bibliog.

Compiled with the help of members of the Cambodian community in southern California this book consists of fifteen stories, a contextual introduction, an appendix offering an introduction to the country and its people, a glossary, and simple line-drawings. The tales are taken from the Gatiloke, an ancient collection of orally transmitted stories, written down in the late 19th century, translated by the venerable Kong Chhean and retold by Carrison. These tales were used by monks as sermons or parables, as Gatiloke loosely translated means 'the right way for the people of the world to live'. The themes of human relations, individual responsibility, punishment and reward, killing of animals, greed and ingratitude, etc., are woven into stories such as 'The Polecat and the Rooster' and 'The King and the Buffalo Boy'.

719 **Cambodian legends: Judge Rabbit stories [in] English-Cambodian.**
Prepared by Chandha Sau, Bettie Lou Sechrist, Kry Lay, under the supervision of Betty H. Seal. Sydney: Indo-China Refugee Association (NSW), 1981. 35p. Originally published, Long Beach, California: Long Beach Unified School District, 1978.

Twelve of the popular Cambodian stories of the wise Judge Rabbit and his deeds are presented here in both English and Khmer, providing a useful resource for the Cambodian expatriate community and for those wanting to know more about

Cambodian folklore and legends. The stories were collected as part of the Southeast Asian Learners Project of the Long Beach Unified School District in California, and the text was reproduced in Australia. While the reprinting is fine for the English, it is a little blurry, making the Khmer letters somewhat indistinct. The stories are: 'How Judge Rabbit helped elephant'; 'How Judge Rabbit was trapped and tried to escape'; 'How Judge Rabbit got across the river'; 'Judge Rabbit and the old lady'; 'Judge Rabbit, the tiger, and the men'; 'How Judge Rabbit made friends with the goat'; 'How Judge Rabbit helped his friend the goat'; 'Judge Rabbit and the snail race'; 'How Judge Rabbit saved men from the tiger'; 'How Judge Rabbit escaped once more from the tiger'; 'How Judge Rabbit saved a man and punished a crocodile'; and 'How Judge Rabbit captured the ghost'.

720 **Contemporary Cambodian literature.**
Martine Piat. *Journal of the Siam Society*, vol. 63, part 2 (July 1975), p. 251-59.

A version of a paper presented at the 29th International Congress of Orientalists, held in Paris in July 1973, this is valuable because it discusses popular literature in the period before it was all but wiped out by the Khmer Rouge. Piat looks at how popular literature had expanded markedly in the Lon Nol period just as other literatures declined, due to the ban on Chinese characters being displayed in public and the exodus or massacre of most of Cambodia's Vietnamese population. As the war raged, magic art books believed to give invulnerability rose in popularity, along with escapist melodrama and romance. Cartoons and comic representations of contemporary and classical works alike outnumbered letterpress, and Piat concludes: 'It seems alarming that Cambodia is moving directly from a state of literary incuriosity to the reading of purely commercial literature'.

721 **Contes du Cambodge.** (Tales of Cambodia.)
Auguste Pavie. Paris: Sudestasie, 1988. 262p. Originally published, Paris: Leroux, 1921.

In his several sojourns in Cambodia the great explorer Auguste Pavie made time to record stories from all manner of people who accompanied or played host to him: guides, musicians, poets and even governors and princes. Pavie tells the tales and also reveals something of the circumstances in which they were imparted. The tales included are: 'Les 12 jeunes filles d'Angkor' (The twelve young girls of Angkor); 'Rothisen'; 'Neang Roungay Sack'; 'Neang Kakey'; 'Mea Yoeung'; 'Sanselkey'; 'Vorivong'; and 'Saurivong'. The text is complemented by 101 black-and-white illustrations and 29 colour plates in the Khmer pagoda style.

722 **Contes et légendes du pays khmer.** (Tales and legends from the Khmer country.)
Khing Hoc Dy. Paris: Sudestasie, 1989.

Khing has gathered a wide range of Cambodian popular literature, including tales, legends, songs, sayings, maxims and proverbs. Transmitted orally, chiefly by the elders, many were considered to be outside the literary canon on account of their ribaldry, and so have previously escaped recording efforts that concentrated on works that contained or reinforced moral and religious precepts.

723 **Contes khmers.** (Khmer tales.)
Translated from Cambodian by G. H. Monod. Paris: Cedoreck, 1985. 303p. (Feuilles de l'Inde, no. 9). First published, Mouans-Sarfoux, Alpes-Maritimes, [France]: C.-A. Högman, 1943. (Publications Chitra).

A re-impression of this charming edition – a small tome dedicated to Princess Pingpeang Yukanthor. Each of the eight stories has a Khmer-language title page graced with a woodcut (by an unnamed artist), and woodcut illustrations also appear in the stories themselves: 'Sophea Tonsay' (The rabbit Sophea); 'Thmenh Chey' (He who always has the last word); 'Chau kdang bay' (Rice crust); 'Neang Lomang Romchek' (The daughter of the white elephant); 'Satra Kakey' (The princess with sweet sighs); and 'Sdech Kmeng' (The boy-king). A glossary and notes follow the text.

724 **Contribution à l'histoire de la littérature khmère. Volume 1. Littérature de l'époque 'classique' (XVe-XIXe siècles). Volume 2. Ecrivains et expressions littéraires du Cambodge au XXème siècle.** (Contribution to the history of Khmer literature. Volume 1. Literature of the 'classical' period [15th-19th centuries]. Volume 2. Authors and literary expressions from Cambodia in the 20th century.)
Khing Hoc Dy. Paris: L'Harmattan, 1990-93. 2 vols. bibliog. (Collection Recherches Asiatiques).

A fascinating study of Khmer literature from the end of the Angkor period to the beginning of the 'modern' age. The author was professor of Khmer literature at the University of Phnom Penh from 1967 to 1971, and since then a scholar in France, now with CNRS and the National Institute of Oriental Languages and Civilizations. The text combines extracts and summaries of religious and secular texts, epics, songs, popular stories and riddles with commentaries on their origins, target audience and social significance. The work is essential reading for those who wish to expand their appreciation of Khmer culture beyond the monuments of Angkor and the Royal Ballet.

725 **De la rizière à la forêt: contes khmers.** (From the rice field to the forest: Khmer tales.)
Solange Thierry. Paris: L'Harmattan, 1988. 254p. (La Légende des Mondes).

This is a collection of classical Cambodian tales, some of which the author had translated in 1946 (with F. Martini), some others in previously unpublished translations. They all belong to a corpus published in Khmer between 1965 and 1971 by the Buddhist Institute in Phnom Penh, in eight volumes.

726 **Étude d'un corpus de contes cambodgiens traditionnels: essai d'analyse thématique et morphologique.** (Study of a corpus of traditional Cambodian tales: an attempt at thematic and morphological analysis.)
Solange Thierry. Doctoral thesis, Université de Lille III, Paris, 1976. x, 553p. bibliog. Available from Lille, France: Atelier Reproduction des thèses, Université de Lille III, Paris, 1978.

This is the thesis that Thierry wrote in 1976 on the Cambodian tales, thirty years after she began translating them. It is by far the most sophisticated study of the tales, a subject which has attracted many Khmerologists. She studies what she calls the 'Cambodian expression' and the role of the tales in it, the narrative techniques and the 'systems of representation' as exhibited by the tales. With this wealth of data, one would expect a great inroad into a deeper understanding of Khmer society and the way it expresses itself. But this is not the case because the author is reluctant to discuss the fundamentals of the theoretical approach to the sudy of folk literature. She knows the good authors and the good books but she does not make use of them. This work looks as if it was written before anthropology existed. It is a lost opportunity for a better knowledge, but is still nice reading.

727 **Études sur le Ramakerti (XVI-XVIII siècles).** (Studies on the Ramakerti, 16th-17th centuries.)
Saveros Pou. Paris: École Française d'Extrême-Orient, 1977. 190p.

Contains a description of the structure of the Ramakerti I, and its evolution in the different periods of Cambodian history, followed by a discussion of related lexicological and bibliographical issues, including a lexicon of terms appearing in the text.

728 **Favourite stories from Cambodia.**
David Chandler, exercises by Susan Chandler. Hong Kong: Heinemann Asia, 1978. 46p. (Favourite Stories Series).

Intended for upper primary and lower secondary school students, this collection contains illustrations.

729 **Florilege jörai.** (Jorai anthology of verse.)
Jacques Dournes. Paris: Sudestasie, 1995. 170p.

A precious recording of the oral literature of the Jorai people of the high plateaux of southern Vietnam and Cambodia by Jacques Dournes, who has spent more than thirty years studying the Jorai people in Vietnam. Since they form a small minority group in Cambodia, the text is included in this bibliography.

730 **The friends who tried to empty the sea: eleven Cambodian folk stories.**
Translated by David P. Chandler. Clayton, Victoria: Centre of Southeast Asian Studies, Monash University, 1984. 27p. (Working Papers, no. 8).

For an understanding of recurring themes in Cambodian culture, one would be advised to start with this modest publication, unfortunately with no introduction, footnotes or commentary. David Chandler, well known for his historical works, has translated eleven folk-tales, nine of which were published in Khmer by the Buddhist Institute in Phnom Penh between 1951 and 1974. The tales are: The friends who tried to empty the sea; The wood-cutter and the mouse-king; The four bald men; Why herons and crows are enemies; How the Koun Lok bird got its feathers; The duplicate husband; One thing leads to another; The outwitted father-in-law; The kind man and the tiger; The crocodile, the abbot and the princess; and The vulture, the elephant and the hare.

731 **Guirlande de cpap.** (Garland of cpap.)
Saveros Pou. Paris: Centre de Documentation et de Recherche sur la Civilisation Khmère, 1988.

The *cpap* (sometimes written *chbap*, or *chbab*) is a very popular form of Khmer literature. They are always didactic and written in verses. They deal with general knowledge (gnomic texts), the moral law (the most well known) and royal and state matters, like teaching in politics and ethics. Most Khmers have learned one or several of them and they form a body of 'classical' reference in the same way as Shakespeare or the Bible in English-speaking culture. In the first volume, after a short introduction, Pou reproduces in Khmer handwriting a large collection of them. The second volume includes a transliteration and a French translation. With this welcome addition to her purely linguistic works, Pou is offering an avenue into the thinking and the value system of the Khmers. Although the Khmer language is not always easy she has done a beautiful translation.

732 **La guirlande de joyaux.** (The garland of jewels.)
Recorded and translated into French by François Bizot, with Pali translation by O. von Hinüber. Paris: EFEO, 1994. 234p. (Textes Bouddhiques du Cambodge).

This volume presents the Ratanamala text, an acrostic poem of 108 syllables in homage to the Buddha Dhamma and the Sangha. It is here translated from Khmer by Bizot from the version given to him in 1974 by Gru Suon Chun, killed by the Khmer Rouge the following year. Von Hinüber has provided a translation from the Pali text. This volume bears the following inscription, 'Each publication in the . . . series is a "sursaut de memoire" (jolt of memory) and an act of accusation against the handful of fanatics who endeavoured in 1975 to empty Cambodia of its intellectuals and its peasants, of its traditions and its culture'.

733 **Kampuchea.**
Soth Polin. In: *Newspapers in Asia, contemporary trends and problems*. Edited by J. A. Lent. Hong Kong: Heinemann, 1982. 597p.

A broad presentation of literature as a social occurrence, rather than a literary analysis, this book offers studies on the search for meaning and identity in a rapidly changing region and suggests there are parallels between the phenomenon of literature in the different countries represented. The chapter 'Literature and society in modern Cambodia' looks at the replacement of classical literature by modern literature, the various stages of this literature's development and the relationship between society's literature at the time of writing. (The authors believe that the 'acceleration of history' Cambodia has experienced can thus be partly understood by analysing transformation in modes of thinking.) Style, motivation, method of recording, and publication, influence and other such aspects are simply but thoroughly surveyed.

734 **Légendes cambodgiennes que m'a contées le Gouverneur Khieu.** (Cambodian legends as told to me by Governor Khieu.)
G.-H. Monod. Paris: Éditions Bossard, 1922. 148p.

Governor Khieu, a man very knowledgeable in Khmer literature but otherwise not identified, guided the author in his search to understand the depths of the ancient Khmer spirit. This selection attempts to give a general idea of popular Khmer literature. The six stories retold without commentary are: Le beau-père qui choisit un gendre (The stepfather who chose a gender); Artifices feminis (Feminine artifices); Histoire d'Alev (History of Alev); Kung le Courageux (Kung the brave); Histoire de la perdrix femelle et de la perdrix male (History of the male and female partridges); and La fondation d'Angkor (The foundation of Angkor).

735 **Literature and society in modern Cambodia.**
Jacques Népote and Khing Hoc Dy. In: *Essays on literature and society in South East Asia.* Edited by Tham Seong Chee. Singapore: Singapore University Press, 1981. 360p.

The authors seek to find some explanations for the 'acceleration of history' which took place in what many had thought of as one of the most stable and unified countries on earth. Believing that the impetus for the changes which took place from 1970 was as much cultural as it was political, they analyse transformations in ways of thinking through a study of Cambodia's literature in a social context. To illustrate the importance and implications of the recent transformation, the authors discuss the replacement of classical literature by modern writing, survey the history of this literature and attempt to define the current relationship of literature to society. Chapter headings include: Classical literature and its present state; The premises of modern literature; The impact of printing; Urbanisation and its importance; and The delta influence. This paper utilizes and analyses information both on ancient traditions and contemporary popular culture, to present a rare, insightful and succinct study.

736 **La métrique: cours traité pour la composition des poèmes.** (The metre: a course on the composition of poems.)
Ieng Say. Thesis for the Diploma in Research and Applied Studies, Institut National des Langues et Civilisations Orientales, Paris, Département Asie du Sud-Est, 1985. 135p.

Contains examples of Khmer metre and poetic structures, providing the poems in Khmer followed by a French translation and some with schematic structures.

737 **Mr. Basket Knife: and other Khmer folktales.**
Translated from the Khmer by A. R. Milne, illustrated by Sisowath Kulachad. London: Allen and Unwin, 1972. 62p. (Unesco Collection of Representative Works: Khmer Series).

Translated from a collection published in 1959 by the Buddhist Institute in Phnom Penh, with the expert aid of Judith Jacob. The book consists of eight tales, some probably entirely indigenous and others adaptations of tales from other places, all of which would formerly have been and, to some extent, continue to be, orally transmitted. The stories are: The story of the greedy family; The origin of the tiger; The story of the jackal and the shrimp; The man who knew how to cure a snake bite; The story of Mr. Basket Knife; The trial; The story of brave Kong; and The caterpillar and the crow. Milne provides brief notes on the Khmer text and on some points of his translation.

738 **Oh Cambodia!: poems from the border.**

Compiled by Ashley Thompson. *New Literary History*, vol. 24, no. 3 (Summer 1993), p. 519-44.

The article begins with a historical background of the entangled political, personal, international and humanitarian forces that shaped the plight of Cambodian refugees on the Thai-Cambodian border between 1979 and 1992. The next section 'In Site 2' is a personal account of the author's time in Site 2, the largest border camp, where she taught English from November 1988 to May 1990. It opens with a description of a New Year's Eve dance, the anticipation of freedom and renewal forming in an atmosphere charged with both sexuality and violence. The piece continues with a series of images that attempt to evoke Site 2 – that unimaginable, unspeakable, 'displaced' place that has substance only for those who inhabit it; 'the gesture of goodbye frozen' in a liminal place fixed between memories of the past and imaginings of the future. The writer's class included guitarists and singers, reporters and newswriters, the staff of a women's association, teachers and high school students. And it was characterized primarily by desire: the desire to learn. Eight poems (and one painted story) by the refugees, with commentary, form the end of Thompson's article. These works focus on both resistance and hope. Their spirit is encapsulated in the image of a flying horse (from the painted story), 'a soaring power to surpass all limits, to fly in spite of the bridle and the reins'. The article includes end-notes.

739 **[Palm leaf manuscripts].**

[Microfilmed in Cambodia by Cornell University Libraries, Ithaca, New York].

A microfilming project carried out in the early 1990s, with chief deposits of palm-leaf manuscripts in Phnom Penh filmed and boxed at the National Library of Cambodia, the National Museum of Cambodia and other collections.

740 **Ramaker ou l'amour symbolique de Ram et Seta.** (Ramaker, or the symbolic love of Ram and Seta.)

François Bizot. Paris: École Française d'Extrême-Orient, 1989. 148p. bibliog. (Publications de l'École Française d'Extrême-Orient, no. 155). (Recherches sur le Bouddhisme Khmer, no. 5).

Recorded in 1969 by Bizot from the recounting of Mi Chak, from a manuscript in the southern temple of Angkor Wat. Several months later Mi Chak died as the fires of war reached Angkor. In this volume Bizot presents the *Ramakerti* (Ramayana) text itself, in Khmer, as well as interpretation, photographs and extensive commentary on the composition and narration, and the historical-religious background to the text.

741 **Ramakerti I, II.**

Presented, translated and annotated by Saveros Pou. Paris: École Française d'Extrême-Orient 1979-82. 3 vols. (Publications de l'École Française d'Extrême-Orient, nos. 117 and 132).

In 1937 the Buddhist Institute in Phnom Penh, under the direction of Suzanne Karpelès, published popular editions of various sections of the *Ramakerti*

(Ramayana), numbered 1-10 and 75-80, in the understanding that they were from a single text with some sixty-five missing sections. In the 1970s the Khmer scholar Savaros Pou concluded that these published sections were in fact from two different editions of the great Ramayana story, and she proceeded to develop critical editions and translations of each separately. In 1977 the first version (*Ramakerti I* – dated by Pou to the 16th-17th centuries) appeared in French translation, together with a volume interpreting and analysing this text, and followed two years later by the Khmer text itself. In 1982 the second version (*Ramakerti II* – dated by Pou to the 18th century) appeared in a single volume containing the Khmer text, French translation and annotations.

742 **Reamker (Ramakerti): the Cambodian version of the Ramayana.** Translated by Judith M. Jacob, with the assistance of Kruoch Haksrea. London: Royal Asiatic Society, [1986]. xxxii, 320p. bibliog. (Oriental Translation Fund [Series]. New series, no. 45).

A translation of the Cambodian version of this renowned and vastly influential text of Indian origin, generally known as the Ramayana. The legend of the Ramayana is depicted on bas-reliefs at Angkor, and later on temple frescoes, and is the exclusive subject of Khmer shadow plays. This, the first English translation, was produced with the collaboration of Cambodian Kruoch Haksrea, and revised in the light of new material contained in Saveros Pou's French translation, *Ramakerti I, II* (q.v.), which was published just prior to this work. Additional to the translation, Jacob usefully provides resumés of the narratives, a list of Sanskrit and Pali loan-words left untranslated, a list of proper names, notes, a glossary and a list of preferred readings. The introduction eloquently accounts for the method and meaning of Khmer usage of the epic themes within the story, some of the history of the translated version, and observation on the character of the *Reamker* in the original form.

743 **Réflexion sur la littérature khmère.** (Reflection on Khmer literature.) Vandy Kaon. Phnom Penh: Institut de Sociologie, Sous Comité d'Examen et de Recherche, 1981. iv, 73p. (Littérature et Philologie, Dossier no. SLK 005).

Vandy Kaon, who was at the time President of the Sub-Committee for Examinations and Research, and Director of the Institute of Sociology, Phnom Penh, here presents a reflective essay on the nature and tendencies of Khmer literature, which in 1981 was emerging from the dark days of Pol Pot. He addresses the origins and evolution of Khmer literature, and he describes the principal works, some of which are quoted. Lists of writers and film-makers are given, and footnotes and a bibliography add to the scholarly nature of this valuable item, which deserves to be republished and to be translated into English and into Khmer.

744 **Le roman khmer contemporain.** (The contemporary Khmer novel.) Khuon Sokhampu. Phnom Penh: Centre de Documentation et Recherche, Section Lettres et Culture-Civilisation Khmères de la Faculté des Lettres et Sciences Humaines, Université de Phnom Penh, 1973. 59p.

Presented at the International Colloquium on the Literatures of Southeast Asia, held at the Sorbonne, 16-23 July 1973, this paper was published in Phnom Penh. It lists the output of Khmer novels from 1900 to 1972, divided into three periods: 1900-53, 1953-69, and 1970-72. Khuon Sokhampu identifies two main categories: 'objective' social and critical works, which were not favoured by the colonial régime and blossomed only after 1947; and 'subjective' sentimental, psychological, romantic and detective works. A graphic representation of annual production and a brief bibliography follow the listing. The author was awarded a PhD from Humboldt State University, Arcata, California.

745 **Le roman source d'inspiration de la peinture khmère à la fin du XIXe et au début du XXe siècle: l'histoire de Preah Chinavong et son illustration dans la (sala) de Vat Kieng Svay Krau.** (The novel that served as a source of inspiration for Khmer painters at the end of the 19th and beginning of the 20th centuries: the story of Preah Chinavong and its illustration in the sala of Wat Kien Svay Krau.) Michel Jacq-Hergoualc'h. Paris: École Française d'Extrême-Orient, 1982. 2 vols. map. bibliog. (Publications de l'École Française d'Extrême-Orient, vol. 126).

The story of Preah Chinavong belongs to a genre of Khmer literature which can be classified as novels. Composed and recited by poets with literary talent, the beauty of their language helps to distinguish them from more popular stories. Preah Chinavong is the hero of one of the most well known of such novels. This scholarly work looks at how his story inspired artists during the late 19th and early 20th centuries and studies in detail the depictions of the legend on the walls of the sala (open part of a temple where people come and listen, learn and pray) of the Kien Svay Krau temple at Koki, a village 18 kilometres southeast of Phnom Penh. Volume two contains many sketches and details from the paintings of the legend. Jacq-Hergoualc'h attempts to extrapolate general rules of iconography for Khmer painting of the period.

746 **South-East Asia languages and literatures: a select guide.** Edited by Patricia Herbert & Anthony Milner. Arran, Scotland: Kiscadale Publications, copyright held by The South East Asia Library Group, [1992?]. 182p.

In ten pages of text devoted to Cambodia, two Paris-based Cambodian scholars (Khing Hoc Dy of the Musée de l'Homme, and Mak Phoeun of the Centre National de la Recherche Scientifique [CNRS]) succinctly but admirably summarize the languages and literatures of Cambodia under the following headings: Dating systems; Language; Script; Manuscripts; Printing and development of the press; and Literature. Each section also refers to the major primary works in Khmer, as well to secondary scholarship, the latter being developed into an eight-page bibliography following the text. This guide forms the essential starting-point for any study of these fields for Cambodia as well as for the other countries of Southeast Asia. Patricia Herbert (Oriental Collections, British Library) and Anthony Milner (Arts Faculty, Australian National University) and the British South-East Asia Library Group are to be congratulated for seeing through this splendid example of what they describe as 'a protracted collective effort, with contributions from scholars and librarians'.

747 **Southeast Asian literatures in translation: a preliminary bibliography.**

Philip N. Jenner. Honolulu, Hawaii: [University of Hawaii], 1973. 198p. bibliog. (Asian Studies at Hawaii, 9).

Contains 129 entries for translations of Cambodian literary works, mainly into French. Materials are grouped into topics: General, Folk literature, Inscriptions (Cham), Chronicles (Cham), Pre-modern prose and poetry, Modern prose (Vietnam), Modern poetry (Vietnam) and Drama (Vietnam). Items include some translations into English; otherwise they are translated into French. Literary criticisms, inventories and anthologies are included as well as individual works, and folk literature includes some folk-tales of upland minorities. The selection concentrates on works available at the University of Hawaii. Some works are briefly annotated, and those most useful for teaching purposes are asterisked. [David G. Marr with Kristine Alilunas-Rodgers]

The cucumber king.
See item no. 681.

Cambodian culture since 1975: homeland and exile.
See item no. 768.

Arts and Cultural Heritage

748 **The age of Angkor: treasures from the National Museum of Cambodia.**
Michael Brand and Chuch Phoeurn, introduction by Pich Keo. Canberra: Australian National Gallery, 1992. 112p. bibliog. (Studies in Asian Art, no. 1).

Excellent both as an introduction to Khmer art and as a reference for those already familiar with it. Predominantly a catalogue of an exhibition of the same title at the Australian National Gallery, each piece is beautifully photographed and annotated. The Age of Angkor exhibition held in 1992 was a landmark of co-operation and cultural communication between Australia and Cambodia and coincided with a politically loaded period of recent Cambodian history. Australia's Minister for Foreign Affairs and Trade introduces the book. Pich Keo, director of the National Museum of Cambodia, provides a brief history of his institution, the museum building itself, and the problems it faces. Michael Brand of the Australian National Gallery provides a very readable introduction to Khmer sculpture, covering, amongst other topics, the significance of Angkor to the Cambodian people, and a history of the Khmer empire's expression in art. Thirty-five pieces appear in the catalogue including figures, architectural features and ritual objects, in bronze and stone.

749 **Ancient Cambodian sculpture.**
Sherman E. Lee. [New York]: Asia Society, [1969]. 115p. map. bibliog. (An Asia House Gallery Publication).

Catalogue of an exhibition selected by Sherman E. Lee, and shown in the Asia House Gallery in the autumn of 1969 as an activity of the Asia Society. The author, former director of the Cleveland Museum of Art, claims that this text is '. . . a kind of personal memoir for an exhibition' for which he was the curator. However, it was designed to help the North American public appreciate Khmer art and, despite being a slim volume, fulfils its intention amply. The preface acknowledges a debt to previous French studies, and some of the conclusions drawn are now superseded, but the thirteen-page historical and artistic synopsis is a succinct guide to the sixty-one pieces, all of which are shown. Styles are identified, techniques explored and details as specific even as the treatment of stone surfaces are pointed out. A brief chronology and basic map precede the catalogue, where smaller reproductions of the photographs are accompanied by a descriptive paragraph which refers to each piece's crafting, style and iconography.

750 **Ancient Cambodia.**
Donatello Mazzeo and Chiara Silvi Antonini, foreword by Han Suyin. London: Reader's Digest Association, 1978. 191p. 2 maps. bibliog. A translation of *Civiltà Khmer* (Khmer civilization). (Monuments of Civilization).

In the coffee-table tradition, this is a beautifully presented book, with impressive photographs flanked by large-type text and brief excerpts from Chou Ta-Kuan's 13th-century notes on Cambodian culture. The authors present their study with an awareness of an 'Europeanism' that 'still lurks' within their discipline. They include an unusual chapter on foreign travellers' preconceptions and records upon visiting Angkor. They briefly examine some monuments contemporaneous with Angkor, statuary, religious life and links between hydraulic works and architecture. Extensively examined are a few of the major monuments such as Banteay Srei and the Bayon. Other features of the book are a recommended-reading list, dates of rulers, events, monuments and dominant styles at Angkor in relation to worldwide architecture and a personal philosophical foreword.

751 **Angkor et dix siècles d'art khmer.** (Angkor and ten centuries of Khmer art.)
Catalogue produced under the direction of Helen I. Jessup and Thierry Zéphir. Paris: Réunion des Musées Nationaux, 1997. 368p.

The catalogue of a major exhibition of Cambodian items from the collections of the Guimet Museum and the National Museum of Cambodia, held at the Grand Palais in Paris, 31 January-26 May 1997 and at the National Gallery of Art in Washington, DC, 29 June-28 September 1997. Black-and-white and colour photographs of 117 pieces are each accompanied by short commentaries. Extensive notes, diagrams, maps and a glossary add to the research value of this catalogue, though regretfully no index is provided. The exhibition itself became the topic of quite a diplomatic and cultural wrangle as different Cambodian ministers and officials gave and then withdrew permission for the pieces to leave the country.

752 **Angkor Vat par la règle et le compas.** (Angkor Wat as drawn with a ruler and compass.)
René Dumont. Metz, France: Editions Olizane, 1996. 91p. (Études Orientales/Péninsule).

The author is an architect who has worked at the Conservation Office in Siem Reap and taught at the University of Fine Arts before the Khmer Rouge period. He was inspired by the work done in the 1930s by Matila Ghyka on the Golden Measure, and the study on proportions in the antique and classical arts of Europe. He has determined that Khmer temples were built on the basis of a unit, which may be measured by the width of the first door of the monument. He thinks the original unit was probably measured on the central statue, which has everywhere disappeared. The book is mostly composed of figures drawn only with a ruler and a compass, tentatively retracing the steps taken on the floor of the future temple by the Khmer architects, using a rope and a pole. Simple graphic solutions are proposed to understand how complex designs could be developed. Dumont has touched on something of the brainwork behind the building of the temples.

753 **Angkor Vat: description graphique du temple.** (Angkor Wat: graphic description of the temple.)
Guy Nafilyan with collaboration from Alex Turletti, Mey Than, Dy Proeng and Vong Von. Paris: École Française d'Extrême-Orient, 1969. 32p. (Publications de l'École Française d'Extrême-Orient. Mémoires Archéologiques, no. 4).

With 113 plates of illustrations and plans, this tome represents the most thorough presentation of the temple from EFEO, and provides the basis for almost all further work on this masterpiece of Cambodian architectural art.

754 **Angkor Wat: time, space and kingship.**
Eleanor Mannikka. Honolulu, Hawaii: University of Hawaii Press, 1996. 360p.

In her exploration of Angkor Wat the author found that the key to understanding the temple lay in the measurement system used by its original builders. By translating metres into cubits, she uncovered a highly sophisticated system of philosophical and religious principles expressed in the temple measurements themselves. The measurements connect the temple to the stars and the cosmos, bridge the gap between human and divine realms, and help unite the king and his deity – in short, they define how time, space, kingship, and divinity exist inseparably from each other. The volume includes 207 pages of illustrations.

755 **Angkor, the serenity of Buddhism.**
Photographs and an essay by Marc Riboud, with an introduction by Jean Lacouture, an essay by Jean Boisselier, and captions by Madeleine Giteau. London: Thames and Hudson, 1993. 159p. A translation of *Angkor, sérénité bouddhique*, Paris: Imprimerie Nationale, 1992.

A truly magnificent pictorial work. Riboud, of Magnum photo-agency fame, visited Angkor in 1968, 1969, 1981 and finally in 1990, when the majority of the photographs were taken. The black-and-white, grainy images, shot with Leica cameras and Leitz lenses, powerfully and yet wistfully evoke the temples and the atmosphere of Angkor with its passing parade of the local people living their lives. Giteau's captions are erudite and informative, but the textual pieces disappoint by comparison, particularly Lacouture's florid and overly self-absorbed introduction.

756 **Angkor: art and civilization.**
Bernard Philippe Groslier and Jacques Arthaud, translated from the French by Eric Ernshaw Smith. London: Thames & Hudson, 1966. rev. ed. 236p. maps. bibliog.

Like his father, to whom he dedicates the book, Bernard Philippe Groslier was a curator of Angkor. Aimed at providing a succinct visual conspectus of Khmer civilization, his authoritative writing is vigorous and expressive. The entire text is enriched by over 100 excellent black-and-white photographs by Arthaud, occasionally interspersed with poetic passages taken from inscriptions. The main body of writing is broken into two major chapters, and these, in turn, are broken into short readable paragraphs. 'The men of Angkor' moves from climate and geography to religion, with some sections such as 'Psychology and mentality of Khmers' being rather dated, and far from 'politically correct'. 'The stones of Angkor', as well as offering studies of particular temples, speculates on daily life around Angkor, and moves on to 'The temple' as a concept. An extensive appendix includes: a synoptic table of parallel events and periods around the world; a brief summary of Khmer iconography and a five-page section identifying 'Main stages in the development of Khmer Art' which would make a simple but informative guide to the temples and pieces in the National Museum of Cambodia.

757 **Angkor: the hidden glories.**

Michael Freeman and Roger Warner, edited and designed by David Larkin. Boston, Massachusetts: Houghton Mifflin, 1990. 253, [3]p. maps. bibliog. (A David Larkin Book).

The short intense paragraphs of this book are written in an intimate, occasionally narrative style, making one feel as if one is discovering the temples with the authors. Cultural analysis is presented as a story rather than a dry history. Freeman's unforgettable photographs not only capture the temples but also some moments of contemporary Cambodia. The Khmer empire is recreated on the page, with extracts from inscriptions and suppositions about their setting and psychology. An understanding of the temples, 'talismans on massive scale', and their purpose, significance and architectural features are covered in the chapter 'The Magic Mountain'. Angkor Wat and the Bayon are the only temples discussed in detail but their study is broad. The authors visited Angkor in 1989, but the impressions they record in this book, both visual and verbal, still remain fresh today.

758 **Angkor.**

Claude Jacques, preface by Federico Mayor, photographs by Guy Nafilyan and Luc Ionesco. Paris: Bordas, 1992.

We have many books on Angkor with good colour photographs. It is difficult not to produce a high-quality book and not to have good photographs with such a tremendous subject. But the photographs are those of architects trained at the old French Conservation of Angkor. They are scholars in their own right. Jacques, as an epigraphist, is bent on reconstructing, piece by piece, a history of the successive realms and cities centred in this area, around the 9th-13th centuries. Although it would be an illusion to present a continuous history, some parts and some developments may be gathered from epigraphy and archaeology. Chinese sources, with the notable exception of Chou Ta-Kuan, do not say very much. Jacques has elected to show first some aspects of Khmer art, then proceed with a cautious approach of 'Angkor before Angkor', trying to characterize the polities which started to create monuments in the region of Angkor. He follows the several displacements of monuments created by the kings to serve as symbolic centres of their polity. The photographs and the drawings are very useful to help illustrate the chronological sequence of monuments that we see together, as if they were of the same age. With its annexes, this book is more than a beautiful coffee-table gift. It is an introduction to a (fragmented) history.

759 **Angkor.**
Henri Stierlin. Fribourg, Switzerland: Office du Livre, 1972. bibliog. (Architecture Universelle).

A scholarly treatment (in French) of the Angkor temples from the point of view of their architectural features. Numerous plans and black-and-white photographs provide the backdrop for the textual analysis of the development of Cambodian urbanism and its architectural expression up to the period of Jayavarman VII (1181-1219). This volume is one of an attractively produced and established series emphasizing ancient architectural traditions.

760 **L'art khmer primitif.** (Primitive Khmer art.)
Henri Parmentier. Paris: G. Vanoest, 1927. 2 vols. (Publications de l'École Française d'Extrême-Orient, nos. 21 & 22).

Although individual temples had been studied, Parmentier presented this work as the first attempt to develop an overview of Khmer art, dividing it into two very distinct styles, breaking at the beginning of the 9th century. Certain features were identified as common to all dated temples from the earlier period, and undated ones which matched these features were then placed into this category. Each monument is given a detailed description, and graphic and photographic representation. In the end, Parmentier selected the term 'primitive Khmer art' in preference to 'pre-Angkor' or 'Indo-Khmer', which had been used earlier, as he believes they refer too closely either to its origins or to its later development.

761 **L'art khmer: les grandes étapes de son évolution.** (Khmer art: main stages in its evolution.)
Gilberte de Coral Rémusat, with a preface by George Coedès. Paris: Vanoest, 1951. 2nd ed. 136p. First published, Paris: Les Éditions d'Art et d'Histoire, 1940. (Études d'Art et d'Ethnologie Asiatiques).

This was the first volume to appear in the new series, edited by Victor Goloubew, inspired by the 'Ars Asiatica' of former times. Using Stern's method of chronologically dating Cambodian architectural monuments, the author (one of Stern's students) herself categorizes (chiefy according to motif) the decorative elements recorded in the photographic collection of the Guimet Museum. Here she reviews the historical and religious background of Angkor before proceeding to present a discussion, copiously illustrated, of the various forms: architecture, lintels, columns, facades, false doors and pillars, bas-reliefs, human and animal sculpture, followed by a chronological summary of the twelve styles identified and a conclusion. A table of the principal monuments grouped by styles clarifies the findings. Unfortunately many of the illustrations, taken in the field in the early days of photography, do not live up to the significance of the text. Many are small and somewhat over-exposed making it difficult to discern the details under discussion.

762 **The art of Indochina, including Thailand, Vietnam, Laos and Cambodia.**
Bernard Philippe Groslier, translated by George Lawrence. New York: Crown Publishers, [1962]. 261p. maps. bibliog. (Art of the World, Non-European Cultures: the Historical, Sociological and Religious Backgrounds). A translation of *Indochine: carrefour des arts* (Indochina: crossroads of the arts).

As a volume in the 'Art of the world' series the focus is defined as 'Non-European cultures, the historical, sociological and religious backgrounds'. The book is actually deeper in some areas and not nearly as broad as the title would suggest. The main focus of the text is on Angkor, with a brief overview of the art and architecture of the region from very early human evidence to the beginning of the present modern period. As Groslier stated in the preface '. . . our study is bound sometimes to be excessively detailed, and at other times to expose desperate gaps'. Groslier has deliberately left out Burma although 'he feels logically it should have been included'. Chapters are devoted to Pre-history, China and India, Funan, Chenla, Angkor, The Khmer empire, Indochina around and beyond Angkor, The decline of Angkor, Thai conquest, and Vietnamese conquest, discussed in the traditional 'monuments and empires' style, with the introduction setting the geographical and anthropological scene.

763 **Arts et Archéologie Khmers: Revue des Recherches sur les Arts, les Monuments et l'Ethnographie du Cambodge, Depuis les Origines Jusqu'à Nos Jours.** (Khmer Art and Archaeology: Research on the Arts, Monuments and Ethnography of Cambodia, From the beginning Until Our Day.)
Edited by George Groslier. Paris: Challamel, 1921/22-26. 2 vols.

This beautiful review is the brain-child of George Groslier. He obtained support from the Ministry of the Colonies, for the creation in 1919 of the École des arts cambodgiens (School of Cambodian Arts), of which he was the head. This review was Groslier's instrument to agitate for more funds. He managed to secure powerful patrons and started a very ambitious programme of protecting works of arts, resurrecting the craftsmanship which had produced them, and the scholarly study of them. Significantly the secretary of the review was Philippe Stern (q.v.), who later wrote important essays which succeeded in incorporating some chronological order into the architectural history of Angkor. In the first issue, G. Groslier draws a dramatic picture of the derelict state of the Khmer monuments, 800 of them being, he said, away from Angkor, in remote places, threatened by mediocre building techniques, the fragility of the sandstone, human neglect or indifference, the wild growth of vegetation, and the inaccessibility of many in fever-ridden areas. The EFEO, created in Hanoi in 1901, had very few resources and was busy all over Indochina. What it could do was a far cry from what was needed, argued Groslier who obviously was listened to in the higher circles of the colonial administration. He was doing all by himself what the international community later proclaimed was needed in 1991, after twelve years of voluntary blindness – starting to work to protect and save Angkor as a part of the world heritage, having taken into account that the cost of such an endeavour is beyond the financial capacities of Cambodia. The articles published in this journal were written by the best experts in the field and their value is great today. Later the bulletin of the EFEO, *Bulletin de l'École Française d'Éxtrême-Orient* (q.v.), took charge of these studies but the role of G. Groslier in instigating them should not be overlooked.

764 **Le Bayon d'Angkor et l'évolution de l'art khmer: étude et discussion de la chronologie des monuments khmers.** (The Bayon of Angkor and the evolution of Khmer art: study and discussion of the chronology of Khmer monuments.)
Philippe Stern. Paris: Paul Geuthner, 1927. xii, 217p.

Stern concentrates his attention on the Bayon, which he suggests was constructed during the first half of the 11th century, some 150 years later than had previously been posited. As a result of this shift, he comes up with a new chronology for Khmer art, which he categorizes into two main Angkor styles, the second epoch commencing with the Bayon. Clear differences are noted in material, plan, architectural features and sculpture. Thirty-two black-and-white photographs grace the text.

765 **Le Bayon d'Angkor Thom: bas-reliefs.** (The Bayon of Angkor Thom: bas-reliefs.)
Published through the Commission Archéologique de l'Indochine, from documents collected by the Henri Dufour Mission and Charles Carpeaux. Paris: Ernest Leroux, 1913. 1 vol. (various pagination). Available also on microfilm (low reduction). At head of title: Ministère de l'Instruction Publique et des Beaux-Arts.

Valuable documentation is presented on the magnificent bas-reliefs of the Bayon, recorded before major restoration work by the EFEO, and before significant later deterioration and damage, making this collection especially important.

766 **Le Bayon.** (The Bayon.)
Jean Dumarçay. Paris: École Française d'Extrême-Orient, 1967-73. 2 vols. maps. bibliog. (Publications de l'École Française d'Extrême-Orient. Mémoires Archéologiques, no. 3).

The Bayon with its haunting faces has rivalled Angkor Wat as the most popular image of Khmer culture. This is the most thorough scholarly archaeological account of the temple. The first volume, with an atlas and some sixty-eight plates was published in 1967. The second volume, which did not appear until some six years later, contains an essay on the archaeological history of the temple by Jacques Dumarçay (q.v.) and a record of its inscriptions by Bernard Philippe Groslier (q.v.).

767 **Cambodia: restoration and revival.**
Edited by Heather A. Peters. Special issue of *Expedition,* vol. 37, no. 3 (1995). 64p. bibliog.

Features articles by specialists on the Cambodian social and cultural revival which has taken place since 1979. The fields they comment on include anthropology, archaeology, art history and environment. A region and country map are provided. Temple plans, chronologies, bibliographies, detailed photographs and impressionistic pictures accompany the relevant articles. The authors have presented thoughtful work in a concise form, often including less common material. Beautifully presented, this magazine provides information for both area specialists and newcomers with a genuine interest in Cambodian culture. The contents are: 'The Angkorean temple-mountain: diversity, evolution, permanence' by Thierry Zéphir; 'Two thousand years of engineering genius on the Angkor Plain' by Richard A. Engelhardt, 'Angkor:

planning for sustainable tourism' by David Bowden; 'The play of the gods: a photo essay on Khmer dance training' by David A. Feingold; and 'Cambodian history through Cambodian museums' by Heather A. Peters. *Expedition* is published by the University of Pennsylvania Museum of Archaeology and Anthropology.

768 **Cambodian culture since 1975: homeland and exile.**
Edited by May M. Ebihara, Carol A. Mortland, and Judy Ledgerwood. Ithaca, New York: Cornell University Press, 1994. 194p. bibliog. (Asia, East by South).

Contains the following contributions: 'Khmer literature since 1975' by Khing Hoc Dy; 'Khmer traditional music today' by Sam-Ang Sam; 'The revival of masked theater, "Lkhaon Khaol", in Cambodia' by Bill Lobban; 'Cambodian Buddhist monasteries in Paris: continuing tradition and changing patterns' by Milada Kalab; 'Khmer Buddhists in the United States: ultimate questions' by Carol A. Mortland; 'Khmer proverbs: images and rules' by Karen Fisher-Nguyen; 'Metaphors of the Khmer Rouge' by John Marston; 'Gender symbolism and culture change: viewing the virtuous woman in the Khmer story "Mea Yoeng"' by Judy Ledgerwood; 'Sharing the pain: critical values and behaviors in Khmer culture' by John Marcucci; 'Cultural consumption: Cambodian peasant refugees and television in the "First World"' by Frank Smith. As indicated, Cambodian culture is here viewed in anthropological terms to include many aspects of social behaviour. The principal concern is with the refugee communities but the chapters by Lobban and Khing Hoc Dy offer a glimpse, albeit a fleeting one, of cultural revival in Cambodia itself.

769 **Charpentes et tuiles khmères.** (Khmer framework and rooftiles.)
Jacques Dumarçay. Paris: École Française d'Extrême-Orient, 1973. 87, lxxx, [42]p. bibliog. (Publications de l'École Française d'Extrême-Orient. Mémoires Archéologiques, 8).

Dumarçay diverges from studies of individual temples to look more broadly at the details of tiles and framework, his essay complemented by 77 illustrated plates and 113 figures.

770 **The civilization of Angkor.**
Madeleine Giteau, [translated from the French by Katherine Watson]. New York: Rizzoli, 1976. 279p. bibliog. A translation of *Angkor, un peuple, un art* (Angkor, a people, an art).

As the chapter headings reveal, this book emphasizes Angkor and the former Khmer empire as a living civilization, rather than a collection of archaeological ruins. 'Life in the provinces' looks at diverse details from village housing, to social structures, to hairstyles. 'Life in Angkor' gives a reconstruction of an ancient urban area. 'Life in the palace' presents suggestions about the social and political structure and atmosphere of Angkor's administration; and 'Life in the temples and ceremonials' identifies figures, such as hermits, scholars and ascetics, as well as providing a more general picture of the role of religion. The appendix contains glossaries on Brahman and Buddhist iconography and Khmer and Sanskrit terms. Giteau refers constantly to bas-reliefs (which are beautifully reproduced in the book), to texts and to continuing Khmer traditions in support of her informed and frequently original understandings.

771 **La collection khmère.** (The Khmer collection.)
Henri Marchal. Hanoi: École Française d'Extrême-Orient, 1939. 170p. bibliog. At head of title: Musée Louis Finot.

Although long out of print, and of limited distribution even in its day, this book retains its value. Marchal, director of Angkor Conservation, here provides a fifty-seven-page introduction to Khmer sculpture, as well as a chronology, bibliography and catalogue to the collection in the EFEO's Louis Finot Museum in Hanoi, with twelve plates.

772 **La convalescence des arts cambodgiens.** (The convalescence of Cambodian art.)
George Groslier. Hanoi: Imprimerie d'Extrême-Orient, 1919. 22p.

This small work heralded a renaissance of Cambodian craftwork. The text is the conclusion of several pieces published in 1918 in the *Revue Indochinoise* (q.v.). It describes the new school, the École des arts cambodgiens (School of Cambodian Arts), with its departments devoted to drawing, carving, smelting, woodwork, carpentry, etc. in the form of a progress report. For more results of these efforts, see the journal *Arts et Archéologie Khmers* (q.v.). The same kind of rejuvenation of craftwork was happening again in Cambodia from 1991-93.

773 **The cultural history of Angkor.**
Text and photographs by Henri Stierlin, [translated by Erika Abrams]. London: Aurum Press, 1984. 94p. map. (Great Civilizations). First published, Geneva: Edito-Service S. A., 1983. A translation of *Le monde d'Angkor* (The world of Angkor), Paris: Princesse, 1979.

The author chooses a small number of the major monuments to summarize and surmise about the styles and periods of Angkor architecture and some of the political history of the Khmer empire. Floor plans, black-and-white photographs and geometrical charts provide the backing for a discussion of the development of Cambodian urbanism and its architectural expression up to the period of Jayavarman VII. Stierlin looks at how Indian influence on the whole region took local forms, with small passages on Champa, Thailand and Burma. The descriptive yet light style of writing is very evocative, and so may give a reader who has not been to Angkor an impression of how it might affect them. The pictures are diverse, including bronzes, stone figures and dancers as well as temples, although the quality of reproduction is mixed. Providing information without being overly academic, this book would be very suitable for an introduction to Angkor, or as material for school projects.

774 **Cultural sites of Burma, Thailand, and Cambodia.**
Jacques Dumarçay and Michael Smithies. Kuala Lumpur: Oxford University Press, 1995. 127p. maps. bibliog.

Written by Dumarçay, retired architect from the EFEO and Smithies, a former academic resident in Southeast Asia. The introduction provides an overview of three of the main ancient civilizations of mainland Southeast Asia – their influences and local adaptations of dominant cultural and technological forms. Significant sites, predominantly religious, in each of the three regions are described, and are placed in historical, cultural and geographical context. The Cambodian sites dealt with are: Sambor Prei Kuk, Wat Phu, Roluos, Angkor and Phnom Penh. The architectural description and chronological accounts are excellent, but the cultural significance is not so well explored. Many fine photographs, plans and axonometric drawings supplement the three main sections, as does the interesting concluding chapter 'The organization of space in Continental South-East Asia'.

775 **Culture Khmère.** (Khmer Culture.)
Paris: CEDORECK, 1981- . twice-yearly.

This small journal was part of the initiative to stimulate a Cambodian cultural revival during the difficult early days of post-Khmer Rouge reconstruction. As well as the journal, a number of out-of-print titles were republished, and courses held to teach the Khmer language. CEDORECK Director, Nouth Narang, returned to Cambodia in 1991 and was appointed Minister of Culture and Fine Arts. There were plans to reconstitute the publishing programme in Cambodia, but these do not appear to have eventuated.

776 **Dance in Cambodia: beyond the killing fields.**
Karen Swenson. *Dance Magazine*, October 1990, p. 50-52.

Though only a short piece, this has value in showing the revival of this important feature of Cambodia's cultural life.

777 **Danses cambodgiennes.** (Cambodian dances.)
Sappho Marchal. [Saigon]: La Revue d'Extrême-Asie, 1931. new ed. 52p.

This edition in booklet form is a revised version of that first published in the journal *La Revue d'Extrême-Asie* in 1931. Marchal discusses the history, setting, movements, costume, characters and music, principally of the Royal Ballet, complementing the text with black-and-white line-drawings. She concludes with a section on the degeneration of the dance since the time it was admired by Rodin on the Ballet's tour to France in 1908.

778 **Danses d'Indochine.** (Dances of Indochina.)
Raymond Cogniat. Paris: Chroniques du Jour, 1932. 89p. (Découverte du Monde).

Sixty beautiful full-page black-and-white photographs (twenty-one from Cambodia) comprise the major part of this work. Dancers are shown performing with the bas-reliefs of Angkor Wat as a backdrop, and at the Royal Palace in Phnom Penh. Lao, Vietnamese and other ethnic minority dancers are also shown.

779 **Danseuses cambodgiennes, anciennes & modernes.** (Cambodian dancers, ancient and modern.)
Text and drawings by George Groslier, preface by Charles Gravelle, music compiled by M. Tricon. Paris: A. Challamel. 178, [2]p.

This book represents an act of adoration for the young girls who dance in the Royal Ballet. Groslier describes a training session, and discusses the girls' recruitment (they are offered by their family) and their schooling. They have a very painful life in fact. The reader is shown the dancers' costumes, jewels, and the way they dress and make-up. He then comments on the life of the dancers, most of whom are actually quite eager to get married and leave the Palace. The drawings are touching and the whole book is permeated by a keen observation coupled with an enormous love for what these brave girls are achieving in the matter of grace, excellence and kindness.

780 **Le décor et la sculpture khmers.** (Khmer decoration and sculpture.) Henri Marchal. Paris: Vanoest; Les Éditions d'Art et d'Histoire, 1951. 134p. bibliog. (Études d'Art et d'Ethnologie Asiatique, no. 3).

Sculpture and decoration play a crucial role in Khmer architecture. As Marchal notes, 'it would seem that the Khmers who constructed these splendid monuments . . . had an instinctive horror of bare surfaces devoid of ornamentation'. Marchal details the elements and motifs used particularly in ancient times, but concludes with a chapter on their appearance in contemporary times (the text was completed in June 1945). Some 109 line-drawings and 263 photographs provide ample illustration of the subject under discussion.

781 **Earth in flower: an historical and descriptive study of the classical dance drama of Cambodia.**
Paul Cravath. PhD thesis, University of Hawaii, 1985. 2 vols. (659 leaves). Also available in microform, Ann Arbor: University Microfilms International.

This extensive text examines evidence for: pre-Angkor formal dance; sculptural and epigraphical evidence from the Angkor period; dance under the influence of the various rulers from 1860 onwards; the mythological foundations of dance tradition; training, costumes, life style and music; and the ritual function of dance. The author's sources are personal observation, inscriptions (mentioning dancers), earlier French studies and regional historians' analyses. Whilst acknowledging a debt to Coedès (q.v.), major theories of the latter are refuted, such as 'the orthodox view of an historical Indianization of Southeast Asia'. Instead Cravath emphasizes a continuity of indigenous cultural forms. As well as following William Solheim's culture interpretation, he also analyses the mythology of the dance drama from a Jungian approach. Detailed historical, technical, analytical and anecdotal data on numerous aspects of Khmer dance are presented in this considered work.

782 **First International Scholars Conference on Cambodia: selected papers.**
Chhang Song, conference chairman; Russell A. Judkins, editor. Geneseo, New York: Anthropology Dept., State University of New York at Geneseo, 1988. ix, 73p. bibliog. (Papers in Anthropology).

The First International Conference on Khmer Culture was held on Capitol Hill in Washington, DC, from 24 April to 26 April 1985, sponsored by Save Cambodia, Inc., and funded by the National Endowment for the Humanities. The conference organizers managed to get good representation from a range of scholars, including May Ebihara, Franklin Huffman and Bernard Philippe Groslier (qq.v.), all of whom provided short papers.

783 **A golden souvenir of Angkor.**
Text and photography by Michael Freeman. Bangkok: Asia Books, 1992. [79]p.

Although based in London, Freeman has managed to visit the region frequently and to publish a number of both scholarly and touristic works. This work falls somewhere between the two genres, being a reasonably priced presentation of some 100 or so photographs of Angkor, some of particular appeal, which a higher quality production would have shown to better advantage. Freeman complements his images with informative captions and a ten-page introduction, setting the photographs in their historical and cultural context. The book serves the top end of the souvenir market.

784 **Guide du Musée national de Phnom-Penh.** (Guide to the National Museum of Phnom Penh.)
Madeleine Giteau. Phnom Penh: Office National du Tourisme, 1960. 58p.

The National Museum of Cambodia was established in 1917 by George Groslier (q.v.), and it is truly one of the world's gems of architecture. A representation in modern form of traditional themes of Khmer architecture, its finials soar to the sky, especially at sunset, and the russet tones of the walls resonate with the different angles of the sun throughout the day. Prepared by the curator, Madeleine Giteau, in 1960 for the National Office of Tourism, this guide remains one of the most succinct yet useful introductions both to the collection itself and to ancient Cambodian art in general. Some sixty-two items are given catalogue entries, and twenty are also accompanied by black-and-white photographic plates, though these are of poor quality reproduction.

785 **Hand woven textiles of South-east Asia.**
Sylvia Fraser-Lu. Singapore: Oxford University Press, 1992. 230p. 3 maps.

If one is searching for a thorough coverage of Khmer textiles then this text will disappoint. But it does contain a small section on Cambodian textiles that may provide the reader with enough information for an overview on the subject and, until the definitive work on Khmer textiles appears, it may have to suffice. The author has a profound knowledge of Southeast Asian textiles, but Cambodian textiles are not her forté and, at the time of the book's completion, she had never visited Cambodia. Illustrations depict traditional dress (*sampot*), a loom and a modern wall hanging made by Khmer refugees in the Thai border camps. The work contains a brief historical overview that says little of the tradition of weaving and textiles in Cambodia. However, the book is well designed, enjoyable to read and informative (on other countries), looking at textiles in relation to the dynamics of the societies throughout history.

786 **Iconographie du Cambodge post-angkorien.** (Iconography of post-Angkor Cambodia.)
Madeleine Giteau. Paris: École Française d'Extrême-Orient, 1975. 381p. map. bibliog. (Publications de l'École Française d'Extrême-Orient, no. 100).

Madeleine Giteau, as Director of the National Museum of Cambodia in Phnom Penh in the pre-Khmer Rouge era, had the opportunity to turn her attention to the post-

Angkor period, previously neglected, and somewhat disparaged as Thai provincial art of little interest. Aside from around 100 statues in the storehouse of the Conservation of Angkor office in Siem Reap, several significant items in the National Museum, and a handful in provincial museums, the majority of items she registered were still in situ in temples or in modern monasteries. From her analysis of this corpus, Giteau posits a tentative chronology, identifying three distinct stylistic periods – Srei Santhor to the beginning of the 17th century, the 17th and 18th centuries, and the 19th to early 20th centuries – and she provides 118 photographs and a number of drawings showing details of styles. One of the many appendices contains 'Rules for statues of Buddha' written in 1544.

787 **Indian sculpture: masterpieces of Indian, Khmer, and Cham art.** Photographs by W. and B. Forman, text by M. M. Deneck, translated by Iris Urwin. London: Spring Books, 1962. 34, [14]p. bibliog.

Because much Khmer art and religion has close links and parallels with that of India, Cambodia has frequently been termed part of Greater India, particularly by Indian scholars. In this presentation of Indian sculpture, one chapter and around 120 of the 264 plates are devoted to Khmer and Cham sculpture, the vast majority of which being Khmer. Deneck, of the Guimet Museum, where the Khmer pieces in this book are held, introduces the artwork with two chapters on 'The development of Indian sculpture' and 'The spread of Indian thought'. The plates are entirely black-and-white, often showing details or alternative views of the one piece. Notes provide details for each item, including size, artistic style and original location. Their symbolism and significance, however, are not treated individually, but covered in the brief introductory chapter. This book may therefore be more suitable for those already familiar with, and fond of, Khmer sculpture. *The Age of Angkor: treasures from the National Museum of Cambodia* (q.v.), an exhibition catalogue from the National Gallery of Australia, serves better to introduce Khmer art.

788 **Inventaire descriptif des monuments du Cambodge.** (Descriptive inventory of Cambodian monuments.) E. Lunet de Lajonquière. Paris: Ernest Leroux, 1902-11. 3 vols. maps. bibliog. (Publications de l'École Française d'Extrême-Orient, nos. 4, 8 & 9). Available on microfilm 87/7086 (P).

The author was an army officer attached to the EFEO. On foot, on horseback, and by boat he travelled all over Cambodia and Eastern Siam in order to gather data on ancient Khmer monuments, some 910 of which are listed here. This book remains a mine of observations and also provides information on the state of conservation almost a century ago; the same survey today would make an interesting comparison. Among his many observations is that the building and the decorative carvings of a monument are two very distinctive phases, sometimes separated, he says, 'by generations'. The book contains a hypothetical reconstruction of Preah Vihear by Demoineau. One of the most striking achievements of this extraordinary work is the map. It shows the nuclear zone of the Angkor polity as lying between the Tonle Sap Lake and the Dangrek Range, further north, concentrated along the two main Angkor roads, leading northwest to Phimai and the Semun river. The country south of the Tonle Sap Lake, which forms the main part of what we now call Cambodia, was not really included.

789 **Khmer art in stone.**
Pich Keo. Phnom Penh: National Museum of Cambodia and JSRC Printing House, [1994?]. 38p. bibliog.

'A walk-through guide to the main styles of Khmer art as seen in the stone pieces on display' providing a good basic introduction to Khmer art and to the National Museum of Cambodia collection. It is written by the then director of the museum, the only qualified archaeologist in Cambodia among the museum staff to have survived the Pol Pot era. He provides one or more examples of each of eleven major styles of Khmer art from the 7th to 13th centuries as shown in black-and-white photographs from the museum archives, and line-drawings taken from Boisselier's *La statuaire khmère et son évolution* (q.v.). The book is on sale at the museum, and proceeds go towards its restoration.

790 **Khmer ceramics from the Kamratan collection in the Southeast Asian Ceramics Museum, Kyoto.**
Hiroshi Fujiwara, introduction by Dawn F. Rooney. Singapore: Oxford University Press, 1990. xvi, 111p. bibliog. (The Asia Collection). A translation of *Kumeru Okoku no koto*.

The Kamratan Collection, comprising 138 pieces owned by Hiroshi Fujiwara, was exhibited in 1989 at the Toyama Museum of Fine Art, Japan. Both a catalogue and reference work, this book contains at least one photograph of each piece, a sixteen-page introduction by Khmer ceramics expert Dawn Rooney, a bibliography, figures and two maps. Most of the photographs are excellent, with muted backgrounds allowing the pieces' true colours to appear, but a few shots seem unfocused. Rooney's introduction is in many ways a summary of her previous more extensive studies, here with specific reference to the Kamratan pieces. A concise outline is given of Khmer ceramic types: cooking ware, storage, and ritual pieces; their influences, including importation of Chinese glaze technology and local adaptation of foreign traditions; and technical evidence in the finds revealing manufacturing methods. The distinctive characteristics of Khmer ceramics are discussed – from clays, glazes and forms, to decoration and detail – making the entire work highly useful for scholars, potters, and art collectors alike.

791 **Khmer ceramics, 9th-14th century.**
Compiled by the Southeast Asian Ceramic Society, edited by Diana Stock. Singapore: Southeast Asian Ceramic Society, 1981. 140p. bibliog.

This book was published to coincide with an exhibition of 120 pieces of Khmer ceramics put on by the Southeast Asian Ceramic Society. In addition to a colour catalogue of the objects, it includes four essays which place them in a social and regional context. Bernard Grocher provides a broad coverage of many aspects of Khmer ceramics, such as determining where and when Khmer ceramics were made, their methods of manufacture, and how pieces were utilized and therefore displayed. Roxanna Brown addresses the form and glazes of 11th- and 12th-century objects from the Korat Plateau. Dawn Rooney refers specifically to pieces in the catalogue in order to speculate on religious, funerary and utilitarian uses, and cross-references her ideas to bas-reliefs at Angkor. An engaging history of the rulers of Cambodia and their building programmes as well as stories and philosophies of the country's past is provided by Malcolm MacDonald, excerpted from his book *Angkor and the Khmers* (q.v.). These informative and thought-provoking essays are matched by the excellent photographs of bowls, zoomorphic lime pots, storage jars, funerary urns and other pieces.

792 **Khmer ceramics.**
Dawn Rooney. Singapore: Oxford University Press, 1984. xv, 245p. bibliog. (Oxford in Asia Studies in Ceramics).

Presented as 'the first comprehensive study' this work examines the background, influences, characteristics, shapes and uses of different types of Khmer ceramics in easily readable language. It is copiously illustrated with photographs, unfortunately mostly in black-and-white, depriving the reader of the lustre and tones of the corpus. Rooney includes valuable information on such points as: the social and religious context of ceramics; firing techniques; the tools used; ceremonial traditions; and the associated meanings of animal figures. The text refers to the 108 plates specifically, and is accompanied by small profile drawings of some pieces. Tiles, figures, animal forms, storage jars, bells, pots, conch shell forms, small boxes and bottles are all represented. Tables show the clay types, glaze types and iron oxide content of glazes as well as a comparative Khmer/Chinese chronology and a worldwide list of public galleries and museums holding Khmer ceramics.

793 **Khmer classical dance songbook.**
[Compiled] by Amy Catlin, English translations by Sam-Ang Sam, Chan Moly Sam, and Amy Catlin. Van Nuys, California: Apsara Media for Intercultural Education, 1992. xiv, 126p. bibliog.

Published for Cambodians living in the United States, this book contains songs, unaccompanied, with Western and number notation. Khmer words with the romanized forms, and English translation are provided.

794 **Khmer court dance: a comprehensive study of movements, gestures, and postures as applied techniques.**
Chan Moly Sam, edited by Diana Schnitt. Newington, Connecticut: Khmer Studies Institute, 1987. xii, 140p. bibliog.

As intended by the author, a former dancer, this book provides a 'comprehensive study of movements, gestures and postures as applied techniques'. She created the study out of a concern about the role of Khmer court dance when removed from its homeland, and laments the proliferation of inauthentic or incomplete teaching in refugee camps and emigrant communities. Chapters briefly document the career of court dancers, private student traditions in France and the United States, modern basic training procedure in Cambodia, technique and hand language. No new analyses are offered, but the material provided forms an authoritative handbook. Postures, gestures, hand and foot positions are all illustrated and described, or matched with good clear photographs. Staves showing drum patterns for different routine exercises are added, as well as an excellent glossary of Khmer terms.

795 **Khmer folk dance.**
Sam-Ang Sam, Chan Moly Sam. Newington, Connecticut: Khmer Studies Institute, 1987. x, 121p. map. bibliog.

A slim volume of immense importance in the effort to maintain Cambodian cultural tradition, compiled by two expatriate Cambodian dancers and musicians, who have done much to revive the forms in the United States. The data originates from various sources, but is largely based on the authors' own experiences and recollections from years of involvement in the field. Much emphasis is placed on the role of the University of Fine Arts and the Conservatory of Performing Arts in training and educating dancers. The book is intended to enable the reconstruction of performances outside Cambodia, and is by no means an exhaustive catalogue of dance, or a social analysis. It provides fundamental information about the meaning, mood and methods of twenty dances, including the Peacock of Pursat, Candle, Good Crops and Chhayam dances. Transcriptions of the music and percussion for almost all the pieces, as well as notes on costume, movement and gesture, and the authors' professionalism, contribute to the book's practical and documentary significance.

796 **Khmer sculpture and the Angkor civilization.**
Madeleine Giteau, translated from the French by Diana Imber, photographs by Hans Hinz. London: Thames & Hudson, 1965. 301p. maps. bibliog.

A beautifully laid-out Thames & Hudson edition, half of which is made up of good clear photographs of statuary, bas-relief panels, lintels and ritual objects. They are divided by material – bronze, stone and wood – with pieces in each of these media from pre-Angkor, Angkor and post-Angkor periods. Additional to a religious and historical perspective which suggests the social purposes of sculpture, the conditions that gave rise to its creation and the various influences on art, Giteau provides a descriptive analysis of the pieces themselves. Describing Khmer art as 'subtle, gay and measured', the scope of her work is limited only by what archaeological evidence remains, with consequently scant coverage of furniture or wooden architecture. Amongst features in the appendix is a catalogue of pieces according to subject matter such as animals, costume, vehicles or vegetation, which would be particularly useful for researchers.

797 **Looting in Angkor: one hundred missing objects = Cent objets disparus: pillage à Angkor.**
Paris: ICOM (International Council of Museums) in co-operation with the École Française d'Extrême-Orient, 1993. 102p.

ICOM has for many years been a vehicle for museum professionals and others, in over 120 countries, to work together to combat illegal traffic in cultural property, and it helped elaborate the 1970 UNESCO Convention on the means of prohibiting the illicit import, export and transfer of ownership of cultural property. The monuments at Angkor have been exposed to vandalism and plunder for centuries, at a particularly alarming rate over the last twenty years. This booklet is intended to assist identification of around 100 of the most important stolen pieces. Eerily reading like a catalogue of physical violations, a photograph and details of each piece are categorized as: Objects stolen from the depot of the Conservation d'Angkor; Objects which have completely disappeared; Statues, isolated heads and various pieces; or Heads removed from statues, with bodies remaining at the depot. Additional to this entreating list, moving introductory passages are provided by (then) Prince Norodom Sihanouk, the President of ICOM, the Director of the EFEO, and Bruno Dagens on 'The plight of Khmer art'. Beautifully designed, the purpose of the publication is international mobilization on behalf of Khmer art, of value to all humanity. 'Measures taken in the fight against illicit traffic of cultural property' by ICOM, UNESCO and Interpol are documented following the list, including information on how to report a theft or a find.

798 **Les monuments du Cambodge: études d'architecture khmère.** (The monuments of Cambodia: studies of Khmer architecture.)
L. Delaporte, introduction; annotation of the plates by the Musée Indo-Chinois du Trocadéro. Paris: Ernest Leroux, 1924. 2 vols. At head of title: Ministère de l'Instruction Publique et des Beaux-Arts, Commission Archéologique de l'Indo-Chine.

Based on documents collected on missions led by Delaporte in 1873 and 1882-83, and on the complementary mission by Faraut in 1874-75. No less than eighteen monuments are depicted with incredible drafting skills – some as plans, others in perspective. The use of light and shadow creates at times an almost photographic rendition, especially in the case of the Bayon, which is the most extensively documented, as the focus of the viewer is led from the construction of the whole to the minute details of ornamentation and architectural features. If, by the process of naming and recording, possession is claimed, then this book must have functioned in the colonial heyday as a luscious land-title. These images are still selected to grace the pages of today's publications, such as Dagens' *Angkor: heart of an Asian empire*, and Osborne's *River road to China: the Mekong River Expedition 1866-73* (qq.v.).

799 **Les monuments khmers du style du Bàyon et Jayavarman VII.** (Khmer monuments in the style of the Bayon and Jayavarman VII.)
Philippe Stern. Paris: Presses Universitaires de France, 1965. 267p. bibliog. (Publications du Musée Guimet. Recherches et Documents d'Art et d'Archéologie, no. 9).

Stern presents his work as having three themes: the emergence of an internal evolution in the Bayon style (revealing three periods); a method of determining such evolution from combining a study of motifs with dated items; and a study of the great Buddhist sovereign Jayavarman VII. The study is divided into three parts: the evolution of motifs; a study of individual monuments; and a chronological exposition of the results. The research was carried out from 1936 until its publication thirty years later, the text complemented by 211 photographs and 15 plans.

800 **Musée Guimet: catalogue des collections indochinoises.** (Guimet Museum: catalogue of the Indochinese collections.)
Pierre Dupont. Paris: Editions Ernest Leroux, 1934. 192p. bibliog.

Almost 300 pieces are described in this catalogue of the best collection of Khmer and Cham sculpture outside of Cambodia itself, principally taken from the country by Aymonier and Delaporte (qq.v), combined at the Guimet Museum, Paris in 1927, where they were supplemented with finds sent annually by George Groslier (q.v.), including the pieces sent for the 1931 Colonial Exposition. Pierre Dupont wrote the introduction, while J. Auboyer comments on the history of the collection, Philippe Stern (Conservator in Chief at the Guimet) on Khmer statuary, and G. de Coral Rémusat on problems of Cham chronology. Fourteen photographic plates and a floor plan of the museum, are included.

801 **La musique du Cambodge et du Laos.** (The music of Cambodia and Laos.)
Alain Daniélou. Pondichéry, India: Institut Français d'Indologie, 1957. [33], ivp. bibliog. (Publications de l'Institut Français d'Indologie, no. 9).

This well-known musicologist, a specialist on India, sees four different, quite separate, musical systems in Cambodian music. He particularly notes the survival of an Indian musical scale called *gandhana-grana*, which disappeared from India after the 6th century, when the harp was displaced by the lute, a change which did not occur in Southeast Asia. He also remarks that the religious chant (in Buddhist ceremonies) is 'very close to the oldest Vedic psalmody' using only three notes. He studies the composition of orchestras (Pi Phat, Mohori), registering the fact that notes have no names and that musicians do not seem to think they should. He then studies the instruments. He says that village music exhibits a real continuity with the past whereas the Palace music has been lost at some point, and reconstructed on Siamese models, which must have been the repository of the old tradition.

802 **Nang Sbek: théâtre d'ombres dansé du Cambodge.** (*Nang Sbek*: theatre of shadow dance of Cambodia.)
Jacques Brunet. Berlin: Institut International d'Études Comparatives de la Musique, 1969. 17p. (Publication de l'Institut International d'Études Comparatives de la Musique).

A slim volume, and presumably difficult to find these days, this is worth inclusion as it was, until the 1995 publication of *Sbek Thom: Khmer shadow theater* (q.v.), a rare attempt to document this distinctive Cambodian/Thai art form. The first reference to shadow theatre is in a text dating from 1458, although it is undoubtedly considerably more ancient. Brunet points out that Cambodia has in fact two shadow theatres: the large figure *Sbek Thom* (*Nang Sbek*) without moving parts, held aloft in two hands by dancers; and the small figure *Sbek Touch* (*Ayang*) which more closely resembles the shadow puppets of Indonesia and China and are manipulated by sticks. The *Nang Sbek* was considered part of the Cambodian classical theatre and, together with the Royal Ballet, formed part of the Palace ritual as well as entertainment. It had almost died out when Brunet began his research in the 1950s, and it was largely due to his endeavours that the surviving portion of the repertoire in the Siem Reap area was recorded and then taught at the University of Fine Arts in Phnom Penh. As with much other cultural activity, this art form was almost wiped out by the Khmer Rouge, and is now making a painfully slow revival. *Nang Sbek* is the focus of this book and is described in terms of the history, the accessories, the dance, the music, the recitative text, and the representation, with a small section on *Ayang* concluding the text. Photographs show the figures themselves, their creation and even the masters at work.

803 **National seminar on archaeology and fine arts for the development of the Arcafa project (Khmer Republic 13-14-15 November 1973).**
[Phnom Penh]: SEAMEO, 1973. 123p.

The proceedings of a preparatory conference for the purpose of establishing in Phnom Penh an Applied Research Centre for Archaeology and the Fine Arts, organized jointly by the Cambodian government and SEAMEO (Southeast Asia Ministers of Education Organization). Of particular interest are reports of the contemporary scene, such as those on: Khmer literature, by Phet Phanur; Khmer theatre; Classical dance;

Choreography, by Chheng Phon; and the opening speech by Um Samuth, Minister of Culture.

804 **Of gods, kings, and men: bas-reliefs of Angkor Wat and Bayon.**
Text by Albert Le Bonheur; photographs by Jaroslav Poncar and students of the Fachhochschule, Cologne. London: Serindia, 1995. 112p. bibliog.

Dedicated to the memory of George Coedès (q.v.), this book is a new attempt to record and analyse the bas-reliefs of the Angkor Wat and Bayon temples. As the longest known bas-reliefs in the world, 2 metres high and 100 metres long, they have always presented problems for presentation in book form. The 'slit-scan' technique, developed in 1992, which allows for the shooting of one long continuous picture, was used by Jaroslav Poncar and students from Cologne, Germany, for this book. Unfortunately, the format of this standard-sized paperback book compromises the point of the exercise, as most of the images are tiny, stretching over a few pages, and with parts lost in the spine. The front-on lighting, in most cases, has reduced the reliefs to merely graphic linear designs, not allowing shadows to reveal the semi-sculptural qualities which are their defining features. However, the text is excellent, containing both descriptive and interpretative comments on the scenes depicted and, in conjunction with the pictures, makes the book invaluable as a guide to the temples, or as a scholarly work.

805 **Palaces of the gods: Khmer art & architecture in Thailand.**
Smitthi Siribhadra, Elizabeth Moore, photography by Michael Freeman. Bangkok: Asia Books, 1992. 352p. map. bibliog.

As the authors alert us, 'The Northeast (of Thailand) provided the Khmer empire with a line of kings that included two of its greatest, Suryavarman II and Jayavarman VII'. Their book presents twenty-three Khmer temples, now located in Thailand, as a stunning art book, a practical guide, and an historical analysis. Michael Freeman's evocative and atmospheric photographs provide a memorable impression of the architecture and its environment, while the informative text attempts to identify local styles and forms of expression within a Khmer tradition. While the temples are treated individually, introductory chapters provide a background to the history and religion of the Khmers' principal deities, the history of the temples' restoration, sculpture and 'applied arts', and a table showing French periodization of Khmer art. Recent political events and their effect on access to many sites are included within suggested itineraries. Historical photography, architectural reconstructions, details of lintels and pediments etc., give additional richness to this impressive publication. Michael Freeman's *A guide to Khmer temples in Thailand and Laos* (Bangkok: River Books, 199?. 315p.) was developed as a companion to the above more scholarly and artistic title. This handy slim volume presents from that work the essentials of the Khmer temples in Thailand, adding to it those found in present-day Laos. Access and other more touristic information complement notes on the art and architecture of the temples, and some 280 splendid colour photographs, 35 temple plans and 12 town maps.

806 **Passage through Angkor.**
Mark Standen, introduction by John Hoskin. Phnom Penh: Indochina News Corporation, 1994. 231p.

English photographer and photo-journalist Mark Standen has here produced one of the highest quality and most memorable books on the oft-photographed Angkor. Grouped around four themes (birth of a civilization, master builders, ancestral life, and passage of time), Standen's images juxtapose the temples, sculptures and bas-reliefs with the local people carrying out their daily tasks, often in the very same way today. Unusual and even rare shots – like lightning above Angkor Wat – provide some very special treats, all the more so since they were all shot without filters, double-exposure or computer-enhancement, and except one – a bat in flight – without even a flash. Unusual, too, is the knowledgeable and beautifully written introduction by John Hoskin. Published in Cambodia (though produced in Bangkok and printed and bound in Hong Kong), it is also available in French translation.

807 **Phantasmatic Indochina: French colonial ideology in architecture, film and literature.**
Norindr Panivong. Durham, North Carolina: Duke University Press, 1996. 240p.

This reflection on colonial culture argues for an examination of 'Indochina' as a fictive and mythic construct, a phantasmic legacy of French colonialism in Southeast Asia. The author uses post-colonial theory to demonstrate how French imperialism manifests itself not only through physical domination of geographical entities, but also through the colonialization of the imaginary. Unfortunately the volume has no illustrations except for the cover which shows the bas-relief by Alfred Janniot of the 1931 Musée Permanent des Colonies (Permanent Museum of the Colonies) described at the time as a 'gigantic tapestry representing the colonies' economic contribution to France', and discussed in some detail.

808 **Phnom Bakheng: étude architecturale du temple.** (Phnom Bakheng: architectural study of the temple.)
Jacques Dumarçay. Paris: l'École Française d'Extrême-Orient, 1971. 40p. (Publications de l'École Française d'Extrême-Orient. Mémoires Archéologiques, 7).

Dumarçay continues his detailed studies of individual temples with this architectural study, complemented by eighteen illustrated plates and thirty plans.

809 **Rapports entre le premier art khmer et l'art indien.** (Connections between early Khmer art and Indian art.)
Mireille Bénisti. Paris: l'École Française d'Extrême-Orient, 1970. 2 vols. maps. (Publications de l'École Française d'Extrême-Orient. Mémoires Archéologiques, 5).

The first volume contains the text, and the second volume consists of 285 figures illustrating the parallels drawn between early Khmer art and Indian art.

810 **Recherches sur les Cambodgiens d'apres les textes et les monuments depuis les premiers siècles de notre ère.** (Research on the Cambodians according to texts and monuments from the first centuries of our era.)
George Groslier. Paris: Augustin Challamel, 1921. 379p.

This large and ambitious book seeks to analyse Cambodia to the beginning of the 20th century on the basis of indigenous sources, namely texts and monuments. The first part describes the people, their culture and their military organization. The second analyses the monuments, sculptures and architecture, describing the techniques used and their evolution.

811 **Renaissance Culturelle du Cambodge.** (Cultural Renaissance of Cambodia.)
Tokyo: Institute of Asian Cultures, Sophia University, 1989- . irregular.

This journal reports recent activity in the area of cultural reconstruction with assistance from Japan. Chiefly archaeological in emphasis, reflecting the work of Sophia University, Tokyo, it also reports on work in other fields such as publishing and the arts. The text is in English, French, Japanese and Khmer.

812 **Sbek Thom: Khmer shadow theater.**
Pech Kum Kravel; Khmer version edited by Thavro Phim and Sos Kem; English translation by Sos Kem; abridged, adapted and edited by Martin Hatch. [Phnom Penh]: Southeast Asia Program, Cornell University; United Nations Educational, Scientific and Cultural Organization, 1995. 35, 161, 153p.

A study of the Khmer oral musical theatre using large leather-hide shadow figures, sponsored by Cornell University, UNESCO, and Japan Sotoshu Relief Committee. 'I have compiled this book in the hope that it will help to rehabilitate Cambodian culture, a national culture destroyed in a bloody protracted war', the author prefaces this important record. The editors hope that it will provide a stimulus for continuation of such studies, noting that ' . . . some of the observations need to be confirmed and there is much more that can be said about the place of the genre in Khmer history and culture'. There are good, captioned black-and-white photographs of 153 shadow figures, including both scenes and individual characters. A thirty-five-page English text lightly covers many aspects of the tradition including manufacture and care of the *sbek* (the puppets), the accompanying musical instruments, some famous storytellers, the origin and synopsis of stories, and contemplation about the revival and survival of traditions in a changing society. The circumstances of performance, especially the associated moral teachings and rituals, are described and emphasized.

813 **La sculpture khmère ancienne.** (Ancient Khmer sculpture.)
George Groslier. Paris: G. Crès, 1925. ii, 89p. + 155p. of plates of illustration. map. (Collection Française des Arts Orientaux).

A seminal work outlining this complex art. All the pieces except one were photographed and handled, 155 plates showing items that are discussed in the text from a variety of viewpoints. Some chapters address particular forms (statuary, Buddha images, bas-reliefs, decorative sculpture, and bronzes) while others approach technique, iconography, geographic distribution and external influences. Groslier, who was Director of Cambodian Arts in the colonial administration, shows his passion for the subject and revels in 'the grandeur, the strength, the true richness of Khmer sculpture'.

814 **Seven bronzes from Southeast Asia and Indonesia: some applications of science in the study of objets d'art. Part 1. Two Khmer bronzes.**
Brian Heffernan et al., edited by Noel Barnard. Canberra: Australian National Gallery, 1978. x, 92p. map. bibliog. (Research Monograph/Australian National Gallery, no. 1).

This scientific study, not an art history analysis, was conducted in the hope that through the identification of particular characteristics a greater understanding of a piece and its maker(s) may be reached. As the then director of the Australian National Gallery James Mollison prefaced the study, 'objects we designate as "works of art" are both universal and surprisingly limited in range'. It contains general observations, details on how sampling of the pieces was undertaken, elemental analysis of the samples, metallographic examination, radiographic examination, and conclusions. It includes scant information on the historical or religious significance of the two pieces from Cambodia, a Bodhisattva from Sriwijaya (7th-12th century), and an 8th-century statuette. Neither does it advance theories based on the findings. However, it may contain valuable source material for archaeologists, scientists and conservators.

815 **Silverware of South-East Asia.**
Sylvia Fraser-lu. Singapore: Oxford University Press, 1990. 124p. maps. bibliog. (Images of Asia).

Sylvia Fraser-lu here reveals the results of her comprehensive research into the art of silverware in Southeast Asia, dealing significantly with Cambodian silverware in her chapter on Indochina. Notwithstanding its brevity it provides a real insight and understanding of the early development of the art of silver-making and its changing patterns and style through the colonial period and up to 1975. Descriptions are provided of designs, symbolism and the manufacture of the objects. Seventeen drawings depict simple designs mixed with indigenous and foreign influences, and six photographs show more elaborate works of silver. Five sketches illustrate the common patterns seen on Cambodian silverware. The brief bibliography exhibits the scarcity of sources on this topic.

816 **South East Asia and China: art, interaction and commerce.**
Edited by Rosemary Scott and John Guy. London: Percival David Foundation of Chinese Art; Singapore: Sun Tree Pub., 1995. 287p. maps.

Contains papers presented at the 17th Percival David Colloquy held in London in 1994. They deal with the period following 1,000 AD, and emphasize recent archaeological excavations.

817 **South-east Asian ceramics: Thai, Vietnamese, and Khmer: from the collection of the Art Gallery of South Australia.**
Dick Richards, photography by Clayton Glen. Kuala Lumpur: Oxford University Press, 1995. 212p. bibliog. (The Asia Collection).

The Art Gallery of South Australia, Adelaide, has a fine collection of Southeast Asian ceramics, here described and discussed by Dick Richards, accompanied by 79 colour photographs, 101 black-and-white illustrations and 2 maps. The monochrome Khmer ware contrasts markedly with the more familiar tones of Thai and Vietnamese ceramics.

818 **La Statuaire khmère et son évolution.** (Khmer statuary and its evolution.)
Jean Boisselier. Saigon: École Française d'Extrême-Orient, 1955. 2 vols. bibliog. (Publications de l'École Française d'Extrême-Orient, no. 7).

On the basis of work carried out since 1934 in Cambodia (at the Albert Sarraut Museum, Phnom Penh and at the Angkor Conservation, Siem Reap) and in France (at the Guimet Museum), and building on the pioneering efforts of Stern in establishing a chronology for the construction of the temples, Boisselier here presents his stylistic and chronological analysis of statuary, divided into thirteen styles. Volume one contains the text, with the emphasis on human forms analysed by their principal elements, costume and technique. Commentary on foreign influences and his chronology are followed by appendices on the bronzes, on unresolved problems, and on relevant texts and inscriptions. Volume two consists entirely of 114 black-and-white plates.

819 **La statuaire préangkorienne.** (Pre-Angkor statuary.)
Pierre Dupont. Ascona, Switzerland: Artibus Asiae, 1955. 240p. map.

Devoted to an analysis of Khmer statuary prior to the 9th century, this study covers the kingdoms of Chenla and Funan, in present-day Cambodia as well as in Cochinchina, part of eastern Thailand and South Annam. The text is complemented by some forty-six pages of fine black-and-white plates, most with two or three pictures per page.

820 **Tâ Kèo: étude architecturale du temple.** (Ta Keo: architectural study of the temple.)
Jacques Dumarçay. Paris: l'École Française d'Extrême-Orient, 1971. (Publications de l'École Française d'Extrême-Orient. Mémoires Archéologiques, 6).

A wealth of material on this single temple is provided here. Dumarçay provides an architectural study of the temple, and this is complemented by an atlas, fifty-five plates and forty-one plans.

821 **Le temple d'Içvarapura (Banteay Srei, Cambodge).** (The temple of Içvarapura, Banteay Srei, Cambodia.)
Architectural study by Henri Parmentier; images by Victor Goloubew; inscriptions and history by Louis Finot. Paris: G. Van Oest, 1926. x, 138p. bibliog. (Publications de l'École Française d'Extrême-Orient. Mémoires Archéologiques, no. 1).

Considered by many to be the jewel among Cambodian temples, this 'Fortress of the women' lies far enough away from the town of Siem Reap to carry something of the attraction of the elusive – all the more so since even in early 1995 tourists going there were attacked, and several people were even killed, evidently by the Khmer Rouge, and minefields have been laid right up to the temple itself. But its exquisite carvings in pinkish stone still hold an allure. For many this book may be as close as they will come for the foreseeable future.

822 **The temples of Angkor: monuments to a vanished empire.**
Miloslav Krása, photographs by Ján Cifra, translated by Joy Turner. London: A. Wingate, [1963]. 211, [61]p. bibliog.

Claiming that 'Angkor is a name, the meaning of which is often indefinite and hazy, and whose connotations have far exceeded the boundaries of its original meaning', the author delineates nine principal artistic styles to lead to a factual presentation of Angkor's history. Each period outline is accompanied by a map, temple floor plan and black-and-white photographs, as well as a detailed description of layout. The introductory chapters are brief, covering the history of the states of the Khmer temple, Angkor as a metropolis and so on. The book shows its age with chapters such as 'The smile and the mask' and 'The mystery of Angkor'. It relies heavily on established theories, especially the 13th-century journals of Chou Ta-Kuan, but despite its romanticism the book contains important information presented in simple language.

823 **Traditional musical instruments of Cambodia.**
Khmer text and photographs by Keo Dorivan, Yun Theara, Y Lina and Mao Lenna, supervised by Bill Lobban; Khmer text edited by Hun Sarin; English text edited by Catherine Geach. [Phnom Penh]: UNESCO, 1994. 167p.

An important contribution to documenting surviving musical traditions compiled by students at the Royal University of Fine Arts, Phnom Penh, under the supervision of Australian ethnomusicologist, Bill Lobban, and edited by Hun Sarin (former Dean of the Faculty of Music) and Catherine Geach (British music teacher in Cambodia). Some forty-six instruments are described – nine string, nine wind, twenty-seven percussion and one mixed string and wind, including some unusual Cambodian instruments, such as conch shells (*kyang sang*), buffalo horn (*sneng*) and leaf (*slek*) as well as a wide range of gongs, flutes and drums. Aside from textual descriptions, drawings, and photographs of the instruments being played, the book provides some notations and details of how the instruments are made, maintained and tuned for performance today and as shown on bas-reliefs from Angkor. Subsidy and printing for this work were provided by the Japan Sotoshu Relief Committee (JSRC). The text is in parallel Khmer and English.

824 **Trends in Khmer art.**
Jean Boisselier, edited by Natasha Eilenberg. Ithaca, New York: Southeast Asia Program, Cornell University, 1989. 118p. bibliog. (Studies on Southeast Asia). A revised translation of *Tendances de l'art khmer*.

By the art historian and author of *La statuaire khmère et son évolution* (Khmer statuary and its evolution) (q.v.), this guide to twenty-four pieces in the National Museum of Cambodia aims to present them without 'erudition and architectural terms'. Using a stylistic analysis inherited from Philippe Stern, Boisselier discusses each piece in detail: its context, importance, technique of manufacture and stylistic characteristics. A couple of pages each on religion and history precede the light, but soundly researched, studies of the pieces. As the author himself states in the preface, the work is intended, and would be very appropriate, for ' . . . art lovers, visitors to the Phnom Penh museum, students of Khmer art . . . '.

Voyage au Cambodge: l'architecture khmer. (Journey to Cambodia: Khmer architecture.)
See item no. 101.

Le Cambodge. (Cambodia.)
See item no. 126.

Documents graphiques de la conservation d'Angkor: 1963-1973. (Graphic documents of the conservation of Angkor.)
See item no. 130.

Safeguarding and development of Angkor.
See item no. 135.

Indian cultural influence in Cambodia.
See item no. 161.

Le roman source d'inspiration de la peinture khmère à la fin du XIXe et au début du XXe siècle: l'histoire de Preah Chinavong et son illustration dans la (sala) de Vat Kieng Svay Krau. (The novel that served as a source of inspiration for Khmer painters at the end of the 19th and beginning of the 20th centuries: the story of Preah Chinavong and its illustration in the sala of Wat Kien Svay Krau.)
See item no. 745.

Musée Guimet: catalogue des collections indochinoises. (Guimet Museum: catalogue of the Indochinese collections.)
See item no. 800.

Le cinquantenaire de l'ÉFEO: compte rendu des fêtes et cérémonies. (The fiftieth anniversary of the EFEO: report of the festivals and ceremonies.)
See item no. 839.

Cambodia dance.
See item no. 913.

The tenth dancer.
See item no. 953.

Cambodian traditional music in Minnesota.
See item no. 960.

Homrong.
See item no. 961.

The music of Cambodia.
See item no. 962.

America's ethnic performing arts: Cambodian.
See item no. 972.

Customs and Ceremonies

825 **Le Cambodge, années vingt: à l'ombre d'Angkor.** (Cambodia in the 1920s: in the shadow of Angkor.)
Léon Busy. [Rueil-Malmaison, France]: Conseil Général Hauts-de-Seine 92, [1992]. 199p.

Chiefly comprising colour illustrations, this volume was conceived around the autochromes and films produced by Léon Busy for the Albert Kahn 'Archives of the Planet', and black-and-white photographs made for the Government General of Indochina.

826 **Cérémonies des douze mois: fêtes annuelles cambodgiennes.** (Ceremonies of the twelve months: Cambodian annual festivals.)
[Phnom Penh]: Commission des Moeurs et Coutumes du Cambodge, [19??]. 77p.

A rough photocopied reprint of this is available in the markets of Phnom Penh, with handwritten corrections of faded words and page numbers (as the bottom of the pages have been lost in the copying process) and it carries the stamp of ownership of the Buddhist Institute, whose library was ransacked – most probably in 1975 and again in 1979. It is marvellous to be able once again to acquire this valuable piece of documentation of a range of religious, royal and traditional local ceremonies, many of which (such as the water festival and the kite festival) are being revived in Cambodia today. The text, long out of print, is accompanied by simple line-drawings by Srey Chuon, and represents a summary of rites and ceremonies prepared by seven members of the Commission on the Mores and Customs of Cambodia, headed by Eveline Porée-Maspéro.

827 **Cérémonies privées des Cambodgiens.** (Private ceremonies of the Cambodians.)
Commission des Moeurs et Coutumes du Cambodge. Paris: Centre de Documentation et de Recherche sur la Civilisation Khmère, 1985. 81p. bibliog.

One of the major efforts of documentation carried out by the Commission on the Mores and Customs of Cambodia, under the direction of Eveline Porée-Maspéro. The commission based this work not on observation, but on documents submitted to it in response from monks, teachers, officials and peasants living in different parts of the country. Members of the commission then added their own comments and explanations. Customs are organized into ten sections: Fortune and misfortune (including the calendar); Rites and symbols common to many ceremonies; The household; Birth; The cutting of the topknot; Retreat into the shadows (on the onset of menstruation); Ordination; Marriage; Illness; and Death. Simple line-drawings illustrate the text, here republished by Cedoreck.

828 **Costumes et parures khmers d'après les devata d'Angkor-Vat.** (Khmer costumes according to the devata of Angkor Wat.)
Sappho Marchal. Paris, Brussels: Librairie Nationale d'Art et d'Histoire, 1927. 110p.

Describes the folding of cloth, hairstyles and jewellery of the female goddess figures depicted in the bas-reliefs of Angkor Wat, accompanied by simple line-drawings.

829 **The customs of Cambodia.**
Chou Ta-Kuan, translated into English by J. Gilman D'Arcy Paul from the French version by Paul Pelliot of Chou's Chinese original. Bangkok: The Siam Society, 1993. 3rd ed. xx, 77p. A translation of *Chên-la fêng tu chi*.

This famous work is endlessly referred to by historians, writers and scholars on Cambodia as it is one of the few remaining texts contemporary with the 'Age of Angkor'. Chou Ta-Kuan (Zhou Daguan in Pinyin transliteration) was a Chinese diplomat who visited Cambodia in 1296. As an observer of the still-powerful empire under the rule of Indravarman III, Chou made note of diverse aspects of local life from fermented drinks to the three religious groups. The entries are short, and often tell as much of a Chinese official's view of society as of the people he observes. Notes on features such as provincial government, materials used in boat building and housing, products of the country, cooking utensils, behaviour of women etc., make this work potentially valuable to a range of readers. This edition includes photographs, etchings, a map, and a chronology of Khmer art. Unfortunately, Pelliot's valuable commentary was not included in the English edition. A recent presentation in simple language is *Reporting Angkor: Chou Ta-Kuan in Cambodia 1296-1297* by Robert Philpotts (London: Blackwater Books, 1996. 92p. maps. bibliog.).

830 **Étude sur les rites agraires des Cambodgiens.** (Study into the agrarian rites of Cambodians.)
Eveline Porée-Maspéro. Paris: Mouton, 1962-69. 3 vols. (xix, 988p.) maps. bibliog. (Monde d'Outre-Mer, Passé et Présent. Première Série. Études, no. 14).

Noting the paucity of previous studies on the beliefs and practices of the majority of the population, the author sought to elucidate the subject by examining Cambodian texts as well as French accounts of archaeology and religion that treat it in passing. However, she states that the principal sources were in fact the domestic workers in her household, who came from various provinces, which she visited in their presence, and the monks from Wat Tuk Thla, 23 kilometres from Phnom Penh, on the road to Kampot, where she built a house and spent considerable periods of time. In addition, the documentation collected by the Commission des Moeurs et Coutumes de Cambodge (Commission on the Mores and Customs of Cambodia – of which she was the head from 1943-50) were also crucial to the research, which was carried out over many years. An indispensable foundation for any serious study of rural Cambodia, the work has resonances even in today's new urban society. An index is included.

831 **Fêtes et cérémonies royales au Cambodge d'hier.** (Festivals and royal ceremonies in the Cambodia of yesterday.)
Paul Fuchs. Paris: L'Harmattan, 1991. 153p.

A fascinating documentation of the ceremonies performed by members of the royal family prior to 1970. Ironically, when this book was published in 1991 it seemed that most of these rituals had passed away, but many are being revived in the re-established Kingdom of Cambodia.

832 **Mémoires sur les coutumes du Cambodge de Tcheou Ta-Kouan.** (Essays on Cambodian customs by Chou Ta-Kuan.)
Paul Pelliot. Paris: Adrien Maisonneuve, 1997. 178p. bibliog. Published under the auspices of the Académie des inscriptions et belles-lettres with support from the CNRS. (Oeuvres Posthumes de Paul Pelliot, no. 3).

Paul Pelliot's work on Chou Ta-Kuan's manuscript was originally published in 1951. It included not only the translation, which is more widely known, and has since been retranslated into English by J. Gilman D'Arcy Paul (q.v.), but also extensive annotation, which has not yet appeared in English. This edition consists of four parts: The tradition of the text; The *Tch'eng tchai tsa ki*; The transcriptions of Cambodian words in the text; and The interpretation of the text. This final part of the manuscript was left incomplete by Pelliot in 1924, and has been edited in this publication to give some slight clarifications and additions to the original.

833 **Popil: objet rituel cambodgien.** (Popil: a ritual Cambodian object.)
Solange Thierry. Paris: Centre de Documentation et de Recherche sur la Civilisation Khmère, 1984. 128p. Published with the support of the UNESCO International Fund for the Promotion of Culture/Fonds International pour la Promotion de la Culture de l'UNESCO. Title also appears in Khmer. (Bibliothèque Khmère: Série A: Textes et Documents, no. 2).

Except for royal ceremonies, Khmer religious rituals are relatively devoid of sacred objects. However, the popil, a kind of candle-holder, is commonly used and appears to have precise meaning in different ceremonies. Thierry discusses the collection of popil at the Musée de l'Homme (Museum of Man), Paris, looking at: their manufacture and transmission; the written and oral tradition concerning popils; their ritual function, in which ceremonies they are used, when and by whom; and descriptions of popils: their materials, form and decoration. The work includes an appendix depicting different popils, their decorations and their design. It is a useful text for serious students of Khmer culture and religious practices.

834 **A taste of Indochina.**
Jan Castorina and Dimitra Stais. Sydney: Hodder & Stoughton, 1995. 160p.

Compiled by two food writers, formerly of the *Australian Womens' Weekly*, this cookbook is attractively presented and easy to use. It opens with descriptions of the basic ingredients used in the recipes and instructions on how to make your own curry pastes and condiments. The recipes are divided into types of dishes, rather than into the regions they originate from, and in fact, no origins are given. More 'Indochina-inspired' than authentic, many recipes are 'hybrids', such as 'Thai pesto' and 'cinnamon sausage baguette'. The majority of dishes are meat-based, although some good tofu and vegetable dishes are included. The recipes are presented with a pure delight in the flavours and ingredients but without any attempt to understand, or educate the cook about the culture from which they come.

835 **Vie quotidienne dans la péninsule indochinoise à l'époque d'Angkor (800-1300).** (Everyday life in the Indochinese peninsula in the Angkor period, 800-1300.)
Louis Frédéric. [Paris]: Hachette, 1981. 414p. map. bibliog.

For the general French reader, Louis Frédéric, who has written widely on Asian, particularly Indian, culture and religion, here reconstructs daily life in Indochina (including Burma) during the Angkor period. The initial introductory chapters are given general references to the principal sources rather than specific annotation to the wide range of French and English scholarly writings referred to in the later chapters, which cover aspects such as political ideology and government, economy and commerce, everyday life, the king and soldiers, and spiritual and religious life. The book is written in a very readable easy style.

The calling of the souls: a study of the Khmer ritual Hau Bralin.
See item no. 403.

The ritual space of patients and traditional healers.
See item no. 447.

First International Scholars Çonference on Cambodia: selected papers.
See item no. 782.

Libraries and Books, Art Galleries, Museums and Archives

836 **Archives in Cambodia: neglected institutions.**
Peter Arfanis and Helen Jarvis. *Archives and Manuscripts*, vol. 21, no. 2 (1993), p. 253-62.

The authors are both Australians who have worked to help restore the information infrastructure of Cambodia in the 1990s – Peter Arfanis in the National Archives (for which he was awarded a gold medal by the Cambodian government in 1997) and Helen Jarvis in the National Library. Here they discuss: The importance of archives in developing countries; History of the Library and Archives; The National Archives today; and What can be done?

837 **Book sector study of Cambodia: final summary report.**
Paul Eastman and Tony Read. London: International Book Development Ltd.; Ottawa: CODE (Canadian Organization for Development through Education), 1992. 150, [3]p. bibliog.

An unusual work in its focus on the printing and publishing sector, including paper and raw materials, manufacturing and distribution.

838 **Catalogue of Library Holdings.**
Phnom Penh: Cambodia Development Resource Institute (CDRI), Documentation and Information Resource Center, 1993- . irregular.

CDRI is one of the major research and documentation institutes in Cambodia, with an emphasis on issues of development and management. This catalogue has been produced from a database developed using the UNESCO database CDS/ISIS.

839 **Le cinquantenaire de l'ÉFEO: compte rendu des fêtes et cérémonies.** (The fiftieth anniversary of the EFEO: report of the festivals and ceremonies.)
Louis Malleret. Paris: École Française d'Extrême-Orient, 1953. 176p. (École Française d'Extrême-Orient. Hors Série).

This anniversary volume provides important documentation of the work of EFEO in its colonial heyday. Its activities in Cambodia began in 1900 with the inventory of monuments carried out by Lunet de Lajonquière and Aymonier (qq.v.). In 1901 a permanent institution was established followed by the Commission of Antiquities in 1905. With the 1907 return from Thai control to Cambodia of the three western provinces including Angkor, the EFEO's activities blossomed, with 780 monuments and 1,000 inscriptions noted within the Angkor Park established in 1908. A documentation centre was built up with a considerable collection of books, rubbings, manuscripts, photographs and artefacts to complement the Museum's collection. Chapter two describes the celebrations in Cambodia, held on 15 November 1951, and announces the formation of the quadripartite commission established to determine ownership of the valuable holdings and assets of EFEO in the various parts of Indochina, as the inevitable French departure was realized and decisions were made as to what to hand over to Cambodian control, and what to take back to France.

840 **Directory of libraries & documentation centres in Cambodia.**
Prepared by the Information Resources Sectoral Group. Phnom Penh: Cooperation Committee for Cambodia; Cambodia Development Resources Institute, 1993- . annual.

Prepared by the Information Resources Sectoral Group, an informal forum for the exchange of information and expertise among people working in libraries and documentation centres, both governmental, inter-governmental and non-governmental, formed under the inspiration of Rosemary Harbridge, an 'Australian Volunteer Abroad' working at the Cooperation Committee for Cambodia (CCC). Some forty-five agencies are listed, almost double the number reported in the first (1993) edition. The work has been published in both Khmer and English editions.

841 **Études indochinoises.** (Indochinese studies.)
George Coedès. *Bulletin de la Société des Études Indochinoises*, NS, vol. 26, no. 4 (1951), p. 437-62.

An established orientalist renders homage to the work of the École Française d'Extrême-Orient (EFEO – French School of Far Eastern Studies) relating to Indochina, from its foundation in 1901. Besides providing a capsule history of a significant colonial institution, this essay conveys some of the atmosphere of French approaches to the Vietnamese, Khmer, Lao and Cham, especially their pre-colonial past, just at the time when France was losing its grip. [David G. Marr with Kristine Alilunas-Rodgers]

842 **The National Library of Cambodia: surviving seventy years.**
Helen Jarvis. *Libraries and Culture*, vol. 30, no. 4 (Fall 1995), p. 391-408.

Written to mark the seventieth anniversary of the National Library of Cambodia, established together with the National Archives in 1922, the article describes the collections, the staffing and the buildings over the period. Archival documents in France, Vietnam and Phnom Penh, as well as interviews and questionnaires with present and former staff were employed in this study. Of particular significance are the appointment of the first Cambodian director, Pach Chhoeun, in 1945 by the Japanese administration, and the fate of the library under the Khmer Rouge, when its grounds were used to keep pigs and its shelves to house cooking and eating utensils.

Education in Cambodia notes and suggestions.
See item no. 667.

Mass Media

843 **The 1994 media guide.**

Editorial work by Nicole O'Brien and Jacqui Park, with assistance and translation by So Naro, Khem Verak and Tharry. Phnom Penh: Khmer Journalists Association, 1994. 60p.

Published with the assistance of AusAID, the aid organization of the Australian government. A valuable update of the work done in the early 1990s by Susan Aitkin, this is a bilingual publication containing background information on the Cambodian media organizations. Details of various media in Cambodia, both local and foreign, are provided, including personal names, addresses, circulation, frequency of publication and a brief description for some. There is a section providing details about the Khmer Journalists Association (KJA) itself, established in December 1993. Although widely regarded as the first such body, there was in existence a journalists' association under the PRK and SOC, and several alternative associations have subsequently been established. KJA joined the International Federation of Journalists (IFJ) in April 1994.

844 **Hollywood on the Mekong: life with video.**

John Eli Shapiro. *Film Comment*, no. 28 (Sep./Oct. 1992), p. 2-6.

A valuable description of the vibrant film and video scene in Cambodia in the early 1990s. The first Cambodian Film and Video Festival, held in November 1990, revealed some 157 production companies had been established. Shapiro, a US film-maker and writer, describes the production routines on minimal budgets (around US$2-3,000 for a 2-hour feature video, or around US$15,000 for a feature film), and the editing at the Ministry of Culture's Film Department. Interviews are included with film-makers Meng C. Muong and Haim Ivong.

845 **IMMF Dispatch.**

Bangkok: Indochina Media Memorial Foundation, 1995- . quarterly.

The Indochina Media Memorial Foundation (IMMF) was established to honour the memory of all those journalists killed in Indochina by fostering and nurturing the profession in Vietnam, Cambodia, Laos and Thailand. It solicits donations from organizations and individuals, runs training programmes and tries to arrange fellowships and exchanges. Denis Gray and Dominic Faulder are the co-presidents, with Ruth Gerson in 1996 becoming editor of the *Dispatch*, the newsletter of the IMMF. Annual subscription costs US$25.00 (at the time of writing) from IMMF, Room 503 Panavongs Building, 104 Suriwong Road, Bangkok 10500, Thailand.

846 **Radio UNTAC of Cambodia: winning ears, hearts and minds.**
Zhou Mei. Bangkok: White Lotus, 1994. 129p.

The author, a Singaporean journalist, was from October 1992 to September 1993, as Deputy Director of the Division of Information and Education of UNTAC, in charge of dissemination of information, most especially Radio UNTAC. The blurb states: 'this book offers an away from the microphone account of "mission" work; in the process it records a country in transition as Cambodians defied the bullets and reached for peace via the ballots'. It is unfortunate that the author decided to devote so much of her text to petty personal snippets and in-jokes, so that the record of this unusual exercise is rather lost in one large gossip column. From 9 November 1992 to 22 September 1993 Radio UNTAC broadcast on MW 918 kHz, through a transmitter and mast made available by the State of Cambodia. From mid-1992 to mid-1993 a second channel, on the Voice of America frequency, was rented at US$610 per hour from the US Information Agency in Thailand. Some 350,000 radios were donated from Japan and distributed in all provinces except Phnom Penh by UNTAC soldiers. Radio UNTAC's studio complex cost over US$3 million and consisted of six state-of-the-art studios installed in rented premises occupied only seven weeks before the election, and some of the equipment was never even used before the complex was dismantled four months later, when the UNTAC operation came to an end.

The war against free speech: letter from Human Rights Watch and the new Cambodian Press Law.
See item no. 521.

Kampuchea.
See item no. 733.

Literature and society in modern Cambodia.
See item no. 735.

Periodicals and News Sources

847 **Agence Khmère de Presse.** (Khmer Press Agency.)
Phnom Penh: Agence Khmère de Presse, 1993- . daily. Title in Khmer and French; text in English. Also issued in Khmer and French.

A daily stencilled publication in three languages (Khmer, English and French) carrying government press statements and official reports. The AKP is attached to the Ministry of Information. Since 1993 the former name has been revived, but during the PRK period it was known as SPK (*Sapordamean Kampuchea*).

848 **Australian Cambodian Quarterly.**
Sydney: Australian Cambodian Support Committee, 1987- . quarterly.

A support group of representatives from various Australian trade unions and other NGOs involved in providing aid to Cambodia met regularly and produced this compilation of news articles and reports as part of their campaign around three objectives: to restore aid to Cambodia; to recognize the People's Republic of Kampuchea as the government of Cambodia; and to bring the Khmer Rouge to justice for their crimes against humanity. Until 1989 it was known as the *Australia Kampuchea Quarterly.*

849 **Bulletin/FUNCINPEC ANS.**
Bangkok: Office of the Personal Representative of HRH Prince Norodom Sihanouk, President of FUNCINPEC and Supreme Commander of the ANS, 1984- . irregular.

Editorial, chronology, FUNCINPEC and ANS (Sihanoukist National Army), news in brief, intelligence report and document sections comprise each issue. Issues are numbered monthly, but normally published bi-monthly. The publication continued after 1991 from Phnom Penh. A related publication is a newsletter released from the King's office in Beijing containing his comments on events unfolding in 'his kingdom'.

850 **Bulletin de l'École Française d'Extrême-Orient.** (Bulletin of the French School of Far Eastern Studies.)
École Française d'Extrême-Orient. Hanoi, Saigon, Paris: École Française d'Extrême-Orient, 1901-11. quarterly; 1912- . irregular.

Together with the EFEO's series of publications the *BEFEO* forms an essential tool for those wishing to study Cambodia in any depth. In the *Bulletin* the many French scholars working on, and in, Indochina published most of their initial findings, and reports were made of the programmes and activities of the EFEO. It is still published, although appearing more infrequently than it did in the heyday of French colonial scholarship. Indexes appear in *BEFEO* nos. 21 (1921), 32 (1932) and in the fiftieth anniversary special issue (1953).

851 **Bulletin de la Société des Études Indochinoises.** (Bulletin of the Society of Indochinese Studies.)
Saigon: Société des Études Indochinoises, 1883-1923; 1926-75?. quarterly.

The *Bulletin of the Society of Indochinese Studies* (Saigon) represented the aspirations of French scholars and their native protégés to master the history and geography of the countries of the Indochina Union, although it was compelled to take second place to the *Bulletin de l'École Française d'Extrême-Orient* (q.v.) from 1901. Indexes were published in 1933, 1952, 1958 and 1962. [David G. Marr with Kristine Alilunas-Rodgers]

852 **Bulletin of Concerned Asian Scholars.**
Boulder, Colorado: BCAS, 1968- . quarterly.

Published initially by the Committee for Concerned Asian Scholars, with the statement: 'We first came together in opposition to the brutal aggression of the United States in Vietnam and to the complicity or silence of our profession with regard to that policy. Those in the field of Asian studies bear responsibility for the consequences of their research and the political posture of their profession. We are concerned about the present unwillingness of specialists to speak out against the implications of an Asian policy committed to ensuring American domination of much of Asia . . .'. Later continuing as an independent refereed journal, *BCAS* has for thirty years provided a forum for scholarly analysis and debate. The developments in postwar Indochina, particularly in Cambodia under the Khmer Rouge, and the later intervention of Vietnam in Cambodia, provided perhaps the greatest issue of contention and polemic among colleagues who had previously been in agreement. Volume 21, nos. 2-4 (1989) provides a review of 'BCAS past and present' as well as being a 'Special twentieth anniversary issue on Indochina and the War'.

853 **Cambodge Soir.** (Evening Cambodia.)
Phnom Penh: Cambodge Soir, 1995- . 3 issues per week.

Appearing three times a week since 8 May 1995, this publication provides for the French-speaking public in Phnom Penh a cross between daily news and analysis.

854 **Cambodia Daily.**

Phnom Penh: Cambodia Daily, 1993- . 5 issues per week.

A small (A4-sized) newspaper filling a real gap for English speakers in Phnom Penh, providing news and notices of events around town, previously gained from word of mouth or from notice boards at the Cooperation Committee for Cambodia. Photographs, hard news stories and analysis as well as advertisements also manage to get packed into its few pages, along with Khmer- and Japanese-language versions of the main stories. It is edited by Bernard Krisher, an American journalist who has visited Cambodia many times since the 1960s, and who developed a close relationship with Sihanouk, including helping to write and edit some of his works. Support is given by Japan Relief for Cambodia and American Assistance for Cambodia, and news is provided free of charge from a number of agencies. The first issue was dated 20 August 1993, but the volume number changes every 100 issues, so that Monday 31 March 1997 is described as Volume 10, Issue 1. Subscriptions are available from The Cambodia Daily, 50B Street 240, Phnom Penh, Cambodia (US$100 per year plus postage at the time of writing).

855 **The Cambodia Times.**

Phnom Penh: Cambodia Times, 1992- . weekly. Also issued in Khmer.

One of the first English-language newspapers to be published in postwar Cambodia, it appeared in July 1992 within days of the *Phnom Penh Post* (q.v.). The *Cambodia Times* is printed in Malaysia and published by a Malaysian company. It has tended to take a relatively pro-CPP position, particularly in the 1993 election campaign. Its Khmer-language counterpart was printed in Phnom Penh on modern equipment supplied from Malaysia. See *Cambodia Times on the Net* (q.v.) for the Internet version.

856 **The CICP Newsletter.**

Phnom Penh: Cambodian Institute for Cooperation and Peace, 1994- . monthly.

A monthly newsletter consisting largely of summaries of addresses on topics related to security, foreign policy and development. It is a valuable record of CICP's activities and of the thinking of prominent Cambodian and visiting foreign politicians, academics and other experts. CICP is a newly established think-tank with close links to the government, promoting the integration of Cambodia into ASEAN. Its director is Kao Kim Hourn.

857 **Daily Report: East Asia.**

Washington, DC: Foreign Broadcast Information Service, 1988- .

An invaluable contemporary source for original foreign-language newspaper and radio broadcasts. It is a publication of the Foreign Broadcast Information Service which collects, translates, disseminates and analyses foreign open-source information on behalf of the US government.

858 **Indochina Chronicle.**

Edited by Keith Ervin, Christopher Jenkins (et al.). Washington, DC; Berkeley, California: Indochina Resource Center, 1971-77. fortnightly, then irregular.

Beginning in July 1971 as a fortnightly compilation of article reprints, translations of documents and trip reports, the *Indochina Chronicle* from no. 15 (1 May 1972) tended to concentrate on one topic per issue, for example heroin traffic, political prisoners, the Paris peace negotiations, refugees, postwar reconstruction, and attempts at diplomatic normalization. About three-quarters of total coverage deals with Vietnam, the remainder with Cambodia and Laos. The viewpoint is consistently critical of US government policy and performance. Fifty-five issues appeared until March 1977, when the publication was renamed *Southeast Asia Chronicle* and coverage expanded accordingly. [David G. Marr with Kristine Alilunas-Rodgers]

859 **Indochina Chronology.**

Berkeley, California: Institute of East Asian Studies, University of California, 1982- . quarterly.

Designed as a research tool, teaching aid and reliable information source on current developments in Vietnam, Cambodia and Laos, a bibliographical source of book and periodical materials, and a news source of academic activity in the field. Accordingly, the publication is divided into areas, country chronologies, bibliography (including official statements and periodicals), conferences, names in the news etc. Every issue has a country chronology, so Cambodia is always featured even if that issue does not carry longer articles focusing on Cambodia. The chronologies record such events as the granting of loans, passing of laws and agricultural or natural disaster. Editor Douglas Pike has performed a valuable and mammoth task in keeping this publication going for so many years, and in building up the associated archive.

860 **Indochina Issues.**

Edited by the staff of the Indochina Project. Washington, DC: Indochina Project, 1979-Aug. 1991. quarterly.

Funded by a grant from the Christopher Reynolds Foundation, the board of advisors has included figures such as the Mayor of Minneapolis, the Chairman of the International Commission of Jurists, and Members of Congress. It has frequent, in-depth coverage of Cambodian issues, namely conflict, politics, the humanitarian situation, international negotiations on the withdrawal of Vietnamese troops from Cambodia and the balances of power behind the personal news stories. It is a good source of news analysis and opinion, with Gareth Porter and Elizabeth Becker (qq.v.) among its regular contributors.

861 **Kambuja: Monthly Illustrated Review.**

Phnom Penh: [s.n], 1965-[70?]. monthly.

A large, glossy, coffee-table style magazine of a bygone era. It captures the pretty face of Sihanouk's time, which many older Cambodians from the élite or even middle classes recall as a golden age of wealth, stability, social services and infrastructure development. The layout is organized by Events of the month, e.g. Audience with Her Majesty the Queen, Visit by Sir Malcolm MacDonald. Most of the coverage is of *Samdech Preah* (Prince) Sihanouk opening public buildings, national congresses and train lines. News events are presented somewhat like fashion shows, with many photographs and few words. Some fairly biting political cartoons and the occasional report of US bombing or the surrender of a Khmer Rouge rebel, suggest the underlying turbulence of the time. Leading figures in the social, political and humanitarian community of Cambodia appear frequently, adding to the magazine's value as a historical resource.

862 **Kampuchea Démocratique Bulletin d'Information.** (Democratic Kampuchea News Bulletin.)
Beijing: L'Ambassade du Kampuchea Démocratique, 1979- .
Description based on: no. 50-80 (Sept. 1980); title from caption.
Available on microfilm, [s.l.: s.n.]. 35 mm. Some issues have title in English: *Democratic Kampuchea News Bulletin.*

Comprises press releases by the Khmer Rouge government in exile in Beijing, particularly focusing on alleged attacks by the Vietnamese on government forces.

863 **Kampuchea Suriya.** (Shining Cambodia.)
Phnom Penh: Buddhist Institute, 1927-1948.

This Khmer-language journal had a profound impact in establishing the Cambodian literary canon of texts, printing for the first time for public distribution, reading and study a range of religious and secular, classical, folk and modern texts, formerly available only within the religious and palace institutions. It is currently being reprinted in Cambodia, with assistance from Japan.

864 **Péninsule: Études Interdisciplinaires sur l'Asie de Sud-Est Péninsulaire.** (Peninsula: Interdisciplinary Studies on the Southeast Asian Peninsula.)
Paris: Cercle de Culture et de Recherches Laotiennes, 1980- . irregular.

Although published by an association with a Laotian focus, this publication venture has Jacques Népote (q.v.) as its director, and includes some of his own and other writings that have a regional or even specifically Cambodian perspective. Book reviews complement scholarly articles in some issues, while others are composed of a single text.

865 **Phnom Penh Post.**
Phnom Penh: Michael Hayes, 10 July 1992- . fortnightly.

Proclaimed as independent and the first English-language newspaper in Cambodia since the war (though appearing within a few days of *The Cambodia Times* which also claims to be the first). Publisher Michael Hayes (a US citizen living in Phnom Penh) has managed to publish a widely read and respected paper. Although irregular to start, it has been on a consistent fortnightly schedule since and has included some colour photographs. A vigorous letters page and an editorial policy that allows exchange of opinion in articles contributes to its appeal, and it has a wide international circulation. Each issue has a centrefold street map and contains classified advertisements including job vacancies. At the time of writing, international subscriptions are US$120 per 26 issues (1 year) from Phnom Penh Post Publishing Ltd., PO Box 12-1074, Soi Suan Phlu Post Office, 10121 Bangkok, Thailand. E-mail address pppost@worldmail.com.kh[.] An Internet version is also available – *Phnom Penh Post [online]* (q.v.).

866 **La Revue Indochinoise.** (The Indochinese Review.)
Hanoi: F.-H. Schneider, 1893-1925.

Hill in his *Index indochinensis* (q.v.) notes that the *Revue Indochinoise*, published as it was by an individual (F.-H. Schneider) had a more wide-ranging and eclectic character than the journals published by semi-official societies, much less by government bodies. It was founded in August 1893 and published until 1925, under variations of the title and various series.

867 **Sangkum: Revue Politique Illustrée.** (Sangkum: Illustrated Political Review.)
[Phnom Penh]: Norodom Sihanouk, 1965-70. monthly.

With the director being Norodom Sihanouk himself, this is a positive, if not self-congratulatory journal reporting the achievements of his government. The issues contain editorial opinion, reports of development projects, letters from the people with his replies, humour and political reports.

868 **Seksa Khmer.** (Khmer Studies.)
Paris: CEDORECK, 1980- . annual. Title also in Cambodian.

An academic journal in Cambodian, English and French, with a variety of articles on linguistics, religion, traditional medicine etc. Together with reprinting Cambodian texts and books on Cambodia in French, this journal was another important initiative of CEDORECK, directed by Nouth Narang, who returned to Cambodia from France after the 1991 Paris Agreements to become Minister of Culture and Fine Arts.

869 **Sereika: la Voix du Cambodge Libre.** (Sereika: Voice of Free Cambodia.)
Cormeilles-en-Parisis, France: Sereika, 1976- . monthly. Imprint varies: Sucy-en-Brie, France until September 1984; Paris, October 1984- . French and Khmer.

Sam Rainsy, notable in Cambodian politics in the 1990s as Minister of Finance and founder of the Khmer Nation Party, previously produced, from France, this magazine of the resistance, containing reports from refugees as to the nature of the Khmer Rouge régime, news items such as border incidents, and international communications between the DK government and foreign states.

870 **Southeast Asian Affairs.**
Singapore: Institute of Southeast Asian Studies, 1974- . annual.

This annual publication from ISEAS contains essays on 'The region' and on individual countries, either review and comment on major developments in the year under review (the year prior to that given in the title), or on topical problems of concern, by a range of scholars and specialists, some who have held visiting fellowships with ISEAS. Regrettably without indexes, but generally well annotated, these annual reviews provide a good starting-point for research into contemporary politics of Southeast Asia, Cambodia included. The 1996 issue, for example, carries two articles on Cambodia: 'Cambodia: a year of consolidation' by Harish Mehta; and 'Cambodia's post-cold war dilemma: democratization, armed conflict and authoritarianism' by Sorpong Peou.

871 **Summary of world broadcasts: Part 3 – Asia-Pacific.**
Reading, England: BBC Monitoring, 1993- . daily.

A daily account of material monitored from foreign media, providing an invaluable contemporary account of events as they happen. Some transcripts or translations of print reports are published verbatim, while others are highlights or summaries of items. It is also available in full or in sections online in machine-readable form and through a closed user group on the Internet via File Transfer Protocol (FTP).

872 **Transdex Index.**
United States Joint Publications Research Service. Ann Arbor, Michigan: University Microfilms International, 1975- . monthly.

This is a monthly cumulation of translations by the Joint Publications Research Service, from materials originally published outside the United States, including Cambodia. Material covered includes serials, broadcasts and speeches. Each issue contains: a series index; a publications index (of all titles included in the current issue); a key-word frequency list; a key-word index to significant words in titles: and a personal name index (author or subject). UM Transdex order numbers are also included. An annual cumulative index is available on microfiche. *Transdex Index* continues *Transdex: Bibliography and Index to the United States Joint Publications Research Service (JPRS) Translations*, which in turn absorbed *Bibliography-Index to Current US JPRS Publications. China & Asia (Exclusive of Near East).* Other items of interest in the Transdex series are *East Asia: Southeast Asia* (Arlington, Virginia: Joint Publications Research Service and Foreign Broadcast Information Service, 1987- . [JPRS Report]. irregular) and *Daily Report, East Asia* (q.v.).

Annales: Université Royale des Beaux-arts. (Annals: Royal University of Fine Arts.)
See item no. 122.

Réalités Cambodgiennes. (Cambodian Realities.)
See item no. 222.

News From Kampuchea: Journal of the Committee of Patriots of Democratic Kampuchea.
See item no. 273.

Cahiers d'Études Franco-Cambodgiens. (Franco-Cambodian Studies.)
See item no. 373.

Mon-Khmer Studies: a Journal of Southeast Asian Languages.
See item no. 394.

Bulletin Administratif au Cambodge. (Administrative Bulletin of Cambodia.)
See item no. 452.

Journal Officiel de l'Indo-Chine Française. (Official Journal of French Indochina.)
See item no. 464.

Annuaire Statistique du Cambodge. (Statistical Annual of Cambodia.)
See item no. 648.

Statistical Yearbook for Asia and the Pacific/Annuaire Statistique pour l'Asie et le Pacifique.
See item no. 652.

Arts et Archéologie Khmers: Revue des Recherches sur les Arts, les Monuments et l'Ethnographie du Cambodge, Depuis les Origines Jusqu'à nos Jours. (Khmer Art and Archaeology: Research on the Arts, Monuments and Ethnography of Cambodia, From the Beginning Until Our Day.)
See item no. 763.

Culture Khmère. (Khmer Culture.)
See item no. 775.

Renaissance Culturelle du Cambodge. (Cultural Renaissance of Cambodia.)
See item no. 811.

IMMF Dispatch.
See item no. 845.

Encyclopaedias, Directories and Reference Works

873 **Cambodia: a country study.**
Edited by Russell R. Ross. Washington, DC: Federal Research Division, Library of Congress, 1990. 3rd ed. xxxvi, 362p. maps. bibliog. Research completed December 1987. (DA Pam Area Handbook Series, 550-50).

A most useful and comprehensive reference book on Cambodia, compiled by a team under the auspices of the Library of Congress, and relatively recent (though unfortunately it has not been updated since 1987 (the imprint date of the first edition) even though this is called the third edition. Lengthy chapters by named authors, few of whom are recognized scholars in their field, provide a more interesting view than the usual anonymous handbook, but show the bias expected for a book prepared for the United States Army. Comprehensive bibliographies for each chapter, a thorough (eighteen-page) index and extensive tables, figures, maps and photographs make this a useful first port of call for information or research on Cambodia, though many important areas (such as culture and art) are omitted or treated only in passing. Chapters include: 'Historical setting' by Donald M. Seekins; 'The society and its environment' by Robert K. Headley Jr.; 'The economy' by Tuyet L. Cosslett; 'Government and policy' by Rinn-Sup Shinn; and 'National security' by Frank Tatu. This title is also available for access through the Internet at the World Wide Web site of the Library of Congress – http://1cweb2.loc.gov/frd/cs/cbtoc.html.

874 **The catalog and guide book of Southeast Asian coins and currency. Volume I: France.**
Howard A. Daniel, III. Portage, Ohio; Camden, South Carolina: BNR Press, 1978. 2nd ed. 140p.

This well-organized volume focuses on French colonial coins and paper money issued in Indochina, and by banks in Thailand with authorization to issue notes up to 1954. It also contains a section on tokens containing French language or denomination which circulated in Southeast Asia. While not all of the photographs are clear, students of colonial iconography, in addition to the numismatic community, will find this presentation of interest. [David G. Marr with Kristine Alilunas-Rodgers]

875 **Les clés du Cambodge.** (The keys to Cambodia.)
Raoul M. Jennar. Paris: Maisonneuve & Larose, 1995. 328p. maps. bibliog.

An enormously valuable contribution – really the only up-to-date reference tool on Cambodia of any substance. Jennar has expanded beyond his usual area of commentary but applies his familiar enthusiasm and depth of understanding. The volume is divided into several parts: facts and figures, including pen pictures of the Royal House and the Khmer Rouge; historical mileposts, adding to a comprehensive chronology since 1835, results of all the elections, including lists of elected delegates and government ministers; Cambodian profiles, with brief biographical sketches of over 450 contemporary figures; and a bibliography of over 1,100 titles, with particular strength in contemporary history and politics. Jennar states his reasons for compiling this text as: 'providing less superficial access for foreigners to Cambodia and Cambodians'; to repatriate historical sources and information, which form the ballast for an organized society and state, so that Cambodians may begin to reappropriate their destiny; and 'to offer to Cambodians the means for a true debate on their future . . . and so it contains facts and raw information that Cambodians may interpret in their own way'. In so doing he has added valuable ballast to his own work on Cambodia, which before 1995 (with the publication of this book and his compilation of the constitutions of Cambodia since 1953) had concentrated on interpretation of events as they were taking place rather than the more considered reflection we see here. It is to be hoped that an English edition will be published.

876 **Dictionary of the modern politics of South-East Asia.**
Michael Leifer. London: Routledge, 1995. 271p.

This new title does not quite meet the bill printed on its cover – 'The essential companion for the traveller in Asia' – but it does most adequately fulfil what the title claims to provide. Cambodia accounts for some forty-seven entries, from the Brevié Line (marking the sea boundary between Cambodia and Vietnam) to the Vietnam War, and includes entries on major political figures, parties, and events and incidents. A list of 'Further reading' is provided, with ten titles recommended for Cambodia. It is a well laid-out ready reference tool on modern politics in the region.

877 **Encyclopedia of Asian history.**
Editor in chief, Ainslie T. Embree. New York: Charles Scribner's Sons; London: Collier Macmillan, 1988. 4 vols.

The main entry on Cambodia amounts to less than three pages of text, by David Chandler (q.v.). The other major section is a series of entries on Angkor, by Ian Mabbett (q.v.). The index points to some ten other entry points, though not all that relate to Cambodia are shown here. Some undistinguished photographs, maps and tables accompany the text.

878 **Gazetteer of Cambodia.**
Prepared by Geographic Department of the Council of Ministers. Phnom Penh: Geographic Department of the Council of Ministers, 1994. Provisional Release. 3 vols. map.

One of the handful of valuable new reference materials to be published in Cambodia, updating the most recent gazetteer, *Cambodia: official standard names approved by the United States Board on Geographic Names* (Washington, DC: Geographic Names Division, US Army Topographical Command, 1971. xi, 392p.). It contains the names of villages, arranged by subdistrict, district and province. Names are in Khmer script and in transliterated form (using the US Board of Geographic Names romanization system, which unfortunately uses rather non-familiar names, relying as it does on an extensive use of diacritic marks to enable reverse transliteration). Latitude and longitude are given as well as a systematic code for each village. The gazetteer was produced from a survey carried out in 1992-93 by the cartographic team of UNTAC which listed some 12,000 villages but gave only a non-standard English rendition of the name and no geographic co-ordinates. Accordingly, considerable follow-up work was required to gather the information for this gazetteer, and field studies were carried out in all provinces except Preah Vihear and Mondulkiri due to transport and security problems. Funded by the United Nations Fund for Population Activities (UNFPA), the gazetteer is published in both hard-copy and machine-readable form. It is available from Geographic department, No. 4, Street 65, Sangkat Srah Chak, Khand Don Penh, Phnom Penh, Cambodia.

879 **A guide to reference materials on Southeast Asia.**
Donald Clay Johnson. New Haven, Connecticut: Yale University Press, 1970. 160p.

This work contains only sixteen entries for Cambodia plus others on Indochina.

880 **Major political events in Indo-China 1945-1990.**
D. J. Sagar. Oxford; New York: Facts on File, 1991. 230p. maps. bibliog.

This work is mainly composed of a detailed chronology of the more significant military, political and economic events concerning Cambodia, Laos and Vietnam from 1945 to 1990, together with brief biographies of leading figures involved, and appendices of tables, relevant documents and extended notes. A small glossary and brief bibliography are also included. There is little attempt by the author to make an analysis of events, except in a brief eighteen-page introduction which doubles as a preface and overview of the chronology. Some readers will therefore find the book unsatisfying, but its direct and straightforward style make it a useful reference, especially suited for undergraduates and senior secondary students.

881 **Stanley Gibbons stamp catalogue: Part 21. Southeast Asia.**
London: Stanley Gibbons Publications Ltd, 1985. 260p.

This popular catalogue of the world's stamps has some thirty-six pages devoted to Cambodia, listing 1,419 stamps issued from 1951 to 1994. Those issued previously are recorded under Part 6, France. As well as giving the exact date of issue, denomination, title, colour, size and price per sheet, the catalogue has black-and-white reproductions of most series. Short paragraphs of the historical and administrative background set the stage for each period, and subjects selected for stamps themselves provide an

1975 were printed at the Government Printing Office in Paris. No stamps were issued during the Democratic Kampuchea period, as there were neither currency nor postal services under Khmer Rouge rule. From August 1979 to June 1981 some stamps from earlier periods were overprinted 'PRK', but seem not to have been actually used for postal use. In early 1980 the riel was reintroduced as the equivalent of one kilogram of rice, and on 10 April several stamps were issued (probably printed in Moscow), and rudimentary postal services were resumed, although even in 1997 these are still slow, sporadic and unreliable. From 1982 most Cambodian stamps were printed in Havana, Cuba, though some were produced at the Litho State Printing Works in Moscow.

882 **Your guide to the United Nations in Cambodia.**
Phnom Penh: Cambodia Communications Institute, [1995?]. 61p.

Published in commemoration of the fiftieth anniversary of the United Nations, principally for Cambodians to understand the role of the various UN agencies working in Cambodia. It is a directory of their officers, addresses and activities, and was developed as a training exercise in the early days of Cambodia Communications Institute, a project of the Royal Government of Cambodia and UNESCO's International Programme for the Development of Communication.

Cambodia, the reemergence of new opportunities: business and investment handbook.
See item no. 587.

Directory of humanitarian assistance in Cambodia.
See item no. 636.

Guide du Musée National de Phnom-Penh. (Guide to the National Museum of Phnom Penh.)
See item no. 784.

Directory of libraries & documentation centres in Cambodia.
See item no. 840.

The 1994 media guide.
See item no. 843.

Asia: a selected and annotated guide to reference works.
See item no. 883.

Bibliographies

883 **Asia: a selected and annotated guide to reference works.**
G. Raymond Nunn. Cambridge, Massachusetts; London: M. I. T. Press, 1971. 233p.

The fact that Nunn manages to find only eight titles to list for Cambodia in his total of 975 reference books listed indicates the paucity of works published up until 1971.

884 **Bibliographie critique des oeuvres parues sur l'Indochine française: un siècle d'histoire et d'enseignement.** (Critical bibliography of works on French Indochina: a century of history and teaching.)
Robert Auvade. Paris: Maisonneuve & Larose, 1965. 153p.

This volume has two distinct parts: the first is concerned with the establishment of archives and libraries in Indochina, providing commentary on principal sources and bibliographies; while the second is a critical selection of works concerning education and scholarship, as well as literary and scientific institutions and endeavours. Some items are accompanied by listings of their location in Parisian libraries. The main bibliography is followed by a listing of complementary sources without annotation, and a classified index where the 230 titles (of which 150 have been analysed) are grouped under 13 headings.

885 **Bibliographie de l'Indochine française, 1913-1935.** (Bibliography of French Indochina, 1913-35.)
Paul Boudet, Rémy Bourgeois. Paris: Maisonneuve, 1967. 4 vols. in 5. Originally published, Hanoi: Imprimerie d'Extrême-Orient, 1929-43.

This series of volumes forms one of the most valuable bibliographic aids to study of Indochina. Boudet (Director of Archives and Libraries for French Indochina), ably assisted by Bourgeois, followed on from the pioneering work of Cordier (q.v.), preparing volumes for 1913-26, 1927-29 and then 1930, and 1931-35. Part I (271p.) lists publications alphabetically by subjects – from 'Abrasin' to 'Zootechnie', and brief annotations sometimes accompany the core bibliographical information. Part II

(75p.) provides an alphabetical index of authors as well as of titles of anonymously written works. Articles have been culled from approximately sixty periodicals from 1912 to 1926, with the thirty most frequently cited ones listed (p. vi-vii). Volume 2 (*1927-1929*, Hanoi, 1931, 240p.), which includes references from over eighty periodicals and publications from years prior to 1929, and Volume 3 (*1930*, Hanoi, 1933, 196p.) follow similar formats, with some modifications. Volume 4 was published in two separate volumes: *1931-1935* (published by Boudet and Bourgeois under the auspices of the Gouvernement Général de l'Indochine, Direction des Archives et des Bibliothèques, Hanoi, 1943, 496p.) supplies an index of authors and anonymous works; *1930-1935* (with 'française' dropping out after 'Indochine' in the title), providing the subject index, was published by Boudet's widow in 1967 (Paris, 708p.). Beginning with Volume 3, works in Vietnamese, Cambodian and Lao were included, as were articles from foreign journals, with nearly 200 source periodicals listed in Volume 4 (p. I-VII). Library cataloguing information is included in Volumes 1 and 4.

886 **Bibliography of Asian Studies: Subject Bibliography.**
Boston, Massachusetts: Association for Asian Studies, 1941- . annual.

For many years this publication has provided comprehensive listing of publications in the field of Asian Studies. Its editors regularly scan Library of Congress Print Catalogues, National Union Catalogues and other bibliographies, as well as around 500 Asian Studies periodicals and 900 general periodicals which contain articles relevant to Asian Studies. Editorial quality is high, and the scope of the citations broad. The major problem has been its chronic lateness. A cumulation for 1941-65 was published by G. K. Hall in 1970.

887 **Bibliotheca Indosinica: dictionnaire bibliographique des ouvrages relatifs à la peninsule indochinoise.** (Bibliotheca Indosinica: a bibliographic dictionary of works related to the Indochinese peninsula.)
Henri Cordier. New York: B. Franklin, [1967]. 5 vols. in 3. (Burt Franklin Bibliographic and Reference Series, no. 106). Originally published, Paris: Imprimerie Nationale, Leroux, 1912-15. 4 vols. (Publications de l'École Française d'Extrême-Orient, nos. 17-20).

Cambodia is dealt with in columns 2649-2770. The bibliography includes coverage of geography, ethnology and anthropology, climate and meteorology, population, government, jurisprudence, history, archaeology, epigraphy, religion, science and industry, the arts, language and literature, bibliographies, beliefs and customs, and voyages. See *Publications de l'EFEO* vol. 18 (1932) for an index to the bibliography prepared by Mme. M.-A. Roland-Cabaton. Its successor is *Bibliographie de l'Indochine française, 1913-1935* (q.v.).

888 **Cambodia: a bibliography.**
Compiled by Zaleha Tamby. Singapore: Institute of Southeast Asian Studies, 1982. 61p. (Library Bulletin. Institute of Southeast Asian Studies, no. 12).

Based exclusively on the ISEAS collection, the bibliography contains 691 items, including both books and journals and also a large number of indexed articles, including those from newspapers. They are overwhelmingly in English. The subject emphasis reflects that of the Institute on politics and international relations, and some material which is otherwise hard to find is listed, such as documents relating to economic and social development planning and press communiqués, though they are rather difficult to locate among the large number of ephemeral news stories. No annotations are provided, but personal and subject indexes to the items are included.

889 **Cambodia: an annotated bibliography of its history, geography, politics, and economy since 1954.**
Mary L. Fisher. [Cambridge, Massachusetts]: Center for International Studies, Massachusetts Institute of Technology, 1967. 66p.

Prepared originally as part of a seminar in bibliographic research at Simmons College School of Library Science, Boston, Massachusetts, this work is a useful account of the readily available English-language material on Cambodia in the late 1960s, both books and journal articles. Fisher focuses her work on modern history, geography, politics and economy, and makes a specific point of excluding the archaeological and Angkor material. Holdings locations are given to items in the Library of Congress and major Boston libraries. An author-title index assists finding items, which are grouped into categories: Interdisciplinary materials; Geography; History; Independence – documents and commentary; Domestic politics and government; and Economics. Appendices list additional important Cambodian serials, and additional works (presumably located after the completion of the main text).

890 **Cambodia: books in Khmer.**
Canberra: National Library of Australia, 1962- .

The National Library of Australia has published a number of lists over the years of Cambodian items coming into its collection. These include New Title Lists, Current Awareness Bulletins, and Bibliographies to the Coedès and Luce Collections as well as this occasional listing.

891 **Catalogue du fonds khmer.** (Catalogue of the Khmer collection.)
Au Chhieng. Paris: Imprimerie Nationale, 1953. xiii, 307p.

Some 350 separate entries are described in this catalogue of Khmer-language holdings in the Bibliothèque Nationale. The Khmer 'fonds' (collection) was established on the donation of eight titles by the Academie des Inscriptions et Belles-Lettres in 1965, just two years after France formally established itself in Cambodia. However, the earliest Khmer text was deposited in the library even earlier, wrongly assigned to the Thai 'fonds'. More than 350 individual texts are described, as some entries detail a number of related items. Each entry is given title and beginning and concluding lines and colophon as well as some brief indication of its contents. The listing is followed by several indexes, including titles, and broad subject areas (with the majority of texts being either religious in nature or technical manuals in astrology, magic, medicine and other rituals). The work was published with support from CNRS.

892 **Catalogue to the Cambodiana collection.**
Phnom Penh: National Library of Cambodia, 1994. 26 leaves.

The first attempt to provide a published catalogue from a database of the NLC's collection. Produced using the UNESCO software, CDS/ISIS, only English- and French-language items were included as the earlier versions did not have Khmer-language capacity.

893 **Contribution à la bibliographie du Cambodge contemporain: XIXeme & XXeme siècles.** (Contribution to the bibliography of contemporary Cambodia: 19th and 20th centuries.)
Roland Thomas. Phnom Penh: Centre de Documentation et de Recherches de la Faculté des Lettres & des Sciences Humaines, January 1975. 101p.

An extract from the author's doctoral thesis submitted to the University of Paris VII on the development of the Cambodian economy, this bibliography represents an important source on publications on Cambodia in French and English available in Phnom Penh on the eve of the Khmer Rouge takeover. The titles are arranged in an idiosyncratic classification within which items are presented in chronological sequence, in order to provide an overview of the development of scholarship in each field. Locations are provided to the three major libraries in Phnom Penh – the Buddhist Institute, the National Library of Cambodia, and the Faculty of Arts of the University of Phnom Penh. An author index and a list of periodicals held at the Buddhist Institute and National Library of Cambodia are included, providing essential data for the establishment of these collections.

894 **Doctoral Dissertations on Asia: An Annotated Journal of Current International Research.**
Compiled and edited by Frank Joseph Shulman. Ann Arbor, Michigan: Association of Asian Studies, University of Michigan, 1975-77; 1980- . semi-annual.

Shulman lists doctoral dissertations or the equivalent, including those in progress as well as completed dissertations. The majority are in the United States and Canada, although Australia and Asia are also well represented. Information includes the name and university of the author and, in certain cases, contact address, pagination, and citation to *Dissertation abstracts international.* Non-English-language titles are translated into English. The Winter/Summer 1990 issue (vol. 13, nos. 1–2), for example, lists over 150 references under 'Indochina'. No cumulative index is published. Readers are referred to earlier issues and other references for retrospective information. For those wishing to purchase a copy of a dissertation, the University Microfilms International number or other information is provided. [David G. Marr with Kristine Alilunas-Rodgers]

895 **Guide to resources on Southeast Asia within the United States.**
Indochina Studies Program. New York: Indochina Studies Program, Social Science Research Council, 1992. unpaginated.

Twenty-four libraries and archives responded to a questionnaire designed to elicit information about opening hours, access, technical facilities, collection details, and the availability (or not) of periodicals, recordings, photographs and artefacts. A companion volume to this guide is available, entitled *Guide to resources on Southeast Asia outside of the United States* (New York, 1992), but its value is limited because only fifteen institutions of disparate significance responded to the questionnaire; only one of those, the Centre des Archives d'Outre-Mer, in Aix-en-Provence, France, contains substantial holdings relating to Indochina/Cambodia. Neither volume contains an index. [David G. Marr with Kristine Alilunas-Rodgers]

896 **Index indochinensis: an English and French index to Revue Indochinoise, Extrême-Asie, Extrême-Asie-Revue Indochinoise, and La Revue Indochinoise Juridique et Économique.**
Compiled by Ronald D. Hill. Hong Kong: Centre of Asian Studies, University of Hong Kong, 1983. 155p.

Reader in Geography at the University of Hong Kong, Hill has put together a most useful index in English to several of the major French colonial periodicals dealing with Indochina. Minor articles, book reviews, notices and official acts have been omitted. The index is a classified one, arranged according to the primary classes of the Library of Congress system, and then by region or country. Additional entries are included on individuals. Thus Cambodian entries are to be found throughout.

897 **Indochina: a bibliography of the land and people.**
Compiled by Cecil C. Hobbs et al. Westport, Connecticut: Greenwood, 1970. 367p. Originally published, Washington, DC: Library of Congress, 1950.

Produced by the Library of Congress in 1950 to meet the demand on the library's services as government and private interest in Indochina grew in the United States. The listed items are primarily held in the Library of Congress, with a preference for materials published since 1930, including some in Russian and Vietnamese. Within major and minor subject classes, items are arranged alphabetically by author. Library of Congress call numbers are given when available, otherwise the item's location in another library is provided. The subject classes are: Bibliographies, handbooks etc.; Description and travel; Geography (including maps); Political history and biography; Foreign relations; Government and law; Economics; Social conditions; Language, literature and folklore; Art and archaeology; Music and dancing; Periodicals; and Newspapers. Publications in Russian and Vietnamese are listed separately. In contrast to most items with the 'Indochina' rubric, a substantial balance of Cambodian material to general, Lao and Vietnamese materials is maintained.

898 **Inventaire des livres imprimés khmers et thaï du fonds George Coedès.** (Inventory of Khmer and Thai printed books from the collection of George Coedès.)
Manuel Mauriès, with the collaboration of Élisabeth Vernier. Paris: Bibliothèque Nationale, 1991. 535p.

One part of the valuable collection of the great scholar George Coedès was acquired by the Department of Manuscripts of the Bibliothèque Nationale in 1970. The printed works, consisting of 281 Khmer-language volumes and 1,129 Thai-language volumes published between 1883 and 1969, was in 1974 transferred to the Department of Foreign Acquisitions, and in 1991 this catalogue was published on the basis of contributions made by various scholars and experts including: Christiane Rageau (q.v.); the present Minister of Culture and Fine Arts, Nouth Narang (q.v.); and Manuel Mauriès, who wrote the preface to the Khmer section. Another part of the collection, including a substantial number of offprints and unpublished papers, was acquired by the National Library of Australia where it forms the Coedès Collection.

899 **Kampuchea: sozialhistorische bibliographie zu Kampuchea von der Vorgeschichte bis 1954.** (Kampuchea: sociohistorical bibliography of Kampuchea up to 1954.)
Walter Aschmoneit. Munster, FRG: SZD-Verlag, 1981. xiii, 184p. Spine title: Kampuchea-Bibliographie.

This is the first volume of what later appeared as a stand-alone database. It includes 2,860 titles (articles, monographs and serials), of which 2,010 are solely on Cambodia arranged in the following order: bibliographies; Southeast Asia; ancient Cambodia; Angkor; and the colonial period. The later periods of Cambodian history are also included in the computer-readable database.

900 **Selected resources: people from Cambodia, Laos, Vietnam.**
Compiled by Judy Lewis. Folsom, California: Southeast Asia Community Resources Center, 1993. 221p.

Compiled for the Ninth Annual Southeast Asia Education Fair held on 20 March 1993, at Folsom Codova Unified School District, California. The work contains 500 items, including 140 theses written since 1975 on topics relating to education and specific ethnic groups. The Cambodian section has 135 items – mainly on refugees, though also including some classics such as those by Mouhot, Chandler and Huffman (q.v.). Teaching resources and items for students are given separate listings, making it a most useful resource for schools. Judy Lewis intends to update it every two years or so, and requests comments and suggestions.

901 **Southeast Asia catalog.**
Cornell University Libraries, [compiled under the direction of Giok Po Oey]. Boston, Massachusetts: G. K. Hall, 1976. 7 vols.

Cornell University boasts the strongest collection of Southeast Asian library materials in the United States. While in no way equalling the breadth and depth of its Indonesian and Vietnamese holdings, nor of course the legal deposit collection of the Bibliothèque Nationale in France, Cornell's Cambodian collection is still significant, particularly for the late 1950s and 1960s, and over 1,000 items were reported in the 1976 Western monographs volume, and a further 400 in the 1983 supplement. Serials, newspapers, maps and vernacular monographs are also listed. Each item is represented by a single entry, filed according to rules for main entry by format and then by country. No indexes are provided. This volume was published in commemoration of the twenty-fifth anniversary of the Cornell University Southeast Asia Program.

902 **Southeast Asia subject catalog of Cornell University Libraries.**
Edited by Cecil Hobbs. Boston, Massachusetts: G. K. Hall, 1970. 6 vols.

This catalogue contains some 76,000 cards relating to 'bibliographic citations to books, pamphlets, journal articles, theses, microfilms and other materials' held in the Orientalia Division of the Library of Congress as of 1969, which amount to approximately 350 periodicals and newspapers, mostly in Western languages. Twenty-one cards, some handwritten, are arranged in vertical columns on each page by alphabetical order of author within each subject heading. Not all the cards reproduce well and subject headings do not stand out clearly. Subsequently, A. Kohar Rony compiled *Southeast Asia: Western-language periodicals in the Library of Congress* (q.v.) listing holdings as of December 1974 in a 'Bibliography' arranged alphabetically and an 'Index' by subject and issuing body arranged by country and region. [David G. Marr with Kristine Alilunas-Rodgers]

903 **Southeast Asia: Western-language periodicals in the Library of Congress.**
Compiled by A. Kohar Rony. Washington, DC: Library of Congress, 1979. 201p.

The guide lists the Library of Congress holdings in one alphabetical sequence according to main entry (title or in some cases issuing body). Some references are given from alternative forms. Indexes are provided to titles filed under names of countries and regions, with well over 100 entries listed under Cambodia, and many relevant titles under Indochina and Southeast Asia. The cut-off date for adding entries and information was December 1974.

904 **Southeast Asian periodicals: an international union list.**
Compiled by G. Raymond Nunn, with contributions from David Wyatt, Charles Bryant, Do Van Anh [and] Elsie Liow. London: Mansell, 1977. 456p.

A list of some 26,000 periodicals with almost 200 listed under Cambodia. Locations are given with specific holdings information for major libraries in the United States, Britain, France, Cambodia and Vietnam. The Cambodian titles were collected by Steve O'Harrow from the catalogue of the National Library of Cambodia in 1970, and in 1974 the NLC reported further holdings information.

905 **Southeast Asian research tools: Cambodia.**
Charles F. Keyes. [Honolulu, Hawaii]: Southeast Asian Studies, Asian Studies Program, University of Hawaii, 1979. xv, 70p. (Southeast Asia Paper, no. 16, part VIII).

This volume is one in a series prepared by the Committee on Research Materials on Southeast Asia (CORMOSEA) in the United States, with funding from the National Endowment for the Humanities, which were conceived to revise and expand the 1970 guide of Donald Clay Johnson (q.v.). Charles F. Keyes was responsible for the volumes on Thailand and Laos as well as Cambodia. Although itself now well out of date, Keyes' bibliographical listing still has value for the researcher, particularly those working on the colonial period of Cambodia's history. He identifies 271 sources on Cambodia considered to be research tools. The listing was compiled on the basis of his own knowledge in the field of Southeast Asian studies, from library searching and from a questionnaire to scholars, only three of whom contributed suggestions for Cambodia, 'indicative of the almost-negligible attention [then] given to Cambodia by English-language specialists'. The sources are arranged in two groups – by form (for general items) and then by subject – and many items are given a brief notice, often an excerpt from another bibliography or review or a comment from one of the three scholars. The listing is preceded by a useful eight-page 'Bibliographic status report for Cambodia' with recommendations for needed reference tools to be produced. Sadly, despite the marked growth in publications on Cambodia, almost none of these reference tools have been superseded.

906 **Vietnamese, Cambodian and Laotian newspapers: an international union list.**

Compiled by G. Raymond Nunn and Do Van Anh. [Taipei, Japan: Cheng-wen Publishing Company]; distributed by Chinese Materials and Research Aids Service Center, 1972. xiii, 104p. bibliog.

This union list was compiled principally on the basis of holdings in the Bibliothèque Nationale in Paris and the National Library and General Library, both in Saigon, supplemented by holdings in research libraries in the United States, Australia, Britain and elsewhere. This publication is an outgrowth from Nunn's more general work on reference resources, and he acknowledges the support given to that effort by SEADAG, supplemented here by support from the University of Hawaii. Newspapers in various languages are included – French, Khmer, Chinese and Vietnamese for the majority – and indication is given of specific library holdings. The information on Cambodian newspapers was largely gathered by Professor Stephen O'Harrow, who surveyed the newspaper holdings at the National Library in Phnom Penh in 1970, and partially by Michael Vickery, whose list of Cambodian newspapers was utilized. There are 142 Cambodian newspapers listed, without notes on their content, but almost all with their location in libraries around the world provided, along with brief notes about the series and condition of such holdings. The work is a useful resource for historians or sociologists examining popular culture, although many of the titles are no longer to be found in Phnom Penh.

907 **Vietnam.**

David G. Marr, with the assistance of Kristine Alilunas-Rodgers. Oxford: ABC-Clio, 1992. lxxviii, [394]p. (World Bibliographical Series, 147).

A recent comprehensive bibliography on Vietnam by one of the world's foremost scholars on 20th-century Vietnamese history, this work is essential for serious research on Cambodia, as its index reveals some sixty items under the entry for 'Cambodia', and Cambodia is frequently also mentioned in many other items of broader 'Indochina' or 'Southeast Asia' focus. David Marr brings to the art of bibliography a keen observer's eye and a depth of background that makes the entries themselves fascinating reading.

Bibliographie des voyages dans l'Indochine française du IXe au XIXe siècle. (Bibliography of travels in French Indochina from the 9th to the 19th centuries.)
See item no. 66.

Bibliographie botanique de l'Indochine. (Botanical bibliography of Indochina.)
See item no. 104

Bibliographie botanique indochinoise de 1970 à 1985: documents pour 'La flore du Cambodge, du Laos et du Viêtnam'. (Indochinese botanical bibliography: documents for 'The flora of Cambodia, Laos and Vietnam'.)
See item no. 105.

Inscriptions of Kambuja.
See item no. 163.

Nouvelles inscriptions du Cambodge. (New inscriptions from Cambodia.)
See item no. 167.

La première guerre d'Indochine (1945-1954): bibliographie. (The first Indochina War, 1945-54: bibliography.)
See item no. 208.

America and the Indochina wars, 1945-1990: a bibliographical guide.
See item no. 226.

The wars in Vietnam, Cambodia, and Laos, 1945-1982: a bibliographic guide.
See item no. 238.

Selected, annotated, English-language bibliography of the Kampuchean revolution.
See item no. 280.

Bibliography of the peoples and cultures of mainland Southeast Asia.
See item no. 348.

An annotated bibliography of Cambodia and Cambodian refugees.
See item no. 356.

Refugee Abstracts.
See item no. 368.

Selected bibliography on Cambodia in Western languages: (August 1981), and, First supplement (November 1984).
See item no. 397.

Facing history and ourselves – holocaust behavior: an annotated bibliography.
See item no. 492.

Bibliography of statistical sources on Southeast Asia, c. 1750-1990.
See item no. 649.

Bibliography of the geology and mineral resources of Democratic Kampuchea, the Lao People's Democratic Republic, and the Socialist Republic of Viet-Nam, 1951-1975: with supplement 1976-77.
See item no. 654.

Bibliographie des traductions françaises des littératures du Viêt-Nam et du Cambodge. (Bibliography of French translations of the literature of Vietnam and Cambodia.)
See item no. 714.

South-East Asia languages and literatures: a select guide.
See item no. 746.

Southeast Asian literatures in translation: a preliminary bibliography.
See item no. 747.

Cambodia: a country study.
See item no. 873.

Les clés du Cambodge. (The keys to Cambodia.)
See item no. 875.

A guide to reference materials on Southeast Asia.
See item no. 879.

Southeast Asian periodicals: an international union list.
See item no. 904.

Cambodia bibliography: bibliography in progress.
See item no. 974.

Films and Videos

908 **Ankor-Cambodia Express.**

Producers: Lek Kitiparaporn and Richard Randall. Director: Alex King (alias Lek Kitiparaporn). Writer: Roger Crutchly and Kailan. Photography: Roberto Forges Davanzati. Music: Stelvio Cipriani. Cast: Robert Walker (Andrew Cameron), Nit Alisa (Meing), Lui Leung Wai (Mitr Saren), Sorapong Chatri (Porn Pen), Woody Strode (Woody), Christopher George (MacArthur), Suchao Pongwilai (Montro), Nancy Kwan (Sue). [Bangkok?]: Monarex Hollywood Corporation, 1982. 96 min.

'Andrew Cameron, an American journalist, sneaks away from a Khmer Rouge news conference to convince Meing, his Vietnamese fiancée, to escape, but she cannot leave her mother and fears Mitr Saren, a Khmer official who has saved her for himself. An old friend, Montri, charges Cameron to publish film of a massacre, but both are caught and tortured by Mitr Saren. Cameron finally signs a confession that he works for the C.I.A.; he is promptly deported. Three years later, having exhausted diplomatic channels, he comes back, determined to rescue Meing himself . . . [with the assistance of] the renegade American officer "MacArthur", who leads a private army in the hills and blames the press for losing Vietnam . . . [When Cameron] goes in search of Meing, he is trapped and about to be executed . . . [but, after escaping he] swims across the boundary river, carrying Meing, whispering his happiness into her ear. Only several minutes after he has collapsed on the far bank does he realize that she is dead.' [Comments available.] From *Vietnam War Films: Over 600 Feature, Made-for-TV, Pilot and Short Movies, 1939-1992, from the United States, Vietnam, France, Belgium, Australia, Hong Kong, South Africa, Great Britain and Other Countries* © 1994 Jean-Jacques Malo and Tony Williams by permission of McFarland & Company, Inc., Jefferson NC 28640.

909 **Apocalypse now.**
Producer and director: Francis Ford Coppola. Writers: John Milius and Francis Ford Coppola, based on Joseph Conrad's *Heart of Darkness*. Photography: Vittorio Storato. Music: Carmine Coppola and Francis Coppola. Editor: Richard Marks. Cast: Martin Sheen (Capt. Benjamin Willard), Marlon Brando (Col. Walter E. Kurtz), Robert Duvall (Col. Kilgore), Frederic Forrest (Chief), Albert Hall (Chief), Sam Bottoms (Lance Johnson), Larry Fishburne (Clean), Dennis Hopper (Photojournalist), G. D. Spradlin (G-2 General), Harrison Ford (Intelligence Officer), Francis Ford Coppola (Film Crew Director). USA: United Artists; Distributor: Zoetrope, 1979. 153 min.

Perhaps the quintessential Vietnam War moving image is the scene of the US helicopters swooping down on a Vietnamese village to Wagnerian strains. 'In Vietnam, Capt. Willard is given a top secret mission: to seek out the stronghold of a renegade U.S. Army officer, Col. Kurtz, who has formed his own army of deserters and mercenaries, and is engaging in unauthorized military activities. Willard, with a support team, must locate Col. Kurtz and "terminate with extreme prejudice" the colonel's activities. The mission takes Willard and his team on a treacherous river journey, on which they witness a series of events bringing home the atrocities, absurdity, and confusion of the war. Crossing into Cambodia, they become involved in a confused night time firefight. With his team virtually obliterated, Willard arrives at Col. Kurtz's headquarters, finding a group of soldiers reverted to savagery, engaged in brutal rituals. In an extended interview with Col. Kurtz, Willard sees the extent to which the experience of war and the exercise of power have allowed Col. Kurtz to surrender completely to his "dark side", and Willard comes to understand Kurtz's appreciation of the "genius" of savagery. In alternate endings to the film, Willard either (1) orders an air strike on Kurtz's headquarters, terminating both the colonel and his dark command (35 mm version); (2) leaves without ordering the air strike (70 mm version); (3) terminates Kurtz and accedes to the dead colonel's position as godlike leader of what has become a primitive warrior-tribe; (4) goes back to the States to tell Kurtz's wife what he tried to accomplish, but then decides not to tell her the truth. Note: Only the first two endings were released.' From *Vietnam War Films: Over 600 Feature, Made-for-TV, Pilot and Short Movies, 1939-1992, from the United States, Vietnam, France, Belgium, Australia, Hong Kong, South Africa, Great Britain and Other Countries* © 1994 Jean-Jacques Malo and Tony Williams by permission of McFarland & Company, Inc., Jefferson NC 28640.

910 **Back to Kampuchea.**
Martin Duckworth and Jean Roach-Marcotte. New York: 1982. 57 min.

A Cambodian taxi driver in the United States 'returns to his homeland to search for his remaining family and to learn more about happenings, following the terror of Pol Pot's regime'. Reproduced from Helen W. Cyr's *A Filmography of the Third World 1976-1983: An Annotated List of 16 mm Films* (1985) with kind permission of Scarecrow Press Inc., Metuchen, New Jersey; London.

911 **Cambodia – Kampuchea.**
Producer and director: James G. Gerrand. Writer: James G. Gerrand. Editor: Stewart Young. Narrator: Stuart Littlemore. [Australia]: James G. Gerrand [producer], [1988]. 1 videocassette (VHS) 57 min. colour with black-and-white sequences. Sequel to *Cambodia: the prince & the prophecy*. Available from sole copyright holder James G. Gerrand, 48 Tryon Road, Lindfield, NSW 2070 Australia. Tel/fax (612) 9416-1018.

A documentary of the Khmer Rouge in power; their overthrow by the Vietnamese and subsequent refugee exodus and formation of resistance. It includes Khmer Rouge and Vietnamese propaganda films and interviews with Prince Norodom Sihanouk.

912 **Cambodia – the betrayal.**
Written and produced by John Pilger, directed and co-produced by David Munro. London: Central Independent Television for ITV, 1990. 49 min. (Viewpoint 90).

'A special report by John Pilger on what he sees as a multi-national conspiracy to return Pol Pot to power in Cambodia. He accuses British and American arms manufacturers of knowingly supplying weapons to the re-emerging Khmer Rouge, and produces evidence that SAS troopers were helping to train the Khmer Rouge in Thailand. He argues that this is an ugly spin-off of British support for the US and that continuing American determination to revenge itself on Vietnam (whose troops liberated Cambodia from Pol Pot) could cause the deaths of millions more innocent Cambodians.' Reproduced from *The British National Film and Video Catalogue*, vol. 29 (1991) with kind permission of BFI Publishing, British Film Institute, 21 Stephen Street, London.

913 **Cambodia dance.**
Ithaca, New York: Cornell University [distributor]. Address of distributor: Cornell University, Audio Visual Resource Centre, 8 Business and Technology Park, Ithaca, New York 14850, 1979. 50 min.

'Features a performance of Cambodian classical and folk dances.' Taken from *The Video Source Book: A Guide to Programs Currently Available on Video*. Edited by Terri Schell. Copyright © 1996, Gale Research. All rights reserved. Reproduced by permission.

914 **Cambodia year ten: a special report by John Pilger.**
Written and produced by John Pilger, directed and co-produced by David Munro. [London]: Central Independent Television for ITV, © 1989. 1 videocassette (VHS, PAL and U-matic) 54 min. colour with black-and-white sequences. Distributor: Educational Film Services. Cassette and container label title: 'Cambodia year 10'. (Viewpoint 89).

Journalist John Pilger returns to Cambodia ten years after the overthrow of Pol Pot, and after his 1979 film *Year zero – the silent death of Cambodia* (q.v.). He reports on the difficulties of the Cambodian people as they face continued isolation and denial of official international reconstruction aid and representation in the United Nations, while the Western powers and China continue to support the coalition of resistance forces, including the Khmer Rouge. The film was nominated for the Media Peace Awards, 1990.

915 **Cambodian doughnut dreams.**
Director: Charles Davis. New York: First Run/Icarus Films [distributor]. Address of distributor: 153 Waverly Place, New York 10014, 1990. 27 min.

'Three Cambodians who escaped the horrors of Pol Pot, work in Los Angeles doughnut shops, 80 percent of which are owned or operated by Cambodians, and try to build new lives and dreams in America.' Taken from *The Video Source Book: A Guide to Programs Currently Available on Video*. Edited by Terri Schell. Copyright © 1996, Gale Research. All rights reserved. Reproduced by permission.

916 **Cambodia: the Angkor mystery.**
Narrators: J. English Smith, William Keane. William Dale Jennings [distributor]. Released by: Trend Film Corp., PO Box 69680, Los Angeles, California 90067, 1970. 15 min.

'Uses close-up photography to show the ruins of Angkor Wat and Angkor Thom in Cambodia, and describes the Khmer civilization that created these fifteenth century structures. Includes excerpts from ... [Mouhot's observations when he saw] the jungle-infested ruins in 1860.' Taken from *The National Union Catalog: Motion Pictures and Filmstrips, 1968-72* (1973), JW Edwards Publishers Inc, Ann Arbor, Michigan.

917 **Cambodia: the prince & the prophecy.**
Producer and director: James G. Gerrand. Editor: Stewart Young. Narrator: Stuart Littlemore. [Australia]: James G. Gerrand [producer], [1987]. 1 videocassette (VHS) 78 min. colour with black-and-white sequences. Part 1 of a 2-part film study; part 2 entitled *Cambodia – Kampuchea*. Available from sole copyright holder James G. Gerrand, 48 Tryon Road, Lindfield, NSW 2070 Australia. Tel/fax (612) 9416-1018.

A documentary study of: Cambodia's decline after the achievements of the Angkor kings; the contrast between Cambodia's Indianized culture and its worldly and expansionist Vietnamese neighbours whose culture derives from China; the history of Sihanouk's rise and domination of politics through the 1950s and 1960s until his overthrow in 1970; and the five years of war that destroyed Cambodia and brought the Khmer Rouge to power in 1975.

918 **Cambodia: the struggle for peace.**
Derry, New Hampshire: Chip Taylor Communications [distributor]. Distributor's address: 15 Spollett Drive, Derry, New Hampshire 03038 USA, 1991. 47 min. Juvenile.

'The history of this southeast Asian country is presented including the upheavals caused by American bombing raids during the Vietnam War and the Khmer Rouge holocaust of the 1970's. Focuses on the struggle of the country to overcome these disasters. An inspiring tribute to the triumph of the human spirit over adversity.' Taken from *The Video Source Book: A Guide to Programs Currently Available on Video*. Edited by Terri Schell. Copyright © 1996, Gale Research. All rights reserved. Reproduced by permission.

919 **Cambodia: year one.**
Producer and narrator: John Pilger. Director: David Munro. London: Associated Television for ITV, 1980. 60 min.

Reviews the advances made during the first year of the new government with the help of thirty-five million dollars in relief aid. Together with *Year zero – the silent death of Cambodia* (q.v.) these two television programmes made millions of people aware of the horrors of the Pol Pot régime, and of the international politicking that denied recognition to the government that replaced it. Munro's haunting footage and Pilger's direct and challenging words combine to make a powerful statement.

920 **Cambodia.**
[Reporter, Mike Carey]. [Milsons Point, New South Wales: SBS TV, 1991?]. 1 videocassette (VHS, PAL) (63 min.). colour. [Part 1] (36 min.) – [Part 2] (24 min.). (Dateline).

Winner of the Media Peace Prize, 1991/92 (Television), this film looks at the reasons the four warring factions in Cambodia had for adopting the United Nations peace plan.

921 **Crisis Cambodia.**
Producer: Andrew Quicke. Director: Frank Dynes. Photographer: Neil Davis. Editor: Richard Neribam. Sound: Andre Ailes. Commentary: John Willy. Visnews Productions for the International Red Cross, Switzerland, [1976?]. 15 min.

'Shows scenes of refugees crowding into Phnom Penh before it fell to Khmer-Rouge forces. Shows the work of the sponsors in hospitals and refugee camps. Intended for non-specialist audiences.' Reproduced from *The British National Film and Video Catalogue*, vol. 14 (1976) with kind permission of BFI Publishing, British Film Institute, 21 Stephen Street, London.

922 **Dragon sky.**
Producers: Michael Safra, Serge Silverman. Director: Marcel Camus. Screenplay: Jacques Viot. Photography: Raymond Le Moigne. Editor: Andree Feix. Music: Maurice Jarre. Cast: Narie Hem, Sam Elm Nop Nem, Skarine, Bopha Devi, Saky Sbong. Loper Pictures [distributor], 1962. 35 mm. 95 min. Filmed on location in Cambodia. French title *L'oiseau de paradis*.

'In Cambodia, Sok, a young and imaginative boy, leaves the Buddhist priesthood to seek a more adventurous life. Tith, a friendly fortune-teller, gives him a bird of paradise which leads him to the Royal Palace at Pnompenh [sic]. There, in an ancient temple, Sok finds Dara, a beautiful dancer in the Imperial Ballet. When she leaves the dance company to take part in ritual celebration, Sok follows her to Angkor Wat, the city of temples, and declares his love for her. Dara is also sought by Khem, a wealthy businessman. When Khem learns of her love for Sok, his jealousy erupts into violence, and Dara falls to her death . . . [or] commits suicide. Sok is injured by Khem, and upon seeing the dead body of his beloved Dara, Sok also dies. The two are reunited in death, as in the legendary love story of Rama and Sita.' Taken from *The American Film Institute Catalog: feature films 1961-70*. Edited by Richard P. Krafsur. Copyright © 1976, R.R. Bowker. All rights reserved. Reproduced by permission.

923 **The eagle, the dragon, the bear and Kampuchea.**
Producer: Bruce Palling. Director: John Sheppard. Camera: Bill Brayne, David Waterston. Sound: Christian Wangler, Ron Yoshida. Editor: David Gladwell. Civic Square, Australian Capital Territory: Ronin Films (distributor), [198?]. 1 videocassette (VHS) ca. 65 min. colour.

'Examines what life is like for ordinary people of Kampuchea after three decades of conflict involving America, China and the Soviet Union. A third of its population is missing, presumed dead and its economy is in a state of collapse.' Reproduced from *The British National Film and Video Catalogue*, vol. 14 (1976) with kind permission of BFI Publishing, British Film Institute, 21 Stephen Street, London.

924 **[Films].**
Norodom Sihanouk. 1966-95.

Prince/King Norodom Sihanouk has devoted much energy to realizing his passion for film-making. Between 1966 and 1995 he made at least twenty-six feature films. They are of the romantic, nostalgic genre, often interweaving traditional folk-tales with modern political situations, revealing much about his view of an ideal world where all-powerful rulers dispense beneficence to a poor and grateful people, and single-handedly ward off dangers. Sihanouk himself and his family members are nearly always to be found in the cast. Raoul Jennar, in *Les clés du Cambodge* (The keys to Cambodia) (q.v.) lists the titles as: *Apsara*, 1966; *La forêt enchantée* (The enchanted forest), 1967; *Le petit prince du peuple: Prachea Komar* (The little prince of the people: Prachea Komar), 1967; *Ombre sur Angkor* (Shadow over Angkor), 1968; *La joie de vivre* (The joy of life), 1968; *Rose de Bokor* (Rose of Bokor), 1969; *Crépuscule* (Twilight), 1968; *Tragique destin* (Tragic destiny), 1969; *La cité mystérieuse* (The mysterious city), 1987; *Adieu, mon amour* (Goodbye, my love), 1988; *La comtesse de Norkorom* (The countess of Norkorom), 1989; *Je ne te reverrai plus, ô mon bien-aimé Kampuchea!* (I shall never see you again, oh my beloved Kampuchea!), 1990; *Le phare qui éclair notre voie* (The beacon that lights our way), 1991; *Mon village au coucher du soleil* (My village at sunset), 1992, winner of the Prix Spécial at the Saint Petersburg Festival in 1994; *La fleur champa de Battambang* (The champa flower of Battambang), 1992; *Le fantôme de ma femme bien-aimée* (The phantom of my beloved wife), 1993; *Un Crésus sauveteur de femmes pauvres* (A Croesus saviour of poor women), 1993; *Les quatres éléments* (The four elements), 1993, a ballet film; *Fatalité* (Fatality), 1994; *Revoir Angkor . . . et mourir* (To see Angkor again . . . and die), 1994; *Un paysan et une paysanne en détresse* (Peasants in distress), 1994; *Robin-des-Bois khmer* (Khmer Robin Hood), 1994; *Nostalgie de la Chine* (Nostalgia for China), 1995; *Une ambition réduite en cendres* (An ambition reduced to cinders), 1995; *Bouddha, Dhamma, Sangkha le seul refuge* (Buddha, Dharma, Sangkha the sole refuge), 1995; and *Les derniers jours du Colonel Savath* (The last days of Colonel Savath), 1995.

925 **Foreign correspondent.**
Sydney: Australian Broadcasting Commission/Corporation, 1992- . Available from ABC TV Library Sales, GPO Box 9994, Sydney NSW, 2001 Australia.

A series of occasional programmes on Cambodia including: 'Problems facing UN peacekeeping force in Cambodia' (Mar. 1992); 'Gem stone trade on Thai-Cambodia border' (Sept. 1992); 'UN in Cambodia' (Feb. 1993); 'Cambodian refugees returning home' (Feb. 1993); 'Khmer Rouge oppose peace deal in Cambodia' (May 1993); 'Australian soldiers take care of Cambodian street kids' (June 1993); 'Political manoeuvring in Cambodia after the elections' (June 1993); 'Continuing civil unrest in Cambodia' (May 1994); 'Corruption in Cambodian army' (Nov. 1994); 'Defection of Khmer Rouge members to Cambodian government' (May 1995); and 'Corruption in Cambodian government' (Sept. 1995).

926 **Four corners.**
Sydney: Australian Broadcasting Commission/Corporation, 1989- . Available from ABC TV Library Sales, GPO Box 9994, Sydney NSW 2001, Australia.

Another series of occasional programmes on Cambodia produced by ABC TV, including: 'Cambodia's foreboding' (Sept. 1989); 'Gambling with genocide' (Nov. 1992); and 'Survivors of the killing fields' (July 1995).

927 **Front line.**
Producer and director: David Bradbury. Writers: David Bradbury, Bob Connolly. Photographer: David Perry. Music: Midnight Oil, Denise Wykes, Lindsay Lei. Editor: Stewart Young. Sydney, 1979. 56 min. Sponsors: Australian Film Commission, Tasmanian Film Corporation, Australian War Memorial.

'A documentary on Neil Davis, an Australian cameraman correspondent who filmed the Vietnam War at the frontline for eleven year's from 1964 to the fall of Saigon in 1975. Combines interviews with Davis with footage shot by him, and other archival film.' Reproduced from *Australian Films 1979-81* (1981) with kind permission of the National Library of Australia, Canberra.

928 **House of the spirit: perspectives on Cambodian health care.**
Directors: Ellen Bruno, Ellen Kuras. Interviewer, Ellen Bruno. Music: Chinary Ung. Translator: Sary Tauv. New York: American Friends Service Committee, © 1984. 1 videocassette (U-matic) 42 min. colour. Available from 15 Rutherford Place, New York, USA.

Mostly in English – with some Khmer dialogue voiced over in English – this film was recorded at a workshop with Cambodian migrants in the United States on the subject of the traditional Cambodian health-care system.

929 **Kampuchea after Pol Pot.**
Director: Mark Stiles. Canberra: Australian Freedom From Hunger Campaign, © 1982. 1 videocassete (U-matic) 48 min. colour. Title in Khmer and English. Also available as 2 film reels 50 min., 16 mm. Australian Distributor: Oceania Media Network; US Distributor: First Run/Icarus, 153 Waverly Place, New York, NY 10014, USA.

The Australian Freedom from Hunger Campaign (AFFHC) was one of the first aid agencies to set up programmes beyond distribution of emergency relief. With two other agencies it established a permanent presence in Phnom Penh, the Joint Australian Non-Government Organisation Office. 'Focuses on the first three years of emergency and effort in [the People's Republic of] Kampuchea and the problems of international politics which threatened . . .' the revival of the country. Taken from *The Video Source Book: A Guide to Programs Currently Available on Video.* Edited by Terri Schell. Copyright © 1996, Gale Research. All rights reserved. Reproduced by permission.

930 **Khmer! Khmer!: Cambodia in conflict.**
Sydney: James Gerrand in co-operation with ABC, 1971. 1 videocassette (U-matic) 64 min. colour. Available from sole copyright holder James G. Gerrand, 48 Tryon Road, Lindfield, NSW 2070 Australia. Tel/fax (612) 9416-1018.

A study of the life, culture, history and politics of Cambodia, concentrating on the leadership of Norodom Sihanouk. Issues raised include the threatened domination of Cambodia by Vietnam and the spread of the Vietnam War into Cambodia.

931 **The killing fields.**
Producer: David Puttnam. Director: Roland Joffé. Photography: Chris Menges. Graphics: John Gorham, Howard Brown. Editor: Jim Clark. Music: Mike Oldfield. [London]: Goldcrest Films and Television, © 1984. 1 videocassette (VHS) ca. 130 min. colour. Issued also as motion picture. Cast: Sam Waterston (Sydney Schanberg), Haing S. Ngor (Dith Pran). (An Enigma Production).

Based on articles by Sydney Schanberg in *The New York Times Magazine* in 1980, this film won three Oscars and eight British Academy Awards. Produced by David Puttnam and with screenplays by Bruce Robinson, it tells the story of Dith Pran and Sydney Schanberg from August 1973 as they cover the war in Cambodia as journalists for *The New York Times*, through the liberation of Phnom Penh by Khmer Rouge troops, Schanberg's departure with Pran left behind, and Pran's horrific personal experiences under Pol Pot rule and subsequent flight from Cambodia, until October 1979 when they meet again in a refugee camp on the border between Thailand and Cambodia. The term 'killing fields' has since been applied particularly to the Khmer Rouge execution grounds, which provide one of the most shocking and grotesque parts of the film, but the film actually goes back much further than that, and the killing fields wrought by the American bombing and the frenzied civil war before 17 April 1975 take up a large part of the film, setting the stage for the horror that follows in this riveting account of the relationship between two men as the world disintegrates around them.

932 **The last God-King: the lives and times of Cambodia's Sihanouk.**
Producer/director/writer: James Gerrand. Sydney: Film Australia, 1996. 1 × 58, and 1 × 60 min., total 118 min. Available from sole copyright holder: James Gerrand, 48 Tryon Road, Lindfield, NSW 2070 Australia. Tel/fax (612) 9416-1018.

This two-part documentary for television is the latest by independent film-maker, James Gerrand, who has documented Cambodia's vicissitudes since the 1960s, with a special emphasis on the varying roles played by Sihanouk. Gerrand here presents rich material from four exclusive interviews in which Sihanouk looks back over the fifty-five years since he was appointed king by the French colonialists in 1941. Sihanouk's reveries are interspersed with a wealth of valuable archival footage and with interviews with other Cambodians and Cambodia watchers. As Sihanouk, seriously ill with cancer but now in remission, draws close to what must be the end of his extraordinary life, Gerrand focuses on two people as the keys to the future – Hun Sen and Sam Rainsy, painted somewhat as black and white alternatives.

933 **Lateline.**
Sydney: Australian Broadcasting Commission/Corporation, 1990- . Available from ABC TV Library Sales, GPO Box 9994, Sydney 2001, NSW Australia.

Occasional programmes on Cambodia including: 'Cambodia burns' (Feb. 1990); 'Cambodia votes' (May 1993); and 'Bleak future of Cambodia' (June 1994).

934 **The lost idol.**
Producer: P. Sumon. Director: P. Chanlong. Writers: Tony S. Suwart and James Phillips based on a story by Bunchurt Dhavee, Tony S. Suwat and Alex Buannakh. Photography: Visidh S. Stone. Music: Anuwat Suebsuwan. Editor: P. Charles. Cast: Eric Estrada (Sgt. Kurt), James Phillips (Lt. Oliver), Mara Chason (Kate). [Bangkok?]: Shappireo Glickenhaus Entertainment [distributor], 1990. 102 min.

'Two hundred soldiers from the 140th Infantry Battalion left behind after the fall of Saigon make their way toward Thailand. While fighting their way through Cambodia, the surviving twenty soldiers find an abandoned temple. The corrupt commander, Lt. Oliver, loots the temple and forces his men to carry a golden idol with them to a cache. The senior enlisted soldier, Sgt. Kurt, argues against carrying the idol, but the officer insists. After the idol is safely hidden away, Lt. Oliver machine-guns his own men. Kurt is wounded, but escapes. The remainder of the film deals with events eight years later when Oliver returns to recover the idol. Oliver enlists the support of a Red Cross worker, Kate, and the Khmer Rouge to find his men who he insists are still alive in Kampuchea. . . . Oliver and his unwitting allies then fight their way into Kampuchea and attempt to recover the idol from the occupying North Vietnamese. The North Vietnamese capture Oliver and his group. The film climaxes with a pitched battle between the North Vietnamese and the insurgent Khmer Rouge. During the struggle Oliver, Kate, the North Vietnamese, and the idol are lost. Only Kurt and some of the Khmer Rouge survive. The final scene shows Kurt walking away from the battle and philosophizing on the results of war.' [Commentary available.] From *Vietnam War Films: Over 600 Feature, Made-for-TV, Pilot and Short Movies, 1939–1992, from the United States, Vietnam, France, Belgium, Australia, Hong Kong, South*

Africa, Great Britain and Other Countries © 1994 Jean-Jacques Malo and Tony Williams by permission of McFarland & Company, Inc., Jefferson NC 28640.

935 **The Mekong.**

An RKO Pictures/BBC-TV co-production. Los Angeles: Churchill Films, 1986. 1 videocassette 57 min. colour. Issued as U-matic 3/4 in. or Beta 1/2 in. or VHS 1/2 in. (River Journeys).

Documents the journey of a former Vietnam War correspondent up the Mekong River after peace had been restored to the region. William Shawcross, a British journalist, set out from the Mekong delta in Vietnam, travelling along the river into Cambodia, in order to discover how the area was recovering now that the war had ended. In Cambodia, his impressions were of a country still haunted by its brutal past, slowly recovering from its ordeal – the footage of street scenes in the capital and interviews with survivors of the Pol Pot period testify to this image. Shawcross also made a short trip to Angkor Wat.

936 **The ninth circle.**

Czechoslovakia; Cambodia: Production Company: Barrandov Studios, ca. 1988.

Produced for the tenth anniversary of the overthrow of Pol Pot, this romantic film celebrates the reconstruction of the country and records the continuing threat from the Khmer Rouge. It contains evocative scenes of Cambodia's lakes, waterfalls, mountains and temples, including Angkor Wat. Near panic was caused during the filming, when actors dressed as Khmer Rouge soldiers were seen in the streets of Phnom Penh.

937 **No retreat, no surrender II.**

Producer: Roy Horan. Director: Corey Yuen. Writers: Roy Horan, Keith Strandberg and Maria Elena Cellino. Photography: Nicholas Von Sternberg. Music: Kevin Sewelson. Editors: Allan Poon and Kevin Sewelson. Cast: Loren Avedon (Scott Wylde), Max Thayer (Mac Jarvis), Cynthia Rothrock (Terry), Patra Wanthivanond (Sulin Nguyen), Perm Hongsakul (Gen. Nguyen), Nirut Sirijunya (Col. Sol Nol), Matthias Hues (Yuri). [Bangkok?]: Shapiro Glickenhaus Entertainment [distributor], 1989. 92 min.

'American Scott Wylde stumbles into Thailand to renew a liaison with Sulin, daughter of an expatriate South Vietnamese general who has sought refuge in Thailand but who assists through his ministrations and contacts the "Khmer Resistance" (the term "Khmer Rouge" is not used) to Vietnamese occupation in Cambodia. . . . Yuri, the Soviet advisor . . . [kidnaps Sulin to use as] bait to lure in the old general so that he may be assassinated. Yuri has, alas, not reckoned on the formidable kickboxing powers of Scott and his resolve to retrieve his "fiance". Scott rounds up a decadent but game comrade, Mac, who, together with their martial girlfriend, Terry the chopper pilot, spirits Scott and a dufflebag full of automatic weapons into Cambodia and the very midst of the Soviet area of operations. They try to recruit the local Khmer commander, Colonel Sol Nol, . . . but the guerrilla camp disintegrates during an artillery attack. Further adventures befall the plucky band as they pursue the luckless Sulin "up Death Mountain". Finally, in a great shootout and deathbrawl, the unfortunate Terry gives her life to save Scott, who beats the . . . [evil Yuri], wraps him up in the . . . [Soviet] flag, drags him behind a jeep, feeds him to crocodiles, and then sets fire to him after gunning down 3,648 ferocious AK-toting campguards.' [Commentary available.] From *Vietnam War Films: Over 600 Feature, Made-for-TV, Pilot and Short Movies, 1939-1992, from the United States, Vietnam, France, Belgium, Australia, Hong Kong, South Africa, Great Britain and Other Countries* © 1994 Jean-Jacques Malo and Tony Williams by permission of McFarland & Company, Inc., Jefferson NC 28640.

938 **Our children didn't come home.**

Written and directed by Luke Bracken. [Brisbane: Film Queensland], 1996. 60 min.

This is a low-budget documentary on the 1994 kidnapping and killing of Kellie Wilkinson, Tina Dominy and Dominic Chappell as they were driving from Phnom Penh to Sihanoukville, where Wilkinson and Chappell ran a restaurant. Interviews with officials and with friends and family of Wilkinson and footage from Cambodia, including the trial of one of the supposed kidnappers – a Khmer Rouge soldier – are supplemented by a number of scenes of re-enactment of their fate in which Wilkinson is played by her sister Brigette, while her twin brother Sean plays Chappell. This gives a particularly poignant edge to this story of three young Westerners working in Cambodia whose lives ended in a tragic way, evidently not long after they were captured, but whose families went through months of trauma as both the Cambodian and Australian governments grappled with whether to engage in ransom negotiations or to attack the Khmer Rouge base where they were presumed to be still held. Luke Bracken, an independent film-maker, took on the project, raising funds from Profile Press media agency, Film Queensland and SBS, while much of the labour was donated.

939 **The people of the rice fields.**

Produced and directed by Rithy Panh.

A film of Rithy Panh's return to his native Cambodia, focusing on the symbiotic relationship between rice and human beings. Only a passing nod is made to recent political events.

940 **Peter Jennings from the killing fields.**

Producer: ABC News, 1986. 160 min. Distributor: MPI Home Video, 161015 108 Avenue, Orland Park. ILL. 60462.

'An in depth report of the continuing conflict in Southeast Asia since US troops departed in 1975. The news team visited the killing fields; interviewed government and ex-government leaders, military commanders and US politicians about the explosive situation in Cambodia.' Taken from *The Video Source Book: A Guide to Programs Currently Available on Video.* Edited by Terri Schell. Copyright © 1996, Gale Resarch. All rights reserved. Reproduced by permission.

941 **The postman goes to war.**
Producer: Jean-Jacques Vital, Andre Cotton. Director: Claude Bernard-Aubert. Screenplay: Rene Hardy, Claude Bernard-Aubert, Claude Accursi, Pascal Jardin. Photography: Marcel Grignon. Editor: Gabriel Rongier. Music: Georges Garvarentz. Cast: Charles Aznavour, Daniel Ceccaldi, Jaques Richard, Maria Minh, Helmut Schneider, Jess Hahn, Franco Fabrizi, Doudou Babet, Lucien Barjon. France: Trans-Lux Distributing Corp. [distributor], 1967. 35 mm. 95 min. Filmed in Cambodia . Based on the book by Gaston-Jean Gautier, *Le facteur s'en va-t-en guerre*, Paris, 1966.

'Thibon, a resourceful Parisian postman, enlists for the French-Indochina War and is sent to Cambodia. He soon becomes disenchanted with the war, however, and is injured in a mine explosion. Thibon is released from the infirmary, and his regiment receives orders to defend Dien Bien Phu, but the group is captured by the Communists. They manage to escape, narrowly missing news of the armistice. Thibon returns to France with a Cambodian woman with whom he has fallen in love.' Taken from *The American Film Institute Catalog: feature films 1961-70*. Edited by Richard P. Krafsur. Copyright © 1976, R.R. Bowker. All rights reserved. Reproduced by permission.

942 **The prospects for peace.**
Produced and directed by Mike Carey, camera by Tim Rayment. Sydney: SBS Television, 1991. 1 videocassette (35 + 9 mins.). (Dateline).

This represents one of a number of programmes filmed for the Australian Special Broadcasting Service (SBS) on Cambodia, particularly by Mike Carey. *The prospects for peace* was made in the week leading up to the October 1991 Paris Peace Conference, and it opens with Sihanouk saying 'let bygones be bygones', in support of removing any reference to genocide in the documents, and Ranariddh saying it was necessary to settle 'or fight to the last Cambodian'. Foreign Minister of SOC, Hor Nam Hong, states that the new government may seek redress, and that the agreements do mean abandonment of the people who suffered at the hands of the Khmer Rouge. Interviews are held with Khmer Rouge officials in Site 8, including Mei Mann who admitted mistakes, but denied that the Khmer Rouge ever committed genocide. In conclusion, the United Nations is presented as a cage for the tiger, and as Cambodia's only hope. The film contains important footage for an understanding of the different views of the period. It is followed by a studio interview of the Australian Foreign Minister, Gareth Evans, by Dateline's Paul Murphy.

943 **Public enemy number one.**
Producers: David Bradbury, Stewart Young. Associate Producer: Bob Connolly. Sponsor: Creative Development Branch, Australian Film Commission. Director: David Bradbury. Writer: David Bradbury. Photography: Niels van t'Hoff. Music: James Moginie. Editor: Stewart Young. Sound: Jan Gerrand. Distributor: Ronin Films, Sydney, 1980. 60 min. 16 mm. In colour with black-and-white sequences.

'Biography of expatriate Australian journalist, Wilfred Burchett. Uses documentary footage and interviews with Wilfred Burchett to trace his career, which [was] largely that of a war correspondent . . . since the 2nd World War. His support for . . . [the Vietnamese against Western powers, including Australia, led to his Australian passport being withdrawn.] Includes extensive footage of Burchett's long association with Indo-China.' Reproduced from *Australian Films 1979-81* (1981) with kind permission of the National Library of Australia, Canberra. For a sympathetic series of essays on his life and work see *Burchett reporting the other side of the world 1939-1983*, edited by Ben Kiernan, with a preface by John Pilger (London: Quartet, 1986. 315p.), containing a chapter, 'Put not thy trust in princes: Burchett on Kampuchea', by Ben Kiernan.

944 **Rebuilding the temple: Cambodians in America.**
A film by Claudia Levin and Lawrence Hott, edited by Sharon Sachs. Assistant Producer: Diane Garey. Cinematographer: Buddy Squires. Music by Richard Einhorn, performed by the Sam-Ang Sam Ensemble. Florentine Films, United States, 1991. 58 mins. 1 videocassette (NTSC). Major funding from the National Endowment for Humanities. Funding also from the State Humanities Councils of Massachusetts, Rhode Island, California, Oregon and Texas and from the Boston Globe Foundation.

A thoughtful and artful piece about the challenges faced by Cambodian refugees beginning new lives in the United States. It examines religion as a focal point for the Khmer community and as a living storehouse of cultural identity in the face of American lifestyle and the trauma of surviving the Pol Pot régime. A wide variety of American Cambodians, including the eminent monk Maha Ghosananda, musicologist Sam-Ang Sam, journalist Dith Pran and a young bride, share their thoughts about their faith, families, identities and 'home'. Anthropologists Judy Ledgerwood and Carol Mortland are among American professionals who offer further insight into the Khmer refugee community. Background to the events which led Cambodians to flee their homeland and background to Cambodian cultural traditions are succinctly interwoven with the interviews. Rare footage, traditional music and poetry are utilized sensitively throughout, making this a most accessible film, which through its subtle, original, and respectful treatment, holds much for both those familiar with, or new to, the subject.

945 **Return to year zero: a special report by John Pilger.**
Written and produced by John Pilger, directed and co-produced by David Munro. London: Central Independent Television for ITV, © 1993. 1 videocassette (VHS). colour with black-and-white sequences. Cassette and container label title: *Cambodia: return to year zero*. Distributor: Educational Film Services.

Presented in two parts: in the first John Pilger revisits Cambodia looking at social conditions; and in the second part he examines the re-emergence of the Khmer Rouge, accorded new legitimacy as a partner in the 1991 Paris Peace Agreements.

946 **Return to Year Zero?**
Producer: David A. Feigold. Director: Shari Robertson. Assistant Producer: Steve Clark-Hall. Camera: Barry Ackroyd. [London?]: Ishi Film Production for Channel 4 Television, 1989. 39 min. (Dispatches).
To mark the tenth anniversary of the overthrow of Pol Pot, this film examines Margaret Thatcher's claim that the Khmer Rouge is 'under new management'. Visits are made to: Site 8, an official camp under Khmer Rouge influence; and to Borei, under total Khmer Rouge control and off limits to international agencies, where some 8,000 refugees have been moved. Interviews with defectors and also with officials within the camps and within the PRK government reinforce the continuing danger posed by the Khmer Rouge.

947 **Roving Report.**
Produced by WTN Productions, 1979-91, distributed by WTN Library.
Regularly featuring Cambodian stories for screening on British television, for example, 8920A *Cambodia: securing a future*, 1989. 8½ min. See particularly 7946A, 8007B, 8044, 8114A, 8137A, 8318A, 8421B, 8546A, 8645A, 8646A, 8805D, 8903B, 8920A, 8925C, 8940A, 8947A, 9015A, 9043B, 9113B, 9120D, 9136A. (Source: *The British national film catalogue*. London: British Film Institute, 1963-1983, 1984-).

948 **Samsara.**
A film by Ellen Bruno. Camera: Ellen Kuras and Wah Ho Chan. Sound: Etienne Sauret. Department of Communication, Stanford University, Stanford, California, 1989. 1 videocassette (VHS). (28 min.) colour. In English, Khmer and French, with English subtitles.
According to the credits, this film is 'based on the memories and stories of Cambodians in the United States and Cambodia' and on *The teachings of Buddha* (Tokyo: Bukkyo Dendo Kyokai, 1966). It is a solemn work, intended to evoke the image of the wheel of endless suffering, turning through cycles of life, death and rebirth. Haunting music and lyrical rural images of drought and rain, and fascinating Cambodian recollections and impressions, are overlaid with rather sonorous passages from the Buddhist texts. The personal anguish of Cambodians even ten years after the Khmer Rouge were overthrown is painted sharply, while the Vietnamese are depicted as ranking equally as the enemy, in the old image of Cambodia as the victim caught between the tiger and the crocodile.

949 **The secrets of S-21.**
Director: David Okuefuna. Editor: Jane Greenwood. Camera: Jeremy Pollard. London: BBC Productions, 1996. 1 videocassette (VHS). 30 min. (The Works).
This documentary film reports the work of the Photo Archive Group in restoring the negatives of some 6,000 photographs of prisoners held at Tuol Sleng Prison during the DK régime. Some 14,200 prisoners are listed as having gone through Tuol Sleng, only 7 of whom survived. Two of the survivors are interviewed, along with two of the prison staff (one guard and one listkeeper). During 1996 further photographs have come to light.

950 **Silent sentinels: coward's war.**
Director: David A. Feingold. Producer: David A. Feingold, Deborah La Gorce Kramer. Associate Producer: Dean Slotar. Editor: Tony Pound. Ophidian Productions, 1996. 55 mins. Subtitles by SBS (Australia), 1996.

Documenting Cambodia's greatest humanitarian plight – the mines that threaten and destroy, while denying land for cultivation. Interviews with mine clearers and with carers of the victims are featured as well as discussion of the needed political campaign to prevent continued laying of mines by all sides.

951 **Swimming to Cambodia [videorecording].**
Producer: R. A. Shafransky. Director: Jonathan Demme. Writer: Spalding Gray. Photography: John Bailey. Music: Laurie Anderson. Editor: Carol Littleton. Cast: Spalding Grey (himself). Cinecom (US Distributor), 1987. 87 min.

'This is a splicing together of several performances by Gray of his monologue that centers on his small part in Roland Joffé's *The Killing Fields* (1984). Gray – an actor, performance artist and monolinguist – roams freely from discoursing on the Khmer Rouge to his thoughts on the bordellos of Thailand. He is filmed sitting on a chair behind a small table. His minimalist props are his microphone, a glass of water, a notebook, a pointer and two maps behind him. There is an occasional slide and a brief clip from *The Killing Fields.*' [Commentary available.] From *Vietnam War Films: Over 600 Feature, Made-for-TV, Pilot and Short Movies, 1939-1992, from the United States, Vietnam, France, Belgium, Australia, Hong Kong, South Africa, Great Britain and Other Countries* © 1994 Jean-Jacques Malo and Tony Williams by permission of McFarland & Company, Inc., Jefferson NC 28640.

952 **The Tan Family, March–April 1995.**
Writer and Director: Rithy Panh. Cinematographer: Prom Mesar. Editor: Marie-Christine Rougerie. Production Co-ordinator: Ros Sareth in collaboration with Atria, Centre de Production Audiovisuelle (Cambodia), Atelier Varan-Cambodge, and UNICEF. La Sept-Arte & Formation Films Ltd., 1995. 1 videocassette (VHS). 30 min. (The UN-Official Version).

'This land is my land . . . Last month I wanted to go fishing with the others. But they told me here people didn't go fishing together . . . you went alone . . . I had never been in the water. I was a child of the camps. I was afraid. The water's deep, I'm scared of the snakes and the forest . . . Since I was twelve I lived in the camps where we relied on the agencies. We had food, but no freedom to go where we pleased. When we returned to Cambodia we didn't know how to survive. We didn't know how to fish, we had no experience. But when we wanted people to go fishing with us they wanted nothing to do with us . . . Now there is only one job, that of being a soldier. I feel like a crab in a basket. There is no escape . . . If the war doesn't end, what will become of us? We may have enough to eat while we wait until the war ends. Then we will be happy.' So we hear the Tan family in Sre Ampil Village, Battambang province, spoken in their own voices with English subtitles – representing the 372,000 repatriated by the United Nations in 1992-93. The story is a tragic one and the film leaves very little scope for optimism as these people face physical difficulties of relocation as well as hostility from those who stayed behind in conditions of grinding poverty. This is part three of a series on the United Nations' activities around the world.

953 **The tenth dancer.**

Writer and Director: Sally Ingleton, Singing Nomads Productions. Civic Square, Australian Capital Territory: Ronin Films, © 1993. 1 videocassette (VHS). 52 min. colour.

A sensitive and beautiful film on the revival of traditional Cambodian dance after the overthrow of the Pol Pot régime. Ingleton focuses her study on Em Theay, one of the few survivors of the Royal Ballet, over ninety per cent of whom are thought to have perished under the Khmer Rouge, and Sok Chea, one of the new dancers being trained for a principal role. We see the dancers' demanding régime of rehearsal and discipline, their life of extreme poverty in the Ministry of Culture's housing block, and we hear their reminiscences of times past, both good and bad, including the New Year of 1975, as described by Em Theay, who died in 1995: 'Under Pol Pot we were all without hope. We thought we wouldn't be able to come back. Now it's as if the flame is back. Before, during the Pol Pot time it had been extinguished. I had no energy to create the movements. It seemed like I was in a dream. Now I have the light to live. Just like a tree that is coming into bud and beginning to bloom'. The film's footage is all the more precious because Em Theay has died since the film was made.

954 **Which way home.**

Producer: Hal McElroy. Director: Karl Shultz. Writer: Michael Laurence. Photography: Ellery Ryan. Music: Bruce Rowland. Editor: Henry Danger. Cast: Cybill Shepherd (Karen Parsons), John Waters (Steve Hannah), John Ewart, Ruben Santiago-Hudson, Marc Gray, Andy Tran, Adrian Kwan, Mark Ngo, Alina Kwan, Anna Ngo, Thuy Le Kim, Paul Gittins (Charlie), Michael Morrissey (Grafton), Bioletta Ngo (Bon Sopral), Ho Le Kinh (Vin Soprala), Timothy Smith (David). USA Australia New Zealand. Distributor TNT-TV, 1990. 141 min. Made for TV.

'Karen Parsons is an American Red Cross nurse in Cambodia during the Vietnam and Khmer Rouge War. She is in the process of evacuating Phnom Penh when a rocket attack on the hospital kills a Cambodian man and wife medical team who happen to be Karen's closest friends. She promises to take care of the couple's children and attempts to evacuate them via Army helicopter. She fails. She decides to take the children to Thailand by driving across Cambodia. Before they get to the border their jeep is stolen and the oldest child, Ben, is killed by the Khmer Rouge. In Thailand Karen plans to buy her way onto a boat full of other refugees with hopes of being "found" by the U.S. Navy. . . . In the attempt to get out of the camp they are followed by a group of Vietnamese children. While the Cambodian children are reluctant to accept the Vietnamese as part of the group, Karen lets them come along. It is only through time that the children accept one another. Steve Hannah is an owner and captain of a boat out of Darwin, Australia . . . [who takes on Karen and the children, rescuing them] from pirates. . . . The rest of the narrative is centred around the debate whether to leave the children at one of the many refugee camps between Thailand and Australia or to take them to Australia. In their journey they are met with several obstacles both man-made and natural. They are attacked by pirates and lose their cargo, one of the Cambodian children (Sudi) becomes ill and eventually dies, and in a storm, a day out of Australia, they are rescued by the Australian coast guard. In the process of this journey Steve gets close to Karen and the children and decides to take them to Darwin. . . . They finally make it to Darwin and the children are placed in quarantine, Karen is deported back to the United States and Steve is left swearing that he will find Karen as soon as he knows that the children are safe.' [Commentary available.] From *Vietnam War Films: Over 600 Feature, Made-for-TV, Pilot and Short Movies, 1939-1992, from the United States, Vietnam, France, Belgium, Australia, Hong Kong, South Africa, Great Britain and Other Countries* © 1994 Jean-Jacques Malo and Tony Williams by permission of McFarland & Company, Inc., Jefferson NC 28640.

955 **The white page.**

Writer, Producer and Director: Ho Quang Minh. Assistant Producer: Tran Thanh Hung. Music: Dam Linh. Photography: Le Dinh An. Vina played by Phuong Dung. Switzerland; Vietnam: MHK Films, [1991?]. 1 videocassette (VHS). 94 min.

This film is a recreation of life and death as experienced under the Khmer Rouge. It tells the story of a Cambodian woman (Vina) and her two small children returning to Phnom Penh from abroad after the victory of the Khmer Rouge in response to an appeal from her husband to come back now that the motherland has been freed to help build the new revolutionary Cambodia. After arriving at Pochentong airport in their new Western clothes they are left abandoned. The plane flies away and they sit for what seems like hours on the steps until a jeep pulls up with cadres who treat them rudely and take them to sleep for the night in the National Museum. In the morning they are taken away to the 17th April Commune to begin their new and horrifying experiences. As well as the dramatic personal story, familiar in broad terms as told by many others in book and film, this film conveys considerably more because it has a number of extended contextual sequences, including speeches by officials on the motivation and doctrine of the 'farsighted and all powerful' *Angkar* (the Organization) that rules their lives, and discussions between the woman and her husband, a Khmer Rouge cadre, on the merits of the revolution and the role of the individual and the family. The film ends in 1979 as Vina returns to Phnom Penh and finds that her husband had been imprisoned at Tuol Sleng and executed. We are shown the beginnings of the rebuilding of Cambodia. It is all spoken in Khmer (with subtitles) giving extra verisimilitude. The film was made by a Vietnamese company, and the principal actors all have Vietnamese names.

956 **World in action.**

UK: Granada TV, 1979- .

Occasional reports on Cambodia, such as *Siege of Phnom Penh* (1975), *Cambodia year one: life after death* (1980), and *Cambodia year one: the aid crisis* (198?) all directed by Michael Beckham, and photographed by George Turner.

957 **Year zero – the silent death of Cambodia.**
Reporter: John Pilger. Director: David Munro. Sound: Peter Rann, Steve Phillips. Research: Nick Clayton. London: Associated Television for ITV, 1979. 60 min. 16mm.

A report on the régime of the Khmer Rouge in Cambodia, and the massive slaughter and famine which swept the country after their takeover in 1975. This film made a tremendous impact on the viewing public, and resulted in unprecedented individual contributions for humanitarian aid in Cambodia, while at the same time becoming part of the campaign for official recognition of the PRK government and for government assistance for the massive reconstruction needed.

958 **Your shadow is mine.**
Producer: Pierre Courau. Director: Andre Michel. Screenplay: Jean-René Huguenin, Fabbri, Madeleine Courau. Photography: Edmond Sechan. Editor: Jean-Michel Gautier. Music: Maurice Jarre. Cast: Jill Hayworth, Michel Ruhl, Ruos Vanny, Marcel Pagliero, Clotilde Joano, Catherine Zago, Madame Pung-Peng-Cheng, Philippe Forquet. France; Italy: Continental Distributing Inc. [distributor], 1962. 90 min. 35 mm. Filmed on location in Cambodia. French name – *Ton Ombre est la mienne*.

'Devi is a French girl who has been raised by a native Cambodian family since she was found wandering in the forest 12 years ago. She looks forward to marrying Rahit, the son of her foster mother, but her idyllic existence is shattered when government officials return her to her brother, Philippe Bergerat, who has been searching for her since the Japanese attacked their family's plantation in 1943. Determined to win Devi's love, Philippe excludes everything else from his life, including his unhappy wife, Anne, but his need for spiritual love soon becomes a physical desire for his sister. When Rahit arrives, the frightened Devi agrees to run away with him. As they make their way back to the village, Philippe takes pursuit in his car. The youngsters hide in the forest, and Philippe drives after them, but he is killed when his car skids off the road and crashes into some trees.' Taken from *The American Film Institute Catalog: feature films 1961-70*. Edited by Richard P. Krafsur. Copyright © 1976, R. R. Bowker. All rights reserved. Reproduced by permission.

Hollywood on the Mekong: life with video.
See item no. 844.

Recorded Music

959 **Cambodia: royal music.**

[Recordings by Jacques Brunet]. Ivry sur Seine, France: Auvidis, 1989. 1 sound disc digital, stereo. (UNESCO Collection: Musics and Musicians of the World = Musiques et Musiciens du Monde). Originally published in record format as 'Royal music of Cambodia', International Music Council, 1971.

A compact disc analog recording. It was recorded in 1970 by Cambodian music expert Jacques Brunet, who also wrote the notes (in French and English) giving essential information about the cultural origins, instruments, history and significance of the music. The six pieces recorded here are performances by various royal orchestras, recorded with the authorization of Her Majesty the Queen. The musicians used the oldest instruments, and the women's choir was increased to its former size for this recording. At the time of the recording, the Royal Palace maintained a retinue of 36 musicians, 35 dancers and 300 pupils. Brunet identifies the art of this music as specifically and necessarily royal, religious, and élite. The pieces are: 'Buong Suong', 'Hang Meas' (The sacred golden bird), 'Pey Keo', 'Salamar', 'Phat Cheay' and 'Sampong', and 'Soy Sar Kat'. Brunet collected a wide range of Cambodian music during the 1950s and it would be interesting to find out if Brunet's archives are publicly available. See also Brunet's chapters on Cambodia in *Traditional dance and music of South East Asia*, edited by Mohd. Taib Osman.

960 **Cambodian traditional music in Minnesota.**

Kent, Ohio: World Music, [198?]. 1 sound cassette analog. Recorded 17 April 1982, in St. Paul and 16 April 1983, in Minneapolis. Various performers.

The recording is accompanied by eleven pages of programme notes with bibliographical references and texts with English translations.

961 **Homrong.**

Musicians of the National Dance Company of Cambodia. [England]: Real World Records, 1991. 1 compact disc digital. Real World Records no. R W MC18. Recorded at Real World Studios, England, 2 and 11 July 1990.

Traditional and contemporary Cambodian songs, arranged and performed by the Musicians of the National Dance Company of Cambodia. The contents are: 'Breu Peyney'; 'Leng suan'; 'Homrong'; 'Tep monorom dance'; 'Nor kor reach'; 'Luok phsar'; 'Tropangpeay'; 'Preah Chinnavong'; 'Bohrapha'; and 'Mohori bompay'.

962 **The music of Cambodia.**

Concept by Eckart Rahn. Recorded and produced by David and Kay Parsons. Co-produced by Bill Lobban, Yon Khien, Pik Tum Kravel, Eng Bunthan and Kim San. Commentary written by John Schaefer. Tucson, Arizona: Celestial Harmonies, 1993-94. 3 sound discs (CD) digital Celestial Harmonies: 13074-2 (vol. 1), 13075-2 (vol. 2), 13076-2 (vol. 3). Vol. 1 recorded inside Angkor Wat, vol. 2 in Phnom Penh.

A magnificent collection of a wide range of Cambodian music with extensive notes and commentaries, a beautifully presented box and booklets, printed, as proclaimed repeatedly, 'on recycled paper'. Volume one, '9 gong gamelan' was recorded in Angkor Wat, and half of the playing time is devoted to the Taam Ming ensemble of Siem Reap. Volume two, 'Royal court music', and volume three, 'Solo instrumental music', were recorded in Phnom Penh. The latter includes a number of rare specifically Cambodian instruments such as the 'kse diev' gourd, the 'chapey dang veng' long-necked lute, the oboe-like 'sralai' and the 'kloy' bamboo flute, some of which date from before the period of Angkor, which commenced in 802 AD. The collection is true to the considerable reputation that the Celestial Harmonies label has developed, and a tribute to those involved in its production. These include the musicians who are all individually named in the programme notes, the producer David Parsons, a New Zealand composer with a profound interest in, and knowledge of Asian music, and Bill Lobban, an Australian ethnomusicologist who worked in Cambodia as a volunteer for some years, and who says 'you can do nothing in Cambodia without having music . . . from healing to dying; from breaking new ground to ceremonies for 7 and 100 days after death'.

Audio and Braille Books

963 **Borany's story [sound recording].**
Borany Kanal as told to Adrienne Jansen, read by Niborom Young. Wellington, New Zealand: Radio New Zealand, Replay Radio, © 1989. 1 sound cassette analog.

A brief autobiography of a survivor of the Cambodian 'holocaust'. For more details see item no. 314.

964 **Cambodian witness [sound recording]: the autobiography of Someth May.**
Someth May, edited and with an introduction by James Fenton, read by Basil Johnson. North Hobart: Hear A Book, 1993. 9 sound cassettes (ca. 13 hr.), 2 track, mono. Recorded from the edition published, London: Faber & Faber, 1988.

Another autobiographical account of life under the Khmer Rouge. For more details see item no. 316.

965 **Down highway one [sound recording]: journeys through Vietnam and Cambodia.**
Susan Downie. Enfield, New South Wales: Royal Blind Society. sound cassettes, 15/16 ips, 4 track, mono.

An account of the Australian journalist Sue Downie's journey along Highway One through Vietnam and Cambodia. For more details see item no. 70.

966 **The gates of ivory [sound recording].**
Margaret Drabble, read by Frances Dharmalingam. Victoria Park, Western Australia: Association for the Blind of Western Australia, 1992. 17 sound cassettes (1,414 min.), 1 7/8 ips, 2 track, mono. For print-handicapped readers. Recorded, London: Viking, 1991.

The third work of a series, revisiting the characters of the preceding two novels, *The radiant way* and *A natural curiosity*. For more details see item no. 688.

967 **The killing fields [sound recording].**
Christopher Hudson, read by Alice Paton. Melbourne: Royal Victorian Institute for the Blind. Tertiary Resource Service, 1988. 2 sound cassettes (9 hr.), 15/16 ips, 4 track, mono. Recorded, London: Pan Books, 1984. Recorded for student use. Requires special playback equipment. Tone-indexed.

Christopher Hudson retells the story of Dith Pran and Sydney Schanberg from August 1973 onwards as they cover the war in Cambodia as journalists for *The New York Times*, through the liberation of Phnom Penh by Khmer Rouge troops, Schanberg's departure with Pran left behind, and Pran's horrific personal experiences under Pol Pot rule and subsequent flight from Cambodia, until October 1979 when they meet again in a refugee camp on the border between Thailand and Cambodia. For more details see item no. 322.

968 **The land in between [braille]: the Cambodian dilemma.**
[Maslyn Williams]. Burwood, New South Wales: Royal Blind Society of New South Wales, 1970. 5 vols of interline braille. Transcribed, New York: Morrow, 1970 [c1969].

A thoughtful account of the author's visit to Cambodia in the late 1960s. For more details see item no. 86.

969 **Stay alive my son [braille].**
Pin Yathay with John Man. South Yarra, Victoria: Louis Braille Productions, 1989. 8 vols. of braille, embossed one side. Transcribed, London: Bloomsbury, 1987. An adaptation of *L'utopie meurtrière* (The murderous utopia).

This is the story of Pin Yathay and his wife and young son under Khmer Rouge rule, and the difficult decision he and his wife made to leave their sick child behind in a Khmer Rouge hospital when they fled the country. For more details see item no. 333.

970 **Surviving the killing fields [sound recording].**
Haing S. Ngor, read by Crawford Logan. Oxford: Oasis Audio Books, © 1990. 12 sound cassettes (18 hrs.), 1 7/8 ips, 2 track, mono, stereo. Dolby processed. Oasis Audio Books: OAS 90041.

A survivor of the Cambodian holocaust, Haing Ngor tells the story of his life and the terrible suffering he and his family endured under Pol Pot rule. For more details see item no. 335.

971 **Vietnam, Laos & Cambodia [braille]/[sound recording]: a travel survival kit**.

Daniel Robinson and Joe Cumming. Enfield, New South Wales: Royal Blind Society, 199?. Braille edition/sound recording. Transcribed and recorded from the printed edition, Hawthorn, Victoria: Lonely Planet, 1991.

Braille and sound recording editions of this popular travel guide. For more details see item no. 61.

Colloquial Cambodian: a complete language course.
See item no. 380.

Modern spoken Cambodian.
See item no. 393.

Internet Sites and Databases

972 **America's ethnic performing arts: Cambodian.**
Sam-Ang Sam and Chan Moly Sam. Available online at **http://asdg-99.umd.edu/cambodia**[.] (Last accessed on 23 October 1997.)

A prototype multimedia guided tour, with music presented by Sam-Ang Sam (q.v.) and dance by Chan Moly Sam (q.v.). Photographs, sound and video animations are included for those with the appropriate sound and video cards and browsers. It contains order information for videotapes and CDs, and a bibliography.

973 **Angkor Wat Internet: Cambodian cyber culture.**
Available online at **http://www.angkorwat.org** (Copyright 1996). (Last accessed on 23 October 1997.)

This site contains many links to Cambodia-related resources and they are grouped under different headings, such as Internet, Education, General Information and Culture & Arts. The design of the interface is simple and it is easy to search.

974 **Cambodia bibliography: bibliography in progress.**
Walter H. Aschmoneit. Osnabrück, Germany: Walter H. Aschmoneit, 1992. 173p.

A bibliographic database, which in 1995 contained some 6,500 items. It was developed from his 1981 printed publication *Kampuchea: Sozialhistorische bibliographie zu Kampuchea von der Vorgeschichte bis 1954* (q.v.), but is being continually updated to include new material. The author appeals for contributions of further titles to be sent to him, and he encloses a sheet for completion and submission to him at the following address: c/o Rosl Kuhlmann, Goldstr. 31, D-4500, Osnabrück, Germany. The database was developed using Ashton Tate's Rapidfile software.

975 **Cambodia: a country study.**
Available online at **http://lcweb2.loc.gov/frd/cs/khtoc.html**[.] (Last accessed on 23 October 1997.)

A valuable reference work on Cambodia of the same title (q.v.) prepared for the United States Army and available on the Internet.

976 **Cambodia Times on the Net.**
Available online at **http://www.jaring.my/at-asia/cam_at_asia/camb_times/ct_list.html** (Copyright 1995, 1996, 1997).

The Internet version of the first English-language newspaper to be published in postwar Cambodia, *The Cambodia Times*. For more details see item no. 855.

977 **The Cambodian Genocide Program.**
Available online at **http://www.yale.edu/cgp** and at **http://www-cgp.silas.unsw.edu.au**[.] (Last version modified 1 May 1997.)

The Cambodian Genocide Program (CGP), centred at Yale University, aims to document the tragedy of the Pol Pot régime when at least twenty per cent of the Cambodian population are believed to have died. This homepage provides a link to The Documentation Center of Cambodia as well as findings from the CGP. A suite of databases known as CGDB (Cambodian Genocide Data Bases) using the software of UNESCO called CDS/ISIS has been developed for the Cambodian Genocide Program. It is possible to search the databases on this homepage, and they include bibliographical, biographical, geographical and photographic data relevant to the Khmer Rouge genocide from 1975-79, including over 5,000 photographs of victims at the Tuol Sleng prison, and locations of over 100 burial sites in 10 provinces. The CGDB is available for purchase on CD-ROM from Dr Helen Jarvis, SILAS, University of New South Wales, Sydney, NSW 2052, Australia.

978 **Cambodian Human and Natural Resources.**
Available online at **http://www.idrc.org.sg/cambodia/**[.] (Last version seen modified on 8 January 1997.)

This site is part of the homepage of the International Development Research Centre's Asia Regional Office in Singapore. The IDRC programme in Cambodia aims to 'support the rebuilding of Cambodia institutional capacity for good governance and sustainable development'.

979 **Cambodian Information Center Homepage.**
Available online at **http://www.best.com/~cambodia/**[.] (Last version seen modified on 14 July 1997.)

This site provides 'many links to Cambodian information as well as homepages of Khmer and friends around the world'. The coverage is quite comprehensive and it includes services offered by the CIC (Cambodian Information Center), academic papers about Cambodia and news etc.

980 **CCCNet – Cambodia.**
Available online at **http://www.pactok.net.au/projects/pactok/cccnet.htm**[.] (Last accessed on 23 October 1997.)

The Cooperation Committee for Cambodia (CCC) is a membership organization for NGOs working in Cambodia to help co-ordinate assistance to the Cambodian people. This homepage provides detailed information about CCC, such as its background, environment, objectives, activities and about CCCNet management. CCCNet–Cambodia is one of the projects of Pactok where partnerships are formed with organizations in the countries of the region who wish to set up a local network. Pactok is a low-cost electronic mail network designed to serve the NGO movement in the Asia-Pacific region. Pactok makes it possible for individuals, educational institutions, community groups and NGOs to exchange information with other people and groups of similar interest locally, nationally or across the globe.

981 **city.net Cambodia.**
Available online at **http://city.net/countries/cambodia**[.] (Last accessed on 23 October 1997.)

This site provides links to related web sites for travellers to Cambodia, such as country information, destinations, news and media, and travel and sights. It should be very useful for travellers who want to know more about Cambodia before they go there.

982 **Country Information – Cambodia.**
Available online at **http://www.ait.ac.th/Asia/infocom.html**[.] (Last version seen modified on 9 November 1995.)

The site is maintained by the Asian Institute of Technology, Bankok. It provides links to information about Cambodia, including news, projects, organizations, facts and news groups.

983 **Cyberspace Cambodia.**
Available online at **http://garnet.berkeley.edu/~net-al/net.html**[.] (Last version seen modified on 1 July 1996.)

This site has been created by a Cambodian student studying in the United States. This homepage aims to organize and evaluate Cambodian information on the Internet. The topics are arranged in alphabetical order so it is very easy to search. The coverage is the most comprehensive when compared with homepages of a similar kind.

984 **The digital archive of Cambodian holocaust survivors.**
Available online at **http://www.cybercambodia.com/dachs/**[.] (Last version seen modified on 22 July 1997.)

'The idea of spreading the awareness of Cambodia holocaust which had happened twenty years ago rooted in the Soc.Culture. Cambodia newsgroup.' This page is a digital archive of the stories of Cambodian holocaust survivors. The aim of this homepage is to appeal to the public to join in the preservation and protection of the memories of the Cambodian holocaust survivors. Besides information about the holocaust, there are also materials about Cambodia in general. Some of the pages take a while to download because of the images.

985 **The Documentation Center of Cambodia.**
Available online at **http://www.yale.edu/cgp/dccam/dccam1.htm**[.] (Last accessed on 23 October 1997.)

The Documentation Center of Cambodia (DCCAM) is a non-profit-making international non-governmental organization (NGO) which exists to facilitate training, research and documentation relating to the genocide carried out by the Khmer Rouge in Cambodia. This site has text-only documents and provides links to other sites related to the Cambodian Genocide Program.

986 **Ethnologue Database: Cambodia.**
Available online at **http://www.sil.org/ethnologue/countries/Camb.html**[.] (Last accessed on 23 October 1997.)

This site 'provides indices to the Ethnologue database (12th ed., 1992)'. The part about Cambodia includes a brief description of the country and the eighteen languages spoken in Cambodia, with details like number of speakers, location, dialects, linguistic affiliation and other sociolinguistic and demographic data.

987 **Lonely Planet Destinations: Cambodia.**
Available online at **http://www.lonelyplanet.com.au/dest/sea/camb.htm** (Copyright 1996). (Last accessed on 23 October 1997.)

Lonely Planet Publications has been publishing travel guides, phrasebooks, travel atlases and videos since the 1970s. It now has over 150 travel guides in print. The online version provides detailed information about Cambodia, relating to topics such as environment, history, economy, culture, events, and attractions, and offering travel tips, pictures and links to other sites about travelling in Cambodia.

988 **Phnom Penh Post [online].**
Available online at **http://www.vais.net/~tapang/ppp/**[.] (Last accessed on 23 October 1997.)

The major articles from the most widely read English-language newspaper from Cambodia is available promptly on the Internet. For more details of its coverage see item no. 865.

989 **Signposts to Asia and the Pacific: Contacts – Cambodia.**
Available online at **http://www.signposts.uts.edu.au/contacts/Cambodia/index.html**[.] (Last updated 2 May 1997.)

Links are provided to a range of media, NGOs and human rights organizations active in Cambodia.

990 **Suorsdey magazine.**
Available online at **http://www.cybercambodia.com/suorsdey**[.] (Last accessed on 23 October 1997.)

An electronic journal or e-zine published in California, and carrying fiction and articles of general interest. Mail address: 1850 Redondo Ave, Long Beach, California, 90804, USA.

991 **USAID assistance for Cambodia.**
Available online at **http://www.info.usaid.gov/countries/kh.html**[.] (Last version seen modified on 11 June 1997.)

USAID offered assistance to Cambodia to support Cambodian Non-Communist (CNC) groups in northwest Cambodia and then moved to support the UN-sponsored peace process and to direct support for rehabilitation and economic growth in the post-election period. This homepage contains a brief background of USAID, its programme and results, and figures of USAID assistance.

992 **The world factbook page on Cambodia.**
Available online at **http://www.odci.gov/cia/publications/nsolo/factbook/cb.htm**[.] (Last accessed on 23 October 1997.)

An online compendium of facts, figures and the flag. It was taken offline in 1996 due to hacking into the then site, considered to be sensitive by the CIA, but is now back online at an apparently more secure site.

993 **World Wide Web Virtual Library: Cambodia.**
Available online at **http://iias.leidenuniv.nl/wwwvl/southeas/cambodia.html**[.] (Last accessed on 23 October 1997.)

The authoritative homepage linking sites on Cambodia from around the world, as reported to the International Institute of Asian Studies at Leiden University, the Netherlands. This forms part of the Asian Studies World Wide Web Virtual Library maintained by the Australian National University. The Cambodia homepage includes links to such important news and discussion groups such as camnews.org, camdisc.org and soc.culture.cambodia.

Summary of world broadcasts: Part 3 – Asia-Pacific.
See item no. 871.

Gazetteer of Cambodia.
See item no. 878.

Indexes

There follow three separate indexes: authors (personal and corporate); titles; and subjects. Title entries are italicized and refer either to the main titles, or to many of the other works cited in the annotations. The numbers refer to bibliographical entry rather than page numbers. Individual index entries are arranged in alphabetical sequence.

Index of Authors

B

C

D

E

H

I

M

N

O

P

T

U

V

W

Y

Z

Index of Titles

D

E

H

I

J

K

L

M

S

T

U

V

Index of Subjects

Q

R

S

Map of Cambodia

This map shows the more important towns and other features.

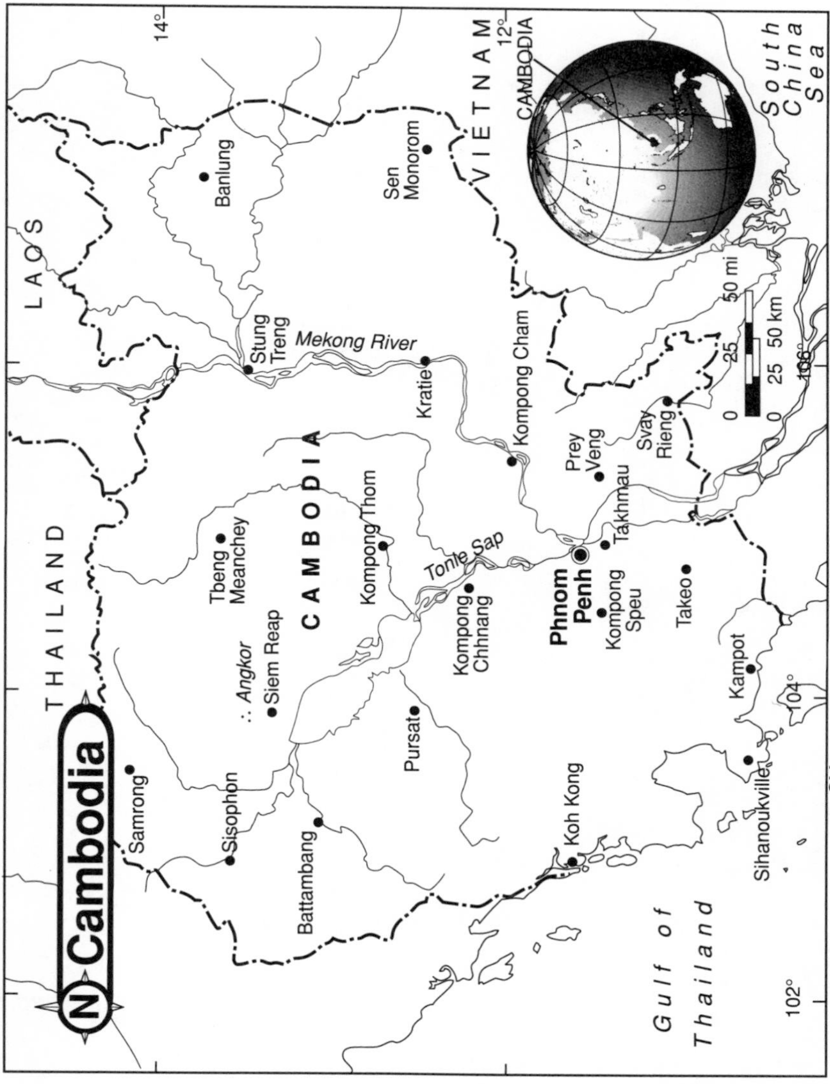

ALSO FROM CLIO PRESS

INTERNATIONAL ORGANIZATIONS SERIES

Each volume in the International Organizations Series is either devoted to one specific organization, or to a number of different organizations operating in a particular region, or engaged in a specific field of activity. The scope of the series is wide-ranging and includes intergovernmental organizations, international non-governmental organizations, and national bodies dealing with international issues. The series is aimed mainly at the English-speaker and each volume provides a selective, annotated, critical bibliography of the organization, or organizations, concerned. The bibliographies cover books, articles, pamphlets, directories, databases and theses and, wherever possible, attention is focused on material about the organizations rather than on the organizations' own publications. Notwithstanding this, the most important official publications, and guides to those publications, will be included. The views expressed in individual volumes, however, are not necessarily those of the publishers.

VOLUMES IN THE SERIES

1 *European Communities*, John Paxton
2 *Arab Regional Organizations*, Frank A. Clements
3 *Comecon: The Rise and Fall of an International Socialist Organization*, Jenny Brine
4 *International Monetary Fund*, Anne C. M. Salda
5 *The Commonwealth*, Patricia M. Larby and Harry Hannam
6 *The French Secret Services*, Martyn Cornick and Peter Morris
7 *Organization of African Unity*, Gordon Harris
8 *North Atlantic Treaty Organization*, Phil Williams
9 *World Bank*, Anne C. M. Salda
10 *United Nations System*, Joseph P. Baratta
11 *Organization of American States*, David Sheinin
12 *The British Secret Services*, Philip H. J. Davies
13 *The Israeli Secret Services*, Frank A. Clements